Jim Fleming 10/11/95

IRELAND

ON THE BALL

Donal Cullen

IRELAND

ON THE BALL

A Complete Record of the
International Matches of the
Republic of Ireland Soccer Team
March 1926 to June 1993

ELO PUBLICATIONS
October 1993

First published in Ireland, October 1993, by
Elo Publications
Reuben Avenue, Dublin 8

ISBN 0 9519593 5 2

Typesetting by Diskon Technical Services Ltd.
48 Reuben Avenue, Dublin 8.
Book designed by Patrick Funge
and printed at the Elo Press Ltd.,
49 Reuben Avenue, Dublin 8.
Bound by PD Finishers Ltd., Dublin 12.

CONTENTS

Dedication

This book is dedicated
to the memory of my father
Sean Cullen
and a friend
John O'Reilly

Acknowledgements

This book would not have been possible without the co-operation of my family whose patience and understanding over the years helped me.

My main research was done in Pearse Street Library and my thanks go to the staff there for their help. A special thank you to Jimmy who was of great assistance in digging out all the newspapers and material I requested. (I still don't know your surname!)

There are many others who have helped me and a list of those appear in Appendix K with due thanks. This list was compiled just after we slaughtered (!) Lithuania 2-0 and so those people who sent me material after that will not appear on the list but my thanks go to them in advance.

Finally I must thank my friend Shay Blair and the staff of Elo Press for their work in getting this book into print. Again a special thanks must go to Josephine and Margaret who spent hours typesetting my scribbles so others could read them.

Donal Cullen

How To Use The Book

All matches follow a basic statistical format which should be easily understood. However, as I have tried to keep each report as concise as possible, I have employed several devices to eliminate repetition. Also for the sake of uniformity I have used certain titles to encompass various names. The explanations are as follows:

MATCH NUMBER – Acts as a simple reference but also as a device to prevent mentioning it in the report (e.g. Ireland's 250th match . . .)

COMPETITIONS – For uniformity the World Cup and European Championship titles are used throughout and include the competitions run under previous names.

TEAMS – Again for uniformity the Republic of Ireland is used throughout even though this title only dates from 1954. This title is shortened to Ireland on occasions except where a distinction is necessary. When playing outside the Republic, the Irish team is always given as the "away" side even at neutral venues.

GOALSCORERS – A number of goalscoring disputes have arisen and these are explained in GOAL SCORING DISPUTES below and at the end of the Match Reports.

TEAM LINE-OUTS – Both sides are given in formation (see FORMATIONS below) with the Irish team detailing the player's full name (where known), the club he was playing for at that time and his cap count. Where a player was on loan from another club, that club's name is given. The player's name is generally the one he was known by and not necessarily his full name (e.g. Francis Stapleton was always called Frank Stapleton). Nicknames are not used.

MANAGER – The figure after the manager's name indicates the number of games he managed.

FORMATIONS – Where no formation figure is given then the Irish team lined out in a standard 2-3-5 formation. These formations, which exclude the goalkeeper, are to show how the Irish team lined out:

2-3-5: RB, LB; RH, CH, LH; RW, IR, CF, IL, LW.
4-2-4: RB, CD, CD, LB; MF, MF; RW, CF, CF, LW.
4-3-3: RB, CD, CD, LB; MF, MF, MF; RW/CF, CF, CF.
4-4-2: RB, CD, CD, LB; MF, MF, MF, MF; CF, CF.
4-5-1: RB, CD, CD, LB; MF, MF, MF, MF, MF; CF.
5-1-4: RB, CD, SW, CD, LB; MF; RW, CF, CF, LW.
5-2-3: RB, CH, SW, CH, LB, MF, MF, W/CF, CF, CF.

CF = Centre Forward, CH = Centre Half (later Central Defender), IL = Inside Left, IR = Inside Right, LB = Left Back, LH = Left Half, LW = Left Winger, MF = Midfielder, RB = Right Back, RH = Right Half, RW = Right Winger, SW = Sweeper, W = Winger.

GOALSCORING DISPUTES – Conflicting reports credit different people with the same goal or certain goals as own goals. In all these disputes I have gone for the best explanation but naturally these decisions are arbitrary.

Own goals are, in the main, clear but the determining of these could be open to question. Two examples serve to explain the difficulty: the goal scored by Paz for Uruguay against Ireland in 1986 could just as easily have been given as an own goal by McCarthy. The reason it was not given as an own goal was because Paz's shot could just as easily have gone in without the deflection. The own goal credited to Staunton against England in 1991 could be credited to Dixon of England, who has claimed it. However, it is highly unlikely that Dixon's shot would have gone in without the deflection. While these explanations are subjective, they serve for the purpose of this book.

Foreword

Football fans are a happy and gregarious bunch. They tend to make a very long week-end out of a match they've been at involving their favourite team.

They'll go somewhere, anywhere, but usually their own local to discuss the finer merits of their win or bemoan their loss. But always they will move thoughts on to the next match and discuss the team's further chances. And all this, of course, with a suitable lubrication of libations – usually pints – to ease the vocal chords into stunning rhetoric.

But often the mood becomes reflective. Suddenly a current player's ability will be compared with a giant of the past. Records will be trotted out and argued about. How many times someone had played for Ireland. Had he played in the famous matches against England?. Had he scored?. And if he had not who had?

Debate and argument like this has been known to go on for months. And now all the conjecture can be resolved, all the confusion sorted out by reference to this publication assembled with such care and industry.

It is truly a triumph of love over labour. A fascinating compilation of all the facts and figures, scores, scorers and players on every Irish International team that ever played since the initial game away to Italy in 1926 right up to the present year and the World Cup games against the Baltic countries concluding with Lithuania in June '93.

We owe an enormous debt of gratitude to the author for his arduous work in trawling through all the records of the past to present this outstanding register of international matches and players that is going to prove quite invaluable as an important work of reference and as a means of settling the arguments that are always springing up in pubs and clubs about who played for Ireland in what match – and who was in goal for the opposition.

We will all have our preferences for a look backwards through the years. I will want to refresh my mind with looking up our World Cup game of 1934 against Belgium when as a boy I saw one of my heroes, the wonderful Paddy Moore score all four goals to snatch a miraculous draw in Dalymount.

And then what about that sensational win over England at Goodison Park with Con Martin and Peter Farrell getting the goals but 'Eggo' not getting a call-up on his own Everton ground. A lot of bets have been laid and lost on who took Tommy's left wing position.

I shall, of course, want to look up the details of who exactly played in the first international I broadcast a commentary on. That was against Argentina in 1951 and the South Americans won by a goal after a great display from their goalkeeper, a fellow with a huge moustache named Rugilo.

It's hard to put down a book like this. I will also want to check on Johnny Giles's first match for Ireland against Sweden in 1959. The Swedes had reached the 1958 World Cup final against Brazil who played Pele for the first time. But a stunning goal by Giles into the goal at the school end saw the Irish edge out the Swedes and send the crowd into ecstasies.

But in 1957 a goal at the other end, the Tramway end, saw John Atyeo head a late equaliser for England that knocked Ireland out of the World Cup and knocked both the crowd and this commentator speechless.

This book will give the times and the details of all these and all the rest including of course the great act of redemption when one goal from the head of Ray Houghton in the European Finals in Stuttgart sent England to defeat and the Irish there dancing with delight.

But to be honest this is a production I will go through from beginning to end and get great enjoyment from. I think we all owe a vote of thanks to its author. It is a pleasure for me to send him my congratulations on a great job well done.

Philip Greene

Match Reports
1926-1993

Match No. 1 ITALY Away

Sunday 21st March, 1926 – Turin

ITALY (3) 3 Baloncieri 13, Magnozzi 36, Bernardini 44
REP. OF IRELAND (0) 0

Ref: Ruoff (Switzerland) **Ground:** Motovelodromo **Att:** 12,000

Italy: G. de Pra, V. Rosetta, U. Caligaris, A. Janni, F. Bernardini, C. Bigatto, L. Conti, A. Baloncieri, G. della Valle, M. Magnozzi, M. Tansini.

Ireland: Harry Cannon (Bohemians 1), Frank Brady (Fordsons 1), Jack McCarthy (Bohemians 1), Mick Foley (Shelbourne 1), Denis Doyle (Shamrock Rovers 1), James Connolly (Fordsons 1), John Joe Flood (Shamrock Rovers 1), Joe Grace (Drumcondra 1), Fran Watters (Shelbourne 1), Bob Fullam (Shamrock Rovers 1), Jack Fagan (Shamrock Rovers 1). **Captain:** Mick Foley.

The Irish team left Dublin on Wednesday and arrived in Italy on Saturday. This long journey had its effect on the game and the Italians dominated the first half. Baloncieri opened the scoring with a powerful drive and Magnozzi added a second when an Irish move broke down. A minute before the break Bernardini scored with a powerful close range shot. The Irish improved in the second half and created two good chances, one of which resulted in both Flood and de Pra being knocked unconscious. Both resumed later, after treatment.

Match No. 2 ITALY "B" Home

Saturday 27th April, 1927 – Dublin

REP. OF IRELAND (1) 1 Fullam
ITALY "B" (0) 2 Munerati (2)

Ref: Langenus (Belgium) **Ground:** Lansdowne Road **Att:** 20,000

Ireland: Frank Collins (Jacobs 1), Alec Kirkland (Shamrock Rovers 1), Frank Brady (Fordsons 2), William Glen (Shamrock Rovers 1), Mick O'Brien (Derby County 1), Tommy Muldoon (Aston Villa 1), Billy Lacey (Shelbourne 1), Harry Duggan (Leeds United 1), C. Martin (Bo'ness United 1), Bob Fullam (Shamrock Rovers 2), Joe Kendrick (Everton 1). **Captain:** Frank Brady.

Italy "B": M. Gianni, M. Zanello, D. Bellini, P. Genovesi, L. Burlando, A. Giordani, F. Munerati, A. Vojak, P. Pastore, E. Rivolta, L. Cevenini.

A frantic opening saw Pastore hit the crossbar and Fullam have a header saved by Gianni before Ireland opened the scoring after 6 minutes. Kendrick beat Giordani and crossed for Martin to shoot. The centre-forwards shot was blocked but the ball rebounded to Fullam who shot high into the net.

The Italians fought back and Pastore had a header kicked off the line by Brady. Before the interval Zanello was knocked unconscious when a free kick by Fullam hit him in the head. He was carried off and replaced by a substitute (there is no mention of this in Italian records).

In the second half Rivolta, Pastore and Vojak set up Munerati to shoot and when this was blocked the winger followed up to score. With 10 minutes left Munerati scored a soft goal to give the Italians victory.

Match No. 3 BELGIUM Away

Sunday 12th February 1928 – Liege

BELGIUM (2) 2 R. Braine 39, Ledent 41
REP. OF IRELAND (0) 4 White 55, 75, Lacey 57, Sullivan 79 (pen.)

Ref: Kingscott (England) **Ground:** Standard Liege Stadium **Att:** 25,000

Belgium: L. Vandenbergh, A. Swartenbroeks, N. Hoydonckx, H. Van Averbeke, F. Van Halme, G. Boesman, C. Elst, P. Braine, R. Braine, F. Ledent, J. Diddens.

Ireland: Harry Cannon (Bohemians 2), Jeremiah Robinson (Bohemians 1), Jack McCarthy (Bohemians 2), Joe Kinsella (Shelbourne 1), Jack Sullivan (Fordsons 1), Paddy Barry (Fordsons 1), Jack Byrne (Bray Unknowns 1), Billy Lacey (Shelbourne 2), Jimmy White (Bohemians 1), Charlie Dowdall (Fordsons 1), Joseph Golding (Shamrock Rovers 1). **Captain:** Jack McCarthy.

With the defence on both sides playing well there were few scoring chances until Pierre Braine headed in Van Averbeke's cross. Francois Ledent added a second for Belgium before the break.

The start of the second half was delayed due to a sudden thunder storm during the interval. On the resumption the Irish adapted well to the conditions and after 10 minutes White scored. Lacey equalised when he scored from 17 yards and Golding set up White for a third. White could have had a hat-trick when he was clean through but the goalkeeper made a fine save at his feet.

Vandenbergh was injured later on and was forced to leave the field; a team-mate replacing him in goal. The deputy 'keeper was beaten once – a penalty (awarded for handball) by Sullivan.

Match No. 4 BELGIUM Home

Saturday 20th April, 1929 – Dublin

REP. OF IRELAND (1) 4 Flood (3), D. Byrne
BELGIUM (0) 0

Ref: Westwood (England) **Ground:** Dalymount Park **Att:** 15,000

Ireland: Tom Farquharson (Cardiff City 1), Jim Maguire (Shamrock Rovers 1), John Burke (Shamrock Rovers 1), William Glen (Shamrock Rovers 2), Mick O'Brien (Walsall 2), Paddy Barry (Fordsons 2), Jimmy Bermingham (Bohemians 1), John Joe Flood (Shamrock Rovers 2), David Byrne (Shelbourne 1), Charlie Dowdall (Barnsley 2), Robert Egan (Dundalk 1). **Captain:** John Burke.

Belgium: L. Somers, T. Nouwens, N. Hoydonckx, H. Van Averbeke, F. Van Halme, G. Boesman, P. Braine, M. Vanderbauwhede, R. Braine, J. Moeschal, J. Diddens.

The first half was dominated by Belgium and the Irish should have been two goals down before the break. That they were not was a combination of poor Belgian finishing and some excellent goalkeeping by Farquharson. It was Ireland, however, who went in at the break a goal in front when Byrne sent in Flood to score two minutes before the interval.

That goal seemed to unsettle Belgium for as they continued to dominate the second period they again lacked finish. Raymond Braine had a certain goal blocked on the line by Maguire but other than that their shooting was poor.

Ireland went two-up after 73 minutes. Farquharson's long kick out was headed on by Bermingham to Byrne, who outpaced the defence and shot past the static Somers.

O'Brien and Dowdall sent Flood in for the third and Flood completed his hat-trick following a pass by Bermingham.

Match No. 5 BELGIUM Away

Sunday 11th May, 1930 – Brussels

BELGIUM (1) 1 Bastin 20
REP. OF IRELAND (1) 3 Dunne 32, 57, Flood 77.

Ref: Melcon (England) **Ground:** Parc Astrid **Att:** 15,000

Belgium: A. Badjou, T. Nouwens, N. Hoydonckx, P. Braine, A. Hellemans, J. de Clercq, L. Versyp, F. Adams, M. Vanderbauwhede, J. Moeschal, D. Bastin.

Ireland: Tom Farquharson (Cardiff City 2), Billy Lacey (Shelbourne 3), Jack McCarthy (Bohemians 3), William Glen (Shamrock Rovers 3), Mick O'Brien (Norwich City 3), F. McLoughlin (Fordsons 1), Harry Duggan (Leeds United 2), John Joe Flood (Shamrock Rovers 3), Jimmy Dunne (Sheffield United 1), Fred Horlacher (Bohemians 1), Joseph Golding (Shamrock Rovers 2). **Captain:** Mick O'Brien.

Bad weather and poor finishing again disrupted the Belgians although they took an early lead when Bastin scored with a hooked shot. Twelve minutes later Jimmy Dunne equalised for the Irish and left the scores even at the break; a fair reflection of the play.

The Irish were more dominant in the second half and won the game with goals from Dunne and Flood.

Match No. 6 SPAIN Away

Sunday 26th April, 1931 – Barcelona

SPAIN (1) 1 Arocha 38
REP. OF IRELAND (1) 1 Moore 35

Ref: Romanhino (Portugal) **Ground:** Montjuich Stadium **Att:** 100,000

Spain: Zamora, Ciriaco, Quincoces I, Marti, Sole, Castillo, Piera, Goiburu, Samitier, Arocha, Gorostiza.

Ireland: Tom Farquharson (Cardiff City 3), George Lennox (Dolphin 1), Paddy Byrne (Dolphin 1), Jeremiah Robinson (Dolphin 2), Harry Chatton (Shelbourne 1), Sean Byrne (Bohemians 1), John Joe Flood (Shamrock Rovers 4), Charlie Dowdall (Cork 3), Paddy Moore (Shamrock Rovers 1), Charlie Reid (Brideville 1), Peter Kavanagh (Glasgow Celtic 1). **Captain:** John Joe Flood.

The game kicked off 40 minutes late due to the pre-match Athletics and Rugby exhibitions. Spain pressured early on and Piera struck the crossbar with a shot. From a breakaway Flood passed to Moore who scored with a neat chip over Zamora's head.

Spain equalised when, following a scramble, Arocha headed in a centre from Piera.

In the second half a light rain made the ground slippy. With 10 minutes left, Samitier raced in as Farquharson gathered the ball. The goalkeeper held his ground and the centre-forward bounced off him. The referee awarded a penalty but Farquharson got to Gorostiza's spot-kick and fisted it away.

Match No. 7 SPAIN Home

Sunday 13th December, 1931 – Dublin

REP. OF IRELAND (0) 0
SPAIN (3) 5 Regueiro 6, 34, Arocha 40, 80, Vantolra 88

Ref: Langenus (Belgium) **Ground:** Dalymount Park **Att:** 35,000

Ireland: Tom Farquharson (Cardiff City 4), George Lennox (Shelbourne 2), Larry Doyle (Dolphin 1), William Glen (Shamrock Rovers 4), Harry Chatton (Dumbarton 2), F. McLoughlin (Cork 2), John Joe Flood (Shamrock Rovers 5), Patsy Gallagher (Falkirk 1), David Byrne (Shamrock Rovers 2), Fred Horlacher (Bohemians 2), Peter Kavanagh (Glasgow Celtic 2). **Captain:** Harry Chatton.

Spain: Blasco, Ciriaco, Zabalo, Leoncito, Gamborena, Roberto, Vantolra, L. Regueiro, Samitier, Arocha, Gorostiza.

The Irish had no answer to Spain's speedy passing game and fell behind to an early goal by Regueiro. Vantolra's cross was fisted away by Farquharson but it fell to Regueiro's feet and he scored.

Ireland's best spell followed this goal. Horlacher struck the crossbar with a shot while a header by Byrne seemed to cross the goal-line before Blasco saved at the second attempt.

A fine Spanish move involving Leoncito, Gamborena and Samitier ended with Regueiro scoring with a right-footed drive. Arocha added a third following a dribble by Samitier, five minutes before the break.

Spanish pressure continued in the second half and Arocha scored the fourth when he headed in Vantolra's cross.

Vantolra (who wore a beret) raced away, cut inside and scored the fifth goal from close range.

NOTE: Spanish records show goalscorers as: L. Regueiro (2), Vantolra, Samitier and Arocha.

Match No. 8 — HOLLAND — Away

Sunday 8th May, 1932 – Amsterdam

HOLLAND (0) 0
REP. OF IRELAND (1) 2 Joe O'Reilly 20, Moore 48

Ref: **Ground:** De Meer Stadium Att: 30,000

Holland: Vander Meulen, Weber, Van Run, Paauwe, Anderiessen, Van Heel, Wels, Volkers, Lagendaal, Mol, Van Nellen.

Ireland: Mick McCarthy (Shamrock Rovers 1), Jimmy Daly (Shamrock Rovers 1), Paddy Byrne (Shelbourne 2), Joe O'Reilly (Brideville 1), Mick O'Brien (Watford 4), Owen Kinsella (Shamrock Rovers 1), Billy Kennedy (St. James's Gate 1), Alex Stevenson (Dolphin 1), Paddy Moore (Shamrock Rovers 2), Fred Horlacher (Bohemians 3), Jimmy Kelly (Derry City 1). **Captain:** Mick O'Brien.

The Irish team, using short-passing, showed better control and understanding than the Dutch, and deserved their victory. The Dutch nearly opened the scoring when Lagendaal shot against an upright. That was against the run of play and the Irish pressure was rewarded when O'Reilly scored with a long, hard, swerving shot.

Ireland's second goal came soon after the break when Kelly and Kennedy gave Moore the chance to score from 25 yards with a hard low shot.

Match No. 9 — BELGIUM — Home

Sunday 25th February, 1934 – Dublin (World Cup)

REP. OF IRELAND (1) 4 Moore 27, 48, 56, 75
BELGIUM (2) 4 Capelle 13, S. Vanden Eynde 26, F. Vanden Eynde 47, 63

Ref: Crew (England) **Ground:** Dalymount Park **Att:** 28,000

Ireland: Jim Foley (Cork 1), Miah Lynch (Cork Bohemians 1), Tom Burke (Cork 1), Paddy Gaskins (Shamrock Rovers 1), Joe O'Reilly (Aberdeen 2), Joe Kendrick (Dolphin 2), Billy Kennedy (St. James's Gate 2), David Byrne (Coleraine 3), Paddy Moore (Aberdeen 3), Tim O'Keeffe (Cork 1), Jimmy Kelly (Derry City 2). **Captain:** Paddy Gaskins.

Belgium: A. Vande Wijer, J. Pappaert, P. Smellinckx, J. Van Ingelghem, F. Welkenhuyzen, D. Bourgeois, L. Versyp, J. Brichaut, J. Capelle, A. Saeys, S. Vanden Eynde. **Subs:** F. Vanden Eynde for S. Vanden Eynde (37 mins).

Remembered most for Paddy Moore's goalscoring exploits, Ireland's first truly competitive game turned out to be a hard, tough but enjoyable encounter. With World Cup points at stake the football was not pretty, although there was little complaint from the £1,700 gate.

Belgium got two early goals. First, Versyp dispossed Burke near the backline and crossed for the unmarked Capelle to score easily. Then, a lob from Versyp was knocked in the air. Foley came out but only succeeded in punching the ball to the feet of Stanley Vanden Eynde who lobbed it back into the empty net.

A minute later Moore raced onto a through ball from Kelly. As Welkenhuyzen and Pappaert closed on him from both sides, Moore shot, as he was tackled, and scored.

Belgium regained their two goal lead after the break when substitute Francois Vanden Eynde (he replaced Stanley Vanden Eynde who broke his leg in the first half) scored. A cross from Van Ingelghem flew across the box, past 4 defenders, and came to Saeys. He cut inside and squared the ball for the substitute to score.

Moore again replied quickly when he reached a cross from Kennedy before Vande Wijer and scored. Moore equalised when he latched onto a high cross by Kelly and steered the ball home.

A pass by Brichaut allowed Vanden Eynde to beat Lynch and score past the advancing Foley but again Moore equalised. A corner was cleared out to Kendrick and when he lobbed the ball back into the area Moore headed home.

Match No. 10 HOLLAND Away

Sunday 8th April, 1934 – Amsterdam (World Cup)

HOLLAND (1) 5 Smit (2), Bakhuys (2), Vente
REP. OF IRELAND (1) 2 Squires, Moore

Ref: **Ground:** De Meer Stadium **Att:** 38,000

Holland: Van Male, Weber, Van Run, Pellikaan, Anderiesen , Van Heel, Wels, Vente, Bakhuys, Smit, Mijnders.

Ireland: Jim Foley (Cork 2), Paddy Gaskins (Shamrock Rovers 2), Paddy Byrne (Drumcondra 3), Joe O'Reilly (Aberdeen 3), Harry Chatton (Cork 3), Joe Kendrick (Dolphin 3), Billy Kennedy (St James's Gate 3), Johnny Squires (Shelbourne 1), Paddy Moore (Aberdeen 4), Billy Jordan (Bohemians 1), Paddy Meehan (Drumcondra 1). **Subs:** Fred Horlacher (Bohemians 4), for Jordan (40 mins), **Captain:** Paddy Gaskins.

Ireland were the better team in the first half but suffered a blow before the break when Jordan went off with an ankle injury. His replacement, Horlacher, was only just on the field when Holland scored. A cross from Wels was knocked into the net by Smit. Two minutes later Moore set up an easy chance for Squires to level the score.

Early in the second half Ireland went ahead. Dutch goalkeeper Van Male was slow in clearing the ball and Moore ran in to shoulder him and the ball into the net. Such challenges were legal at that time and the goal stood.

Moore had a chance to put the Irish further ahead but his lob shot just went over. On 65 minutes a break by Mijnders from the halfway line set up Bakhuys to equalise with a shot which went in off the post.

In the final ten minutes the Dutch scored three more goals to give them a flattering victory. Bakhuys headed them in front, Vente added another and Smit scored the fifth with a glorious drive.

Match No. 11 **HUNGARY** **Home**

Sunday 16th December, 1934 – Dublin

REP. OF IRELAND (1) 2 J. Donnelly, Bermingham (pen)
HUNGARY (2) 4 Avar (2), Vincze, Markos

Ref: Langenus (Belgium) **Ground:** Dalymount Park **Att:** 25,000

Ireland: Jim Foley (Glasgow Celtic 3), Paddy Gaskins ((Shamrock Rovers 3), Paddy Bermingham (St James's Gate 1), Paddy O'Kane (Bohemians 1), Charlie Lennon (St James's Gate 1), Fred Horlacher (Bohemians 5), R. Griffiths (Walsall 1), Joey Donnelly (Dundalk 1), Alf Rigby (St James's Gate 1), Paddy Moore (Aberdeen 5), Bill Fallon (Notts County 1). **Captain:** Paddy Gaskins.

Hungary: J. Hada, J. Vago, L. Sternberg, G. Seres, G. Szucs, A. Szalay I, I. Markos, J. Vincze, I. Avar, L. Cseh II, P. Titkos. **Subs:** A. Szabo, for Hada (half-time), J. Gyori for Seres (half-time).

Ireland began well and forced four corners in the first 15 minutes. This pressure did not yield a goal and on 18 minutes O'Kane was penalised for what looked like a good tackle on Cseh. As the Irish protested the award, the free kick was quickly taken and came to Titkos who crossed in for Avar to score.

On 28 minutes Foley came to punch away a corner but was challenged by Vincze who forced him to fist the ball into the roof of the net for the Hungarians second.

Seven minutes later, following a brilliant passing movement involving Rigby, Donnelly and Fallon, Donnelly reduced the arrears when he knocked home Fallon's low cross.

The start of the second half was delayed as Gaskins protested the use of three subs by Hungary. In the end only Szabo was allowed but Gyori also stayed on. Avar had to resume instead of Solty.

Hungary began well but gradually the Irish got on top and equalised when Sternberg handled a headed pass by Moore to Rigby and Bermingham scored from the resultant penalty.

Further Irish pressure looked like bringing victory but on 65 minutes Moore was carried off injured while Gaskins was also injured but played on.

On 83 minutes Avar scored with a fine low shot and two minutes later a misunderstanding in the Irish defence allowed Markos to run through and score the fourth.

The Irish Team in Switzerland in 1935

Match No. 12 **SWITZERLAND** **Away**

Sunday 5th May,1935 – Basle

SWITZERLAND (0) 1 Weiler 62 (pen)
REP. OF IRELAND (0) 0

Ref: Berenek (Austria) **Ground:** St Jacob's Stadium **Att:** 23,000

Switzerland: Bizzozzero, Minelli, Gobet, Defago, Weiler II, E. Müller, Amado, Poretti, Kielholz, Bösch, Jaeck.

Ireland: Jim Foley (Glasgow Celtic 4), Paddy Gaskins (Shamrock Rovers 4), Leo Dunne (Manchester City 1), Paddy O'Kane (Bohemians 2), Charlie Lennon (St James's Gate 2), Freddie Hutchinson (Drumcondra 1), Jimmy Daly (Shamrock Rovers 2), Plev Ellis (Bohemians 1), Alf Rigby (St James's Gate 2), Joey Donnelly (Dundalk 2), Paddy Monahan (Sligo Rovers 1). **Captain:** Paddy Gaskins.

Ireland opened their two-match European tour with this defeat by Switzerland. The Swiss, who were the better team on the ground, went close twice in the first half when Kielholz struck the crossbar and Poretti being denied by a timely tackle by Dunne. The Irish came close with headers by Rigby and Donnelly.

The second half was dominated by Switzerland but Ireland suffered a series of injury blows. Monahan and Hutchinson were injured and the latter went off to get treatment. When the left half resumed, Gaskins went off with a leg injury only to return at outside right, Daly dropping back to full back.

A breakaway by Amado resulted in a cross to Kielholz, who looked to be well offside as he received the ball. The winger must have thought so too because he hesitated. Taking this hesitation as an offside decision by the referee, Dunne picked the ball up and, to the amazement of the players, the referee awarded a penalty which was tucked away by Swiss captain Weiler.

In the last minute Dunne and O'Kane sent Ellis away on the right wing. The inside right beat Minelli and sent in a hard cross shot which eluded Bizzozzero, hit the upright and went wide, just as Donnelly threw himself forward and missed the ball by inches.

Jim Foley collects safely as Switzerland attack

Bizzozzero (Switzerland) is beaten to the ball, but the ball goes wide

Match No. 13 — GERMANY — Away

Wednesday 8th May, 1935 – Dortmund

GERMANY (1) 3 Damminger 31, 47, Lehner 88
REP. OF IRELAND (1) 1 Ellis 19

Ref: Krist (Czechoslovakia) **Ground:** Kampfbahn Rote Erde **Att:** 35,000

Germany: F. Buchloh, P. Janes, W. Tiefel, P. Zielinski, L. Goldbrunner, J. Bender, E. Lehner, O. Siffling, A. Lenz, L. Damminger, J. Fath.

Ireland: Jim Foley (Glasgow Celtic 5), Paddy Gaskins (Shamrock Rovers 5), Leo Dunne (Manchester City 2), Paddy O'Kane (Bohemians 3), Charlie Lennon (St James's Gate 3), Freddie Hutchinson (Drumcondra 2), Plev Ellis (Bohemians 2), Paddy Moore (Aberdeen 6), Alf Rigby (St James's Gate 3), Joey Donnelly (Dundalk 3), Paddy Monahan (Sligo Rovers 2). **Captain:** Paddy Gaskins.

Both sides opened nervously and there was little goalmouth action early on. After 15 minutes Moore tested Buchloh with a hard shot but four minutes later Ireland got a shock opening goal. A free kick on the halfway line was taken by Gaskins, who sent a hard shot into the box. As the ball came into the area it was challenged for by Ellis, German fullback Tiefel and goalkeeper Buchloh. The ball came off the heads of Ellis and Tiefel, leaving Buchloh stranded, and bounded into the net.

The Germans equalised when they were awarded a free kick for a foul on Lehner by Dunne. The winger took the free himself which Foley knocked onto the crossbar and when it bounced down Damminger tapped it into the net.

At half-time both O'Kane and Foley were found to be carrying injuries and after the break O'Kane went to outside right with Ellis going to right half. This switch upset the side and Germany capitalised to score twice more.

Following a great run and measured cross by Lehner, Ludwig Damminger was left with a simple tap in for his second goal. Then, with two minutes to go, Lehner broke from midfield and unleashed a thunderbolt of a shot from 30 yards which ended up in the roof of the net.

Match No. 14 — HOLLAND — Away

Sunday 8th December, 1935 – Dublin

REP. OF IRELAND (3) 3 Ellis 13, Horlacher 32, 35
HOLLAND (2) 5 Bakhuys 1, Van Nellen 15, 48, Drok 69, Smit 88

Ref: Bauwens (Germany) **Ground:** Dalymount Park **Att:** 22,000

Ireland: William Harrington (Cork 1), William O'Neill (Dundalk 1), Bill McGuire (Bohemians 1), William Glen (Shamrock Rovers 5), Paddy Andrews (Bohemians 1), Joe O'Reilly (Brideville 4), Plev Ellis (Bohemians 3), Joey Donnelly (Dundalk 4), Paddy Moore (Shamrock Rovers 7), Fred Horlacher (Bohemians 6), Joe Kendrick (Dolphin 4). **Captain:** William Glen.

Holland: L. Halle, B. Caldenhove, B. Weber, G. Van Heel, W. Anderiesen, B. Paauwe, J. Van Nellen, J. Smit, E. Bakhuys, D. Drok, F. Wels.

Straight from the kick-off the Dutch attacked and Glen was harshly penalised for a tackle on Smit. Drok took the free kick and gave the ball to Wels. The winger rounded a defender and crossed for Bakhuys to score.

Halle saved from Horlacher and Kendrick before Ireland got an equaliser. Moore, with an extraordinary jump, met Horlachers high cross with a looping header. As the ball was dropping on the goalline, Ellis raced in and knocked it home before Halle could get to it.

From the kick-off Bakhuys sent Van Nellen clear and he dribbled into position before unleashing a 40 yard shot which found the back of the net. The Dutch almost increased their lead soon after but Drok shot against the post and sent the rebound wide.

Ireland got an equaliser when Moore's jump allowed Horlacher to smack a 25 yard volley home off the underside of the crossbar. Three minutes later, Donnelly sent Ellis clear to cross for Horlacher to head Ireland into the lead.

Holland started the second half well and chances fell to Smit and Drok before Van Nellen equalised with an overhead kick from Wels's corner. A minute later Glen was brought down in the box and Ireland were awarded a penalty. O'Reilly's spot kick was saved at the second attempt by Halle.

Following this the Dutch regained the lead when Bakhuys and Smit set up Drok to score with a speedy shot on the run. With 2 minutes to go Drok had another shot parried by Harrington. The ball fell to Bakhuys who passed to Wels. The wingers high cross was met with a downward header by Smit and although Andrews stopped it the referee ruled it had crossed the line.

Match No. 15 — SWITZERLAND — Home

Tuesday 17th March, 1936 – Dublin

REP. OF IRELAND (1) 1 Dunne 34
SWITZERLAND (0) 0

Ref: Langenus (Belgium) **Ground:** Dalymount Park **Att:** 32,000

Ireland: William Harrington (Cork 2), William O'Neill (Dundalk 2), Bill Gorman (Bury 1), William Glen (Shamrock Rovers 6), Charlie Turner (Southend 1), Joe O'Reilly (Brideville 5), Plev Ellis (Bohemians 4), Joey Donnelly (Dundalk 5), Jimmy Dunne (Arsenal 2), Fred Horlacher (Bohemians 7), Jimmy Kelly (Derry City 3). **Captain:** William Glen.

Switzerland: G. Schlegel, S. Minelli, W. Weiler, F. Defago, F. Jaccard, E. Müller, E. Diebold, L. Kielholz, A. Frigerio, J. Spagnoli, G. Aeby.

Ireland were much the more superior team and had it not been for the excellent goalkeeping of Schlegel they could have won by a bigger margin. The Irish were not happy with the rugged defending of the Swiss and this too accounted for the lack of goals.

Schlegel saved two shots from Horlacher, headers from O'Reilly and Dunne, two more shots from Horlacher and a shot form Dunne before Aeby and Spagnoli forced Harrington into action.

After 34 minutes a mistake by Jaccard put Ellis in possession. The winger gave the ball to Dunne in the clear. The centre-forward rounded the goalkeeper and shot to the empty goal only for the ball to be blocked on the line by Minelli. Horlacher quickly seized on the rebound and squared the ball back in for Dunne to tap it home.

Dunne could have added a second but was pulled back in the process of shooting into an open goal – an infringement the referee did not see.

Kielholz had a chance at the start of the second half to score but missed. Dunne and Ellis had further chances as had Frigerio near the end but in the end Ireland had to settle for one goal.

Match No. 16 — HUNGARY — AWAY

Sunday 3rd May, 1936 – Budapest

HUNGARY (1) 3 Sarosi 7, 48 (pen), Sas 75
REP. OF IRELAND (2) 3 Dunne 12, 68, Joe O'Reilly 19

Ref: Bruell (Czechoslovakia) **Ground:** Hungaria Uti Stadium **Att:** 20,000

Hungary: A. Szabo, G. Futo, K. Deri, I. Bela Magda, J. Turay, J. Dudas, F. Sas, J. Vincze, G. Sarosi, L. Cseh II, T. Kemeny. **Subs:** J. Hada for Szabo (half-time).

Ireland: William Harrington (Cork 3), William O'Neill (Dundalk 3), Bill Gorman (Bury 2), William Glen (Shamrock Rovers 7), Con Moulson (Lincoln City 1), Joe O'Reilly (Brideville 6), Harry Duggan (Leeds United 3), Joey Donnelly (Dundalk 6), Jimmy Dunne (Arsenal 3), Owen Madden (Cork 1), Bill Fallon (Notts County 2). **Captain:** William Glen.

Ireland began their three-match tour of Europe with this magnificent draw against a strong Hungarian side. The Irish long-ball tactics and wingers troubled the Hungarians who played a short-passing game.

Hungary had a good opening and Harrington was in action early on. After seven minutes Sas got away and, from the corner flag, sent in a low cross which Sarosi dispatched into the net. Five minutes later O'Reilly sent a long ball forward to Dunne. The centre-forward took it in his stride, ran on a few yards and sent in a powerful shot which found the back of the net. Seven minutes later Ireland were awarded a free kick 30 yards out. Joe O'Reilly stepped up to take it and surprised everyone when he drove it high into the net.

Three minutes into the second half Moulson handled the ball in the box and Sarosi scored from the spot. Ireland took the lead again when Dunne scored with a magnificent 20 yards shot.

Immediately after this goal the bad weather, which had hung over the city for days, unleashed a heavy shower. This suited the Hungarins better and with 15 minutes to go Sas cut inside and shot. Harrington had it covered but the ball glanced off O'Reilly's body and into the net.

Three days later the Irish played a Rhineland XI in Cologne and were beaten 4-1; Dunne scoring the Irish goal.

Match No. 17 — LUXEMBOURG — Away

Saturday 9th May, 1936 – Luxembourg

LUXEMBOURG (0) 1 Mart 59 (pen)
REP. OF IRELAND (1) 5 Dunne 9, 86, J. Donnelly 65, Kelly 71, 87

Ref: Bauwens (Germany) **Ground:** Municipal Stadium **Att:** 8,000

Luxembourg: J. P. Hoscheid, J. P. Frisch, V. Majerus, J. Schmit, A. Kieffer, J. Fischer, O. Stamet, A. Schmit, L. Mart, R. Geib, T. Speicher.

Ireland: William Harrington (Cork 4), William O'Neill (Dundalk 4), Bill Gorman (Bury 3), William Glen (Shamrock Rovers 8), Con Moulson (Lincoln City 2), Joe O'Reilly (Brideville 7), Harry Duggan (Leeds United 4), Joey Donnelly (Dundalk 7), Jimmy Dunne (Arsenal 4), Plev Ellis (Bohemians 5), Jimmy Kelly (Derry City 4). **Captain:** William Glen.

A hard pitch spoilt a good game which was dominated by Ireland. The visitors took the lead when Dunne headed in an O'Reilly free kick. Ellis, Duggan and Dunne, again, had further chances as had Stamet for Luxembourg, before the break.

Ireland continued to press in the second period but an infringement by Moulson gave Mart the chance to equalise with a penalty kick.

After 20 minutes Dunne fed Donnelly and the inside right scored with a 20 yard shot. Dunne set up Ireland's third when he passed to Kelly and the winger scored with a glorious shot. O'Reilly went close with another shot, which was just over, before Dunne and Kelly wrapped up a splendid victory.

Match No. 18 — GERMANY — Home

Saturday 17th October, 1936 – Dublin

REP. OF IRELAND (2) 5 J. Donnelly 25, 69, Davis 35 (pen), 76, Geoghegan 59
GERMANY (2) 2 Kobierski 26, Szepan 32

Ref: Webb (Scotland) **Ground:** Dalymount Park **Att:** 28,000

Ireland: Jim Foley (Glasgow Celtic 6), William O'Neill (Dundalk 5), Bill Gorman (Bury 4), Joe O'Reilly (St James's Gate 8), Charlie Turner (Southend 2), Hugh Connolly (Cork 1), Plev Ellis (Bohemians 6), Joey Donnelly (Dundalk 8), Tom Davis (Oldham Athletic 1), Paddy Moore (Shamrock Rovers 8), Matty Geoghegan (St James's Gate 1), **Captain:** Charlie Turner.

Germany: H. Jakob, R. Muenzenberg, A. Munkert, J. Rodzinski, L. Goldbrunner, A. Kitzinger, E. Lehner, O. Siffling, K. Hohmann, F. Szepan, S. Kobierski.

The Irish tactics of stopping the German short-passing game, combined with magnificent displays by the Irish defence and forward line, especially Moore, paved the way for a famous victory.

An end-to-end game exploded into life after 25 minutes with 4 goals in a ten minute spell. Moore sent a pass out to Geoghegan on the wing. The winger sent in a low cross which found Donnelly and he scored with a low shot.

Within a minute the Irish were caught cold and when Lehner's cross found Kobierski, the winger scored with a low shot from close range.

A shot by Moore hit an upright before Germany went in front. Kobierski was sent clear on the wing and his cross was scrambled clear to Szepan who scored with a fast shot. Ireland equalised when Turner and O'Reilly sent Davis dashing in on goal. As he was about to score, Goldbrunner brought him down for a penalty. Davis got up and scored from the spot himself.

Ireland should have had another penalty when Geoghegan was brought down in the box and Germany almost got a goal when Kobierski's chip shot was saved by Foley.

Despite an early escape at the start of the second half, it was a half of Irish pressure. After 14 minutes an accurate cross by Moore was headed clear by a defender. Ellis headed the ball back to the far post where Geoghegan flung himself at it and the ball went in off his chest. Geoghegan could have had another goal but he headed wide with a free header from 6 yards.

On 69 minutes a cross by Moore was headed on by Ellis to Donnelly. The inside-rights shot was deflected into the net by Muenzenberg but Donnelly claimed the goal as it was going in anyway.

Seven minutes later Moore dribbled through the defence and sent in a powerful shot from 25 yards. Jakob parried it but was unable to hold the ball and, as the ball dropped on the line, Davis ran in to slide it home.

Match No. 19 — HUNGARY — Home

Sunday 6th December, 1936 – Dublin

REP. OF IRELAND (1) 2 Fallon, Davis (pen)
HUNGARY (2) 3 Titkos, Vincze, Toldi

Ref: Nattrass (England) **Ground:** Dalymount Park **Att:** 27,000

Ireland: Jim Foley (Glasgow Celtic 7), William O'Neill (Dundalk 6), Bill Gorman (Bury 5), Joe O'Reilly (St James's Gate 9), Charlie Turner (Southend 3), Con Moulson (Notts County 3), Plev Ellis (Bohemians 7), Joey Donnelly (Dundalk 9), Tom Davis (Oldham Athletic 2), Paddy Moore (Shamrock Rovers 9), Bill Fallon (Notts County 3),. **Captain:** Charlie Turner.

Hungary: J. Palinkas, G. Polgar, J. Vago, J. Turay, G. Szucs, J. Dudas, L. Cseh II, J. Vincze, G. Sarosi, G. Toldi, P. Titkos. **Subs:** A. Szabo for Palinkas.

In an exciting game Ireland pressured the Hungarian goal for long periods but lost because they were not able to combat the visitors superb teamwork. The Irish took the lead after 20 minutes when a pass intended for Davis was back-headed by Polgar to Fallon. The winger shot past the goalkeeper from 22 yards to score.

Moore went off with an eye injury and, while he was receiving treatment, Hungary scored twice in a minute. After 36 minutes Foley saved, but could not hold a free kick, and Titkos pounced to score. Then a harmless-looking cross from Dudas was allowed to go the Vincze who had no trouble in adding another. Before the break Toldi missed a great chance to get a third.

Three minutes into the second half a low cross form Cseh was taken on the run by Toldi. The inside left side-stepped a tackle by O'Neill and went on to score past the advancing Foley.

Although Hungary came close to scoring twice more, what followed was almost continious Irish pressure. Szucs was penalised for handball and Davis got one back from the penalty spot. Ireland might have had a second penalty when Donnelly was fouled in the box but the referee played advantage and Donnelly went on but missed.

Match No. 20 **SWITZERLAND** **Away**

Monday 17th May, 1937 – Berne

SWITZERLAND (0) 0
REP. OF IRELAND (1) 1 Dunne 30

Ref: Lewington (England) **Ground:** Wankdorf Stadium **Att:** 25,000

Switzerland: Bizzozzero, Minelli, G. Lehmann, Liniger, Vernati, Lörtscher, Bickel, P. Aebi, Rupf, Karcher, G. Aebi.

Ireland: Tommy Breen (Manchester United 1), William O'Neill (Dundalk 7), Johnny Feenan (Sunderland 1), Joe O'Reilly (St James's Gate 10), Charlie Turner (Southend 4), Con Moulson (Notts County 4), Johnny Brown (Coventry City 1), Davy Jordan (Wolves 1), Jimmy Dunne (Southampton 5), Paddy Farrell (Hibernian 1), Bill Fallon (Notts County 4). **Captain:** Charlie Turner.

The Swiss began very well and threatened the Irish goal on several occasions. Tommy Breen brought off some good saves and this, combined with some poor finishing, kept the Irish goal intact.

After Karcher had shot wide when sent clear, Dunne had a chance when he broke through the defence but his shot was saved. Fallon and Rupf had further chances and Jordan headed just over following a cross from Fallon.

In another breakaway, Ireland attacked down the middle. Jordan gave the ball to Dunne and the centre-forward scored with a splendid low shot from 20 yards.

At the start of the second half Dunne nearly got a second but headed inches wide. Georges Aebi came close for Switzerland when his shot struck the crossbar and in the last minute Bickel had a great chance but his shot struck the post.

The Irish panel which played against Switzerland at Berne in 1937. The same team played against France 6 days later – The first time an Irish team was unchanged for consecutive games.
Players Standing (L to R): *Johnny Feenan, Mick McCarthy (Shamrock Rovers), Joe O'Reilly, Charlie Turner, Tommy Breen and Con Moulson.*
Kneeling (L to R): *Johnny Brown, Davy Jordan, Jimmy Dunne, William O'Neill, Paddy Farrell and Willie (Bill) Fallon.*

Ireland's captain, Charlie Turner, meets his Swiss counterpart, Serverino Minelli

Ireland's Joe O'Reilly clears from Swiss winger Georges Aebi. Irish players from left to right are William O'Neill, Tommy Breen, Joe O'Reilly and Charlie Turner

Match No. 21 FRANCE Away

Sunday 23rd May, 1937 – Paris

FRANCE (0) 0
REP. OF IRELAND (0) 2 Jordan 52, Brown 58

Ref: Krist (Czechoslovakia) **Ground:** Colombes Stadium **Att:** 16,688

France: Di Lorto, Ben Bouali, Diagne, Bourbotte, Meuris, Delfour, Lauri, Ignace, Courtois, Frutuoso, Aston.

Ireland: Tommy Breen (Manchester United 2), William O'Neill (Dundalk 8), Johnny Feenan (Sunderland 2), Joe O'Reilly (St James's Gate 11), Charlie Turner (Southend 5), Con Moulson (Notts County 5), Johnny Brown (Coventry City 2), Davy Jordan (Wolves 2), Jimmy Dunne (Southampton 6), Paddy Farrell (Hibernian 2), Bill Fallon (Notts County 5). **Captain:** Charlie Turner.

The game opened at a terrific pace. Ireland were slow to settle on a perfect pitch and in the hot conditions the French dominated the first twenty minutes. French winger Lauri had three chances to score in that period but Breen saved one, another hit the underside of the crossbar and the third was a penalty for handball after 12 minutes which he hit straight at Breen and the goalkeeper saved well.

Ireland came more into the game following this initial French attack and chances fell to Fallon, Farrell, Brown and Dunne. At the other end Courtois had a shot rebound off a post and, as Breen came out to clear, Ignace shot just over the crossbar.

During the break the Irish altered their forward line with Dunne, who was tightly marked, changing places with Jordan. This change had an immediate effect on the match. After 7 minutes Brown's right wing cross found Moulson up in support of the attack. The left half then gave it to Jordan and the "new" centre-forward took the ball on a few yards before shooting on the run to give Di Lorto no chance of saving.

The French pressed forward to get an equaliser but a long pass downfield from O'Reilly found Dunne who transfered it to Jordan. The latter lobbed the ball over Meuris to Brown and the winger scored the second.

Dunne nearly had a third soon after but the goalkeeper saved well. The French had two late chances but Courtois had a shot saved by Breen and Ignace hit the post.

Match No. 22 — NORWAY — Away

Sunday 10th October, 1937 – Oslo (World Cup)

NORWAY (1) 3 Kvammen 30, 64, Martinsen 78
REP. OF IRELAND (1) 2 Geoghegan 37, Dunne 49

Ref: Bauwens (Germany) **Ground:** Ullevaal Stadium **Att:** 19,000

Norway: T. Blohm, R. Johannesen, O. Holmsen, F. Ulleberg, N. Eriksen, R. Holmberg, O. Frantzen, R. Kvammen, A. Martinsen, M. Isaksen, A. Brustad.

Ireland: George McKenzie (Southend 1), Joe Williams (Shamrock Rovers 1), Mick Hoy (Dundalk 1), Joe O'Reilly (St James's Gate 12), Charlie Turner (Southend 6), Owen Kinsella (Shamrock Rovers 2), Tom Donnelly (Drumcondra 1), Joey Donnelly (Dundalk 10), Jimmy Dunne (Shamrock Rovers 7), Billy Jordan (Bohemians 2), Matty Geoghegan (St James's Gate 2). **Captain:** Charlie Turner.

In this first leg of the qualifying group for the 1938 World Cup, Ireland came away with a good result but should have been well beaten by a dominant Norwegian side whose star was inside right Kvammen. The Irish, who had been travelling for four days, looked tired and only good goalkeeping from McKenzie kept the Norwegians at bay.

In excellent conditions the Norwegians opened at terrific speed and, following many escapes, the Irish goal finally fell when Kvammen knocked home a corner kick. However the Irish responded well and, after Dunne had a shot saved, Geoghegan shot home the equaliser following good work by O'Reilly.

Isaksen and Martinsen both had chances to put Norway ahead before Martinsen was fouled in the box and the referee awarded a penalty. Holmberg hit the spot-kick against the post and it went wide.

Four minutes into the second half an Irish attack ended with Dunne shooting in Jordan's pass for the lead. More Norwegian pressure followed before Kvammen equalised when he put away Brustad's cross.

The Irish came close to grabbing a lead again through Geoghegan and Dunne before Isaksen set up Martinsen to score the winner from close range. Norway finished the stronger and had a number of chances to increase the score before the final whistle blew.

Match No. 23 NORWAY Home

Sunday 7th November, 1937 – Dublin (World Cup)

REP. OF IRELAND (1) 3 Dunne 10, K. O'Flanagan 62, Duggan 88
NORWAY (2) 3 Kvammen 16, 33, Martinsen 49

Ref: Gibbs (England) **Ground:** Dalymount Park **Att:** 27,000

Ireland: George McKenzie (Southend 2), William O'Neill (Dundalk 9), Bill Gorman (Bury 6), Joe O'Reilly (St James's Gate 13), Charlie Turner (Southend 7), Tom Arrigan (Waterford 1), Kevin O'Flanagan (Bohemians 1), Harry Duggan (Newport County 5), Jimmy Dunne (Shamrock Rovers 8), Johnny Carey (Manchester United 1), Tommy Foy (Shamrock Rovers 1). **Captain:** Charlie Turner.

Norway: S. Nordby, R. Johannesen, O. Holmsen, K. Henriksen, N. Eriksen, R. Holmberg, K. Eeg, R. Kvammen, A. Martinsen, O. Frantzen, J. Hval.

A very entertaining game, with a real cup-tie atmosphere, saw Norway qualify for the 1938 World Cup finals, 6-5 on aggregate. The game was played in a very sporting manner and the large attendance responded with the famous "Dalymount Roar". For the first time both sides wore numbered jerseys.

Norway set out to defend their first-leg lead but after five minutes Turner and Carey sent Kevin O'Flanagan in to score but the referee ruled it out for offside. Five minutes later Duggan headed on Foy's cross for Dunne to head the opening goal.

Duggan had another chance before Norway went on the offensive when a mistake in defence allowed Holmberg to set up Kvammen and the latter scored with a high shot into the roof of the net.

Carey shot across the goal and had a header just over before Norway got a second on a breakaway. Martinsen beat Gorman and drew McKenzie before shooting. O'Neill got back and cleared off the line but the ball fell to Kvammen who worked his way into the box and scored.

Before the break Duggan, Foy and Kvammen all had chances but failed. Four minutes into the second period Frantzen sent Martinsen away to score off a post. Kvammen came close soon after to completing his hat-trick but shot wide.

Carey sent an O'Flanagan corner wide before a cross by Foy was back-headed by Dunne for O'Flanagan to score. O'Flanagan had another chance soon after but so had Martinsen, Kvammen and Hval. With two minutes to go Turner sent Carey in and from the latters cross Duggan shot home the equaliser.

Match No. 24 CZECHOSLOVAKIA Away

Wednesday 18th May, 1938 – Prague

CZECHOSLOVAKIA (1) 2 Nejedly 3 (pen), 46
REP. OF IRELAND (1) 2 Davis 42, Dunne 89

Ref: Barlassina (Italy) **Ground:** AC Sparta Stadium **Att:** 17,000

CSSR: Planicka, Burgr, Davcik, Kostalek, Boucek, Kopecky, Riha, Simunek, V. Bradac, Ludl, Nejedly.

Ireland: George McKenzie (Southend 3), Paddy Gaskins (St James's Gate 6), Bill Gorman (Bury 7), Joe O'Reilly (St James's Gate 14), Matt O'Mahoney (Bristol Rovers 1), Charlie Turner (West Ham United 8), Kevin O'Flanagan (Bohemians 2), Jimmy Dunne (Shamrock Rovers 9), Tom Davis (Tranmere Rovers 3) Johnny Carey (Manchester United 2), Tim O'Keeffe (Waterford 2). **Captain:** Charlie Turner.

Despite the fact that they were down to ten men for most of the second half, Czechoslovakia should have won this encounter as they were the better attacking side. Ireland put up a good performance but were unsettled by an early goal when Nejedly scored from the penalty spot after handball by Gorman. Following this Bradac had a shot over, Nejedly shot wide and Simunek hit the post with another shot.

Three minutes before the break Ireland got an equaliser. Davis gathered a cross from O'Keeffe and, seeing that the two centre-backs misread each others intentions, he ran between them and scored from close range.

Czechoslovakia got a great start to the second half when, from the kick-off, Nejedly raced away, beat two or three men and scored a brilliant solo goal.

The Irish fought back and forced the Czechs to defend. Nejedly was hurt and went off; he did not return. Boucek was injured later and forced to leave the field; he resumed at outside right. Meanwhile Riha came close when his shot struck the bar.

In the last minute, Dunne received the ball in the Czech half. Despite being a long way out he sent in a long range shot which completely beat Planicka and found the net. A magnificient goal.

Match No. 25 — POLAND — Away

Sunday 22nd May, 1938 – Warsaw

POLAND (3) 6 Piontek (2), Wodarz (2), Wilimowski, Wasiewicz

REP. OF IRELAND (0) 0

Ref: Majorsky (Hungary) **Ground:** Military Stadium **Att:** 40,000

Poland: Madejski, Szczepaniak, Galecki, Gora, Wasiewicz, Dytko, Piec I, Piontek, Wilimowski, Scherfke II, Wodarz.

Ireland: George McKenzie (Southend 4), Paddy Gaskins (St James's Gate 7), Bill Gorman (Bury 8), Joe O'Reilly (St James's Gate 15), Matt O'Mahony (Bristol Rovers 2), Charlie Turner (West Ham United 9), Kevin O'Flanagan (Bohemians 3), Jimmy Dunne (Shamrock Rovers 10), Tom Davis (Tranmere Rovers 4), Johnny Carey (Manchester United 3), Tim O'Keeffe (Waterford 3). **Subs:** William Harrington (Cork 5), for McKenzie (69 mins). **Captain:** Charlie Turner.

Ireland suffered their heaviest pre-war defeat in this first meeting with Poland. Irish newspaper reports credit Piontek with four goals and Wodarz with two but official Polish records give the goalscorers as listed above. Thus there are doubts about certain goalscorers and so the match report only includes names of known scorers.

Ireland started well and had three early chances. After 12 minutes Piontek opened the scoring with a fine low drive to the right hand corner of the net. Ireland continued to attack and chances fell to Davis and Carey before Wodarz got Polands second goal after 30 minutes. Dunne had two further chances to pull a goal back but 2 minutes before the break Poland got a third following a quick counter-attack.

Five minutes into the second half a fine bout of passing ended with a fourth goal and, while Carey and Davis had more chances, a fine solo run gave Poland a fifth score. McKenzie was injured trying to save and was replaced by Harrington. Near the end a strong cross-cum-shot by Wodarz was left by the substitute goalkeeper, who thought it was going over. Instead the ball found the top right-hand corner of the net.

Match No. 26 — SWITZERLAND — Home

Sunday 18th September, 1938 – Dublin

REP. OF IRELAND (3) 4 Bradshaw (2), Dunne, T. Donnelly

SWITZERLAND (0) 0

Ref: Mortimer (England) **Ground:** Dalymount Park **Att:** 31,000

Ireland: George McKenzie (Southend 5), Bill Gorman (Bury 9), Mick Hoy (Dundalk 2), Joe O'Reilly (St James's Gate 16), Matt O'Mahoney (Bristol Rovers 3), Dick Lunn (Dundalk 1), Tom Donnelly (Shamrock Rovers 2), Jimmy Dunne (Shamrock Rovers 11), Paddy Bradshaw (St James's Gate 1), Johnny Carey (Manchester United 4), Bill Fallon (Notts County 6). **Captain:** Jimmy Dunne.

Switzerland: Huber, Minelli, G. Lehmann, Springer, Vernati, Lörtscher, Bickel, T. Abegglen, Amado, Walaschek, G. Aeby.

The start of the game was delayed by ten minutes when the Swiss refused to play unless they were allowed to obstruct forwards while defending their goal. It was a rule which was dropped the previous season but, on agreement with Jimmy Dunne, the referee allowed the Swiss to use such tactics.

Within 20 seconds, however, the Swiss were a goal down . From the kick-off Dunne played a one-two with Donnelly and shot weakly at goal. Huber picked the ball up and, as he kicked it out, Bradshaw ran in, blocked the kick out with his foot and the ball bounced into the goal.

After 8 minutes Ireland got another when Dunne nodded home a corner by Fallon. There followed chances for Fallon and Bradshaw before Bradshaw headed in Dunnes cross after 20 minutes for the third goal.

Bradshaw and Dunne had more chances before Abegglen forced McKenzie into a full length save. Aeby had another chance but was denied by some good defending by Gorman. On the whole Ireland had dominated the first period and the story was the same after the break.

Carey headed wide as did Donnelly soon after the restart. Ireland got a fourth goal when Donnelly sent Fallon clear on the wing. The winger sent a low cross across the goal for Donnelly to sweep it in at the far post. Near the end Aeby shot against the post with McKenzie punching away the rebound. Aeby had one last chance but shot across the goal with nobody there to finish.

Match No. 27 — POLAND — Home

Sunday 13th November, 1938 – Dublin

REP. OF IRELAND (2) 3 Fallon 10, Carey 12, Dunne 68
POLAND (1) 2 Wilimowski 15, Piontek 75

Ref: Bauwens (Germany) **Ground:** Dalymount Park **Att:** 34,295

Ireland: George McKenzie (Southend 6), Bill Gorman (Bury 10), Mick Hoy (Dundalk 3), Joe O'Reilly (St James's Gate 17), Matt O'Mahony (Bristol Rovers 4), Dick Lunn (Dundalk 2), Kevin O'Flanagan (Bohemians 4), Jimmy Dunne (Shamrock Rovers 12), Paddy Bradshaw (St James's Gate 2), Johnny Carey (Manchester United 5), Bill Fallon (Notts County 7),. **Captain:** Jimmy Dunne.

Poland: E. Madejski, W. Szezepaniak, A. Galecki, W. Gora, E. Nyc, E.Dytko, L. Piontek, I. Piec, J. Wostal, G. Wodarz, E. Wilimowski. **Subs:** Mrugala for Madejski (14 minutes), Madejski resumed in goal when Mrugala was injured on 46 minutes).

Ireland, thanks to a superior first half performance, scored two goals in the first 15 minutes but could have had four before Poland pulled a goal back, inspiring them into a better second half display. A heavy shower restricted good football but it was an exciting clean game.

O'Flanagan had an early opening when set up by Carey and Dunne but shot into the side netting. After 10 minutes Bradshaw challenged Madejski and the ball fell loose for Carey to shoot. Carey's shot was blocked but Fallon put away the rebound. Two minutes later Carey headed in a Fallon corner to put Ireland two up.

Ireland continued to press and another challenge on Madejski, this time by O'Flanagan, gave Bradshaw the chance to put the ball into the net. However the Polish goalkeeper was injured and the goal disallowed for offside. Madejski went off and Mrugala took over in goal.

Poland pulled a goal back a minute later. Wostal sent in a hard shot which McKenzie knocked into the air and Wilimowski followed up to head home. Ireland kept pressing and Bradshaw shot two good chances wide before the interval.

Mrugala was injured in a clash with Bradshaw at the beginning of the second period and Madejski had to re-take his place in goal. He was beaten for the third time when Dunne headed a corner by O'Flanagan into the net. With 15 minutes to go McKenzie dropped a shot from Wilimowski and Piontek shot home past a group of players.

Match No. 28 **HUNGARY** **Home**

Sunday 19th March, 1939 – Cork

REP. OF IRELAND (1) 2 Bradshaw 14, Carey 87
HUNGARY (1) 2 Zsengeller 35, Kollath 50

Ref: **Ground:** The Mardyke **Att:** 18,000

Ireland: George McKenzie (Southend 7), Bill Gorman (Brentford 11), Mick Hoy (Dundalk 4), Joe O'Reilly (St James's Gate 18), Charlie Turner (West Ham United 10), E. Weir (Clyde 1), Kevin O'Flanagan (Bohemians 5), Jimmy Dunne (Shamrock Rovers 13), Paddy Bradshaw (St James's Gate 3), Johnny Carey (Manchester United 6), Tommy Foy (Shamrock Rovers 2). **Captain:** Jimmy Dunne

Hungary: A. Szabo, L. Koranyi, S. Biro, G. Lazar, B. Sarosi III, I Balogh I, S. Adam, G. Zsengeller, F. Kollath, I. Kiszely, L. Gyetvai.

The lack of something akin to a "Dalymount Roar" in this first full international in Cork seemed to affect the players. After a bright opening quarter, which yielded a goal, the Irish seemed to lose heart and allowed Hungary back into the game. Only a late rally salvaged a draw.

In an impressive opening Carey and Foy had early chances before Koranyi gave away an unnecessary corner. Foy took the flag kick and Bradshaw stooped down to head it into the net.

After this nearly all the play was Hungary's. Both Gyetvai and Kiszely were denied goals by McKenzie while Kollath hit a post and Adam sent the rebound wide of an open goal. Adam, though, had a hand in the equaliser when his ball in behind the Irish defence allowed Kollath to race through, control the ball and shoot past McKenzie.

Hungary went ahead early in the second half when Lazar and Kollath put Zsengeller in to shoot past the advancing goalkeeper. Near the end Ireland staged a late recovery and were rewarded with an equaliser. Dunne and Carey sent Foy away in the clear. The winger found Bradshaw who fed it up for Carey to smack the ball home with a great shot.

A panoramic view of the Mardyke during the Ireland versus Hungary match in 1939. The picture above left shows Kevin O'Flanagan going on the attack, while the picture on the right shows Bradshaw scoring the opening goal

Match No. 29 HUNGARY Away

Thursday 18th May, 1939 – Budapest

HUNGARY (1) 2 Kollath 41, Sarosi 86
REP. OF IRELAND (0) 2 K. O'Flanagan 53, 80

Ref: **Ground:** MTK Stadium **Att:** 25,000

Hungary: A. Szabo, K. Kis, S. Biro, A. Szalay, G. Szucs, I. Balogh, J. Szanto, G. Sarosi, F. Kollath, I. Kiszely, A. Nagy.

Ireland: George McKenzie (Southend 8), William O'Neill (Dundalk 10), Mick Hoy (Dundalk 5), Joe O'Reilly (St James's Gate 19), Matt O'Mahoney (Bristol Rovers 5), E. Weir (Clyde 2), Kevin O'Flanagan (Bohemians 6), Jimmy Dunne (Shamrock Rovers 14), Paddy Bradshaw (St James's Gate 4), Johnny Carey (Manchester United 7), Bill Fallon (Sheffield Wednesday 8). **Captain:** Jimmy Dunne.

Both sides played exciting football despite very hot conditions. There were chances at both ends early on before Fallon was forced to retire with concussion. When he resumed he immediately set up a chance for Dunne which Szabo saved.

Kollath had two chances before O'Neill was injured and had to change places with O'Reilly. Four minutes before the interval Hungary opened the scoring when Kollath netted from close range. Bradshaw almost equalised minutes later but, after beating three defenders, he delayed his shot and the chance was lost.

Eight minutes into the second half O'Flanagan equalised with a great 25 yard shot. Hungary pressed again for the lead but with ten minutes to go Carey put O'Flanagan free again. The winger took the ball on the run and beat Szabo with another shot from outside the box.

Urged on by a passionate crowd Hungary pressed for the equaliser. O'Neill collapsed with the heat but returned soon after leaving the field for treatment. With four minutes remaining Sarosi got the equaliser after some great play.

Hungary tried for a winner but the Irish defence held out for a draw which, on the overall play, they deserved.

Match No. 30 GERMANY Away

Tuesday 23rd May, 1939 – Bremen

GERMANY (1) 1 Schön 38
REP. OF IRELAND (0) 1 Bradshaw 65

Ref: Remke (Denmark) **Ground:** Weser Stadium **Att:** 35,000

Germany: H. Jakob, P. Janes, J. Streitle, A. Kupfer, H. Rohde, A. Kitzinger, E. Lehner, W. Hahnemann, J. Gauchel, H. Schön, W. Arlt.

Ireland: George McKenzie (Southend 9), William O'Neill (Dundalk 11), Mick Hoy (Dundalk 6), Joe O'Reilly (St James's Gate 20), Matt O'Mahoney (Bristol Rovers 6), E. Weir (Clyde 3), Kevin O'Flanagan (Bohemians 7), Jimmy Dunne (Shamrock Rovers 15), Paddy Bradshaw (St James's Gate 5), Johnny Carey (Manchester United 8), Bill Fallon (Sheffield Wednesday 9). **Captain:** Jimmy Dunne.

A capacity crowd packed the stadium long before the kick-off for Germany's first full international in Bremen. Germany were using this game as preparation for the 1940 Olympic football tournament and all eleven players would be eligible for that competition.

In a fast and exciting first half both sides had good scoring chances. Hahnemann shot against the post from a pass by Schön, Dunne then got a chance when Jakob dropped a free-kick by Bradshaw but the goalkeeper recovered as Dunne rushed in.

On 35 minutes Dunne was injured when he collided with Rohde and had to leave the field. Three minutes later McKenzie saved a shot by Lehner but the ball came out to Kupfer who crossed high into the box. Gauchel headed it on to Schön and he drove the ball into the net with a first time shot.

The second half was a disappointment after the hectic opening period but after ten minutes Dunne returned on the left wing while O'Flanagan moved to centre forward and Bradshaw took Dunne's place at inside right.

Three minutes later Carey had chance but Jakob saved at the expense of a corner. Eventually the good Irish play had its reward. Fallon sent a nice cross into the box and Bradshaw got to it before the goalkeeper and headed in the equaliser.

The 1940 Olympics were not held as World War Two started four months later and the Irish did not resume international soccer until the end of the conflict.

International Record	**P**	**W**	**D**	**L**	**F**	**A**
1926-1939	30	11	8	11	65	66
Home	13	5	3	5	34	32
Away	17	6	5	6	31	34

World Cup Record	**P**	**W**	**D**	**L**	**F**	**A**
1934-1939	4	0	2	2	11	15
Home	2	0	2	0	7	7
Away	2	0	0	2	4	8

Leading Goalscorers		**Most Capped Players**	
Jimmy Dunne	13	Joe O'Reilly	20
Paddy Moore	7	Jimmy Dunne	15
Paddy Bradshaw	4	William O'Neill	11
Tom Davis		Bill Gorman	
Joey Donnelly		Joey Donnelly	10
John Joe Flood		Charlie Turner	

Penalties awarded to Ireland 5 (4 scored, 1 saved)

Sullivan	v Belgium	1928	scored
Bermingham	v Hungary	1934	scored
O'Reilly	v Holland	1935	saved
Davis	v Germany	1936	scored
Davis	v Hungary	1936	scored

Penalties awarded against Ireland 7 (4 scored, 2 saved, 1 miss)

Gorostiza, Spain	1931	saved
Weiler, Switzerland	1935	scored
Sarosi, Hungary	1936	scored
Mart, Luxembourg	1936	scored
Lauri, France	1937	saved
Holmberg, Norway	1937	miss
Nejedly, Czechoslovakia	1938	scored

Hat-tricks for Ireland

John Joe Flood	3 goals	v Belgium	1929
Paddy Moore	4 goals	v Belgium	1934

Leading Goalscorers against Ireland

4 Reidar Kvammen, Norway
3 Eberhard Bakhuys, Holland
Leonard Piontek, Poland
Dr. Gyorgy Sarosi, Hungary
Jaap Smit, Holland
Arocha, Spain

Match No. 31 PORTUGAL Away

Sunday 16th June, 1946 – Lisbon

PORTUGAL (3) 3 Araujo 7, Rogerio 17, Peyroteo 20
REP. OF IRELAND (0) 1 Jack O'Reilly 55

Ref: **Ground:** Stadium of Light **Att:** 60,000

Portugal: Joao Azevedo, Alvaro Cardoso, Serafim das Neves, Mariano Amaro, A. Feliciano, F. Ferreira, M. Lourenco, A. Araujo, F. Peyroteo, F. Coiado, Rogerio de Carvalho. **Subs:** A. Bentes for Rogerio.

Ireland: Edward Courtney (Cork United 1), Billy McMillan, (Belfast Celtic 1), Tommy Aherne (Belfast Celtic 1), Johnny Carey (Manchester United 9), Jackie Vernon (Belfast Celtic 1), Peter Farrell (Shamrock Rovers 1), Jack O'Reilly (Cork United 1), Josiah Sloan (Arsenal 1), Davy Walsh (West Bromwich Albion 1), Jimmy McAlinden (Portsmouth 1), Tommy Eglington (Shamrock Rovers 1). **Subs:** Con Martin (Glentoran 1), for Courtney (30 mins). **Captain:** Peter Farrell.

Playing against a strong wind in the first half, which made ball control difficult, Ireland conceded three early goals to a faster and technically superior Portuguese side.

Portugal got an early goal when Rogerio beat the Irish defence and crossed for Araujo to score. Rogerio scored a second with a terrific drive after he had beaten McMillan and Vernon. Rogerio was also involved in the third goal when his cross found Peyroteo and the centre forward headed in off the upright.

Courtney was hurt in trying to save this last effort and went off to be replaced by Martin. The Portuguese also brought on a substitute when Bentes replaced Rogerio amid howls of protest from the crowd. Near the interval McAlinden and Walsh had chances but both efforts were well saved by Azevedo.

Ireland, with the wind behind them in the second half, dominated the play and attacked from the start. The Portuguese seemed content to 'sit' on their lead which was reduced by one when Sloan set up Jackie O'Reilly to score. Ireland pressed for more and McAlinden had a shot saved by Azevedo as had Eglington a few minutes later. The match ended with Martin saving from Bentes and Azevedo saving an effort by Walsh.

Match No. 32 SPAIN Away

Sunday 23rd June, 1946 – Madrid

SPAIN (0) 0
REP. OF IRELAND (1) 1 Sloan 37

Ref: Wartburg (Switzerland) **Ground:** Metropolitano **Att:** 45,000

Spain: Eizaguirre, Jugo, Aparico, Huerte, Ipina, Gonzalvo III, Gainza, Cesar, Martin, Panzio, Iriondo. **Subs:** Zarra for Martin (35 min).

Ireland: Con Martin (Glentoran 2), Billy McMillan (Belfast Celtic 2), Tommy Aherne (Belfast Celtic 2), Johnny Carey (Manchester United 10), Jackie Vernon (Belfast Celtic 2), Peter Farrell (Shamrock Rovers 2), Jack O'Reilly (Cork United 2), Josiah Sloan (Arsenal 2), Davy Walsh (West Bromwich Albion 2), Jimmy McAlinden (Portsmouth 2), Tommy Eglington (Shamrock Rovers 2). **Captain:** Peter Farrell.

Ireland, playing some good football, dominated the first half and, thanks to some excellent defending, achieved their first away victory over Spain.

Spain opened nervously and although they got through the defence on a few occasions Con Martin brought off some good saves while Gainza was off target in other chances. The Irish took the lead when Sloan received a pass from O'Reilly, beat Aparico and scored with a low shot. Three minutes later Walsh forced another opening but shot wide.

The Spanish started the second half with constant attacks on the Irish goal which continued right through the rest of the match. Martin was in superb form, denying several Spaniards and, even when he was beaten, McMillan was back to kick the ball off the line. Sloan, McMillan, McAlinden and Vernon were all injured with Sloan leaving the field for treatment, resuming with his head bandaged. Near the end a shot by Panzio seemed to beat Martin but the goalkeeper stuck out a leg and deflected the ball out for a corner.

The Players who toured Iberia in 1946
Front Row (left to right): *M. O'Flanagan (Bohemians), J. O'Reilly (Cork Utd.), D. Walsh (West Bromwich Albion), J. McAlinden (Portsmouth), W. McMillan (Belfast Celtic), T. Eglington (Shamrock Rovers), J. Sloan (Arsenal).*
Back Row *E. Courtney (Cork Utd.), J. Carey (Manchester Utd.), J. Vernon (Belfast Celtic), C. Martin (Glentoran), P. Farrell (Shamrock Rovers), E. Gannon (Shelbourne), T. Aherne (Belfast Celtic).*

Match No. 33 — ENGLAND — Home

Monday 30th September, 1946 – Dublin

REP. OF IRELAND (0) 0
ENGLAND (0) 1 Finney 82

Ref: Webb (Scotland) **Ground:** Dalymount Park **Att:** 31,988

Ireland: Tommy Breen (Shamrock Rovers 3), Bill Gorman (Brentford 12), Billy Hayes (Huddersfield 1), Johnny Carey (Manchester United 11), Con Martin (Glentoran 3), Willie Walsh (Manchester City 1), Kevin O'Flanagan (Arsenal 8), Paddy Coad (Shamrock Rovers 1), Michael O'Flanagan (Bohemians 1), Alex Stevenson (Everton 2), Tommy Eglington (Everton 3). **Captain:** Johnny Carey.

England: F. Swift, L. Scott, G. Hardwick, B. Wright, N. Franklin, H. Cockburn, T. Finney, R. Carter, T. Lawton, W. Mannion, R. Langton.

Despite heavy rain a huge crowd turned up at Dalymount Park two hours before kick-off, to see this first visit by England to the Irish Republic. What they saw was a thrilling match. The Irish out-played England with the defence subduing the English forward line and it was left to the two wingers, Langton and Finney, to give England a victory they did not deserve on the run of play.

England started well, forcing two corners which came to nothing. Finney set up Carter for a shot which Breen saved well. The Irish forced the English to fight for every ball and began to master the conditions. Stevenson shot through a crowd of players but Swift saved. The O'Flanagan brothers combined well and Kevin raced through on Michael's pass. Swift came out and clashed with the inside-right, the ball coming loose for Scott to knock it out for a corner to prevent Stevenson from scoring.

At the start of the second half Hayes was injured and Ireland were basically reduced to ten fit men as he never recovered. Hayes went out to the right wing, Carey took over at left back, Coad dropped back into Carey's position while Kevin O'Flanagan moved to inside right.

These changes did not seem to affect the Irish as they began much as they finished the first half. Eglington had an early chance but shot wide. England then had a good opening but Langton shot across the goal, although Carey had it covered in case of trouble.

The O'Flanagans had further chances when Kevin shot wide and Michael hit the side netting. After an hours play a movement on the left between Eglington and Stevenson set up the winger to race through and beat Swift with a grand shot which hit the crossbar and went over.

Further Irish pressure followed but with 8 minutes left England scored the only goal of the game. A good run by Langton down the left ended when his shot was parried by Breen to Lawton who gave it to Finney to score. The Irish tried for an equaliser but the closest they came was a free kick by Stevenson which was blocked by the English wall.

Match No. 34 — SPAIN — Home

Sunday 2nd March, 1947 – Dublin

REP. OF IRELAND (2) 3 D. Walsh 16, 79, Coad 23
SPAIN (1) 2 Zarra 26, 59

Ref: Barrick (England) **Ground:** Dalymount Park **Att:** 42,102

Ireland: Tommy Breen (Shamrock Rovers 4), John McGowan (Cork United 1), Johnny Carey (Manchester United 12), Peter Farrell (Everton 3), Con Martin (Leeds United 4), Willie Walsh (Manchester City 2), Kevin O'Flanagan (Arsenal 9), Paddy Coad (Shamrock Rovers 2), Davy Walsh (West Bromwich Albion 3), Alex Stevenson (Everton 3), Tommy Eglington (Everton 4), **Captain:** Johnny Carey.

Spain: Eizaguirre, Querejata, Curta, Gonzalvo III, Sans, Nando, Epi, Arsa, Zarra, Herrerita, Gainza.

The severe winter of 1947 had restricted football games both here and in Britain so when Spain came over to play Ireland a big crowd turned up, packing Dalymount Park to its limits. Such was the interest in the game that some of the attendance spilled out onto the touchlines and this almost led to the game being abandoned completely.

The snow and frost of the previous weeks had left the pitch in a bad state. One half, shadowed by the stand, was very hard while the other, exposed to the sunshine, had turned into a quagmire. The Irish adapted better to the conditions and played well.

After only 5 minutes play the game was held up due to encroachment by the crowd. Play was resumed soon after with Spain testing Breen with shots from Herrerita and Epi. After 16 minutes Stevenson's cross was headed on by Coad for Davy Walsh to deflect the ball into the net with his head.

Spain came close to equalising when Epi had the ball kicked off his foot on the goalline by Carey before Ireland got a second goal. Kevin O'Flanagan beat Nando and his shot was deflected to Coad who scored easily. Three minutes later Gainza intercepted a pass from McGowan intended for Martin. The winger raced away, found Zarra easily and the centre-forward scored with a well placed shot.

After 35 minutes Ireland were awarded a free on the touchline. Kevin O'Flanagan was unable to clear the crowd to take it so Mr. Barrick ordered both teams off the field until the touchlines could be cleared. A delay of 25 minutes followed as the Gardai managed to get the lines clear and the groundsmen re-lined them.

The teams reappeared after this break and played out the rest of the half and then Mr. Barrick turned both teams around to play on. The second "half" began with Spanish attacks and after 14 minutes they equalised. A mistake by Farrell put Gainza clear again. The winger easily beat the Irish offside trap and found Zarra who beat the advancing Breen with a low shot.

Spain continued to press and Herrerita and Gainza were both wide with good efferts. Ireland came close with a long range effort by Martin and a shot by Davy Walsh. With 11 minutes to go Davy Walsh got the winner when he headed home a high cross from Coad.

Match No. 35 PORTUGAL Home

Sunday 4th May, 1947 – Dublin

REP. OF IRELAND (0) 0
PORTUGAL (2) 2 Jesus Correia, Araujo

Ref: Pearse (England) **Ground:** Dalymount Park **Att:** 31,618

Ireland: Tommy Breen (Shamrock Rovers 5), Billy Gorman (Brentford 13), Billy Hayes (Huddersfield 2), Willie Walsh (Manchester City 3), Johnny Carey (Manchester Uniter 13), Peter Farrell (Everton 4), Kevin O'Flanagan (Arsenal 10), Paddy Coad (Shamrock Rovers 3), Davy Walsh (West Bromwich Albion 4), Alex Stevenson (Everton 4), Tommy Eglington (Everton 5). **Captain:** Johnny Carey.

Portugal: Joao Azevedo, Alvaro Cardoso, F. Ferreira, Mariano Amaro, A. Feliciano, F. Moreira, A. Jesus Correia, A. Araujo, F Peyroteo, J. Travacos, Rogerio de Carvalho.

Portugal started very well and were a goal up in twelve minutes when Peyroteo passed out to Jesus Correia and the winger scored with a bullet-like drive. The Irish seemed to recover from this early reverse and Walsh had two chances to equalise while Stevenson was denied a certain goal when his shot was blocked on the line by a defender. A minute later Stevenson was brought down in the box after beating Feliciano but the penalty claim was ignored. Two minutes later Peyroteo set up Araujo who scored with a lovely left-footed strike.

After this second goal Portugal seemed content to defend their lead but a minute into the second half Feliciano handled in the box and a penalty was awarded. Hayes took the spot kick but sent it well wide. A minute later Stevenson was again brought down in the area but the referee waved play on.

It was all Ireland in this second period but the could not breach the Portuguese defence. Ireland's best chance fell to Stevenson when he was sent clear by Davy Walsh's pass but the inside left shot straight at the advancing goalkeeper.

Match No. 36 PORTUGAL Away

Sunday 23th May, 1948 – Lisbon

PORTUGAL (2) 2 Peyroteo 22, Albano 26
REP. OF IRELAND (0) 0

Ref: **Ground:** Stadium of Light **Att:** 50,000

Portugal: F. Barrigana, Serafim das Neves, Alberto de Jesus, C. Canario, A. Feliciano, F. Ferreira, A. Jesus Correia, M. Vasques, F. Peyroteo, J. Travacos, Albano Pereira. **Subs:** J. Machado for Canario (28 mins).

Ireland: George Moulson (Lincoln City 1), Johnny Carey (Manchester United 14), Con Martin (Leeds United 5), Willie Walsh (Manchester City 4), Kevin Clarke (Drumcondra 1), Peter Farrell (Everton 5), Benny Henderson (Drumcondra 1), Paddy Coad (Shamrock Rovers 4), Davy Walsh (West Bromwich Albion 5), Alex Stevenson (Everton 5), Tommy Eglington (Everton 6). **Captain:** Johnny Carey.

On a very hot day Ireland had a good start with both Davy Walsh and Eglington having early chances. There was some good football being played by both sides and it was against the general run of play that Portugal scored their two goals.

After 22 minutes the Irish worked the ball out to the left wing but Peyroteo nipped in, intercepted a pass and sent in a screaming drive which beat Moulson. From the kick-off Ireland attacked and Davy Walsh set up Coad to shoot over.

On 26 minutes Travacos gave the ball to Jesus Correia who sent a high lobbing cross into the box. Moulson was caught in two minds before coming out but Albano got to it first and scored. Ireland had several chances coming up to the break but could not get the break through.

The second half was dull and punctuated with fouls. The Portuguese were unable to beat Ireland's offside trap and were constantly caught. The Portuguese press found this tactic "unsporting" but in fact there were few real chances created. Peyroteo had a header saved by Moulson and Coad had a shot saved by Barrigana. Late in the game Travacos and Jesus Correia had chances but the Irish defence coped well with them.

Match No. 37 — SPAIN — Away

Sunday 30th May, 1948 – Barcelona

SPAIN (1) 2 Igoa 32, 71
REP. OF IRELAND (1) 1 Moroney 24

Ref: Szel (France) **Ground:** Montjuich Stadium **Att:** 65,000

Spain: Eizaguirre, G. Alonso, Aparicio, Gonzalvo II, Alconero, Nando, Juncosa, Panizo, Cesar, Igoa, Epi. **Subs:** Aldecoa for Juncosa.

Ireland: George Moulson (Lincoln City 2), Johnny Carey (Manchester United 15), Con Martin (Leeds United 6), Willie Walsh (Manchester City 5), Kevin Clarke (Drumcondra 2), Peter Farrell (Everton 6), Alex Stevenson (Everton 6), Paddy Coad (Shamrock Rovers 5), Davy Walsh (West Bromwich Albion 6), Tommy Moroney (West Ham United 1), Benny Henderson (Drumcondra 2). **Captain:** Johnny Carey.

Ireland and Spain returned to the stadium which had hosted their first encounter 17 years ago, with Spain recording their first victory on Spanish soil against the Irish.

Ireland almost scored in the first minute when Carey sent Davy Walsh in. The centre-forward squared the ball to Coad whose shot was brilliantly saved by Eizaquirre. Moroney had another chance but shot wide. Spain had been restricted to long range efforts but, using their superior speed, came close with a header by Panizo and a Juncosa shot.

It was against the run of play that Ireland took the lead. Eizaguirre turned a shot by Stevenson around the post and from the corner Davy Walsh headed against the underside of the crossbar. The ball bounced down on the line and a melee developed. There was some confusion before the referee awarded a goal which was credited to Moroney. Spain equalised following a corner of their own – Igoa rising to head home.

Ireland had rather better of the play until half-time but the second half began with a constant siege of the Irish goal. Moulson parried a shot by Igoa and saved on the ground as Cesar tried to shoot home the rebound. Igoa had another header cleared off the line before he got a second goal when he availed of confusion in the Irish defence to knock home substitute Aldecoa's cross. Spain then employed time-wasting tactics to ensure victory and the closest Ireland came to an equaliser were shots by Henderson and Martin.

Match No. 38 — SWITZERLAND — Home

Sunday 5th December, 1948 – Dublin

REP. OF IRELAND (0) 0
SWITZERLAND (0) 1 F. Bickel 53

Ref: Reader (England) **Ground:** Dalymount Park **Att:** 25,563

Ireland: George Moulson (Lincoln City 3), Johnny Carey (Manchester United 16), Tom Keane (Swansea 1), Eddie Gannon (Notts County 1), Con Martin (Aston Villa 7), Peter Farrell (Everton 7), John O'Driscoll (Swansea 1), Paddy Coad (Shamrock Rovers 6), Davy Walsh (West Bromwich Albion 7), Alex Stevenson (Everton 7), Tommy Eglington (Everton 7). **Captain:** Johnny Carey.

Switzerland: Jucker, Gyger, Neury, Lanz, Eggimann, Bocquet, Antenen, Tamini, F. Bickel, Maillard, Amado.

Ireland dominated the play for most of the game against a poor Swiss side but again the shooting of the forwards let them down. The Irish had a number of chances early on with Eglington shooting wide after a mistake by Lanz. A back pass by Bocquet beat the goalkeeper but went wide and a shot by Stevenson was saved at the foot of the post.

Switzerland then came into the picture with Amado having a shot saved and Antenen being denied by Moulson. Jucker brought off an equally good save at the other end to deny O'Driscoll. Ireland's best chance fell to Martin when he took a free kick which went through Juckers hands and hit the post.

The second half went much like the first with Farrell and O'Driscoll bringing good saves out of Jucker. With 8 minutes gone the Swiss got a surprise goal. A free kick was awarded against Carey, 30 yards out. Bickel took the free and sent in a low shot which passed by a number of defenders, hit Moulson's arm and spun into the net.

The Swiss almost had a second a minute later but Tamini's shot, which beat Moulson, was headed off the goal-line by Keane. Ireland tried hard for an equaliser but their best chance was a free kick by Carey which was saved by Jucker.

Match No. 39 — BELGIUM — Home

Sunday 24th April, 1949 – Dublin

REP. OF IRELAND (0) 0
BELGIUM (0) 2 Mees 56, Mermans 84

Ref: Sdez (France) **Ground:** Dalymount Park **Att:** 28,018

Ireland: Willie Hayes (Limerick 1), Johnny Carey (Manchester United 17), Lar O'Byrne (Shamrock Rovers 1), Eddie Gannon (Sheffield Wednesday 2), Con Martin (Aston Villa 8), Willie Walsh (Manchester City 6), John O'Driscoll (Swansea 2), John Lawlor (Drumcondra 1), Brendan Carroll (Shelourne 1), Paddy Coad (Shamrock Rovers 7), Gerry Malone (Shelbourne 1). **Captain:** Johnny Carey.

Belgium: H. Meert, L. Aernaudts, R. Gillard, J. VanderAuwera, J. Henriet, V. Mees, V. Lemberechts, H. Coppens, J. Mermans, F. Chaves, R. Thirifays.

The Irish suffered their first defeat at the hands of Belgium in a game which contrasted sharply with the previous meetings. Whereas in previous games between the two nations the Irish forwards scored freely the problem here was the lack of finish in the forward line.

Belgium, who deserved victory on the run of play, almost scored following their first corner but O'Byrne cleared off the line from Mermans. Further chances fell to Coppens, which Hayes saved, and Chaves who shot wide. Carey had a free kick saved under the crossbar while Coad and O'Driscoll gave Carroll a great chance but he shot wide with only Meert to beat. Mermans, Chaves and Thirifays also shot wide in further Belgium attacks. Before half-time Coad took a pass from Lawlor and as he moved in on goal he was forced wide to shoot into the side netting.

On 56 minutes Belgium took the lead. Mees sent a high ball into the box. Martin, Hayes and Mermans rose to meet it but it passed over all of them and bounced into the net. Ireland fought back after this reverse with Carroll shooting across the goalmouth from a narrow angle, Malone being denied by Meert and Coad shooting wide. At the other end Thirifays and Mermans were stopped by Hayes while Coppens had a header hit the post.

Belgium's second goal was a beauty. Thirifays and Coppens set up Mermans and the centre-forward hit it first time right into the corner of the net. Near the end Belgium could have had a third but Hayes made a tremendous save to deny Mermans.

Match No. 40 — PORTUGAL — Home

Sunday 22nd May, 1949 – Dublin

REP. OF IRELAND (1) 1 Coad 35 (pen)
PORTUGAL (0) 0

Ref: Le Foll (France) **Ground:** Dalymount Park **Att:** 28,108

Ireland: Tommy Godwin (Shamrock Rovers 1), Johnny Carey (Manchester United 18), Tom Keane (Swansea 2), Eddie Gannon (Sheffield Wednesday 3), Con Martin (Aston Villa 9), Tommy Moroney (West Ham United 2), Peter Corr (Everton 1), Paddy Coad (Shamrock Rovers 8), Davy Walsh (West Bromwich Albion 8), Daniel McGowan (West Ham United 1), Tommy Eglington (Everton 8). **Subs:** Peter Farrell (Everton 8) for D. Walsh (35 minutes) (Davy Walsh returned 4 minutes later for Farrell). **Captain:** Johnny Carey.

Portugal: F. Barrigara, V. Mendes, Serafim das Neves, C. Canario, F. Antunes, F. Ferreira, A. Ferreira, M. Vasques, J. Mota, J. Travacos, Rogerio de Carvalho.

Many of the international teams that had visited Ireland on previous occasions had done so having had their squad together for some days. Portugal were no exception and travelled to Ireland having beaten Wales 3-2 a week before. Ireland had been denied such squad sessions for many games. Often players had to travel after playing a League game the day before and such was the case that a players performance depended not so much on his stamina but on the state of the Irish sea.

However, by the time the squad had been prepared for this game the League season was already over in England and the selected players were able to train together for a few days and work on tactics etc. The fact that Ireland achieved its first win in six games and turned in an excellent performance could largely be put down to this. Unfortunately Ireland was to be denied such luxuries for many years.

Portugal were on the defensive for most of the game and so Ireland had the majority of the play. Barrigara denied Eglington and Moroney early on while Felix Antunes had to head a corner by Corr off the line. On 35 minutes Walsh was brought down in the box and a penalty was awarded. Walsh went off injured, was replaced by Farrell, but returned 4 minutes later! Coad, after consultation with trainer and captain Carey, scored with the spot-kick.

A minute into the second half Davy Walsh almost got a second but his effort hit the crossbar. Coad brought a good save from Barrigara. The nearest Portugal came to scoring was when Armando Ferreira's corner was punched out by Godwin to Rogerio. Godwin seemed to be wrong footed as the winger sent in a powerful shot but the goalkeeper reacted well and caught the ball to deny Portugal an equaliser.

Match No. 41 — SWEDEN — Away

Thursday 2nd June, 1949 – Stockholm (World Cup)

SWEDEN (2) 3 S. Andersson 17 (pen), Jeppson 37, Liedholm 69

REP. OF IRELAND (1) 1 D. Walsh 9

Ref: Baert (Belgium) **Ground:** Resunda Stadium **Att:** 38,000

Sweden: K. Svensson, K. E. Andersson, E. Nilsson, K. Rosen, K. Nordahl, S. Andersson, E. Johnsson, G. Gren, H. Jeppson, H. Carlsson, N. Liedholm.

Ireland: Tommy Godwin (Shamrock Rovers 2), Johnny Carey (Manchester United 19), Tom Keane (Swansea 3), Eddie Gannon (Sheffield Wednesday 4), Con Martin (Aston Villa 10), Tommy Moroney (West Ham United 3), John O'Driscoll (Swansea 3), Paddy Coad (Shamrock Rovers 9), Davy Walsh (West Bromwich Albion 9), Daniel McGowan (West Ham United 2), Tommy Eglington (Everton 9). **Captain:** Johnny Carey.

The first post-war World Cup created a lot of interest worldwide, especially in Sweden who were the Olympic Soccer champions. Swedish football was on a high and, with a 3-1 victory over England a month earlier, they went into the competition with great confidence.

The match was played in a constant drizzle and, despite early attacks by Sweden it was Ireland who scored first. O'Driscoll lobbed a high ball into the area. Knut Nordahl missed it, giving Davy Walsh the chance to run in and score from an acute angle. Eight minutes later Sweden equalised. A header by Carlsson was booted away by Martin. The ball fell to Johnsson who sent it back into the area and a melee developed before the referee awarded a penalty against Martin for handball. Sune Andersson scored from the spot. The Swedes got a second eight minutes before the interval. Carlsson broke away and fed Johnsson to cross in for Jeppson to score.

Svensson in the Swedish goal did not have a lot to do but in the second half he was tested by a long range shot from O'Driscoll which he did well to turn away for a corner. Godwin had earlier saved a good effort from Jeppson but was beaten for a third time when Liedholm headed home a free by Gren.

Match No. 42 **SPAIN** **Home**

Sunday 12th June, 1949 – Dublin

REP. OF IRELAND (1) 1 Martin 14 (pen)
SPAIN (3) 4 Zarra 30, 36, Basora 35, Igoa 86

Ref: Ellis (England) **Ground:** Dalymount Park **Att:** 30,171

Ireland: Tommy Godwin (Shamrock Rovers 3), Johnny Carey (Manchester United 20), Tom Keane (Swansea 4), Peter Farrell (Everton 9), Con Martin (Aston Villa 11), Tommy Moroney (West Ham United 4), Peter Corr (Everton 2), Eddie Gannon (Sheffield Wednesday 5), Davy Walsh (West Bromwich Albion 10), Daniel McGowan (West Ham United 3), Jim Hartnett (Middlesbrough 1). **Captain:** Johnny Carey.

Spain: Eizaguirre, V. Asensi, Antunez, Lozano, Gonzalvo III, Puchades, Basora, Venancio, Zarra, Artigas, Gainza. **Subs:** Igoa for Artigas.

On this hot summers day Spain overwhelmed Ireland with their attacking football and cancelled out Martin's early penalty with a three goal salvo in 6 minutes.

Spain attacked from the kick-off. Basora tricked his way past Keane and sent Venancio clear in the first minute. Venancio's shot was stopped by Godwin but rebounded out to Basora whose shot was tipped away for a corner by the goalkeeper. In another attack Gainza, the man of the match, beat Carey and shot across the goalmouth – Zarra just failing to add the finish. On 14 minutes Keane took a free kick and as the ball came into the box Antunez pushed McGowan. Referee Arthur Ellis gave a penalty and, despite Spanish protests, Martin put it away. A minute later Zarra's header hit a post and Artigas had another effort saved by Godwin.

After half an hour Spain started their scoring spree. Gonzalvo lobbed a ball into the area and Zarra ran in to direct his header against the post and in. Six minutes later Gainza sent a ball up to Zarra on the back line. The centre forward beat Martin and ran in on goal before setting up Basora to score. Straight from the re-start Zarra got possession again, gave the ball to Venancio and raced through to accept the inside-right's return pass to score from close range. After this tempers rose and in ensuing "play" Zarra and Antunez were injured while Artigas was taken off with a knee injury to be replaced by Igoa. A minute from the break Corr had a good shot just over.

The second half was scrappy and the football was a poor comparison to that of the first period. Spain started well and Venancio had an effort just wide. On the hour Gannon and Farrell changed positions with each other to alter the attack. This tactic, which they had tried in the first half after the third Spanish goal, seemed to have had some effect on the forward line as, almost immediately Walsh and Farrell sent Hartnett clear to shoot across the goal. Ireland had more of the play which followed but in the last few minutes Spain renewed their attack. Igoa shot wide and Gainza hit the post with another shot before Gonzalvo passed in for Igoa to score with a low drive.

Match No. 43 **FINLAND** **Home**

Thursday 8th September, 1949 – Dublin (World Cup)

REP. OF IRELAND (2) 3 Gavin 35, Martin 44 (pen), 68
FINLAND (0) 0

Ref: Evans (England) **Ground:** Dalymount Park **Att:** 22,479

Ireland: Tommy Godwin (Shamrock Rovers 4), Johnny Carey (Manchester United 21), Tommy Aherne (Luton Town 3), Eddie Gannon (Sheffield Wednesday 6), Con Martin (Aston Villa 12), Tommy Moroney (West Ham United 5), Johnny Gavin (Norwich City 1), Arthur Fitzsimons (Middlesbrough 1), Brendan Carroll (Shelbourne 2), Peter Desmond (Middlesbrough 1), Tommy O'Connor (Shamrock Rovers 1). **Subs:** Pat Daly (Shamrock Rovers 1) for Carroll (25 mins). **Captain:** Johnny Carey.

Finland: T. Sarnola, K. Martin, E. Saarnio, V. Asikainen, T. Pylkkönen, E. Beijar, H. Svahn, S. Myntti, A. Rytkönen, J. Vaihela, K. Lehtovirta.

Ireland gained their first World Cup victory thanks to a penalty and two goals from corner kicks. That they did not score more was due largely to Sarnola. The Finnish goalkeeper brought off good saves to deny Desmond, Moroney, O'Connor and Carroll before Fitzsimons nearly scored a brilliant goal. The inside-right dribbled past three defenders, rounded the goalkeeper and lobbed the ball towards goal only for Gavin to head it wide in trying to make sure. Later, Desmond played a one-two with Fitzsimons and had a shot saved by Sarnola.

On 25 minutes Carroll was injured and replaced by Daly. The substitute went to centre-half with Martin taking over at centre-forward – his sixth different position while playing for Ireland. Finland's best chance fell soon after when Asikainen sent Rytkönen in but Godwin saved well.

After 35 minutes Ireland went ahead when a corner by Gavin slipped through the goal-keepers hands and ended up in the goal. Just before half-time Asikainen brought Desmond down in the box and Martin scored with the resulting penalty.

Arthur Fitzsimons made his international debut in the 3-0 victory over Finland. He was denied a debut goal by Gavin.

The second half contained few highlights but mid-way through Martin headed home another corner for Ireland's third goal. Martin was denied a hat-trick when Sarnola brought off a good save near the end.

Match No. 44 **ENGLAND** **Away**

Wednesday 21st September, 1949 – Liverpool

ENGLAND (0) 0
REP. OF IRELAND (1) 2 Martin 33 (pen), Farrell 85

Ref: Mowat (Scotland) **Ground:** Goodison Park **Att:** 51,047

England: B. Williams, B. Mozley, J. Aston, B. Wright, N. Franklin, J. Dickinson, P. Harris, J. Morris, J. Pye, W. Mannion, T. Finney.

Ireland: Tommy Godwin (Shamrock Rovers 5), Johnny Carey (Manchester United 22), Tommy Aherne (Luton Town 4), Willie Walsh (Manchester City 7), Con Martin (Aston Villa 13), Tommy Moroney (West Ham United 6), Peter Corr (Everton 3), Peter Farrell (Everton 10), Davy Walsh (West Bromwich Albion 11), Peter Desmond (Middlesbrough 2), Tommy O'Connor (Shamrock Rovers 2). **Captain:** Johnny Carey.

The English selectors used this game to "blood" some new players for the forthcoming British Championship which would also serve as a World Cup qualification group. They gave debuts to two forwards, Harris and Pye and it was Pye who had the first chance of the game. Finney beat Willie Walsh and sent Mannion away to cross for Pye to head just wide. Finney then set up Mannion who shot wide and Pye was denied when "Bud" Aherne made an interception. Davy Walsh had a chance at the other end but Williams saved.

After 33 minutes of almost continuous English pressure O'Connor released Desmond who raced into the box. Mozley, caught for pace, brought him down from behind and referee Mowat awarded a penalty. Martin blasted the spot kick at goal but Williams guessed correctly and got his hands to the shot. However the ball spun out of his hands and into the goal such was the power of the kick.

Ireland took heart from this and Davy Walsh and Desmond had chances before the break.

On the resumption England went all out for an equaliser and had many chances. England captain Billy Wright tested Godwin who had to dive full length to save. Godwin also denied Harris while Aherne stopped Pye from scoring by kicking the ball off his toe. A curling free kick by Harris hit the underside of the bar, bounced down and was cleared away. A fierce shot by Morris was saved by Godwin while Martin twice cleared his lines,

England did not let up but Ireland still managed a few breakaways and from one of these the Irish got a second goal. O'Connor received the ball when an English attack broke down. The winger broke away with Farrell and drew some defenders before his pass put Farrell clear to run in on goal. As Williams advanced, Farrell chipped the ball over the goalkeeper's head and it bounced into the net.

England did not recover from this late blow and went down to their first home defeat by a non-British side. It was also their first defeat at Goodison Park.

The Irish team which beat England 2-0 at Goodison Park in 1949.
Back Row (L. to R): *Con Martin, Tommy Aherne, Tommy Godwin, Tommy Moroney and Willie Walsh.*
Seated (L to R): *Peter Corr, Tommy O'Connor, Johnny Carey, Peter Desmond, Peter Farrell and Davy Walsh.*

Match No. 45 **FINLAND** **Away**

Sunday 9th October, 1949 – Helsinki (World Cup)

FINLAND (0) 1 Vaihela 89
REP. OF IRELAND (0) 1 Farrell 65

Ref: Bronkhorst (Holland) **Ground:** Olympiastadion **Att:** 13,000

Finland: M. Laaksonen, K. Martin, E. Saarnio, V. Asikainen, T. Pylkkönen, E. Beijar, J. Vaihela, S. Myntti, Y. Asikainen, V. Teräs, H. Saarinen.

Ireland: Tommy Godwin (Leicester City 6), Johnny Carey (Manchester United 23), Tommy Aherne (Luton Town 5), Jimmy Coffey (Drumcondra 1), Con Martin (Aston Villa 14), Tommy Moroney (West Ham United 7), Johnny Gavin (Norwich City 2), Peter Farrell (Everton 11), Davy Walsh (West Bromwich Albion 12), Peter Desmond (Middlesbrough 3), Tommy O'Connor (Shamrock Rovers 3). **Captain:** Johnny Carey.

After an even first half Ireland had slightly the better of the play in the second. A mistake by Laaksonen allowed Davy Walsh to score what looked like a good goal but the referee ruled it out for a foul on the goalkeeper. Irish pressure continued but a break the length of the field ended with Y. Asikainen hitting a tremendous shot off the crossbar.

Ireland took the lead when Coffey gave to Farrell and the inside-right beat a defender before shooting past Laaksonen. Ireland tried for a second but in the last minute a group of Finnish forwards rushed in for a cross. The ball and a couple of Irish defenders ended up in the net. Despite Irish protests the goal was given, credited to Vaihela.

Match No. 46 — SWEDEN — Home

Sunday 13th November, 1949 – Dublin (World Cup)

REP. OF IRELAND (0) 1 Martin 61 (pen)
SWEDEN (2) 3 Palmer 4, 40, 68

Ref: Ling (England) **Ground:** Dalymount Park **Att:** 41,031

Ireland: Tommy Godwin (Leicester City 7), Johnny Carey (Manchester United 24), Tommy Aherne (Luton Town 6), Willie Walsh (Manchester City 8), Con Martin (Aston Villa 15), Reg Ryan (West Bromwich Albion 1), Peter Corr (Everton 4), Peter Farrell (Everton 12), Davy Walsh (West Bromwich Albion 13), Peter Desmond (Middlesbrough 4), Tommy O'Connor (Shamrock Rovers 4). **Captain:** Johnny Carey.

Sweden: T. Lindberg, K. E. Andersson, E. Nilsson, O. Ahlund, K. Nordahl, K. Rosen, E. Jönsson, K. Palmer, H. Jeppson, S. Andersson, S. Sundkvist.

Ireland needed a victory to force a play-off with Sweden for a place in the 1950 World Cup finals. A goal after only 4 minutes and another before half-time killed off their chances while another strike mid-way through the second half gave 19 year old Kalle Palmer a hat-trick, the first ever scored against the Republic of Ireland.

An early chance fell to Sundkvist who shot across the goal. However in the next attack the winger's cross landed at Palmer's feet and the inside-right scored with a good shot. Following this Ireland pressed hard for an equaliser and threatened the Swedish goal for long periods. A good ball from Davy Walsh found Corr running into the box but from two yards the winger hit the crossbar. Corr again struck the bar with a free kick a few minutes later and in between these efforts Jeppson was denied when Godwin saved with his feet. Lindberg was in action at the other end saving a Davy Walsh effort. Ireland's best effort of the half was when they were awarded an indirect free in the box, 6 yards from goal. The Swedes brought all their players back to defend the goal-line. Desmond squared the free to Carey and his shot seemed to strike a hand before it was cleared.

Five minutes before half-time Sweden worked their way up the pitch. As the ball came to Palmer a whistle sounded. The Irish defenders stopped but the centre-forward ran on and scored. The referee signalled that the goal stood as the whistle had apparently come from the crowd.

Ireland pulled a goal back 16 minutes into the second half when Nordahl held Davy Walsh in the box and from the penalty Martin scored.

The Irish began to tire in this second period (some of them had played the day before for their club sides) and Sweden got a third goal when Carey was pressured into kicking the ball across his own goal giving Palmer the chance to complete his hat-trick. A late reshuffle which saw Martin go to centre-forward, Carey to centre-half, Farrell to left-half and Ryan to right back did not help and Ireland suffered their first World Cup home defeat.

International Record	P	W	D	L	F	A
1946-1949	16	5	1	10	16	26
Home	9	3	0	6	9	15
Away	7	2	1	4	7	11

International Record	P	W	D	L	F	A
1926-1949	46	16	9	21	81	92
Home	22	8	3	11	43	47
Away	24	8	6	10	38	45

World Cup Record	P	W	D	L	F	A
1934-1949	8	1	3	4	17	22
Home	4	1	2	1	11	10
Away	4	0	1	3	6	12

Number of players capped by Ireland 139
Number of goalscorers for Ireland 33

Leading Goalscorers		Most Capped Players	
Jimmy Dunne	13	Johnny Carey	24
Paddy Moore	7	Joe O'Reilly	20
Con Martin	5	Jimmy Dunne	15
Paddy Bradshaw	4	Con Martin	
Tom Davis		Bill Gorman	13
Joey Donnelly		Davy Walsh	
John Joe Flood		Peter Farrell	12

Penalties awarded to Ireland 11 (9 scored, 1 saved, 1 miss)

Penalties awarded against Ireland 8 (5 scored, 2 saved, 1 miss)

Number of nations played: 16

Hat-tricks for Ireland
John Joe Flood 3 goals v Belgium 1929
Paddy Moore 4 goals v Belgium 1934

Hat-tricks against Ireland
Kalle Palmer Sweden 3 goals 1949

Leading Goalscorers against Ireland
4 Reidar Kvammen, Norway
Telmo Zarraonandia Montoya "Zarra", Spain

Irish Captains
14 Johnny Carey
8 Charlie Turner
5 Jimmy Dunne, Paddy Gaskins
4 William Glen
2 Peter Farrell, Mick O'Brien
1 Frank Brady, John Burke, Harry Chatton, John Joe Flood, Mick Foley, Jack McCarthy

The Irish and Belgian teams line-up before the start of the game in the Century Stadium in 1950. The last half hour of this game was played under floodlights.
The Irish team from left to right is: *Con Martin, Mattie Clarke, Tommy Moroney, Tommy Godwin, Willie Walsh, Arthur Fitzsimons, Bobby Duffy, Martin Colfer, Terry Murray, Thomas Aherne and Reg Ryan*

Match No. 47 — BELGIUM — Away

Wednesday 10th May, 1950 – Brussels

BELGIUM (3) 5 Mermans (3) De Hert, Chaves
REP. OF IRELAND (0) 1 Duffy

Ref: Bronkhorst (Holland) **Ground:** Century Stadium **Att:** 25,000

Belgium: H. Meert, A. Vaillant, P. Anoul, J. Vander Auwera, L. Carre, V. Mees, R. Coppens, F. Chaves, J. Mermans, A. De Hert, G. Mordant.

Ireland: Tommy Godwin (Leicester City 8), Mattie Clarke (Shamrock Rovers 1), Tommy Aherne (Luton Town 7), Willie Walsh (Manchester City 9), Con Martin (Aston Villa 16), Tommy Moroney (West Ham United 8), Terry Murray (Dundalk 1), Arthur Fitzsimons (Middlesbrough 2), Bobby Duffy (Shamrock Rovers 1), Reg Ryan (West Bromwich Albion 2), Martin Colfer (Shelbourne 1). **Captain:** Con Martin

The Irish defence, missing Johnny Carey for the first time since the war, conceded an early goal after 3 minutes. De Hert sent Mordant clear and the winger raced away to cross for De Hert. The inside-left drew Godwin and set up Mermans to score. An Irish free kick almost brought an equaliser when Ryan tapped the ball to Moroney who shot over. Belgium's second came when Mermans and Martin missed a ball and Chaves was sent clear. The forward gave the ball to De Hert and the inside-left ran in to score with a low shot from 20 yards. On the half-hour Godwin was pressured by Chaves, when coming for a corner, and could only palm the ball out to Mermans who scored easily.

The Irish captain Con Martin shakes hands with his Belgian counterpart before the game in Brussels in 1950

Eleven minutes into the second half Mordant beat the Irish defence and gave the ball to Mermans. The centre-forward gave it to Chaves who ran in, beat two defenders and shot home Belgiums fourth. Ireland pulled one back when Murray sent Colfer's cross back to Duffy and the centre-forward headed home with 18 minutes to go. However, Mermans completed his hat-trick when Godwin parried a shot from Mordant and the centre-forward was first onto the loose ball to score.

Match No. 48 **NORWAY** **Home**

Sunday 26th November, 1950 – Dublin

REP. OF IRELAND (1) 2 Carey 24 (pen), D. Walsh 61
NORWAY (2) 2 Bredesen 6, Andresen 11

Ref: Pearce (England) **Ground:** Dalymount Park **Att:** 31,215

Ireland: Tommy Godwin (Leicester City 9), Sean Fallon (Glasgow Celtic 1), Tommy Aherne (Luton Town 8), Eddie Gannon (Sheffield Wednesday 7), Johnny Carey (Manchester United 25), Tommy Moroney (West Ham United 9), Christy Giles (Doncaster Rovers 1), John Lawlor (Doncaster Rovers 2), Davy Walsh (West Bromwich Albion 14), Reg Ryan (West Bromwich Albion 3), Tommy Eglington (Everton 10). **Captain:** Johnny Carey.

Norway: T. Torgersen, B. Spydevold, H. Boye-Karlsen, G. Hansen, T. Svenssen, T. Olsen, G. Thoresen, P. Bredesen, V. Andresen, R. Hvidsten, W. Olsen.

Ireland had early chances by "Kit" Lawlor and Walsh before Norway took a shock lead. Thoresen forced a corner and from the flag kick Bredesen hit it first time into the net. Norway got a second five minutes later when Bredesen drew Carey out to the right and crossed for the unmarked Andresen to head home. Andresen got the ball in the net for a third time soon after but it was ruled out as he was offside.

Irish team left to right: *Johnny Carey, Tommy Godwin (hidden), Sean Fallon, Tommy Moroney, John (Kit) Lawlor, Christy Giles, Eddie Gannon, Thomas 'Bud' Aherne, Tommy Eglington, Davy Walsh and Reg Ryan*

After 29 minutes "Kit" Lawlor was taken down in the box by Svenssen and, in the absence of the regular penalty taker Con Martin, captain Carey took the penalty and scored. Ireland continued to press with Lawlor almost in twice and Ryan having a header saved. Just at half-time Andresen had a great shot which hit the post and rebounded across the goalmouth.

In the second half Norway had early chances with Bredesen and Thoresen shooting wide but in general the play was with Ireland. On 61 minutes Davy Walsh dived to head in a hard cross from Gannon for the equaliser. Ryan had an effort saved by Torgersen while later Lawlor beat the Norwegian goalkeeper but Svensson cleared off the line. Ryan had two late chances but both were saved by Torgersen.

Match No. 49 — ARGENTINA — Home

Sunday 13th May, 1951 – Dublin

REP. OF IRELAND (0) 0
ARGENTINA (0) 1 Labruna 54

Ref: Leafe (England) **Ground:** Dalymount Park **Att:** 40,000

Ireland: Fred Kiernan (Shamrock Rovers 1), Johnny Carey (Manchester United 26), Tommy Aherne (Luton Town 9), Reg Ryan (West Bromwich Albion 4), Con Martin (Aston Villa 17), Peter Farrell (Everton 13), Alf Ringstead (Sheffield United 1), Jim Higgins (Birmingham City 1), Davy Walsh (Aston Villa 15), John Lawlor (Doncaster Rovers 3), Tommy Eglington (Everton 11). **Captain:** Johnny Carey.

Argentina: M. Rugilo, J. Allegri, J. Figueras, N. Yacono, U. Faina, E. Gutierrez, M. Boye, N. Mendez, J. Benevidez, A. Labruna, F. Loustau. **Subs:** G. Perez for Figueras (39 mins).

A disappointing match saw Ireland dominate for most of the time but the big attendance left frustrated as the Irish attack was thwarted again by bad luck and tenacious defending.

In the first minute Walsh played a one-two with Ringstead but was prevented from scoring when he was hustled off the ball. "Kit" Lawlor then set up Ringstead who shot across goal while Ryan had another shot which went over. Argentina then had a couple of chances with Labruna's shot saved and an overhead kick by Benevidez wide. Higgins next put Eglington clear for a shot on goal but Rugilo saved at the expence of a corner. Labruna and Boye had other chances for Argentina before Rugilo saved at the feet of "Kit" Lawlor.

Argentina began the second half very well with Boye twice coming near before the Argentinian goalkeeper saved twice from Lawlor and Walsh. With 9 minutes gone Mendez sent a through ball to Labruna, who was played on-side by Aherne. The inside-left had no trouble in scoring and placed a low shot wide of Kiernan. Kiernan denied Loustau another goal soon after and Benevidez had the ball in the net twice more but both efforts were ruled out as the centre-forward was offside. Boye should have scored a second but shot over after beating Kiernan. Ryan had a chance for an equaliser near the end but his header was saved by Rugilo.

Match No. 50 — NORWAY — Away

Wednesday 30th May, 1951 – Oslo

NORWAY (1) 2 Wong Sorensen 14, Hvidsten 55
REP. OF IRELAND (1) 3 Farrell 17, Ringstead 67 Coad 82

Ref: Jorgensen (Denmark) **Ground:** Ullevaal Stadium **Att:** 20,900

Norway: E. Kihle, B. Spydevold, H. Boye-Karlsen, T. Olsen, T. Svenssen, E. Laerum, R. Hvidsten, P. Bredesen, G. Dylowad, O. Wong Sorensen, K. Skifjeld.

Ireland: Fred Kiernan (Shamrock Rovers 2), Tommy Clinton (Everton 1), Tommy Aherne (Luton Town 10), Reg Ryan (West Bromwich Albion 5), Johnny Carey (Manchester United 27), Tommy Moroney (West Ham United 10), Alf Ringstead (Sheffield United 2), Tim Cunneen (Limerick 1), Davy Walsh (Aston Villa 16), Peter Farrell (Everton 14), Martin Colfer (Shelbourne 2). **Subs:** Paddy Coad (Shamrock Rovers 10), for Cunneen (42 min). **Captain:** Johnny Carey.

Norway opened up well but were restricted to one goal in the first half due to a combination of good Irish defending and poor Norwegian finishing.

Norway took the lead when Bredesen took advantage of Dylowad's knock-on to race clear and cross for Wong Sorensen to net easily. Three minutes later Ireland equalised. Ryan set off on a brilliant solo run which ended with a defender making an interception. As the ball ran loose, with Ryan in chase, Farrell ran onto it and blasted a right footed shot into the net.

The Norwegians should have had at least another goal before the break but 10 minutes into the second half Hvidsten got a deserved second from a breakaway. Ireland had lost the services of Cunneen in the first half due to a hip injury and had brought Coad on at inside-right. This substitution seemed to revive the Irish attack in the second half and on 22 minutes they equalised again. A header by Ringstead was caught by the goalkeeper after it had crossed the line. The referee consulted the linesman before awarding the goal. With 8 minutes to go a great left-footed shot from Coad, about 20 yards from goal, found the top corner of the net for a winner.

Match No. 51 — WEST GERMANY — Home

Wednesday 17th October, 1951 – Dublin

REP. OF IRELAND (2) 3 Posipal (O.G.), 9 Fitzsimons 40, Glynn 85
WEST GERMANY (0) 2 Morlock 63, F. Walter 75

Ref: Ling (England) **Ground:** Dalymount Park **Att:** 29,451

Ireland: Fred Kiernan (Southampton 3), Sean Fallon (Glasgow Celtic 2), Tommy Aherne (Luton Town 11), Tommy Moroney (West Ham United 11), Florrie Burke (Cork Athletic 1), Peter Farrell (Everton 15), Alf Ringstead (Sheffield United 3), Arthur Fitzsimons (Middlesbrough 3), Dessie Glynn (Drumcondra 1), Reg Ryan (West Bromwich Albion 6), Tommy Eglington (Everton 12). **Captain:** Peter Farrell.

West Germany: A. Turek, J. Streitle, W. Kohlmeyer, P. Mebus, J. Posipal, E. Schanko, F. Gerritzen, A. Preissler, M. Morlock, F. Walter, R. Herrmann.

Five years after the end of the Second World War West Germany resumed international fixtures and travelled to Dublin to play its fifth post-war game. Most of the side was inexperienced but their captain, Fritz Walter, had been capped in 1940 while Jakob Streitle was a survivor of the Ireland-Germany meeting in Bremen in 1939. However, the German team had a total of 60 caps while the Irish total was one less.

The game started with Ryan outwitting two defenders and sending in a shot which Turek saved. Herrmann had a shot wide before Ireland took an early lead. A long through ball from Glynn found Fitzsimons running in on goal. As Turek advanced to cut out the danger, Posipal came across but in trying to clear he sent the ball high over the goalkeeper and on into the net. West Germany retaliated with a header from Preissler which Kiernan tipped over.

Despite a 30 yard shot from Fitzsimons which went over it was all West Germany and they looked set for an equaliser until they suffered a serious handicap. Fritz Walter was injured in a challenge with Fallon and was forced to leave the field after 35 minutes. Five minutes later ten-man Germany conceded another goal. Ringstead sent a pass to Fitzsimons who tricked the German defenders and unleashed a thunderbolt of a shot from the edge of the area which flew past Turek and into the net. A minute before the break Fitzsimons almost had another but his shot hit the underside of the crossbar and bounced back into play before being cleared.

Fritz Walter reappeared at the start of the second half but it was Ireland who had the better of the chances early on. A good save by the German goalkeeper denied Fitzsimons and the same player was involved again when his shot, which finished off a good move involving Eglington and Ryan, was blocked by a defender. Gradually West Germany began to dominate the play and both Morlock and Preissler had shots saved by Kiernan before some good play by Fritz Walter set up Morlock to score with a good shot from the edge of the box. Morlock and Herrmann had further chances later while, at the other end, another fine move resulted in Eglington shooting across goal with Glynn just failing to get a finishing touch.

On 75 minutes Fritz Walter equalised when a cross by Gerritzen was not properly cleared and the German captain sent a terrific shot into the back of the net. A few minutes later Walter had another chance but Kiernan saved his header.

With five minutes to go Farrell broke from defence and gave the ball to Eglington on the left. The winger, on the half-way line, sent a high cross into the area and found Glynn. Glynn controlled the ball with his shoulder, rounded Turek, and slipped the ball home.

With time running out Germany continued to press and in the last minute Walter played a one-two with Herrmann before sending in a fierce drive from 35 yards which Kiernan did well to turn around the post for a corner. Gerritzen took the corner and found the head of Streitle who planted the ball in the back of the net. However the referee, amidst some confusion, indicated that he had already blown for full time as the ball was coming across and no goal was awarded.

Match No. 52 — WEST GERMANY — Away

Sunday 4th May, 1952 – Cologne

WEST GERMANY (1) 3 Posipal 31, O. Walter 77, Termath 87
REP. OF IRELAND (0) 0

Ref: Ellis (England) **Ground:** Mungersdorf Stadium **Att:** 75,000

West Germany: K. Adam, E. Retter, W. Kohlmeyer, J. Posipal, J. Streitle, E. Schanko, B. Klodt, J. Röhrig, O. Walter, R. Herrmann, B. Termath. **Subs:** G. Stollenwerk for Herrmann (43 mins).

Ireland: Fred Kiernan (Southampton 4), Tommy Aherne (Luton Town 12), Sean Fallon (Glasgow Celtic 3), Eddie Gannon (Sheffield Wednesday 8), Con Martin (Aston Villa 18), Peter Farrell (Everton 16), Alf Ringstead (Sheffield United 4), Arthur Fitzsimons (Middlesbrough 4), Shay Gibbons (St Patrick's Athletic 1), Reg Ryan (West Bromwich Albion 7), Tommy Eglington (Everton 13). **Captain:** Peter Farrell.

A good performance by the Irish team was not enough to halt a superior German side in the second half. The Irish had a number of chances but the failure of the forward line to capitalise on these in the first half led to their downfall.

The Germans had an early chance when Farrell was dispossessed but Herrmann shot wide. Ireland were playing well in the first half-hour and an attack involving Gibbons, Fitzsimons and Ringstead was stopped when Adam cleared. After 19 minutes Fitzsimons sent Gibbons away but the referee had already blown for offside when the striker put the ball in the net. Just after the half-hour Herrmann headed the ball down to Posipal and the right-half scored with a fierce shot from 22 yards. Not long afterwards Eglington crossed to the unmarked Fitzsimons but the inside right missed a good chance. Two minutes from the break Herrmann was injured in a challenge with Fallon and had to be replaced.

At the start of the second half Termath almost scored but Gannon got back to clear. Fitzsimons had a shot blocked by Kohlmeyer but in general it was all Germany. Posipal had a shot saved before Germany had two good claims for penalties turned down. First Aherne brought Ottmar Walter down in the box and the same player stopped another shot with his arm but both claims were ignored by the referee. Kiernan stopped another Ottmar Walter shot but was beaten a minute later by the same player when he sent a screaming 25 yard shot into the corner of the net. Three minutes from the end a cross-cum-shot by Termath also found the net for Germany's third.

Match No. 53 — AUSTRIA — Away

Wednesday 7th May, 1952 – Vienna

AUSTRIA (4) 6 A. Huber (3), Haummer, Dienst (2)
REP. OF IRELAND (0) 0

Ref: Reinhardt (West Germany) **Ground:** Praeter Park **Att:** 60,000

Austria: J. Musil, R. Röck, E. Happel, G. Hanappi, E. Ocwirk, K, Koller, E. Melchior, K. Decker, R. Dienst, A. Huber, W. Haummer.

Austria's Robert Dienst gets between Ireland's Frank O'Farrell and Con Martin to head goalwards. Karl Decker looks on. (Photo: Votavafoto)

Ireland: Fred Kiernan (Southampton 5), Sean Fallon (Glasgow Celtic 4), Tommy Aherne (Luton Town 13), Eddie Gannon (Sheffield Wednesday 9), Con Martin (Aston Villa 19), Frank O'Farrell (West Ham United 1), Alf Ringstead (Sheffield United 5), Arthur Fitzsimons (Middlesbrough 5), Reg Ryan (West Bromwich Albion 8), Peter Farrell (Everton 17), Tommy Eglington (Everton 14). **Captain:** Peter Farrell.

A brilliant display of attacking football by both sides should have yielded many more goals but a hat-trick by Adolf Huber in only 4 minutes decided the contest in Austria's favour.

Ireland started well, forcing Happel to head over his own crossbar in their first attack. From the resulting corner the ball fell to the unmarked Fitzsimons but he shot wide. Austria replied with shots from Ocwirk, Melchior and Haummer all of which were dealt with by Kiernan.

With 22 minutes gone Haummer sent in a hard shot which Kiernan could only palm out to Decker who gave it to Huber to score. A minute later a cross by Melchior fell to Huber who netted again. Two minutes later he completed his hat-trick. On 36 minutes Melchior and Huber sent Haummer in for Austria's fourth.

On the half-hour Austria's Karl Koller clears from Ireland's Reg Ryan. (Photo: Votavafoto)

Ireland were not out of it and kept plugging away. Fitzsimons broke through the Austrian defence and squared the ball for Eglington but the winger missed the ball completely. Then Eglington forced an opening and raced away. He rounded the goalkeeper and laid the ball back for Ryan only to have Happel to intercept it, saving a certain goal.

The second half continued much as the first with many chances at both ends but two goals by Dienst sealed victory for the Austrians.

Match No. 54 SPAIN Away

Sunday 1st June, 1952 – Madrid

SPAIN (4) 6 Coque 3, Gainza 10, Cesar 13, Basora 43, 70, Panizo 67

REP. OF IRELAND (0) 0

Ref: Leafe (England) **Ground:** Chamartin Stadium **Att:** 75,000

Spain: Ramallets, J. M. Martin, P. Biosca, Sequer, Munoz, Puchades, Basora, Coque, Cesar, Panizo, Gainza.

Ireland: Jimmy O'Neill (Everton 1), Sean Fallon (Glasgow Celtic 5), Tommy Aherne (Luton Town 14), Peter Farrell (Everton 18), Con Martin (Aston Villa 20), Reg Ryan (West Bromwich Albion 9), Alf Ringstead (Sheffield United 6), Paddy Coad ((Shamrock Rovers 11), Davy Walsh (Aston Villa 17), Arthur Fitzsimons (Middlesbrough 6), Tommy Eglington (Everton 15). **Captain:** Peter Farrell.

Ireland were completely outplayed by a brilliant Spanish side in which each of the five forwards scored. Ireland had a good start with Eglington and Walsh shooting over before Spain opened the scoring with their first attack. Gainza sent Panizo away up the wing and when his cross arrived in the box Coque had an easy task of shooting home.

Ireland were still playing well but a pass by Fallon was intercepted by Gainza. The winger ran on and beat the advancing goalkeeper for the second goal. Gainza was also involved in the third when he broke through and set up Cesar to score. Spain began to dominate the game and even though Fitzsimons forced Ramallets into a good save Basora scored a fourth when he lobbed the ball over O'Neill.

At the start of the second half Coque went off injured and while he was off the field receiving attention, Fitzsimons broke free but was taken down in the box for a penalty. Martin hit the spot-kick against the crossbar and when it bounced back Fitzsimons shot against the post. The ten-man Spain got a fifth goal when O'Neill failed to hold a corner from Gainza and Panizo pounced to score. Coque resumed with his arm in a sling but was still able to set up Basora to score again. Nine minutes later Farrell got the ball in the Spanish net but the goal was ruled out for offside.

Match No. 55 FRANCE Home

Sunday 16th November, 1952 – Dublin

REP. OF IRELAND (1) 1 Fallon 24

FRANCE (0) 1 Piantoni 67

Ref: Alsteen (Belgium) **Ground:** Dalymount Park **Att:** 40,000

Ireland: Jimmy O'Neill (Everton 2), Seamus Dunne (Luton Town 1), Tommy Aherne (Luton Town 15), Peter Farrell (Everton 19), Johnny Carey (Manchester United 28), Sean Cusack (Limerick 1), Johnny Gavin (Norwich City 3), Arthur Fitzsimons (Middlesbrough 7), Sean Fallon (Glasgow Celtic 6), Reg Ryan (West Bromwich Albion 10), Tommy Eglington (Everton 16). **Captain:** Johnny Carey.

France: C. Ruminski, L. Gianessi, R. Marche, Ferry, R. Jonquet, A. Penverne, R. Kopa, J. Ujlaki, A. Strappe, R. Piantoni, S. Curyl.

French winger Kopa (No. 7) puts the ball into the net, but Irish appeals for offside were upheld by the Referee.
Other players in picture are (L to R): *Reg Ryan (on ground, far left), Johnny Carey, Sean Cusack, Tommy Aherne, Peter Farrell and Jimmy O'Neill.*

As with the visit of Spain in 1947, the huge interest in the visit of an attractive side to this country resulted in the capacity of Dalymount Park being stretched to its limits. Again the crowds spilled onto the touchlines and even though this caused some problems it did not result in any major disruptions. It should be noted that following this there were calls for a new soccer stadium to be built but these calls were only to be echoed in years to come.

The French played some brilliant football and dominated the play for most of the game but determined battling by the Irish brought them a share of the spoils.

After two minutes the Irish defence was split wide open and Ujlacki was left unmarked in the box. Ujlaki shot but O'Neill dived full length and palmed it away only for Strappe to shoot over. Fitzsimons had a shot saved and Kopa had the ball in the net but was offside in further chances. France began to pepper the Irish goal with shots forcing O'Neill into a string of fine saves. Curyl had the ball in the net again but he used a hand. It was against this run of play that Ireland grabbed a lucky goal. Fallon headed a Gavin cross goalwards and, as the goalkeeper struggled to get to it, Jonquet deflected it into the net.

A back pass by Ryan was intercepted by Strappe soon after but O'Neill brought off a fine save to deny him an equaliser. Despite this Ireland began to get on top and another Fallon header was saved.

Ireland had a lucky escape when Carey, having been beaten by Strappe, used his arm to prevent the ball going further but the referee, apparently unsighted, ignored French appeals for a penalty. The game then went through a ugly patch as players kicked and punched each other with the referee appearing not to notice. One incident which could not have escaped his attention was the sight of a French player running for dear life while an angry Irishman tried to catch him. However sanity was restored and before the break Eglington and Ryan had shots saved by the French goalkeeper.

The second half began with chances at both ends and Ireland came close when a header by Gavin beat Ruminski but went wide. The French equaliser when it came was a brilliant goal. Ujlaki sent over a beautiful cross and Piantoni met it with a bullet-like drive which gave O'Neill no chance. Further chances gave Kopa moments to win the match but he was denied by O'Neill while Cusack had Ireland's last chance with a shot which was deflected for a corner.

Match No. 56 **AUSTRIA** **Home**

Wednesday 25th March, 1953 – Dublin

REP. OF IRELAND (0) 4 Ringstead 46, 53, Eglington 74, O'Farrell 80
AUSTRIA (0) 0

Ref: Ellis (England) **Ground:** Dalymount Park **Att:** 40,000

Ireland: Jimmy O'Neill (Everton 3), Seamus Dunne (Luton Town 2), Joseph Lawler (Fulham 1), Peter Farrell (Everton 20), Johnny Carey (Manchester United 29), Frank O'Farrell (West Ham United 2), Alf Ringstead (Sheffield United 7), Arthur Fitzsimons (Middlesbrough 8), Davy Walsh (Aston Villa 18), Reg Ryan (West Bromwich Albion 11), Tommy Eglington (Everton 17). **Captain:** Johnny Carey.

Austria: P. Schweda, K. Stotz, K. Kowanz, G. Hanappi, E. Ocwirk, K. Koller, F. Kominek, T. Wagner, A. Huber, E. Stojaspal, F. Zechmeister. **Subs:** F. Pelikan for Schweda (31 mins), P. Halla for Huber (33 mins).

Another great display of attacking football by both sides again produced a flattering scoreline for the home side, but, as in 1952, when Austria won 6-0, the home side deserved victory.

Davy Walsh had an opening shot saved and then had a second shot strike the post. In an even first half both goalkeepers were kept busy. Ocwirk (twice) and Kominek were denied by O'Neill with Schweda stopping O'Farrell and Fitzsimons. The Austrian goalkeeper was injured in saving a shot from Walsh and had to be replaced. Austria also brought on Halla, despite Irish protests. The substitute forced O'Neill into a good save before half-time.

Ireland went ahead just after the break. A free kick by "Robin" Lawler was missed by Walsh and Stotz and bounced up for Ringstead to head it home. A minute later Fitzsimons knocked a Ryan shot onto the bar while, later still, Carey came out of defence to send in a long range shot for Pelikan to save. The substitute goalkeeper was beaten again when a curling shot by Eglington struck the crossbar, bounced down and Ringstead was there to head in again. Ringstead nearly had

Jimmy O'Neill has the situation well in hand but Jackie Carey and Seamus Dunne are there just in case

O'Farrell's shot has goalkeeper Pelikan well beaten to register an Irish goal in the 4-0 victory over Austria.

The Austrian keeper has better luck this time and his flying leap fells an onrushing Irish forward.

a hat-trick but he only just missed a pass from Walsh. At the other end Stojaspal hit the crossbar and Hanappi shot wide.

A switch of positions in the Irish side saw Ryan and Eglington swop places. This switch had an immediate effect as Ryan set up Eglington to score with a well placed shot. Six minutes later O'Farrell sent a long range shot through a crowd of players. Pelikan saw it too late and it nestled in the back of the net without much reaction. Late in the game Halla hit the crossbar, Zechmeister had a shot saved and Fitzsimons had a goal ruled out for offside.

Match No. 57 — FRANCE — Home

Sunday 4th October, 1953 – Dublin (World Cup)

REP. OF IRELAND (0) 3 Ryan 58, D. Walsh 83, O'Farrell 88
FRANCE (2) 5 Glovacki 23, Penverne 40, Ujlaki 50, 69, Flamion 72

Ref: Franken (Belgium) **Ground:** Dalymount Park **Att:** 45,000

Ireland: Jimmy O'Neill (Everton 4), Seamus Dunne (Luton Town 3), Tommy Aherne (Luton Town 16), Peter Farrell (Everton 21), Con Martin (Aston Villa 21), Frank O'Farrell (West Ham United 3), Arthur Fitzsimons (Middlesbrough 9), Tommy Moroney (Evergreen United 12), Davy Walsh (Aston Villa 19), Reg Ryan (West Bromwich Albion 12), Tommy Eglington (Everton 18). **Captain:** Peter Farrell.

France: R. Vignal, L. Gianessi, R. Marche, A. Penverne, R. Jonquet, J. Marcel, J. Ujlaki, L. Glovacki, R. Kopa, R. Flamion, R. Piantoni.

The game started at a brisk pace but it was 14 minutes before there was a shot on target and that was a high back-pass by Penverne which forced Vignal to save at the expence of a corner. Then, from a Martin free kick, Walsh punched the ball towards goal only for the French keeper to save superbly. The infringement went unnoticed by the referee. O'Neill made an equally good save to deny Ujlaki but, from a corner by Kopa, Glovacki got possession and scored.

Play swung from one end to the other following this goal. Chances fell to Walsh, which was saved, and Flamion, whose header was also saved but five minutes before the interval France got a second. A free by Jonquet found Kopa who switched it to Penverne. The right-half ran through the exposed defence and finished with a low shot into the goal.

France started the second period very well and after O'Neill had stopped shots from Kopa and Glovacki, Ujlaki cut through the defence and beat the goalkeeper at the near post with a good

Irish centre-forward Davy Walsh flicks Tommy Moroney's cross past Vignal for Ireland's second goal.

shot. A change of position, which saw Ryan moving to inside-right, Moroney to outside-right and Eglington to inside-left again worked for Ireland. A shot by Ryan was handled by Marcel and a penalty was awarded. Ryan took the spot-kick himself and, although Vignal saved well, Ryan followed up to knock in the rebound.

France resumed on the attack and went 4-1 ahead when O'Neill could only parry a shot from Piantoni to the feet of Ujlaki and the French winger scored easily. The French were subsequently reduced to ten men when their captain Marche, went off the field injured. While he was getting treatment, Flamion finished off a neat move, involving Kopa and Glovacki, for their fifth goal. At that stage the France seemed to relax and with 7 minutes to go Walsh reduced the arrears when he headed in Moroney's cross. Ireland then came close with Fitzsimons and Farrell just off target. Two minutes from the final whistle Eglington and Farrell gave O'Farrell the chance to hit a shot on the run and he beat Vignal to reduce the deficit but not enough to save Ireland from defeat.

Match No. 58 — LUXEMBOURG — Home

Wednesday 28th October, 1953 – Dublin (World Cup)

REP. OF IRELAND (1) 4 Fitzsimons (2), Ryan (pen), Eglington.
LUXEMBOURG (0) 0

Ref: Bond (England) **Ground:** Dalymount Park **Att:** 20,000

Ireland: Jimmy O'Neill (Everton 5), Seamus Dunne (Luton Town 4), Joseph Lawler (Fulham 2), Eddie Gannon (Sheffield Wednesday 10), Noel Cantwell (West Ham United 1), Reg Ryan (West Bromwich Albion 13), Liam Munroe (Shamrock Rovers 1), George Cummins (Luton Town 1), Shay Gibbons (St Patrick's Athletic 2), Arthur Fitzsimons (Middlesbrough 10), Tommy Eglington (Everton 19). **Captain:** Tommy Eglington.

Luxembourg: P. Steffen, J. Speck, R. Lorang-Trinkes, H. Fickinger, L. Spartz, C. Wagner, N. May, J. Meurisse, A. Kohn, R. Weydert, P. Kemp.

A poor game opened quietly and with Luxembourg defending for most of the time the majority of the play was with Ireland. Early play saw Munroe curl a corner against the post. Gibbons got to the rebound but his shot was parried by Steffen and when it fell to the striker again he sent it wide. With 18 minutes gone Fitzsimons moved up along the goal-line. Gibbons made himself available for a pass and in doing so confused the defenders allowing Fitzsimons to skip by three of them, switch the ball to his right foot and score from a narrow angle. Play was poor following this but

Ireland's third goal. Arthur Fitzsimons, far left, has just finished off a fine dribble with a shot which went in off Steffen's body for Ireland's 101st international goal. Running in to make sure is Ireland's Tommy Eglington.

Ryan brought a good save out of Steffen. In one of the few attacks on the Irish goal a long range shot from Kemp was tipped over by O'Neill.

On 48 minutes Ryan got Ireland's second goal from the penalty spot after he had been taken down in the box. Further Irish attacks followed before Gibbons sent Fitzsimons away and the inside-left scored with a low shot which went in off the goalkeeper after 59 minutes. Ireland dominated the remainder of the game and brought Ryan forward to add to the attack. Ireland got a fourth goal when Munroe sent Eglington clear on the wing and when the winger crossed Gibbons crashed a header off the crossbar but the ball fell down to Eglington who shot it home.

Match No. 59 **FRANCE** **Away**

Wednesday 25th November, 1953 – Paris (World Cup)

FRANCE (0) 1 Piantoni 73
REP. OF IRELAND (0) 0

Ref: Van Nuffel (Belgium) **Ground:** Parc des Princes **Att:** 32,265

France: F. Remetter, A. Mihoubi, L. Gianessi, R. Marche, A. Cuissand, J. J. Marcel, J. Ujlaki, A. Strappe, B. M. Abdesselem, R. Piantoni, L. Delarderliere.

Ireland: Jimmy O'Neill (Everton 6), Tommy Clinton (Everton 2), Joseph Lawler (Fulham 3), Eddie Gannon (Sheffield Wednesday 11), Con Martin (Aston Villa 22), Peter Farrell (Everton 22), Alf Ringstead (Sheffield United 8), Reg Ryan (West Bromwich Albion 14), Davy Walsh (Aston Villa 20), Arthur Fitzsimons (Middlesbrough 11), Tommy Eglington (Everton 20). **Captain:** Tommy Eglington.

An excellent match was spoilt somewhat by the failure of both sides to take their chances, a sharp contrast to the previous meeting. An early chance fell to Ben Mohamed Abdesselem but he shot wide as did Fitzsimons at the other end. A good move involving Farrell, Eglington and Walsh set up Ryan to shoot over while, later, Walsh was close but the goalkeeper saved well.

French chances included an Abdesselem shot saved by O'Neill, Clinton saving a certain goal by kicking the ball off the line and Ujlaki having another shot saved.

France had more chances in the second period. Piantoni was stopped by O'Neill, Abdesselem shot wide when well placed and O'Neill brought off saves to deny Piantoni and Strappe. "Robin" Lawler cleared the ball off the line again before Farrell was injured and went to outside-left with Ryan dropping back to left-half. France eventually got the break through but in controversial circumstances. "Robin" Lawler was clearing the ball when Ujlaki crashed into him, making no attempt to play the ball. The ball broke loose for Ujlaki to cross, Clinton misdirected a header and Piantoni scored.

Match No. 60 — LUXEMBOURG — Away

Sunday 7th March, 1954 – Luxembourg (World Cup)

LUXEMBOURG (0) 0
REP. OF IRELAND (0) 1 Cummins 62

Ref: Ausum (Holland) **Ground:** Municipal Stadium **Att:**

Luxembourg P. Steffen, J. Mosar, N. May, S. Caldarelli, C. Wagner, M. Reuter, J. Meurisse, G. Peiffer, A. Kohn, R. Weydert, L. Karier.

Ireland: Ted Scannell (Southampton 1), Tommy Clinton (Everton 3), Tommy Traynor (Southampton 1), Matt Gallagher (Hibernian 1), Con Martin (Aston Villa 23), Pat Saward (Millwall 1), Johnny Gavin (Norwich City 4), Noel Kelly (Nottingham Forest 1), Fred Kearns (West Ham United 1), George Cummins (Luton Town 2), Jim Hartnett (Middlesbrough 2). **Captain:** Con Martin.

Luxembourg had never won a World Cup game but against Ireland's experimental line-up they almost achieved that first victory with a marvellous first-half display. After 4 minutes Meurisse crossed for Kohn to knock the ball into Weydert's path but as the inside-left ran onto it Scannell came out and cleared. Weydert had another chance 7 minutes later but he shot Karier's pass wide. Karier had Luxembourg's next chance when he shot against the post from a narrow angle. Ireland were kept at bay by some good defending but saw a lot of the ball.

The second half started with Kearns skipping through the defence and shooting from an acute angle forcing Steffen to save for a corner. From the corner Kearns got in a great header but it was cleared off the goal line by a defender. The Irish were superior in this half and restricted Luxembourg to a few breakaways. On the hour Kohn got free but shot straight at Scannell who saved. After 62 minutes Cummins beat Wagner and sent a powerful low shot into the net giving Steffen no chance to save. Ireland continued to press and had the majority of the play. Cummins almost had a second goal but Steffen saved at his feet when he was clean through.

Match No. 61 — NORWAY — Home

Sunday 7th November, 1954 – Dublin

REP. OF IRELAND (0) 2 Martin 59, Ryan 66 (pen)
NORWAY (1) 1 W. Olsen 13

Ref: Clough (England) **Ground:** Dalymount Park **Att:** 34,000

Ireland: Jimmy O'Neill (Everton 7), Don Donovan (Everton 1), Joseph Lawler (Fulham 4), Eddie Gannon (Shelbourne 12), Con Martin (Aston Villa 24), Peter Farrell (Everton 23), Fionan Fagan (Manchester City 1), Reg Ryan (Derby County 15), Paddy Ambrose (Shamrock Rovers 1), George Cummins (Luton Town 3), Tommy Eglington (Everton 21). **Captain:** Peter Farrell.

Norway: W. Aronsen, A. Bakker, H. Boye-Karlsen, R. Rygel, T. Svenssen, T. Hernes, P. Fauchald, R. Hvidsten. R. Larsen, H. Hennum, W. Olsen.

Irish President Sean T. O'Kelly is introduced to Tommy Eglington by his captain Peter Farrell. Other Irish players that can be seen are, from right to left: Jimmy O'Neill, Con Martin, Eddie Gannon, 'Robin' Lawlor, George Cummins, Fionan Fagan, Paddy Ambrose and Reg Ryan. This was the first official Republic of Ireland team. Don Donovan is hidden behind Peter Farrell.

Ireland dominated for most of the play but were fortunate to win after conceding an early goal. The Irish forwards had difficulty in breaking down the Norwegian defence and it was left to centre-half Martin, the tallest player in the Irish team, to head the break-through.

Ryan and Ambrose were involved in Ireland's first dangerous move which saw Eglington volley over. After 13 minutes Norway broke away with Olsen. The winger cut in, ran at the heart of the defence and shot. Martin managed to block Olsen's effort but was unable to prevent the winger from getting to the rebound and scoring off the post.

Following this Norway were forced to defend for the rest of the half as Ireland raided constantly. "Robin" Lawler played a one-two with Farrell and put Eglington away. The winger swept past two men and passed in for Ryan to shoot but Aronsen saved well.

This pressure continued after the break with Ryan and Eglington coming close before Ambrose had an appeal for a penalty turned down. Norway's breakaways caused problems and Donovan was forced to head a cross off the goal-line with O'Neill beaten. A Norwegian player performed a similar feat at the other end when Svenssen kicked a Martin header away.

After 59 minutes Martin came up for a corner. Fagan sent a high cross across the goal and Martin came in at the far post and headed home. A minute later Hennum pounced on a mistake by O'Neill and sent a shot goalwards. The ball was going in but Larsen latched onto it and helped it on its way into the goal. However, Larsen had been standing in an offside position and when he put the ball in the referee had no option but to disallow the goal as he was clearly interfering with play. Ireland pressed for a winner and Farrell had a shot saved. Another Norwegian breakaway saw Hennum head against the crossbar. On 66 minutes Ambrose was tackled unfairly from behind in the box

The first official Republic of Ireland team lining up with that of Norway before the game at Dalymount Park in 1954.

and Ryan scored from the penalty spot. Ambrose and Ryan had other chances but both were denied by brilliant saves from Aronsen. Norway had the last chance but Fauchald shot over from a pass by Huidsten.
Note: This was the first time the team played under the title of "Republic of Ireland" which was officially designated to them by FIFA.

Match No. 62 — HOLLAND — Home

Sunday 1st May, 1955 – Dublin

REP. OF IRELAND (0) 1 J. Fitzgerald 79
HOLLAND (0) 0

Ref: Luty (England) **Ground:** Dalymount Park **Att:** 16,680

Ireland: Jimmy O'Neill (Everton 8), Don Donovan (Everton 2), Joseph Lawler (Fulham 5), Peter Farrell (Everton 24), Con Martin (Aston Villa 25), Frank O'Farrell (West Ham United 4), Johnny Gavin (Tottenham Hotspur 5), Paddy Ambrose (Shamrock Rovers 2), Jack Fitzgerald (Waterford 1), Arthur Fitzsimons (Middlesbrough 12), Tommy Eglington (Everton 22). **Captain:** Peter Farrell.

Holland: W. Landman, R. Wiersma, K. Kuys, Steenbergen, C. Vander Hart, J. Klaassens, F. Wilkes, H. Schouten, C. Vander Gijp, T. Timmermans, P. Geel. **Subs:** Bruychere for Vander Gijp (11 mins)

Despite an early save from O'Neill it was Ireland who came closest to scoring. Gavin latched onto Fitzsimons through ball and unleashed a powerful shot. Landman got his hands to it but the ball spun out of his grasp and almost crossed the line before the Dutch goalkeeper made a good recovery. A corner by Eglington gave Ambrose another chance but Landman saved his header. The Dutch made a change after 11 minutes when Bruychere came on at outside-right with Wilkes moving in to replace centre-forward Vander Gijp.

The second half started slowly but an excellent move by Martin, Fitzsimons and Eglington gave Ambrose a chance to send in a good header but again Landman brought off an excellent save. Martin was brought down in the box but the referee refused a penalty and later Martin was inches wide with another effort. On 79 minutes Ireland were awarded a free kick. Martin took it and Jack Fitzgerald met the ball with a bullet-like header which Landman was unable to stop from going into the goal. The last chances fell to O'Farrell and Fitzgerald both of which were saved.

The Irish team which beat Holland 1-0 in 1955, left to right: Peter Farrell, Con Martin, Frank O'Farrell, Johnny Gavin, 'Robin' Lawlor, Tommy Eglington, Arthur Fitzsimons, Jack Fitzgerald, Don Donovan, Paddy Ambrose and Jimmy O'Neill.

Republic of Ireland v. Holland, May, 1955.

Jack Fitzgerald, the Dutch goalkeeper and a Dutch defender watch the Irishman's header enter the net for the only score of the match.

Match No. 63 — NORWAY — Away

Wednesday 25th May, 1955 – Oslo

NORWAY (1) 1 Kotte 39
REP. OF IRELAND (1) 3 Cummins 17, 70, Ringstead 80

Ref: Meissner (West Germany) **Ground:** Bislett Stadium **Att:** 18,574

Norway: W. Aronsen, A. Bakker, R. Berge, T. Olsen, T. Svenssen, T. Hernes, R. Hvidsten, R. Kristiansen, A. Kotte, O. Wong Sorensen, W. Olsen.

Ireland: Jimmy O'Neill (Everton 9), Don Donovan (Everton 3), Joseph Lawler (Fulham 6), Eddie Gannon (Shelbourne 13), Con Martin (Aston Villa 26), Frank O'Farrell (West Ham United 5), Alf Ringstead (Sheffield United 9), George Cummins (Luton Town 4), Sean Fallon (Glasgow Celtic 7), Arthur Fitzsimons (Middlesbrough 13), Dessie Glynn (Drumcondra 2) . **Captain:** Con Martin.

On a small pitch, which in places overlapped the athletics track, Ireland were in control for most of the game and, despite going in at the break all square, had all the play in the second period.

Fallon had three good openings early on before Ireland scored after 17 minutes. A free kick by Martin was half-cleared by Aronsen under pressure from Fallon. The ball fell to Fitzsimons but his shot was blocked and came out to him again. The inside-left tricked the defence into thinking he was about to shoot and instead sent in a high cross which Cummins headed into the goal. Norway pressed hard for an equaliser and 6 minutes before the interval Hvidsten set up Kotte to score from an acute angle. Norway deserved their equaliser and had further chances but Kotte and Willy Olsen both missed easy chances.

Ireland had all the play after the break and peppered the Norwegian goal with shots. Svenssen was forced to leave the field for 12 minutes with a head injury but when he re-appeared Norway were still holding on. After 25 minutes Cummins produced a goal out of the blue when he sent a screaming 25 yard shot straight into the top corner of the net. Ten minutes later a shot from Fitzsimons was punched out to the feet of Ringstead by Aronsen and the winger scored with a left-footed shot.

Match No. 64 — WEST GERMANY — Away

Saturday 28th May, 1955 – Hamburg

WEST GERMANY (1) 2 Waldner 13, Mai 62
REP. OF IRELAND (0) 1 Fallon 67

Ref: Vander Meer (Holland) **Ground:** Vorkspark Stadium **Att:** 50,000

West Germany: H. Kubsch, E. Retter, H. Erhardt, R. Schlienz, R. Hoffmann, K. Mai, E. Waldner, H. Weilbächer, U. Biesinger, J. Röhrig, J. Schäfer.

Ireland: Jimmy O'Neill (Everton 10), Don Donovan (Everton 4), Joseph Lawler (Fulham 7), Eddie Gannon (Shelbourne 14), Con Martin (Aston Villa 27), Peter Farrell (Everton 25), Johnny Gavin (Tottenham Hotspur 6), George Cummins (Luton Town 5), Sean Fallon (Glasgow Celtic 8), Arthur Fitzsimons (Middlesbrough 14), Tommy Eglington (Everton 23) . **Captain:** Con Martin.

West Germany were World Champions and it was the first time Ireland had played one of the holders of the games ultimate prize. As befitting their status, the Germans played excellent football and should have won by more but the 2-1 scoreline also reflected the Irish contribution to an entertaining match.

After 11 minutes Weilbächer accepted a Waldner pass to shoot just wide but two minutes later Waldner ran in and flicked the ball into the net following a Röhrig corner. The first Irish chance came after 28 minutes when Lawler and Eglington combined to set up Fitzsimons for a shot which hit the crossbar. Soon after Waldner had another glorious chance but was foiled by an excellent

Kubsch and Schlienz are put under pressure by George Cummins.

save from O'Neill. After 41 minutes Fitzsimons almost got in again but was stopped at the last moment by an excellent tackle from Schlienz.

Early in the second half Fitzsimons shot across the goal but it was the Germans who were to the fore. After 49 minutes Biesinger forced O'Neill into a save but wasted a good chance as Schäfer was completely unmarked in the box. Then Fallon almost got in but Kubsch managed to grab the ball before it could cross the line. After 62 minutes Mai waltzed his way past three static defenders before crashing a shot into the back of the net. Five minutes later Fitzsimons's through ball was deflected by Schlienz to Gavin and his square ball was scrambled home by Fallon despite the efforts of Erhardt. With 4 minutes left Ireland had a chance to salvage a draw but Cummins was denied by another timely tackle from Schlienz. Schlienz incidentally had only one arm, the result of an accident in 1948.

Match No. 65 YUGOSLAVIA Home

Wednesday 19th October, 1955 – Dublin

REP. OF IRELAND (1) 1 Fitzsimons
YUGOSLAVIA (3) 4 Milutinovic (3), Vaselinovic

Ref: Murdock (England) **Ground:** Dalymount Park **Att:** 22,000

Ireland: Jimmy O'Neill (Everton 11), Albie Murphy (Clyde 1), Joseph Lawler (Fulham 8), Peter Farrell (Everton 26), Con Martin (Aston Villa 28), Frank O'Farrell (West Ham United 6), Alf Ringstead (Sheffield United 10), Arthur Fitzsimons (Middlesbrough 15), Shay Gibbons (St Patrick's Athletic 3), George Cummins (Luton Town 6), Liam Tuohy (Shamrock Rovers 1). **Captain:** Peter Farrell.

Yugoslavia: V. Beara, B. Belin, M. Zekovic, V. Boskov, T. Crnkovic, D. Krstic, Z. Rajkov, B. Vukas, M. Milutinovic, P. Vaselinovic, B. Zebec. **Subs:** Kralj for Beara (82 mins).

There was a lot of public protest over the fact that the FAI had arranged a fixture with a communist state and fans were urged not to turn up to support the visit. Despite these calls (and maybe because of them) a crowd of 22,000 turned up and saw an exciting match which was settled by a first half hat-trick from Milutinovic.

Both sides had early chances but after 10 minutes Frank O'Farrell handled the ball just outside the area and the referee awarded a free kick. Milutinovic stepped up and took it sending the ball into the back of the net. Rajkov had a chance soon after but volleyed straight at O'Neill. After 14 minutes Milutinovic intercepted a back-pass by Martin and ran on to net easily for his second.

Holding a two-goal lead the Yugoslaves decided to defend this margin and thus allowed Ireland back into the match. Beara made good saves to stop Gibbons, Ringstead and Cummins before Fitzsimons took advantage of a mistake by Zebec, who had dropped back to defend, to score with a strong shot. A minute from the interval Rajkov and Vukas sent Milutinovic in to complete his hat-trick.

Milutinovic about to score for Yugoslavia despite the close attention of Con Martin and goalkeeper Jimmy O'Neill. This was his second of the three goals he was to score in the first half. Incidentally Milutinovic played as centre-forward despite wearing the No. 8 shirt.

Ireland played better in the second half. Gibbons had a shot parried by Beara with Crnkovic clearing the rebound. Cummins intercepted a back-pass by Belin but, with only the goalkeeper to beat, shot straight at Beara. Milutinovic almost got a fourth before he sent Vaselinovic clear with a defence-splitting pass after 76 minutes. The inside-left rounded O'Neill and scored. The last chance fell to Milutinovic again but this time O'Neill stuck out a foot and saved a certain goal.

Yugoslavian goalkeeper Beara collects the ball before Shay Gibbons or Arthur Fitzsimons can do any damage.

Match No. 66 — SPAIN — Home

Sunday 27th November, 1955 – Dublin

REP. OF IRELAND (1) 2 Fitzsimons 8, Ringstead 76
SPAIN (2) 2 Pahiño 24, 44

Ref: Ellis (England) **Ground:** Dalymount Park **Att:** 35,000

Ireland: Jimmy O'Neill (Everton 12), Seamus Dunne (Luton Town 5), Noel Cantwell (West Ham United 2), Peter Farrell (Everton 27), Con Martin (Aston Villa 29), Reg Ryan (Derby County 16), Alf Ringstead (Sheffield United 11), Arthur Fitzsimons (Middlesbrough 16), Shay Gibbons (St Patrick's Athletic 4), George Cummins (Luton Town 7), Tommy Eglington (Everton 24). **Captain:** Peter Farrell.

Spain: Carmelo, Guillamon, Campanal II, Mauri, Garay, Segarra, Miguel, Maguregui, Pahiño, Manuel Domenech, Collar. **Subs:** Arteche for Manuel Domenech (37 mins)

Ireland and Spain was always an attractive fixture and, as with previous meetings in Dublin, a huge crowd turned up to see this latest instalment. An official attendance of 35,000 was off the mark as an estimated 5,000 more got in when a sudden surge forced one of the gates. However, there were no serious incidents and the game was not interrupted.

Early Irish pressure yielded a free kick after 8 minutes. Cummins took it quickly and gave it to Ringstead. The wingers cross was half-cleared to Farrell who returned it back for Gibbons to set up Fitzsimons to score with a hard shot into the roof of the net. Further Irish play gave chances to Ringstead and Farrell but Spain got back on terms after 24 minutes. Miguel sent in a hard, low shot which O'Neill stopped but could not hold and Pahiño pounced on the loose ball to score. A minute later Collar had a goal ruled out for offside.

After 37 minutes Arteche came on at inside-right with Maguregui moving to inside-left in a tactical move. Just before half-time Collar broke loose from Dunne and made his way to the back-line before sending over an excellent cross which was headed in by the unmarked Pahiño.

Spain had many chances in the second half. Pahiño shot across goal, Collar had two shots wide and Pahiño sent a powerful header off the crossbar and over. Ireland also had chances and pressured the Spanish goal for long periods. Then, after 29 minutes, a long clearance by Martin fell to Gibbons in the box. The centre-forward was tightly marked by Garay but succeeded in chesting the ball into the path of Ringstead who sent a cracking volley into the goal for the equaliser.

Match No. 67 — HOLLAND — Away

Thursday 10th May, 1956 – Rotterdam

HOLLAND (0) 1 Appel 77
REP. OF IRELAND (0) 4 Fitzsimons 52, 67, Haverty 59, Ringstead 71

Ref: Penning (West Germany) **Ground:** Feynoord Stadium **Att:** 60,000

Holland: De Munck, Wiersma, Vander Hart, Odenthal, Brooymans, Klaassens, Appel, Bosselaar, Koopal, Lenstra, Moulijn.

Ireland: Tommy Godwin (Leicester City 10), Seamus Dunne (Luton Town 6), Noel Cantwell (West Ham United 3), Tommy Dunne (St Patrick's Athletic 1), Con Martin (Aston Villa 30), Frank O'Farrell (West Ham United 7), Alf Ringstead (Sheffield United 12), Arthur Fitzsimons (Middlesbrough 17), Jack Fitzgerald (Waterford 2), Liam Whelan (Manchester United 1), Joe Haverty (Arsenal 1). **Captain:** Con Martin.

Ireland had a nervous opening period and Dutch play should have yielded at least two goals before the break. But four goals in a 20 minute spell of the second half gave the Irish a convincing victory.

Despite early Dutch pressure it was Ireland who had the first real chance when a through ball from Fitzsimons sent Whelan clear to crack a shot off the crossbar. The Dutch then had a great chance. A kick out by Godwin fell for Moulijn who returned the ball back into the area for Koopal to chip over Godwin's head but it went wide. Koopal and Appel had further chances but shot wide

Tommy Godwin makes a great but unavailing attempt to stop Holland's only goal. Extreme left Noel Cantwell, and centre Tommy Dunne.

and when Lenstra did get a shot on target, Cantwell cleared off the line. Cantwell repeated that act when he denied Koopal a certain goal at the start of the second half.

Seven minutes after the interval Ringstead and Whelan sent Fitzsimons racing through. The inside-right beat one tackle, then another, drew the goalkeeper and shot past him for the opening goal. Haverty began and finished the move that gave Ireland a second goal. The winger sent Whelan away to cross in for Ringstead's head. De Munck got his hand to the ball and, as it spun into the air, Haverty leapt up and smashed the ball home with a scissors kick. Eight minutes later Fitzsimons picked the ball up on the half-way line, dribbled past three or four tackles and cracked a 15 yard shot home. Ringstead completed a magnificent 20 minute spell with a fourth goal. Whelan and Fitzsimons played some neat football which led Ringstead to shoot another long-range effort into the Dutch net.

Soon after this Haverty went off to get attention for an ankle injury and it was when Ireland were down to ten men that Appel reduced the arrears with a low drive. Koopal was denied a second goal when Godwin brought off an excellent save near the end.

Match No. 68 DENMARK Home

Wednesday 3rd October, 1956 – Dublin (World Cup)

REP. OF IRELAND (2) 2 Curtis 28, Gavin 44 (pen)
DENMARK (0) 1 A. Jensen 86

Ref: Bond (England) **Ground:** Dalymount Park **Att:** 32,600

Ireland: Jimmy O'Neill (Everton 13), Seamus Dunne (Luton Town 7), Noel Cantwell (West Ham United 4), Tommy Dunne (St Patrick's Athletic 2), Gerry Mackey (Shamrock Rovers 1), Ronnie Nolan (Shamrock Rovers 1), Johnny Gavin (Norwich City 7), Liam Whelan (Manchester United 2), Dermot Curtis (Shelbourne 1), Arthur Fitzsimons (Middlesbrough 18), Joe Haverty (Arsenal 2). **Captain:** Seamus Dunne.

Denmark: K., Joergensen, E. Linde Larsen, V. Nielsen, E. Jensen, O. Hansen, J. Olesen, J. Hansen, K. Lundberg, O. Anderson, A. Jensen, O. Bech Nielsen.

A dull game had an exciting opening when after 12 minutes Mackey jinked his way out of defence. Moving upfield he played a one-two with Curtis to leave a defender stranded. Repeating the move with Curtis to get into the box he fired in a hard shot to the back of the net. It looked a great goal but the referee indicated that he had already blown for a Danish free earlier in the move due to a push by Mackey. Soon after a goal kick was missed by Mackey and Anderson was clear

The Irish team which beat Denmark 2-1 in 1956
Back Row (left to right): *S. Dunne, G. Mackey, T. Dunne, J. O'Neill, N. Cantwell, R. Nolan.*
Front Row: *J. Gavin, L. Whelan, D. Curtis, A. Fitzsimons , J. Haverty.*

to run in on goal and shoot. The centre-forward's shot was tipped away for a corner and from the flag kick Anderson sent a flashing header just wide.

After 28 minutes a hard shot by Fitzsimons struck Ove Hansen and deflected to Curtis who was standing in an offside position. Curtis slammed the ball into the net and to the surprise of the Danes the referee allowed the goal. Mr. Bond stated later that Curtis was offside but not interfering with play as he was standing still! There was a flurry of activity following this goal. A shot by Fitzsimons hit the post and Cantwell cleared a shot by Ove Bech Nielsen off the goal-line. A minute before the break Haverty burst into the box and was taken down by Erling Linde Larsen. Gavin took the resultant penalty which Joergensen turned onto a post but it went into the goal.

The second half was very tedious with the only highlights being a lob shot by Curtis just over and a good shot from Ove Bech Nielsen being saved by O'Neill. With 4 minutes left the Irish goalkeeper came out of his box to clear a ball but Anderson got to it first and sent it back into the area. Aage Jensen headed it in; Seamus Dunne just failing to head clear as it crossed the line.

Match No. 69 WEST GERMANY Home

Sunday 25th November, 1956 – Dublin

REP. OF IRELAND (0) 3 Cantwell 63 (pen) Haverty 87, McCann 89
WEST GERMANY (0) 0

Ref: Murdock (England) **Ground:** Dalymount Park **Att:** 35,000

Ireland: Alan Kelly (Drumcondra 1), Seamus Dunne (Luton Town 8), Noel Cantwell (West Ham United 5), Tommy Dunne (St Patrick's Athletic 3), Gerry Mackey (Shamrock Rovers 2), Ronnie Nolan (Shamrock Rovers 2), Jimmy McCann (Shamrock Rovers 1), Noel Peyton (Shamrock Rovers 1), Dermot Curtis (Shelbourne 2), Arthur Fitzsimons (Middlesbrough 19), Joe Haverty (Arsenal 3). **Captain:** Gerry Mackey

West Germany: H. Kwiatkowski, H. Erhardt, E. Juskowiak, E. Schlebrowski, H. Wewens, K. Mai, H. Rahn, M. Morlock, J. Miltz, H. Schäfer, H. Vollmar. **Subs:** H. Eckel for Schäfer (17 mins).

Despite a dull first half, the Irish were the better team throughout the game and a great second half display enabled Ireland to inflict on West Germany their heaviest defeat since they won the World Cup in 1954.

Ireland had three early chances. Fitzsimons had a header saved, McCann was denied by another save and Curtis's back-header was stopped by the German goalkeeper. Kelly, in the other goal,

Seamus Dunne captained the Irish team to a victory against Denmark in 1956.

Noel Peyton made his international debut against West Germany.

brought off a good save to prevent Morlock from scoring. Haverty was brought down in the box but no penalty was awarded and Kelly saved again to stop Miltz. Curtis headed inches wide before Kwiatkowski brought off a marvellous triple save to stop shots by Fitzsimons, Curtis and Fitzsimons again.

Early in the second half a cross from Nolan was handled in the box but the referee waved play on. After 18 minutes the referee finally awarded a penalty when Erhardt and Wewens sandwiched Curtis just inside the area. Cantwell hit an unstoppable spot-kick out of Kwiatkowski's reach for

German goalkeeper Kwiatkowski saves from Dermot Curtis.

his first goal for Ireland. On 67 minutes Mai raced into the box and shot against the post before Vollmar had Germany's best chance. The German winger received the ball when an Irish corner was cleared and skipped past the last man back, Seamus Dunne. With the rest of the defence trying to get back, Vollmar raced clear to face Kelly one-on-one. The German, in sizing up his options, delayed his shot and Kelly, anticipating this, timed his advance perfectly to save at Vollmar's feet.

With three minutes to go Fitzsimons outwitted the German defence and sent an excellent defence-splitting pass to Haverty. The winger exploited a huge gap in the defence and ran through. As the defenders rushed in on either side to close him down and the goalkeeper advanced to do likewise, Haverty waited until the last moment and knocked the ball past Kwiatkowski into the goal. In the last minute a short corner by "Maxie" McCann found Tommy Dunne who returned it to McCann in space. The winger unleashed a powerful shot from an awkward angle which deflected off Juskowiak's head into the net for Ireland's third.

Match No. 70 — ENGLAND — Away

Wednesday 8th May, 1957 – London (World Cup)

ENGLAND (4) 5 Taylor 9, 18, 40, Atyeo 38, 89
REP. OF IRELAND (0) 1 Curtis 56

Ref: Phillips (Scotland) **Ground:** Wembley Stadium **Att:** 51,000

England: A. Hodgkinson, J. Hall, R. Byrne, R. Clayton, B. Wright, D. Edwards, S. Matthews, J. Atyeo, T. Taylor, J. Haynes, T. Finney.

Ireland: Alan Kelly (Drumcondra 2), Don Donovan (Everton 5), Noel Cantwell (West Ham United 6), Peter Farrell (Everton 28), Gerry Mackey (Shamrock Rovers 3), Pat Saward (Aston Villa 2), Alf Ringstead (Sheffield United 13), Liam Whelan (Manchester United 3), Dermot Curtis (Bristol City 3), Arthur Fitzsimons (Middlesbrough 20), Joe Haverty (Arsenal 4). **Captain:** Peter Farrell

This first ever World Cup tie at Wembley Stadium did not attract a large attendance. Those that turned up, including a large section of Irish supporters, saw England take an early lead. Haynes paved the way for Taylor to take his pass on the run, beat Saward and score with a cracking low

Alan Kelly fails to stop England's third goal. Also in the picture Cantwell (3), Tommy Taylor (9) and Mackey (5).

Alan Kelly dives at the feet of England's Johnny Haynes during the 1957 World Cup match in Wembley. Noel Cantwell jumps to avoid Kelly watched by Gerry Mackey.

shot. Nine minutes later Finney sent Taylor away again, and, with nobody to challenge him, the centre-forward ran 20 yards to score from the edge of the box with a shot that deceived Kelly. Ireland saw a good deal of play after this but could not break down a strong defence and coming up to the break England scored two goals in as many minutes. First, Finney beat Donovan and sent in a cross-cum-shot. Kelly got a hand to the ball, parried it but Atyeo ducked low and nodded the ball home. Taylor then completed his hat-trick when he headed in Finney's corner. Before half-time Atyeo had two further chances but Kelly saved one and the other went just over.

England's performance in the second half was dismal compared to what had gone on in the first. However, Ireland's display improved so much so that they had the majority of the play. Whelan and Curtis set up Fitzsimons to fully test Hodgkinson. The goalkeeper pushed this effort out to Ringstead whose shot was blocked by a host of defenders. After 11 minutes Haverty beat Hall and sent over a beautiful cross which was headed in by Curtis. Ringstead had another effort saved while England had chances when Atyeo shot over and Taylor shot wide. Fitzsimons and Farrell came close and Whelan hit the crossbar before England scored in the last minute. Atyeo began and finished the move when he sent Finney clear and shot home the wingers pass.

Match No. 71 — ENGLAND — Home

Sunday 19th May, 1957 – Dublin (World Cup)

REP. OF IRELAND (1) 1 Ringstead 3
ENGLAND (0) 1 Ayteo 90

Ref: Phillips (Scotland) **Ground:** Dalymount Park **Att:** 47,600

Ireland: Tommy Godwin (Bournemouth 11), Seamus Dunne (Luton Town 9), Noel Cantwell (West Ham United 7), Ronnie Nolan (Shamrock Rovers 3), Charlie Hurley (Millwall 1), Pat Saward (Aston Villa 3), Alf Ringstead (Sheffield United 14), Liam Whelan (Manchester United 4), Dermot Curtis (Bristol City 4), Arthur Fitzsimons (Middlesbrough 21), Joe Haverty (Arsenal 5). **Captain:** Noel Cantwell.

England: A. Hodgkinson, J. Hall, R. Byrne, R. Clayton, B. Wright, D. Edwards, T. Finney, J. Atyeo, T. Taylor, J. Haynes, D. Pegg.

England travelled to Dublin knowing that a draw would see them through to the final stages of the 1958 World Cup. With each group being decided on points only, the English only needed one to be sure. Ireland had two points from two games and victories against England and the part-timers of Denmark would leave them level on points with England, thus forcing a play-off. This was the scenario as both teams lined-up in front of a record crowd at Dalymount Park.

Ireland got a great start with a goal after only three minutes. Hurley found Haverty and his pass went to Fitzsimons via Whelan. The inside-right raced up to the back-line and sent over a high cross which missed a group of players on the near post but came to the unmarked Ringstead who smacked the ball home.

After 7 minutes Atyeo was sent clean through but Godwin came out and saved at his feet. Three minutes later Whelan headed down a cross into the path of Ringstead but the winger shot wide. Fitzsimons had another effort saved by Hodgkinson and the English 'keeper got a hand to a later shot from Haverty. After 22 minutes Taylor was clean through but again Godwin saved at his feet. Edwards, Taylor and Haynes had further chances but in a half dominated by Ireland it was the home side who had the last chance before the break. Hurley and Curtis sent Fitzsimons through and the inside-left's shot was only inches wide.

The first period had produced excellent, passionate, football and this was repeated in the second which saw England pressing for an equaliser. Godwin was in action early saving well from Taylor and Haynes while Seamus Dunne kicked a Clayton shot off the line. Ireland came back with a Ringstead shot which was just wide. With 15 minutes to go Haverty took advantage of confusion in the English defence to shoot towards an empty goal but Billy Wright just managed to dive and deflect the ball away with his head.

As time was slowly running out for England, Taylor missed another chance as did Haverty at the other end. In the countdown to the final whistle the "Dalymount Roar" reached a crescendo as fans waved scarfs, banners, flags, hankies, whatever in an effort to encourage the referee to blow for full-time. The game went into injury time as Finney beat Saward on the standside touchline. Cantwell, expecting Finney to cut in and shoot, held off, allowing the winger space to send in a high cross. The ball went over Taylor and Hurley at the near post for the incoming Atyeo to head it into the net amid a sudden silence. Fans behind the goal felt Atyeo had used his shoulder to put the ball in but the goal stood and England qualified for the Finals.

The real tragedy however came during the following season when the Munich Air disaster claimed the lives of Roger Byrne, Duncan Edwards, David Pegg, Tommy Taylor and Liam Whelan. These were five of eight Manchester United players killed in a total of 23 fatalities which included some of the English newspapers reporters who had covered the match·above.

Match No. 72 **DENMARK** **Away**

Wednesday 2nd October, 1957 – Copenhagen (World Cup)

DENMARK (0) 0
REP. OF IRELAND (0) 2 Cummins 53, Curtis 62

Ref: Schulz (East Germany) **Ground:** Idraetspark **Att:** 28,000

Denmark: H. From, E. Linde Larsen, V. Nielsen, F. Nielsen, P. Andersen, J. Olesen, P. Pedersen, E. Jensen, F. A. Hansen, C. Mosegaard, P. Kjaer.

Ireland: Tommy Godwin (Bournemouth 12), Seamus Dunne (Luton Town 10), Noel Cantwell (West Ham United 8), Pat Saward (Aston Villa 4), Charlie Hurley (Sunderland 2), Frank O'Farrell (Preston 8), Alf Ringstead (Sheffield United 15), Arthur Fitzsimons (Middlesbrough 22), Dermot Curtis (Bristol City 5), George Cummins (Luton Town 8), Joe Haverty (Arsenal 6). **Captain:** Noel Cantwell.

Ireland's first visit to Copenhagen ended controversially when an angry crowd gathered outside the stadium to protest against the Irish tactics of 'sitting' on a two-goal lead. Some of the 'tactics' were mis-interpreted by the Danes but their anger was such that the Irish squad, officials and pressmen had to be shepherded away from the ground by a back route.

Denmark had a good first half and tested Godwin with shots from Kjaer, Mosegaard and Flemming Nielsen before Ringstead came close at the other end. Pedersen and Olesen had further Danish chances before the break.

Ireland opened the second half positively. Fitzsimons worked his way down the field and fired inches wide. On 53 minutes Ringstead put Fitzsimons in possession. The inside-right, with his back to goal, turned and crossed high into the area for Cummins to meet it with a powerful header and send it into the net. Danish protests led to the referee consulting his linesman before awarding the goal. Six minutes later Fitzsimons again crossed for Cummins to head in again but this time the referee ruled it out for offside. The referee was having a poor game and this was one of a number of strange decisions he made during the match as there seemed nothing wrong with the strike. However, three minutes after this, Ireland scored again. O'Farrell found Cummins near the goal-line. The inside-left worked his way into the box and squared the ball for Curtis to score.

After this initial assault, the Irish decided to defend their lead and thus allowed Denmark back into the game. It was from this point that the Danish crowd became frustrated and among the incidents which brought the wrath of the crowd were Irish players going down "injured" on the pitch, keeping possession of the ball and, not least of which, some strange refereeing decisions. Denmark had three late chances; Pedersen's effort was saved by Godwin, Olesen was wide with another effort while Hurley made a goal-line clearance to deny another Dane.

As Curtis stumbles, Cummins moves on to his pass to shoot home Irelands second goal against Poland in Katowice. (Photo: CAF/PAP)

Match No. 73 **POLAND** **Away**

Sunday 11th May, 1958 – Katowice

POLAND	**(1) 2**	Cieslik 25, Zientara 74
REP. OF IRELAND	**(1) 2**	Curtis 12, Cummins 49

Ref: Romain (Austria) **Ground:** Slaski Stadium **Att:** 100,000

Poland: Szymkowiak, Florenski, Korynt, Wozniak, Gawlik, Zientara, Jezierski, Jankowski, Cieslik, Soporek, Lentner. **Subs:** Suszczyk for Gawlik (39 mins).

Ireland: Tommy Godwin (Bournemouth 13), Seamus Dunne (Luton Town 11), Noel Cantwell (West Ham United 9), Ronnie Nolan (Shamrock Rovers 4), Charlie Hurley (Sunderland 3), Pat Saward (Aston Villa 5), Alf Ringstead (Sheffield United 16), George Cummins (Luton Town 9), Dermot Curtis (Bristol City 6), Arthur Fitzsimons (Middlesbrough 23), Joe Haverty (Arsenal 7). **Captain:** Noel Cantwell.

Nearly twenty years after their visit to Poland, Ireland returned to renew a rivallary which would continue intermittently over the next three decades. Soccer had always played a major part in Polish life and Ireland's first visit behind, what Churchill called the 'Iron Curtain', attracted a crowd of 100,000.

Despite a scorching hot day (the temperature was over 80°c) Ireland did most of the attacking and scored after 12 minutes when Curtis headed home a great cross from Ringstead. Poland equalised with a marvellous solo goal. Cieslik worked his way forward and, as Hurley came out to challenge, a sudden burst of speed left Ireland's centre-half for dead. Taking it on Cieslik sent in a cracking shot which found the back of the net.

It had been pretty even during the first half but Ireland had the better of exchanges in the second period and got a goal after 4 minutes. Curtis dribbled to the back-line, cut inside Wozniak and squared the ball for Cummins to hit it on the run into the net. Poland came back again and got the equaliser when Zientara broke from defence and raced on to Suszczyk's through ball to score.

Match No. 74 **AUSTRIA** **Away**

Wednesday 14th May, 1958 – Vienna

AUSTRIA (1) 3 Körner II 20, Buzek 59, Hamerl 79,
REP. OF IRELAND (0) 1 Curtis 70

Ref: Wyssling (Switzerland) **Ground:** Praeter Park **Att:** 35,000

Austria: R. Szanwald, P. Halla, E. Happel, F. Swoboda, G. Hanappi, K. Koller, W. Horak, H. Sanekovitsch, J. Buzek, A. Körner II, J. Hamerl. **Subs:** W. Schleger for Swoboda.

Ireland: Jimmy O'Neill (Everton 14), Seamus Dunne (Luton Town 12), Noel Cantwell (West Ham United 10), Mick McGrath (Blackburn Rovers 1), Charlie Hurley (Sunderland 6), Pat Saward (Aston Villa 6), Alf Ringstead (Sheffield United 17), George Cummins (Luton Town 10), Dermot Curtis (Bristol City 7), Arthur Fitzsimons (Middlesbrough 24), Joe Haverty (Arsenal 8). **Captain:** Noel Cantwell.

Sanekovitsch and Buzek had early efforts before Austria took the lead after 20 minutes. Horak found his way to the back-line and his cross was knocked on by Buzek for Körner to score with a low shot. A few minutes later Sanekovitsch rounded O'Neill but his shot was kicked off the line by Seamus Dunne. Ireland had few chances but were playing well.

After 59 minutes Buzek challenged Hurley in the air. The Irish centre-half won the battle but his header back to O'Neill was short and Buzek ran onto it and shot past O'Neill. Austria were playing great football in this second half and it was against the run of play that Ireland scored. A corner by Ringstead was cleared out to Dunne and he gave it back to the winger in space. Ringstead sent in a high cross for Curtis to head a goal back for Ireland. Nine minutes later a corner by Horak was headed into the net by Hamerl for Austria to regain their two-goal lead. Horak went off injured soon after and for the last few minutes Ireland tried hard for another goal against 10-man Austria. Haverty, Fitzsimons and Ringstead all had chances but could not score.

Austria's third goal headed in by Josef Hamerl, not in picture. Players left to right: Helmut Sanekovitsch, Jimmy O'Neill, Johann Buzek, Mick McGrath, Charlie Hurley and Karl Koller. (Photo: Votavafoto)

Match No. 75 POLAND Home

Sunday 5th October, 1958 – Dublin

REP. OF IRELAND (2) 2 Cantwell 26 (pen), 31
POLAND (2) 2 Pol 17, 19

Ref: Clough (England) **Ground:** Dalymount Park **Att:** 23,000

Ireland: Jimmy O'Neill (Everton 15), Seamus Dunne (Luton Town 13), Noel Cantwell (West Ham United 11), Mick McGrath (Blackburn Rovers 2), Shay Keogh (Shamrock Rovers 1), Pat Saward (Aston Villa 7), Alf Ringstead (Sheffield United 18), Arthur Fitzsimons (Middlesbrough 25), Dermot Curtis (Ipswich Town 8), George Cummins (Luton Town 11), Joe Haverty (Arsenal 9). **Subs:** Tommy Taylor (Waterford 1), for O'Neill (65 mins). **Captain:** Noel Cantwell.

Poland: E. Szymkowiak, S. Florenski, R. Korynt, J. Wozniak, G. Gawlik, E. Zientara, E. Pol, W. Majewski, S. Hachorek, M. Norkowski, K. Basziewicz.

Poland made a good start and Pol had an early angled shot saved by O'Neill. Curtis had a chance at the other end but shot well over. The quiet opening was shattered after 17 minutes when Poland scored twice in as many minutes. Basziewicz sent in a low cross which was going away from O'Neill. The goalkeeper came out and managed to get a hand to the ball but only succeeded in shoving it to Pol's feet for the forward to score. The same players were involved in Poland's second. Basziewicz sent in another low centre which spun out of O'Neill's hands and Pol was there again to score.

Ireland fought back and Curtis shot wide before Fitzsimons was sandwiched between Korynt and Wozniak in the box and Cantwell shot home the penalty which was awarded. Five minutes later Cantwell came up for a corner which was cleared out by Wozniak. The ball fell for Cummins to send it back into the box and Cantwell volleyed it home as it came down off Ringstead.

The second half was poor and there were few highlights. O'Neill brought off a brilliant save to stop Hachorek but in doing so he was injured and was replaced by Taylor.

Match No. 76 CZECHOSLOVAKIA Home

Sunday 5th April, 1959 – Dublin (European Championship)

REP. OF IRELAND (2) 2 Tuohy 21, Cantwell 41 (pen)
CZECHOSLOVAKIA (0) 0

Ref: Van Nuffel (Belgium) **Ground:** Dalymount Park **Att:** 42,000

Ireland: Jimmy O'Neill (Everton 16), Brendan McNally (Luton Town 1), Noel Cantwell (West Ham United 12), Mick McGrath (Blackburn Rovers 3), Charlie Hurley (Sunderland 5), Pat Saward (Aston Villa 8), Alf Ringstead (Sheffield United 19), Tommy Hamilton (Shamrock Rovers 1), Christy Doyle (Shelbourne 1), George Cummins (Luton Town 12), Liam Tuohy (Shamrock Rovers 2). **Captain:** Noel Cantwell.

CSSR: I. Stacho, J. Tichy, G. Mraz, S. Pluskal, J. Popluhar, T. Bubernik, J. Brumovsky, A. Moravcik, L. Kacani, P. Molnar, T. Kraus. **Subs:** J. Hildebrandt for Mraz (18 mins)

The first European Nations Cup attracted only just over half the countries entitled to compete and, with the competition being run on a knock-out system, a preliminary round was needed to reach a final 16. Ireland and Czechoslovakia were picked out to play this round; the winners to meet Denmark in the first round proper.

The first leg of this meeting was played at Dalymount Park and a big crowd turned up for this first visit by a Czech side. Ireland attacked from the start hoping to build a good lead to take with them to Czechaslovakia. After 19 minutes Cummins met a Ringstead cross and headed against the post, but two minutes later another header, this time by Tuohy, found the net following a cross by Hamilton. Seven minutes later Hamilton's lob was tipped over by Stacho. Ireland continued on the attack and four minutes before the interval they got a free. Cummins took it but it was cleared out to him again. The inside-left again lobbed it into the box where Hildebrandt, under no pressure, handled the ball. Cantwell placed the spot-kick well out of Stacho's reach and into the corner of the net.

Czechlovakia saw a good deal of play after the interval but rarely threatened the Irish goal. Ireland, however, had a great chance. Cantwell put Hamilton through on-side, catching the entire Czech defence napping. But Hamilton, with only the goalkeeper to beat, shot weakly and Stacho saved. Near the end a hard shot from Brumovsky smacked against the crossbar for the Czechs only real chance.

Match No. 77 — CZECHOSLOVAKIA — Away

Sunday 10th May, 1959 – Bratislava (European Championship)

CZECHOSLOVAKIA (1) 4 Stacho 4 (pen), Bubernik 57, Paulovic 67, Dolinsky 75

REP. OF IRELAND (0) 0

Ref: Barberan (France) **Ground:** Tehelne Pole Stadium **Att:** 60,000

CSSR: I. Stacho, J. Tichy, J. Popluhar, L. Novak, S. Matlak, T. Bubernik, L. Paulovic, A. Scherer, V. Bubnik, L. Kaconi, M. Dolinsky.

Ireland: Jimmy O'Neill (Everton 17), Richard Whittaker (Chelsea 1), Noel Cantwell (West Ham United 13), Frank O'Farrell (Preston 9), Charlie Hurley (Sunderland 6), Mick McGrath (Blackburn Rovers 4), Alf Ringstead (Sheffield United 20), Tommy Hamilton (Shamrock Rovers 2), Arthur Fitzsimons (Lincoln City 26), George Cummins (Luton Town 13), Liam Tuohy (Shamrock Rovers 3). **Captain:** Noel Cantwell.

Straight from the kick-off Ireland attacked with Fitzsimons running through the defence before giving Hamilton a great chance but the inside-right shot wide with only Stacho to beat. Three minutes later Ireland were a goal down. Paulovic chased a ball which appeared to be going out. Stopping it right on the line, he sent a looping cross over Hurley's head for Bubernik to head past O'Neill but O'Farrell stopped it from crossing the line with his hands and a penalty was given. The Czech goalkeeper, Stacho, came upfield and scored with the spot-kick. Both teams had chances following this. Cummins shot across goal, Dolinsky shot over and Fitzsimons had a header brilliantly saved by Stacho. Near the interval Bubernik had a free kick wide and at half-time Czechoslovakia were 1-2 down on aggregate.

Ireland started the second half well. Tuohy found McGrath in the clear and when the left-halfs cross came into the box Tuohy met it with a firm header which Stacho saved well. The Irish though concentrated on defence, giving Czechoslovakia the majority of the play. After 12 minutes a corner by Scherer was missed by O'Neill and Bubernik headed in the aggregate equaliser. Ten minutes later Dolinsky crossed in for Paulovic to net. The Czechs were reduced to 10 men after 70 minutes when Tichy was stretchered off injured but still managed a fourth goal when Dolinsky was unmarked in the box to score.

Match No. 78 — SWEDEN — Home

Sunday 1st November, 1959 – Dublin

REP. OF IRELAND (2) 3 Giles 16, Curtis 24, 53

SWEDEN (2) 2 Börjesson 7, Berndtsson 12

Ref: Holland (England) **Ground:** Dalymount Park **Att:** 40,250

Ireland: Noel Dwyer (West Ham United 1), Joe Carolan (Manchester United 1), Noel Cantwell (West Ham United 14), Mick McGrath (Blackburn Rovers 5), Charlie Hurley (Sunderland 7), Pat Saward (Aston Villa 9), Fionan Fagan (Manchester City 2), Johnny Giles (Manchester United 1), Dermot Curtis (Ipswich Town 9), George Cummins (Luton Town 14), Joe Haverty (Arsenal 10). **Captain:** Noel Cantwell.

Sweden: B. Nyholm, O. Bergmark, S. Axbom, T. Jonsson, Ä. Johansson, S. Parling, B. Berndtsson, H. Thillberg, A. Simonsson, R. Börjesson, B. Salomonsson.

The World Cup finalists travelled to Dublin having beaten England 3-2 at Wembly on Wednesday. Scorer of two of the goals against England was Agne Simonsson and he was expected to be the main danger to Ireland. Simonsson had a very quiet game and the reason for that was a superb display by Hurley who had spent much of the previous 24 hours travelling to the game!

Sweden got off to a great start. An Irish attack broke up and Simonsson and Börjesson were left in the clear. Playing a series of one-two's they worked their way up the field before Börjesson sent in a hard shot. Dwyer had it covered but the ball deflected off McGrath, wrong-footing the goalkeeper, and went into the net. Five minutes later the ball was played out to Berndtsson and he caught everybody out by curling the ball with the outside of his foot into the net. Ireland were back into the game four minutes later. Fagan's lob into the area was cleared out to him again and the winger sent in another cross. This time the headed clearance fell for Giles 30 yards out and before it reached the ground the inside-right volleyed it straight into the top of the net. Ireland equalised on 24 miniutes. Saward and Cantwell started the move which led to Curtis giving Giles possession. Giles swung a long ball out to Haverty. The winger had Cumins in close attendance and was able to use his presence to get around Bergmark. Haverty sent in a brilliant cross for Curtis to time his jump perfectly and place a header into the net.

Ireland had two further goals ruled out for offside before they got the winning goal 8 minutes into the second half. Cummins got possession from a Saward throw-in and worked his way past two defenders on the by-line before squaring the ball for Curtis to chip the ball over Nyholm.

Dermot Curtis beats Swedish goalkeeper Nyholm with a chipped shot from a Cummins pass for the winning goal against Sweden in 1959.

	P	W	D	L	F	A
International Record	**P**	**W**	**D**	**L**	**F**	**A**
1950-1959	32	14	6	12	55	65
Home	17	9	5	3	36	24
Away	15	5	1	9	19	41
International Record	**P**	**W**	**D**	**L**	**F**	**A**
1926-1959	78	30	15	33	136	157
Home	39	17	8	14	79	71
Away	39	13	7	19	57	86
World Cup Record	**P**	**W**	**D**	**L**	**F**	**A**
1934-1959	16	5	4	7	31	35
Home	8	3	3	2	21	17
Away	8	2	1	5	10	18

EuropeanChampionship Record

	P	W	D	L	F	A
1959	2	1	0	1	2	4
Home	1	1	0	0	2	0
Away	1	0	0	1	0	4

Number of players capped by Ireland	193
Number of goalscorers for Ireland	49 (+ 1 own goal)
Number of nations played	20

Leading Goalscorers		**Most Capped Players**	
Jimmy Dunne	13	Con Martin	30
Dermot Curtis	7	Johnny Carey	29
Arthur Fitzsimons		Peter Farrell	28
Paddy Moore		Arthur Fitzsimons	26
Alf Ringstead		Tommy Eglington	24
Con Martin	6	Joe O'Reilly	20
George Cummins	5	Alf Ringstead	
Davy Walsh		Davy Walsh	

Penalties awarded to Ireland 20 (16 scored, 2 saved, 2 missed)
Penalties awarded against Ireland 9 (6 scored, 2 saved, 1 missed)

Hat-tricks for Ireland

John Joe Flood	3 goals	v Belgium	1929
Paddy Moore	4 goals	v Belgium	1934

Hat-tricks against Ireland

Kalle Palmer, Sweden	3 goals	1929
Jef Mermans, Belgium	3 goals	1950
Adolf Huber, Austria	3 goals	1952
Milos Milutinovic, Yugoslavia	3 goals	1955
Tommy Taylor, England	3 goals	1957

Irish Captains
19 Johnny Carey
12 Peter Farrell
8 Noel Cantwell, Charlie Turner
5 Jimmy Dunne, Paddy Gaskins, Con Martin
4 William Glen
2 Tommy Eglington, Mick O'Brien
1 Frank Brady, John Burke, Harry Chatton, Seamus Dunne, John Joe Flood, Mick Foley, Jack McCarthy, Gerry Mackey

Own goals for Ireland
Josef Posipal, West Germany 1951

Own goals by Irish players
None

Leading goalscorers against Ireland
4 Reider Kvammen, Norway
Telmo Zarraonandia Montoya "Zarra", Spain
Jef Mermans, Belgium

Match No. 79 — CHILE — Home

Wednesday 30th March, 1960 – Dublin

REP. OF IRELAND (1) 2 Cantwell 16 (pen), Curtis 80
CHILE (0) 0

Ref: Aston (England) **Ground:** Dalymount Park **Att:** 17,000

Ireland: Noel Dwyer (West Ham United 2), Joe Carolan (Manchester United 2), Noel Cantwell (West Ham United 15), Ronnie Nolan (Shamrock Rovers 5), Charlie Hurley (Sunderland 8), Pat Saward (Aston Villa 10), Fionan Fagan (Derby County 3), Johnny Giles (Manchester United 2), Dermot Curtis (Ipswich Town 10), George Cummins (Luton Town 15), Joe Haverty (Arsenal 11). **Captain:** Noel Cantwell.

Chile: Coloma, Eyzaguirre, Navarro, Luco, Raul Sanchez, Rodriguez, Moreno, Fouilloux, Juan Soto, Leonel Sanchez, Musso.

Chile came to Dublin to play their third game of a 5 match tour of Europe. The weather they encountered was not to their liking and the cold was matched by constant heavy rain which not only reduced the attendance but also turned the pitch into a quagmire.

The visitors had a good start when Moreno found Fouilloux on the goal-line and he crossed in for Leonel Sanchez to shoot inches wide. Giles had a shot blocked by Raul Sanchez and Nolan had another shot saved before Curtis almost scored in spectular fashion. Nolan set Cummins up and when the inside-left crossed Curtis dived forward knocking the ball over with his heel. After 16 minutes Saward played the ball through a gap in defence and as Cummins ran onto it he was brought down in the box by Eyzaguirre. The referee awarded a penalty and Cantwell sent the goalkeeper the wrong way with his kick.

Up until then Chile had played some nice football but following the penalty they began to foul regularly. Haverty and Fagan suffered most and despite warnings from the referee the Chileans continued. Juan Soto almost got in for an equaliser but shot wide while Cantwell sent in a tremendous shot at the other end which Coloma turned out for a corner. Some of the Irish players began to indulge in fouling and Fagan was lucky when, after taking Musso down in the penalty area, the referee waved play on.

The second half was littered with fouls which made constructive football difficult. Moreno had a shot which was deflected for Dwyer to save well. Moreno had another chance but his free kick was well saved again. Eyzaguirre was booked for persistant fouls on Haverty before Giles had two efforts wide and Cummins had a shot punched over the bar by the goalkeeper. After 35 minutes Saward gave a lovely pass to Curtis. The centre-forward hit a lovely shot from the edge of the area which hit the underside of the crossbar and bounced down over the line. Ireland nearly had a third goal near the end when Giles's free kick found the head of Curtis, only a few yards from goal, but the forward knocked the ball straight into Coloma's hands.

Match No. 80 — WEST GERMANY — Away

Wednesday 11th May, 1960 – Düsseldorf

WEST GERMANY (0) 0
REP. OF IRELAND (1) 1 Fagan 30

Ref: Ellis (England) **Ground:** Rheinstadion **Att:** 51,000

Germany: G. Sawitzki, W. Giesemann, H. Erhardt, W. Schulz, F. Wenauer, I. Porges, B. Steffen, A. Schmidt, A. Brülls, H. Haller, H. Vollmar.

Ireland: Noel Dwyer (West Ham United 3), Seamus Dunne (Luton Town 14), Ronnie Nolan (Shamrock Rovers 6), Mick McGrath (Blackburn Rovers 6), Charlie Hurley (Sunderland 9), Pat Saward (Aston Villa 11), Ambrose Fogarty (Sunderland 1), Noel Peyton (Leeds United 2), Dermot Curtis (Ipswich Town 11), George Cummins (Luton Town 16), Fionan Fagan (Derby County 4). **Captain:** Pat Saward.

Ireland began it's continental tour with this eighth meeting with Germany. The previous seven games had gone with the home side and with Germany undefeated at home for three years their manager decided to experiment; playing three new players.

Germany had a nervous opening and the Irish had the majority of the play early on. The first chance, though, fell to Germany after 5 minutes when Haller's diving header was punched over by Dwyer. Dunne twice cleared his line before Fogarty had a shot deflected by Porges for a corner. After 30 minutes Sawitzki punched away a cross under pressure but the ball fell to Fagan and, although it was on his 'wrong' foot, he slammed it into the net. Germany came more into the game following this set-back and Haller had a good chance but shot over. In the last minute of the half a shot by Curtis was parried by Sawitzki who recovered well to save Fagan's follow-up.

The second-half belonged to Germany for long periods. After 5 minutes Haller beat two defenders and crossed for Brülls to net but the centre-forward was offside. Haller shot wide before Ireland had a good spell which saw Cummins shoot over, Fagan having a shot saved and Peyton come close twice. Germany's final efforts saw Vollmar hit the crossbar and Dwyer saving from Brülls and Haller.

Match No. 81 — SWEDEN — Away

Wednesday 18th May, 1960 – Malmö

SWEDEN (3) 4 Simonsson 25, 30, S.Dunne (o.g.) 43, Börjesson 89

REP. OF IRELAND (0) 1 Fagan 77 (pen)

Ref: Bronkhurst (Holland) **Ground:** Malmö Stadium **Att:** 31,339

Sweden: B. Nyholm, O. Bergmark, H. Mild, T. Jonsson, A. Johansson, S. Parling, B. Berndtsson, O. Ohlsson, A. Simonsson, R. Börjesson, L. Backman.

Ireland: Noel Dwyer (West Ham United 4), Seamus Dunne (Luton Town 15), Ronnie Nolan (Shamrock Rovers 7), Mick McGrath (Blackburn Rovers 7), Charlie Hurley (Sunderland 10), Pat Saward (Aston Villa 12), Dermot Curtis (Ipswich Town 12), Ambrose Fogarty (Sunderland 2), Noel Cantwell (West Ham United 16), George Cummins (Luton Town 17), Fionan Fagan (Derby County 5). **Subs:** Noel Peyton (Leeds United 3) for Cantwell (43 mins), Maurice Swan (Drumcondra 1), for Dwyer (half-time). **Captain:** Noel Cantwell.

Sweden had only lost one home game since 1955 and that was the World Cup Final against Brazil. So when Ireland came to Malmö to play it's final game of the tour the Swedes expected their team to avenge their defeat at Ireland's hands last November.

Ireland forced a number of openings early on but did not bother Nyholm as their shooting was off. After 15 minutes Cantwell was injured in a collision with the Swedish goalkeeper and was basically a passenger from then until he was replaced. After 25 minutes Börjesson passed in for Simonsson to score and 5 minutes later Jonsson and Börjesson gave Simonsson an easy chance to score his second. On 43 minutes Berndtsson tried to 'nut-meg' Dunne but the ball hit the right backs leg and spun into the net.

Dwyer injured his elbow during the first half and did not re-appear after the interval; Swan making his international debut. Fogarty had an early shot wide before Sweden had three great chances in a 6 minute spell mid-way through the half. First Simonsson shot wide when well placed. Then a shot by Berndtsson spun out of Swan's hands but Simonsson slipped when trying to shoot. Finally Backman shot against the post. After 77 minutes Curtis was brought down in the box by Johansson and Fagan shot home the penalty. In the last minute a hard back pass by Dunne was only tipped by Swan and Börjesson nipped to tap the ball into the net.

Match No. 82 WALES Home

Wednesday 28th September, 1960 – Dublin

REP. OF IRELAND (1) 2 Fagan 28, 72 (pen)
WALES (1) 3 Jones 26, 53, Woosnam 65

Ref: Best (USA) **Ground:** Dalymount Park **Att:**

Ireland: Noel Dwyer (Swansea 5), Phil Kelly (Wolves 1), John O'Neill (Preston 1), Mick McGrath (Blackburn Rovers 8), Charlie Hurley (Sunderland 11), Pat Saward (Aston Villa 13), Fionan Fagan (Derby County 6), Johnny Giles (Manchester United 3), Peter Fitzgerald (Leeds United 1), Noel Peyton (Leeds United 4), Joe Haverty (Arsenal 12). **Captain:** Pat Saward

Wales: G. Vearncombe, S. Williams, G. Williams, V. Crowe, M. Nurse, C. Baker, T. Medwin, P. Woosnam, G. Moore, R. Vernon, C. Jones.

Wales first ever game in Dublin saw them end Ireland's 8 game undefeated run at home. In a very entertaining match Ireland had the majority of the play but the forwards were tightly marked and lacked penetration.

Ireland, playing against a stiff breeze, started well but did not trouble Vearncombe unduly. After 26 minutes Jones won a corner. As Medwin came across to take it Jones went into the box and took up a centre-forward position. This move must have unsettled the Irish defence because when Medwin's flag-kick came over, Jones rose unmarked to head home. Two minutes later Ireland equalised with a superb goal. Kelly took a quick free and gave the ball to Fagan on the wing. The winger cut inside Graham Williams and ran in on goal. Then, from 30 yards out, he sent a powerful left-footed shot which dipped just under the crossbar and landed in the net. Ireland finished the half on top but had few shots on target.

Wales started the second period on the attack and Jones came close when his header hit the post. After 6 minutes Peter Fitzgerald came equally close with his effort just wide but two minutes later Wales scored. A corner by Vernon again found Jones unmarked and he headed in. Twelve minutes later Vernon gave to Jones. The winger beat McGrath and crossed in for Woosnam to first-time it to the net. Ireland pulled a goal back when Giles was tripped by Stuart Williams in the box and Fagan scored from the spot.

Match No. 83 NORWAY Home

Sunday 6th November, 1960 – Dublin

REP. OF IRELAND (2) 3 Fagan 28, P. Fitzgerald 39, 83
NORWAY (1) 1 Hennum 2

Ref: Bowman (Scotland) **Ground:** Dalymount Park **Att:** 26,000

Ireland: Noel Dwyer (Swansea 6), Phil Kelly (Wolves 2), Noel Cantwell (West Ham United 17), Johnny Fullam (Preston 1), Charlie Hurley (Sunderland 12), Pat Saward (Aston Villa 14), Fionan Fagan (Derby County 7), Peter Fitzgerald (Leeds United 2), Dermot Curtis (Ipswich Town 13), Johnny Giles (Manchester United 4), Joe Haverty (Arsenal 13). **Captain:** Noel Cantwell

Norway: A. Hansen, A. Bakker, J. Kramer, A. Natland, T. Svenssen, R. Johansen, B. Borgen, R. Jensen, H. Hennum, R. Birger Pedersen, A. Berg.

Ireland attacked straight from the kick-off and the ball passed from Fullam to Saward to Curtis to Haverty and the winger crossed in for Fitzgerald to have a great header saved by Hansen. Ninety seconds later Hurley was caught out by a through ball from Natland and slipped, sending Hennum clear. The centre-forward took the ball on the run and burst the back of the net with a tremendous shot. The Norwegians then enjoyed their best spell of the game and had the ball in the net again but Berg was offside. Ireland then took over and Fitzgerald had two efforts expertly saved before Fagan equalised with another brilliant goal. Kelly passed to Fagan and the winger cut in-field before shooting powerfully into the net giving the Norwegian goalkeeper no chance. Six minutes before the interval Jensen worked his way to the by-line but was dispossessed by Giles who brought the ball out of the area and sent a long ball up to Haverty. The winger raced away, played a one-two with Curtis and crossed in for Fagan. The cross found Fagan flat-footed but he managed to get in a good shot which Hansen saved but the ball fell to Fitzgerald and he netted with a first-time shot. Giles finished off an entertaining half with another shot which was saved.

Ireland continued their good work after the break with Fitzgerald having a shot blocked and a header wide. Saward sent another shot inches wide. Fagan thumped a 25 yard shot off the foot of the post and Fitzgerald was denied again when sent clear only to hesitate and be dispossessed. Ireland settled back after that initial burst and Norway came into the game again but threatened little. Seven minutes from the end Giles set up Fitzgerald to score again and in the last minute Hurley cleared off the line from Pedersen.

Match No. 84 — SCOTLAND — Away

Wednesday 3rd May, 1961 – Glasgow (World Cup)

SCOTLAND (2) 4 Brand 14, 40, Herd 59, 85
REP. OF IRELAND (0) 1 Haverty 52

Ref: Guique (France) **Ground:** Hampden Park **Att:** 46,696

Scotland: L. Leslie, B. Shearer, E. Caldow, P. Crerand, B. McNeill, J. Baxter, J. McLeod, P. Quinn, D. Herd, R. Brand, D. Wilson.

Ireland: Noel Dwyer (Swansea 7), Brendan McNally (Luton Town 2), Noel Cantwell (Manchester United 18), Andy McEvoy (Blackburn Rovers 1), Charlie Hurley (Sunderland 13), Pat Saward (Huddersfield Town 15), Johnny Giles (Manchester United 5), Ambrose Fogarty (Sunderland 3), Dermot Curtis (Ipswich Town 14), George Cummins (Luton Town 18), Joe Haverty (Arsenal 14). **Captain:** Noel Cantwell

Scotland dominated this game for long periods and restricted Ireland to only three goal chances in an overall disappointing display.

The home side attacked from the start with McLeod forcing Dwyer into making a good save early on. After 14 minutes Hurley headed out a free kick from Caldow only for Brand to return it to the back of the net with a speedy shot. After 21 minutes a free kick from Cummins hit the crossbar with Leslie beaten. Five minutes from the interval a move up the Irish right saw Baxter and Herd combine to put Brand in and he beat Dwyer with a great shot.

Ireland's best period of the game came after the break when they pulled a goal back through Haverty who shot home a Giles cross. However, Scotland regained their two-goal lead when Quinn's pass was shot home by Herd. Fogarty had a shot saved by Leslie but when the ball ran loose Haverty missed a 'sitter' when he shot wide. The last word went to Scotland when Herd forced the ball home after a cross from Wilson was not held by Dwyer.

Match No. 85 — SCOTLAND — Home

Sunday 7th May, 1961 – Dublin (World Cup)

REP. OF IRELAND (0) 0
SCOTLAND (2) 3 Young 4, 16, Brand 86

Ref: Grandin (Belgium) **Ground:** Dalymount Park **Att:** 36,000

Ireland: Noel Dwyer (Swansea 8), Phil Kelly (Wolves 3), Noel Cantwell (Manchester United 19), Andy McEvoy (Blackburn Rovers 2), Charlie Hurley (Sunderland 14), Mick Meagan (Everton 1), Fionan Fagan (Derby County 8), Johnny Giles (Manchester United 6), Peter Fitzgerald (Leeds United 3), George Cummins (Luton Town 19), Joe Haverty (Arsenal 15). **Captain:** Noel Cantwell

Scotland: L. Leslie, B. Shearer, P. Crerand, E. Caldow, B. McNeill, J. Baxter, J. McLeod, P. Quinn, A. Young, R. Brand, D. Wilson.

Noel Dwyer saves at the feet of Brand. Other players looking on are (from left): Charlie Hurley, Noel Cantwell, Mick Meagan and Andy McEvoy.

Ireland produced one of their poorest performances and lost to a Scottish team which had a boost of two early goals. Lacking passion, the team was jeered at by the crowd but those two early goals had 'killed' the game as a contest.

After 4 minutes Brand headed on a cross to Young. The centre-forward was in an off-side position and the linesman raised his flag. However Young played on and headed past Dwyer. The referee ignored the flag and awarded the goal. There was also some controversy about Scotland's second goal. Brand and Kelly raced after a ball which appeared to have crossed the back line before Brand crossed for Young to shoot into the net. This time there was no flag and the referee gave the goal.

Ireland had only two real chances in the entire match. First, a Cummins pass gave Fagan room to send in a pile-driver of a shot which hit Leslie in the stomach and was cleared. The goalkeeper was crippled by this blow but recovered after treatment. Then Fitzgerald managed to get free and send in another powerful shot which Leslie did well to turn out for a corner. Basically these were incidents out of the ordinary and although Ireland saw a lot of the ball the forwards were too tightly marked to do anything . Four minutes from the end Young sent Brand in to score Scotland's third.

Alex Young, extreme left, shoots home his and Scotland's second goal against Ireland at Dalymount Park in 1961. Other players in picture are: Ralph Brand (No. 10), Charlie Hurley (No. 5), David Wilson, Noel Dwyer, Phil Kelly, Mick Meagan and Noel Cantwell (No. 3).

Match No. 86 **CZECHOSLOVAKIA** **Home**

Sunday 8th October, 1961 – Dublin (World Cup)

REP. OF IRELAND (1) 1 Giles 40
CZECHOSLOVAKIA (1) 3 Scherer 3, Kvasnak 61, 69

Ref: Holland (England) **Ground:** Dalymount Park **Att:** 26,000

Ireland: Noel Dwyer (Swansea 9), Phil Kelly (Wolves 4), Noel Cantwell (Manchester United 20), Ronnie Nolan (Shamrock Rovers 8), Charlie Hurley (Sunderland 15), Mick McGrath (Blackburn Rovers 9), Peter Fitzgerald (Chester City 4), Ambrose Fogarty (Sunderland 4), Frank O'Neill (Shamrock Rovers 1), Johnny Giles (Manchester United 7), Joe Haverty (Blackburn Rovers 16). **Captain:** Noel Cantwell

CSSR: V. Schrojf, J. Tichy, Hledik, Popluhar, S. Pluskal, J. Masopust, T. Pospichal, A. Scherer, R. Kucera, A. Kvasnak, V. Masek.

Ireland opened well and in an even first half both sides had chances. But the Czechs took command after the break and only the woodwork denied them a bigger margin of victory. Again the Irish team was subjected to jeering from the crowd as the Czech 4-2-4 system frustrated their efforts.

After 3 minutes a slick passing move between Hledik and Kucera put Scherer in the clear to have a shot. The Czechs shot seemed to be covered by Dwyer but it deflected off Hurley into the goal. Czech records credit the goal to Scherer. O'Neill had two good chances after this but failed with both before Czechoslovakia began to dominate. Kucera beat Hurley on the edge of the box but shot over with only the goalkeeper to stop him. Pospichal had a header over as had Cantwell at the other end. Giles nearly caught out the Czech goalkeeper with a 30 yard lob but Schrojf saved just under his crossbar. Kucera had another shot cleared by Hurley and Giles brought a good save from Schrojf before the inside-left got Ireland's equaliser. Haverty found O'Neill who gave the

Vilem Schrojf managed to get hands to Johnny Giles's shot but could not prevent it from going into the net for Ireland's only goal.

Hurley comes up for a corner but Schroif makes a timely clearance.

ball out to Fitzgerald, now on the left wing. Fitzgerald rolled the ball into Giles's path and from 30 yards out the inside-left cracked a great shot into the net. Just before the break Kvasnak missed a 'sitter' when he mis-kicked right in front of goal for Dwyer to save easily.

The second period belonged to Czechoslovakia. Kucera had an early effort saved before thumping another shot off the post. Masek hit the crossbar just before the Czechs got a second. Kucera sent in a fiercly-hit shot which Dwyer stopped but could not hold and Kvasnak was first to the rebound to tap it home. Masek struck the crossbar again and Giles was inches over with further chances. On 69 minutes Kvasnak headed in a Masek corner for the Czech's third goal.

Match No. 87 — CZECHOSLOVAKIA — Away

Sunday 29th October, 1961 – Prague (World Cup)

CZECHOSLOVAKIA (4) 7 Kvasnak 8, 36, Scherer 24, 75, Jelinek 30, Pospichal 57, Masopust 61

REP. OF IRELAND (0) 1 Fogarty 56

Ref: Lundell (Sweden) **Ground:** Strahove Stadium **Att:** 30,000

CSSR: V. Schrojf, J. Hledik, J. Tichy, S. Pluskal, J. Popluhar, J. Masopust, T. Pospichal, A. Scherer, A. Kvasnak, J. Adamec, J. Jelinek.

Ireland: Noel Dwyer (Swansea 10), Phil Kelly (Wolves 5), Noel Cantwell (Manchester United 21), Ronnie Nolan (Shamrock Rovers 9), Charlie Hurley (Sunderland 16), Mick McGrath (Blackburn Rovers 10), Frank O'Neill (Shamrock Rovers 2), Ambrose Fogarty (Sunderland 5), Peter Fitzgerald (Chester City 5), Johnny Giles (Manchester United 8), Joe Haverty (Blackburn Rovers 17). **Captain:** Noel Cantwell

Czechoslovakia needed a victory to force a play-off with Scotland for a place in the World Cup Finals. Straight from the kick-off the Czechs attacked and for the first 20 minutes they rained shot after shot on the Irish goal. After 8 minutes Pospichal broke through the Irish defence and crossed for Kvasnak to open the scoring. The Czechs continued to press and got a second goal when Scherer headed in a high cross from Jelinek. The winger got another 6 minutes later when he raced away from the half-way line, beat five defenders and smashed an 18 yard shot into the net. In another 6 minutes Kvasnak shot home Jelineks pass for the fourth goal. The Irish had been overrun in the first half and were restricted to two chances both of which were missed by Haverty.

The Irish team when it arrived at Prague. Back Row from left to right: J. Wickham (Secretary F.A.I.), C. Hurley, N. Cantwell, W. P. Murphy (Irish Independent), N. Dwyer, J. Fullam, R. Nolan, P. Kelly, J. Younger, R. J. Doran, S. Prole, A. Byrne, Dist. Justice E. O Riain. Front row: Billy Lord, J. Haverty, F. O'Neill, J. Giles, A. Fogarty, M. McGrath and P. Fitzgerald.

The second half was less frenetic and Ireland enjoyed a brief spell of attacking football. Hurley and Fitzgerald gave Fogarty a chance but he shot over. However, after 50 minutes, Giles put Fitzgerald away and when his cross came over Fogarty scored from close range. From the re-start Pospichal worked his way up-field and from 20 yards scored. A soft goal as Dwyer seemed to think the shot was going wide and did not react. Four minutes later Pospichal and Scherer set up Masopust to score from close range. Scherer got a seventh goal for the Czechs when a defensive mistake allowed him to round Dwyer and slot the ball home.

Match No. 88 — AUSTRIA — Home

Sunday 8th April, 1962 – Dublin

REP. OF IRELAND (0) 2 Cantwell 48, Tuohy 59
AUSTRIA (1) 3 Buzek 43, Hirnschrodt 58, E. Hof 64

Ref: Gulde (Switzerland) **Ground:** Dalymount Park **Att:** 32,434

Ireland: Alan Kelly (Preston 3), Tony Dunne (Manchester United 1), Tommy Traynor (Southampton 2), Pat Saward (Huddersfield Town 16), Charlie Hurley (Sunderland 17), Mick Meagan (Everton 2), Alfie Hale (Aston Villa 1), Johnny Giles (Manchester United 9), Noel Cantwell (Manchester United 22), Dermot Curtis (Ipswich Town 15), Liam Tuohy (Newcastle United 4). **Subs:** Dinny Lowry (St Patrick's Athletic 1), for Kelly (34 mins). **Captain:** Charlie Hurley

Austria: G. Fraydl, J. Windisch, K. Stotz, E. Strobl, I. Puschnik, K. Koller, H. Hirnschrodt, E. Hof, J. Buzek, A. Knoll, R. Flögel. **Subs:** E. Hasenkopf for Windisch, J. Rafreider for Hirnschrodt, E. Fiala for Flögel.

Although Ireland suffered its fifth consecutive defeat the teams performance was an improvement on what had gone on before. The match opened with Hof having a shot saved by Kelly's knees, and Curtis forcing Fraydl to parry his shot and diving on the rebound before Cantwell could get to it. Buzek brought another fine save from Kelly at the expense of a corner and from that corner Buzek's header was cleared by Meagan. After 23 minutes Kelly made a magnificent save to stop a shot by Hof but in doing so he landed badly and hit his head on the ground. Kelly tried to play on after treatment but was suffering from double vision and had to retire with Lowry taking his place in goal. Before that Hurley had headed Tuohys free kick into the net but the goal was ruled out due to offside against Curtis. Saward and Hurley had further efforts before Buzek headed in a cross to give Austria the lead.

On the resumption Tuohy brought a good save from Fraydl in the first minute. Two minutes later Ireland were level. Cantwell sent in a hard cross from the touch-line which went over Fraydl, hit the far post and went into the goal. A corner by Saward gave Hurley another chance but his header just went over. After 58 minutes a shot by Buzek was knocked to Hof by Lowry. The inside-right knocked the ball back across goal and Hirnschrodt knocked it in. A minute later Ireland equalised when Cantwell's shot bounced off the crossbar and Tuohy headed it in. Five minutes later Austria were back in front when a long ball out of defence by Puschnik found Erich Hof in the clear. Hurley raced back but Hof cut inside him and went on to beat Lowry. Giles had a late chance of an equaliser but missed a good opportunity.

Match No. 89 — ICELAND — Home

Sunday 12th August, 1962 – Dublin (European Championship)

REP. OF IRELAND (2) 4 Tuohy 11, Fogarty 41, Cantwell 65, 76
ICELAND (1) 2 R. Jonsson 37, 86

Ref: Smith (Wales) **Ground:** Dalymount Park **Att:** 20,246

Ireland: Alan Kelly (Preston 4), Tony Dunne (Manchester United 2), Tommy Traynor (Southampton 3), Pat Saward (Huddersfield Town 17), Charlie Hurley (Sunderland 18), Mick Meagan (Everton 3), Alfie Hale (Doncaster Rovers 2), Johnny Giles (Manchester United 10), Noel Cantwell (Manchester United 23), Ambrose Fogarty (Sunderland 6), Liam Tuohy (Newcastle United 5). **Captain:** Charlie Hurley

Rikharour Jonsson scores for Iceland, Kelly can only watch as the ball hits the net

Iceland: H. Danielsson, A. Njalsson, B. Felixson, G. Arnason, H. Felixson, S. Jonsson, S. Agustsson, T. Beck, R. Jonsson, E. B. Schram, T. Jonsson.

Both sides had early chances with Danielsson saving at the feet of Cantwell and Dunne clearing a shot off the Irish goal-line. However the majority of the play was in one direction – towards the Icelandic goal which fell after 11 minutes when Tuohy stooped low to head home Giles's cross. Kelly had then to save at Beck's feet before Cantwell had a shot saved by Danielsson and Tuohy headed just wide. Agustsson had a curling shot headed out by Hurley in further play. After half an hour Tuohy was denied a certain second goal when Njalsson handled on the goal-line and a penalty was awarded. Cantwell, successful in his last four spot-kicks kicks for Ireland, hit the penalty against the crossbar but it bounced down for Fogarty to net. However the goal was ruled out as Cantwell was adjudged to be offside. Seven minutes later Hurley dallied on the ball, caught between two options (pass or clearance) and was robbed by Rikharour Jonsson who shot home the equaliser. Four minutes from half-time a cross from Traynor was headed goalwards by Cantwell. Danielsson made a good save but the ball ran loose and Fogarty was quickly on to it to put Ireland into the lead again.

Ten minutes into the second half Thorour Jonsson almost got an equaliser but failed to connect in front of goal. Ireland however again had the upper hand with Danielson saving an effort from Cantwell, diving at Hale's feet to prevent the winger from getting through and making a superb save to stop a 25 yard shot from Giles. After 20 minutes Fogarty passed in to Cantwell who placed a low shot out of Danielson's reach and into the net. Eleven minutes later Cantwell outjumped Danielson and Felixson to head home Hale's cross. Four minutes from the end the visitors were awarded a free kick. Thorour Jonsson took it and as he did the Irish defence moved out 'en masse' leaving three forwards apparently offside. Rikharour Jonsson stroked the ball home and the referee gave the goal.

Match No. 90 — ICELAND — Away

Sunday 2nd September, 1962 – Reykjavik (European Championship)

ICELAND (0) 1 Arnason 59
REP. OF IRELAND (1) 1 Tuohy 38

Ref: Nielsen (Norway) **Ground:** Laugardalsvöllur **Att:** 9,100

Iceland: H. Danielsson, A. Njalsson, B. Felixson, G. Arnason, J. Stefanson, S. Jonsson, S. Agustsson, T. Beck, R. Jonsson, E. B. Schram, T. Jakobsson.

Ireland: Alan Kelly (Preston 5), Brendan McNally (Luton Town 3), Tommy Traynor (Southampton 4), Ronnie Nolan (Shamrock Rovers 10), Charlie Hurley (Sunderland 19), Pat Saward (Huddersfield Town 18), Dermot Curtis (Ipswich Town 16), Ambrose Fogarty (Sunderland 7), Noel Cantwell (Manchester United 24), Noel Peyton (Leeds United 5), Liam Tuohy (Newcastle United 6). **Captain:** Charlie Hurley

Ireland dominated the first half but seldom troubled Danielsson in a poor game. Seven minutes before the break Peyton gave to Curtis who beat Felixson and cut in along the back line. Thinking he was about to shoot, the defenders closed on him but Curtis chipped the ball over to the in-rushing Tuohy who headed it into the top of the net. Iceland had a brief attacking spell following this and Rikharour Jonsson had the ball in the net but it was ruled out for offside. Ireland also had a goal ruled out for the same reason in the second period but Iceland drew level when Arnason shot home from close range.

Match No. 91 — SCOTLAND — Home

Sunday 9th June, 1963 – Dublin

REP. OF IRELAND (1) 1 Cantwell 6
SCOTLAND (0) 0

Ref: Howley (England) **Ground:** Dalymount Park **Att:** 26,000

Ireland: Alan Kelly (Preston 6), Tony Dunne (Manchester United 3), Tommy Traynor (Southampton 5), Andy McEvoy (Blackburn Rovers 3), Charlie Hurley (Sunderland 20), Mick McGrath (Blackburn Rovers 11), Johnny Giles (Manchester United 11), Paddy Turner (Glasgow Celtic 1), Noel Cantwell (Manchester United 25), Noel Peyton (Leeds United 6), Joe Haverty (Blackburn Rovers 18). **Sub:** Ambrose Fogarty (Sunderland 8), for Peyton (44 mins). **Captain:** Noel Cantwell

Scotland: T. Lawrence, A. Hamilton, D. Holt, F. McLintock, B. McNeill, J. Baxter, W. Henderson, D. Gibson, J. Millar, D. Law, D. Wilson. **Subs:** I. St. John for Millar (44 mins).

Ireland's 45th international at Dalymount Park was played on a very hot summers day. Despite the heat the Irish turned in a magnificent performance.

Ireland began well and after 6 minutes a corner by Haverty fell for Turner who mis-kicked but Cantwell was there to sweep the ball past Lawrence. A minute later Millar played a one-two with Law and sent in a powerful shot which Kelly tipped over. In another minute Giles brought a good save out of the Scottish goalkeeper at the other end. Cantwell and Peyton had other chances as Ireland had the better of the play in the first half. A minute before the interval St. John came on for Millar and Law and Gibson switched positions in an effort to disrupt the Irish defence. Ireland were forced to use a substitute when Peyton retired with a head injury just on the break.

Fogarty had the first effort of the second half, which Lawerence tipped over, but in general it was Scotland who had the majority of the chances. Law had three excellent opportunities. First he was sent clear but shot wide. Then he was stopped by Traynor as he was about to score and last he was sent clear again but Kelly saved. Ireland had two efforts with a cross by Fogarty going right across the goal and Giles heading a Haverty cross against the bar. Late efforts saw Turner shoot straight at Lawrence when put clear and Hurley heading another Law shot off the line.

Austria's Ernst Fiala on the ball with Ireland's Ray Brady closing in. In the background is Johnny Giles. (Photo: Vovtavafoto)

Match No. 92 **AUSTRIA** **Away**

Wednesday 23rd September, 1963 – Vienna (European Championship)

AUSTRIA (0) 0
REP. OF IRELAND (0) 0

Ref: Gere (Hungary) **Ground:** Praeter Park **Att:** 26,800

Austria: G. Fraydl, P. Vargo, W. Glechner, E. Hasenkopf, R. Oslansky, K. Koller, R. Flögel, E. Hof, H. Nemec, E. Fiala, J. Hörmayer.

Ireland: Alan Kelly (Preston 7), Willie Browne (Bohemians 1), Tommy Traynor (Southampton 6), Ray Brady (Queens Park Rangers 1), Charlie Hurley (Sunderland 21), Mick McGrath (Blackburn Rovers 12), Johnny Giles (Leeds United 12), Ronnie Whelan (St Patrick's Athletic 1), Dermot Curtis (Exeter City 17), Ambrose Fogarty (Sunderland 9), Liam Tuohy (Shamrock Rovers 7). **Captain:** Charlie Hurley.

Ireland came away from a rain-soaked Vienna with their first-ever scoreless draw. Despite the fact that there were few highlights and Ireland came close to winning the game near the end, the visitors were delighted with the result.

Ireland came to defend and succeeded in restricting the Austrians to only a few shots on target. During the first half Fiala had three good chances, two of which he missed while the third was saved by Kelly's knee. The Irish did not venture forward too much and only threatened with long range shots from Giles and Hurley. The Irish captain was booked just after half-time and became the first Irish player to be so cautioned in the European Championships.

The second half was as miserable as the weather but Ireland had a number of chances. Whelan was put clean through but elected to shoot early rather than to run on and make sure and Fraydl saved. Near the end Curtis was also twice put through but he too shot at the goalkeeper. The best chance of the match fell to Fogarty and he was only denied by a magnificent save from the Austrian goalkeeper.

Austrian goalkeeper Gernot Fraydl saves from Ireland's Dermot Curtis with Austria's Erich Hasenkopf in close attendance. (Photo: Votavafoto)

Match No. 93 AUSTRIA Home

Sunday 13th October, 1963 – Dublin (European Championship)

REP. OF IRELAND (1) 3 Cantwell 44, 89 (pen), Koller (o.g.) 65,
AUSTRIA (1) 2 Koleznik 39, Flögel 82

Ref: Poulsen (Denmark) **Ground:** Dalymount Park **Att:** 40,000

Ireland: Alan Kelly (Preston 8), Tony Dunne (Manchester United 4), Tommy Traynor (Southampton 7), Ray Brady (Queens Park Rangers 2), Charlie Hurley (Sunderland 22), Mick McGrath (Blackburn Rovers 13), Johnny Giles (Leeds United 13), Andy McEvoy (Blackburn Rovers 4), Noel Cantwell (Manchester United 26), Ambrose Fogarty (Sunderland 10), Joe Haverty (Millwall 19). **Captain:** Charlie Hurley.

Austria: G. Fraydl, P. Vargo, W. Glechner, E. Hasenkopf, J. Frank, K. Koller, W. Koleznik, H. Jank, J. Buzek, H. Nemec, R. Flögel.

The second leg of this tie was a rough game but one filled with incident and atmosphere. The official attendance was 40,000 but many got in without paying and this overcrowding caused problems. There were five pitch invasions which not only stopped play but could have led to the abandoning of the match.

Early shots from Fogarty and Koleznik went wide while one from Cantwelll was saved before McGrath was forced to retire with a head injury after 16 minutes. McEvoy took over at left-half. Cantwell and Giles had efforts wide before a 37th minute header from Buzek was saved by Kelly. Two minutes later Austria took the lead when Koleznik accepted a pass from Frank, cut inside and shot powerfully home. Ireland equalised in the dying minutes of the half. A through ball from Fogarty gave Cantwell the chance to blast a shot at goal. Fraydl made a tremendous save to keep it out but the ball ran loose to Haverty whose shot hit the underside of the crossbar and bounced back into play. Both Haverty and Cantwell rushed forward and Cantwell headed into the empty net.

During the break there was a pitch invasion which kept the players in their dressing rooms for 20 minutes and when they came back McGrath was with them. He went to outside right but was nothing more than a 'passenger'. After 62 minutes Giles curled a shot around the wrong side of the post. Three minutes later Fogarty headed on a corner from Haverty which hit Koller on the chest and spun into the net; resulting in another pitch invasion. When the pitch was cleared chances fell to Giles, Cantwell and Haverty all of which came close. With 8 minutes left a cross from Koleznik was deflected into the path of Flögel who hit a stunning first time shot to the back of the net. In the last minute Haverty broke up the left and crossed over into the box. Frank tried to clear but in his attempt he handled the ball and the referee immediately pointed to the spot. Another pitch invasion followed and it was at least two minutes before sanity was restored. This did nothing to help Cantwell, who had missed his last penalty for Ireland, but he held his nerve and sent Fraydl the wrong way with a powerful left-footed shot to the roof of the net. Amid chaotic scenes the pitch was invaded again then cleared. 'Injury' time was played but there were no further chances and Ireland qualified for the quarter finals of the European Nations Championship.

Match No. 94 SPAIN Away

Wednesday 11th March, 1964 – Seville (European Championship)

SPAIN (4) 5 Amancio 13, 30, Fuste 15, Marcelino 33, 88
REP. OF IRELAND (1) 1 McEvoy 22

Ref: Van Nuffel (Belgium) **Ground:** Sanchez Pizjuan Stadium **Att:** 27,200

Spain: J. A. Iribar, F. M. Rivilla, I. Calleja, I. Zoco, F. Olivella, J. M. Fuste, Amancio, J. M. Pereda, Marcelino, J. M. Villa, C. Lepetra.

Ireland: Alan Kelly (Preston 9), Theo Foley (Northampton Town 1), Tommy Traynor (Southampton 8), Ray Brady (Queen's Park Rangers 3), Charlie Hurley (Sunderland 23), Mick Meagan (Everton 4), Johnny Giles (Leeds United 14), Andy McEvoy (Blackburn Rovers 5), Alfie Hale (Doncaster Rovers 3), Ambrose Fogarty (Hartlepools United 11), Joe Haverty (Millwall 20). **Captain:** Charlie Hurley.

On a wet and muddy pitch Spain outplayed Ireland for most of the game. Spain eased up in the second half but controlled the game throughout and scored a fifth goal near the end. The game was played in a constant downpour of rain.

After 13 minutes Amancio intercepted a Hurley pass and ran on to beat Kelly with a strong shot for the first goal. Two minutes later a powerful shot from Fuste gave Kelly no chance and Spain were two up. Ireland pulled a goal back when McEvoy took a Giles pass on the run, controlled it and shot past Iribar. Eight minutes later a cross by Villa was smashed into the net by Amancio and then the winger set up Marcelino to put Spain four-one ahead.

The second half was less hectic and there were few chances. McEvoy forced two openings but could not score. Near the end Marcelino's shot was deflected into the net by Traynor to complete the scoring.

Match No. 95 — SPAIN — Home

Wednesday 8th April, 1964 – Dublin (European Championship)

REP. OF IRELAND (0) 0
SPAIN (1) 2 Zaballa 24, 87

Ref: Versyp (Belgium) **Ground:** Dalymount Park **Att:** 38,100

Ireland: Alan Kelly (Preston 10), Tony Dunne (Manchester United 5), Willie Browne (Bohemians 2), Ray Brady (Queen's Park Rangers 4), Charlie Hurley (Sunderland 24), Johnny Fullam (Shamrock Rovers 2), Johnny Giles (Leeds United 15), Andy McEvoy (Blackburn Rovers 6), Noel Cantwell (Manchester United 27), Paddy Turner (Glasgow Celtic 2), Alfie Hale (Doncaster Rovers 4). **Captain:** Charlie Hurley.

Spain: J. A. Iribar, F. M. Rivilla, I. Calleja, I. Zoco, F. Olivella, J. M. Fuste, P. Zaballa, J. M. Pereda, Marcelino, J. M. Villa, C. Lepetra.

Ireland, needing 4 goals, started on the attack but it was Spain who had the best of the early chances with Villa having a shot saved and Zoco shooting wide. While Ireland pressed for a goal their defence was left exposed and Spain exploited this to score the first goal. A long throw-out by Iribar sent Lepetra away. The winger exchanged passes with Marcelino before sending over a perfect cross which Zaballa headed home easily. Pereda had two further efforts which were wide and saved and, at the other end, both McEvoy and Cantwell shot over when well placed.

A minute into the second half a Zaballa cross was blocked out to Pereda who hit a fierce shot at goal from 20 yards. Kelly got both his hands to the ball and deflected it onto the top of the net for a corner. Five minutes later a free kick by Fuste hit Fullam on the head but was prevented from going in by another excellent save from Kelly. Zaballa and Pereda had further chances but Kelly kept them out. The Irish had switched Giles and Turner at the start of the second period but it had little effect. Iribar was not troubled much but a Cantwell header from a Giles free kick forced him into a good save. Three minutes from the end another excellent cross from Lepetra was headed superbly into the net by Zaballa.

Match No. 96 — POLAND — Away

Sunday 10th May, 1964 – Cracow

POLAND (1) 3 Faber 25, Wilim II 63, Szoltysik 76
REP. OF IRELAND (1) 1 Ambrose 35

Ref: Kainer (Austria) **Ground:** Wisla Stadium **Att:** 60,000

Poland: Kornek, Szczepanski, Lysko, Bazan, Oslizlo, Nieroba, Faber, Gzel, Szoltysik, Musiatek, Lentner. **Subs:** Wilim II for Gzel (33 mins).

Alan Kelly and Tony Dunne combine to foil this Polish attack. In the background Theo Foley looks on as Kelly comes out the worst. (Photo: Caf/Pap)

Ireland: Alan Kelly (Preston 11), Theo Foley (Northampton Town 2), Tony Dunne (Manchester United 6), Ray Brady (Queen's Park Rangers 5), Charlie Hurley (Sunderland 25), Fred Strahan (Shelbourne 1), Johnny Giles (Leeds United 16), Andy McEvoy (Blackburn Rovers 7), Paddy Ambrose (Shamrock Rovers 3), Johnny Fullam (Shamrock Rovers 3), Joe Haverty (Millwall 21). **Subs:** Noel Dwyer (Swansea 11), for Kelly (55 mins). **Captain:** Charlie Hurley.

Poland, playing a 4-2-4 formation, dominated the first fifteen minutes and in that time Musiatek shot wide twice when clean through, Faber had a shot over, Nieroba shot against the post and Gzel was stopped by Kelly when again put clear. After 20 minutes Szoltysik shot against the crossbar again but five minutes later the Poles scored. Brady's pass across his area was intercepted by Gzel who passed in for Faber to net. Ireland had been seeing a good deal of the ball and after 35 minutes got an equaliser. A long ball from Strahan was taken by McEvoy and controlled instantly. McEvoy beat two men, played a one-two with Ambrose and then sent the centre-forward through with a lovely pass. The goalkeeper came out and clashed with Ambrose, the ball running free. Ambrose was quickly on his feet and blasted the ball into the goal.

Kelly was injured saving a shot by Faber in the second half and was replaced by Dwyer. Poland still had the majority of the play but McEvoy was denied a goal when his shot beat Kornek but was kicked off the goalline by Lysko. After 63 minutes a misunderstanding between Hurley and Dwyer left Wilim free to score Polands second. McEvoy had a shot saved and Ambrose had a goal ruled out before Szoltysik and Musiatek combined for Szoltysik to score from an acute angle.

Match No. 97 — NORWAY — Away

Wednesday 13th May, 1964 – Oslo

NORWAY (0) 1 Eriksen 53
REP. OF IRELAND (2) 4 Hurley 3, 63, Giles 10, McEvoy 77

Ref: Malka (West Germany) **Ground:** Ulleval Stadium **Att:** 14,354

Norway: S. Andersen, E. Hagen, E. Stakseth, R. Johansen, F. Thorsen, T. Andersen, B. Borgen, A. Pedersen, P. Kristoffersen, O. Nielsen, R. Jensen. **Subs:** L. Eriksen for Jensen (23 mins).

Ireland: Noel Dwyer (Swansea 12), Theo Foley (Northampton Town 3), Tony Dunne (Manchester United 7), Ray Brady (Queen's Park Rangers 6), Fred Strahan (Shelbourne 2), Johnny Fullam (Shamrock Rovers 4), Johnny Giles (Leeds United 17), Andy McEvoy (Blackburn Rovers 8), Charlie Hurley (Sunderland 26), Paddy Ambrose (Shamrock Rovers 4), Joe Haverty (Millwall 22). **Captain:** Charlie Hurley.

Despite the scoreline, this was a hard-fought victory played in brilliant sunshine throughout. The decisive factor was an excellent opening ten-minute spell in which Ireland scored twice and could have had another goal. With 3 minutes gone Haverty raced down the wing and crossed in for Hurley to shoot home. Three minutes later Hurley met a corner from Giles with a bullet-like header which the goalkeeper turned on to a post and out.

In another four minutes Haverty again crossed in for Giles to send a powerful shot from the edge of the box into the corner of the net. After 23 minutes Jensen was injured and replaced by Eriksen. This change seemed to restore the Norwegian attack which subsequently came close when Nielsen's header was cleared off the line by Foley. At the other end McEvoy ended a Giles dribble by planting the ball in the net but the referee disallowed it for offside.

Early in the second half Giles was taken down in the box but the referee only awarded an indirect free which came to nothing. After 8 minutes Pedersen put Borgen through and the wingers cross was put in by the substitute Eriksen. Soon after Dwyer denied Nielsen an equaliser. After 18 minutes a long ball from Brady hit a defender on the back and fell for Hurley to send a high lobbing shot over the goalkeeper and into the net. Ireland got a fourth goal when a lovely through ball from Giles put McEvoy clear and he beat the goalkeeper with a shot which found the corner of the net.

Match No. 98 — ENGLAND — Home

Sunday 24th May, 1964 – Dublin

REP. OF IRELAND (0) 1 Strahan 42
ENGLAND (2) 3 Eastham 9, Byrne 22, Greaves 56

Ref: Davidson (Scotland) **Ground:** Dalymount Park **Att:** 40,000

Ireland: Noel Dwyer (Swansea 13), Tony Dunne (Manchester United 8), Noel Cantwell (Manchester United 28), Fred Strahan (Shelbourne 3), Willie Browne (Bohemians 3), Mick McGrath (Blackburn Rovers 14), Johnny Giles (Leeds United 18), Andy McEvoy (Blackburn Rovers 9), Eddie Bailham (Shamrock Rovers 1), Paddy Ambrose (Shamrock Rovers 5), Joe Haverty (Millwall 23). **Subs:** Ronnie Whelan (St Patrick's Athletic 2) for Haverty (5 mins). **Captain:** Noel Cantwell.

England: T. Waiters, G. Cohen, R. Wilson, G. Milne, R. Flowers, B. Moore, P. Thompson, J. Greaves, J. Byrne, G. Eastham, B. Charlton.

On another sunny afternoon Ireland were almost totally outplayed by an England side preparing for the World Cup in two years time. Again the scoreline looks deceptive, for had England taken their chances they could have won by a much bigger margin.

Ambrose had the first chance of the game when he forced Waiters to dive and save his shot but after 5 minutes Haverty went off with an ankle injury to be replaced by Whelan. Four minutes later Milne put Byrne through. The centre-forward held off Browne and sent in a shot which bounced off Dwyer's leg for Eastham to snap up the rebound and blast it into the roof of the net. After 12 minutes Byrne sent Greaves through but with only Dwyer to beat he delayed his shot and the goalkeeper saved. Byrne had another shot right across the goal before he scored England's second. Milne gave to Greaves who worked his way right up to the goalline before squaring the ball back for Byrne to score at his second attempt. Cantwell switched with Browne and Whelan with Ambrose in an effort to stem the English attacks but the English came close twice more with Cohen shooting wide and Byrne hitting the underside of the crossbar. Three minutes before the break Ireland got a goal from an unexpected move. Strahan got possession on the half-way line and moved forward. The English defenders backed off him, expecting the pass but Strahan kept moving, by-passing Wilson and Moore, and shot from the edge of the penalty area into the net.

Ireland started the second half well with Strahan having two shots wide and Bailham shooting against the post. After 11 minutes Thompson and Byrne sent Eastham away. The inside-left carried the ball up to the back-line and sent over a high cross which found Greaves at the far post. The ball came to the inside-right at a difficult angle but Greaves met it first time and flashed it into the net. Greaves had three further chances but lacked his usual finish and, although Giles and Bailham had chances near the end, England ran out easy winners.

Match No. 99 — POLAND — Home

Sunday 25th October, 1964 – Dublin

REP. OF IRELAND (1) 3 McEvoy 26, 82, Mooney 81
POLAND (2) 2 Lubanski 20, Pol 22

Ref: Clements (England) **Ground:** Dalymount Park **Att:** 25,100

Ireland: Noel Dwyer (Swansea 14), Theo Foley (Northampton Town 4), Tony Dunne (Manchester United 9), Fred Strahan (Shelbourne 4), Noel Cantwell (Manchester United 29), Mick McGrath (Blackburn Rovers 15), Frank O'Neill (Shamrock Rovers 3), Andy McEvoy (Blackburn Rovers 10), Jackie Mooney (Shamrock Rovers 1), Jackie Hennessy (Shelbourne 1), Joe Haverty (Glasgow Celtic 24). **Captain:** Noel Cantwell.

Poland: Kornek, Szczepanski, Oslizlo, Bazan, Orzechowski, Grzegorczyr, Banas, Brychczy, Pol, Lubanski, Faber. **Subs:** Foetyn for Kornek.

On Poland's last visit to Dublin they had caught Ireland with two goals in as many minutes mid-way through the first half. History repeated itself as a quiet first half exploded into life after 20 minutes.

The first chance of the game fell to Cantwell whose header from Haverty's free kick beat Kornek but was cleared off the line by Banas. The game was played at a leisurely pace for the first fifteen minutes but after 20 minutes Pol put Lubanski through to run on and shoot past Dwyer. Two minutes later Pol brushed past Strahan and McGrath, played a one-two with Lubanski and shot home Poland's second goal. As in 1958 Ireland fought back and got a goal after 26 minutes. McGrath sent a long ball forward to Hennessy but it hit the inside-left's heel and deflected into open space. However, McEvoy was quickly on to it. Taking it in his stride he rounded Kornek and, from a difficult angle, shot the ball into the net off the far post. Both Pol and McEvoy had other chances but at the break Poland were 2-1 ahead.

Early in the second half Kornek was injured in a challenge with Hennessy and was replaced by Foetyn. Poland had two early opportunities with Banas having his shot kicked off the line by Foley and Dwyer denying Lubanski with a superb save. Ireland, though, were dominant and both Haverty and McEvoy hit the woodwork. After 63 minutes McEvoy had another chance when Hennessy's shot was deflected to him but again he was denied by the woodwork when his lob shot hit the underside of the crossbar. Banas got in a shot at the other end but Dwyer deflected it on to the post before Ireland got two goals in a minute. A long cross from Dunne sailed over Orzechowski's head for Mooney to run onto it and flick the ball over Foetyn for the equaliser. Then, a minute later, Mooney met a Foley cross with a powerful header which Foetyn could only parry out for McEvoy to return it to the net. Late in the game McEvoy was denied a hat-trick when he flicked O'Neill's shot goalwards but Szczepanski made a goal-line clearance.

Match No. 100 — BELGIUM — Home

Sunday 24th March, 1965 – Dublin

REP. OF IRELAND (0) 0
BELGIUM (1) 2 McEvoy (o.g.) 15, Jurion 60

Ref: Bogaerts (Holland) **Ground:** Dalymount Park **Att:** 20,252

Ireland: Alan Kelly (Preston 12), Theo Foley (Northampton Town 5), Mick Meagan (Huddersfield Town 5), Mick McGrath (Blackburn Rovers 16), Fran Brennan (Drumcondra 1), Jackie Hennessey

(Shelbourne 2), Frank O'Neill (Shamrock Rovers 4), Oliver Conmy (Peterborough United 1), Jackie Mooney (Shamrock Rovers 2), Andy McEvoy (Blackburn Rovers 11), Liam Tuohy (Shamrock Rovers 8). **Captain:** Theo Foley

Belgium: J. Nicolay, G. Heylens, R. Willems, A. Sulon, J. Cornelis, G. Sulon, J. Jurion, J. Verheyen, P. Van Himst, F. Vermeyen, W. Puis.

A weakened Irish team began well with Mooney having two good openings both of which were stopped by the goalkeeper. But, after 15 minutes, a piece of bad luck affected the Irish team to such an extent that Belgium had the majority of the play for the rest of the game. A pass from Puis was deflected to McEvoy near the goal. McEvoy, in attempting a back-pass to Kelly, put the ball wide of his goalkeeper and, with Kelly flat-footed, the ball rolled into the net. Following this the Belgians saw a lot of the ball but indulged in too much passing which resulted in neither goal being threatened.

The second half was a bit more lively and, after 15 minutes, Jurion cut in-field and unleashed a 25 yards drive which flew past Kelly on its way into the net. The visitors could have had a third when Verheyen put Vermeyen through but Kelly brought off a brilliant save. After 75 minutes Conmy brought the best out of Nicolay when his angled shot was turned away for a corner.

Match No. 101 — SPAIN — Home

Wednesday 5th May, 1965 – Dublin (World Cup)

REP. OF IRELAND (0) 1 Iribar (o.g.) 63
SPAIN (0) 0

Ref: Callaghan (Wales) **Ground:** Dalymount Park **Att:** 40,772

Ireland: Pat Dunne (Manchester United 1), Shay Brennan (Manchester United 1), Tony Dunne (Manchester United 10), Mick McGrath (Blackburn Rovers 17), Charlie Hurley (Sunderland 27), Jackie Hennessey (Shelbourne 3), Frank O'Neill (Shamrock Rovers 5), Johnny Giles (Leeds United 19), Noel Cantwell (Manchester United 30), Andy McEvoy (Blackburn Rovers 12), Joe Haverty (Bristol Rovers 25). **Captain:** Noel Cantwell

Spain: J. A. Iribar, F. Rivilla, F. Olivella, I. Zoco, S. Reija, J. Glaria IV, J. A.Ufarte, V. Guillot, Marcelino, Adelardo, C. Lepetra.

A jubilant Noel Cantwell (9), Republic of Ireland's centre-forward, races out of goal after Frank O'Neill's beautifully placed free kick was helped into the net by Spanish goalkeeper Iribar to give Ireland a well deserved 1-0 success in the World Cup qualifier at Dalymount Park.

Ireland's captain Noel Cantwell shakes hands with his Spanish counterpart Fernando Olivella before the start of the 1965 World Cup match at Dalymount Park.

Originally drawn in a group which also included Syria, Ireland were to play four games to decide who would qualify for the finals in England. Syria were unable to compete so FIFA decided that Spain and Ireland should play each other with points deciding the finalist. Therefore a victory for Ireland would guarantee them a play-off, at least.

Ireland went all-out for victory and after 8 minutes Hurley headed a Giles free into the net. However the goal was ruled out for a foul by Cantwell. Three minutes later Cantwell sent McEvoy running clear in on goal. Iribar came out and saved at his feet with Zoco clearing the rebound before O'Neill could get to it. Spain then began to press with Adelardo, Ufarte and Marcelino all having chances coming up to the break but were denied by good goalkeeping and poor finishing.

Lepetra came close in the second half when his shot from an acute angle was kicked out for a corner, and it was against the run of play that Ireland scored. Ireland were awarded a free kick for a foul on Giles near the touchline. O'Neill took it and sent a high ball into the box. Cantwell, closely marked by Zoco, was unable to get to it but Iribar misjudged his jump and, although he got his hands to it, the ball slipped form his grasp and bounced down into the net. Following this Adelardo shot wide and McEvoy into the side netting. In the closing stages Guillot, Adelardo and Glaria all had chances but Ireland kept them out and held on for a crucial victory.

Match No. 102 **SPAIN** **Away**

Wednesday 27th October, 1965 – Seville (World Cup)

SPAIN (2) 4 Pereda 40, 44, 58, Lepetra 63
REP. OF IRELAND (1) 1 McEvoy 26

Ref: Freitas (Portugal) **Ground:** Sanchez Pizjuan **Att:** 29,452

Spain: A. Betancort, F. Rivilla, F. Olivella, I. Zoco, S. Reija, J. Glaria IV, J. A. Ufarte, J. M. Pereda, Marcelino, L. Suarez, C. Lepetra.

Ireland: Pat Dunne (Manchester United 2), Theo Foley (Northampton Town 6), Tony Dunne (Manchester United 11), Mick McGrath (Blackburn Rovers 18), Noel Cantwell (Manchester United 31), Mick Meagan (Huddersfield Town 6), Frank O'Neill (Shamrock Rovers 6), Andy McEvoy (Blackburn Rovers 13), Eric Barber (Shelbourne 1), Johnny Giles (Leeds United 20), Joe Haverty (Shelbourne 26). **Captain:** Noel Cantwell

Spain, needing a win, began well and layed seige to the Irish goal for the first 15 minutes. In that time Glaria shot over, Pereda had a shot cleared off the line by Foley and Marcelino had a header turned onto the bar by Pat Dunne. Ireland weathered that storm and after 19 minutes were awarded a free kick on the edge of the area for obstruction on Barber. O'Neill took it quickly and layed it off to McGrath who cracked the ball home. However the referee ordered a re-take as it was taken too quickly. After 26 minutes another Irish free kick was passed out to Giles whose pin-point cross was volleyed home by McEvoy for the lead goal. Spain were rattled by this goal but 5 minutes from the break a cross from Lepetra eluded Marcelino and Cantwell and ran on for Pereda to shoot powerfully home. Then just before half-time a quickly taken Spanish free kick allowed Zoco to run through and shoot. Pat Dunne stopped it but Pereda followed up to score.

Spain again began on the attack with Pereda forcing Pat Dunne into an early save and Cantwell clearing a shot from Ufarte off the goal-line. After 58 minutes Pereda chased a long ball into the box and scored from a difficult angle. Five minutes later Lepetra shot home from 18 yards to seal the match for Spain. Giles and O'Neill had efforts for a consolation goal but the nearest each side came to scoring again was when Suarez had a shot taken off the line by Cantwell.

Match No. 103 — SPAIN — Neutral

Wednesday 10th November, 1965 – Paris (World Cup play-off)

SPAIN (0) 1 Ufarte 79
REP. OF IRELAND (0) 0

Ref: Schwinte (France) **Ground:** Colombes Stadium **Att:** 35,731

Spain: A. Betancort, F. Rivilla, F. Olivella, I. Zoco, S. Reija, J. Glaria IV, L. Suarez, J. A. Ufarte, J. M. Pereda, Marcelino, C. Lepetra.

Ireland: Pat Dunne (Manchester United 3), Shay Brennan (Manchester United 2), Tony Dunne (Manchester United 12), Theo Foley (Northampton Town 7), Noel Cantwell (Manchester United 32), Mick Meagan (Huddersfield Town 7), Frank O'Neill (Shamrock Rovers 7), Eamonn Dunphy (York City 1), Andy McEvoy (Blackburn Rovers 14), Johnny Giles (Leeds United 21), Joe Haverty (Shelbourne 27). **Captain:** Noel Cantwell

The venue for this play-off was to raise some controversy in years to come. Both London and Paris were offered as venues and the cash-starved FAI accepted a Spanish proposal that the Irish would receive the gate receipts if the game was played in Paris. The FAI probably took a realistic view of this match and with defeat likely against a vastly superior side decided to get something out of this fixture. On reflection it was a bad decision as it turned out to be a virtually home game for Spain with 30,000 Spaniards turning up in Paris to cheer their team on.

The Spanish supporters had not much to cheer about early on as Ireland forced a number of openings. Giles headed a Foley free kick wide and McEvoy headed over from Giles cross before Spain had a great chance. Suarez split the Irish defence wide open to send Ufarte in but the latter wasted the chance by shooting wide. Back came Ireland with O'Neill shooting just over and then, after 32 minutes, Giles chipped a pass to McEvoy. The centre-forward blasted a shot past Betancort but it hit Zoco on its way in and deflected out for a corner. Near the interval Pat Dunne was forced into action to deny Glaria and Zoco.

Spain had dominated play in the first half and this continued in the second period with Ireland playing a defensive game relying on breakaways. Pereda and Ufarte had early chances as had Giles and McEvoy but in general play was mainly in the Irish half. Pat Dunne brought off a double save to stop Marcelino and Ufarte before Foley was injured and had to leave the field. On his return, 11 minutes from the end at inside-right, Spain scored. Suarez sent Pereda away and he beat Tony Dunne before crossing in for Suarez. The latter swung a boot at it but missed and with Cantwell and Meagan wrong-footed the ball ran on for the unmarked Ufarte to shoot past Pat Dunne. Late in the game Suarez was denyed a second goal when Pat Dunne saved well.

Match No. 104 — WEST GERMANY — Home

Wednesday 4th May, 1966 – Dublin

REP. OF IRELAND (0) 0
WEST GERMANY (2) 4 Haller 5, Beckenbauer 19, Overath 55, 72

Ref: Mullen (Scotland) **Ground:** Dalymount Park **Att:** 16,091

Ireland: Pat Dunne (Manchester United 4), Theo Foley (Northampton Town 8), Fred Strahan (Shelbourne 5), Mick McGrath (Bradford City 19), Charlie Hurley (Sunderland 28), Jackie Hennessy (Shelbourne 4), Frank O'Neill (Shamrock Rovers 8), Ray Treacy (West Bromwich Albion 1), Bobby Gilbert (Shamrock Rovers 1), Eamonn Dunphy (Millwall 2), Joe Haverty (Shelbourne 28). **Subs:** John Keogh (Shamrock Rovers 1) for Foley (10 mins). **Captain:** Charlie Hurley.

Germany: J. Maier, F. Lutz, W. Schulz, H-D Höttges, J. Kurbjuhn, F. Beckenbauer, H. Haller, J. Grabowski, U. Seeler, W. Overath, H. Hornig.

West Germany strolled to an easy victory; their first in Dublin. After 5 minutes Hornig beat Foley and sent Haller in for the opening goal. In another 5 minutes Foley was forced to leave the field after crashing into some railings near the stand. Keogh, a late call-up, was brought on but after 19 minutes Beckenbauer played a one-two with Seeler and scored Germany's second. Ireland had few chances but Gilbert's shot in front of goal was deflected for a corner. Seeler, at the other end, also missed a chance in front of goal when he shot over. Near the interval Treacy rounded Maier but was forced wide and the chance was lost while Hurley headed a Strahan cross over.

The second half belonged to West Germany. Haller and Overath had good strikes before Haller sent Overath in to shoot home the third goal. Haverty and Hurley came near before Overath got free again and shot in the fourth through the goalkeepers legs.

Match No. 105 — AUSTRIA — Away

Sunday 22nd May, 1966 – Vienna

AUSTRIA (0) 1 Seitl 75
REP. OF IRELAND (0) 0

Ref: Gere (Hungary) **Ground:** Praeter Park **Att:** 33,000

Austria: R. Pichler, W. Gebhardt, W. Glechner, W. Stamm, W. Ludescher, E. Ullmann, W. Skocik, H. Hirnschrodt, W. Seitl, R. Flögel, A. Macek. **Subs:** T. Parits for Hirnschrodt (55 mins).

Ireland: Alan Kelly (Preston 13), Shay Brennan (Manchester United 3), Tony Dunne (Manchester United 13), Mick McGrath (Bradford City 20), Charlie Hurley (Sunderland 29), Mick Meagan (Huddersfield Town 8), Frank O'Neill (Shamrock Rovers 9), Johnny Fullam (Shamrock Rovers 5), Noel Cantwell (Manchester United 33), Johnny Giles (Leeds United 22), Joe Haverty (Shelbourne 29). **Captain:** Charlie Hurley.

On a stifling hot day Ireland played a defensive game relying on the odd breakaway. Both teams were to suffer from the oppressive heat but Austria, who dominated the game throughout, started well. Ullmann shot a 30 yard free kick against the underside of the crossbar and Seitl had a good opportunity from a Macek knock-down but shot against the post. The heat restricted the football following this but Meagan twice cleared his lines in dangerous Austrian moves.

Austria's Walter Seitl shoots into an empty net for the only goal of the game.
Also in the picture are Alan Kelly and Tony Dunne. (Photo: Votavafoto)

Austrian goalkeper Roman Pichler can only stand and watch as a Giles shot hits the crossbar. (Photo: Votavafoto)

Austria's Walter Seilt challenges Alan Kelly despite being surrounded by Irishmen.
Players from left: *Shay Brennan, Charlie Hurley, Kelly, Seitl, Mick Meagan and Tony Dunne.*
(Photo: Votavafoto)

Two minutes into the second half Glechner shot a 25 yard free kick into the goal but the referee ordered a re-take as he was not ready. After 75 minutes McGrath under-hit a long back-pass to his goalkeeper, allowing Seitl to run onto it, beat Meagan and shoot past Kelly. Ireland had two chances to equalise near the end. First Giles smacked a shot off the crossbar with Haverty wrong-footed in front of goal from the re-bound and then Hurley shot over.

Match No. 106 — BELGIUM — Away

Wednesday 25th May, 1966 – Liege

BELGIUM (2) 2 Van Himst 4, Vanden Boer 24
REP. OF IRELAND (1) 3 Cantwell 19, 48, Fullam 68

Ref: Schwinte (France) **Ground:** Standard Liege Stadium **Att:** 3,000

Belgium: J. Trappeniers, G. Heylens, J. Plaskie, M. Lemoine, J. Cornelis, J. Jurion, G. Vanden Boer, L. Semmeling, J. Stockman, P. Van Himst, W. Puis.

Ireland: Alan Kelly (Preston 14), Shay Brennan (Manchester United 4), Tony Dunne (Manchester United 14), Mick McGrath (Bradford City 21), Charlie Hurley (Sunderland 30), Mick Meagan (Huddersfield Town 9), Eric Barber (Shamrock Rovers 2), Johnny Fullam (Shamrock Rovers 6), Noel Cantwell (Manchester United 34), Johnny Giles (Leeds United 23), Joe Haverty (Shelbourne 30). **Captain:** Charlie Hurley.

Ireland returned to the scene of its first-ever victory when, 38 years ago, on a rain-soaked pitch they beat their hosts 4-2 with a great second-half display. History repeated itself when, in the midst of a continual downpour (in sharp contrast to the previous Sunday) they again came from behind to record a victory.

After 4 minutes Lemoine put Semmeling away and when he crossed in, Van Himst was there to head past Kelly. Both teams had opened brightly and after 19 minutes Cantwell got possession when a Belgian attack broke down. Cantwell gave the ball to Dunne who brought it well into the Belgian half before threading a lovely through-ball for Cantwell to beat the offside trap, round the goalkeeper and score. Five minutes later Belgium were back in front when Vanden Boer curled a 25 yard shot beyond Kelly and into the net. Coming up to the break Cantwell again got free and shot past Trappeniers only to see his effort cleared off the line by a defender.

Three minutes after the interval Meagan sent Barber up the wing with a fine pass. Barber crossed in for Cantwell and the centre-forward beat Plaskie before shooting low into the net. Soon after Giles crossed in with Hurley just failing to connect with a diving header. Another Giles cross found Fullam's head perfectly and the inside-right headed down into the net for the winner.

Match No. 107 — SPAIN — Home

Sunday 23rd October, 1966 – Dublin (European Championship)

REP. OF IRELAND (0) 0
SPAIN (0) 0

Ref: Carlsson (Sweden) **Ground:** Dalymount Park **Att:** 37,000

Ireland: Alan Kelly (Preston 15), Shay Brennan (Manchester United 5), Noel Cantwell (Manchester United 35), Mick Meagan (Huddersfield Town 10), Tony Dunne (Manchester United 15), Johnny Giles (Leeds United 24), Jimmy Conway (Fulham 1), Frank O'Neill (Shamrock Rovers 10), Andy McEvoy (Blackburn Rovers 15), Ray Treacy (West Bromwich Albion 2), Tony O'Connell (Dundalk 1). **Captain:** Noel Cantwell. **Formation:** 4-2-4.

Spain: Iribar, Sanchis, F. Santamaria, Reija, Glaria IV, Violeta, Vava, Luis, Ansola, Marcial, Paquito.

A disappointing and sometimes rough game ended in a scoreless draw. Kelly had early saves to stop Luis and Vava while Conway had a good shot on the turn wide. In a game of few highlights it was Spain who came close near the break with Vava hitting the crossbar and Luis having a shot saved by Kelly.

Kelly was also in action early in the second half saving from Ansola and Marcial while Glaria shot a good chance over. After 62 minutes Giles knocked a free kick to Cantwell whose shot was destined for the net until Iribar brought off a great save. Nine minutes later a header from McEvoy was cleared off the line by Violeta. Shortly before the final whistle Kelly again saved from Luis and Vava.

Match No. 108 — TURKEY — Home

Wednesday 16th November, 1966 – Dublin (European Championship)

REP. OF IRELAND (0) 2 O'Neill 59, McEvoy 74
TURKEY (0) 1 Ogun 88

Ref: Sorensen (Denmark) **Ground:** Dalymount Park **Att:** 20,000

Ireland: Pat Dunne (Manchester United 5), Shay Brennan (Manchester United 6), Charlie Hurley (Sunderland 31), Mick Meagan (Huddersfield Town 11), Tony Dunne (Manchester United 16), Jimmy Conway (Fulham 2), Eamonn Dunphy (Millwall 3), Frank O'Neill (Shamrock Rovers 11), Johnny Giles (Leeds United 25), Andy McEvoy (Blackburn Rovers 16), Joe Haverty (Shelbourne 31). **Captain:** Charlie Hurley. **Formation:** 4-2-4.

Turkey: Ali, Talet, Fehuri, Seref, Ercan, Yilmaz, Ogun, Ayhan, Fevzi, Nevzat, Faruk.

Turkey came to defend and rarely threatened the Irish goal except late in the game. The Turkish defensive play caused Ireland a lot of problems and, although the home side remained encamped in the Turkish half for long periods throughout the game, they could not find a way through.

McEvoy had an early chance but shot over and Ali made good saves to stop Giles and Conway. There were few clear-cut chances in this first period but three minutes before the break Dunphy's flashing header from O'Neill's cross forced Ali into an excellent save.

Irish domination continued after the turn-around and Haverty and Giles had efforts that just went wide. Another Haverty shot beat Ali but Erlan headed it off the line. Fourteen minutes into the half Ireland finally got the goal their play deserved. A free kick, for a foul on Haverty, was quickly knocked out to O'Neill who, from 20 yards out, thumped the ball into the net, via a deflection from Hurley. Three minutes later Turkey almost drew level when Ayhan was sent clear but he shot wide from a good position. After 74 minutes Haverty gave a short corner to Giles and when the latter sent over a perfect cross McEvoy spun around to knock the ball home with a great left-footed shot. The Turks then abandoned their defensive posture and created a number of late chances. Two minutes from the end, Talet and Faruk set up Ogun to score from close range. A minute later a Yilmaz shot brought a good save from Kelly this being the last chance of the game.

Match No. 109 — SPAIN — Away

Wednesday 7th December, 1966 – Valencia (European Championship)

SPAIN (2) 2 Jose Maria 21, Pirri 40
REP. OF IRELAND (0) 0

Ref: Roomer (Holland) **Ground:** Mestalla Stadium **Att:** 20,000

Spain: Iribar, Sanchis, F. Gallego, Reija, Paquito, Violeta, Pirri, Jara, Ansola, Luis, Jose Maria.

Ireland: Alan Kelly (Preston 16), Shay Brennan (Manchester United 7), Charlie Hurley (Sunderland 32), John Dempsey (Fulham 1), Tony Dunne (Manchester United 17), Eamonn Dunphy (Millwall 4), Mick Meagan (Huddersfield Town 12), Frank O'Neill (Shamrock Rovers 12), Jimmy Conway (Fulham 3), Alfie Hale (Waterford 5), Joe Haverty (Shelbourne 32). **Captain:** Charlie Hurley. **Formation:** 4-2-4.

Spain dominated the game from start to finish and, with the Irish forwards restricted to the odd breakaway, Iribar did not have a single shot to save. The few Irish chances fell mainly to Haverty, who was off-target twice, and O'Neill, who also shot wide. If Iribar was inactive the same could not be said of his opposite number who produced a string of marvellous saves to keep the scoreline down.

For the opening half-hour Spain kept Ireland in their half and peppered the Irish goal with shot after shot. Luis had the best of these chances but was off-target with one while his second was saved by Kelly. After 21 minutes Pirri worked his way through the Irish defence and sent the ball out to Jose Maria. The pass was a bad one and when the winger picked the ball up he was near the corner flag. Brennan came across but Jose Maria beat him and, from a difficult angle, curled the ball into the far corner of the net. Spain continued to press and were denied a penalty when Hurley handled in the box. However, a minute later, Spain added a second. A free kick by Sanchis was claimed by Kelly who was prevented from grasping it by obstruction on the part of Luis. The ball fell from the goalkeepers hands and Pirri was there to put it into the roof of the net.

The second half was a repeat of the first except there were no goals. Jara had an early shot on the run which hit the crossbar, Jose Maria dribbled through the Irish defence only to shoot over while Pirri had a close range effort stopped by Kelly. Ten minutes from the end Pirri beat Kelly but his 35 yard shot hit a post and went wide.

Match No. 110 — TURKEY — Away

Wednesday 22nd February, 1967 – Ankara (European Championship)

TURKEY (1) 2 Ayhan 35, Ogun 80
REP. OF IRELAND (0) 1 Cantwell 89

Ref: Roumenchev (Bulgaria) **Ground:** May 19 Stadium **Att:** 35,000

Turkey: Ali, Talet, Ercan, Sukru, Fehmi, Ayhan, Seref, Ergun, Ogun, Abdullah, Faruk.

Ireland: Alan Kelly (Preston 17), Joe Kinnear (Tottenham Hotspur 1), Charlie Hurley (Sunderland 33), Al Finucane (Limerick 1), Mick McGrath (Bradford City 22), Mick Meagan (Huddersfield Town 13), Johnny Giles (Leeds United 26), Frank O'Neill (Shamrock Rovers 13), Charlie Gallagher (Glasgow Celtic 1), Noel Cantwell (Manchester United 36), Eamonn Dunphy (Millwall 5). **Captain:** Charlie Hurley. **Formation:** 5-1-4.

Ireland adopted the Turkish defensive game used in the match in Dublin and played five at the back, using Finucane as a sweeper.

Turkey swept into attack and Abdullah was narrowly wide with their first effort. A corner by Faruk was fumbled by Kelly and Kinnear had to kick the ball off the line to prevent a goal. Ireland's best effort came when O'Neill's high cross into the box was headed down by Hurley for Dunphy to blast over. Turkey eventually went into a deserved lead when a cross by Ercan caught Kelly and Hurley in two minds and Ayhan slipped in to score.

Seref almost got in for an early goal in the second half but Meagan got back to deny him. Soon after Dunphy was injured and this affected his game. After 80 minutes Dunphy was unable to stop Faruk (now on the right) and the winger's cross was headed home by Ogun. Late in the game Giles brought off a fine save from Ali but the Turkish goalkeeper was beaten seconds from the end when Giles and Finucane set up Cantwell to score, from close range, with a flick shot.

Match No. 111 — CZECHOSLOVAKIA — Home

Sunday 21st May, 1967 – Dublin (European Championship)

REP. OF IRELAND (0) 0
CZECHOSLOVAKIA (1) 2 Finucane (o.g.) 16, V. Masny 47

Ref: Schaut (Belgium) **Ground:** Dalymount Park **Att:** 8,500

Ireland: Alan Kelly (Preston 18), Theo Foley (Northampton Town 9), John Dempsey (Fulham 2), Al Finucane (Limerick 2), Charlie Hurley (Sunderland 34), Mick Meagan (Huddersfield Town 14), Charlie Gallagher (Glasgow Celtic 2), Andy McEvoy (Blackburn Rovers 17), Ray Treacy (West Bromwich Albion 3), Eamonn Dunphy (Millwall 6), Oliver Conmy (Peterborough 2). **Coach/Captain:** Charlie Hurley. **Formation:** 2-3-5.

Czechoslovakia: I. Viktor, J. Lala, K. Majernik, J. Popluhar, V. Taborsky, J. Geleta, A. Kvasnak, J. Szikora, V. Masny, J. Adamac, D. Kabat.

A dull match with few highlights failed to excite the small rain-soaked crowd. Early in the game McEvoy shot into the side netting but after 16 minutes Czechoslovakia took the lead. Adamac gave the ball out to Szikora who shot first time. The shot looked as if it was going wide but it hit Finucane and ended up in the goal. Three minutes later Kabat had another chance but shot over. Ireland's two best chances fell to Treacy in a three-minute spell. First, after 24 minutes, his header was saved by Viktor then he deflected a Finucane cross past the Czech goalkeeper but it bounced wide. Near the end of the half Kelly made good saves to stop Adamec (twice) and Kabat.

The second half was as bad as the first and the only real highlight was the Czech's second goal. A bad pass by Finucane allowed Szikora time to work his way into the box before slipping the ball to Masny who scored easily.

Match No. 112 CZECHOSLOVAKIA Away

Wednesday 22nd November, 1967 – Prague (European Championship)

CZECHOSLOVAKIA (0) 1 Dempsey (o.g.) 58
REP. OF IRELAND (0) 2 Treacy 65, O'Connor 86

Ref: Vetter (East Germany) **Ground:** Slavia Stadium **Att:** 10,000

Czechoslovakia: A. Kramerius, J. Lala, J. Popluhar, V. Taborsky, A. Horvath, J. Geleta, J. Levicky, J. Szikora, L. Kuna, J. Jurkanin, V. Vrana.

Ireland: Alan Kelly (Preston 19), Joe Kinnear (Tottenham Hotspur 2), John Dempsey (Fulham 3), Charlie Hurley (Sunderland 35), Mick Meagan (Huddersfield Town 15), Jimmy Conway (Fulham 4), Eamonn Dunphy (Millwall 7), Eamonn Rogers (Blackburn Rovers 1), Oliver Conmy (Peterborough 3), Ray Treacy (Charlton Athletic 4), Turlough O'Connor (Fulham 1). **Coach/Captain:** Charlie Hurley. **Formation:** 4-3-3.

Czechosolvakia went into the last game in Group One needing only a draw to be sure of a place in the Quarter Finals. Ireland came to defend, remembering their last visit to Prague six years ago.

Early Czech pressure resulted in three corners in as many minutes. After 11 minutes Jurkanin was put through following a mistake by Hurley but shot wide when well placed. The same player had two further chances soon after but Kelly brought off two great saves to deny him. The nearest Ireland came to a goal in the first half was a shot by Conmy which was saved by Kramerius. Coming up to the break a Kuna header hit the crossbar and a free kick by Pupluhar was only just wide.

Ireland showed more attacking spirit in the second half but soon after the restart Kinnear was forced to clear a Popluhar effort off the line. After 13 minutes Levicky chased a long ball from Lala up the wing. Meagan went with the winger and, getting to the ball first, clipped it back into his own area. The rest of the defence was in full retreat to cover the treat of the Czech forwards and when the ball fell to the feet of Dempsey he was unable to steady himself. In trying to clear the ball he instead shot over Kelly and into the net. However in another seven minutes Ireland were level. Conmy broke from defence and gave the ball to Rogers. Conmy ran on expecting the return pass but Rogers switched it out to Conway on the other wing. The latter found Dunphy and he crossed in for Treacy to head home. Eight minutes later Szikora was injured after a tackle by Hurley and was carried off with a broken leg. Ten-man Czechoslovakia settled for defence but this proved to be their undoing. With four minutes left Treacy robbed Popluhar on the edge of his own area and crossed in for O'Connor to score with a diving header. Dunphy and Rogers were booked during the game.

Match No. 113 POLAND Home

Wednesday 15th May, 1968 – Dublin

REP. OF IRELAND (0) 2 Dempsey 52, Hale 89
POLAND (2) 2 Lubanski 5 (pen), Jarosik 24

Ref: Jennings (England) **Ground:** Dalymount Park **Att:** 30,000

Ireland: Alan Kelly (Preston 20), Joe Kinnear (Tottenham Hotspur 3), Mick Meagan (Huddersfield Town 16), Charlie Hurley (Sunderland 36), Tommy Carroll (Ipswich Town 1), Eamonn Dunphy (Millwall 8), Johnny Fullam (Shamrock Rovers 7), Eamonn Rogers (Blackburn Rovers 2), Oliver Conmy (Peterborough 4), John Dempsey (Fullam 4), Ray Treacy (Charlton Athletic 5). **Subs:** Alfie Hale (Waterford 6), for Rogers (72 mins). **Coach/Captain:** Charlie Hurley. **Formation:** 4-3-3.

Poland: H. Kostka, Bazan, S. Oslizto, W. Winkler, J. Gmoch, H. Latocha, J. Zmijewski, B. Bula, W. Lubanski, A. Jarosik, E. Faber.

Ireland had two early chances when Rogers shot over from 20 yards and Dempsey hustled Kostka into a mistake only for Gmoch to clear off the line. Poland's first attack came after 5 minutes. A cross from the left was handled by Hurley and Lubanski scored from the resultant penalty. A lot of scrappy play followed before Jarosik brought out a good save from Kelly. After 24 minutes Jarosik mis-hit a cross from Zmijewski, the ball hit Hurley and spun into the net. Ireland staged a recovery before the interval with Dempsey having his header saved by Kostka.

Seven minutes into the second period Dempsey had better luck when his header, from Fullam's high cross, could only be helped into the net by the beaten goalkeeper. Following this Dempsey moved back into defence with Hurley taking over at centre-forward. Hurley was soon in action forcing Kostka into a fine save to stop his blistering 25 yard shot. Conmy was just over with a similar effort soon after while Treacy had a header saved by the Polish goalkeeper. Hale replaced Rogers and took over from Hurley up front. Treacy got in another header but this time was denied by a post. A minute from the end Dunphy skirted past four defenders and sent over a hanging cross for Hale to head home the equaliser.

Match No. 114 — POLAND — Away

Wednesday 30th October, 1968 – Katowice

POLAND (0) 1 Lubanski 60

REP. OF IRELAND (0) 0

Ref: **Ground:** Slaski Stadium **Att:** 20,000

Poland: H. Kostka, Rudnow, Florenski, W. Winkler, A. Musial, E. Wilczek, B. Blaut, J. Zmijewski, W. Lubanski, J. Sadek, R. Gadocha.

Ireland: Alan Kelly (Preston 21), Tommy Carroll (Ipswich Town 2), Charlie Hurley (Sunderland 37), John Dempsey (Fullham 5), Tony Dunne (Manchester United 18), Eamonn Dunphy (Millwall 9), Johnny Fullam (Shamrock Rovers 8), Eamonn Rogers (Blackburn Rovers 3), Frank O'Neill (Shamrock Rovers 14), Alfie Hale (Waterford 7), Ray Treacy (Charlton Athletic 6). **Subs:** Mick Smyth (Shamrock Rovers 1), for Kelly (61 mins). **Coach/Captain:** Charlie Hurley. **Formation:** 4-3-3.

A meagre crowd turned up to see a poor game. The first 15 minutes contained few highlights but Kelly made a good save to deny Lubanski and then recovered to save the follow-up from Sadek. Hurley and Hale had chances at the other end but both were off target. Coming up to the break Lubanski had another shot saved by Kelly who also denied Gadocha by deflecting his shot out for a corner with his foot.

The second half was scrappy. Lubanski got a good header to a Zmijewski cross but again Kelly saved. Sadek also had two efforts stopped by Kelly before Poland scored. Carroll passed a ball straight to the unmarked Lubanski and, with Kelly out of position, the Pole had little difficulty in scoring. Kelly, who had started the game with a knee injury, went off and Smyth took over in

The Irish team which lost 0-1 to Poland in Katowice in 1968
Players left to right: *John Dempsey, Tony Dunne, Eamonn Rogers, Alfie Hale, Johny Fullam, Alan Kelly, Frank O'Neill, Tommy Carroll, Eamonn Dunphy, Ray Treacy and Charlie Hurley. (Photo: PAPLCAF)*

goal. Soon after Treacy had a shot saved by Kostka but following that there were few chances and the last half-hour was played out without incident.

Unfortunately whilst the game was in progress the FAI secretary, Joseph Wickham, suffered a heart attack which proved fatal.

Match No. 115 — AUSTRIA — Home

Sunday 10th November, 1968 – Dublin

REP. OF IRELAND (0) 2 Rogers 81, Hale 86
AUSTRIA (1) 2 Redl 15, E. Hof I 51

Ref: Davidson (Scotland) **Ground:** Dalymount Park **Att:** 18,000

Ireland: Alan Kelly (Preston 22), Joe Kinnear (Tottenham Hotspur 4), Tommy Carroll (Ipswich Town 3), Johnny Fullam (Shamrock Rovers 9), John Dempsey (Fulham 6), Jackie Hennessy (St Patrick's Athletic 5), Frank O'Neill (Shamrock Rovers 15), Eamonn Dunphy (Millwall 10), Alfie Hale (Waterford 8), Johnny Giles (Leeds United 27), Eamonn Rogers (Blackburn Rovers 4). **Subs:** Jimmy Conway (Fulham 5), for Hennessy (54 mins). **Captain:** Johnny Giles. **Formation:** 2-3-5.

Austria: W. Fuchsbichler I, W. Gebhardt, G. Sturmberger, J. Eigenstiller, H. Russ, J. Ettmaier, R. Horvath, E. Hof I, A. Fritsch, H. Köglberger, H. Redl. **Subs:** G. Herreither for Fuchsbichler (8 mins), H. Mätzler for Köglberger (79 mins).

Ireland began well with Fuchsbichler making a double save to foil O'Neill. The Austrian goalkeeper injured a finger while saving and had to be replaced by Herreither. The substitute was soon tested by a Hale header but he saved well. After 15 minutes the Irish defence was exposed when Eigenstiller broke a tackle from Carroll and sent Horvath away. Horvath combined with Fritsch and the latter slipped the ball in for Redl to score easily. Austria had few attacking moves but just after the half-hour Köglberger had a goalbound shot deflected for a corner. From the flag kick Fritsch shot wide and soon after Köglberger was sent clear by Hof only for Kelly to save. After 41 minutes Dempsey headed an O'Neill corner against the bar while at the other end Horvath shot wide when well placed.

Ireland dominated the second period but conceded a second goal soon after the restart. Hof played a one-two with Redl and placed the ball wide of Kelly and into the net. Conway came on for Hennessy and took up a defensive position allowing Dempsey to go forward. Hale was just wide with a header, O'Neill similarly with a 25 yard shot and Rogers hit the post with another effort before Ireland got a goal back. A cross by Dunphy caught in the wind and sailed away from the goal towards the waiting Rogers. The winger, on the edge of the box, met the ball with a bullet-like volley which flashed past the static Herreither. Three minutes later Dempsey bundled the Austrian goalkeeper over the line as he saved a shot by Giles but the referee awarded a free out. After 86 minutes O'Neill and Rogers put Giles running in on goal. Avoiding a couple of defenders he sent in a shot against the post with Hale following up to knock the rebound home. Late chances fell to Ettmaier (who shot against the crossbar) and Giles (shot saved) to win the game but a draw was a fair result.

Match No. 116 — DENMARK — Home

Wednesday 4th December, 1968 – Dublin (World Cup)

REP. OF IRELAND (1) 1 Giles 40 (pen)
DENMARK (1) 1 Wiberg 18

Ref: Syme (Scotland) **Ground:** Dalymount Park **Att:**
Abandoned after 51 minutes

Ireland: Alan Kelly (Preston 23), Tommy Carroll (Ipswich Town 4), Tony Dunne (Manchester United 19), John Dempsey (Fulham 7), Charlie Hurley (Sunderland 38), Johnny Fullam (Shamrock Rovers

10), Frank O'Neill (Shamrock Rovers 16), Eamonn Dunphy (Millwall 11), Alfie Hale (Waterford 9), Johnny Giles (Leeds United 28), Eamonn Rogers (Blackburn Rovers 5). **Coach/Captain:** Charlie Hurley. **Formation:** 2-3-5.

Denmark: K. Engedal, J. Larsen, H. J. Christiansen, L. Sorensen, H. M. Jensen, E. Sandvad, K. Praest, B. Jensen, N. Holmstrom, F. Wiberg, U. le Fevre.

Due to the foggy conditions the game kicked off almost half an hour late. The referee saw an improvement in the weather but as the game progressed it got worse and six minutes into the second half he abandoned the game as he could not see his linesmen. What those attending the match saw were only brief glimpses of players darting in and out of mist.

Denmark scored first through Wiberg although only the player himself and those behind the goal know how. Ireland equalised when the referee awarded a penalty for handball against Henning Munk Jensen. Giles scored from the spot-kick even though Engedal guessed correctly.

The Danes were willing to replay the game the next day but the officials were unable to agree and the fixture was not played until the next season.

Match No. 117 — CZECHOSLOVAKIA — Home

Sunday 4th May, 1969 – Dublin (World Cup)

REP. OF IRELAND (1) 1 Rogers 15
CZECHOSLOVAKIA (0) 2 Kabat 51, Adamec 65

Ref: Ribeiro (Portugal) **Ground:** Dalymount Park **Att:** 32,002

Ireland: Alan Kelly (Preston 24), Shay Brennan (Manchester United 8), Charlie Hurley (Sunderland 39), John Dempsey (Chelsea 8), Paddy Mulligan (Shamrock Rovers 1), Al Finucane (Limerick 3), Johnny Giles (Leeds United 29), Frank O'Neill (Shamrock Rovers 17), Mick Leech (Shamrock Rovers 1), Ray Treacy (Charlton Athletic 7), Eamonn Rogers (Blackburn Rovers 6). **Subs:** Eoin Hand (Portsmouth 1), for Leech (44 min). **Coach/Captain:** Charlie Hurley. **Formation:** 4-2-4.

CSSR: Vencel, K. Dobias, Plass, A. Horvath, V. Hagara, J. Szikora, A. Kvasnak, B. Vesely, J. Jurkanin, J. Adamec, D. Kabat. **Subs:** Hrdlicka for Szikora.

Ireland's 25th World Cup match turned out to be a very bad tempered affair with Leech being carried off following a dreadful tackle by Plass. There were several punch-ups, notably between Finucane and Horvath, but surprisingly no bookings. Of the actual play Ireland had a brilliant opening 45 minutes but the second half belonged to the Czechs.

Leech was in action early challenging Vencel for a cross. The goalkeeper dropped the ball and Leech shot towards goal only to have a defender clear. Rogers and the Czech Dobias were off target with further efforts before Ireland took the lead. Treacy latched on the Giles through ball and beat the offside trap before shooting across goal. The ball came to O'Neill, racing in from the opposite side, and he crossed first-time for Rogers to score with a firm downward header. The Irish continued to press but a series of fights broke out and this culminated in Leech being stretchered off to be replaced by Hand who took over at centre-forward.

Ireland were not in the second half as Czechoslovakia came out attacking. After 51 minutes Brennan deflected a cross by Jurkanin onto the post and Kabat had no trouble putting the rebound in. Treacy was just over with another shot before the Czechs got what proved to be the winner. Jurkanin put Adamec racing in on goal and the latter outpaced the defence before shooting past Kelly into the goal.

Match No. 118 — DENMARK — Away

Tuesday 27th May, 1969 – Copenhagen (World Cup)

DENMARK (1) 2 O. Soerensen 35, 67
REP. OF IRELAND (0) 0

Ref: Arkhipov (USSR) **Ground:** Idraetspark **Att:** 26,195

Denmark: K. Engedahl, J. Larsen, T. Nielan, C. Andersen, H. M. Jensen, N. Moller, B. Jensen, O. Soerensen, O. Madsen, L. Sorensen, U. le Fevre.

Ireland: Alan Kelly (Preston 25), Shay Brennan (Manchester United 9), Al Finucane (Limerick 4), John Dempsey (Chelsea 9), Paddy Mulligan (Shamrock Rovers 2), Billy Newman (Shelbourne 1), Eamonn Dunphy (Millwall 12), Ray Treacy (Charlton Athletic 8), Mick Leech (Shamrock Rovers 2), Don Givens (Manchester United 1), Eamonn Rogers (Blackburn Rovers 7). **Subs:** Frank O'Neill (Shamrock Rovers 18), for Newman (55 mins). **Captain:** John Dempsey. **Formation:** 4-2-4.

Irelands last visit to Copenhagen had provoked some Danes in the crowd to violence due to the Irish tactics of 'sitting' on a two-goal lead. Whilst not using the same tactics in this game the Irish play (admittedly at times rugged) provoked one lady to run onto the pitch and assault John Dempsey while in another incident a bottle was thrown at Paddy Mulligan when he wrestled Ole Soerensen to the ground. The game was at times rough and this probably influenced these two incidents. Madsen of Denmark and Dempsey of Ireland were booked.

Leech got the first chance of the game after 12 minutes when Dunphy set him up to shoot just over. Two minutes later le Fevre put Soerensen in and he beat 3 tackles before shooting; Kelly saving at the expense of a corner. Treacy shot over from 25 yards as did Andersen, from 30 yards, at the other end before the Danes scored. A mistake by Mulligan allowed Bent Jensen to break from the half-way line to the Irish penalty area. There he beat Newman and passed in for Ole Soerensen to net.

A minute into the second half Givens picked up a loose ball, burst into the Danish box and his low shot would have found the net had Engedahl not got a hand to it to deflect it out for a corner. Charlie Hurley, Ireland's Coach, brought on O'Neill as a winger with Treacy dropping back to mid-field. The Irish, though, conceded a second goal when Madsen made a great run before setting up Ole Soerensen to get his second goal.

Match No. 119 — HUNGARY — Home

Sunday 8th June, 1969 – Dublin (World Cup)

REP. OF IRELAND (0) 1 Givens 59
HUNGARY (1) 2 A. Dunai II 23, Bene 80

Ref: Loraux (Belgium) **Ground:** Dalymount Park **Att:** 17,286

Ireland: Alan Kelly (Preston 26), Shay Brennan (Manchester United 10), Al Finucane (Limerick 5), Paddy Mulligan (Shamrock Rovers 3), Tony Dunne (Manchester United 20), Jimmy Conway (Fulham 6), Eamonn Dunphy (Millwall 13), Eamonn Rogers (Blackburn Rovers 8), Mick Leech (Shamrock Rovers 3), Charlie Hurley (Bolton Wanderers 40), Don Givens (Manchester United 2). **Subs:** Frank O'Neill (Shamrock Rovers 19), for Hurley (half-time). **Coach/Captain:** Charlie Hurley. **Formation:** 4-3-3.

Hungary: A. Szentmihalyi, B. Kaposzta, K. Meszöly, L. Szucs, K. Ihasz, J. Göröcs, F. Albert, S. Zambo, F. Bene, A. Dunai II, M. Kozma. **Subs:** J. Farkas for Kozma (70 mins).

The opening half, played in warm sunshine, produced little constructive football. Hungary opened well with Szucs testing Kelly twice. The visitors had the better of things during that opening period and went ahead mid-way through it. Antal Dunai sent in a cross which was headed down by Albert to Göröcs on the edge of the box. Göröcs sent the ball wide for Bene to run onto it and shoot. Kelly saved but the ball spun out of his hands and, although Mulligan cleared it, the ball struck Bene again and rolled across the goal for Dunai to score.

At half-time Hurley decided to bring on O'Neill up front, and 4 minutes into the half Conway volleyed Brennans cross over. A minute later Dunphy put Leech clear but the latter's shot was saved by the goalkeeper. After 59 minutes Dunphy robbed Zambo on the edge of the Irish box and sent O'Neill away. The winger sprinted into the Hungarian half, beat Szucs and crossed in for Givens to chest the ball down before shooting past Szentmihalyi. Kelly saved an Albert header and Szentmihalyi a Leech shot before Hungary got the winner, ten minutes from the end, when a cross from Farkas was volleyed home first-time by Bene.

Match No. 120 SCOTLAND Home

Sunday 21st September, 1969 – Dublin

REP. OF IRELAND (1) 1 Givens 27
SCOTLAND (1) 1 Stein 8

Ref: Burtenshaw (England) **Ground:** Dalymount Park **Att:** 27,000

Ireland: Alan Kelly (Preston 27), Shay Brennan (Manchester United 11), Al Finucane (Limerick 6), Paddy Mulligan (Shamrock Rovers 4), Mick Meagan (Drogheda 17), Jimmy Conway (Fulham 7),Johnny Giles (Leeds United 30), Eamonn Rogers (Blackburn Rovers 9), Don Givens (Manchester United 3), Alfie Hale (Waterford 10), Ray Treacy (Charlton Athletic 9). **Captain:** Mick Meagan. **Manager:** Mick Meagan (1). **Formation:** 4-3-3.

Scotland: E. McGarr, J. Greig, R. McKinnon, P. Stanton, T. Gemmell, B. Bremner, P. Cormack, B. Moncur, W. Henderson, C. Stein, J. Hughes. **Subs:** J. Herriot for McGarr (24 mins), W. Callaghan for Gemmell (half-time).

Ireland entered a new era when the FAI appointed Mick Meagan as National Team Manager. Previous 'managers' were no more than coaches but this new position left team selection, tactics etc. to the managers discretion. This new step was counter-balanced by an old problem as most of the players (on both sides) had played hard league games the day before. This was to have an effect on the match as the second half had a very'tired' look about it.

The first half, in which Ireland dominated the play for long spells, was very entertaining. After 6 minutes Rogers's curling free kick was saved brilliantly by McGarr. Two minutes later Scotland launched its first attack and scored. A shot by Bremner was blocked by Mulligan back to him. The mid-fielder knocked the ball back to Stanton who blasted a shot at goal. Kelly dived and got a hand to the shot but was unable to recover in time to prevent Stein from putting in the rebound. Ireland responded well to this set-back. Rogers had another free kick wide and Treacy had a header off-target as the Irish attacked. After 18 minutes a long-range shot by Cormack beat Kelly but hit a post. Both Moncur (from Givens shot) and Brennan (from Cormack) were forced to clear their lines before McGarr was injured while saving from Givens. Herriot came on but was beaten straight away by a Rogers header which was kicked off the line by Greig. After 27 minutes Hale found Givens in the box and even though the centre-forwards first shot was saved he followed up to put the ball into the net. Giles came close with another effort on the half-hour but was wide. Just before the break Givens went off injured but resumed after the interval.

Scotland replaced Gemmell with Callaghan for the second half. Callaghan went to right back with Greig switching over to Gemmell's berth. Conway and Treacy had early efforts for Ireland before Scotland began to attack. Hughes had a good shot wide after 10 minutes. Fifteen minutes from the end Kelly brought off a marvellous double save when first he blocked a shot by Cormack and then denied Stein from the rebound. Two late chances fell to the visitors when Kelly saved from Stanton and Callaghan shot wide when in a good position. Hughes of Scotland and Brennan of Ireland were booked during the game.

Match No. 121 CZECHOSLOVAKIA Away

Tuesday 7th October, 1969 – Prague (World Cup)

CZECHOSLOVAKIA (3) 3 Adamec 9, 37, 44
REP. OF IRELAND (0) 0

Ref: Lo Bello (Italy) **Ground:** Sparta Stadium **Att:** 32,879

CSSR: I. Viktor, J. Pivarnik, V. Migas, A. Horvath, V. Hagara, A. Kvasnak, L. Kuna, B. Vesely, J. Jurkanin, J. Adamec, D. Kabat. **Subs:** K. Jokl for Jurkanin, Hrivnak for Migas.

Ireland: Kevin Fitzpatrick (Limerick 1), Shay Brennan (Manchester United 12), Al Finucane (Limerick 7), Paddy Mulligan (Shamrock Rovers 5), Tommy Carroll (Ipswich Town 5), Joe Kinnear (Tottenham Hotspur

Joe Kinnear.

Terry Conroy.

Ireland's Eamonn Rogers and Hungary's Antol Dunai watch as Mihaly Kozma clears the ball.

5), Jimmy Conway (Fulham 8), Oliver Conmy (Peterborough 5), Don Givens (Manchester United 4), Alfie Hale (Waterford 11), Terry Conroy (Stoke City 1). **Subs:** Johnny Fullam (Shamrock Rovers 11), for Givens (half-time). **Captain:** Shay Brennan. **Manager:** Mick Meagan (2). **Formation:** 4-3-3.

Ireland were completely outplayed by the Czechs. In 9 minutes a long ball from Migas was flicked into the centre by Kabat for Adamec to score. After 37 minutes a free kick by Kvasnak was squared for Adamec to send a bullet-like shot into the back of the net. The Czech centre-forward completed his hat-trick in the dying seconds of the half when Jurkanin chested a Vesely corner into his path and he scored with a shot from 15 yards.

At half-time Fullam came on for Givens. Fullam went to mid-field while Conmy moved into the forward line. This seemed to be a containing move and it was effective as there were no goals in the second period although Kvasnak missed a simple chance after 65 minutes.

Match No. 122 — DENMARK — Home

Wednesday 15th October, 1969 – Dublin (World Cup)

REP. OF IRELAND (1) 1 Givens 8
DENMARK (0) 1 B. Jensen 85 (pen)

Ref: Patterson (Scotland) **Ground:** Dalymount Park **Att:** 19,603

Ireland: Alan Kelly (Preston 28), Joe Kinnear (Tottenham Hotspur 6), Tony Byrne (Southampton 1), Paddy Mulligan (Shamrock Rovers 6), Shay Brennan (Manchester United 13), Jimmy Conway (Fulham 9), Eamonn Dunphy (Millwall 14), Eamonn Rogers (Blackburn Rovers 10), Terry Conroy (Stoke City 2), Don Givens (Manchester United 5), Ray Treacy (Charlton Athletic 10). **Captain:** Shay Brennan. **Manager:** Mick Meagan (3). **Formation:** 4-3-3.

Denmark: K. Poulsen, J. Larsen, E. Nielsen, K. Thorst, H. M. Jensen, N. Moeller, K. Praest, A. Michaelsen, B. Jensen, J. Andersen, S. Roemer. **Subs:** P. Madsen for Roemer.

A match in which Ireland should have had a comfortable victory ended in a disappointing draw. After 8 minutes Rogers exchanged passes with Dunphy before sending over a cross which Givens took down before shooting past Poulsen. The first half was basically one-way traffic as Ireland missed chance after chance. The best of them fell to Dunphy 2 minutes before half-time when he shot past Poulsen only for the ball to roll wide.

The second half saw Ireland miss a string of good opportunities. Treacy had one effort cleared from the goal-line by Henning Munk Jensen, Rogers had another magnificently saved by Poulsen, while Byrne, Treacy and Conroy missed other chances. With 5 minutes to go Madsen broke clear and was taken down in the box by Kelly. The referee pointed to the spot and Bengt Jensen slotted in the equaliser.

Match No. 123 — HUNGARY — Away

Wednesday 5th November, 1969 – Budapest (World Cup)

HUNGARY (1) 4 Halmosi 31, Bene 48, Puskas 72, Kocsis 81
REP. OF IRELAND (0) 0

Ref: Jakse (Yugoslavia) **Ground:** NEP Stadium **Att:** 23,620

Hungary: G. Tamas, J. Kelemen, M. Pancsics, L. Szucs, K. Ihasz, J. Göröcs, Z. Halmosi, L. Fazekas, F. Bene, A. Dunai II, S. Zambo. **Subs:** L. Puskas for Dunai, L. Kocsis for Göröcs.

Ireland: Alan Kelly (Preston 29), Shay Brennan (Manchester United 14), John Dempsey (Chelsea 10), Paddy Mulligan (Chelsea 7), Tony Dunne (Manchester United 21), Jimmy Conway (Fulham 10), Joe Kinnear (Tottenham Hotspur 7), Eamonn Dunphy (Millwall 15), Eamonn Rogers (Blackburn Rovers 11), Terry Conroy (Stoke City 3), Don Givens (Manchester United 6). **Subs:** Ray Treacy (Charlton Athletic 11) for Conroy (40 mins). **Captain:** Tony Dunne. **Manager:** Mick Meagan (4). **Formation:** 4-4-2.
Sendings off: John Dempsey (Ireland) 85 mins, Lajos Szucs (Hungary) 89 mins.

Another poor showing by Ireland who, despite a brief opening attack, failed to trouble Tamas in the home goal. After 19 minutes a shot by Halmosi was saved at the expense of a corner. This was one of a string of corners Hungary forced as they pressured the Irish goal and after 31 minutes they finally scored from one of them, when Halmosi took advantage of some confusion in the Irish area to score. The half ended with Dunai missing a good chance from 8 yards out.

Three minutes after the interval, Ihasz sent Zambo away. The winger beat Dunne and crossed in for Bene to score with a fierce shot. After 72 minutes a free kick by Kelemen was headed goalwards by Fazekas. The ball was looping away from Kelly but he got hands to it only for Puskas to race in and shoot home the rebound. Kocsis added a fourth 9 minutes later. In the last 10 minutes Dempsey was annoyed at the referee awarding a foul against him on Bene and threw the ball at the official who then sent him off. In the final minutes Szucs received his marching orders for a foul on Treacy.

International Record	**P**	**W**	**D**	**L**	**F**	**A**
1960-1969	45	12	8	25	52	92
Home	25	8	6	11	34	44
Away	19	4	2	13	18	47
Neutral	1	0	0	1	0	1

International Record	**P**	**W**	**D**	**L**	**F**	**A**
1926-1969	123	42	23	58	188	249
Home	64	25	14	25	113	115
Away	58	17	9	32	75	133
Neutral	1	0	0	1	0	1

World Cup Record	**P**	**W**	**D**	**L**	**F**	**A**
	30	6	6	18	40	72
Home	15	4	5	6	27	29
Away	14	2	1	11	13	42
Neutral	1	0	0	1	0	1

EuropeanChampionship Record	**P**	**W**	**D**	**L**	**F**	**A**
	14	5	3	6	16	24
Home	7	4	1	2	11	9
Away	7	1	2	4	5	15

Number of players capped by Ireland	241
Number of goalscorers for Ireland	65 (+ 3 own goals)
Number of nations played	25

Leading Goalscorers		**Most Capped Players**	
Noel Cantwell	14	Charlie Hurley	40
Jimmy Dunne	13	Noel Cantwell	36
Dermot Curtis	8	Joe Haverty	32
Arthur Fitzsimons	7	Johnny Giles	30
Paddy Moore		Con Martin	
Alf Ringstead		Johnny Carey	29
Andy McEvoy	6	Alan Kelly	
Con Martin		Peter Farrell	28
George Cummins	5	Arthur Fitzsimons	26
Fionan Fagan		Tommy Eglington	24
Davy Walsh		Mick McGrath	22

Penalties awarded to Ireland 26 (21 scored, 2 saved, 3 missed)
Penalties awarded against Ireland 11 (8 scored, 2 saved, 1 missed)

Hat-tricks for Ireland

John Joe Flood	3 goals	v Belgium	1929
Paddy Moore	4 goals	v Belgium	1934

Hat-tricks against Ireland

Kalle Palmer, Sweden	3 goals	1949
Jef Mermans, Belgium	3 goals	1950
Adolf Huber, Austria	3 goals	1952
Milos Milutinovic, Yugoslavia	3 goals	1955
Tommy Taylor, England	3 goals	1957
Jesus Maria Pereda, Spain	3 goals	1965
Josef Adamec, Czechoslovakia	3 goals	1969

Irish Captains

23	Noel Cantwell
21	Charlie Hurley
19	Johnny Carey
12	Peter Farrell
8	Charlie Turner
5	Jimmy Dunne, Paddy Gaskins, Con Martin
4	William Glen
2	Shay Brennan, Tommy Eglington, Mick O'Brien, Pat Saward
1	Frank Brady, John Burke, Harry Chatton, John Dempsey, Seamus Dunne, Tony Dunne, John Joe Flood, Mick Foley, Theo Foley, Johnny Giles, Jack McCarthy, Gerry Mackey, Mick Meagan.

Own goals for Ireland

Josef Posipal, West Germany	1951
Karl Koller, Austria	1963
Jose Angel Iribar, Spain	1965

Own goals by Irish players

Seamus Dunne for Sweden	1960
Andy McEvoy for Belgium	1965
Al Finucane for Czechoslovakia (H)	1967
John Dempsey for Czechoslovakia (A)	1967

Irish Players sent-off

John Dempsey v Hungary	1969

Leading goalscorers against Ireland

4	Reider Kvammen, Norway
	Telmo Zarraonandia Montoya "Zarra", Spain
	Jef Mermans, Belgium
	Andrej Kvasnak, Czechoslovakia
	Josef Adamec, Czechoslovakia

Match No. 124 POLAND Away

Wednesday 6th May, 1970 – Poznan

POLAND (2) 2 Kozerski 9, Szoltysik 25
REP. OF IRELAND (0) 1 Givens 55

Ref: **Ground:** Warta Stadium **Att:** 35,000

Poland: H. Kostka, H. Latocha, R. Strzalkowski, S. Oslizto, Z. Anczok, Z. Szoltysik,, L. Cmikiewicz, B. Bula, M. Kozerski, W. Lubanski, A. Jarosik. **Subs:** W. Winkler for Oslizto (half-time), A. Olek for Cmikiewicz (half-time).

Ireland: Alan Kelly (Preston 30), Joe Kinnear (Tottenham Hotspur 8), Tony Byrne (Southampton 2), Paddy Mulligan (Chelsea 8), Tommy Carroll (Ipswich Town 6), Eamonn Dunphy (Millwall 16), Eoin Hand (Portsmouth 2), Johnny Giles (Leeds United 31), Jimmy Conway (Fulham 11), Terry Conroy (Stoke City 4), Don Givens (Manchester United 7). **Subs:** Shay Brennan (Manchester United 15) for Carroll (half-time), Ray Treacy (Charlton Athletic 12) for Conway (half-time). **Captain:** Johnny Giles. **Manager:** Mick Meagan (5). **Formation:** 4-3-3.

Ireland's first match of its two-game tour ended in another defeat. Poland played a weakened side but were still too good for the Irish and were only denied a bigger win by Kelly's goalkeeping.

Lubanski forced the first opening but shot wide after 7 minutes. Two minutes later a good pass from Bula was picked up by Kozerski who shot past Kelly; the ball going in off a post. After 16 minutes Kozerski was denied a second goal when Kelly saved well. Ireland's one real chance of the first half came after 24 minutes when Mulligan headed a Conway cross against the bar. A minute later another good cross from Bula was finished to the back of the net by Szoltysik. Near the end of the half Kelly made a good save to stop Jarosik form adding a third.

Mick Meagan made two substitutions during the break, moved Mulligan into midfield, Hand to central defence and Dunphy into Hand's first-half berth. These alterations seemed to have the desired effect when, in 10 minutes, a good cross from Conroy allowed Givens in to pull a goal back. In the closing stages, however, Poland came closest to adding to their tally but were unable to beat Kelly who brought off a string of fine saves.

Match No. 125 WEST GERMANY Away

Saturday 9th May, 1970 – West Berlin

WEST GERMANY (1) 2 Seeler 18, Löhr 82
REP. OF IRELAND (0) 1 Mulligan 86

Ref: Boström (Sweden) **Ground:** Olympic Stadium **Att:** 60,000

West Germany H. Wolter, B. Patzke, W. Weber, W. Schulz, B. Vogts, J. Grabowski, F. Beckenbauer, W. Overath, U. Seeler, G. Müller, J. Löhr. **Subs:** P. Dietrich for Grabowski (half-time), S. Held for Overath (76 mins).

Ireland: Alan Kelly (Preston 31), Shay Brennan (Manchester United 16), Eoin Hand (Portsmouth 3), Tony Byrne (Southampton 3), John Dempsey (Chelsea 11), Tommy Carroll (Ipswich Town 7), Paddy Mulligan (Chelsea 9), Johnny Giles (Leeds United 32), Jimmy Conway (Fulham 12), Don Givens (Luton

Town 8), Terry Conroy (Stoke City 5). **Subs:** Eamonn Dunphy (Millwall 17), for Conway (58 mins), Ray Treacy (Charlton Athletic 13) for Givens (87 mins). **Captain:** Johnny Giles. **Manager:** Mick Meagan (6). **Formation:** 5-2-3.

Ireland suffered its second successive 1-2 defeat but the two games were totally different. The poor showing in Poland was more a result of lack of preparation and teamwork than anything. But with three days in which to get together, train and discuss tactics Ireland showed a great improvement.

Ireland kicked off and sent the ball out to Conroy. His cross was headed on by Giles for Mulligan to head against the post. Ireland continued to press and allowed the Germans few attacks. After 18 minutes a corner by Overath found Seeler and his header went into the net via a deflection from Hand. However, Ireland kept up their battling display and restricted the Germans to two Seeler efforts both of which were stopped by Kelly.

As in the first half, Ireland almost scored in the opening seconds of the second – Givens bursting through to shoot wide. After 68 minutes Seeler had another header wide but still Ireland battled away. With 8 minutes to go Löhr stuck out a leg and deflected a shot from Held past Kelly for Germany's second goal. Müller almost got another a minute before Muligan headed in a cross from Dunphy for Ireland's goal. Near the end of the game Beckenbauer was booked for a foul on Hand.

Match No. 126 — POLAND — Home

Wednesday 23rd September, 1970 – Dublin

REP. OF IRELAND (0) 0
POLAND (2) 2 Stachurski 27, Szoltysik 41

Ref: Lyden (England) **Ground:** Dalymount Park **Att:** 24,000

Ireland: Alan Kelly (Preston 32), Shay Brennan (Waterford 17), John Dempsey (Chelsea 12), Eoin Hand (Portsmouth 4), Tony Byrne (Southampton 4), Eamonn Dunphy (Millwall 18), Paddy Mulligan (Chelsea 10), Mick Lawlor (Shamrock Rovers 1), Steve Heighway (Liverpool 1), Ray Treacy (Charlton Athletic 14), Terry Conroy (Stoke City 6). **Subs:** Tony O'Connell (Bohemians 2), for Lawlor (half-time), Mick Kearns (Oxford United 1), for Kelly (76 mins), Alfie Hale (Waterford 12) for Heighway (85 mins). **Captain:** Shay Brennan. **Manager:** Mick Meagan (7). **Formation:** 4-3-3.

Poland: W. Grotynski, W. Stachurski, J. Wyrobek, J. Gorgon, A. Musial, Z. Szoltysik, B. Blaut, L. Cmikiewicz, J. Marx, W. Lubanski, R. Gadocha.

Polands first victory in Dublin was never in doubt when after taking a 2-nil lead before half-time, they 'sat' on it for the second half, denying the Irish a chance to recover as they had against Polish teams in earlier visits.

After 7 minutes Kelly stopped but could not hold a shot from Cmikiewicz and Dempsey cleared. Four miutes later a curling shot from Heighway was just touched around the post for a corner by Grotynski. The Polish goalkeeper stopped another Heighway effort soon after with Kelly doing the same with a shot from Szoltysik. After 27 minutes Stachurski caught Kelly out with a shot out of the blue from 35 yards for the opening goal. Musial tried a similar effort 3 minutes after but Kelly tipped it over the bar. From the corner Byrne was forced to clear a Lubanski effort off the line. Lawlor had a shot at the other end deflected over the bar by Conroy before Poland scored again. A shot by Blaut was blocked to Szoltysik who found a gap and burst through to flick the ball past Kelly. Coming up to the break both Lawlor and Treacy hit the frame of the goal with good chances.

The second half was poor as Poland defended their lead. The best Irish chances fell to Dempsey (two headers wide) and Heighway (a shot over the bar), but in general neither goalkeeper was troubled unduly.

Match No. 127 SWEDEN Home

Wednesday 14th October, 1970 – Dublin (European Championship)

REP. OF IRELAND (1) 1 Carroll 43 (pen)
SWEDEN (0) 1 Brzokoupil 61

Ref: Halles (France) **Ground:** Dalymount Park **Att:** 30,000

Ireland: Alan Kelly (Preston 33), Tommy Carroll (Ipswich Town 8), John Dempsey (Chelsea 13), Tony Byrne (Southampton 5), Tony Dunne (Manchester United 22), Eamonn Dunphy (Millwall 19), Paddy Mulligan (Chelsea 11), Mick Lawlor (Shamrock Rovers 2), Steve Heighway (Liverpool 2), Don Givens (Luton Town 9), Terry Conroy (Stoke City 7). **Subs:** Joe Kinnear (Tottenham Hotspur 9), for Carroll (70 mins), Ray Treacy (Charlton Athletic 15), for Givens (83 mins). **Captain:** Tony Dunne. **Manager:** Mick Meagan (8). **Formation:** 4-3-3.

Sweden: S. G. Larsson, H. Selander, K. Kristensson, B. Nordqvist, R. Grip, T. Svensson, J. Olsson, L. Eriksson, I. Danielsson, O. Grahn, B. Larsson. **Subs:** D. Brzokoupil for Danielsson.

Ireland turned in an excellent first half performance but faded badly in the second period and were lucky not to lose.

The Irish began well and took the game to the Swedes. After 6 minutes a great cross by Dunphy was missed by three Irish players in the box. Conroy followed this with a shot that was just wide. Heighway then had two chances. His first shot, from 25 yards, went wide while his second forced Larsson, the goalkeeper, into a good save. Ireland had claims for a penalty turned down when Mulligan was tripped in the box but 2 minutes before the break they were awarded one when Dempsey was brought down in the area. Carroll's spot-kick gave Sven Gunnar Larsson no chance.

Sweden dominated the play after the interval and should have had more than the one goal. Brzokoupil took advantage of some poor defending to fire home the equaliser. In a sometimes rough half Sweden twice were denied by the woodwork. Both Nordquist (Sweden) and Givens (Ireland) were booked before Givens was injured and had to be replaced near the end.

Match No. 128 SWEDEN Away

Wednesday 28th October, 1970 – Stockholm (European Championship)

SWEDEN (0) 1 Turesson 75
REP. OF IRELAND (0) 0

Ref: Kazakov (USSR) **Ground:** Fotbollstadion **Att:** 11,922

Sweden: R. Hellström, H. Selander, K. Kristensson, B. Nordqvist, R. Grip, T. Svensson, B. Larsson, J. Olsson, L. Eriksson, O. Grahn, D. Brzokoupil. **Subs:** T. Turesson for Brzokoupil (63 mins), C. Cronqvist for Grip (67 mins).

Ireland: Alan Kelly (Preston 34), Shay Brennan (Waterford 18), John Dempsey (Chelsea 14), Tony Byrne (Southampton 6), Paddy Dunning (Shelbourne 1), Eamonn Dunphy (Millwall 20), Al Finucane (Limerick 8), Mick Lawlor (Shamrock Rovers 3), Steve Heighway (Liverpool 3), Ray Treacy (Charlton Athletic 16), Terry Conroy (Stoke City 8). **Captain:** Shay Brennan. **Manager:** Mick Meagan (9). **Formation:** 4-4-2.

Ireland came to defend and rarely came out of their own half. Their tactics of slowing the game down and passing back not only frustrated the crowd but the home side also. There were few real chances and Kelly was in action only once when saving a shot from Grahn.

A half-time lashing by outgoing Swedish manager, Orvar Bergmark, seemed to rouse his charges as there was an improvement in the overall quality of play. But still Ireland defended well although Kelly was now seeing a lot more action. Sweden got the only goal of the match when a pass from Eriksson split the Irish defence and Turesson had an easy task to shoot past Kelly.

Match No. 129 ITALY Away

Tuesday 8th December, 1970 – Florence (European Championship)

ITALY (2) 3 De Sisti 21 (pen), Boninsegna 42, Prati 84
REP. OF IRELAND (0) 0

Ref: Schaut (Belgium) **Ground:** Stadio Comunale **Att:** 44,754

Italy: E. Albertosi, T. Burgnich, M. Bertini, R. Rosato, G. Facchetti, P. Cera, A. Mazzola, G. De Sisti, A. Domenghini, R. Boninsegna, P. Prati.

Ireland: Alan Kelly (Preston 35), Shay Brennan (Waterford 19), John Dempsey (Chelsea 15), Tony Byrne (Southampton 7), Paddy Dunning (Shelbourne 2), Eamonn Dunphy (Millwall 21), Al Finucane (Limerick 9), Eamonn Rogers (Blackburn Rovers 12), Terry Conroy (Stoke City 9), Don Givens (Luton Town 10), Ray Treacy (Charlton Athletic 17). **Subs:** Mick Lawlor (Shamrock Rovers 4), for Dunphy (36 mins). **Captain:** Shay Brennan. **Manager:** Mick Meagan (10). **Formation:** 4-3-3.

Ireland used the same tactics against Italy they had used to frustrate Sweden previously. These tactics almost worked in the last game but against the Italians their function was to keep the scoreline down. However, Ireland managed to force a few openings and with a bit more adventure could have shocked the World Cup runners-up.

Prati and Domenghini had early shots off target before Facchetti forced Kelly into the first of a string of saves; his shot being tipped over by the goalkeeper. After 13 minutes Conroy set up Dunning to shoot from long range. Albertosi fumbled the shot but recovered in time to stop it crossing the line. Two minutes later Kelly fumbled a shot from De Sisti but he too recovered to stop it. After 21 minutes the referee awarded a penalty to Italy when Brennan handled in the box and De Sisti scored from the spot. Rogers tested Albertosi again before Italy scored again. Boninsegna capitalised on a mistake by Dempsey, rounded Kelly and scored easily. A minute before the break Mazzola had another goal disallowed for handball.

Treacy shot over from a few yards early in the second half as Ireland showed more attacking spirit. However, Kelly was kept busy and had to bring off good saves twice to stop Boninsegna. Six minutes from time Prati converted a pass from De Sisti from close in to give Italy a deserved victory.

Match No. 130 ITALY Home

Monday 10th May, 1971 – Dublin (European Championship)

REP. OF IRELAND (1) 1 Conway 23
ITALY (1) 2 Boninsegna 15, Prati 59

Ref: Schulenburg (East Germany) **Ground:** Lansdowne Road **Att:** 25,000

Ireland: Alan Kelly (Preston 36), Joe Kinnear (Tottenham Hotspur 10), Paddy Mulligan (Chelsea 12), Tony Byrne (Southampton 8), Tony Dunne (Manchester United 23), Eamonn Dunphy (Millwall 22), Johnny Giles (Leeds United 33), Eamonn Rogers (Blackburn Rovers 13), Steve Heighway (Liverpool 4), Don Givens (Luton Town 11), Jimmy Conway (Fulham 13). **Subs:** Al Finucane (Limerick 10) for Rogers (half-time). **Captain:** Johnny Giles. **Manager:** Mick Meagan (11). **Formation:** 4-3-3.

Italy D. Zoff, T. Burgnich, P. Cera, R. Rosato, G. Facchetti, M. Bertini, M. Corso, A. Mazzola, G. De Sisti, R. Boninsegna, P. Prati.

The Irish opened strongly and kept the visitors in their own half for the first 10 minutes. However, it was the Italians who had the first real scoring opportunity when Mazzola's powerful shot was well saved by Kelly. The visitors then took the lead. As Byrne protested a free kick awarded against him it was quickly taken and found Mazzola. He crossed in and Boninsegna sent a nice header into the back of the net. Irelands reply came 8 minutes later when Conway ran in to meet Dunphy's free kick with a powerful header which Zoff could only parry into the net. Soon after Heighway went off to get attention after being elbowed in the face but a 10-man Ireland still pressured the Italian goal. Giles put Conway in for another chance but this time his goalbound shot was deflected by an Italian defender for a corner. From the corner Rogers found Givens whose header was just over. Ireland finished on the up with Zoff making a last-gasp save to stop Conway.

During the break Finucane replaced the injured Rogers. The substitute went into defence with Mulligan moving up to midfield. Again Ireland started well but after 14 minutes they fell behind as a result of another set-piece. This time Boninsegna headed down Mazzola's free kick for Prati to shoot home. Ireland tried hard for an equaliser but the tough Italians kept them out. Late in the game Giles had a great shot saved by Zoff and at the other end Boninsegna shot wide when well placed. In a game littered with fouls only one player was booked – Bertini of Italy.

Match No. 131 AUSTRIA Home

Sunday 30th May, 1971 – Dublin (European Championship)

REP. OF IRELAND (0) 1 Rogers 49 (pen)
AUSTRIA (3) 4 Schmidradner 4 (pen), Kodat 11, J. Dunne (o.g.) 31, Starek 71

Ref: Hoberg (Norway) **Ground:** Dalymount Park **Att:** 16,000

Ireland: Alan Kelly (Preston 37), Tony Byrne (Southampton 9), Tony Dunne (Manchester United 24), Eoin Hand (Portsmouth 5), Jimmy Dunne (Fulham 1), Eamonn Dunphy (Millwall 23), Eamonn Rogers (Blackburn Rovers 14), Jimmy Conway (Fulham 14), Don Givens (Luton Town 12), Ray Treacy (Charlton Athletic 18), Steve Heighway (Liverpool 5). **Subs:** Noel Campbell (St Patrick's Athletic 1) for Dunphy (half-time), Jimmy Holmes (Coventry City 1) for Givens (74 mins). **Captain:** Tony Dunne. **Manager:** Mick Meagan (12). **Formation:** 4-2-4.

Austria: H. Rettensteiner, J. Schmidradner, G. Sturmberger, J. Eigenstiller, W. Kriess, G. Starek, N. Hof, J. Ettmaier, J. Hickersberger, W. Kreuz, K. Kodat. **Subs:** R. Schlagbauer for Kriess (78 mins).

A poor performance by Ireland who went a goal down after 4 minutes. A cross by Kreuz was deflected via Dunphy and Hand to Kodat. The winger knocked the ball over Byrne's head but the Irishman knocked it away with his hands and Schmidradner converted the resultant penalty. Ireland's best chance came a minute later when Treacy intercepted a bad back-pass only for Rettensteiner to bring off a fine save. After 11 minutes Kreuz headed down a corner from Hickersberger for Kodat to sweep the ball home. Givens did manage to find the Austrian net but the goal was ruled out for offside. A minute later a hard low cross by Ettmaier was deflected into his own goal by Jimmy Dunne.

Four minutes after the interval Byrne was taken down in the area by Hof and Rogers reduced the arrears with a well taken penalty. However Austria regained their three goal margin when a fine run by Hickersberger drew Kelly out. The Austrian flicked the ball past him for Ettmaier to shoot. As the ball headed goalwards Starek ducked low and flicked it on with his head into the net. Near the end Holmes had a good shot saved by the goalkeeper.

Match No. 132 AUSTRIA Away

Sunday 10th October, 1971 – Linz (European Championship)

AUSTRIA (3) 6 Jara 11,85, Pirkner 41, Parits 45, 52, 89
REP. OF IRELAND (0) 0

Ref: Göppel (Switzerland) **Ground:** Linzer Stadium **Att:** 20,000

Austria: A. Antrich, J. Schmidradner, G. Sturmberger, J. Eigenstiller, P. Pumm, R. Horvath, N. Hof, J. Ettmaier, H. Pirkner, T. Parits, K. Jara.

1971 Austria 6-0 Ireland
Adolf Antrich saves from Ireland's Mick Leech as Mick Martin looks on.
(Photo: Votavafoto)

1971 Austria 6-0 Ireland
Ireland's Tommy McConville challenges Austria's Thomas Parits watched by John Herrick.
(Photo: Votavafoto)

1971 Austria 6-0 Ireland
Austria's Hans Pirkner follows up to put away his saved penalty. Neither Paddy Roche nor Mick Gannon can do much to prevent it. (Photo: Votavafoto)

Ireland: Paddy Roche (Shelbourne 1), Mick Gannon (Shelbourne 1), Al Finucane (Limerick 11), Tommy McConville (Dundalk 1), John Herrick (Cork Hibernians 1) Mick Kearin (Shamrock Rovers 1), Paddy Mulligan (Chelsea 13), Mick Martin (Bohemians 1), Frank O'Neill (Shamrock Rovers 20), Mick Leech (Shamrock Rovers 4), Turlough O'Connor (Dundalk 2). **Subs:** Damien Richardson (Shamrock Rovers 1) for Kearin (53 mins), Alfie Hale (Waterford 13) for Martin (69 mins). **Captain:** Al Finucane. **Manager:** Liam Tuohy (1). **Formation:** 4-3-3.

Irelands new manager got off to a bad start when his weakened team suffered another 6-0 defeat at the hands of Austria. Ireland had some promising moves but lacked a finishing touch.

After 11 minutes a great ball from Ettmaier put Schmidradner away. The latter worked his way to the touchline before sending over a high cross which was headed in by Jara. Roche was kept busy after this and brought off some good saves before Herrick was adjudged to have handled a shot by Parits in the area, giving Austria a penalty. Pirkner's spot-kick was saved by Roche but the goalkeeper could do nothing when the taker followed up to shoot home the rebound. O'Neill managed to force an opening and his shot was turned out for a corner. In the dying seconds of the half Parits scored Austrias third with a great shot from outside the area.

Seven minutes into the second half Parits got his second goal when he outpaced McConville and Finucane prior to shooting past Roche. Pumm was denied a goal by a good save from Roche while Hof shot against the post. In the final 5 minutes Jara shot home a pass from Horvath and Ettmaier sent Pirkner away to set up Parits to complete his hat-trick. There was one booking – Richardson for a foul on Sturmberger.

1971 Austria - Ireland

Thomas Parits shoots past Paddy Roche to complete his hat-trick and score Austria's sixth goal. (Photo: Votavafoto)

Match No. 133 IRAN Neutral

Sunday 11th June, 1972 – Recife (Brazilian Independence Cup))

IRAN (1) 1 Hessenali 10
REP. OF IRELAND (0) 2 Leech 63, Givens 67

Ref: Angonese (Italy) **Ground:** Santa Cruz Stadium **Att:** 10,500

Iran: Nasser, Ibraim, Majia, Jafar, Mustafa, Parviz, Mehdi, Javad, Hessenali, Hassein, Safar.

Ireland: Alan Kelly (Preston 38), Joe Kinnear (Tottenham Hotspur 11), John Dempsey (Chelsea 16), Paddy Mulligan (Chelsea 14), Tommy Carroll (Birmingham City 9), Noel Campbell (Fortuna Cologne 2), Mick Martin (Bohemians 2), Eamonn Rogers (Charlton Athletic 15), Ray Treacy (Swindon Town 19), Mick Leech (Shamrock Rovers 5), Don Givens (Luton Town 13). **Subs:** Turlough O'Connor (Dundalk 3) for Leech (78 mins). **Captain:** Paddy Mulligan. **Manager:** Liam Tuohy (2). **Formation:** 4-3-3.

Ireland's first victory in 20 games was achieved on Brazilian soil against Asian opponents in a tournament organised by the Brazilian FA to celebrate their 150th year of Independence.

Iran were quickly on the offensive and got a goal after 10 minutes when Hessenali scored with a curling shot from just inside the box. Iran continued to press and Kelly was in action through the rest of the half.

In the second half Iran began to tire. However, after an hour's play Parviz broke through the Irish defence and scored only for the referee to disallow the goal as Parviz had fouled an Irish player on his way through. The Iranians objected strongly to this decision and as they argued with the referee the Irish broke downfield and equalised. Leech exchanged passes with Campbell to put himself away. Leech rounded a defender and knocked the ball, past the advancing goalkeeper, into the net. Four minutes later Givens pounced on a mistake by Ibraim to shoot home the winner. The Irish finished on the up and deserved their victory.

Match No. 134 ECUADOR Neutral

Sunday 18th June, 1972 – Natal (Brazilian Independence Cup)

ECUADOR (1) 2 Coronel 36, Lasso 78
REP. OF IRELAND (1) 3 Rogers 12, Martin 61, O'Connor 88

Ref: Kitabjan (France) **Ground:** New Lake Stadium **Att:**

Ecuador: Maldonado, Pelaez, Camacho, Guerrero, Ortiz, Bolanos, Lasso, Coronel, Estupinam, Guime, Herrera. **Subs:** Moralez for Herrera.

Ireland: Alan Kelly (Preston 39), Joe Kinnear (Tottenham Hotspur 12), John Dempsey (Chelsea 17), Paddy Mulligan (Chelsea 15), Tommy Carroll (Birmingham City 10), Noel Campbell (Fortuna Cologne 3), Mick Martin (Bohemians 3), Eamonn Rogers (Charlton Athletic 16), Ray Treacy (Swindon Town 20), Mick Leech (Shamrock Rovers 6), Don Givens (Luton Town 14). **Subs:** Turlough O'Connor (Dundalk 4) for Treacy (half-time), Miah Dennehy (Cork Hibernians 1) for Leech. **Captain:** Paddy Mulligan. **Manager:** Liam Tuohy (3). **Formation:** 4-3-3.
Sending off: Don Givens (Ireland) 64 mins.

Both sides went all out for victory and after 12 minutes Givens was fouled just outside the penalty area. Rogers took the resultant free kick and sent it directly into the goal for the opening score. After 36 minutes Coronel again exposed the weak Irish defence when he dribbled past three defenders before shooting home the equaliser.

The Irish had the better of the second period and went ahead again when Givens put Martin through and he shot past Maldonado. Twelve minutes from the end Ecuador equalised with a scrambled goal from Lasso. In the last 2 minutes a long kick out from Kelly found O'Connor in the clear. He ran on and as the goalkeeper advanced, he shot past him for the winner. Givens had been sent off for rough play 24 minutes earlier.

Match No. 135 CHILE Neutral

Wednesday 21st June, 1972 – Recife (Brazilian Independence Cup)

CHILE (0) 2 Caszely 60, Fouilloux 68
REP. OF IRELAND (0) 1 Rogers 79

Ref: Arpi (Brazil) **Ground:** Isle of Retiro Stadium **Att:**

Chile: Neff, Machuca, Azocar, Angulo, Arias, Lara, Peralta, Carvallo, Crisosto, Caszely, Veliz. **Subs:** Fouilloux for Crisosto, Espinoza for Veliz.

Ireland: Alan Kelly (Preston 40), Joe Kinnear (Tottenham Hotspur 13), John Dempsey (Chelsea 18), Paddy Mulligan (Chelsea 16), Tommy Carroll (Birmingham City 11), Noel Campbell (Fortuna Cologne 4), Mick Martin (Bohemians 4), Eamonn Rogers (Charlton Athletic 17), Ray Treacy (Swindon Town 21), Miah Dennehy (Cork Hibernians 2), Turlough O'Connor (Dundalk 5). **Subs:** John Herrick (Cork Hibernians 2) for Carroll (82 mins). **Captain:** Paddy Mulligan. **Manager:** Liam Tuohy (4). **Formation:** 4-3-3.
Sending off: Turlough O'Connor (Ireland) 75 mins.

The first half was evenly balanced with both sides on the attack. Ireland's best chances fell to O'Connor, who shot just wide, Treacy, who headed over and Martin, who was stopped at the last moment by a great save from Neff.

Chile had the better of a rough second half and went ahead when Fouilloux's through ball was slammed into the net by Caszely. Caszely returned the compliment for Fouilloux to put Chile 2 nil ahead. After 75 minutes O'Connor was sent off for a foul on Azocar. Four minutes later Rogers headed in a cross from Martin to pull a goal back. Ireland tried hard for an equaliser but the best effort of the closing period fell to Lara whose shot was brilliantly saved by Kelly.

Match No. 136 PORTUGAL Neutral

Sunday 25th June, 1972 – Recife (Brazilian Independence Cup)

PORTUGAL (2) 2 Peres 35, Nene 37
REP. OF IRELAND (1) 1 Leech 38

Ref: Coerezza (Argentina) **Ground:** Isle of Retiro Stadium **Att:** 13,000

Portugal: Jose Henrique, Artur, Humberto, Messias, Adolfo, Peres, Matine, Toni, Eusebio, Nene, Artur Joege. **Subs:** Mourinho for Jose Henrique, Jamie Graca for Nene.

Ireland: Alan Kelly (Preston 41), Joe Kinnear (Tottenham Hotspur 14), John Dempsey (Chelsea 19), Paddy Mulligan (Chelsea 17), Tommy Carroll (Birmingham City 12), Noel Campbell (Fortuna Cologne 5), Mick Martin (Bohemians 5), Eamonn Rogers (Charlton Athletic 18), Ray Treacy (Swindon Town 22), Mick Leech (Shamrock Rovers 7), Don Givens (Luton Town 15). **Subs:** Turlough O'Connor (Dundalk 6) for Treacy. **Captain:** Paddy Mulligan. **Manager:** Liam Tuohy (5). **Formation:** 4-3-3.

Ireland needed to beat Portugal by five clear goals to qualify for the final stages but it was the Portuguese who dominated the game against a tired Irish side.

All the goals came in a four minute spell in the first half. Peres received the ball just outside the Irish box and sent a powerful shot beyond Kelly into the roof of the net. Two minutes later a mistake by Mulligan let Nene in and he shot past the advancing Kelly. A minute after that a pass from Treacy sent Leech away. Leech beat one man, ran on and shot past Jose Henrique.

Portugal dominated the second half and Ireland rarely threatened with the result that Portugal were rather easier winners than the scoreline suggests.

Match No. 137 USSR Home

Wednesday 18th October, 1972 – Dublin (World Cup)

REP. OF IRELAND (0) 1 Conroy 82
USSR (0) 2 Puzach 55, Kolotov 65

Ref: Hoberg (Norway) **Ground:** Lansdowne Road **Att:** 25,000

Ireland: Alan Kelly (Preston 42), Joe Kinnear (Tottenham Hotspur 15), Tommy McConville (Waterford 2), Eoin Hand (Portsmouth 6), Tommy Carroll (Birmingham City 13), Noel Campbell (Fortuna Cologne 6), Mick Martin (Bohemians 6), Eamonn Rogers (Charlton Athletic 19), Steve Heighway (Liverpool 6), Ray Treacy (Swindon Town 23), Terry Conroy (Stoke City 10). **Subs:** Mick Leech (Shamrock Rovers 8) for Rogers (62 mins). **Captain:** Alan Kelly. **Manager:** Liam Tuohy (6). **Formation:** 4-3-3.

USSR: V. Pilgui, R. Dzodzvashvili, M. Khurtsilava, V. Kaplichny, E. Lovchev, V. Kolotov, V. Muntyan, V. Semenov, V. Fedotov, A. Puzach, G. Euryuzhikhin. **Subs:** E. Rudakov for Pilgui.

Kelly was in action early saving twice from Muntyan. At the other end Conroy was stopped by Pilgui and Treacy was brought down in the box without penalty. Kelly again made a vital stop to foil Fedotov and later Euryuzhikhin. Coming up to the break Rogers curled a free kick around the wall only for Pilgui to make a good save at the expense of a corner.

Soon after the re-start Heighway sent a dangerous cross right across the face of the goal forcing Dzodzvashvili to put it out for a corner. The Soviets had the better of this half but their first goal came out of the blue, when Fedotov found Puzach in the clear and the latter shot home. Minutes later Puzach sent Kolotov away to net but the referee disallowed the goal as Kolotov had pushed an Irish player on his way. Tuohy brought on Leech for Rogers altering the formation to 4-2-4. The now weakened midfield was exposed soon after when Kolotov finished off a good move by Puzach and Muntyan although the midfielder looked offside when he headed home Muntyan's pass. Euryuzhikhin and Puzach had further chances and Kinnear came close with a header at the other end before Conroy got a pass from Leech and sent a bullet-like drive to the back of the net for Ireland's goal.

Match No. 138 — FRANCE — Home

Wednesday 15th November, 1972 – Dublin (World Cup)

REP. OF IRELAND (1) 2 Conroy 28, Treacy 75
FRANCE (0) 1 Larque 66

Ref: Rasmussen (Denmark) **Ground:** Dalymount Park **Att:** 30,000

Ireland: Alan Kelly (Preston 43), Joe Kinnear (Tottenham Hotspur 16), Paddy Mulligan (Crystal Palace 18), Tommy McConville (Waterford 3), Jimmy Holmes (Coventry City 2), Eoin Hand (Portsmouth 7), Johnny Giles (Leeds United 34), Tony Byrne (Southampton 10), Terry Conroy (Stoke City 11), Ray Treacy (Swindon Town 24), Don Givens (Queen's Park Rangers 16), . **Subs:** Noel Campbell (Fortuna Cologne 7) for Byrne (64 mins), Turlough O'Connor (Bohemians 7), for Conroy (89 mins). **Captain:** Johnny Giles. **Manager:** Liam Tuohy (7). **Formation:** 4-3-3.

France: G. Carnus, J. Broissart, C. Quittet, M. Tresor, J-P. Rostagni, J-N. Huck, J-P. Adams, C. Loubet, H. Revelli, J-M. Larque, G. Bereta. **Subs:** Molitor for Loubet (64 mins).

This match was to prove a watershed for Irish soccer. The game in this country was on the decline due, in part, to the fact that the international team had not won a home game for six years. There were other reasons of course but if there was to be any hope for this 'foreign' game in Ireland then it must be with the recovery of the national side. Therefore, before the tie kicked-off, Liam Tuohy told his players that the result was not only vital for Ireland's World Cup chances but for the game in Ireland as a whole. Although the Irish team was to have its ups and downs in the coming years, this was the beginning of a recovery.

Ireland had a shaky start with Kinnear sending a back pass past Kelly but also wide of the target. Then Revelli headed a Rostagni cross just wide and a smashing shot from Larque flew just over. The French had made the early running and their best chance of this opening period fell to Revelli who shot against the post. Ireland regained its composure to launch their own attacks and their first shot on target produced their first goal. A free by Giles was knocked into the air by Tresor. Giles was quickly on to it and headed it into the area. A French defender headed it down but Conroy controlled it before smashing a great shot off the underside of the crossbar and into the goal. Ireland continued to press with Byrne and Giles setting up Givens for a shot which Carnus saved well. The French now began to look shaky and Tresor over-hit a back pass which Carnus had to save at the last moment. Coming up to half-time another effort from Conroy smacked against the crossbar while Carnus was forced to turn a Tresor deflected header out for a corner.

The Irish pressure continued in the second half but after 66 minutes French substitute Molitor, who had only been on the field for 2 minutes, sent a lovely cross into the goalmouth for Larque to volley home. However, Ireland still forced the pace and a free by Giles was headed by Conroy towards goal only for Carnus to parry it to Mulligan who shot over. After 75 minutes a long ball out of defence was chased by Hand and Rostagni. The Irishman got to the ball just before the defender, turned inside him and crossed high into the area. The ball came to Treacy awkwardly as he ran in but he lept into the air and flicked the ball over the goalkeeper with the back of his head for the winning goal. Giles and Conroy had other late chances but the Irish then contained the French until the referee blew for full time after about 4 minutes injury time.

Match No. 139 USSR Away

Sunday 13th May, 1973 – Moscow (World Cup)

USSR (0) 1 Onischenko 58
REP. OF IRELAND (0) 0

Ref: Dalberg (Sweden) **Ground:** Lenin Stadium **Att:** 70,000

USSR: V. Pilgui, R. Dzodzvashvili, V. Kaplichny, M. Khurtsilava, E. Lovchev, V. Kolotov, V. Muntyan, V. Kuznetzov, A. Andreasan, V. Onischenko, O. Blokhin. **Subs:** S. Olchanski for Muntyan, V. Fedotov for Andreasan.

Ireland: Alan Kelly (Preston 44), Tommy Carroll (Birmingham City 14), Paddy Mulligan (Crystal Palace 19), Tommy McConville (Waterford 4), Jimmy Holmes (Coventry City 3), Eoin Hand (Portsmouth 8), Johnny Giles (Leeds United 35), Mick Martin (Manchester United 7), Terry Conroy (Stoke City 12), Ray Treacy (Swindon Town 25), Don Givens (Queen's Park Rangers 17), . **Subs:** Tony Byrne (Southampton 11) for Giles (half-time), Miah Dennehy (Nottingham Forest 3) for Conroy (Half-time). **Captain:** Johnny Giles. **Manager:** Liam Tuohy (8). **Formation:** 4-3-3.

The Soviets began on the attack and forced Ireland to defend for most of the half. Despite the pressure the Irish defence restricted the Soviets to a few openings. Kolotov brought a brilliant save from Kelly after 14 minutes and near the break the Irish goalkeeper again spectacularly saved, this time from a shot by Muntyan. The Irish had one effort – a Givens shot which was saved by Pilgui.

During the break Giles and Conroy were forced to withdraw with hamstring trouble; their places being taken by Byrne and Dennehy. Ireland opened well but despite some promising attacks they failed to trouble Pilgui. Kelly on the other hand was kept busy and, within a minute of Andreasan shooting over from a good position, he was beaten for the only goal. A cross from Muntyan was missed by Carroll and Onischenko ran on to it to shoot past the Irish goalkeeper. Further Soviet chances fell to Blokhin and Onischenko but Kelly made fine stops to deny them a second goal.

Match No. 140 POLAND Away

Wednesday 16th May, 1973 – Wroclaw

POLAND (1) 2 Lubanski 44, 81
REP. OF IRELAND (0) 0

Ref: Kunz (East Germany) **Ground:** Olympic Stadium

Poland: M. Szeya, A. Szymanowski, H. Wieczorek, M. Bulzacki, A. Musial, L. Cmikiewicz, Kraska, Kasztelan, B. Masztaler, W. Lubanski, R. Gadocha. **Subs:** J. Banas for Masztaler (29 mins), H. Kasperczak for Kasztelan (67 mins), K. Kmiecik for Banas (74 mins).

Ireland: Alan Kelly (Preston 45), Tommy Carroll (Birmingham City 15), Paddy Mulligan (Crystal Palace 20), Tommy McConville (Waterford 5), Jimmy Holmes (Coventry City 4), Eoin Hand (Portsmouth 9), Mick Martin (Manchester United 8), Mick Lawlor (Shamrock Rovers 5), Miah Dennehy (Nottingham Forest 4), Ray Treacy (Swindon Town 26), Don Givens (Queen's Park Rangers 18). **Subs:** Gerry Daly (Manchester United 1) for Lawlor (half-time), Turlough O'Connor (Bohemians 8) for Dennehy (67 mins). **Captain:** Paddy Mulligan. **Manager:** Liam Tuohy (9). **Formation:** 4-3-3.

Ireland began well but Poland had the first chance of the match when Kraska shot wide. Martin forced Szeya into his only save soon after when his powerful shot was well held. Ireland faded badly after that and Lubanski could have had a hat-trick after half an hour. First he shot a pass from Kraska wide, then he was denied by a briliant save from Kelly and a last-minute tackle from Hand stopped him again. A minute from the break another shot from Lubanski was turned out for a corner by Kelly and from Gadocha's flag-kick the Polish forward finally netted when he knocked the ball in at the near post.

The second half was more of the same but saw less scoring opportunities. Banas had a shot just over and a Gadocha free kick hit the frame of the goal. With nine minutes left another free kick this time from Lubanski found the net when the forward sent a dipping 35 yard shot over Kelly and into the goal.

Match No. 141 — FRANCE — Away

Saturday 19th May, 1973 – Paris (World Cup)

FRANCE (0) 1 Chiesa 79
REP. OF IRELAND (0) 1 Martin 84

Ref: Rainea (Rumania) **Ground:** Parc des Princes **Att:** 40,463

France: G. Carnus, R. Domenech, C. Quittet, M. Tresor, J-P. Rostagni, H. Michel, J-P. Adams, L. Floch, H. Revelli, J-M. Larque, G. Bereta. **Subs:** Chiesa for Larque.

Ireland: Alan Kelly (Preston 46), Tommy Carroll (Birmingham City 16), Paddy Mulligan (Crystal Palace 21), Tommy McConville (Waterford 6), Jimmy Holmes (Coventry City 5), Mick Martin (Manchester United 9), Eoin Hand (Portsmouth 10), Tony Byrne (Southampton 12), Miah Dennehy (Nottingham Forest 5), Ray Treacy (Swindon Town 27), Don Givens (Queen's Park Rangers 19). **Subs:** John Herrick (Shamrock Rovers 3) for Carroll (25 mins). **Captain:** Paddy Mulligan. **Manager:** Liam Tuohy (10). **Formation:** 4-3-3.

Before this tour Liam Tuohy had indicated his intention to resign as manager of Ireland due to pressure of business and so this was to be his last game in charge. As it turned out it was the best away performance under his control and gained Ireland its first World Cup away point for twelve years.

In the first quarter of an hour Irish pressure saw Treacy shooting over passes from Hand and Martin. The Irish spoilt many French moves and their only shot of note came on 21 minutes when Bereta fired well over. After 25 minutes Carroll went off with a leg injury and was replaced by Herrick. The French also used a substitute but no sooner had Chiesa come on the field than he was booked for not waiting for the officials permission! In the latter stages of the half Revelli forced Kelly into a good save, Bereta shot a good chance over under pressure from Herrick and Revelli hit the post.

Irelands impressive display continued in the second period but with 11 minutes to go Chiesa found space in the goalmouth to flick in a corner from Floch. Five minutes later Ireland were level. Dennehy outwitted a couple of defenders and thumped a shot off the crossbar. As the ball rebounded out there was Martin to score with a downward header. Both Givens and Treacy were booked during the game as well as the unfortunate Frenchman.

Match No. 142 | **NORWAY** | **Away**

Wednesday 6th June, 1973 – Oslo

NORWAY (0) 1 Paulsen 69
REP. OF IRELAND (1) 1 Dennehy 17

Ref: Hirviniemi (Finland) **Ground:** Ullevaal Stadium **Att:** 11,084

Norway: G. Karlsen, E. Meirik, J. Birkelund, P. Pettersen, S. Slinning, J. Christiansen, J. Vold, T. E. Johansen, H. Sunde, H. E. Paulsen, T. Lund.

Ireland: Alan Kelly (Preston 47), Tommy Carroll (Birmingham City 17), Mick Martin (Manchester United 10), Paddy Mulligan (Crystal Palace 22), Jimmy Holmes (Coventry City 6), Gerry Daly (Manchester United 2), Miah Dennehy (Nottingham Forest 6), Tony Byrne (Southampton 13), Terry Conroy (Stoke City 13), Ray Treacy (Swindon Town 28), Don Givens (Queen's Park Rangers 20). **Subs:** Damien Richardson (Gillingham 2) for Byrne (half-time), Eamonn Fagan (Shamrock Rovers 1) for Treacy (79 mins). **Captain:** Paddy Mulligan. **Manager:** Sean Thomas (1). **Formation:** 4-3-3.

The Irish put up a poor showing against an all-amateur Norwegian side.

After 17 minutes Treacy headed Carrolls cross into the path of Dennehy and he shot home from 10 yards. Kelly was twice in action in the first half saving a shot from Vold and a header from Lund.

A good second-half opening saw Givens and Holmes shoot over and Daly shooting wide but Norway came back with Kelly saving at the feet of Sunde. After 69 minutes a shot by Lund crashed off the crossbar but Paulsen followed up to head in the rebound.

Sean Thomas had taken over as care-taker manager for this match only.

Match No. 143 | **POLAND** | **Home**

Sunday 21st October, 1973 – Dublin

REP. OF IRELAND (1) 1 Dennehy 31
POLAND (0) 0

Ref: Matthewson (England) **Ground:** Dalymount Park **Att:** 25,000

Ireland: Peter Thomas (Waterford 1), Joe Kinnear (Tottenham Hotspur 17), Terry Mancini (Queens Park Rangers 1), Paddy Mulligan (Crystal Palace 23), Jimmy Holmes (Coventry City 7), Mick Martin (Manchester United 11), Eoin Hand (Portsmouth 11), Tony Byrne (Southampton 14), Terry Conroy (Stoke City 14), Ray Treacy (Swindon Town 29), Don Givens (Queen's Park Rangers 21). **Subs:** Miah Dennehy (Nottingham Forest 7) for Conroy (10 mins), Mick Kearns (Walsall 2) for Thomas (half-time), Alfie Hale (Waterford 14) for Givens (84 mins). **Captain:** Paddy Mulligan. **Manager:** Johnny Giles (1). **Formation:** 4-3-3.

Poland: J. Kalinowski, J. Gut, W. Zmuda, M. Bulzacki, A. Szymanowski, L. Cmikiewicz, K. Deyna, H. Kasperczak, G. Lato, Z. Kapka, R. Gadocha. **Subs:** J. Domarski for Kapka (half-time), K. Kmierik for Lato (73 mins).

Ireland kicked off a new international season with a new manager but also with an old difficulty. The Poles came fresh from their historic 1-1 draw with England whereas Ireland's players had travelled the night before after playing for their league clubs on Saturday. It says much for the new manager and his professional approach that this problem was not to occur again. Giles was injured and was unable to play. It was to be the first of only six games he would miss until he retired from playing in 1979.

After 2 minutes Treacy headed a free from Conroy wide and 3 minutes later Gadocha put Gut away to cross in for Deyna whose shot was brilliantly saved, at the expense of a corner, by Thomas. The injury-prone Conroy had to leave the field with a twisted knee and was replaced by Dennehy who was soon in action sending a shot past Kalinowski only for Gut to head it over

Ireland 1-0 Poland
Ireland's Tony Byrne tries to stop Poland's Robert Gadocha.

on the goal-line. Further chances fell to Givens, Martin and Hand who were all off target as was Kasperczak following a mistake by Holmes. After 31 minutes a perfectly floated free kick from Kinnear found Dennehy whose glancing header flew past Kalinowski and on into the net. Late in the half Treacy was given a great chance from a pass by Byrne but his weak shot was easily dealt with by the Polish goalkeeper.

Kearns came on for the injured Thomas at half-time and, with a tired Ireland forced to defend for most of the second period, he was kept busy. His best save came 15 minutes from the end when a Polish move up the left stretched the Irish defence. A quick flick into the centre found Gadocha in the clear only 10 yards out. The winger struck his shot well but Kearns reacted quickly and managed to turn the shot around the post.

Match No. 144 — BRAZIL — Away

Sunday 5th May, 1974 – Rio de Janeiro

BRAZIL (0) 2 Leivinha 50, Rivelino 56
REP. OF IRELAND (0) 1 Mancini 70

Ref: Velasquez (Colombia) **Ground:** Maracana Stadium **Att:** 74,696

Brazil: Leao, Ze Maria, Luis Pereira, Marinho Perez, Marinho Chagas, Carbone, Rivelino, Paulo Cesar, Jairzinho, Cesar Augusto, Leivinha.

Ireland: Peter Thomas (Waterford 2), Joe Kinnear (Tottenham Hotspur 18), Paddy Mulligan (Crystal Palace 24), Terry Mancini (Queens Park Rangers 2), Jimmy Holmes (Coventry City 8), Eoin Hand (Portsmouth 12), Johnny Giles (Leeds United 36), Mick Martin (Manchester United 12), Terry Conroy (Stoke City 15), Ray Treacy (Preston 30), Don Givens (Queen's Park Rangers 22). **Subs:** Tony Dunne (Bolton Wanderers 25) for Holmes (half-time), Gerry Daly (Manchester United 3) for Treacy (half-time). **Captain:** Johnny Giles. **Manager:** Johnny Giles (2). **Formation:** 4-3-3.

Brazil dominated the match for long spells but a good opening period saw Ireland come close with Holmes shooting into the side netting and Givens just failing to connect with a great cross from

Conroy. Generally it was one-way traffic as Leivinha was off target with two headers. Rivelino had a shot wide and another saved by Thomas. Coming up to half-time Brazil increased the pressure and Marinho Perez burst past several Irish players before shooting against a post.

Five minutes into the second half a reshuffled Irish side conceded a goal when Leivinha shot past Thomas. In another 6 minutes Rivelino had added a second with a tremendous long-range strike. Ireland pulled a goal back when Mancini sent a powerful header to the back of the net following an accurate free kick from Giles. Two late chances saw shots from Paulo Cesar and Hand off target.

Match No. 145 — URUGUAY — Away

Wednesday 8th May, 1974 – Montevideo

URUGUAY (2) 2 Morena 16, 26
REP. OF IRELAND (0) 0

Ref: Barreto (Uruguay) **Ground:** Centenario Stadium **Att:** 40,000

Uruguay: R. Fernandez, Jauregui, Masnik, Forlan, Pavoni, Cardaccio, Jimenez, Mantegazza, F. Morena, Gomez, R. Corbo. **Subs:** Millar for Mantegazza, Alvarez for Gomez.

Ireland: Mick Kearns (Walsall 3), Joe Kinnear (Tottenham Hotspur 19), Paddy Mulligan (Crystal Palace 25), Terry Mancini (Queens Park Rangers 3), Tony Dunne (Bolton Wanderers 26), Eoin Hand (Portsmouth 13), Johnny Giles (Leeds United 37), Mick Martin (Manchester United 13), Terry Conroy (Stoke City 16), Jimmy Conway (Fulham 15), Don Givens (Queen's Park Rangers 23). **Subs:** Gerry Daly (Manchester United 4) for Givens (73 mins). **Captain:** Johnny Giles. **Manager:** Johnny Giles (3). **Formation:** 4-3-3.

Uruguay were quickly on the attack and scored twice in the first half-hour. Subsequently Ireland forced them on the defensive with some good play but they failed to beat Fernandez in the home goal.

Match No. 146 — CHILE — Away

Sunday 12th May, 1974 – Santiago

CHILE (0) 1 Valdez 57
REP. OF IRELAND (1) 2 Hand 43, Conway 76

Ref: **Ground:** Nacional Stadium **Att:**

Chile: Vallehos, Machuca, Quintano, Figueroa, Arias, Valdez, Paez, Reynoso, Caszely, Ahumada, Veliz. **Subs:** Garcia for Machuca, Lara for Valdez, Gamboa for Caszely, Castro for Veliz.

Ireland: Mick Kearns (Walsall 4), Joe Kinnear (Tottenham Hotspur 20), Paddy Mulligan (Crystal Palace 26), Terry Mancini (Queens Park Rangers 4), Tony Dunne (Bolton Wanderers 27), Eoin Hand (Portsmouth 14), Johnny Giles (Leeds United 38), Mick Martin (Manchester United 14), Terry Conroy (Stoke City 17), Jimmy Conway (Fulham 16), Don Givens (Queen's Park Rangers 24). **Captain:** Johnny Giles. **Manager:** Johnny Giles (4). **Formation:** 4-3-3.
Sendings-off: Don Givens (Ireland) 60 mins, Carlos Reynoso (Chile) 60 mins.

Ireland finished off its three-match tour of South America with this victory over Chile. Ireland opened the scoring just before half-time when Hand headed home a corner from Giles. Chile equalised when a shot from Caszely struck an upright and Valdez followed up to help it over the line. After an hour both Givens and Reynoso were sent off after a punch-up. The visitors got the winning score when Mulligan raced up the field, beat several tackles and crossed in for Conway to shoot past Vallehos. Chile tried desperately for an equaliser in the closing stages but some sound defending and great goalkeeping kept them out.

Match No. 147 USSR Home

Wednesday 30th October, 1974 – Dublin (European Championship)

REP. OF IRELAND (2) 3 Givens 23,30,70
USSR (0) 0

Ref: Axelryd (Sweden) **Ground:** Dalymount Park **Att:** 35,000

Ireland: Paddy Roche (Manchester United 2), Joe Kinnear (Tottenham Hotspur 21), Paddy Mulligan (Crystal Palace 27), Terry Mancini (Arsenal 5), Jimmy Holmes (Coventry City 9), Mick Martin (Manchester United 15), Johnny Giles (Leeds United 39), Liam Brady (Arsenal 1), Steve Heighway (Liverpool 7), Ray Treacy (Preston 31), Don Givens (Queen's Park Rangers 25). **Captain:** Johnny Giles. **Manager:** Johnny Giles (5). **Formation:** 4-3-3.

USSR: V. Pilgui, S. Nikulin, V. Kaplichny, S. Olshansky, E. Lovchev, V. Matvienko, V. Kolotov, V. Veremeev, V. Onischenko, V. Fedotov, O. Blokhin. **Subs:** V. Fedorov for Veremeev (58 mins).
Sendings-off: Terry Mancini (Ireland) 32 mins, Vladimir Kaplichny (USSR) 32 mins.

In the first quarter of an hour Ireland created three good openings. A Giles free kick gave Mancini the first chance but his effort was just wide. Treacy then headed a Martin cross into the path of Givens but he too shot wide. Givens was pulled down in the box when about to head in a Giles cross but no penalty was awarded. Then after 23 minutes the striker scored his first goal. Giles swept a long ball out to Kinnear on the wing. The right back had time to send a perfect cross into the goalmouth and Givens ducked between two defenders to steer the ball well out of Pilgui's reach and on into the corner of the net. Blokhin had a shot over 4 minutes later but in Irelands next meaningful attack they scored again. A long throw-in by Heighway was flicked on by Treacy for Givens. The ball was intercepted and headed back to Treacy who in turn knocked it to the near post where Givens hooked it home. The Irish continued to press and soon after, as Giles prepared to take a free kick, Mancini and Kaplichny were involved in a scuffle. Mancini 'floored' the Soviet and was ordered off as was Kaplichny after he had received treatment. The Irish lost much of their composure after this as Martin dropped back to replace Mancini and Onischenko almost capitalised on defensive confusion soon after but shot over when well placed. Late in the half Heighway had a shot well saved by Pilgui.

The Soviets went all-out for goals at the start of the second period, but it was Brady who had the first effort when his 30 yard shot was saved by Pilgui. Roche saved shots from Blokhin and Onischenko and also parried a shot from Fedotov with Kolotov shooting the rebound wide. After 25 minutes Givens raced on to a Giles free kick and headed the ball down past Pilgui into the far corner of the net for his hat-trick. This exciting international ended with a volley from Giles which forced the Soviet goalkeeper into a finger-tip save. As well as the two sendings-off, Matvienko was booked for a foul on Brady.

Match No. 148 TURKEY Away

Wednesday 20th November, 1974 – Izmir (European Championship)

TURKEY (0) 1 Martin (o.g.) 56
REP. OF IRELAND (0) 1 Givens 63

Ref: Srodecki (Poland) **Ground:** Stade d'Ataturk **Att:** 67,000

Turkey: Yasin, Alphaslan, Ismail, Ziya, Zekeriya, Mehmet Fuji, Selcuk, Engin, Mehmet Buyuk, T. Cemil, Metin. **Subs:** Osman for Mehmet Fuji (80 mins).

Ireland: Paddy Roche (Manchester United 3), Joe Kinnear (Tottenham Hotspur 22), Paddy Mulligan (Crystal Palace 28), Eoin Hand (Portsmouth 15), Tony Dunne (Bolton Wanderers 28), Mick Martin (Manchester United 16), Johnny Giles (Leeds United 40), Liam Brady (Arsenal 2), Steve Heighway (Liverpool 8), Don Givens (Queen's Park Rangers 26), Terry Conroy (Stoke City 18). **Subs:** Miah Dennehy (Nottingham Forest 8) for Conroy (86 mins). **Captain:** Johnny Giles. **Manager:** Johnny Giles (6). **Formation:** 4-3-3.

Don Givens followed up his hat-trick against USSR with Ireland's only goal in Turkey.

Johnny Giles, player, Captain and Manager of the Irish team.

Ireland set out from the start to defend in the hope of coming out of this encounter with a point. Despite a hostile atmosphere they succeeded in holding the Turks scoreless at the break after surviving some intense pressure. The two best scoring opportunities fell to Turan Cemil. First he was put clear by a through ball from Metin only to waste a good chance by shooting into the side netting then a mistake by Giles again put him in the clear but this time he was stopped when Roche saved at his feet. Irelands best chance of the half fell to Conroy whose shot was well saved by Yasin.

Eleven minutes into the second half a corner by Metin was headed into his own net by Martin under pressure from Cemil. Four minutes later a long ball by Ziya was headed down by Mehmet Buyuk giving Metin a clear shot on goal only for Roche to make a brilliant save. In a further 3 minutes Ireland were level. Giles broke down the left wing and sent over a cross which was missed by the sweeper giving Givens enough time to control the ball before shooting past Yasin from the edge of the box. Givens had another chance late in the game but this time the Turkish goalkeeper made a good save.

Match No. 149 — WEST GERMANY "B" — Home

Tuesday 11th March, 1975 – Dublin

REP. OF IRELAND (0) 1 Conway 89
WEST GERMANY "B" (0) 0

Ref: Homewood (England) **Ground:** Dalymount Park **Att:**

Ireland: Paddy Roche (Manchester United 4), Joe Kinnear (Tottenham Hotspur 23), Mick Martin (Manchester United 17), Eoin Hand (Portsmouth 16), Tony Dunne (Bolton Wanderers 29), Noel Campbell (Fortuna Cologne 8), Gerry Daly (Manchester United 5), Liam Brady (Arsenal 3), Steve Heighway (Liverpool 9), Ray Treacy (Preston 32), Don Givens (Queen's Park Rangers 27). **Subs:** Terry

Conroy (Stoke City 19) for Treacy (half-time), Jimmy Conway (Fulham 17) for Campbell (65 mins), Miah Dennehy (Nottingham Forest 9) for Daly (83 mins). **Captain:** Tony Dunne. **Manager:** Johnny Giles (7) (Alan Kelly). **Formation:** 4-3-3.

West Germany "B": R. Kargus, M. Kaltz, G. Zimmermann, U. Kliemann, H. Konopka, B. Nickel, E. Beer, J. Pirrung, W. Seel, D. Müller, F. Keller.

The Germans came to Dublin expecting to play a "B" International. When they found out their opposition was the Irish "A" team they were not pleased but did not object to the game going ahead. The game itself had other anomalies. Johnny Giles was unable to attend but picked the side for Alan Kelly to take charge of. Giles's team had one late defection when Mulligan pulled out injured and Kelly was forced to play Martin in defence with Daly coming in at mid-field. Giles intended using Daly and Conroy as substitutes during the break but it was a sub used by Kelly who proved the match-winner. One last anomaly was that this game was listed as a representative game but in 1985 the FAI up-graded it to a full international and thus is included in this book as such.

The first chance of the game fell to Heighway who headed over after Kargus had punched away a cross from Kinnear. The German goalkeeper was in action again saving from Martin while Kliemann robbed Brady of a goal with a last minute tackle. Ireland had the lions share of the play but shortly before the interval the Germans had three good openings. A free kick by Zimmermann was just over, Roche saved a shot from Keller and Müller was put clear only to shoot wide as Roche advanced.

The Irish started the second half much as they had started the first. Givens set up Daly but he shot over while at the far end Roche saved twice from Beer and Keller. After 70 minutes Givens shot past Kargus only for the ball to hit the post and rebound back to the German goalkeeper. Not long afterwards another Givens shot was parried by Kargus with Conroy firing the rebound wide. In the last minute a clearance by Konopka was knocked down by the head of Hand for Conway to blast a volley into the German net.

Match No. 150 SWITZERLAND Home

Saturday 10th May, 1975 – Dublin (European Championship)

REP. OF IRELAND (2) 2 Martin 2, Treacy 29
SWITZERLAND (0) 1 Müller 73

Ref: Schiller (Austria) **Ground:** Lansdowne Road **Att:** 50,000

Ireland: Paddy Roche (Manchester United 5), Joe Kinnear (Tottenham Hotspur 24), Paddy Mulligan (Crystal Palace 29), Eoin Hand (Portsmouth 17), Tony Dunne (Bolton Wanderers 30), Mick Martin (Manchester United 18), Johnny Giles (Leeds United 41), Liam Brady (Arsenal 4), Terry Conroy (Stoke City 20), Ray Treacy (Preston 33), Don Givens (Queen's Park Rangers 28). **Captain:** Johnny Giles. **Manager:** Johnny Giles (8). **Formation:** 4-3-3.

Switzerland: E. Burgener, G. Guyot, M. Heer, L. Bizzini, R. Hasler, E. Rutschmann, H-P Schild, J. Kuhn, R. Botteron, K. Müller, D. Jeandupeux.

As the Irish team became more successful so more people wanted to see them play. Thus the FAI were swamped with requests for tickets. This interest emphasised the teams progress under Giles because the public now expected victory and even the Swiss coach stated he would be happy with a draw. Irish strength at home would be a telling factor in future games and would provide a solid base to build on.

Soon after the start Treacy intercepted a pass out of defence by Heer and played a one-two with Conroy before sending over a cross which was knocked into the roof of the net with a diving header by Martin. Another one-two, this time between Mulligan and Treacy, gave Givens a chance but his shot was saved. Givens and Treacy were combining well and their next effort was only scrambled away at the last moment. The only Swiss chance of any note during this half was a 30 yard shot by Botteron which was saved by Roche. After 27 minutes Conroy put Givens through. Although Bizzini tried to pull him back in the box, Givens shook him off only to shoot just wide. Two minutes later Conroy again set up Givens for a shot which hit the goalkeeper and bounced out for Treacy to thump the ball into the net with his left foot. Late in the half a corner by Giles was headed on by Treacy for Givens at the far post but the latters stabbed shot was turned out for another corner by Burgener.

The second half started with a curling 30 yard effort by Giles which Burgener again saved at the expense of a corner. Givens got in for another chance soon after but the Irish then settled for containment of their two goal lead. This policy brought the ire of the huge attendance down on the Irish especially after first Bizzini fluffed an excellent scoring chance and then Jeandepeux set up Müller to reduce the arrears with a good shot. Although there were to be no more scoring chances the spectacle of the Irish team hanging on for a single-goal victory in a match which should have been won comfortably did not bring the expected plaudits from press and public.

Match No. 151 — USSR — Away

Sunday 18th May, 1975 – Kiev (European Championship)

USSR (2) 2 Blokhin 11, Kolotov 28
REP. OF IRELAND (0) 1 Hand 79

Ref: **Ground:** Central Stadium **Att:** 100,000

USSR: E. Rudakov, A. Konkov, M. Fomenko, V. Troshkin, V. Matvienko, L. Buryak, V. Muntyan, V. Veremeyev, V. Onischenko, V. Kolotov, O. Blokhin. **Subs:** S. Reshko for Muntyan, V. Fedorov for Veremeyev.

Ireland: Paddy Roche (Manchester United 6), Joe Kinnear (Tottenham Hotspur 25), Paddy Mulligan (Crystal Palace 30), Eoin Hand (Portsmouth 18), Tony Dunne (Bolton Wanderers 31), Mick Martin (Manchester United 19), Johnny Giles (Leeds United 42), Liam Brady (Arsenal 5), Steve Heighway (Liverpool 10), Don Givens (Queen's Park Rangers 29), Terry Conroy (Stoke City 21). **Captain:** Johnny Giles. **Manager:** Johnny Giles (9). **Formation:** 4-3-3.

Ireland faced a Soviet XI entirely composed of players from Dynamo Kiev who had won the European Cup-Winners-Cup final four days earlier. Full of confidence and backed by a capacity crowd the Soviets (or Ukrainians) totally overwhelmed the Irish.

Switzerland 1-0 Ireland 1975
A shot by Daniel Jeandepeux beats both Eoin Hand and Paddy Roche but went wide.

After 11 minutes a corner by Giles was cleared by Matvienko to Veremeyev. With the Irish players funneling back the Soviets launched an all-out attack and Veremeyev fed Blokhin who shot through Kinnears legs past the stranded Roche. Two minutes later Roche made a good save to deny Blokhin a second. Ireland had a brief foray into the Soviet box soon after but Conroy headed wide and Givens shot straight at Rudakov when clean through. Most of the pressure however was at the other end and Roche again saved from Blokhin. After 29 minutes the Irish defence was caught out again when Kolotov came steaming in to plant a diving header into the back of the net following a cross from Veremeyev.

The Soviets kept up the pressure in the second half and should have had a third goal when Roche dropped a cross but Onischenko shot into the side netting. Blokhin was again denied by the Irish goalkeeper while Kinnear cleared another shot off the line. After 79 minutes Ireland got a goal out of the blue. A free kick from Giles fell perfectly for Givens to head over the advancing goalkeeper and Hand shot home. This goal unsettled the home team and two minutes from the end Conroy got on to the end of a Giles corner but headed into the side netting. The Soviets deserved a bigger margin of victory but like the Ireland – Swiss game they were forced near the end to hold on.

Match No. 152 — SWITZERLAND — Away

Wednesday 21st May, 1975 – Berne (European Championship)

SWITZERLAND (0) 1 Elsener 76
REP. OF IRELAND (0) 0

Ref: Cesar (Portugal) **Ground:** Wankdorf Stadium **Att:** 20,000

Switzerland: E. Burgener, G. Guyot, S. Trinchero, L. Bizzini, P. Fischbach, E. Rutschmann, J. Kuhn, R. Hasler, R. Botteron, K. Müller, D. Jeandupeux. **Subs:** H-J Pfister for Rutschmann (half-time), R. Elsener for Müller (70 mins).

Ireland: Paddy Roche (Manchester United 7), Tony Dunne (Bolton Wanderers 32), Paddy Mulligan (Crystal Palace 31), Eoin Hand (Portsmouth 19), Jimmy Holmes (Coventry City 10), Mick Martin (Manchester United 20), Johnny Giles (Leeds United 43), Liam Brady (Arsenal 6), Terry Conway (Stoke City 22), Ray

Switzerland 1-0 Ireland 1975
The only goal. Rudolf Elsener takes advantage of an Irish defensive mix-up to shoot home the Swiss winner with Giles and Martin powerless to prevent it.

Treacy (Preston 34), Don Givens (Queen's Park Rangers 30). **Subs:** Gerry Daly (Manchester United 6) for Giles (79 mins). **Captain:** Johnny Giles. **Manager:** Johnny Giles (10). **Formation:** 4-3-3.

A very entertaining game had a slow start with the first real chance coming to Ireland after 30 minutes. Martin broke up the right, beat two defenders and smacked in a low cross which the in-rushing Treacy only just failed to get a touch to. Brady followed this with a long range shot which just went wide. Both teams were playing well but a minute before the interval Jeandupeux should have scored but shot wide when clean through.

Swiss finishing was poor and after 47 minutes Müller knocked a Fischbach cross over the bar with only Roche to beat from close range. Two minutes later Pfister sent a powerful down-ward header goalwards only for Roche to make a brilliant stop at the butt of the upright. Conroy set up Givens and Treacy at the other end but both shot wide while Pfister wasted another opportunity when he shot over from close range following a cross from Bizzini. Roche saved well at the feet of Jeandupeux, Brady was just over with a well hit shot and Holmes cleared a Jeandupeux header off the line before the Swiss got the only goal of the match. Both Hand and Conroy went for a cross from Botteran and got in each others way with the result that the ball fell loose for Elsener to shoot past Roche. Soon after Giles went off with a leg injury and his replacement, Daly, had a chance near the end but his header from Conroy's cross went over. Late in the game Brady fired another long-range shot wide. Ireland's 75th defeat was a disappointment as it virtually ended their chances of qualifying for the European Championship quarter-finals.

Match No. 153 — TURKEY — Home

Wednesday 29th October, 1975 – Dublin (European Championship)

REP. OF IRELAND (3) 4 Givens 27, 32, 36, 88
TURKEY (0) 0

Ref: Martinez (Spain) **Ground:** Dalymount Park **Att:** 23,000

Ireland: Paddy Roche (Manchester United 8), Tony Dunne (Bolton Wanderers 33), Paddy Mulligan (West Bromwich Albion 32), Eoin Hand (Portsmouth 20), Jimmy Holmes (Coventry City 11), Mick Martin (West Bromwich Albion 21), Johnny Giles (West Bromwich Albion 44), Liam Brady (Arsenal 7), Steve Heighway (Liverpool 11), Ray Treacy (Preston 35), Don Givens (Queen's Park Rangers 31). **Subs:** Terry Conroy (Stoke City 23) for Heighway (half-time), Joe Kinnear (Brighton 26) for Dunne (83 mins). **Captain:** Johnny Giles. **Manager:** Johnny Giles (11). **Formation:** 4-3-3.

Turkey: Yasin, Sabahattin, Ismail, Fatih, Kadir, Alpaslan, Engin, Necati, Ali Kemal, Gökmen, T. Cemil. **Subs:** Zafor for Ismail (33 mins), Rasim for Yasin (39 mins).
Sendings-off: Mick Martin (Ireland) 79 mins, Alpaslan Eratli (Turkey) 79 mins.

Ireland finished off their group with their biggest win for 22 years. Givens four goals also equalled a 41 year-old record for most goals in a match. It was a successful end to a campaign which began brightly but faded out in the final run-in despite this finale.

Holmes set up Martin for the first chance of the match but the midfielders finishing was weak. Other openings came to Heighway and Treacy, who also finished poorly, before Turkey missed a 'sitter'. Hand left a cross from Ali Kemal to Roche but Gökmen nipped in only to head wide. Six minutes later Ireland went ahead. A cross from Mulligan was headed down by Treacy for Givens. The latter controled it, shook off the attention of a defender and shot home powerfully from a narrow angle. Five minutes later Treacy tussled with Yasin for a cross from Dunne. The Turkish goalkeeper could only punch the ball to Givens who headed home his second. Givens completed his hat-trick in nine minutes when Heighway sent Treacy away to send in a perfect cross and Givens nodded it in. Whilst not a dirty game the Turks lost their captain and goalkeeper with injuries – the latter carried off after a challenge by Treacy.

Yasin's deputy, Rasim, was then involved in an incident which almost led to the game being abandoned. Three minutes after the break the Turkish goalkeeper was suddenly pelted with missiles from the crowd behind his goal. The referee stopped the game as Gardai raced to control the situation. The game was stopped a second time four minutes later and the referee was set to abandon the match should the trouble re-occur. Thankfully it did not. However these stoppages plus another three minutes delay when getting the floodlights lit meant the game was to stretch to an extra 13 minutes of 'lost' time. These interruptions seemed to disrupt the Irish and Turkey came more into the game. After 61 minutes they were awarded a free kick just outside the penalty area and Alpaslan curled the ball over the wall and into the net. The referee disallowed the goal as the free was indirect but neither team were aware of that! Five minutes later Givens sent Treacy clear in the box. As the latter attempted to round the goalkeeper, Rasim took him down and a penalty was awarded. Holmes's spot-kick was turned onto a post by Rasim who recovered in time to save the left-backs effort from the rebound. After 79 minutes Martin and Alpaslan were involved in a punch-up and both received their marching orders. The Spanish referee also booked two Turks in the course of the game. Two minutes before the belated final whistle Mulligan crossed in for Givens to side-foot a volley into the back of the net to finish off an incident-packed international.

Match No. 154 — NORWAY — Home

Wednesday 24th March, 1976 – Dublin

REP. OF IRELAND (2) 3 Brady 25, Holmes 36 (pen), Walsh 61
NORWAY (0) 0

Ref: Partridge (England) **Ground:** Dalymount Park **Att:** 20,000

Ireland: Mick Kearns (Walsall 5), Tony Grealish (Orient 1), Mick Martin (West Bromwich Albion 22), Jimmy Holmes (Coventry City 12), Ray O'Brien (Notts County 1), Jimmy Conway (Fulham 18), Noel Campbell (Fortuna Cologne 9), Liam Brady (Arsenal 8), Steve Heighway (Liverpool 12), Mickey Walsh (Blackpool 1), Don Givens (Queen's Park Rangers 32). **Subs:** Ray Treacy (Preston 36) for Givens (81 mins). **Captain:** Mick Martin. **Manager:** Johnny Giles (12). **Formation:** 4-3-3.

Norway: T. R. Jacobsen, H. Skuseth, S. Grondalen, R. Ottesen, S. Slinning, S. Kvia, T. E. Johansen, A. Olsen, S. Thunberg, F. R. Vadahl, G. Hoyland. **Subs:** A. Dokken for Olsen (81 mins).

Ireland had the lion's share of the play and it was Heighway who forced the first opening with an exciting run and shot which was deflected over the bar. O'Brien forced Jacobsen into his first save with a shot while another shot, this time from Brady was just wide. Norway's only real chance came soon after when an error by O'Brien allowed Olsen's ball to find Hoyland but Kearns made a good save from the wingers shot. A mistake in the Norwegian defence allowed Walsh to latch on to a poor back pass but his powerful shot hit the butt of the upright and went out. A minute later Heighway, Martin, Grealish and Campbell combined well to set up Brady who beat two men before shooting powerfully home from 20 yards. After 36 minutes Givens was fouled in the area by Ottesen when going for a cross from Grealish and Holmes sent Jacobsen the wrong way with the resultant penalty.

Tony Grealish made his debut against Norway.

Ireland were awarded a second penalty 4 minutes after the break when a header from Givens was handled on the goal-line by Olsen. Givens took the spot-kick himself but it hit the goalkeepers foot and he was prevented from scoring from the rebound. After 61 minutes Walsh controlled an then turned on a cross from Conway before rifling a shot into the corner of the net. Givens had another opportunity, shortly before he went off injured, but his header was saved by Jacobsen.

Match No. 155 POLAND Away

Wednesday 26th May, 1976 – Poznan

POLAND (0) 0
REP. OF IRELAND (2) 2 Givens 4, 11

Ref: Poucek (Czechoslovakia) **Ground:** Warta Stadium **Att:** 15,000

Poland: J. Tomaszewski, H. Wawrowski, P. Janas, W. Zmuda, W. Rudy, Z. Garlowski, H. Kasperczyk, Z. Boniek, G. Lato, A. Szarmach, K. Kmiecik. **Subs:** J. Mowlik for Tomaszewski (half-time), Jakobczak for Garlowski (half-time), J. Benigier for Boniek (half-time).

Ireland: Mick Kearns (Walsall 6), Tony Grealish (Orient 2), Paddy Mulligan (West Bromwich Albion 33), Jimmy Holmes (Coventry City 13), Ray O'Brien (Notts County 2), Jimmy Conway (Fulham 19), Mick Martin (West Bromwich Albion 23), Liam Brady (Arsenal 9), Terry Conroy (Stoke City 24), Mickey Walsh (Blackpool 2), Don Givens (Queen's Park Rangers 33). **Subs:** Ray Treacy (Preston 37) for Walsh (31 mins), Miah Dennehy (Walsall 10) for Conway (half-time). **Captain:** Paddy Mulligan. **Manager:** Johnny Giles (13). **Formation:** 4-3-3.

Ireland got an early goal when O'Brien and Givens put Conroy away on the wing. Conroy's cross was not dangerous but Tomaszeswski made a total hash of collecting it and when the ball ran loose Givens was at hand to knock it into the goal. A second mistake, seven minutes later, gave Ireland another goal. A bad kick out by the Polish goalkeeper allowed Martin to gain possession ahead of Boniek. Martin gave the ball to Walsh who knocked a perfect through ball to Givens who beat the offside trap and went on to beat Tomaszewski for a second time. Kearns was then forced into action when Mulligan mis-cued a cross from Lato forcing the goalkeeper to tip the ball over. Polish finishing was poor and Boniek, Szarmach and Lato were all guilty of bad misses in this half.

Walsh had gone off injured during the half and Conway also went off during the break with double vision. Giles brought on Dennehy up front with Conroy dropping back to midfield. Dennehy missed an early chance before he combined with Conroy to set up Givens only for the latter to be denied by a superb save from Mowlik. Szarmach again demonstrated his poor finishing when he was put clear in the box only to shoot across goal. Polands nearest chance of a goal was a shot by Jakobczak which was palmed onto the post by Kearns who recovered well to smother the rebound.

Match No. 156 ENGLAND Away

Wednesday 8th September, 1976 – London

ENGLAND (1) 1 Pearson 44
REP. OF IRELAND (0) 1 Daly 57 (pen)

Ref: Alexander (Scotland) **Ground:** Wembley Stadium **Att:** 51,000

England: R.Clemence, C. Todd, R. McFarland, B. Greenhoff, P. Madeley, R. Wilkins, T. Cherry, T. Brooking, S. Pearson, C. George, K. Keegan. **Subs:** G. Hill for George (65 mins).

Ireland: Mick Kearns (Walsall 7), Paddy Mulligan (West Bromwich Albion 34), David O'Leary (Arsenal 1), Mick Martin (West Bromwich Albion 24), Jimmy Holmes (Coventry City 14), Gerry Daly (Derby County 7), Johnny Giles (West Bromwich Albion 45), Liam Brady (Arsenal 10), Steve Heighway (Liverpool 13), Don Givens (Queen's Park Rangers 34) Terry Conroy (Stoke City 25). **Captain:** Johnny Giles. **Manager:** Johnny Giles (14). **Formation:** 4-3-3.

This was an important World Cup warm-up game for both countries and it was Ireland who showed the better form. Indeed had it not been for some poor finishing the visitors might have run out comfortable winners.
Two minutes after the kick-off Givens climbed highest to head a Mulligan cross just wide. Both sides defences then came to the fore and it was not until mid-way through the half that Brady shook off his marker to shoot into the side netting. Mulligan again set up Givens who outwitted McFarland before sending a shot just wide of the far post. Another Brady shot whistled over the bar before England put in a storming closing 15 minutes. Brooking and Cherry had shots saved by Kearns and Wilkins should have scored with a 6 yard header but it went over. Pearson had a close-range shot saved by Kearns before George and Keegan set up Pearson to score with a close-range side-foot volley into the roof of the net.

Ireland again took up the play after the break and Conroy's header from Giles' free kick was only just over. Conroy got kicked in the face by accident whilst heading over and went off the field to get treatment. As his head was being bandaged behind Clemence's net Ireland equalised. Heighway cut inside Todd and ran in on the English goal. He beat Cherry on the edge of the area but was taken down by Wilkins in full flight and a penalty was awarded. Daly took the spot-kick and sent Clemence the wrong way. Conroy resumed before England restarted the game. After 61 minutes another break by Heighway saw him smack a shot towards goal. Clemence managed to get a fist to the ball but only succeeded in punching the ball to Givens who shot weakly wide. Late in the game Keegan almost got in but O'Leary made a great tackle to deny him and England an undeserved winner.

Match No. 157 — TURKEY — Away

Wednesday 13th October, 1976 – Ankara

TURKEY (0) 3 B. Cemil 51, 71, Isa 65
REP. OF IRELAND (2) 3 Stapleton 3, Daly 14, Waters 80

Ref: Cayic (Yugoslavia) **Ground:** May 19 Stadium **Att:** 35,000

Turkey: Rasim, Alpaslan, Turgay, Ismail, Ali Cemil, B. Kemal, Fatih, Isa, Ali Kemal, B. Cemil, Mehmet.
Subs: Rasit for Mehmet (70 mins)

Ireland: Mick Kearns (Walsall 8), Joe Waters (Grimsby Town 1), Paddy Mulligan (West Bromwich Albion 35), Mick Martin (West Bromwich Albion 25), Jimmy Holmes (Coventry City 15), Gerry Daly (Derby County 8), Johnny Giles (West Bromwich Albion 46), Liam Brady (Arsenal 11), Terry Conroy (Stoke City 26), Don Givens (Queen's Park Rangers 35), Frank Stapleton (Arsenal 1). **Captain:** Johnny Giles. **Manager:** Johnny Giles (15). **Formation:** 4-3-3.

The May 19 Stadium had an artificial base covered by grass which needed some familiarising with before being played on. The Irish appeared to have mastered it early on but subsequently there were numerous mistakes and slips which the Turks took advantage of to score three times. The influence of the pitch, however, could not excuse some bad play in midfield from the Irish which allowed the Turks back into the match but the overall play made for a thrilling game.

Ireland got off to a great start when Stapleton headed in a Giles free kick at the near post. Givens and Martin then had chances before the visitors scored again. Daly found Givens out on the wing and the latter got past Ali Cemil before squaring the ball back for Daly to score with the outside of his boot. Turkey kicked-off again and went straight into attack with Holmes dispossesing Ali Kemal in the box. Inexplicably the referee awarded a penalty for the tackle but Fatih's spot-kick was saved by Kearns. The Turks then began to dominate and the Irish goalkeeper was kept busy for the rest of the half notably bringing off superb saves to stop B. Cemil and Ali Kemal.

The Turks renewed their attacks after the interval and within 6 minutes had pulled a goal back. As Mulligan was taking the ball out of defence he slipped and the ball rolled to B. Cemil. The Turk broke clear and hammered the ball into the net. The home side continued to press and Kearns was forced to make good saves to stop B. Cemil and Ali Kemal while Holmes stopped another Turk with a timely tackle. Isa sent a shot whizzing past the post before he scored the equaliser. A cross by Fatih was headed away by Giles but only as far as Isa who returned it to the net with a superb volley. By this time the Irish were completely out of it and 6 minutes later Turkey went ahead. Kearns mis-judged the flight of the ball from an Ali Kemal corner and it sailed over his head for B. Cemil, at the far post, to nod it down into the net. Therefore it came as a surprise when the Irish suddenly rallied and began to control the game's last quarter. With 10 minutes left Daly and Giles put Waters free on the right. As Waters shaped up to cross, Rasim advanced to cut it off but the Irish right-back sent in a powerful shot which deceived the goalkeeper and Rasim was only able to help it over the line. The match almost had a dramatic conclusion when, 3 minutes from the end, B. Cemil weaved his way through the Irish defence and shot across the goal; the ball going just the wrong side of the post.

Match No. 158 — FRANCE — Away

Wednesday 17th November, 1976 – Paris (World Cup)

FRANCE (0) 2 Platini 48, Bathenay 88
REP. OF IRELAND (0) 0

Ref: Maksimovic (Yugoslavia) **Ground:** Parc des Princes **Att:** 50,000

France: D. Baratelli, G. Janvion, C. Lopez, M. Tresor, M. Bossis, D. Bathenay, M. Platini, R. Keruzore, D. Rocheteau, B. Lacombe, D. Six. **Subs:** O. Rouyer for Lacombe (73 mins).

Ireland: Mick Kearns (Walsall 9), Paddy Mulligan (West Bromwich Albion 36), David O'Leary (Arsenal 2), Mick Martin (West Bromwich Albion 26), Jimmy Holmes (Coventry City 16), Gerry Daly (Derby County 9), Johnny Giles (West Bromwich Albion 47), Liam Brady (Arsenal 12), Steve Heighway (Liverpool 14), Don Givens (Queen's Park Rangers 36), Frank Stapleton (Arsenal 2). **Subs:** Mickey Walsh (Blackpool 3), for Stapleton (63 mins). **Captain:** Johnny Giles. **Manager:** Johnny Giles (16). **Formation:** 4-3-3.

For the first time Ireland entered a World Cup competition full of confidence and with realistic ambitions of qualifying for the finals. The foundations for this optimism lay with a strong home record which would prove invaluable if this form was translated to away games. Unfortunately it was not and Ireland's World Cup quest would end in another false dawn.

An undistinguished match saw Ireland contain France in the first period. Irish forward play created two openings with Brady firing in a left-footed shot which was saved and Givens shooting wide from a Brady cross. France had few good openings and their frustration manifested itself when Lacombe made a dreadful tackle on O'Leary for which he was booked. As tempers became frayed coming up to the break O'Leary was also shown the yellow card for another foul while Kearns was cautioned for time wasting.

The Irish goalkeeper was in action early in the second half when he just managed to push a Platini free kick around the post. The corner came to nothing but in trying to launch another attack Giles was robbed by Six who then put Platini in the clear to open the scoring. Three minutes later France had the ball in the net again when Tresor finished off a great move but the referee ruled the goal out as Bathenay was adjudged to have handled the ball. After 57 minutes Brady skipped past two men and crossed over for Stapleton to head the ball into the net. The referee disallowed this goal for offside. It was a debatable decision and the first of a number that were to plague Ireland in this and the next World Cups. For the rest of the match the visitors pressed forward with Daly and Giles coming close before they were caught out by a counter-attack which ended with Bathenay netting with a 20 yard shot from a pass by Platini.

Mickey Walsh who came on as a substitute for Stapleton in the second half.

Match No. 159 SPAIN Home

Wednesday 9th February, 1977 – Dublin

REP. OF IRELAND (0) 0
SPAIN (1) 1 Satrastegui 10

Ref: Hunting (England) **Ground:** Lansdowne Road **Att:** 25,000

Ireland: Mick Kearns (Walsall 10), Mick Martin (West Bromwich Albion 27), David O'Leary (Arsenal 3), Jimmy Holmes (Tottenham Hotspur 17), Ray O'Brien (Notts County 3), Noel Campbell (Fortuna Cologne 10), Tony Macken (Derby County 1), Liam Brady (Arsenal 13), Steve Heighway (Liverpool 15), Don Givens (Queen's Park Rangers 37), Frank Stapleton (Arsenal 3). **Subs:** Gerry Peyton (Fulham 1) for Kearns (half-time). **Captain:** Mick Martin. **Manager:** Johnny Giles (17). **Formation:** 4-3-3.

Spain: Miguel Angel, Capon, B. Migueli, Pirri, Cortabarria, Villar, Satrustegui, Asensi, Camacho, Quini, Rojo I. **Subs:** Olmo for Cortabarria (half-time), Idigoras for Quini (half-time), Ramos for Pirri.

Spain got an early goal when Pirri passed to the overlapping Capon and when the latter crossed over Satrustegui sent a dipping header over Kearns into the net. Ireland then launched a series of attacks but the Spanish defence was not troubled. Ireland's best chances of the half fell to Stapleton who had two headers, from crosses by Brady and Heighway, saved well by Miguel Angel.

The visitors sat back on their lead after the break and Ireland dominated the second period. A quick free kick by Brady put Holmes in but a bad bounce ruined his shot which went wide. Brady almost got through also but was barged off the ball when about to shoot. In the last few minutes Heighways cross was headed on by Stapleton for Givens to blast a shot off the upright with the rebound being cleared.

Match No. 160 FRANCE Home

Wednesday 30th March, 1977 – Dublin (World Cup)

REP. OF IRELAND (1) 1 Brady 10
FRANCE (0) 0

Ref: Linemayr (Austria) **Ground:** Lansdowne Road **Att:** 48,000

Ireland: Mick Kearns (Walsall 11), Paddy Mulligan (West Bromwich Albion 37), David O'Leary (Arsenal 4), Mick Martin (West Bromwich Albion 28), Jimmy Holmes (Tottenham Hotspur 18), Gerry Daly (Derby County 10), Johnny Giles (West Bromwich Albion 48), Liam Brady (Arsenal 14), Steve Heighway (Liverpool 16), Ray Treacy (West Bromwich Albion 38), Don Givens (Queen's Park Rangers 38). **Captain:** Johnny Giles. **Manager:** Johnny Giles (18). **Formation:** 4-3-3.

France: A. Rey, G. Janvion, P. Rio, C. Lopez, T. Tusseau, D. Bathenay, M. Platini, C. Synaeghal, D. Rocheteau, B. Lacombe, O. Rouyer.

A crowd of 48,000 packed Lansdowne Road to see Ireland beat France and put themselves in a great position to qualify for the finals. Officialy there was an all-ticket crowd of 36,000 but, as with earlier visits by France, a bigger-than-expected crowd turned up despite the fact that the game was shown live on television.

The Irish dictated the play from the kick-off and got the boost of an early goal. After 10 minutes a free kick from Giles was headed clear by Lopez but only to Brady who was 30 yards from goal. The French defence moved quickly out of the box to catch Treacy and Givens offside but Brady advanced, broke through past Lopez and Bathenay and raced into the area to slide the ball under the advancing Rey. Bathenay had a chance soon after but his powerful shot was just over. That came against the run of play because it was Ireland who were forcing the openings. After 22 minutes Givens, for once on-side, was taken down by Janvion but the referee waved play on. Four minutes later a 25 yard shot by Giles cannoned off the woodwork, flew up into the air and when it came down Givens headed over. The French then had three good openings. Lopez sent Synaeghal clear on the wing but his shot from an acute angle was turned into the side netting by Kearns. From the corner, which was cleared, Bathenay, Rocheteau and Synaeghal combined in a

Liam Brady slides the ball past Rey in the French goal and turns with his arms in the air to accept the applause.

lightning-quick move which ended with Rocheteau flashing a 20 yard shot just past the post. A minute later Bathenay curled a brilliant free kick towards the top corner of the goal but Kearns brilliantly tipped it away to safety. The French offside trap denied Giles a goal when he shot home a pass by Givens only to see the linesman's flag up not against him but Daly.

The second half was as exciting as the first. After 5 minutes a 20 yard shot from Brady was tipped over by Rey. However it was France who had the lions share of the play and after 70 minutes Platini had their best chance. A bad pass from Mulligan was intercepted by the French midfielder who raced away with only Kearns to beat. But, as Platini sized up his opportunity, O'Leary suddenly appeared to save the situation with a timely tackle, knocking the ball out for a corner. French pressure continued with Rocheteau shooting just wide and a header from Platini also just off target. The Irish were reduced to clearing the ball upfield and out into touch for the final ten minutes before the referee blew the full-time whistle. Rio and Daly were booked in the last few minutes as the tension rose.

Match No. 161 — POLAND — Home

Sunday 24th April, 1977 – Dublin

REP. OF IRELAND (0) 0
POLAND (0) 0

Ref: Mathewson (England) **Ground:** Dalymount Park **Att:** 20,000

Ireland: Ron Healey (Cardiff City 1), Paddy Mulligan (West Bromwich Albion 38), Mark Lawrenson (Preston 1), Jimmy Holmes (Tottenham Hotspur 19), Ray O'Brien (Notts County 4), Mick Martin (West Bromwich Albion 29), Johnny Giles (West Bromwich Albion 49), Jimmy Conway (Manchester City 20),

Terry Conroy (Stoke City 27), Ray Treacy (West Bromwich Albion 39), Mickey Walsh (Blackpool 4). **Subs:** Miah Dennehy (Walsall 11) for Lawrenson (85 mins). **Captain:** Johnny Giles. **Manager:** Johnny Giles (19). **Formation:** 4-3-3.

Poland: J. Tomaszewski, M. Dziuba, W. Zmuda, H. Wieczorek, C. Boguszewicz, H. Kasperczak, B. Masztaler, K. Deyna, G. Lato, A. Szarmach, S. Terlecki. **Subs:** Z. Boniek for Deyna (half-time).

A poor game with few highlights. Neither side seemed to make the effort to lift the game and the big attendance (officially 13,500) only saw two good chances and a few half-chances. Giles sent a 30 yard shot just over before Ireland had their only goalscoring opportunity. After 15 minutes a brilliant cross from Holmes found Treacy at the far post but Tomaszewski made a brilliant save to stop his header. Treacy 'put himself about a bit' and was lucky only to be shown the yellow card by a lenient referee who also booked Wieczorek. Healey's only save came 6 minutes later when he stopped a hard shot from Szarmach. Conroy had another shot over and O'Brien chipped a back pass over his own goalkeeper (but wide) before Kasperczak had the visitors best chance. After 37 minutes a corner from Deyna found Szarmach who headed it back only for Kasperczak to shoot over from 10 yards. The second half was as dull as the first with the only highlight being a shot from Martin which went wide.

Match No. 162 — BULGARIA — Away

Wednesday 1st June, 1977 – Sofia (World Cup)

BULGARIA (1) 2 Panov 13, Jeliazkov 76
REP. OF IRELAND (0) 1 Givens 47

Ref: Zlatanos (Greece) **Ground:** Vassil Levski Stadium **Att:** 50,000

Bulgaria: R. Goranov, B. Dimitrov, K. Ivkov, N. Arabov, Z. Vasilev, T. Barzov, K. Borisov, R. Zdravkov, P. Panov, Milanov, T. Tzvetkov. **Subs:** A. Jeliazkov for Barzov (62 mins), A. Aleksandrov for Zdravkov.

Ireland: Mick Kearns (Walsall 12), Paddy Mulligan (West Bromwich Albion 39), David O'Leary (Arsenal 5), Mick Martin (West Bromwich Albion 30), Jimmy Holmes (Tottenham Hotspur 20), Gerry Daly (Derby County 11), Johnny Giles (West Bromwich Albion 50), Liam Brady (Arsenal 15), Steve Heighway (Liverpool 17), Don Givens (Queens Park Rangers 39), Frank Stapleton (Arsenal 4). **Subs:** Noel Campbell (Fortuna Cologne 11), for Daly (79 mins). **Captain:** Johnny Giles. **Manager:** Johnny Giles (20). **Formation:** 4-3-3.
Sendings-off: Mick Martin (Ireland) 80 mins, Noel Campbell (Ireland) 80 mins, Andrej Jeliazkov (Bulgaria) 80 mins, Krasimir Borisov (Bulgaria) 80 mins.

Although the match was played in constant rain, both sides produced some good football which was unfortunately over-shadowed by the refereeing of Niklos Zlatanos and his linesmen. The officials made some 'strange' decisions at a crucial time in the game that almost certainly altered its outcome. As watching French manager Michel Hidalgo said after the match: "I have no doubt that (Ireland) would have won without the referee".

Bulgaria pressured Ireland straight from the kick-off and were awarded a free kick outside the box. Panov curled the free kick around the wall and just over. Heighway and Givens almost got Daly in at the other end but a mistake by Heighway paved the way for the home teams first goal. The Irish wingers pass to Mulligan was intercepted by Tzvetkov who gave the ball to Milanov. He beat O'Leary before knocking the ball in for Panov to blast it into the net with his left foot. Ireland came back with two shots from Heighway which were wide but it was Bulgaria who were playing the better football. Panov worked an opening but his pass went right across the face of the goal without a finishing touch and Kearns made two brilliant saves to stop a header from Milanov and a shot from Panov. Just before the interval Heighway got a cross into the Bulgarian area but just as Givens was about to head it in at the near post he was blatently pushed by Dimitrov. It seemed a clear case for a penalty but the referee ignored the offence. He had earlier turned down a Bulgarian claim for a penalty when the ball struck Martin's arm and possibly that had something to do with it.

Two minutes into the second half Givens headed home a Giles corner to level the scores. This goal disrupted the home sides play and it was Ireland who started to dominate. After 59 minutes Heighway outwitted Dimitrov and sent a high cross to the far post where Daly arrived to knock it back for Giles to hammer home a shot. The referee awarded the goal but, on seeing the linesmans flag raised, disallowed it. The flag was raised presumably for offside but against whom it is impossible to say and this caused some bitterness in the Irish camp. Bulgaria then raised their game with Aleksandrov shooting just over and Jeliazkov heading a great chance wide. After 76 minutes an indirect free was awarded to Bulgaria for what seemed a good tackle by Holmes on Borisov outside the box. Panov again tried to curl the kick around the wall but the ball hit Giles's head and spun towards the net. Kearns managed to adjust himself enough to flap at it but was unable to do anything as Jeliazkov finished it to the net. Two minutes later Aleksandrov, although clearly offside, was allowed to run on and only a great save by Kearns at the forwards feet stopped him from increasing their lead. Daly went off injured and was replaced by Campbell. The substitute was only just on the field when a reckless challenge by Tzvetkov on Stapleton suddenly sparked off a brawl on the touchline in which at least a dozen players were involved. Play was held up for five minutes as order was restored and the referee showed the red card to four players – two from each side. One of those who received his marching orders was Campbell who never even got a kick of the football! This game had one last incident when Givens raced through on a marvellous ball by O'Leary. The Irish striker snatched at the chance and blazed the ball over the bar. Perhaps it is just as well he missed as the linesman had his flag up for an offside decision which was hard to justify. Givens had also been shown the yellow card during the second half before tempers became frayed.

Match No. 163 — BULGARIA — Home

Wednesday 12th October, 1977 – Dublin (World Cup)

REP. OF IRELAND (0) 0
BULGARIA (0) 0

Ref: Gonella (Italy) **Ground:** Lansdowne Road **Att:** 25,000

Ireland: Gerry Peyton (Fulham 2), Paddy Mulligan (West Bromwich Albion 40), David O'Leary (Arsenal 6), Mark Lawrenson (Brighton 2), Jimmy Holmes (Tottenham Hotspur 21), Gerry Daly (Derby County 12), Johnny Giles (Shamrock Rovers 51), Liam Brady (Arsenal 16), Steve Heighway (Liverpool 18), Don Givens (Queens Park Rangers 40), Frank Stapleton (Arsenal 5). **Captain:** Johnny Giles. **Manager:** Johnny Giles (21). **Formation:** 4-3-3.

Bulgaria: S. Staykov, Z. Vasilev, Angelov, K. Ivkov, G. Bonev, A. Kolev, V. Kostov, N. Arabov, S. Dvevizov, P. Panov, T. Tzvetkov. **Subs:** A. Aleksandrov for Tzvetkov (54 mins), N. Grantschanov for Vasilev (71 mins).

Ireland produced some excellent football against a Bulgarian side who had come to defend for a point. The visitors achieved their objective but only due to some tenacious defending and some poor finishing by the home side.

The first half was virtually one-way traffic as the Irish laid siege to Staykov's goal. In a 6 minute spell during the first quarter of an hour Giles had a shot just wide, Stapleton a header over and a shot saved and Daly had another shot wide. Soon after Givens put in a fine run only to shoot wide and Daly took advantage of a Kostov mistake to place another shot off target. After 32 minutes a Giles free kick was headed across goal by O'Leary only for Givens to head over from close range. Three minutes later O'Leary headed a Daly cross over. Later in the half shots from Daly, Heighway and Brady were all off target.

The Bulgarians tightened-up in the second half giving the Irish less opportunities. Givens had two early chances off target again before Peyton was forced into his only save after 65 minutes when he went full length to stop a shot from Aleksandrov. A minute later Stapleton got free of the attentions of Angelov and Ivkov but, with only the goalkeeper to beat, he shot wide. After

68 minutes a cross-cum-shot from Heighway was headed off the line by Bonev. Near the end both sides could have snatched a late winner. After 81 minutes Staykov punched a cross from Mulligan straight to Stapleton but the striker volleyed it over. Four minutes after a free kick from Aleksandrov was bent around the wall beautifully and just skimmed past the post. There were four bookings in the match; O'Leary and Givens for Ireland and Vasilev and Kostov for the visitors.

Match No. 164 — TURKEY — Home

Wednesday 5th April, 1978 – Dublin

REP. OF IRELAND (4) 4 Giles 3, McGee 12, Treacy 18, 23
TURKEY (0) 2 Onder 55, B. Cemil 62

Ref: Alexander (Scotland) **Ground:** Lansdowne Road **Att:** 10,000

Ireland: Gerry Peyton (Fulham 3), David Langan (Derby County 1), Jimmy Holmes (Tottenham Hotspur 22), Noel Synnott (Shamrock Rovers 1), Maurice Daly (Wolverhampton Wanderers 1), Gerry Daly (Derby County 13), Johnny Giles (Shamrock Rovers 52), Ashley Grimes (Manchester United 1), Gerry Ryan (Derby County 1), Ray Treacy (Shamrock Rovers 40), Paul McGee (Queens Park Rangers 1). **Sub:** Synan Braddish (Dundalk 1) for G. Daly (67 mins). **Captain:** Johnny Giles. **Manager:** Johnny Giles (22). **Formation:** 4-3-3.

Turkey: Rasim, Turgay, Erol, Necati, Erdogan, Volkan, Engin, Onder, Sedat, B. Cemil, Ali Kemal. **Subs:** Senol for Rasim (24 mins), Oner for Volkan (half-time), Corkun for Sedat (80 mins).

After 3 minutes Giles curled in a cross from the edge of the box for Treacy to run on to. Treacy lunged at the ball but missed and, with the Turkish goalkeeper positioned for the header, the ball sailed into the far corner of the net. Ireland got a second when Giles curled a free kick into the area but this time McGee got his head to it and flicked it into the net. The Turkish goalkeeper was having a nightmare and Treacy almost scored again but his header was deflected for a corner by a defender. From the corner, taken by Giles, Treacy managed to get in front of Rasim and head the ball past him for the third goal. Five minutes later Treacy headed home his second goal when he finished off a Langan-Synnott move. The Turkish goalkeeper was taken off soon after that. Later Gerry Daly almost got in for a fifth goal and Treacy had an effort cleared off the line by Erol. Erol came closest for Turkey in the first half when his long range free kick had Peyton struggling but the Irish goalkeeper knocked the ball over for an inconclusive corner.

Four minutes after the restart Gerry Daly was taken down by Necati in the box and a penalty was awarded. Daly, the normal penalty taker, let Treacy take it but the Irish striker knocked the ball over the bar. Six minutes later Turkey pulled a goal back when Onder blasted a 20 yard shot into the net. Then after 62 minutes Cemil finished off a good Turkish move by curling the ball home from the edge of the box. Visions of the Turkish come-back in 1976 almost came to fruition minutes later when Cemil dispossessed Synnott in his own half but the Turk could not find the finish this time and Peyton saved. Seven minutes from the end Grimes nearly scored with a powerful shot but Senol knocked it over the crossbar. Two Turks, Engin and Erdogan, were booked during the game.

Match No. 165 — POLAND — Away

Wednesday 12th April, 1978 – Lodz

POLAND (0) 3 Boniek 52, Deyna 60, Mazur 82
REP. OF IRELAND (0) 0

Ref: Schenerell (East Germany) **Ground:** Widzew Stadium **Att:** 35,000

Poland: J. Tomaszewski, A. Szymanowski, R. Wojcicki, W. Zmuda, M. Justek, A. Nawalka, K. Deyna, Z. Boniek, G. Lato, W. Lubanski, A. Szarmach. **Subs:** R. Wojtowicz for Justek (64 mins), W. Mazur for Nawalka (72 mins).

1978 Poland 3-0 Ireland Ireland's Cathal Muckian attempts to try and get through the Polish defence. Players left to right: *Synan Braddish, Kazimierz Deyna, Ashley Grimes, Wladyslaw Zmuda, Muckian and Zbigniew Boniek.*

Ireland: Gerry Peyton (Fulham 4), Eamonn Gregg (Bohemians 1), Mark Lawrenson (Brighton 3), Noel Synnott (Shamrock Rovers 2), Jimmy Holmes (Tottenham Hotspur 23), Ashley Grimes (Manchester United 2), Johnny Giles (Shamrock Rovers 53), Synan Braddish (Dundalk 2), Maurice Daly (Wolverhampton Wanderers 2), Ray Treacy (Shamrock Rovers 41), Cathal Muckian (Drogheda United 1). **Sub:** Jerome Clarke (Drogheda United 1) for Giles (78 mins). **Captain:** Johnny Giles. **Manager:** Johnny Giles (23). **Formation:** 4-4-2.

Poland were on top form throughout and only some excellent goalkeeping from Peyton kept the scoreline down. Soon after the start the Irish goalkeeper made a great save to stop Lubanski. The weakened Irish side set out to contain the Poles and succeeded for the first 45 minutes even though Peyton made further saves to deny Boniek and Szymanowski, twice. Polands best effort of the half was a shot from Deyna which hit the crossbar.

Peyton blotted his display with his only mistake which led to the first goal. A cross from Deyna found Boniek who shot powerfully only for Peyton to parry the ball back to the midfielder who made no mistake with the second chance. Irish attacks were few and they were frustrated by variable offside decisions. However, soon after the goal Grimes put Braddish racing clear on-side only for Tomaszewski to advance and hack the ball away. Braddish had Ireland's best chance when Gregg flicked a Giles free to him only for his shot to be deflected for a corner by a defender. After an hours play Deyna scored with a lovely 25 yard chip shot to put Poland two up. Ten minutes later Deyna should have scored again but his close range shot struck a post. After 82 minutes Szymanowski broke up the right and sent over an inch-perfect cross for Mazur to score with a diving header.

Match No. 166 — NORWAY — Away

Sunday 21st May, 1978 – Oslo

NORWAY (0) 0
REP. OF IRELAND (0) 0

Ref: Fredriksson (Sweden) **Ground:** Ullevaal Stadium **Att:** 11,413

Norway: T. Jacobsen, H. Karlsen, T. Kordahl, E. Aase, T. Pedersen, S. Thumburg, T. E. Johansen, Y. Anderson, A. L. Okland, O. Iversen, H. Thoressen. **Subs:** P. Jacobsen for Thoressen (half-time), G. Hoyland for Okland (60 mins), T. Jacobsen for Anderson (85 mins), J. Birkelund for Kordahl (88 mins).

Ireland: Mick Kearns (Walsall 13), David Langan (Derby County 2), David O'Leary (Arsenal 7), Paddy Mulligan (West Bromwich Albion 41), Jimmy Holmes (Tottenham Hotspur 24), Tony Grealish (Orient 3), Johnny Giles (Shamrock Rovers 54), Liam Brady (Arsenal 17), Steve Heighway (Liverpool 19), Don Givens (Queens Park Rangers 41), Frank Stapleton (Arsenal 6). **Subs:** Ashley Grimes (Manchester United 3), for Brady (23 mins), Mark Lawrenson (Brighton 4) for Langan (half-time), Paul McGee (Queens Park Rangers 2) for Givens (60 mins). **Captain:** Johnny Giles. **Manager:** Johnny Giles (24). **Formation:** 4-3-3.

On a bumpy pitch the home side had the better of the first half of a poor match. An early chance fell to Iversen whose shot from a Thoressen cross was deflected wide by Mulligan. Not long after a good move involving Iversen, Thoressen and Okland ended with another Iversen shot being deflected out for a corner, this time by Langan. Irelands slow build-up was not possible in the conditions and the pitch accounted for injuries to Brady and later Givens, both of whom had to be substituted. Brady's injury was serious and would force him to miss Ireland's next game against Denmark on the following Wednesday. The best chance of the whole game came in the closing stages of the half when an Irish move broke down and Anderson sent Thoresson away. The winger outpaced Langan before cutting a nice ball back for Okland whose shot from 12 yards was sailing into the top corner of the net until Kearns made a wonderful save to tip it over the bar.

During the break Lawrenson came on for Langan with Mulligan switching over to right-back. Despite two early Iversen chances, it was Ireland who had the better of things in this half. Substitute McGee headed a Giles free over and had two other shots only just skimming the crossbar as Irish play improvedd. Two late chances saw a McGee header from a Mulligan cross well saved by the goalkeeper who also did well to stop a powerful downward header from Stapleton in the last minute.

Match No. 167 — DENMARK — Away

Wednesday 24th May, 1978 – Copenhagen (European Championship)

DENMARK (1) 3 H. Jensen 33, B. Nielsen 79 (pen), Lerby 80
REP. OF IRELAND (2) 3 Stapleton 11, Grealish 28, Daly 66

Ref: Beck (Holland) **Ground:** Idraetspark **Att:** 13,000

Denmark: B. Jensen, J. Hansen, H. Munk Jensen, P. Rontved, S. Lerby, M. Olsen, K. Nygaard, J. Sorensen, B. Nielsen, H. Jensen, J. Kristensen. **Subs:** F. Arnesen for Nygaard (66 mins), J. Hojland for Olsen (76 mins).

Ireland: Mick Kearns (Walsall 14), Paddy Mulligan (West Bromwich Albion 42), David O'Leary (Arsenal 8), Mark Lawrenson (Brighton 5), Jimmy Holmes (Tottenham Hotspur 25), Gerry Daly (Derby County 14), Johnny Giles (Shamrock Rovers 55), Tony Grealish (Orient 4), Steve Heighway (Liverpool 20), Don Givens (Queens Park Rangers 42), Frank Stapleton (Arsenal 7). **Subs:** Paul McGee (Queens Park Rangers 3) for Givens (half-time), Eamonn Gregg (Bohemians 2) for Holmes (51 mins). **Captain:** Johnny Giles. **Manager:** Johnny Giles (25). **Formation:** 4-3-3.

As the scoreline suggests this was a magnificent game. Danish manager, Kurt Nielsen, played an attacking formation having been misled by Ireland's poor showing in Norway on Sunday. In that game in Oslo the Irish midfield and attack never really showed but these areas were to be major Irish strengths in a great team performance in Copenhagen.

Ireland had the better of the opening exchanges and after 5 minutes a cross from Mulligan was punched out to the feet of Daly by Birger Jensen, but the Irish midfielder shot a good opening over. A minute later O'Leary ran onto a Giles free kick but he too headed over. Then, after 11 minutes, another cross from Mulligan found Heighway at the far post, who headed the ball down to Givens and he slid the ball to Stapleton who stabbed it home. Soon after Kearns was forced to save at the feet of Benny Nielsen. After 19 minutes the Danish goalkeeper was forced into action when Stapleton and Givens set up Grealish for a shot which Birger Jensen did well to stop. The visitors went two-nil ahead with a great goal. A pass from Stapleton found Mulligan again on the wing but this time instead of crossing the right back fired in a low shot from a narrow angle. The goalkeeper was taken by surprise and only just managed to parry the shot. The rebound fell to

Nygaard who was equally surprised and only succeeded in knocking the ball straight to Heighway. The Irish winger could have shot but heard a shout from Grealish and instead rolled the ball into the latters path for the midfielder to blast home his first Irish goal. The Danes fought back and pulled a goal back 5 minutes later after some constant pressure. A good run up the wing by Kristensen took him to the back line where he crossed in for Nygaard to smash a shot past Kearns and against the crossbar. The ball bounced down and Henning Jensen was there to head in the rebound. Two minutes later Kristensen set up another chance, this time for Sorensen whose 35 yard shot was brilliantly tipped over by Kearns.

There was no let-up in the action for the second half as both sides visited each goal in turn. After 51 minutes Holmes went off with a groin strain and was replaced by Gregg. During the break McGee had come on for Givens. After 58 minutes a slip by Mulligan allowed Nygaard to go free but from nowhere Lawrenson got back to make a vital interception. McGee then broke through a couple of tackles to have his shot saved by Birger Jensen and 2 minutes later Stapleton had a shot which thumped off a post. Ireland regained their two-goal margin when Heighway and McGee combined for the latter to send a low hard pass across the face of the goal for Daly, sliding in at the far post, to convert. Kristensen then missed a 'sitter' before Denmark got back into the game with two goals in a minute. First Henning Jensen raced clear onto a beautiful ball from Kristensen but was taken down by O'Leary in the box. Benny Nielsen scored from the resultant penalty. Then Giles lost the ball to Henning Jensen who found Lerby out on the wing. The full back took the ball in his stride and sent a bullet-like drive from 30 yards straight into the back of the net. Denmark went all-out for a winner in the last ten minutes but Ireland held on for a disappointing point considering the fact that they should have had two. There was one booking during the game – Lawrenson early in the first half.

Match No. 168 — NORTHERN IRELAND — Home

Wednesday 20th September, 1978 – Dublin (European Championship)

REP. OF IRELAND (0) 0
NORTHERN IRELAND (0) 0

Ref: Rion (Belgium) **Ground:** Lansdowne Road **Att:** 46,000

Ireland: Mick Kearns (Walsall 15), Tony Grealish (Orient 5), Mark Lawrenson (Brighton 6), Noel Synnott (Shamrock Rovers 3), Jimmy Holmes (Tottenham Hotspur 26), Gerry Daly (Derby County 15), Johnny Giles (Shamrock Rovers 56), Liam Brady (Arsenal 18), Steve Heighway (Liverpool 21), Paul McGee (Queens Park Rangers 4), Frank Stapleton (Arsenal 8). **Subs:** Mickey Walsh (Everton 5) for Stapleton (54 mins), Don Givens (Birmingham City 43) for Heighway (63 mins). **Captain:** Johnny Giles. **Manager:** Johnny Giles (26). **Formation:** 4-3-3.

Northern Ireland: P. Jennings, P. Rice, A. Hunter, C. Nicholl, S. Nelson, D. McCreery, J. Nicholl, M. O'Neill, S. McIlroy, G. Armstrong, D. Spence. **Subs:** T. Cochrane for Spence (69 mins), Bryan Hamilton for Hunter (72 mins).

The first meeting of the two Irelands was an historic but tedious affair. Both managers were aware of the game's significance but the competition was uppermost in their minds and in that context the result suited the visitors.

Northern Ireland came to defend and it was the Republic who had the early chances. Heighway set up both Stapleton and Holmes in the first ten minutes but in both cases the finish was lacking. The Republic's best chance came after 20 minutes when McGee headed a Brady cross inches wide. Stapleton had another header just over 3 minutes later. McIlroy and O'Neill tried their luck at the other end but after 36 minutes McIlroy and McCreery set up Armstrong who should have scored but his header went just over.

The second half saw fewer openings but McIlroy did manage to get free on an O'Neill pass only for Lawrenson to make a vital tackle to stop him. Late in the game Giles put Givens in but his shot was brilliantly saved by Jennings. In the last minute Givens headed a McGee cross down for Walsh but Chris Nicholl managed to clear the ball away just before the Republic's striker could get to it. Two players were booked during the game – Holmes (the Republic) and Chris Nichol (the North).

Wednesday 25th October, 1978 – Dublin (European Championship)

REP. OF IRELAND (1) 1 Daly 26
ENGLAND (1) 1 Latchford 8

Ref: Aldinger (West Germany) **Ground:** Lansdowne Road **Att:** 50,000

Ireland: Mick Kearns (Walsall 16), Paddy Mulligan (West Bromwich Albion 43), David O'Leary (Arsenal 9), Mark Lawrenson (Brighton 7), Jimmy Holmes (Tottenham Hotspur 27), Gerry Daly (Derby County 16), Tony Grealish (Orient 6), Liam Brady (Arsenal 19), Gerry Ryan (Brighton 2), Don Givens (Birmingham City 44), Paul McGee (Queens Park Rangers 5). **Subs:** Frank Stapleton (Arsenal 9) for McGee (65 mins), Eamonn Gregg (Bohemians 3) for O'Leary (73 mins). **Captain:** Paddy Mulligan. **Manager:** Johnny Giles (27). **Formation:** 4-3-3.

England: R. Clemence, P. Neal, D. Watson, E. Hughes, M. Mills, R. Wilkins, T. Brooking, S. Coppell, P. Barnes, B. Latchford, K. Keegan. **Subs:** P. Thompson for Watson (22 mins), T. Woodcock for Barnes (81 mins).

England opened on the attack and Keegan almost scored soon after kick off when his curling shot was turned over by Kearns. After 8 minutes a corner by Brooking was mis-headed across the goalmouth by Daly and Latchford, standing on the 6 yard line, directed his header down between Holmes and Kearns into the net. Three minutes later Coppell smashed a 20 yard shot off the frame of the goal with Kearns beaten. After 18 minutes Barnes sent Keegan running into the box where Lawrenson pulled him back by the shirt. A penalty should have been awarded but apparently the referee did not notice the infringement. Ireland recovered well and when a cross from Holmes was missed by Latchford, Givens slammed a hurried shot into the side netting. Ireland equalised soon after. O'Leary was obstructed by Keegan as he raced into the English area and a free kick was

The Irish team pictured before the match against England.
Back row, left to right: *Mark Lawrenson, Liam Brady, Gerry Daly, Mick Kearns, Paul McGee, David O'Leary,.*
Front row: *Gerry Ryan, Don Givens, Tony Grealish, Paddy Mulligan, Jimmy Holmes.*

awarded on the left hand side of the box. The defence lined up expecting a high ball in for the strikers but Brady knocked the ball to Daly who was unmarked and he swept it past the advancing defenders into the net. Both sides then had chances coming up to the break with the best of them falling to the visitors. Kearns saved well from Mills following another corner from Brooking and Keegan headed a Barnes cross over.

The second half saw early attempts by McGee, Givens and Ryan before England put in a 20 minute spell of continuous pressure the best effort of which was a Coppell shot which was flicked over by Kearns. Stapleton then headed a Mulligan cross wide before O'Leary had to go off with a groin injury. Mulligan took over at the centre while Gregg went to right back. Soon after this reshuffle Brooking had a shot saved by Kearns legs and when he got the rebound his second shot was cleared off the line by Mulligan. After 84 minutes a Brady cross was challenged for by Stapleton, Clemence and Givens with the latter back heading the ball to Ryan who promptly netted. However, the referee ruled it out for a foul on the goalkeeper. Two minutes from the end Latchford got clear but shot a good chance well over.

Match No. 170 — DENMARK — Home

Wednesday 2nd May, 1979 – Dublin (European Championship)

REP. OF IRELAND (1) 2 Daly 44, Givens 65
DENMARK (0) 0

Ref: Vantrot (France) **Ground:** Lansdowne Road **Att:** 35,000

Ireland: Gerry Peyton (Fulham 5), Eamonn Gregg (Bohemians 4), Paddy Mulligan (West Bromwich Albion 44), Mick Martin (Newcastle United 31), Jimmy Holmes (Tottenham Hotspur 28), Gerry Daly (Derby County 17), Johnny Giles (Shamrock Rovers 57), Liam Brady (Arsenal 20), Austin Hayes (Southampton 1), Frank Stapleton (Arsenal 10), Don Givens (Birmingham City 45). **Subs:** Mickey Walsh (Queens Park Rangers 6) for Hayes (61 mins), Paul McGee (Queens Park Rangers 6) for Givens (71 mins). **Captain:** Johnny Giles. **Manager:** Johnny Giles (28). **Formation:** 4-3-3.

Denmark: O. Kjaer, F. Nielsen, P. Rontved, L. Larsen, S. Lerby, M. Olsen, F. Arnesen, F. Lund, A. Simonsen, B. Nielsen, P. Elkjaer. **Subs:** H. Agerbeck for B. Nielsen (76 mins).

Denmark dominated the first half but their poor finishing was to cost them the game. Early in the match Peyton dropped a cross from Benny Nielsen straight onto the feet of the incoming Simonsen but the Dane completely mis-hit his shot and Peyton recovered to stop the ball from going in. Two minutes later Benny Nielsen headed a Flemming Nielsen free kick on for Arnesen but his shot was well saved by Peyton at the expense of a corner. After 21 minutes another Benny Nielsen pass gave Simonsen another chance but, as Peyton advanced, he shot weakly and the Irish goalkeeper got a hand to the ball to deflect it out for a corner. On the half-hour the Irish lost possession in midfield allowing Simonsen to break past Holmes's tackle only to shoot wide inside the box. After 36 minutes Arnesen got past Gregg only for his cross-cum-shot to be hooked of the line by Mulligan with Martin deflecting the follow-up shot by Benny Nielsen out for a corner. Irish attacks were few so it came as a complete surprise when they scored a minute before the interval. Giles's long ball out to Hayes was controlled instantly by the forward who then crossed in. The ball sped across the goalmouth to Daly at the far post who connected with it first-time with the outside of his left foot. The ball curled around Lerby bounced and found the back of the net leaving Kjaer helpless.

The Danes never really recovered from that psychological blow and it was the Irish who got stronger as the game went on. Six minutes after the break Brady almost caught Kjaer off his line with a 25 yard chip but the Danish goalkeeper managed to get back in time to tip the ball over the bar. Benny Nielsen shot into the side netting and Simonsen missed a 'sitter' before Givens scored Ireland's second with a brilliant header. Stapleton found Daly out on the right and he sent over a perfect cross where Givens timed his jump expertly to send a powerful header back over the stranded Kjaer into the corner of the net. Soon after Mulligan got through the off-side trap to shoot wide as did Stapleton later following a mistake by Rontved. In the final eight minutes Daly chipped the ball over Kjaers head and into the net only for the goal to be disallowed for offside. Daly was brought down in the box by Lerby but no penalty was given. Arnesen had a shot just wide and Elkjaer had a header cleared off the line by Holmes. A hectic finish to a very good game which was at times rough. Benny Nielsen and Lerby were booked for Denmark as was Hayes for Ireland.

Match No. 171 BULGARIA Away

Saturday 19th May, 1979 – Sofia (European Championship)

BULGARIA (0) 1 Tzvetkov 80
REP. OF IRELAND (0) 0

Ref: Bucek (Austria) **Ground:** Vassil Levski Stadium **Att:** 20,000

Bulgaria: Y. Filipov, N. Granchanov, K. Ivkov, I. Iliev, Z. Vassilev, R. Zdravkov, K. Borissov, P. Panov, V. Voinov, A. Jeliazkov, T. Tzvetkov.

Ireland: Gerry Peyton (Fulham 6), Eamonn Gregg (Bohemians 5), David O'Leary (Arsenal 10), Mick Martin (Newcastle United 32), Jimmy Holmes (Tottenham Hotspur 29), Gerry Daly (Derby County 18), Johnny Giles (Shamrock Rovers 58), Liam Brady (Arsenal 21), Steve Heighway (Liverpool 22), Mickey Walsh (Queens Park Rangers 7), Don Givens (Birmingham City 46). **Subs:** Paddy Mulligan (West Bromwich Albion 45) for Holmes (58 mins), Paul McGee (Queens Park Rangers 7) for Walsh (75 mins). **Captain:** Johnny Giles. **Manager:** Johnny Giles (29). **Formation:** 4-3-3.

Ireland returned to Sofia but thankfully not to the trouble of two years ago. The game however was not without incident. In the first quarter of an hour Heighway was hacked down three times as he attempted to get away and on 15 minutes Daly crossed in from the right for Walsh to head the ball into the net. The goal was not allowed as the Irish striker was adjudged to be offside. Panov and Daly had shots saved by each goalkeeper with Peyton making another save to stop a cracking shot from Tzvetkov. Four minutes before the break Heighway was again taken down this time by Granchanov in the box but no penalty was forthcoming. A few minutes later Peyton made a good save to stop Jeliazkov heading in a Voinov cross.

Five minutes after the interval Givens headed a Heighway cross back to Giles but the latters header was over. Bulgaria were the superior team and having had two penalty claims turned down Jeliazkov got in a shot which was brilliantly saved one-handedly by Peyton. Two minutes later Holmes broke his leg in a fair challenge with Iliev. He was carried off in agony to be replaced by Mulligan. As the game entered its last half hour it was all Bulgaria. Peyton made another fantastic save when Granchanov met a Zdravkov cross with a point blank header only for the Irish goalkeeper to turn the ball over for a corner. Another defender, Ivkov broke through the Irish defence but shot wide when well placed. Panov also had a shot off target before Bulgaria finally got the goal they deserved. Tzvetkov knocked the ball out to Panov and ran on for the return leaving Gregg stranded. Panov chipped a ball to Tzvetkov and as it was dropping he hit it on the turn sending it curling across goal to go in off a post. In the final few minutes Peyton saved at Tzvetkov's feet and Brady cracked a shot just wide. Panov and Gregg were booked during the proceedings.

Holmes's injury, compounded by the fact that the plaster put on it was too tight, effectively ended his international career. He made just one more appearance in the Irish team before the FAI granted him a testimonial in 1985.

Eamonn Gregg in action against West Germany at Lansdowne Road. Johnny Giles awaits developments.

Match No. 172 — WEST GERMANY — Home

Tuesday 22nd May, 1979 – Dublin

REP. OF IRELAND (1) 1 Ryan 26
WEST GERMANY (1) 3 Rumminigge 28, Kelsch 81, Hoeness 90

Ref: Courtney (England) **Ground:** Lansdowne Road **Att:** 22,000

Ireland: Gerry Peyton (Fulham 7), Eamonn Gregg (Bohemians 6), David O'Leary (Arsenal 11), Mick Martin (Newcastle United 33), Paddy Mulligan (West Bromwich Albion 46), Tony Grealish (Orient 7), Johnny Giles (Shamrock Rovers 59), Liam Brady (Arsenal 22), Gerry Ryan (Brighton 3), Don Givens (Birmingham City 47), Frank Stapleton (Arsenal 11). **Subs:** Brendan O'Callaghan (Stoke City 1) for Givens (15 mins), Mickey Walsh (Queens Park Rangers 8) for Stapleton (67 mins). **Captain:** Johnny Giles. **Manager:** Johnny Giles (30). **Formation:** 4-3-3.

West Germany: J. Maier, M. Kaltz, B. Cullmann, K-H. Förster, B. Förster, H. Zimmermann, B. Schuster, H. Müller, K-H. Rumminigge, D. Hoeness, K. Allofs. **Subs:** D. Burdenski for Maier (half-time), W. Kelsch for Müller (half-time), C. Memering for Rummenigge (72 mins), J. Hartwig for Zimmermann (72 mins).

The Germans attacked from the start and Schuster put Rumminigge away for a shot that was just wide. Soon after Cullmann stopped Giles as he was about to shoot and the same player also deflected a shot from Stapleton out for a corner. Three minutes later Ryan headed a Gregg cross straight at the goalkeeper. After 15 minutes Givens went off injured and was replaced by Brendan O'Callaghan. Five minutes later Rumminigge sent Dieter Hoeness clear but the latter shot wide under pressure from O'Leary who managed to get back. Brendan O'Callaghan had a header wide before Ireland opened the scoring a couple of minutes later. A corner by Giles found Mulligan unmarked in the box and he crossed in for Ryan to find the top of the net with an overhead kick. In another 2 minutes Germany drew level. Gregg made a mess of an attempted pass back to Peyton and Allofs nipped in to send an outward pass across the area to the inrushing Rumminigge. The forward took it in his stride and threaded his shot along the ground into the goal. The Germans had slightly the better of an entertaining half with other chances falling to Zimmermann, whose shot was kicked off the line by O'Leary, and Müller, who had a shot saved by Peyton.

The Germans also had a good start to the second half with Kelsch's header from a Kaltz corner being cleared off the line by Mulligan. A minute later Allofs was put free by Dieter Hoeness but Peyton made a good save. Ireland then began to dominate and Brady forced a good save out of Burdenski with an 18 yard shot. Another Brady effort from long range, this time a chip, fell on the top of the net. Stapleton went off injured and 4 minutes later Ireland's best chance of the half fell to Grealish whose bullet-like shot was tiped over by Burdenski. Brady had another effort wide before Germany scored twice in the last 9 minutes. A pass by Martin, intended for Brady, was intercepted by Kelch who knocked it around Brady and ran clear. The German ran 45 yards to get to the box and as Peyton advanced and O'Leary closed he chipped the ball over Peyton into the net. In the last few seconds Karl-Heinz Förster hit a long 50 yard pass up into the Irish area. Dieter Hoeness shook off O'Leary and with his outstretched leg he deflected the ball low between Peyton and his left hand post.

This was the last full international played by Johnny Giles whose international career stretched over 20 years. His last official game was played a week later in a UNICEF benefit game when the Republic of Ireland selection drew 0-0 with World Cup winners Argentina. The Irish players were not capped on that occasion.

Match No. 173 — WALES — Away

Tuesday 11th September, 1979 – Swansea

WALES	**(1) 2**	Walsh 24, Curtis 53
REP. OF IRELAND	**(1) 1**	Jones (o.g.) 22

Ref: Stevens (England) **Ground:** Vetch Field **Att:** 6,825

Wales: D. Davies, P. Nicholas, G. Berry, L. Phillips, J. Jones, J. Mahoney, T. Yorath, B. Flynn, I. Walsh, A. Curtis, M. Thomas.

Ireland: Gerry Peyton (Fulham 8), Eamonn Gregg (Bohemians 7), David O'Leary (Arsenal 12), Mick Martin (Newcastle United 34), Paddy Mulligan (Shamrock Rovers 47), Tony Grealish (Luton Town 8), Liam Brady (Arsenal 23), Jerry Murphy (Crystal Palace 1), Gerry Ryan (Brighton 4), Brendan O'Callaghan (Stoke City 2), Frank Stapleton (Arsenal 12). **Captain:** Paddy Mulligan. **Manager:** Johnny Giles (31). **Formation:** 4-3-3.

A competitive game played before a small attendance on a bumpy pitch had a bright opening. In the first 15 minutes a shot from Curtis forced Peyton into a hurried save when it took a vicious bounce off the pitch. O'Leary headed off the line from Jones and Gregg was cautioned for a foul on Walsh. Ireland had an equal share of the play and Brady forced Davies into a finger-tip save to concede a corner. From Brady's flag-kick Jones, under pressure from O'Callaghan, headed the ball into his own net. A couple of minutes later Thomas got over a good cross and Walsh climbed highest to send a powerful downward header past Peyton into the goal for the equaliser. Both sides then saw a lot of the ball and it was not until the closing stages that there was a decent chance – a shot by Walsh which went across the goal only just wide.

Eight minutes after the resumption Nicholas found Walsh who knocked a long ball forward to Curtis. Curtis instantly controlled the ball before turning O'Leary and hammered a low shot into the back of the net. The Welsh then settled to hold that lead allowing Ireland to gain control of the match. A long ball by Brady got Stapleton in but he shot into the side netting. Ryan passed in for Grealish who had a powerful shot blocked by Phillips. After 80 minutes O'Callaghan knocked home a Brady cross but it was ruled out for offside. Near the end Brady had a shot blocked by Yorath and Walsh had a header saved by Peyton.

Match No. 174 **CZECHOSOLAVAKIA** **Away**

Wednesday 26th September, 1979 – Prague

CZECHOSLOVAKIA (2) 4 Ondrus 4, Nehoda 33, Kroupa 71, M. Masny 90
REP. OF IRELAND (0) 1 McGee 89

Ref: Milcenko (USSR) **Ground:** Evzena Rosickeho Strahov **Att:** 12,000

CSSR: Z. Hruska, J. Barmos, A. Ondrus, R. Vojacek, K. Gogh, F. Stambachr, J. Kozak, A. Penenka, M. Masny, Z. Nehoda, M. Gajdusek. **Subs:** J. Pollok for Stambachr (62 mins), K. Kroupa for Panenka (62 mins).

Ireland: Gerry Peyton (Fulham 9), Eamonn Gregg (Bohemians 8), Paddy Mulligan (Shamrock Rovers 48), Pierce O'Leary (Shamrock Rovers 1), John Devine (Arsenal 1), Mick Martin (Newcastle United 35), Tony Grealish (Luton Town 9), Fran O'Brien (Philadelphia Furies 1), Damien Richardson (Gillingham 3), Paul McGee (Queens Park Rangers 8), Terry Donovan (Aston Villa 1). **Subs:** Jeff Chandler (Leeds United 1) for Richardson (83 mins), Ray Treacy (Shamrock Rovers 42) for Donovan (83 mins), John Anderson (Preston 1) for Devine (88 mins). **Captain:** Paddy Mulligan. **Manager:** Johnny Giles (32). **Formation:** 4-3-3.

Ireland were forced to play a depleted side against the holders of the Henri Delaunay Cup. Not surprisingly the Irish suffered a heavy defeat but not without a fight.

The first chance of the match fell to Ireland after a minute. O'Brien's cross was layed back by Richardson into the path of Grealish who slammed a low shot just wide. After 4 minutes Ondrus broke from defence and gave the ball out to Kozak before running on. Kozak's cross was dummied by Nehoda for Ondrus to hit the ball on the run and score. A minute later Masny was denied a second when Peyton made a good save. Grealish then had a shot saved by Hruska and, at the other end, Gajdusek had a shot blocked. Both Grealish and Ondrus shot over before Peyton made a wonderful save to keep out a powerful downward header from Nehoda. A couple of minutes later Peyton brought off an equally fine save to stop a shot from Gajdusek. A minute later Peyton saved a fierce drive by Stambachr but was unable to hold the ball and it came to Nehoda who shot past the prostrated goalkeeper. Peyton got a touch but could not stop it from finding the net. After 42 minutes Richardson flick-headed a Devine cross towards goal only for Hruska to dive and stretch full-length to push the ball around the post. Just before the break Peyton brought off another good save to stop a shot from Nehoda.

Ireland began the second half in great style and a shot by Richardson was deflected wickedly by Ondrus but Hruska managed to change direction to save well. A push by Martin on Kroupa in the area went unnoticed by the referee while Mulligan headed off the line following a shot by Kozak.

Pierce O'Leary made his debut against Czechosolvakia.

Damien Richardson made his third and final appearance for Ireland against Czechosolavakia.

After 71 minutes Pierce O'Leary missed a cross from Gogh which gave Kroupa time to control the ball before blasting a shot into the net. Two minutes after McGee headed on a Richardson cross to Fran O'Brien but as he was about to shoot he was tackled from behind without penalty. Ireland were denied the chance of another penalty when Gogh handled in the box. Instead the referee awarded a free kick on the edge of the area. Richardson knocked the free to Grealish and he found Pierce O'Leary who headed the ball against the far post. Two minutes from the end Devine went off with a leg injury and in the last minute Hreuska and Treacy challenged for a Pierce O'Leary cross. The goalkeeper tried to punch the ball away but only succeeded in finding McGee who returned it to the back of the net. Two minutes into injury time Masny broke clear to shoot home the Czechs fourth goal with the help of a deflection off Anderson. Fran O'Brien and McGee were booked in the first half of an entertaining match.

Match No. 175 — BULGARIA — Home

Wednesday 17th October, 1979 – Dublin (European Championship)

REP. OF IRELAND (1) 3 Martin 40, Grealish 46, Stapleton 83
BULGARIA (0) 0

Ref: Einbeck (East Germany) **Ground:** Lansdowne Road **Att:** 18,000

Ireland: Gerry Peyton (Fulham 10), Paddy Mulligan (Shamrock Rovers 49), David O'Leary (Arsenal 13), Pierce O'Leary (Shamrock Rovers 2), Ashley Grimes (Manchester United 4), Mick Martin (Newcastle United 36), Liam Brady (Arsenal 24), Tony Grealish (Luton Town 10), Steve Heighway (Liverpool 23), Paul McGee (Queens Park Rangers 9), Frank Stapleton (Arsenal 13). **Captain:** Paddy Mulligan. **Manager:** Johnny Giles (33). **Formation:** 4-3-3.

Bulgaria: R. Goranov, Z. Vasilev, G. Dimitrov, G. Bonev, I. Iliev, V. Kostov, T. Barsov, P. Markov, A. Jeliazkov, B. Velitchkov, T. Tzvetkov. **Subs:** K. Kostadinov for Kostov (half-time).

The Irish produced a superb display against a defensively-minded Bulgarian side. After 16 minutes Brady's pass was put into the net by Grealish but he was offside. Eight minutes later another Brady pass found McGee unmarked in the area but the forward's header was well saved by Goranov. Heighway had a shot blocked and Stapleton appeared to be fouled in the box before the visitors had their only real opportunity of a match almost exclusively dominated by Ireland. It came after 28 minutes when a mistake by the otherwise excellent Brady set in motion a Bulgarian move which saw David O'Leary block a 20 yard shot from Tzvetkov. The ball ran loose to Jeliazkov about 10 yards out but his shot was tipped around the post by Peyton. After 40 minutes Brady picked out an unmarked Martin in the area with a tremendous 40 yard cross-field pass. Martin seemed to have lost control as he chested it down but he recovered well to slip past Bonev and crack a low shot into the far corner from a difficult angle. Just before the interval McGee had a chance but shot straight at the goalkeeper.

Thirty seconds after the resumption of play Pierce O'Leary, Brady and Stapleton moved the ball quickly downfield to Grealish. Grealish ran at the defence and tried to play a one-two with McGee. The ball however hit a Bulgarian leg and rebounded back to put Grealish clear in the box. The goalkeeper made a late advance and Grealish placed the ball wide of him into the corner of the net. Stapleton had a header off target, Martin hit the post with a cross-cum-shot and McGee had a header turned onto the crossbar and over by Goranov in further play. Velitchkov and Tzvetkov had half-chances for Bulgaria at the other end while another Brady through ball put Stapleton in but he shot straight at the goalkeeper. Seven minutes from the end Grimes and Brady combined for the latter to send over a perfect cross for Stapleton to beat Goranov at the near post with a great header. Just before the final whistle Brady almost got a fourth but his shot just shaved the outside of a post.

Match No. 176 **USA** **Home**

Monday 29th October, 1979 – Dublin

REP. OF IRELAND	**(0) 3**	Grealish 64, Givens 66, Anderson 68
USA	**(1) 2**	Dibernardo 11, Villa 63

Ref: Farrell (Ireland) **Ground:** Dalymount Park **Att:** 17,000

Ireland: Mick Kearns (Wolverhampton Wanderers 17), Chris Hughton (Tottenham Hotspur 1), Mick Martin (Newcastle United 37), Pierce O'Leary (Shamrock Rovers 3), Ashley Grimes (Manchester United 5), Jerry Murphy (Crystal Palace 2), Tony Grealish (Luton Town 11), Jeff Chandler (Leeds United 2), Steve Heighway (Liverpool 24), Paul McGee (Preston 10), Brendan O'Callaghan (Stoke City 3). **Subs:** Don Givens (Birmingham City 48) for McGee (45 mins), Paddy Mulligan (Shamrock Rovers 50) for Chandler (half-time), John Anderson (Preston 2) for O'Leary (65 mins). **Captain:** Mick Martin. **Manager:** Johnny Giles (34), (Alan Kelly). **Formation:** 4-3-3.

USA: W. Dubose, T. Bellinger, T. Keough, S. Pecher, G. Makowski, A. Dibernardo, R. Cantillo, B. Bandov, L. Nanchoff, G. Villa, M. Liveric. **Subs:** P. Vanderbeck for Dibernardo (57 mins), N. Pesa for Liveric (85 mins).
Sendings-off: Greg Villa (USA) 74 mins.

The visitors made a brilliant start and dominated the match for about 70% of the play. They got an early goal when Nanchoff beat Grimes and sent a high cross over to Dibernardo. The American managed to control the ball, flick it over Martin (who fell) and sent a powerful drive in off the underside of the crossbar. USA continued to dominate and on 27 minutes O'Leary was robbed by Liveric who fired in a shot which Kearns parried. The ball ran loose to Nanchoff who beat Kearns but Martin cleared off the line. Dobernardo was quickly on to the ball as it came out but his shot was again cleared away from the goal-line by Martin. Irish attacks were few but Heighway presented Murphy, McGee and O'Callaghan with good crosses only for the chances to be lost. Just on the stroke of half-time McGee went off with a knee injury to be replaced by Givens.

During the break Alan Kelly, who was in charge in Giles's absence, made another change. Paddy Mulligan came on to partner Pierce O'Leary at the centre of defence with Martin moving up to strengthen the midfield. So as the second half began the Irish midfield was Grealish, Martin and Murphy. Seconds after the restart Givens nodded down for Grimes to shoot on the turn with Dubose forced into a good save. After 56 minutes a Martin cross found Murphy at the near post but he shot over. Seven minutes later Liveric crossed in for Villa to shake off challenges from O'Leary and Grimes before sending a bullet-like drive into the roof of the net. Sixty seconds later O'Callaghan gave a pass to Givens whose cross was cleared badly by Bellinger to Grealish

Don Givens, arms upraised in salute, scores against the USA.

and he smacked a shoulder-high shot to the back of the net. Pierce O'Leary then went off with cramp and was replaced by Anderson. After 66 minutes a Grimes free kick found Heighway on the left touchline. His cross was headed on by O'Callaghan for Givens to get his boot to the ball despite the challenge of Keough and shoot past Dubose. In another couple of minutes Ireland's comeback was complete. Heighways long throw in was headed on by O'Callaghan with the American defence in disarray. The ball ran loose for Grimes who left it for Anderson. The substitute avoided a tackle and hit a shot from 15 yards which went through a crowded area on its way to the net. The visitors then allowed their frustration to manifest itself in a couple of bad tackles for which Nanchoff was booked (for a foul on Grimes) and Villa was sent off (for kicking Anderson). Pecher almost suffered a similar dismissal for arguing the decision. In the final few minutes O'Callaghan had a header just over from Murphy's cross.

Match No. 177 NORTHERN IRELAND Away

Wednesday 21st November, 1979 – Belfast (European Championship)

NORTHERN IRELAND (0) 1 Armstrong 54
REP. OF IRELAND (0) 0

Ref: Daina (Switzerland) **Ground:** Windsor Park **Att:** 15,000

Northern Ireland P. Jennings, J. Nicholl, A. Hunter, C. Nicholl, S. Nelson, M. O'Neill, D. McCreery, V. Moreland, S. McIlroy, G. Armstrong, D. Spence. **Subs:** T. Cassidy for O'Neill (66 mins).

Ireland: Mick Kearns (Wolverhampton Wanderers 18), John Devine (Arsenal 2), David O'Leary (Arsenal 14), Pierce O'Leary (Shamrock Rovers 4), Ashley Grimes (Manchester United 6), Gerry Daly (Derby County 19), Mick Martin (Newcastle United 38), Tony Grealish (Luton Town 12), Steve Heighway (Liverpool 25), Paul McGee (Preston 11), Frank Stapleton (Arsenal 14). **Subs:** Joe Waters (Grimsby Town 2) for Daly (53 mins), Don Givens (Birmingham City 49) for McGee (75 mins). **Captain:** Mick Martin. **Manager:** Johnny Giles (35). **Formation:** 4-3-3.

In sharp contrast to the previous meeting this was a very lively affair, full of attacking football and incident. Since that initial encounter the situation had altered and, with the Republic needing both points to stay in touch, both sides played open football unencumbered by defensive tactics.

Northern Ireland made the better opening with O'Neill forcing Kearns into a good save after 3 minutes. The Republic's goalkeeper was caught out by an in-swinging corner a few minutes later and Martin was forced to head clear from the goalmouth. On 19 minutes Kearns dropped a Jimmy Nicholl cross but he recovered in time to deny Spence. Then the Republic went on the offensive with Heighway beating Jimmy Nicholl and crossing in for McGee to have a good shot turned out for a corner by Jennings. A minute later O'Neill and Spence combined to give Armstrong a great chance but he shot wide form 6 yards out. Grealish then brought another good save from Jennings when the latter turned over the former's volley. Heighway tricked his way past two defenders before his shot too was saved by the North's goalkeeper. After 39 minutes a corner by Daly was met with a powerful header by Stapleton. As the ball sped towards goal, Jennings reacted instantly to tip it over from just under the crossbar. A minute from the break another corner, this time by Heighway, gave Stapleton another header chance but again Jennings made a brilliant one-handed save.

Northern Ireland again took up the running at the start of the second half. In the first few minutes Spence had a shot saved by Kearns and then another deflected wide by Devine. Another deflection denied Chris Nicholl a goal before Daly went off with a head injury. His replacement, Waters, had only just come on when the North scored. A throw-in by Nelson was returned to him via Armstrong and McIlroy. Nelson crossed high into the goalmouth where Kearns was late in going for it and Armstrong darted in to direct his header into the corner of the net. Five minutes later David O'Leary almost got in for an equaliser but Jennings again made a great save at the expense of a corner. Grealish had two late chances but both his shots were stopped by Jennings.

International Record 1970-1979	P	W	D	L	F	A
1970-1979	54	16	12	26	63	79
Home	23	12	5	6	35	22
Away	27	2	7	18	21	50
Neutral	4	2	0	2	7	7

International Record 1926-1979	P	W	D	L	F	A
1926-1979	177	58	35	84	251	328
Home	87	37	19	31	148	137
Away	85	19	16	50	96	183
Neutral	5	2	0	3	7	8

World Cup Record	P	W	D	L	F	A
	38	8	8	22	46	81
Home	19	6	6	7	31	32
Away	18	2	2	14	15	48
Neutral	1	0	0	1	0	1

EuropeanChampionship Record	P	W	D	L	F	A
	33	10	8	15	39	52
Home	17	9	4	4	29	18
Away	16	1	4	11	10	34

Number of players capped by Ireland	291
Number of goalscorers for Ireland	84 (+ 4 own goal)
Number of Nations played	33

Leading Goalscorers		Most Capped Players	
Don Givens	18	Johnny Giles	59
Noel Cantwell	14	Paddy Mulligan	50
Jimmy Dunne	13	Don Givens	49
Dermot Curtis	8	Alan Kelly	47
Arthur Fitzsimons	7	Ray Treacy	42
Paddy Moore		Charlie Hurley	40
Alf Ringstead		Mick Martin	38
Andy McEvoy	6	Noel Cantwell	36
Con Martin		Tony Dunne	33
Gerry Daly	5	Joe Haverty	32
Fionan Fagan		Con Martin	30
Johnny Giles		Johnny Carey	29
Eamonn Rogers		Jimmy Holmes	
Ray Treacy		Peter Farrell	28
Davy Walsh		Terry Conroy	27

Penalties awarded to Ireland 33 (25 scored, 4 saved, 4 missed)

Penalties awarded against Ireland 15 (10 scored, 4 saved, 1 miss)

Hat-tricks for Ireland

John Joe Flood	3 goals	v Belgium	1929
Paddy Moore	4 goals	v Belgium	1934
Don Givens	3 goals	v USSR	1974
Don Givens	4 goals	v Turkey	1975

Hat-tricks against Ireland

Kalle Palmer, Sweden	3 goals	1929
Jef Mermans, Belgium	3 goals	1950
Adolf Huber, Austria	3 goals	1952
Milos Milutinovic, Yugoslavia	3 goals	1955
Tommy Taylor, England	3 goals	1957
Jesus Maria Pereda, Spain	3 goals	1965
Josef Adamec, Czechoslovakia	3 goals	1969
Thomas Parits, Austria	3 goals	1971

Irish Captains

30 Johnny Giles
23 Noel Cantwell
21 Charlie Hurley
19 Johnny Carey
13 Paddy Mulligan
12 Peter Farrell
8 Charlie Turner
5 Shay Brennan, Jimmy Dunne, Paddy Gaskins, Con Martin
4 Tony Dunne, William Glen, Mick Martin
2 Tommy Eglington, Mick O'Brien, Pat Saward
1 Frank Brady, John Burke, Harry Chatton, John Dempsey, Seamus Dunne, Al Finucane, John Joe Flood, Mick Foley, Theo Foley, Alan Kelly, Jack McCarthy, Gerry Mackey, Mick Meagan.

Own goals for Ireland

Josef Posipal, West Germany	1951
Karl Koller, Austria	1963
Jose Angel Iribar, Spain	1965
Joey Jones, Wales	1979

Own goals by Irish players

Seamus Dunne for Sweden	1960
Andy McEvoy for Belgium	1965
Al Finucane for Czechoslovakia (H)	1967
John Dempsey for Czechoslovakia (A)	1967
Jimmy Dunne II for Austria	1971
Mick Martin for Turkey	1974

Irish Players sent-off

John Dempsey v Hungary	1969
Don Givens v Ecuador	1972
Turlough O'Connor v Chile	1972
Don Givens v Chile	1974
Terry Mancini v USSR	1974
Mick Martin v Turkey	1975
Mick Martin v Bulgaria	1977
Noel Campbell v Bulgaria	1977

Leading goalscorer against Ireland

5 Wlodzimierz Lubanski, Poland

Match No. 178 — ENGLAND — Away

Wednesday 6th February, 1980 – London (European Championship)

ENGLAND (1) 2 Keegan 34, 75
REP. OF IRELAND (0) 0

Ref: Scheurell (West Germany) **Ground:** Wembley Stadium **Att:** 92,299

England: R. Clemence, T. Cherry, D. Watson, P. Thompson, K. Sansom, T. McDermott, K. Keegan, B. Robson, L. Cunningham, D. Johnson, T. Woodcock. **Subs:** S. Coppell for Johnson (60 mins).

Ireland: Gerry Peyton (Fulham 11), Chris Hughton (Tottenham Hotspur 2), David O'Leary (Arsenal 15), Mark Lawrenson (Brighton 8), Ashley Grimes (Manchester United 7), Gerry Daly (Derby County 20), Tony Grealish (Luton Town 13), Liam Brady (Arsenal 25), Fran O'Brien (Philadelphia Furies 2), Steve Heighway (Liverpool 26), Frank Stapleton (Arsenal 15). **Subs:** Ron Healey (Cardiff City 2) for Peyton (60 mins), Pierce O'Leary (Shamrock Rovers 5), for D. O'Leary (68 mins). **Captain:** Liam Brady. **Manager:** Johnny Giles (36). **Formation:** 4-4-2.

An unexciting game was highlighted by a spectacular second goal from Keegan. Ireland showed well in the opening few minutes but the first scoring opportunity fell to England's Keegan whose glancing header was wide. After 8 minutes Grimes set up Grealish for a shot which was blocked by Watson with Clemence out quickly to grab the rebound ahead of Stapleton. Peyton subsequently had trouble dealing with some of England's crosses and both Irish centre-backs had to clear from the goalmouth. After 34 minutes Peyton missed another cross, this time from McDermott, allowing Johnson to head back across the face of the goal for Keegan to shoot home past three defenders. Coming up to the break Stapleton's header from a Brady corner caused Clemence some problems before he saved.

Ireland again started the half on the attack and after 7 minutes Stapleton headed just wide from a Brady free kick. Grealish then had a shot saved by Clemence before Heighway beat Sansom and had a shot deflected into the side netting by a defender. After 60 minutes both Peyton and Johnson were injured when they clashed going for a cross from Keegan. As the ball ran loose Cunningham was quickly on to it but his shot was blocked on the line by Lawrenson. Peyton and Johnson were forced to retire with their injuries and were replaced by Healey and Coppell respectively. Three minutes later a cross from Hughton gave Stapleton another headed chance but this too was wide. David O'Leary was replaced by his brother Pierce following an injury to the former. With 15 minutes to go Keegan won a heading duel with Brady in the Irish half and set off towards goal. As the Irish defenders converged on him when he reached the edge of the area, the English captain spotted Healey off his line and chipped the ball over his head into the empty net. This goal virtually 'killed' the game as a contest and there were no further goal attempts of note.

Match No. 179 — CYPRUS — Away

Wednesday 26th March, 1980 – Nicosia (World Cup)

CYPRUS (1) 2 Pantziaras 27, Kaiafas 74 (pen)
REP. OF IRELAND (3) 3 McGee 8, 37, Lawrenson 23

Ref: Sharir (Israel) **Ground:** Bishop Makarios Stadium **Att:** 10,000

Cyprus: F. Stylianou, A. Papacostas, S. Lyssandrou, N. Pantziaros, S. Papadopoulos, F. Neofitou, L. Mauroudis, A. Kissonergis, P. Demetriou, S. Kaiafas, A. Kanaris. **Subs:** M. Tsingis for Demetriou (half-time), P. Theofanos for Kanaris (76 mins).

Ireland: Gerry Peyton (Fulham 12), Tony Grealish (Luton Town 14), David O'Leary (Arsenal 16), Mark Lawrenson (Brighton 9), Ashley Grimes (Manchester United 8), Gerry Daly (Derby County 21), Liam Brady (Arsenal 26), Jerry Murphy (Crystal Palace 3), Steve Heighway (Liverpool 27), Paul McGee (Preston 12), Frank Stapleton (Arsenal 16). **Subs:** Gerry Ryan (Brighton 5) for Heighway (53 mins), Fran O'Brien (Philadelphia Furies 3) for Murphy (72 mins). **Captain:** Liam Brady. **Manager:** Johnny Giles (37). **Formation:** 4-3-3.

Ireland's 11th World Cup campaign began on the island of Cyprus. It was the second game of World Cup 1982 and with the earlier match (between Israel and Northern Ireland) finishing scoreless it was left to Paul McGee to score the first goal of the tournament. For Ireland it was to be another tournament of realistic ambition which would end in bitter disappointment.

Ireland had a great start with a goal after 8 minutes of constant pressure. A pin-point 40 yard ball from Brady found Stapleton running into the 6 yard area. Stapleton knocked the ball back across the goalmouth and McGee powered in to shoot it into the top of the net. The goal was originally given as an own goal by Stefanas Lyssandrou but McGee was in no doubt that it had gone in off his boot. Further Irish pressure had its reward in a second goal after 23 minutes. Lawrenson got possession on the edge of the Irish box and broke upfield. When he reached the half-way line he passed the ball to Brady and ran on. The Irish captain held the ball and then sent it forward for Lawrenson, clear in the Cypriot area, to shoot past Stylianou from close range. Cyprus pulled one goal back when a header from Kaiafas fell to Kissonergis whose shot was blocked by Lawrenson only for Pantziaras to scramble the ball over the line. Eight minutes later Murphy shot home a cross from O'Leary from the edge of the box but the referee disallowed the goal for offside even though the linesman had not flagged. In another couple of minutes O'Leary headed down a Brady cross for McGee to stab the ball home. The half ended with two Brady pile-drivers one of which was saved while the other was just over.

Ireland continued their attacks in the second half despite losing Heighway with an injury after 8 minutes. Stapleton had an early effort off target before a bad back pass from Grimes let Kaiafas in. He shot past Peyton but Grealish got back to clear off the line. Stapleton had a shot from just outside the Cypriot box go over the crossbar and 3 minutes later a shot from Daly was turned onto a post by the goalkeeper. After 64 minutes a header from McGee was turned over for a corner by Stylianou. From Brady's flag-kick Murphy curled a long-range shot off a post and wide. Murphy then had to go of with a twisted ankle before Cyprus scored again. O'Leary obstructed Kaiafas in the box and the referee awarded a penalty although his first decision appeared to be an indirect free kick. Kaiafas took the spot-kick and gave Peyton no chance. Ireland held on for their first World Cup away victory since 1957 but they should have not had to be in that position.

On 15th April Johnny Giles resigned as manager of the Republic of Ireland stating that he wanted to concentrate on managing Shamrock Rovers. Other reasons obviously played a part in his decision but speculation about these can only be conjecture. Giles served Ireland as player and manager for over twenty years and departed having delivered them from the dark ages.

Match No. 180 — SWITZERLAND — Home

Wednesday 30th April, 1980 – Dublin

REP. OF IRELAND (2) 2 Givens 12, Daly 41
SWITZERLAND (0) 0

Ref: Thomas (Wales) **Ground:** Lansdowne Road **Att:** 20,000

Ireland: Gerry Peyton (Fulham 13), David Langan (Derby County 3), Kevin Moran (Manchester United 1), Mark Lawrenson (Brighton 10), Chris Hughton (Tottenham Hotspur 3), Gerry Daly (Derby County 22), Tony Grealish (Luton Town 15), Gary Waddock (Queens Park Rangers 1), Gerry Ryan (Brighton 6), Don Givens (Birmingham City 50), Paul McGee (Preston 13). **Captain:** Tony Grealish. **Manager:** Alan Kelly (1). **Formation:** 4-3-3.

Switzerland: K. Engel, Heinz Hermann, J. Stohler, G. Coutaz, L. Bizzini, M. Schnyder, U. Berberis, R. Botteron, C. Andrey, H. J. Pfister, C. Sulser. **Subs:** M. Weber for Schnyder (half-time), E. Maissen for Andrey (75 mins).

Alan Kelly was appointed manager of Ireland folowing the resignation of Giles. His term of office was not to last long as he was forced to quit the job, due to club commitments, soon after this match. For the record this was his third game in charge (two as Giles's deputy) and all three ended in victory.

Ireland dominated the first half against an apathetic Swiss side. Soon after the kick-off Waddock shot over from 20 yards following a cross from Langan. After 12 minutes Langan found Daly with a long pass up the field. Daly crossed in to the far post and Givens beat Coutaz to head powerfully downwards straight into the corner of the net. Ryan and Givens subsequently missed further opportunities to increase the lead while Grealish had a shot blocked with Ryan just off target with the rebound. Swiss chances were few with Peyton in action twice; saving a cross from Botteron and a shot from Berberis. Four minutes before the interval Ireland scored again. A cross by Langan was knocked into the air by a Swiss defender. As the ball came down Ryan flicked it on with the back of his head for Daly. As the ball bounced Daly turned on it and smacked a shot into the top corner of the net.

The second half was sluggish with only one good Irish scoring chance. That came soon after the restart when a free kick by Daly was headed over by Moran. The Swiss, on the other hand, came into the game a lot more. Pfister had a header saved while Sulser pressured Moran into heading a cross from Pfister into his own net. It could have ruined the defenders debut but a Swiss player was offside and the goal was ruled out. McGee shot a half-chance well wide and Peyton saved from Heinz Hermann before the final whistle blew.

Match No. 181 — ARGENTINA — Home

Friday 16th May, 1980 – Dublin

REP. OF IRELAND (0) 0

ARGENTINA (1) 1 Valencia 28

Ref: Courtney (England) **Ground:** Lansdowne Road **Att:** 30,100

Ireland: Gerry Peyton (Fulham 14), David Langan (Derby County 4), Kevin Moran (Manchester United 2), Pierce O'Leary (Shamrock Rovers 6), Chris Hughton (Tottenham Hotspur 4), Gerry Daly (Derby County 23), Tony Grealish (Luton Town 16), Gary Waddock (Queens Park Rangers 2), Steve Heighway (Liverpool 28), Don Givens (Birmingham City 51), Paul McGee (Preston 14). **Subs:** Ray O'Brien (Notts County 5) for Grealish (half-time), Gerry Ryan (Brighton 7) for Waddock (75 mins). **Captain:** Tony Grealish. **Manager:** Eoin Hand (1). **Formation:** 4-3-3.

Argentina: U. Fillol, J. Olguin, J. Simon, D. Passarella, A. Tarantini, J. Barbas, A. Gallego, D. Maradona, S. Santamroia, R. Diaz, J. D. Valencia. **Subs:** M. Calderon for Diaz (73 mins).

Argentina were the better team overall and deserved their victory. Ireland had few chances but emerged with some credit considering the team was in transition. Eoin Hand took charge of the team on a care-taker basis but was appointed manager after the match.

Ireland started nervously and a mistake by Moran gave Santamrioa a great chance but Peyton saved well. Three minutes later Maradona played a one-two with Valencia to get free but the Irish goalkeeper was out quickly to snuff out the danger. Ireland's only chance of the half came when Daly beat a resolute defence to head a Heighway cross straight at the goalkeeper. After 28 minutes Maradona was fouled by Grealish on the edge of the Irish box. Maradona took the free kick himself and sent a low ball powerfully to the 6 yard area where Jose Daniel Valencia stooped down to glance it well out of Peytons reach with a flashing header. Four minutes later Maradona curled another free kick around the Irish wall but Peyton made a magnificent diving save to tip the ball around the post. Soon after Diaz and Valencia shot good opportunities wide and near the break another free kick from Mardadona went just over.

Hand was forced into a change during the break when Grealish, who injured his groin early in the match, was unable to continue. This weakened the Irish midfield but the second half saw Argentina play a more containing game. The visitors finishing was weak and when chances fell to Barbas, Gallego and Valencia they failed to capitalise. In the final 10 minutes Ireland had its best spell. Daly had a shot saved and Givens a header wide before Daly had the best chance of the second half. McGee headed on a Givens header to put Daly running clear. As the Argentinian goalkeeper came out Daly chipped the ball over his head but the ball bounced wide. Langan (Ireland) and Gallego (Argentina) received yellow cards for fouls in the second half.

Liam Brady, captain of the Republic of Ireland, jumps highest to clear the danger from a Dutch attack.

Match No. 182 HOLLAND Home

Wednesday 10th September, 1980 – Dublin (World Cup)

REP. OF IRELAND (0) 2 Daly 79, Lawrenson 84
HOLLAND (0) 1 Tahamata 57

Ref: Lund-Sorensen (Denmark) **Ground:** Lansdowne Road **Att:** 30,000

Ireland: Gerry Peyton (Fulham 15), David Langan (Birmingham City 5), David O'Leary (Arsenal 17), Pierce O'Leary (Shamrock Rovers 7), Chris Hughton (Tottenham Hotspur 5), Gerry Daly (Coventry City 24), Mark Lawrenson (Brighton 11), Tony Grealish (Luton Town 17), Liam Brady (Juventus 27), Frank Stapleton (Arsenal 17), Don Givens (Birmingham City 52). **Captain:** Liam Brady. **Manager:** Eoin Hand (2). **Formation:** 4-4-2.

Holland: J. Hiele, B. Wijnstekers, M. Vander Korput, R. Spelbos, E. Brandts, D. Schoenaker, J. Peters, F. Thijssen, J. Van Deinsen. T. Van Mierlo, S. Tahamata. **Subs:** J. Metgot for Vander Korput (half-time), W. Vander Kerkhof for Schoenaker (64 mins).

Ireland's new manager brought a new style of play to his side. Dispensing with the slow build-up, Hand opted for a fast attacking policy with players getting forward as much as possible. This tactic almost back-fired against the Dutch but the Irish deserved their victory in a very entertaining match.

Soon after the kick-off a Daly cross was deflected to Stapleton by Spelbos. The Irish strikers' first shot was blocked back out to him but his second effort thumped off the upright. A few minutes later a lovely pass from Grealish put Brady through but Hiele brought off a great save. In the 14th minute a long free kick by Peters found Thijssen running through but his shot hit the bar and went over. David O'Leary stopped Peters from getting in for another chance while, at the other end, Daly was taken down in the box when going for a Givens cross but no penalty was awarded; nor for similar fouls later on Stapleton and Daly, again. After 32 minutes a well-rehearsed free kick saw Brady jumping over the ball, Daly hitting the free to Stapleton who headed down to the in-rushing Brady only for Hiele to make a fine save at the Irish captains feet. A couple of minutes later another free kick, this time by Brady, found Stapletons head again and his goalbound effort was scrambled away for a corner. Four minutes before the break a cross from Brady was headed on by Stapleton only for Lawrenson to shoot badly wide from close range.

The Dutch made a good start to the second half and Spelbos exchanged passes with Peters to have a good shot well saved at the expense of a corner. From the flag-kick the ball was deflected out to Peters whose powerful volley was again saved well by Peyton. A free kick by Van Deinsen was flicked on by Van Mierlo but Peyton reacted quickly to save the ball just before Thijssen could get a finishing touch. After 10 minutes a long ball from Pierce O'Leary dropped down in the box. As the goalkeeper tried to claim it, Daly managed to get to the ball first and leaving the goalkeeper stranded, he placed his shot well only for Thijssen to get back to clear the ball off the goal-line. Two minutes later the Dutch took the lead. Van Mierlo worked his way in along the left side of the box. Breaking a couple of weak tackles he overran the ball. Peyton came out to smother it but the ball rolled loose allowing Van Mierlo to poke it across to the unmarked Tahamata who had no difficulty in scoring. The Irish recovered from the set-back to dominate the rest of the game. Grealish had a bullet-like shot knocked over the bar by Hiele after 18 minutes and a corner by Brady was only just missed by Lawrenson at the far post a few minutes later. After 75 minutes a tremendous run from Brady ended with his shot being deflected out for a corner. Four minutes after this a ball from Hughton, for Stapleton, was knocked up into the air by Van der Korput. As the ball dropped down both Brady and Peters went for it. Brady got there first and knocked the ball inside for Grealish who then played a one-two with Stapleton. Grealish got the return on the edge of the box and as the Dutch came out to play offside he flicked the ball in for Daly to run onto to shoot past the advancing goalkeeper. In another 5 minutes the Irish were ahead. Daly was fouled by Metgot about 30 yards from goal. Brady took the resulting free kick and chiped the ball wide of the Dutch wall where both Lawrenson and David O'Leary were free. Lawrenson ran onto it and met the ball with a diving header which found the bottom corner of the net. In the last few minutes the Dutch tried for an equaliser and they came close when a cross by Tahamata was knocked across the goalmouth by Peters only for Lawrenson to whack it clear. Two Dutchmen were booked, one in each half; Brandts for a foul on Givens and Tahamata for a minor infringement.

Gerry Daly (extreme left) *shoots past the advancing Joop Hiele in the Dutch goal, to level the match.*

Match No. 183 BELGIUM Home

Wednesday 15th October, 1980 – Dublin (World Cup)

REP. OF IRELAND (1) 1 Grealish 42
BELGIUM (1) 1 Cluytens 13

Ref: Rolles (Luxembourg) **Ground:** Lansdowne Road **Att:** 40,000

Ireland: Gerry Peyton (Fulham 16), David Langan (Birmingham City 6), Mark Lawrenson (Brighton 12), Kevin Moran (Manchester United 3), Chris Hughton (Tottenham Hotspur 6), Gerry Daly (Coventry City 25), Tony Grealish (Luton Town 18), Liam Brady (Juventus 28), Steve Heighway (Liverpool 29), Don Givens (Birmingham City 53), Frank Stapleton (Arsenal 18). **Subs:** Paul McGee (Preston 15) for Givens (75 mins). **Captain:** Liam Brady. **Manager:** Eoin Hand (3). **Formation:** 4-3-3.

Belgium: J-M. Pfaff, E. Gerets, L. Millecamps, W. Meeuws, M. Renquin, W. Van Moer, R. Vandereychen, L. Coeck, A. Cluytens, E. Vandenberg, J. Ceulemans. **Subs:** J. Heyligen for Van Moer (84 mins), M. De Wolf for Millecamps (88 mins).

Belgium, through a combination of an effective use of the offside trap and swift attacks, dictated this match from start to finish. Both sides played well and a draw was a fair result of a good, if frustrating, game.

Peyton was in action early saving a wayward back-pass from Hughton and also stopping a good Belgian attack involving Vandereychen and Cluytens. Grealish almost got through at the other end but Renquin made a last gasp tackle to stop him. Soon after Grealish got through again but was offside when he fell in the box under a challenge from Pfaff. The offside trap was to catch out Langan, Daly and Stapleton later in the match. After 13 minutes a pass from Vandenberg was headed on by Van Moer to Cluytens. The latter showed a tremendous burst of speed to leave Hughton and Lawrenson for 'dead' and when Peyton came out, forcing him wide, Cluytens finished well from a narrow angle. Renquin made another good tackle to stop Daly but it was Belgium who had the best of the chances. Peyton kicked away a shot from Vandenberg while Ceulemans shot badly wide when put clear. On 37 minutes a cross from Moran was met by a superb header from Daly with Pfaff making an equally superb one-handed save to turn it over.

Tony Grealish scores Ireland's goal in their 1-1 draw with Belgium.

Three minutes before the break Daly's pass found Brady. As the defence moved out, Brady swept it out to the right. The ball struck a defender but fell to Grealish. The linesman raised his flag but the referee waved play on. Grealish rounded Pfaff and from an acute angle placed his shot into the net ahead of a string of retreating defenders.

The second half was full of tension but few chances and the Belgians settled for containment. The only chance of note came after 7 minutes when a ball from Grealish found Daly in the clear but as the latter controlled the ball Pfaff came out and made a brave save at Daly's feet.

Match No. 184 FRANCE Away

Tuesday 28th October, 1980 – Paris (World Cup)

FRANCE (1) 2 Platini 10, Zimako 77
REP. OF IRELAND (0) 0

Ref: Lamo Castillo (Spain) **Ground:** Parc des Princes **Att:** 46,300

France: D. Dropsey, P. Battison, L. Specht, C. Lopez, M. Bossis, J-F. Larios, J. Tigana, M. Platini, D. Rocheteau, B. Lacombe, D. Six. **Subs:** J. Zimako for Lacombe (66 mins), J. Petit for Platini (74 mins).

Ireland: Gerry Peyton (Fulham 17), David Langan (Birmingham City 7), Mark Lawrenson (Brighton 13), Kevin Moran (Manchester United 4), Chris Hughton (Tottenham Hotspur 7), Mick Martin (Newcastle United 39), Tony Grealish (Luton Town 19), Liam Brady (Juventus 29), Steve Heighway (Liverpool 30), Frank Stapleton (Arsenal 19), Michael Robinson (Brighton 1). **Subs:** Gerry Ryan (Brighton 8) for Martin (78 mins). **Captain:** Liam Brady. **Manager:** Eoin Hand (4). **Formation:** 4-3-3.

The FAI were involved in two controversial incidents in the days leading up to this game. First they made use of the FIFA release ruling to force the English Football League to free the players from Arsenal, Tottenham Hotspur, Coventry City and Birmingham City from League Cup commitments. This was the first time the FAI used this prerogative and while it might have had a damaging affect on player release for non-competitive matches it was a vital precedent. The second controversy involved the case of Michael Robinson who expressed the wish to play for Ireland, the birthplace of his grandmother. FIFA rules only provide for nationality as far as parents but this was circumvented when Roinson's mother took out Irish citizenship thus making him eligible for an Irish passport. It was an abuse of the ruling and one which would bring scorn on the FAI. The FAI would continue to use the rule (as was their right) and be criticised for it even though they were not the only country to take advantage of it. Robinson and the other 'released' players took part in the game which would provide a third controversy.

The French got off to a flying start with Lacombe and Six finding openings before they scored after 10 minutes. From a throw-in by Bossis, Tigana got possession and sent a high curling ball over the head of Hughton for Platini to trap before shooting past the advancing Peyton. Five minutes later Platini sent a great through ball to Lacombe but the French forward completely mishit his shot in front of goal. The opening French onslaught had caught Ireland 'cold' but they recovered to launch their own onslaught on the French goal. After 17 minutes a pass from Langan was knocked back into the path of Grealish by Robinson with Dropsey forced to parry the fiercely-driven shot. A cross by Martin was punched off Robinsons head by Dropsey. Robinson chased after the ball and retrieved it on the back line before giving it to Brady. The Irish captain then worked an opening and when he crossed in there was Robinson again to send in a header which Dropsey saved. Brady then worked another opening a few minutes later when he beat three men before crossing to the far post where both Robinson and Moran got in each others way and missed the ball.

The Irish continued their offensive in the second half and after 10 minutes Grealish found Stapleton who sent a long pass across to Brady. Brady beat one man and sent a through ball for Hughton to run onto. Hughton outpaced the defence and sent in a blistering shot which was again parried by the goalkeeper. A couple of minutes later Heighway got free and sent a perfect cross to the far post where Moran outjumped the goalkeeper and a defender to knock the ball down for Robinson to blast in home. The referee disallowed the goal for handball against Moran but the Irish defender had clearly headed the ball down. The French then caught Ireland twice on the break with Rocheteau shooting wide and having another effort saved by Peyton. Lawrenson also hit the post with a back pass before France scored again. Six and Zimako broke clear from the centre circle and with, only Martin back to cover, Six easily found Zimako who shot past Peyton from 12 yards. Late in the game a shot from Robinson was brilliantly saved by Dropsey and two minutes from the end Ryan shot against the post when the French goalkeeper dropped a cross from Lawrenson.

Match No. 185 — CYPRUS — Home

Wednesday 19th November, 1980 – Dublin (World Cup)

REP. OF IRELAND (4) 6 Daly 11 (pen), 24, Grealish 25, Robinson 29, Stapleton 46, Hughton 65

CYPRUS (0) 0

Ref: Gudmundsson (Iceland) **Ground:** Lansdowne Road **Att:** 22,000

Ireland: Gerry Peyton (Fulham 18), David Langan (Birmingham City 8), Mark Lawrenson (Brighton 14), Kevin Moran (Manchester United 5), Chris Hughton (Tottenham Hotspur 8), Gerry Daly (Coventry City 26), Tony Grealish (Luton Town 20), Liam Brady (Juventus 30), Steve Heighway (Liverpool 31), Frank Stapleton (Arsenal 20), Michael Robinson (Brighton 2). **Subs:** Don Givens (Birmingham City 54) for Robinson (76 mins). **Captain:** Liam Brady. **Manager:** Eoin Hand (5). **Formation:** 4-3-3.

Cyprus: A. Constantino, L. Loucia, S. Lyssandrou, N. Pantziaras, E. Erotokritou, F. Kalotheou, T. Theofanous, A. Miamiliotis, Y. Yiagoudakis, S. Kaiafas, M. Tsingis. **Subs:** K. Kovis for Kaiafas (half-time), L. Mavroudis for Miamiliatis (64 mins).

A very one-sided game saw Ireland create all the openings and could have doubled their winning margin. Early in the match Brady shot wide from a Langan cross but after 11 minutes Ireland scored their first. Robinson, with his back to goal, trapped a Heighway cross but was taken down from behind by Kalotheou. The referee awarded a penalty and, after booking Kalotheou for arguing with the decision, watched as Daly sent the goalkeeper the wrong way from the spot-kick. Soon after Moran had a header cleared off the line by Loucia and Roinson had another header strike the crossbar before Ireland scored again. A corner by Brady was headed on to Lawrenson by Daly. Lawrenson fell as he attempted to turn on the edge of the area and Lyssandrou was in quickly to knock it back towards his own goal where Daly pounced to sweep the ball under the goalkeeper. A minute later a strong run by Hughton ended with his cross from the back line being cleared out to Grealish who sent a first-time shot speeding to the back of the net. In another 4 minutes a cross from Stapleton was also met first time by Robinson whose volley flashed past Constantino. Just before the break Stapleton got to a Langan cross just before Constantino but his header just went wide.

A minute after the break Robinson headed on a Brady pass for Stapleton to run onto and curl the ball over Constantino to the net. Hughton sent another curled shot just wide while Daly's shot hit the crossbar following a pass from Heighway. After 20 minutes Brady's header found Hughton who worked his way into the area, past four tackles, before shooting home with his right foot. Nine minutes later Daly had a shot blocked and Heighway hit the crossbar when the rebound fell to him. Robinson was stretchered off a minute later after an off-ball incident and his place was taken by Givens. In the last few minutes Peyton was forced to bring off his only saves to deny Mavroudis, twice. Daly was booked during the game.

Michael Robinson scored his first international goal against Cyprus.

Match No. 186 — WALES — Home

Tuesday 24th February, 1981 – Dublin

REP. OF IRELAND (1) 1 Grealish 25
WALES (2) 3 Price 34, Boyle 38, Yorath 89

Ref: Reeves (England) **Ground:** Tolka Park **Att:** 15,000

Ireland: Seamus McDonagh (Everton 1), David Langan (Birmingham City 9), Brendan O'Callaghan (Stoke City 4), Jimmy Holmes (Vancouver Whitecaps 30), Chris Hughton (Tottenham Hotspur 9), Gerry Daly (Coventry City 27), Tony Grealish (Luton Town 21), Gary Waddock (Queens Park Rangers 3), Steve Heighway (Liverpool 32), Don Givens (Birmingham City 55), Eamonn O'Keefe (Everton 1). **Subs:** Kevin Moran (Manchester United 6) for Givens (half-time). **Captain:** Tony Grealish. **Manager:** Eoin Hand (6). **Formation:** 4-3-3.

Wales: D. Davies, J. Jones, K. Ratcliffe, P. Price, T. Boyle, T. Yorath, B. Flynn, P. Nicholas, L. James, I. Walsh, K. Harris.

Both sides used this game to try out new players. Wales and Ireland topped their respective World Cup groups and, with important matches the next month, both wanted a boost from this first full international at Tolka Park.

There was a slow start to the match with Heighway forcing the first save from either goalkeeper with a hard 30 yard shot which was well held by Davis. The Welsh came to defend and Givens had a shot blocked in a crowded goalmouth while Waddock volleyed a Heighway corner just wide. After 25 minutes a strong run by Hughton forced a corner. The flag-kick was knocked to Heighway who laid it off to Grealish. The Irish captain spotted Davies off his line and fired a 35 yard shot over his head into the top corner of the net. The visitors then suddenly went on the offensive with Harris smashing a Ratcliffe cross just wide. After 34 minutes Price stole in at the far post to meet James's corner and bury it into the back of the net. Four minutes later Hughton conceded a free kick just outside the box. Yorath took it and sent it curling towards the far post. McDonagh reacted late and could only palm the ball into the air with Boyle getting his head to it to nod it home. For the rest of the half Wales 'sat' on their lead.

During the break Moran came on for Givens with O'Callaghan moving to centre forward. After 55 minutes Waddock had a goalbound shot deflected by Yorath and two minutes later Moran headed wide form Heighway's cross. O'Keefe had another shot deflected away before Harris had two good chances. First he broke clear to shoot over and then he had a second shot into the side netting. In the closing seconds Jones sent Walsh racing clear on goal. McDonagh managed to parry his close range effort but could do nothing when Yorath followed up to hit home the loose ball.

The game had an unfortunate outcome for Eamonn O'Keefe who had declared for Ireland as his grandparents had made him eligible. But when playing for non-league Mossley he had represented Englands semi-pros against Scotland and Holland in 1979. This made him ineligible to play for Ireland according to FIFA but the player fought this and eventually won his case.

Match No. 187 — BELGIUM — Away

Wednesday 25th March, 1981 – Brussels (World Cup)

BELGIUM (0) 1 Ceulemans 87
REP. OF IRELAND (0) 0

Ref: Nazare (Portugal) **Ground:** Heysel Stadium **Att:** 47,000

Belgium: M. Preud'homme, E. Gerets, L. Millecamps, W. Meeuws, M. Renquin, L. Coeck, R. Vandereycken, R. Mommens, A. Cluytens, E. Vandenberg, J. Ceulemans. **Subs:** W. Wellens for Coeck (76 mins), F. Vercauteren for Mommens (85 mins).

Ireland: Seamus McDonagh (Everton 2), David Langan (Birmingham City 10), Mick Martin (Newcastle United 40), Kevin Moran (Manchester United 7), Chris Hughton (Tottenham Hotspur 10), Gerry Daly (Coventry City 28), Tony Grealish (Luton Town 22), Liam Brady (Juventus 31), Steve Heighway (Liverpool 33), Frank Stapleton (Arsenal 21), Michael Robinson (Brighton 3). **Subs:** Mickey Walsh (F.C. Porto 9) for Stapleton (71 mins). **Captain:** Liam Brady. **Manager:** Eoin Hand (7). **Formation:** 4-3-3.

A night of huge disappointment for Ireland as some (more) bad refereeing decisions cost them another World Cup point and would ultimately deny them a place in the finals. It is easy to blame the referee when covering up any shortcomings (Belgium were the better team) but the fact remains that he made two key decisions which totally altered the result, and arguably the outcome of the group.

Ireland set out to contain and frustrate the Belgians early on. This policy succeeded in reducing Belgium to few openings and it was 26 minutes before Coeck and Vandenberg got Ceulemans in with McDonagh saving at the expense of a corner. From Mommens flag-kick, Ceulemans' header beat the goalkeeper but Hughton cleared off the line. In another 15 minutes Gerets got in for a shot which went across the goal and wide. Ireland had few openings due to Belgiums offside trap but just on the interval they were awarded a free kick just outside the area for a foul on Robinson. Brady took the kick and found Stapleton running in to shoot past Preud'homme into the net. There was no flag but the referee backed into a Belgian player on the ground and disallowed the goal. He would later give no reason why he disallowed the strike and, as it is difficult to find fault with the goal, it is presumed it was for a foul on the Belgian player (who he knocked over) as he awarded a free out.

Five minutes after the restart Brady weaved his way past three defenders before shooting from 20 yards with Pred'homme making a good save to keep it out. After 58 minutes a long free kick by Langan found Robinson at the far post but his shot from an acute angle was saved by the goalkeeper. Three minutes later Meeuws found Gerets with a long pass and when the full back crossed hard into the box Ceulemans met it with a good header which McDonagh saved with his legs. Daly shot across the goal and soon after put Robinson away to have a shot turned around the post by the goalkeeper. Gerets had a header saved, Langan cleared off the goal-line from Ceulemans and McDonagh brought off a brilliant save to stop Vandenberg's shot. With 3 minutes to go Gerets 'took a dive' just outside the box and the referee awarded a free kick. The ball had run away from the Belgian full back but his dive was enough to ensure a free. Vandereycken took the kick and sent a shot over the wall but onto the crossbar. The ball flew up into the air and when it dropped down in the 6 yard area Ceulemans climbed above a posse of players to nod the ball home. The free should not have been awarded in the first place and when Raul Joaquim Fernandes Nazare blew for full time Eoin Hand confronted him on the pitch calling him ".......a disgrace and a cheat". It was a cruel end to a match which should have ended in a draw. Just to compound the manager's anger Daly was booked during the game and with two yellow cards (one v Cyprus) he would miss the next World Cup match.

Match No. 188 — CZECHOSLOVAKIA — Home

Wednesday 29th April, 1981 – Dublin

REP. OF IRELAND (1) 3 Moran 19, 72, Stapleton 78
CZECHOSLOVAKIA (0) 1 Masny 54

Ref: Gray (England) **Ground:** Lansdowne Road **Att:** 8,000

Ireland: Seamus McDonagh (Everton 3), David Langan (Birmingham City 11), David O'Leary (Arsenal 18), Kevin Moran (Manchester United 8), John Devine (Arsenal 3), Gerry Daly (Coventry City 29), Mick Martin (Newcastle United 41), Ashley Grimes (Manchester United 9), Kevin O'Callaghan (Ipswich Town 1), Frank Stapleton (Arsenal 22), Mickey Walsh (F.C. Porto 10). **Subs:** Ronnie Whelan (Liverpool 1) for Daly (63 mins). **Captain:** David O'Leary. **Manager:** Eoin Hand (8). **Formation:** 4-3-3.

CSSR: S. Semen, F. Jakubec, L. Radimec, Macela, J. Barmos, J. Kozak, P. Nemec, J. Berger, M. Masny, W. Licka, Z. Nehoda. **Subs:** L. Jurkemik for Macela (half-time), P. Bicovsky for Nemec (half-time).

The Czech saw a lot of the ball but it was the Irish who were more threatening. After 6 minutes Langan shot over from 20 yards and soon after Kevin O'Callaghan had a shot rebound off the frame of the goal. Ireland's early pressure was rewarded after 19 minutes when Moran headed home Martin's accurate free kick. Walsh then had a shot over, O'Leary mis-kicked in front of goal and Grimes had a powerful 20 yard drive pushed away by Semen. Just before half-time Kozak's rocket shot was well stopped by McDonagh and Licka shot wide.

The visitors made a better start to the second half and Nehoda beat Moran before shooting just wide. After 54 minutes Masny ran at the heart of the defence, played a one-two with Berger on the left, then another with Radimec on the right and chipped the ball over McDonagh for the equaliser. Masny had another shot deflected for a corner before Ireland took the lead for the second time. A free kick by O'Callaghan was knocked back to Devine whose curling ball into the area was again met with a brilliant header from Moran. Stapleton headed over from a Grimes free kick before he got the third Irish goal. Moran sent Devine clear on the left and his ball to the near post was hooked home by Stapleton. In the closing 10 minutes Whelan shot into the side netting, Martin had two shots blocked and Stapleton had another shot saved by Semen.

Match No. 189 — WEST GERMANY "B" — Away

Thursday 21st May, 1981 – Bremen

WEST GERMANY "B" (0) 3 Del'Haye 50, Funkel 62, Schröder 64
REP. OF IRELAND (0) 0

Ref: Frickmann (Denmark) **Ground:** Weser Stadium **Att:** 5,000

West Germany "B": N. Nigbur, K-H Geils, M. Koch, P. Steiner, J. Fleer, U. Bittcher, F. Funkel, H. Schröder, K. Del'Haye, D. Müller, H. Willmer. **Subs:** W. Junghans for Nigbur (half-time), K. Pinkall for Willmer (64 mins), S. Gross for Funkel (71 mins), M. Wiesner for Müller (84 mins)

Ireland: Seamus McDonagh (Everton 4), David Langan (Birmingham City 12), David O'Leary (Arsenal 19), Kevin Moran (Manchester United 9), John Devine (Arsenal 4), Gerry Daly (Coventry City 30), Mick Martin (Newcastle United 42), Tony Grealish (Luton Town 23), Kevin O'Callaghan (Ipswich Town 2), Frank Stapleton (Arsenal 23), Michael Robinson (Brighton 4). **Subs:** Gerry Ryan (Brighton 9) for O'Callaghan (57 mins), Terry Donovan (Aston Villa 2) for Robinson (72 mins), Ashley Grimes (Manchester United 10) for Martin (77 mins). **Captain:** Tony Grealish. **Manager:** Eoin Hand (9). **Formation:** 4-3-3.

A dull game played at walking pace in front of a small crowd produced a very one-sided contest. Schröder and Del'Haye set up Funkel for the first chance but he shot weakly and McDonagh saved. A quick free kick by Del'Haye gave Müller another chance but he shot wide. After 21 minutes Müller shot a Willmer cross against the underside of the crossbar and Del'Haye put the rebound wide. Coming up to the break Langan cleared a shot by Funkel off the line.

Five minutes into the second period Bittcher fed Del'Haye on the wing. The German seemed to elbow Devine in the stomach as he cut into the box and, as Devine fell, so did the Irish goal with Del'Haye's shot from 6 yards. Germany got a second when Funkel's shot from Willmer's cross took a deflection off Moran and sent McDonagh the wrong way. Two minutes later Schröder unleashed a tremendous 30 yard drive which found the top of the goal. The only Irish shot of note was an O'Leary effort which was well wide. Both Langan and Devine were booked for fouls during the game.

Match No. 190 — POLAND — Away

Sunday 24th May, 1981 – Bydgoszcz

POLAND (2) 3 Iwan 2, O'Leary (o.g.) 37, Ogaza 66
REP. OF IRELAND (0) 0

Ref: Tatar (Rumania) **Ground:** Zopisya Stadium **Att:** 10,000

Poland: P. Mowlick, M. Dziuba, P. Janas, W. Zmuda, J. Jalocha, B. Buda, J. Kupcewicz, A. Buncol, A. Iwan, R. Ogaza, W. Smolarek. **Subs:** Z. Kapka for Buda (half-time), Skrobowski for Janas (half-time),

Z. Kostrzewa for Mowlick (65 mins), M. Okanski for Smolarek (68 mins), W. Majewski for Dziuba (70 mins)

Ireland: Patrick Bonner (Glasgow Celtic 1), David Langan (Birmingham City 13), David O'Leary (Arsenal 20), Mark Lawrenson (Brighton 15), Chris Hughton (Tottenham Hotspur 11), Tony Grealish (Luton Town 24), Kevin Moran (Manchester United 10), Ashley Grimes (Manchester United 11), Kevin O'Callaghan (Ipswich Town 3), Frank Stapleton (Arsenal 24), Michael Robinson (Brighton 5). **Subs:** Gary Waddock (Queens Park Rangers 4) for Moran (58 mins), Gerry Ryan (Brighton 10) for O'Callaghan (62 mins), Gerry Daly (Coventry City 31) for Grimes (80 mins). **Captain:** Tony Grealish. **Manager:** Eoin Hand (10). **Formation:** 4-3-3.

This was a more lively affair than the German game but still basically a one-sided match, although Ireland showed a bit more attacking play. After 1½ minutes Poland were awarded a free kick near the touchline and Kupcewicz curled the kick into the goalmouth. The ball came to Ogaza whose shot was parried but Iwan followed up to score. Ireland then recovered to launch a number of attacks but the nearest they came to goal was when Stapleton headed on O'Leary's ball towards Moran but Zmuda intercepted to clear. A free kick by Kupcewicz was turned over by Bonner before Kupcewicz and Iwan put Buda in to net but the score was ruled offside. On the half hour O'Leary cleared a shot from Iwan of the line and six minutes later Stapleton headed a Langan free to Robinson who headed just wide. A minute after O'Leary, under pressure from Smolarek, turned a hard low cross from Ogaza into his own net.

Robinson had a chance early in the second half but his shot was saved by Mowlick. After 58 minutes Moran was injured in a tackle with Kupcewicz and replaced by Waddock. Ireland made two other substitutions while Poland used all five of their replacements. After 21 minutes another free kick by Kupcewicz was headed on by Dziuba for Ogaza to head home at the far post. Near the end of the game Kupcewicz had a great chance of a fourth but missed an easy opening.

1981 Poland 3-0 Ireland
The Irish team which lost 0-3 to Poland in 1981. Front to back: *Kevin Moran, David O'Leary, Ashley Grimes, Frank Stapleton, Chris Hughton, Mark Lawrenson* (hidden), *David Langan, Kevin O'Callaghan, Michael Robinson, Patrick Bonner and Tony Grealish. (Photo: PAP/CAF)*

Match No. 191 — HOLLAND — Away

Wednesday 9th September, 1981 – Rotterdam (World Cup)

HOLLAND (1) 2 Thijssen 11, Muhren 65 (pen)
REP. OF IRELAND (1) 2 Robinson 40, Stapleton 71

Ref: Vojtech (Czechoslovakia) **Ground:** Feynoord Stadium **Att:** 50,000

Holland: P. Schrijvers, B. Wijnstekers, E. Brandts, M. Vander Korput, R. Krol, A. Muhren, F. Thijssen, T. La Ling, K. Van Kooten, R. Geeles, J. Rep. **Subs:** J. Peters for Geeles (half-time), R. Vander Kerkhof for La Ling (59 mins)

Ireland: Seamus McDonagh (Bolton Wanderers 5), David Langan (Birmingham City 14), David O'Leary (Arsenal 21), Mark Lawrenson (Liverpool 16), John Devine (Arsenal 5), Mick Martin (Newcastle United 43), Tony Grealish (Brighton 25), Liam Brady (Juventus 32), Steve Heighway (Minnesota Kicks 34), Frank Stapleton (Manchester United 25), Michael Robinson (Brighton 6). **Subs:** Gerry Ryan (Brighton 11) for Heighway (60 mins), Ronnie Whelan (Liverpool 2) for Martin (74 mins). **Captain:** Liam Brady. **Manager:** Eoin Hand (11). **Formation:** 4-3-3.

Seconds after kick off Brady and Stapleton combined to put Devine away on the left. The left back sent a low cross right across the goalmouth for Robinson to slide in and deflect the ball just wide of the near post. However it was the Dutch who made the better openings and after 11 minutes they went ahead when a mistake by Heighway 'gifted' the ball to Thijssen who played a one-two with Van Kooten before shooting powerfully home from 12 yards. The Dutch continued to press with Wijnstekers rifling a 30 yard shot just wide and Muhren having a shot taken off the line by Lawrenson following a cross by Rep. Ireland recovered to launch their own attacks and Martin and Langan forced an opening for Grealish whose long-range shot only just went wide. Two minutes later Ireland were level. Brady sent Heighway clear on the right and his perfectly delivered cross was volleyed into the net by Robinson.

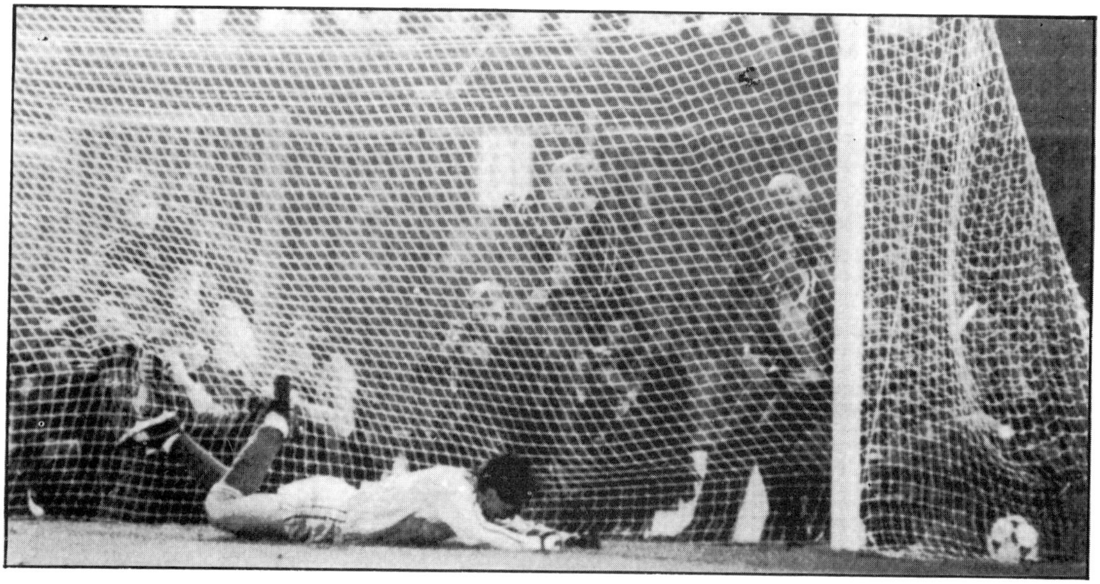

A disappointed Seamus McDonagh just fails to stop Muhren's penalty which restored Holland's lead in Rotterdam.

The Dutch began the second half much as they had started the first. A cross from La Ling was headed down by Van Kooten but McDonagh saved with his legs. Muhren had a chip shot just too high and Rep gave La Ling a great chance but he slipped as he was shooting and the ball went wide of an empty net. After 20 minutes Rep outwitted Langan on the edge of the box and the right back brought the winger down from behind as he sprinted into the area. McDonagh guessed correctly and got a hand to Muhren's penalty but could not keep it out. Six minutes later Lawrenson cut past Muhren and Brandts to get to the back-line. He then cut up along the line and sent a high cross to the far post where the lurking Stapleton scored with a firm downward header. Not long after Whelan and Langan were involved in a move which ended in Robinson heading over the latters cross. Late in the game Lawrenson made a vital tackle to stop Rep from getting in for a goal. The Dutch were awarded a free kick just outside the box but the referee blew for full time before it could be taken. Martin was booked just before he was replaced.

Match No. 192 **FRANCE** **Home**

Wednesday 14th October, 1981 – Dublin (World Cup)

REP. OF IRELAND (3) 3 Mahut (o.g.) 5, Stapleton 25, Robinson 39
FRANCE (1) 2 Bellone 8, Platini 82

Ref: Ericsson (Sweden) **Ground:** Lansdowne Road **Att:** 53,000

Ireland: Seamus McDonagh (Bolton Wanderers 6), David Langan (Birmingham City 15), David O'Leary (Arsenal 22), Kevin Moran (Manchester United 11), Chris Hughton (Tottenham Hotspur 12), Ronnie Whelan (Liverpool 3), Mick Martin (Newcastle United 44), Mark Lawrenson (Liverpool 17), Liam Brady (Juventus 33), Frank Stapleton (Manchester United 26), Michael Robinson (Brighton 7). **Subs:** Don Givens (Neuchatel Xamax 56) for Stapleton (87 mins). **Captain:** Liam Brady. **Manager:** Eoin Hand (12). **Formation:** 4-4-2.

France: J. Castaneda, M. Bossis, P. Mahut, C. Lopez, G. Janvion, R. Girand, J-F Larios, D. Christophe, M. Platini, A. Couriol, B. Bellone. **Subs:** D. Six for Bellone (62 mins), F. Bracci for Mahut (70 mins).

Ireland's hopes for a World Cup Finals place lay with victory in this match but also with the results of France's two remaining home games. In acheiveing the first of these prerequisites a second became clear when Ireland could only match France's goal difference and this was ultimately to cost Ireland it's Finals place.

The game was only five minutes old when Whelan dispossessed Janvion and put Robinson racing down the field. Robinson knocked the ball past Lopez and got into the penalty area before sending over a low cross which was deflected into his own net by Mahut under pressure from Stapleton. Three minutes later a slick passing move saw the French break down the left with Couriol's cross finding Bellone who turned and fired a 20 yard shot to the back of the net. Soon after Bossis burst up the field and let fly with another long-range effort but this time McDonagh beat it down for Langan to shepherd it back to him. At the other end Castaneda did well to turn a Stapleton shot out for a corner and Moran had an overhead kick saved after Robinson had flicked on a Whelan

The Irish team which defeated France 3-2 at Lansdowne Road.
Back row, left to right: *Kevin Moran, Seamus McDonagh, Mark Lawrenson, Ronnie Whelan and David O'Leary.*
Front row: *David Langan, Liam Brady, Frank Stapleton, Chris Hughton, Michael Robinson and Mick Martin.*

corner. After 20 minutes Platini played a one-two with Larios before sending a shot just wide. Five minutes later a shot from Moran was blocked out to Martin on the left side of the box. He sent a high ball back across the goal and although it missed Stapleton, it came to O'Leary on the edge of the 6 yard box. O'Leary could have shot but with two defenders rushing back to cover he squared it to Stapleton who shot high into the far top corner. A minute later Whelan cracked a long-range shot off the crossbar as Ireland began to dominate. Six minutes before the interval a backward header from Robinson intended for Stapleton, was intercepted by Larios who attempted to pass it back to Mahut. Unfortunately his back pass went well wide of the defender and Robinson ran onto it to shoot powerfully from the edge of the area. Castaneda got his hands to the ball but was unable to prevent it from landing in the back of the net.

Ireland made a good start to the second period with Stapleton curling a shot just wide. But it was France who had the better of a poor half. Platini had a 20 yard shot saved by McDonagh after 6 minutes and soon after the French captain was denied again by the Irish goalkeeper. A third effort from Platini was blocked out for a corner by O'Leary and from the flag-kick McDonagh saved at the feet of Larios on the goal-line. With 8 minutes to go Janvion crossed in from the left forcing Hughton to clear in front of the goal. The ball fell to Platini who shot it into the roof of the net from close range. A minute later Stapleton came close at the other end but his shot was deflected out for a corner. Whelan had a shot over before in the final minute a cross from Couriol found Six in the box only for McDonagh to react superbly to turn his shot out for a corner. Liam Brady was shown the yellow card during this half. This was his second booking during the campaign and under FIFA rules it would mean he would miss the first game of the finals if Ireland had qualified. It is ironic that when Ireland did qualify for a major finals FIFA disciplinary rules would deny Brady a place in the tournament.

Match No. 193 — ALGERIA — Away

Wednesday 28th April, 1982 – Algiers

ALGERIA (1) 2 Assad 15, Madjer 64
REP. OF IRELAND (0) 0

Ref: Lambert (France) **Ground:** Olympic Stadium **Att:** 65,000

Algeria: M. Cerbah, C. Merzekane, Medjadi, M. Guendouz, N. Kourichi, F. Mansouri, K. Maroc, L. Belloumi, A. Bourebou, D. Tlemcani, S. Assad. **Subs:** M. Kovichi for Merzekane (half-time), R. Madjer for Tlemcani (half-time), Bensheik for Belloumi (half-time), F. Chebal for Bourebou (63 mins)

Ireland: Patrick Bonner (Glasgow Celtic 2), John Devine (Arsenal 6), Mick Martin (Newcastle United 45), Kevin Moran (Manchester United 12), Ashley Grimes (Manchester United 12), Gerry Daly (Coventry City 32), Tony Grealish (Brighton 26), Gary Waddock (Queens Park Rangers 5), Kevin O'Callaghan (Ipswich Town 4), Frank Stapleton (Manchester United 27), Michael Robinson (Brighton 8). **Subs:** Mickey Walsh (F.C. Porto 11) for Robinson (half-time), Eamonn Deacy (Aston Villa 1) for Moran (70 mins), Gerry Ryan (Brighton 12) for Waddock (75 mins). **Captain:** Tony Grealish. **Manager:** Eoin Hand (13). **Formation:** 4-3-3.

Ireland were in charge for long spells of the game but failed to take advantage of the openings created. Algeria opened nervously but both their goals were the result of some good play.

After 15 minutes Assad played a one-two with Belloumi and outpaced Devine before shooting past Bonner from an acute angle. The goal came against the run of play.

The second half was more physical and both Bourebou and Moran had to leave the field with injuries. Algeria got their second goal when a long ball by Assad from deep inside his own half found Madjer on the right wing. Madjer cut in, tricked his way past Grimes and Stapleton and shot low from the edge of the box. Bonner had it covered but the ball bounced in front of him and slipped through his hands to roll into the net.

Match No. 194 **CHILE** **Away**

Friday 21st May, 1982 – Santiago

CHILE (1) 1 Gamboa 1

REP. OF IRELAND (0) 0

Ref: Ojeda (Chile) **Ground:** Nacional Stadium **Att:** 16,000

Chile: M. Osben, L. Garrido, E. Figueroa, R. Valenzuela, V. Bigorra, C. Rivas, R. Dubo, M. Soto, P. Yanez, M. A. Gamboa, G. Moscoso. **Subs:** M. Galindo for Garrido, J. C. Letelier for Gamboa

Ireland: Seamus McDonagh (Bolton Wanderers 7), Eamonn Deacy (Aston Villa 2), Mick Martin (Newcastle United 46), John Anderson (Preston 3), Mike Walsh (Everton 1), Gerry Daly (Coventry City 33), Tony Grealish (Brighton 27), Liam Brady (Juventus 34), Sean O'Driscoll (Fulham 1), Michael Robinson (Brighton 9), Kevin O'Callaghan (Ipswich Town 5). **Subs:** Mick Fairclough (Dundalk 1) for O'Driscoll (70 mins), Gerry Ryan (Brighton 13) for Robinson (75 mins). **Captain:** Tony Grealish. **Manager:** Eoin Hand (14). **Formation:** 4-3-3.

The decision to undertake a tour of South America, and more especially to include a game against Argentina as part of its itinerary, caused a storm of protest in Britain. The FAI saw no objection to having such a game but their insensibility caused many clubs to withhold their players because, in their view, it was inappropriate that representatives of English clubs should be part of a sporting ocasion with a country which was at war with Britain. The controversey grew when some Irish politicans got involved and the issue developed beyond its soccer origin. The matter was eventually defused when the FAI dropped the Argentina game from its tour plans. A serious rift was averted but, so far as this tour was concerned, the damage had already been done.

Eoin Hand did not want the tour from the start but went along with it when the controversy died down. However, he now had other problems. Most English clubs had left on end-of-the-season tours and player-release was going to be a problem. He scraped together a panel of 15 but with the League of Ireland on tour in New Zealand he was unable to get any more. He was promised some more players as the tour progressed but as far as he knew the tour now only consisted of games against Chile and Brazil. The FAI said they would organise a third game but this was hardly a way to undertake such a venture.

So it was that Ireland kicked off against Chile and immediately suffered a blow when Gamboa burst from midfield to score after a solo run. The game was played at walking pace and neither goal was threatened seriously in subsequent play. Near the end of the game Robinson suffered an ankle injury and was replaced. This injury would force Robinson to return home leaving Hand with only two recognised strikers in the panel.

Match No. 195 **BRAZIL** **Away**

Thursday 27th May, 1982 – Uberlandia

BRAZIL (1) 7 Falcao 32, Socrates 53, 73, Serginho 64, 75, Lusinho 68, Zico 78

REP. OF IRELAND (0) 0

Ref: Arppi Filho (Brazil) **Ground:** **Att:** 60,000

Brazil: Valdir Peres, Leandro, Oscar, Lusinho, Junior, Falcao, Socrates, Zico, Paulo Isidoro, Careca, Eder. **Subs:** Serginho for Careca (half-time), Toninho for Paulo Isidoro (60 mins), Paulo Sergio for Valdir Peres (80 mins), Dirceu for Eder (80 mins)

Ireland: Seamus McDonagh (Bolton Wanderers 8), Eamonn Deacy (Aston Villa 3), Mick Martin (Newcastle United 47), John Anderson (Preston 4), Mike Walsh (Everton 2), Gerry Daly (Coventry City 34), Tony Grealish (Brighton 28), Liam Brady (Juventus 35), Sean O'Driscoll (Fulham 2), Kevin O'Callaghan (Ipswich Town 6), Brendan O'Callaghan (Stoke City 5). **Subs:** Gerry Ryan (Brighton 14) for B. O'Callaghan (70 mins). **Captain:** Tony Grealish. **Manager:** Eoin Hand (15). **Formation:** 4-4-2.

On the 23rd September 1981 Brazil beat a League of Ireland representative side 6-0 in Maceio but as the game was a senior international for Brazil it went down in their records as a 6-0 victory over the Republic of Ireland. Several nations had mistaken the League's XI for the full side but the FAI had always protested about the difference. In 1981 they made sure the mistake was rectified but this served only to cause even more embarrassment when the 'official' Irish team was beaten 7-0 in this game.

Ireland's tour problems continued when the promised extra players never turned up and Eoin Hand was forced to play a weakened side against a team which was not only the 1982 World Cup favourites but was on a run of 16 games without defeat.

Despite the omens Ireland made a good start to the game and succeeded in frustrating the home side with their defensive tactics. The first real opening fell to Ireland when Daly presented Brendan O'Callaghan with a great chance but the forward failed to take advantage of it. After 32 minutes Falcao scored Brazil's first goal with a deflectd shot and this sealed Ireland's fate for the second half.

After 8 minutes a viciously curled corner found Socrates at the far post and he headed home. An identical corner after 19 minutes gave Serginho the chance to head in Brazil's third goal. Two more corners, this time in the 23rd and 28th minutes, were not cleared properly and both Lusinho and Socrates took advantage to add to the scoreline. Serginho and Zico completed the scoring with the latter scoring when a fifth corner caused problems.

Match No. 196 — TRINIDAD & TABAGO — Away

Sunday 30th May, 1982 – Port of Spain

TRINIDAD & TABAGO (1) 2
REP. OF IRELAND (1) 1 Brady

Ref: **Ground:** Arima Stadium **Att:** 6,000

Trinidad and Tobago:

Ireland: Gerry Peyton (Fulham 19), Eamonn Deacy (Aston Villa 4), Mick Martin (Newcastle United 48), Mike Walsh (Everton 3), John Anderson (Preston 5), Gerry Daly (Coventry City 35), Tony Grealish (Brighton 29), Liam Brady (Juventus 36), Johnny Walsh (Limerick United 1), Gerry Ryan (Brighton 15), Brendan O'Callaghan (Stoke City 6). **Subs:** Mick Fairclough (Dundalk 2) for B. O'Callaghan, Sean O'Driscoll (Fulham 3) for Deacy, Kevin O'Callaghan (Ipswich Town 7) for Ryan. **Captain:** Tony Grealish. **Manager:** Eoin Hand (16). **Formation:** 4-4-2.

This game was hastily arranged and with the players 'down' after the Brazilian result it proved an instantly forgetable game for them. Unfortunately this would not prove so back in Ireland as the result served only to fuel the criticism of the venture – a venture which was encouraged to go ahead only weeks before.

On a hot day and a bumpy pitch (which was used in some quarters to excuse the Irish performance although in reality it was a combination of other factors) Brady put Ireland ahead only for the home side to equalise before half-time. The West Indians scored the winning goal in the last 15 minutes.

Match No. 197 — HOLLAND — Away

Wednesday 22nd September, 1982 – Rotterdam (European Championship)

HOLLAND (1) 2 Schoenaker 1, Gullit 65
REP. OF IRELAND (0) 1 Daly 79

Ref: Greer (Czechoslovakia) **Ground:** Feynoord Stadium **Att:** 19,000

Holland: H. Van Breukelen, B. Wijnstekers, J. Metgot, R. Spelbos. H. Stevens, M. Vander Korput, W. Vander Kerkof, D. Schoenaker, R. Gullit, R. Vander Gijp, G. Vanenburg. **Subs:** R. Vander Kerkof for Metgot (half-time), K. Van Kooten for Vanenburg (85 mins)

Ireland: Seamus McDonagh (Bolton Wanderers 9), Mark Lawrenson (Liverpool 18), Mick Martin (Newcastle United 49), David O'Leary (Arsenal 23), Chris Hughton (Tottenham Hotspur 13), Gerry Daly (Coventry City 36), Tony Grealish (Brighton 30), Liam Brady (Sampdoria 37), Tony Galvin (Tottenham Hotspur 1), Frank Stapleton (Manchester United 28), Michael Robinson (Brighton 10). **Subs:** Gary Waddock (Queens Park Rangers 6) for Galvin (75 mins), Mickey Walsh (F.C. Porto 12) for Daly (82 mins). **Captain:** Tony Grealish. **Manager:** Eoin Hand (17). **Formation:** 4-4-2.

Ireland got off to a bad start when they conceded a goal after only 45 seconds. An Irish move broke down and Vander Gijp crossed low and hard in front of the goal for Schoenaker to come in at the far post to shoot home. This was a body-blow from which Ireland never recovered and the Dutch proceeded to dominate the game. Gullit headed a Vanenburg corner wide then the same player had a close range shot brilliantly saved by McDonagh. It was 25 minutes before Ireland created their first opening – Brady passing to Daly only for Van Breukelen to save at the latters feet. Another good save on the part of McDonagh prevented Vanenburg from scoring when he was clear in the box. Coming up to half-time Ireland staged a recovery with Lawrenson's cross causing problems when Vanenburg almost turned it into his own net but the goalkeeper saved. Then a Brady cross gave Daly a chance but he shot into the side netting and in the final minute Stapleton set up Grealish but his carefully placed chip was saved by the Dutch goalkeeper.

Ireland made a better start to the second half and Robinson headed a Brady cross down to Daly whose shot was turned over for a corner. From the flag-kick O'Leary had a great chance in front of goal but could not control the ball. The Irish continued to press but after 20 minutes the Dutch scored again. A long cross-field ball from Stevens was headed on by Schoenaker for Gullit who turned Hughton before firing a shot from the edge of the box into the bottom left corner of McDonaghs net. Three minutes later Willy Vander Kerkof sent Wijnstekers clear but McDonagh saved well at his feet. Galvin went off with a leg injury with Waddock replacing him on the left side of midfield. As the game entered its last quarter Ireland again created some openings. Stapleton headed a Brady cross straight at Van Breukelen and Brady had a shot turned over by the Dutch goalkeeper. Eleven minutes from the end a cross by Waddock was not properly dealt with by the Dutch defence and Brady nipped in ahead of everybody to send a cross to the far post where Daly tapped it home. Two late chances saw Vander Korput's full-blooded drive smash off the bar and a Grealish shot go just wide. Brady was booked just before half-time for a foul on Schoenaker.

Eamonn Deacy played four times for Ireland.

Mark Lawrenson played thirty-eight times for Ireland.

Match No. 198 **ICELAND** **Home**

Wednesday 13th October, 1982 – Dublin (European Championship)

REP. OF IRELAND (1) 2 Stapleton 35, Grealish 73
ICELAND (0) 0

Ref: Rion (Luxembourg) **Ground:** Lansdowne Road **Att:** 21,000

Ireland: Seamus McDonagh (Bolton Wanderers 10), Mark Lawrenson (Liverpool 19), David O'Leary (Arsenal 24), Kevin Moran (Manchester United 13), Mike Walsh (Everton 4), Ronnie Whelan (Liverpool 4), Tony Grealish (Brighton 31), Gary Waddock (Queens Park Rangers 7), Liam Brady (Sampdoria 38), Frank Stapleton (Manchester United 29), Michael Robinson (Brighton 11). **Subs:** Kevin O'Callaghan (Ipswich Town 8) for Brady (64 mins). **Captain:** Tony Grealish. **Manager:** Eoin Hand (18). **Formation:** 4-4-2.

Iceland: T. Bjarnason, V. Halldorsson, O. Oskarsson, S. Jonsson, M. Geirsson, G. Gislason, P. Ormslev, A. Edvaldsson, A. Gudjohnsen, P. Petursson, L. Gudmundsson. **Subs:** R. Margeirsson for Ormslev (42 mins).

The game got off to a slow start with Gudmundsson shooting wide early on. The next chance came after 28 minutes when Stapletons header from Brady's cross forced Bjarnason into a good save. After 35 minutes a long ball from Moran found Robinson deep in the Icelandic half. Robinson knocked the ball back to Whelan who threaded a ball through the defence for Stapleton to run onto and shoot past Bjarnason into the corner of the net. Three minutes later Robinson shot wide before the game entered a rough period following a bad tackle by Walsh on Ormslev, who was stretchered off. Just before the break Stapleton had a header wide and Gislason a weak header saved.

Just after the resumption Brady crossed in for Stapleton only for the latters header to be kicked off the line by Jonsson. After 50 minutes Grealsih headed in a Lawrenson cross but the flag was up for offside. Ten minutes later Gislason fed Gudjohnsen whose shot was saved at the second attempt by McDonagh. Whelan played a one-two with Stapleton before having his shot saved and Grealish shot over after a good move. Iceland's best chance came after 72 minutes when a corner by Petursson flew off O'Leary and came to the unmarked Jonsson at the far post but he headed into the side netting. From the goalkick, which was played back to him, McDonagh sent a long ball forward to Robinson who flicked it on for Grealish to get between Halldorsson and Geirsson and shoot past Bjarnason with the help of a deflection. In the closing stages of the game McDonagh made a good save to deny Petursson while O'Callaghan was denied a certain goal when, after getting clear of three defensive tackles, he was pulled back by the referee for a free kick for the first foul on him. The game was very physical during this half and Waddock (Ireland), Gudjohnsen and Edvaldsson (Iceland) were all booked for rough play.

Match No. 199 **SPAIN** **Home**

Wednesday 17th November, 1982 – Dublin (European Championship)

REP. OF IRELAND (1) 3 Grimes 2, Stapleton 63, 76
SPAIN (1) 3 Maceda 31, Martin (o.g.) 46, Victor 60

Ref: Redelfs (West Germany) **Ground:** Lansdowne Road **Att:** 35,000

Ireland: Seamus McDonagh (Bolton Wanderers 11), John Devine (Arsenal 7), Mick Martin (Newcastle United 50), Mark Lawrenson (Liverpool 20), Chris Hughton (Tottenham Hotspur 14), Tony Grealish (Brighton 32), Liam Brady (Sampdoria 39), Ashley Grimes (Manchester United 13), Kevin O'Callaghan (Ipswich Town 9), Frank Stapleton (Manchester United 30), Michael Robinson (Brighton 12). **Subs:** Mickey Walsh (F.C. Porto 13) for Grealish (60 mins). **Captain:** Tony Grealish. **Manager:** Eoin Hand (19). **Formation:** 4-3-3.

Spain: L. Arconada, Juan Jose, A. Maceda, F. Bonet, J. A. Camacho, Senor, Victor, R. Gordillo, J. C. Pedraza, Santillana, Marcos. **Subs:** E. Martin for Pedraza (74 mins), F. Roberto for Santillana (76 mins).

Ireland began well with Stapleton and Robinson putting Brady in for a right-footed shot which just went wide. A minute later Grealish slid in to beat Gordillo and when the ball ran loose Grimes put Robinson away for a shot which was blocked. Robinson regained possession and rolled the ball back for Grimes to unleash a rocket-like drive from 20 yards which found the top corner of the net. Five minutes later Stapleton could have had a second but, with the ball at his feet in front of the goal, he hesitated and the chance was lost. Grimes and Pedraza had shots saved before Spain equalised. A free kick by Gordillo, on the right of the Irish area, found Maceda unmarked 8 yards out and he volleyed powerfully into the roof of the net. Three minutes later Hughton broke up the left, beat two defenders, and sent in a cross which was headed over by Robinson.

A minute into the second half Victor found Senor racing into the box and the latters low, hard cross-cum-shot eluded McDonagh. Martin, in trying to cut it out, only succeeded in putting the ball into the net with his outstretched leg. After 15 minutes Marcos gained possession in the Irish half, cut inside Martin and sent a through ball into the box for Victor. McDonagh advanced but Victor got around him and waited until Lawrenson committed himself before shooting into the empty net. Grealish then went off with an injury with Walsh coming on at midfield while O'Callaghan had switched from the left wing over to the right at the start of the second period. Grimes headed an O'Callaghan corner wide before the Irish pulled a goal back. Brady sent a high hanging free kick into the box and Stapleton outwitted his marker to send a free header to the back of the net. Minutes later Arconada parried a close-range header from Grimes to the far post where Walsh shot only for the Spanish goalkeeper to save with his knee. Marcos came close at the other end before Ireland equalised with a brilliant goal. Lawrenson found O'Callaghan out by the touchline with a cross-field pass. The winger controlled the ball instantly and beat Gordillo with a drag-back. As he ran on Victor came across to cover but O'Callaghan knocked the ball past him and then, with the outside of his boot, sent a looping cross to the far post where Stapleton met it with a firm downward header. The game still could have had a winner with late chances falling to O'Callaghan, a shot saved by the goalkeeper, and Roberto, whose effort was just wide. This was another very rough game in which six players were booked: Martin (Ireland) and Juan Jose, Bonet, Victor, Marcos and Maceda (Spain).

Match No. 200 — MALTA — Away

Wednesday 30th March, 1983 – Valetta (European Championship)

MALTA (0) 0
REP. OF IRELAND (0) 1 Stapleton 89

Ref: Mathias (Austria) **Ground:** Ta Qali Stadium **Att:** 10,000

Malta: J. Bonello, Emanuel Farrugia, Edwin Farrugia, Mario Farrugia, M. Schembri, J. Holland, S. Demanuele, E. Fabri, M. Degiorgio, R. Xuereb, G. Xuereb.

Ireland: Seamus McDonagh (Bolton Wanderers 12), John Devine (Arsenal 8), Mick Martin (Newcastle United 51), Mark Lawrenson (Liverpool 21), Chris Hughton (Tottenham Hotspur 15), Ronnie Whelan (Liverpool 5), Liam Brady (Sampdoria 40), Gary Waddock (Queens Park Rangers 8), Tony Galvin (Tottenham Hotspur 2), Frank Stapleton (Manchester United 31), Michael Robinson (Brighton 13). **Subs:** Kevin O'Callaghan (Ipswich Town 10) for Galvin (63 mins). **Captain:** Mick Martin. **Manager:** Eoin Hand (20). **Formation:** 4-3-3.

A new surface was being layed at the Ta Qali Stadium which was itself being renovated, when the Irish made their first visit to Malta. What they found was a threadbare pitch littered with building material. Although cleared before the match, the ground was unsuitable for soccer (at any time). The Irish complaints fell on deaf ears but provided an ironic twist as similar complaints about Lansdowne Road (although not nearly as bad as this) were similarly ignored.

The match was played in a gale which not only negated the Irish high ball tactics but also whipped up a sandstorm. After 8 minutes Demanuele made progress down the left before sending over a cross for Raymond Xuereb who miskicked in front of goal. A minute later Brady and Stapleton gave Galvin a chance but he shot wide. Generally it was Ireland to the fore but Devine had to clear a dangerous cross from Emanuel Farrugia off the line after 16 minutes. After half an hour Stapleton took advantage of a defensive error to get in a shot but Bonello was out quickly to save at his feet. Whelan and Waddock came close with other shots with Whelan having another effort wide. A minute before the break Mario Farrugia sent Demanuele clear only for Lawrenson to make a saving tackle.

The second half was all Ireland's as they strove for goals. O'Callaghan passed in for Devine to shoot over from 20 yards and when Robinson headed on Martin's cross, Stapleton's volley was brilliantly saved by Bonello. Hughton had a 25 yard shot saved by the Matlese goalkeeper and Demanuele shot wide before Ireland scored in the final seconds of normal time. Hughton crossed over to the far post where O'Callaghan knocked it back across the 6 yard box. Stapleton, with his back to goal, stretched to stop the ball with his right foot and, with the same foot, back-heeled it into the corner of the net. There was one booking – Brady for a foul on Demanuele in the final minutes. It was his second yellow card which meant he would miss Ireland's next game.

Match No. 201 — SPAIN — Away

Wednesday 27th April, 1983 – Zaragoza (European Championship)

SPAIN (0) 2 Santillana 51, Rincon 89
REP. OF IRELAND (0) 0

Ref: Buttenko (USSR) **Ground:** La Romareda Stadium **Att:** 35,000

Spain: L. Arconada, Juan Jose, A. Maceda, F. Bonet, J. Camacho, Victor, Senor, R. Gordillo, Marcos, Santillana, F. Carrasco. **Subs:** R. Gallego for Victor (half-time), H. Rincon for Carrasco (74 mins)

Ireland: Seamus McDonagh (Bolton Wanderers 13), Mark Lawrenson (Liverpool 22), David O'Leary (Arsenal 25), Mick Martin (Newcastle United 52), Chris Hughton (Tottenham Hotspur 16), Ronnie Whelan (Liverpool 6), Tony Grealish (Brighton 33), Gary Waddock (Queens Park Rangers 9), Ashley Grimes (Manchester United 14), Frank Stapleton (Manchester United 32), Mickey Walsh (F.C. Porto 14). **Subs:** Kevin O'Callaghan (Ipswich Town 11) for Grimes (57 mins), Gerry Daly (Coventry City 37) for Whelan (77 mins). **Captain:** Tony Grealish. **Manager:** Eoin Hand (21). **Formation:** 4-4-2.

Ireland set out from the start to defend and thus had few scoring chances. Spain, however, had many. After 19 minutes a cross from Senor was headed down by Santillana to Marcos who shot over. Carrasco had a shot saved before Lawrenson had Ireland's only chance of the half – a shot wide after combining with Whelan. Just after the half-hour a long-range shot from Gordillo hit the crossbar and when the ball rebounded back Maceda headed a great chance wide. Carrasco sent a header just over and O'Leary blocked a goal-bound shot from the same player as Spain finished the half on the up.

A minute after the interval Gallego burst through the Irish defence to shoot over from 20 yards while a free kick by Gordillo in a dangerous position was blocked by the Irish wall 3 minutes later. After 51 minutes Senor and Juan Jose exchanged passes before laying the ball off to Gallego. The midfielder sent a curling cross into the box where McDonagh and O'Leary missed it with Santillana having an easy task to head home. A minute later Santillana shot over another good chance. After 57 minutes Hand altered his line-up with O'Callaghan coming on as an extra forward player. It was the substitute who set up Ireland's best chance when he got past Juan Jose to send over a high cross. Walsh outjumped Gordillo and Maceda to send a curling header towards the top corner of the net only for Arconada to make a brilliant save. Another substitute, Rincon, got in a powerful shot which McDonagh could not hold and rolled wide. Another good cross from O'Callaghan was just missed by O'Leary before Ireland conceded a second goal in the final minute. A free kick by Gallego was curled into the 6 yard area where Rincon met it with a flashing header to give McDonagh no chance.

Match No. 202 — ICELAND — Away

Wednesday 21st September, 1983 – Reykjavik (European Championship)

ICELAND (0) 0
REP. OF IRELAND (2) 3 Waddock 16, Robinson 21, Walsh 81

Ref: Biguet (France) **Ground:** Laugardalsvollur **Att:** 13,706

Iceland: T. Bjarnason, V. Halldorsson, S. Larusson, S. Jonsson, J. Edvaldsson, J. Gudlaugsson, A. Edvaldsson, P. Ormslev, A. Gudjohnsen, P. Petursson, L. Gudmundsson. **Subs:** A. Eliasson for Gudjohnsen (52 mins), S. Gretarsson for Petursson (81 mins)

Ireland: Seamus McDonagh (Notts County 14), John Devine (Norwich City 9), Mark Lawrenson (Liverpool 23), Kevin Moran (Manchester United 14), Chris Hughton (Tottenham Hotspur 17), Gary Waddock (Queens Park Rangers 10), Tony Grealish (Brighton 34), Liam Brady (Sampdoria 41), Kevin O'Callaghan (Ipswich Town 12), Frank Stapleton (Manchester United 33), Michael Robinson (Liverpool 14). **Subs:** Mickey Walsh (F.C. Porto 15) for Robinson (76 mins). **Captain:** Tony Grealish. **Manager:** Eoin Hand (22). **Formation:** 4-3-3.

Ireland were quickly on the attack with O'Callaghan setting up Waddock for a shot which was deflected wide but it was the home side who had the best chance in the first quarter of an hour. Gudmundsson and Petursson combined to send Gudlaugsson free only for the midfielder to be denied when McDonagh grabbed the ball as he tried to go round him. After 16 minutes Brady weaved his way past two defenders to get to the by-line from where he sent a low cross back across the box. Stapleton was unable to get to it but Waddock, following up, did and sent a hard low shot to the back of the net with the help of a deflection from Larusson. Gudjohnsen shot wide before Ireland got a second goal. Stapleton had a cross blocked near the by-line but sent over another which was met by a diving header from Robinson, giving Bjarnason no chance. Coming up to the break Devine crossed in to give Robinson another headed chance but this time his effort was saved.

A minute into the second half McDonagh made a good save to stop a shot from Gudlaugsson while Petursson was denied a certain goal after 59 minutes when McDonagh turned his volley around the post with his fingertips. However Ireland sealed victory when Brady's short free kick put Hughton free on the left and his perfectly placed cross was headed in at the near post by Walsh. Both Robinson and Ormslev were booked for fouls on opposing goalkeepers.

Match No. 203 — HOLLAND — Home

Wednesday 12th October, 1983 – Dublin (European Championship)

REP. OF IRELAND (2) 2 Waddock 7, Brady 33 (pen)
HOLLAND (0) 3 Gullit 52, 77, Van Basten 67

Ref: Daina (Switzerland) **Ground:** Dalymount Park **Att:** 28,500

Ireland: Seamus McDonagh (Notts County 15), John Devine (Norwich City 10), Mark Lawrenson (Liverpool 24), Kevin Moran (Manchester United 15), Chris Hughton (Tottenham Hotspur 18), Gary Waddock (Queens Park Rangers 11), Tony Grealish (Brighton 35), Liam Brady (Sampdoria 42), Kevin O'Callaghan (Ipswich Town 13), Frank Stapleton (Manchester United 34), Michael Robinson (Liverpool 15). **Subs:** Tony Galvin (Tottenham Hotspur 3) for O'Callaghan (74 mins), Kevin Sheedy (Everton 1) for Grealish (81 mins). **Captain:** Tony Grealish. **Manager:** Eoin Hand (23). **Formation:** 4-3-3.

Holland: P. Schrijvers, B. Wijnstekers, P. Boeve, R. Gullit, J. Silooy, E. Ophof, R. Koeman, W. Vander Kerkhof, A. Van Tiggelen, G. Vanenburg, M. Van Basten. **Subs:** B. Brocken for Van Tiggelen (half-time)

A game of two contrasting halves saw Ireland dominate the first but Holland, thanks to a tactical change, held sway in the second. It was Ireland's first defeat at Dalymount Park for over 12 years and their first competitive home defeat in 11 years.

Ireland began on the attack and after 7 minutes Grealish sent a pass forward to Stapleton who appeared to be fouled as Silooy came in from behind to intercept. The ball ran loose and, as Stapleton held off Silooy, Waddock ran onto it to send a low shot, from outside the box, into the corner of the net. The Dutch had their only chance of the half soon after when Boeve headed a cross from Ophof just past the post. O'Callaghan had a shot saved and Stapaleton headed a Brady cross straight at Schrijvers in ensuing play. After 25 minutes Stapleton's header, from O'Callaghan's corner, beat the Dutch goalkeeper but Willy Vander Kerkhof was on the goal-line to head clear. Another Stapleton header, this time from a Brady cross, was just over before a ball up the touchline by Devine found Stapleton clear on the right wing. As he cut into the area he was taken down by the libero Gullit and from the resulting penalty Brady sent Schrijvers the wrong way.

The Irish renewed their attacks at the start of the second half with Grealish shooting over from a corner by Brady. Then a long clearance by McDonagh went over Silooy's head allowing Robinson to get around Schrijvers only to leave himself with a bad shooting angle. As he tried to square it to the incoming Brady it was cleared by the Dutch defence. After 52 minutes a cross into the area by Koeman was mis-headed by Moran straight to Gullit, now operating in midfield. Gullit hit it first time, McDonagh parried the ball at the near post but Gullit was first onto the rebound and shot through a group of players into the net. Brady brought a good save from Schrijvers before the Dutch equalised when Van Basten stooped to head a Wijnstekers corner into the net, despite an attempted goal-line clearance by Devine. The Irish tried to restore their lead but in going forward they were caught out. A bad pass by Hughton gave Galvin no chance and he had to concede a throw-in. This was taken quickly to Brocken who sent a long ball up to Van Basten. The striker turned Moran and rolled the ball into the path of Gullit who ran into the box before shooting into the corner of the net. There was one booking – Silooy for holding Stapleton's shirt in the first half.

Match No. 204 — MALTA — Home

Wednesday 16th November, 1983 – Dublin (European Championship)

REP. OF IRELAND (3) 8 Lawrenson 24, 64, Stapleton 26 (pen), O'Callaghan 34, Sheedy 74, Brady 76, 80, Daly 88

MALTA (0) 0

Ref: Amundsen (Denmark) **Ground:** Dalymount Park **Att:** 10,000

Ireland: Patrick Bonner (Glasgow Celtic 3), Kieran O'Regan (Brighton 1), Mark Lawrenson (Liverpool 25), Kevin Moran (Manchester United 16), Chris Hughton (Tottenham Hotspur 19), Gerry Daly (Coventry City 38), Kevin Sheedy (Everton 2), Liam Brady (Sampdoria 43), Kevin O'Callaghan (Ipswich Town 14), Frank Stapleton (Manchester United 35), Mickey Walsh (F.C. Porto 16). **Subs:** Jacko McDonagh (Shamrock Rovers 1) for Moran (half-time), Gary Waddock (Queens Park Rangers 12) for Lawrenson (81 mins). **Captain:** Frank Stapleton. **Manager:** Eoin Hand (24). **Formation:** 4-3-3.

Malta: J. Bonello, C. Consiglio, J. Holland, Edwin Farrugia, A. Azzopardi, Emanuel Farrugia, S. Demanuelle, Mario Farrugia, N. Attard, C. Busuttil, E. Spiteri-Gonzi. **Subs:** G. Xuereb for Attard (68 mins), E. Fabri for Mario Farrugia (81 mins)

Ireland finished off their European Championship matches with this record score in their 75th international at Dalymount Park. These eight goals would represent a pinnacle (as far as goalscoring) in Hand's term of office as the next two years would yield only eight more goals in 16 matches.

The game itself was over as a contest by half-time. For the opening quarter Ireland were kept at bay with Bonello producing good saves to deny O'Callaghan, Walsh and Moran. But after 24 minutes Ireland finally broke the deadlock. Brady sent the ball out to the overlapping Hughton who in turn found Walsh in the box. Walsh wriggled free of two tackles to send over a cross which was headed away by Edwin Farrugia. The ball came to Lawrenson, on the edge of the box, who chested it down before shooting home off the post. Two minutes later Stapleton beat Azzopardi to a long ball but was taken down from behind by the full back as he got into the penalty area. Stapleton took the spot-kick himself and sent Bonello the wrong way. After 34 minutes Brady threaded a through ball past three defenders for O'Callaghan to run onto. With Stapleton and Walsh in support, he feigned to cross before firing a low shot to the corner of the net.

The second half was all one-way traffic with Ireland mounting attack after attack. After 64 minutes Brady put Lawrenson in to score again and, 10 minutes later, Brady and Lawrenson combined to set up Sheedy to score from just inside the box. Irelands sixth came when a 25 yard pass from Stapleton found Brady who beat Bonello easily. Another long ball, this time from Sheedy, allowed Brady to beat the offside trap, round a very advanced goalkeeper and steer the ball into the empty net. Daly completed the scoring when Walsh headed a Brady chip to him and he hooked it home in front of goal.

Match No. 205 — ISRAEL — Away

Wednesday 4th April, 1984 – Tel Aviv

ISRAEL (1) 3 Ohana 2, Armeli 62, Sinai 65
REP. OF IRELAND (0) 0

Ref: Lartigot (France) **Ground:** Bloomfield Stadium **Att:** 10,000

Israel: A. Haviv, D. Pisanti, S. Kirat, A. Cohan, G. Lasri, Y. Malmillian, Y. Eckhiz, R. Turk, M. Sinai, Z. Armeli, E. Ohana. **Subs:** N. Barda for A. Cohan (78 mins). N. Cohen for Malmillian (88 mins)

Ireland: Patrick Bonner (Glasgow Celtic 4), John Devine (Norwich City 11), David O'Leary (Arsenal 26), Kevin Moran (Manchester United 17), Ashley Grimes (Coventry City 15), Gary Waddock (Queens Park Rangers 13), Mark Lawrenson (Liverpool 26), Liam Brady (Sampdoria 44), Ronnie Whelan (Liverpool 7), Frank Stapleton (Manchester United 36), Michael Robinson (Liverpool 16). **Subs:** Tony Galvin (Tottenham Hotspur 4) for Whelan (70 mins), Gerry Daly (Coventry City 39) for Robinson (79 mins). **Captain:** Frank Stapleton. **Manager:** Eoin Hand (25). **Formation:** 4-4-2.

Israel got off to a great start when Armeli cut in from the right wing and passed to Ohana who took it in his stride before blasting the ball into the roof of the net from just inside the box. The Irish response was slow and after 21 minutes Robinson headed over a cross from Brady. Robinson returned the compliment to Brady soon after with Brady's shot being saved by Haviv. Grimes set up Whelan for another shot which bounced off Haviv's chest and Stapleton worked a one-two with Lawerson only to have his goal-bound shot deflected away for a corner.

Early in the second half a Devine cross was headed down by Robinson for Whelan but Kirat made a good covering tackle. After 52 minutes another Devine cross found O'Leary's head but the ball hit the post. Ten minutes later Kirat broke up the centre and gave the ball out to Pisanti on the wing. The right back ran to the by-line and sent over a cross for Armeli to send a free header to the back of the net. Stapleton got Whelan in for another chance but the latter shot wide. A minute later a break up the middle again caused problems and when the ball came out to Ohana, on the wing, he beat Devine before getting to the by-line form where he crossed to the far post. There was Sinai and he scored with a marvellous scissors kick. Armeli almost got a fourth goal near the end but missed a good chance.

Match No. 206 POLAND Home

Wednesday 23rd May, 1984 – Dublin

REP. OF IRELAND (0) 0
POLAND (0) 0

Ref: Courtney (England) **Ground:** Dalymount Park **Att:** 8,100

Ireland: Seamus McDonagh(Notts County 16), Kieran O'Regan (Brighton 2), David O'Leary (Arsenal 27), Mick McCarthy (Manchester City 1), Ashley Grimes (Coventry City 16), Pat Byrne (Shamrock Rovers 1), Tony Grealish (West Bromwich Albion 36), Liam Brady (Sampdoria 45), Gerry Ryan (Brighton 16), Frank Stapleton (Manchester United 37), Mickey Walsh (F.C. Porto 17). **Subs:** Jacko McDonagh (Shamrock Rovers 2) for O'Leary (53 mins), Liam Buckley (Shamrock Rovers 1) for Stapleton (79 mins). **Captain:** Frank Stapleton. **Manager:** Eoin Hand (26). **Formation:** 4-4-2.

Poland: J. Mlynarczyk, K. Pawlak, W. Zmuda, R. Wojcicki, M. Ostrowski, A. Buncol, J. Wijas, Z. Boniek, W. Matysik, J. Furtok, W. Smolarek. **Subs:** M. Okanski for Furtok (68 mins)

Ireland's 100th home game turned out to be a very dull event, with the Polish side's defensive tactics blunting the Irish attacks. The visitors had the first chance of the game when Boniek shot wide from Smolarek's cross. A flick header from Stapleton gave Walsh a chance at the other end but the latter shot over and then a Byrne cross gave Stapleton an opening but his weak shot was saved easily. The best chance of the half was created by Boniek who got Pawlak in for a shot which was deflected wide by McCarthy. In the closing minutes both Walsh and Brady were off target with further efforts.

The second half was a bit more lively with Grealish and Brady having early shots over while McDonagh saved a shot from Smolarek at the other end. All the best action though, was confined to the last fifteen minutes. Grealish 'dummied' an O'Regan cross for Brady to have a shot over from just outside the penalty area. Then Buckley crossed in for Grealish to have a good shot saved at the butt of an upright. Byrne next set up Buckley whose 25 yard shot went just wide and in the last few minutes another shot from Buckley again went the wrong side of the post.

Match No. 207 CHINA Neutral

Sunday 3rd June, 1984 – Sapparo (Japan Cup)

PEOPLES REP. OF CHINA (0) 0
REP. OF IRELAND (0) 1 O'Keefe 57

Ref: **Ground:** Maryuama Stadium **Att:**

China:

Ireland: Patrick Bonner (Glasgow Celtic 5), John Anderson (Newcastle United 6), David O'Leary (Arsenal 28), Mick McCarthy (Manchester City 2), Jim Beglin (Liverpool 1), Pat Byrne (Shamrock Rovers 2), Tony Grealish (West Bromwich Albion 37), Gerry Ryan (Brighton 17), Frank Stapleton (Manchester United 38), Mickey Walsh (F.C. Porto 18), Eamonn O'Keefe (Port Vale 2). **Subs:** Gary Howlett (Brighton 1) for Byrne (55 mins). **Captain:** Frank Stapleton. **Manager:** Eoin Hand (27). **Formation:** 4-3-3.

Played as part of the Japan Cup (see Appendix D) this semi-final was Ireland's only full international during the tournament and as it turned out, their only victory.

The only previous meeting between these two nations was an under 21 match in 1983 when Eamonn O'Keefe scored four goals in a 5-1 win. The Chinese goalkeeper on that occasion was Li Fusheng and he was again in goal when O'Keefe scored his first goal for the senior side. Having had a perfectly good goal ruled out five minutes earlier, O'Keefe took a pass from Stapleton and fired home a bullet-like drive in off the underside of the crossbar.

Eamonn O'Keefe, not in picture, scores his first goal for Ireland against the People's Republic of China in the 1984 Japan Cup. No. 8 for Ireland is Tony Grealish.

Match No. 208 **MEXICO** **Home**

Wednesday 8th August, 1984 – Dublin

REP. OF IRELAND (0) 0
MEXICO (0) 0

Ref: Baumann (Switzerland) **Ground:** Dalymount Park **Att:** 5,100

Ireland: Seamus McDonagh (Notts County 17), Kieran O'Regan (Brighton 3), Kevin Moran (Manchester United 18), Mick McCarthy (Manchester City 3), Jim Beglin (Liverpool 2), Pat Byrne (Shamrock Rovers 3), Tony Grealish (West Bromwich Albion 38), Gerry Ryan (Brighton 18), Tony Galvin (Tottenham Hotspur 5), Liam Buckley (Waregem 2), Eamonn O'Keefe (Port Vale 3). **Subs:** Gerry Peyton (Fulham 20) for S. McDonagh (half-time), Chris Hughton (Tottenham Hotspur 20) for O'Regan (half-time), Gerry Daly (Birmingham City 40) for Byrne (half-time), Kevin O'Callaghan (Ipswich Town 15) for Galvin (half-time), Jacko McDonagh (Shamrock Rovers 3) for Hughton (76 mins). **Captain:** Tony Grealish. **Manager:** Eoin Hand (28). **Formation:** 4-3-3.

Mexico: P. Larios, M. Trejo, F. Quirarte, A. Manzo, F. Chavez, C. de los Cobos, E. Lopez Zarza, J. Aquirre, T. Boy, E. de la Torre, L. Flores. **Subs:** R. Amador for Trejo (74 mins), J. Hernandez for Flores (87 mins)

Mexico, at the start of a 6-match European tour, did not want to lose their first game so defended throughout for a draw. This made for a poor spectacle for the small attendance with the only real chance falling to Ireland mid-way through the first half. McCarthy's long throw-in found Moran's head and his powerful effort was well held by Larios on the goal-line. After 35 minutes a shot from Byrne was deflected out for a corner by Manzo and from the flag-kick Galvin had a shot from outside the area saved by the Mexican goalkeeper.

A minute after the break Buckley, O'Callaghan and Daly combined for Hughton to have a shot which was easily saved. The visitors only threat was when a corner by Lopez Zarza was not gathered by Peyton and Quirarte scooped a good chance over the bar. Quirarte was booked during the match and his audible 'no, no, no' at the sight of the yellow card was the only other 'highlight' of a forgetable game.

Ireland's line-out before the match against USSR.
Back row, left to right: *Mark Lawrenson, Seamus McDonagh, Liam Brady, Chris Hughton, Ronnie Whelan, Dave O'Leary.*
Front row: *Michael Robinson, Tony Grealish, John Devine, Mickey Walsh, Tony Galvin.*

Match No. 209 — USSR — Home

Wednesday 12th September, 1984 – Dublin (World Cup)

REP. OF IRELAND (0) 1 Walsh 64
USSR (0) 0

Ref: Keizer (Holland) **Ground:** Lansdowne Road **Att:** 28,000

Ireland: Seamus McDonagh (Notts County 18), John Devine (Norwich City 12), David O'Leary (Arsenal 29), Mark Lawrenson (Liverpool 27), Chris Hughton (Tottenham Hotspur 21), Ronnie Whelan (Liverpool 8), Tony Grealish (West Bromwich Albion 39), Liam Brady (Inter Milan 46), Tony Galvin (Tottenham Hotspur 6), Mickey Walsh (F.C. Porto 19), Michael Robinson (Liverpool 17). **Subs:** Eamonn O'Keefe (Port Vale 4) for Walsh (80 mins). **Captain:** Tony Grealish. **Manager:** Eoin Hand (29). **Formation:** 4-3-3.

USSR: R. Dasaev, T. Sulakvelidze, S. Baltacha, A. Chivadze, S. Aleinikov, A. Demianenko, V. Bessonov, G. Litovchenko, K. Oganesian, O. Blokhin, S. Rodionov. **Subs:** A. Zygmantovich for Bessonov (36 mins), G. Gotsmanov for Oganesian (68 mins)

Interest in Ireland's soccer fortunes was on the decline when the qualifying games for the 1986 World Cup kicked off with this game against the Soviets. The poor performances had obviously had an effect with Lansdowne Road only half full despite an evening kick-off. The crowd of 28,000 was to be the best for any of the four World Cup home games which indicated further decline.

Early chances saw Whelan and Blokhin off target with shots while Walsh had a chip shot over following a one-two with Whelan. After 16 minutes Brady found Devine out by the touchline with a short pass and when the full backs cross came over Robinson sent a flashing header over. Lawrenson made two vital stretching tackles to stop Soviet breaks before Brady sent Galvin away to beat Litovchenko and sent over a cross which was headed wide by Robinson with Walsh only just failing to connect with a follow-up header. Rodionov and Aleinikov had shots wide, the latter after being sent clear following a one-two before a Brady free kick was met by a great header from Walsh only for Dasaev to make a marvellous mid-air save. The visitors finished the half on the attack with

Oganesian, Rodionov and Litovchenko all coming close with good efforts. Four minutes before the break a free kick was laid off for Chivadze to have a shot just over.

The Soviets began the second half well but after 10 minutes Brady broke past two tackles in mid-field to have a long range shot deflected down for Dasaev to save. A minute later a free kick by Blokhin was headed away by Grealish but only as far as Aleinikov on the edge of the area. Aleinikov's shot was deflected by Whelan to Oganesian who shot home as the defence moved out. However the linesman had his flag raised and the goal was ruled out for a very marginal offside decision. A break by O'Leary into the Soviet half saw him play a one-two with Brady then knock the return out to Galvin. The winger raced to the by-line before sending over a great cross which both Dasaev and O'Leary failed to connect with properly. After 19 minutes a Soviet attack broke down and Whelan fed Robinson deep in the Irish half. Robinson got past Aleinikov and raced away up the wing before sending a low cross to Walsh on the edge of the box. Walsh took it in his stride and sent a low shot into the far corner of the net. Three minutes later a long kick out by McDonagh was headed on by Robinson for Walsh but this time his shot was saved on the goal-line by Dasaev. With 10 minutes to go the Soviets turned on the pressure. Chivadze knocked a through ball into Zygmantovich in the box and he layed it off for Blokhin to run onto only for McDonagh to save bravely at his feet. Two minutes later Rodionov headed a great chance wide and McDonagh was forced to tip a Demianenko cross over from underneath the crossbar. Two minutes from the end Rodionov beat Lawrenson on the edge of the area and shot against the crossbar. The ball bounced back into play and came to Litovchenko whose shot from outside the box struck a post. Two minutes into injury time a long kick out by McDonagh found O'Keefe in the Soviet area and he wriggled free of the depleated cover to have a shot saved by Dasaev's legs at the near upright. There was one booking in the game – Baltacha for holding off Galvin when the Irish winger was through on a ball from Brady.

Match No. 210 — NORWAY — Away

Wednesday 17th October, 1984 – Oslo (World Cup)

NORWAY (1) 1 Jacobsen 42
REP. OF IRELAND (0) 0

Ref: Schürev (East Germany) **Ground:** Ullevaal Stadium **Att:** 12,468

Norway: E. Thorstvedt, S. Fjaelberg, A. Hareide, T. Kojedal, P. E. Mordt, E. Soler, P. E. Ahlsen, H. Thoresen, K. K. Herlovsen, A. L. Okland, P. Jacobsen **Subs:** V. Davidsen for Fjaelberg (34 mins), P. Henriksen for Jacobsen (89 mins)

Ireland: Seamus McDonagh (Birmingham City 19), John Devine (Norwich City 13), David O'Leary (Arsenal 30), Mark Lawrenson (Liverpool 28), Chris Hughton (Tottenham Hotspur 22), Ronnie Whelan (Liverpool 9), Tony Grealish (West Bromwich Albion 40), Liam Brady (Inter. Milan 47), Tony Galvin (Tottenham Hotspur 7), Frank Stapleton (Manchester United 39), Michael Robinson (Liverpool 18). **Subs:** Kevin O'Callaghan (Ipswich Town 16) for Whelan (67 mins), Mickey Walsh (F.C. Porto 20) for Robinson (69 mins). **Captain:** Frank Stapleton. **Manager:** Eoin Hand (30). **Formation:** 4-3-3.

After the high of the opening game with the Soviets, Ireland came back down to the ground with a bump with this disappointing result against Norway. Ireland played well but the home side converted one of their chances and in the end that was what counted.

Ireland's opening attacks saw Robinson head a Brady free kick wide, Grealish have a long range shot saved and Stapleton have a shot deflected out for a corner. After 13 minutes Galvin sent a great cross in for Stapleton's head only for Thorstvedt to save on the goalline with his knee. Norway came back with Okland heading a Thoresen cross over and Jacobsen having a shot easily saved by McDonagh. After 25 minutes McDonagh saved a hard shot from Mordt at the near post and from the resulting corner Jacobsen shot over from outside the box. Eight minutes later a corner from Galvin was flick-headed on by Stapleton for Whelan but the latters header was stopped on the line by Thorstvedt. Three minutes from the break Jacobsen broke from the Norwegian half, exchanged passes with Okland and shot low as McDonagh advanced. The Irish goalkeeper got a leg to the ball but could not prevent it from bouncing into the net.

Whelan had an early chance in the second half but delayed his shot from Brady's pass and checked to curl the ball wide. After an hours play Mordt made a fine run to get to the by-line but his cross was missed by two Norwegians with Whelan clearing the loose ball. After 67 minutes O'Callaghan replaced Whelan which altered the formation to a 4-2-4 set-up. (Walsh replaced Robinson 2 minutes later in a straight swap.) After 70 minutes a Grealish pass was flicked on to Brady by Walsh and Brady's shot was deflected into the side netting by a defender. Norway had few chances as Ireland strove for an equaliser but in the 81st minute a cross from Davidsen found Soler whose header beat McDonagh but Lawrenson headed it out for a corner and 2 minutes later, Ahlsen and Okland combined to get Jacobsen in again only for McDonagh to save with his legs. Two minutes from the end Brady met a Devine cross with a diving header which only just bounced wide. While not a dirty game there was a lot of niggling fouls but the referee produced no yellow cards.

Match No. 211 DENMARK Away

Wednesday 14th November, 1984 – Copenhagen (World Cup)

DENMARK (1) 3 Elkjaer 29, 46, Lerby 54
REP. OF IRELAND (0) 0

Ref: Wurtz (France) **Ground:** Idraetspark **Att:** 45,300

Denmark: O. Qvist,J. Sivebaek, I. Nielsen, M. Olsen, S. Busk, J. J. Bertelsen, S. Lerby, F. Arnesen, K. Berggreen, P. Elkjaer, M. Laudrup. **Subs:** J. Molby for Bertelsen (57 mins), K. Brylle for Elkjaer (63 mins)

Ireland: Seamus McDonagh (Notts County 20), Mark Lawrenson (Liverpool 29), David O'Leary (Arsenal 31), Mick McCarthy (Manchester City 4), Jim Beglin (Liverpool 3), Liam Brady (Inter. Milan 48), Tony Grealish (West Bromwich Albion 41), Kevin Sheedy (Everton 3), Tony Galvin (Tottenham Hotspur 8), Frank Stapleton (Manchester United 40), Mickey Walsh (F.C. Porto 21). **Subs:** Kevin O'Callaghan (Ipswich Town 17) for Galvin (Half-time). **Captain:** Frank Stapleton. **Manager:** Eoin Hand (31). **Formation:** 4-3-3.

Denmark opened on the attack which did not let up until soon after their third goal. Ireland were reduced to a few half chances and were lucky not to have suffered a bigger defeat.

In a frenetic opening 20 minutes Arnesen and Lerby had shots off target while Arnesen had good claims for a penalty turned down when Grealish brought him down in the box. McDonagh failed to hold a flicked Laudrup shot but saved at the feet of Berggreen from the rebound. After 13 minutes a Brady corner was flicked over Qvist by Stapleton but Sivebaek cleared off the goal-line. A minute later McDonagh again saved at the feet of Berggreen following a good move by Lerby and Laudrup. After 25 minutes a quick Elkjaer throw-in sent Arnesen racing free into the box but he wasted the chance by shooting over. Four minutes later an attempted Grealish pass to McCarthy was intercepted by Elkjaer who outpaced McCarthy before shooting past McDonagh. Elkjaer almost got another goal soon after but blazed a good chance well over while Ireland came close at the other end when a long throw-in by McCarthy found Stapleton in the 6 yard box but the latter's header was straight at Qvist who saved easily. Just before half-time a Sheedy – Galvin move gave Stapleton another headed chance but again the Danish goalkeeper saved easily.

Forty-eight seconds into the second half the Danes got a second goal with a marvellous move which went the entire length of the pitch. Lerby and Arnesen combined to stop Stapleton near the Danish goalline and gave the ball to Olsen. The Danish captain switched it to the opposite side of the field where Sivebaek broke into the Irish half. Siveback than gave the ball out to Laudrup who beat McCarthy and Beglin to get to the goalline and crossed in for Elkjaer to turn O'Leary before shooting past McDonagh from close range. After 54 minutes Lerby played a one-two with Laudrup, beat Grealish on the right side of the box and ran on to squeeze the ball between McDonagh and his right post for the third goal. A minute later a Danish break from an Irish corner saw Elkjaer and Laudrup combine to send the former completely free with only the goalkeeper to beat. It should have been his hat-trick but he shot a great chance wide. Following this the Danes relaxed and the best chances of the remainder of the game fell to the visitors. After 62 minutes Stapleton knocked a Beglin cross down for O'Callaghan but he shot well over and 6 minutes later Stapleton again headed down a Lawrenson free kick to Sheedy whose falling volley from outside the area was well held by Qvest. Both Galvin and Grealish were booked for fouls on Olsen.

Match No. 212 — ITALY — Home

Tuesday 5th February, 1985 – Dublin

REP. OF IRELAND (0) 1 Waddock 52
ITALY (2) 2 Rossi 4 (pen), Altobelli 17

Ref: Keizer (Holland) **Ground:** Dalymount Park **Att:** 40,000

Ireland: Patrick Bonner (Glasgow Celtic 6), Chris Hughton (Tottenham Hotspur 23), Mark Lawrenson (Liverpool 30), Mick McCarthy (Manchester City 5), Jim Beglin (Liverpool 4), Gary Waddock (Queens Park Rangers 14), Kevin Sheedy (Everton 4), Liam Brady (Inter. Milan 49), Tony Galvin (Tottenham Hotspur 9), Frank Stapleton (Manchester United 41), John Byrne (Queens Park Rangers 1). **Subs:** Paul McGrath (Manchester United 1) for Lawrenson (9 mins), Ronnie Whelan (Liverpool 10) for Galvin (29 mins), Alan Campbell (R.C. Santander 1) for Byrne (76 mins). **Captain:** Frank Stapleton. **Manager:** Eoin Hand (32). **Formation:** 4-3-3.

Italy: F. Tancredi, S. Bagni, P. Vierchowd, G. Scirea, G. Bergomi, A. Cabrini, B. Conti, M. Tardelli, A. di Gennaro, P. Rossi, A. Altobelli. **Subs:** A. Serena for Conti (72 mins), G. Dosena for Rossi (72 mins)

The unsuitability of Dalymount Park for 'big-time' soccer was demonstrated when a huge crowd turned up to see the visit of the World Cup holders. This caught the FAI off guard and with their refusal to open the gates early, a serious crowd problem developed which was only alleviated when a section was allowed onto the touchline in front of the main stand. These events had precedents in the 40's and 50's but by the 80's they should have been eradicated and it was not until after the horrendous Hillsborough disaster that a fundamental change took place in the area of crowd control.

The game's kick-off was delayed by 15 minutes to accommodate the bigger-than-expected crowd and 4 minutes after the start Italy were awarded a penalty. This came about when a Lawrenson pass was blocked by Altobelli to Rossi who returned it to Altobelli in space. As the striker raced into the box he was taken down by Lawrenson and Rossi scored from the spot. Lawrenson injured his arm in the incident and was replaced soon after by McGrath. Another mistake in the Irish defence, this time by McCarthy, allowed Conti in for a shot which was saved by Bonner. But a third mistake, after 17 minutes, was punished by Altobelli. Hughton came out of defence and linked with Brady and Sheedy before losing the ball to Conti in midfield. Conti knocked the ball forward for Altobelli to race clear on the right, cut inside McCarthy and find the bottom corner of the net with a ground shot. Waddock almost got Hughton in for a goal soon after but the right backs shot screwed high and wide. Galvin then went off injured before Hughton had another shot blocked. As the Italians packed their box it was getting difficult to find openings but another blocked shot, this time by McGrath, gave Stapleton a chance with his volley being saved by Tancredi. The best Irish chance of the half came when Stapleton forced Tancredi to punch a Hughton cross straight to Whelan whose shot was deflected for a corner by the outstretched leg of Scirea.

The second half was poor with Italy defending their two-goal lead. That was reduced by one when a quick throw-in by Sheedy found Beglin who, in turn, found Stapleton on the right edge of the Italian box. Stapleton shook off the attentions of Vierchowd and Bagni before rolling the ball into the path of Waddock whose low shot from outside the area found the bottom left-hand corner of Tancredi's net. A free kick from Brady was easily saved by the Italian goalkeeper while the Irish goalkeeper had to save at the feet of Rossi. After having two penalty claims turned down earlier there were howls of protest when a third claim for an apparent push by Tardelli on Sheedy was also turned down on 80 minutes. A minute later Whelan combined with Brady before the former had a hard shot saved by Tancredi. Much of the constructive play was broken up by fouls (34 in all) but there was only one booking – Tardelli for grabbing the ball in the air to prevent Stapleton from getting a free.

Match No. 213 ISRAEL Away

Wednesday 27th February, 1985 – Tel Aviv

ISRAEL (0) 0
REP. OF IRELAND (0) 0

Ref: Como (Italy) **Ground:** Ramat Gan Stadium **Att:** 3,000

Israel: A. Haviv, S. Kirat, A. Cohen, N. Barda, D. Pizanti, M. Sinai, R. Turk, N. Cohen, M. Selecter, Z. Armeli, E. Ohana. **Subs:** Y. Ekhoiz for A. Cohen (half-time), B. Manam for N. Cohen (half-time), R. Rosental for Armeli (half-time).

Ireland: Patrick Bonner (Glasgow Celtic 7), Chris Hughton (Tottenham Hotspur 24), David O'Leary (Arsenal 32), Mick McCarthy (Manchester City 6), Jim Beglin (Liverpool 5), Ronnie Whelan (Liverpool 11), Paul McGrath (Manchester United 2), Gary Waddock (Queens Park Rangers 15), Kevin Sheedy (Everton 5), Frank Stapleton (Manchester United 42), Alan Campbell (R.C. Santander 2). **Subs:** John Byrne (Queens Park Rangers 2) for Stapleton (65 mins). **Captain:** Frank Stapleton. **Manager:** Eoin Hand (33) **Formation:** 4-4-2.

Ireland had the majority of the play but some poor finishing denied them victory. Sheedy twice carved out good openings but there was nobody to finish them off while a Whelan shot was well wide in the opening twenty minutes. After 23 minutes Bonner fumbled a long-range shot from Armeli but Beglin was back to clear before the Israeli forwards could get to it. A free kick from Whelan was headed down by McGrath but Haviv cleared before Stapleton could get to it and before the break McGrath shot wide following good work by Whelan, Stapleton and Sheedy.

Whelan had a volley saved by Haviv and McCarthy got back to stop Rosental from getting through at the start of the second period. After 9 minutes Waddock's shot from outside the box hit the underside of the crossbar and bounced back into play while, 4 minutes later, Whelan headed a Sheedy cross into Campbell's path but the latters weak shot was easily saved. The home sides best chance came after 27 minutes when a corner by Manam found Ohana but his shot was cleared off the line by Hughton. A late chance fell to Byrne but his shot on the turn was just over.

Match No. 214 ENGLAND Away

Tuesday 26th March, 1985 – London

ENGLAND (1) 2 Steven 44, Lineker 75
REP. OF IRELAND (0) 1 Brady 87

Ref: Smith (Scotland) **Ground:** Wembley Stadium **Att:** 34,793

England: G. Bailey, V. Anderson, M. Wright, T. Butcher, K. Sansom, R. Wilkins, B. Robson, T. Steven, M. Hateley, G. Lineker, C. Waddle. **Subs:** G. Hoddle for Robson (67 mins), P. Davenport for Hateley (73 mins)

Ireland: Patrick Bonner (Glasgow Celtic 8), Chris Hughton (Tottenham Hotspur 25), Mick McCarthy (Manchester City 7), Mark Lawrenson (Liverpool 31), Jim Beglin (Liverpool 6), Paul McGrath (Manchester United 3), Gary Waddock (Queens Park Rangers 16), Liam Brady (Inter. Milan 50), Ronnie Whelan (Liverpool 12), Frank Stapleton (Manchester United 43), Eamonn O'Keefe (Port Vale 5). **Subs:** David O'Leary (Arsenal 33) for McGrath (half-time), Kevin O'Callaghan (Portsmouth 18) for Whelan (70 mins), John Byrne (Queens Park Rangers 3) for O'Keefe (79 mins). **Captain:** Frank Stapleton. **Manager:** Eoin Hand (34) **Formation:** 4-4-2.

A dull game had a quiet opening and it was not until a quarter of an hour had gone that the first goal threat developed. Waddle sent a through ball to Robson who failed to control it and McCarthy deflected it towards goal with Bonner forced to tip over. A minute later a long kick out by Bonner was headed on by Stapleton to O'Keefe who managed to get in a shot ahead of Wright which just went past the far upright. Bonner was forced into another finger-tip save from Sansom's strongly-driven shot and then saved a Butcher header with his legs at the expense of a corner; from which Butcher headed over. The Irish goalkeeper made two more saves to deny Hateley before England scored on the stroke of half-time. A long ball by Butcher was headed on by Hateley in the box. The ball bounced off Whelan and Steven capitalized from this mistake to shoot past Bonner from 6 yards.

McGrath did not appear for the second half having been replaced by O'Leary. O'Leary went into defence with Lawrenson moving into midfield. After 6 minutes Whelan and Lawrenson set up Waddock for a curling shot which just went wide. Waddle and Anderson went close for England before they scored again. A long headed clearance by Wright eluded McCarthy allowing Davenport to square the ball into the unmarked Lineker who ran on and chipped the ball over the advancing goalkeeper. In the closing stages Wilkins had a shot saved and Beglin a shot wide before Brady scored a consolation goal. A free kick by O'Leary on the halfway line was played short to Beglin via Brady. Beglin sent a pass forward to Stapleton who flicked it into the path of the inrushing Brady. Brady returned the ball to Stapleton and ran on to accept the return from the Irish captain. Taking the ball in his stride, Brady's shot from an acute angle spun out of Bailey's grasp and went into the net. Beglin was shown the yellow card during the second half for a foul on Hateley.

Match No. 215 — NORWAY — Home

Wednesday 1st May, 1985 – Dublin (World Cup)

REP. OF IRELAND (0) 0
NORWAY (0) 0

Ref: Nemeth (Hungary) **Ground:** Lansdowne Road **Att:** 15,000

Ireland: Patrick Bonner (Glasgow Celtic 9), David Langan (Oxford United 16), Mark Lawrenson (Liverpool 32), David O'Leary (Arsenal 34), Jim Beglin (Liverpool 7), Gerry Daly (Birmingham City 41), Liam Brady (Inter. Milan 51), Gary Waddock (Queens Park Rangers 17), Tony Galvin (Tottenham Hotspur 10), Frank Stapleton (Manchester United 44), Michael Robinson (Queens Park Rangers 19). **Subs:** Ronnie Whelan (Liverpool 13) for Brady (67 mins), Paul McGrath (Manchester United 4) for Langan (83 mins). **Captain:** Frank Stapleton. **Manager:** Eoin Hand (35) **Formation:** 4-3-3.

Norway: E. Thorstvedt, S. Fjaelberg, T. Kojedal, A. Hareide, H. H. Henriksen, K. E. Herlovsen, P. E. Ahlsen, H. Thoresen, E. Soler, A. L. Okland, U. Moen. **Subs:** A. Erlandsen for Herlovsen (58 mins), P. Jacobsen for Moen (87 mins)

A disappointing result for Ireland and, it must be said, for Norway as both sides had chances to win the game. An early opportunity saw Thoresen and Moen set up Okland for a shot which curled over the bar. Brady almost got Robinson in at the other end but Thorstvedt saved at the forwards feet while O'Leary blocked a shot from Herlovsen. After 29 minutes a move up the right saw Langan feed Daly whose cross was met on the volley by Galvin only for Thorstvedt to make a brilliant one-handed save on the goal-line. Ten minutes before the break Thoresen played a one-two with Okland on the half-way line and burst clear. But, as Bonner advanced, he elected to chip the goalkeeper and Bonner made a great save to turn the ball out for a corner.

Bonner denied Thoresen again, 2 minutes into the second half, when he saved the Norwegian captain's defelected shot. A minute later a free kick from Daly was headed goalwards by O'Leary forcing Thorstvedt into another save. A shot from Stapleton was also saved as was a header by Moen from a free kick by Thoresen. After 12 minutes a cross from Galvin was headed back across goal by Stapleton and O'Leary for Brady to thump a shot against the crossbar. As the ball rebounded into play Stapleton headed it into the net. However, the goal was ruled out by the referee as the linesman had his flag raised for either a foul or offside. Three minutes later a clearance from the Norwegian defence was headed on by Moen to put Okland sprinting clear from halfway. Again Bonner was faced with a one-on-one situation but this time he stayed on his goal-line and brought off another good save although the Norwegians finishing was poor.

Manager Eoin Hand decided to resign after the game but was persuaded to stay on by the players.

Match No. 216 — SPAIN — Home

Sunday 26th May, 1985 – Cork

REP. OF IRELAND (0) 0
SPAIN (0) 0

Ref: Gaechter (Switzerland) **Ground:** Flower Lodge **Att:** 12,000

Ireland: Seamus McDonagh (Gillingham 21), David Langan (Oxford United 17), David O'Leary (Arsenal 35), Mick McCarthy (Manchester City 8), Chris Hughton (Tottenham Hotspur 26), Gerry Daly (Birmingham City 42), Gary Waddock (Queens Park Rangers 18), Liam Brady (Inter. Milan 52), Tony Galvin (Tottenham Hotspur 11), Alan Campbell (R.C. Santander 3), Michael Robinson (Queens Park Rangers 20). **Subs:** Tony Grealish (West Bromwich Albion 42) for Galvin (25 mins), Kieran O'Regan (Brighton 4) for Hughton (65 mins), Pat Byrne (Shamrock Rovers 4) for Langan (81 mins). **Captain:** Liam Brady. **Manager:** Eoin Hand (36) **Formation:** 4-3-3.

Spain: A. Zubizarretta, M. Gerardo, A. Maceda, A. Goicoechea, J. Camacho, Victor, R. Gallego, R. Gordillo, Marcos, Santillana, H. Rincon. **Subs:** Caldere for Gallego (70 mins), J. Alberto for Gordillo (76 mins), M. Sarabia for Santillana (85 mins), Marina for Marcos (85 mins)

Ireland's first international in Cork for 46 years turned out to be a dour struggle with little for the large attendance to enthuse about.

Play for the first 30 minutes was inconsequental with the only attempts of note being a McCarthy header which was easily saved and a Rincon header wide. On the half hour Langan set up Grealish for a shot which was deflected wide by a defender. From the resulting corner another McCarthy header was easily dealt with by the goalkeeper. The nearest Ireland came to scoring in the first half was when a free kick by Daly curled over the wall but went just wide.

The second half began well with McCarthy heading a Brady free kick just over the crossbar. Then Brady, taking advantage of a Robinson knock-down, rounded Zubizarretta and crossed over for Grealish to head wide. A minute later McDonagh brought off a great save to turn away Marcos's header from Gerardo's cross although the referee had already blown for offside. Brady was again in the thick of things when he skipped past Gerardo and Victor to set up Robinson for an angled shot which was well saved by Zubizarretta. In the closing stages Campbell's header and shot were saved, O'Leary's tackle stopped Rincon getting through and O'Regan had a shot again saved by Zubizarretta.

Match No. 217 — SWITZERLAND — Home

Sunday 2nd June, 1985 – Dublin (World Cup)

REP. OF IRELAND (2) 3 Stapleton 7, Grealish 33, Sheedy 57
SWITZERLAND (0) 0

Ref: Bergamo (Italy) **Ground:** Lansdowne Road **Att:** 17,300

Ireland: Seamus McDonagh (Gillingham 22), David Langan (Oxford United 18), David O'Leary (Arsenal 36), Mick McCarthy (Manchester City 9), Jim Beglin (Liverpool 8), Gerry Daly (Birmingham City 43), Tony Grealish (West Bromwich Albion 43), Liam Brady (Inter. Milan 53), Kevin Sheedy (Everton 6), Frank Stapleton (Manchester United 45) Michael Robinson (Queens Park Rangers 21). **Subs:** Ronnie Whelan (Liverpool 14) for Daly (half-time). Paul McGrath (Manchester United 5) for Grealish (63 mins). **Captain:** Frank Stapleton. **Manager:** Eoin Hand (37) **Formation:** 4-4-2.

Switzerland: K. Engel, A. Geiger, H. Ludi, R. Wehrli, C. In-Albon, A. Egli, U. Barberis, H. Hermann, M. Descastel, C. Matthey, M. Braschler. **Subs:** E. Burgener for Engel (23 mins), G. Bregy for Barberis (59 mins)

Ireland got off to a great start with a rehearsed set-piece move after 7 minutes. Sheedy floated a free kick over to the far side of the box where the unmarked Langan knocked it back across the face of the goal. Daly missed the ball at the near post but it rolled on for Stapleton to net at the far albeit from an offside position. Five minutes later Egli headed on a long throw-in from Hermann for Matthey to send a flashing volley just wide. Ireland began to dominate and after 16 minutes Brady sent a perfect through ball to put Sheedy clear in the box only for Engel to make a brilliant save with his legs. Engel was injured in a clash with Grealish and was replaced by Burgener after 23 minutes. Ten minutes later a long high pass from Daly was back-headed onto a post by Grealish and the ball rolled back across and over the goal-line.

Daly was injured just before the half-time whistle and did not reappear for the second half. His replacement, Whelan, almost got a third goal within half a minute of the restart but his shot was well held by Burgener. Ireland did get a third goal when McDonagh's long kick allowed Sheedy to race clear of the Swiss offside trap. Chesting the ball down, he cooly slotted the ball wide of the goalkeeper and into the net. The Swiss brought on an extra forward, Bregy, who came close to scoring twice. First his free kick just curled wide and then his fiercely-hit shot from outside the box forced McDonagh into a fine diving save. Late in the game Stapleton headed a Beglin cross wide when well placed and a parting shot from Matthey curled wide.

Match No. 218 SWITZERLAND Away

Wednesday 11th September, 1985 – Berne (World Cup)

SWITZERLAND (0) 0
REP. OF IRELAND (0) 0

Ref: Aladren (Spain) **Ground:** Wankdorf Stadium **Att:** 24,000

Switzerland: K. Engel, A. Geiger, C. In-Albon, H. Hermann, A. Egli, M. Schällibaum, P. Perret, G. Bregy, M. Koller, R. Lüthi, C. Matthey. **Subs:** J. P. Brigger for Schällibaum (75 mins)

Ireland: Seamus McDonagh (Sunderland 23), Chris Hughton (Tottenham Hotspur 27), David O'Leary (Arsenal 37), Mick McCarthy (Manchester City 10), Jim Beglin (Liverpool 9), Gerry Daly (Birmingham City 44), Liam Brady (Inter. Milan 54), Mark Lawrenson (Liverpool 33), Kevin Sheedy (Everton 7), Frank Stapleton (Manchester United 46) Tony Cascarino (Gillingham 1). **Subs:** Paul McGrath (Manchester United 6) for Daly (66 mins), Kevin O'Callaghan (Portsmouth 19) for Sheedy (70 mins). **Captain:** Frank Stapleton. **Manager:** Eoin Hand (38) **Formation:** 4-4-2.

*Switzerland 0-0 Ireland 1985. Robert Lüthi gets above everybody to have a header saved by McDonagh. Irish players (*in white, from left*): Cascarino, McCarthy, Beglin, Sheedy and O'Leary (*No. 5*).*

Both sides were going through a bad spell and this return meeting only served to emphasise their problems. A poor game saw many passes going astray and the few scoring chances wasted.

Early incidents saw Matthey mis-kick in front of goal and McDonagh saving a long range effort from Hermann. After 21 minutes a cross by Hughton was missed by In-Albon and Cascarino's snatched shot went wide. Five minutes later Cascarino got his head to a Brady free kick but his long range effort was easily saved by Engel. Coming up to the break the home side had three great chances but failed to convert them. A long kick by Engel was missed by O'Leary allowing Bregy to run clear but O'Leary redeemed his error by getting back to make a saving tackle. Then a Bregy corner flew across the goal with Hermann just failing to make contact on the goal-line. Six minutes from the interval In-Albion shot over from point blank range following a free kick by Schällibaum.

Switzerland 0-0 Ireland 1985
Jim Beglin and David O'Leary cover a shot from Georges Bregy as Robert Lüthi looks on.

Five minutes into the second half Hughton had a shot saved by Engel after weaving through the Swiss cover. McDonagh saved a long range shot from Bregy and a Lüthi header before another Bregy corner flashed across the goalmouth without a finishing touch. After 65 minutes Sheedy's long range shot was saved and 5 minutes later, Cascarino got on the end of another Brady free kick to have a shot on the turn into the side netting. On 76 minutes a Cascarino cross was headed on by McGrath for O'Callaghan to have a net-bound shot defelected out for a corner by Perret. Three minutes after that a Beglin cross found Stapleton unmarked only a few yards out but he lunged at the shot and Engel saved easily. Matthey, Koller and Brigger failed to find the net with late chances while in the last minute Stapleton did only for the referee to blow for offside. The frustration of the players manifested itself in a foul count of 52 which yielded three bookings – Hughton and Beglin for Ireland and Brigger for the home side.

Match No. 219 USSR Away

Wednesday 16th October, 1985 – Moscow (World Cup)

USSR (0) 2 Cherenkov 60, Protasov 89
REP. OF IRELAND (0) 0

Ref: Casarin (Italy) **Ground:** Lenin Stadium **Att:** 103,000

USSR: R. Dasayev, G. Morozov, A. Demianenko, A. Chivadze, A. Bubnov, S. Aleinikov, G. Gotsmanov, A. Zavarov, F. Cherenkov, O. Protasov, O. Blokhin. **Subs:** G. Kondratiev for Blokhin (55 mins), V. Bessanov for Zavarov (83 mins)

Ireland: Seamus McDonagh (Notts County 24), Chris Hughton (Tottenham Hotspur 28), David O'Leary (Arsenal 38), Mark Lawrenson (Liverpool 34), Mick McCarthy (Manchester City 11), Jim Beglin (Liverpool 10), Gary Waddock (Queens Park Rangers 19), Tony Grealish (West Bromwich Albion 44), Liam Brady (Inter. Milan 55), Frank Stapleton (Manchester United 47) Tony Cascarino (Gillingham 2). **Subs:** Ronnie Whelan (Liverpool 15) for Grealish (71 mins), Kevin O'Callaghan (Portsmouth 20) for Beglin (79 mins). **Captain:** Frank Stapleton. **Manager:** Eoin Hand (39) **Formation:** 5-3-2.

Ireland turned in one of their better away performances but still lost to a Soviet team defending an unbeaten home record in the World Cup.

Hughton and Waddock had early shots off target in a bright opening. After 13 minutes Ireland should have had a penalty when Beglin was taken down in the area by Chivadze but the referee waved play on. The Soviets then took control with Blokhin setting up Cherenkov for a shot which was saved and Gotsmanov having a cross-cum-shot turned over by McDonagh. Coming up to half-time Ireland went on the offensive with Grealish only just stopped at the last moment by a saving tackle from Chivadze and Brady having a shot blocked after playing a one-two with Stapleton.

Nine minutes into the second half McDonagh did well to stop a long range shot from Blokhin with Lawrenson clearing the rebound. On the hour Protasov got away from Lawrenson on the half-way line and raced away to cross over for the unmarked Cherenkov to shoot past McDonagh. Whelan almost equalised, soon after coming on, when he latched on to a deflected shot from Brady but could only force the goalkeeper into turning the ball out for a corner. From the Irish flag-kick the Soviets launched an immediate counter-attack with Zavarov and Kondratiev combining to get Demianenko in but McCarthy deflected the latter's shot into the side netting. With 8 minutes left Stapleton headed wide from Brady's free kick. In the last minute good play by Cherenkov and Bessanov allowed Gotsmanov to round McDonagh and cross in for Protasov to score with a diving header which might have hit McCarthy on it's way in.

After the game Eoin Hand announced that he would be resigning as manager after the final game against Denmark.

Match No. 220 DENMARK Home

Wednesday 13th November, 1985 – Dublin (World Cup)

REP. OF IRELAND (1) 1 Stapleton 6
DENMARK (1) 4 Elkjaer 7, 76, Laudrup 49, Sivebaek 59

Ref: Wöhrer (Austria) **Ground:** Lansdowne Road **Att:** 15,154

Ireland: Seamus McDonagh (Wichita Wings 25), Kevin Moran (Manchester United 19), Mark Lawrenson (Liverpool 35), David O'Leary (Arsenal 39), Jim Beglin (Liverpool 11), Paul McGrath (Manchester United 7), Tony Grealish (West Bromwich Albion 45), Liam Brady (Inter. Milan 56), Kevin Sheedy (Everton 8), Frank Stapleton (Manchester United 48) Tony Cascarino (Gillingham 3). **Subs:** Pat Byrne (Shamrock Rovers 5) for Grealish (30 mins), Michael Robinson (Queens Park Rangers 22) for Sheedy (69 mins). **Captain:** Frank Stapleton. **Manager:** Eoin Hand (40) **Formation:** 4-4-3.

Denmark: T. Rasmussen, J. Sivebaek, S. Busk, M. Olsen, I. Nielsen, J. Molby, S. Lerby, J. Olsen, K. Berggreen, M. Laudrup, P. Elkjaer. **Subs:** J. J. Bertelsen for Lerby (59 mins), F. Arnesen for M. Olsen (70 mins)

Republic of Ireland v Denmark
Front row, left to right: *David O'Leary, Tony Grealish, Frank Stapleton, Kevin Moran and Liam Brady.*
Back row: *Seamus McDonagh, Paul McGrath, Tony Cascarino, Mark Lawrenson, Kevin Sheedy and Jim Beglin.*

Note: The Irish defence was Moran and O'Leary in the centre with Lawrenson as sweeper and Beglin at left back. McGrath played on right side of midfield but was the token right back.

Eoin Hand's last game in charge ended with his heaviest competitive defeat and Ireland's biggest home defeat since 1971. Denmark completely outplayed the home side despite conceding an early goal.

After 6 minutes Stapleton headed a Lawrenson ball down to Grealish on the half way line. Grealish sent it forward to Cascarino who tricked his way past Busk before sending over a perfect cross for Stapleton to head powerfully past Rasmussen. A minute later Sivebaek exchanged passes with Lerby and Berggreen in a run up the Irish left, beat Beglin and crossed in for Elkjaer to shoot home the equaliser from close range. Soon after Molby got Elkjaer in again but, after beating Moran and Lawrenson, his shot failed to beat McDonagh. After 10 minutes Elkjaer again shook off his marker, Moran, and made his way into the box before passing to Berggreen who was taken down from behind by Lawrenson as he was about to shoot. The referee, however, saw nothing wrong and waved play on. Lawrenson made two saving tackles to stop Elkjaer and Laudrup from getting through while, at the opposite end, Ireland had three chances late in the half. Rasmussen punched a Brady cross off Stapleton's head, Cascarino headed another Brady cross wide and Byrne sent McGrath in for a ground shot which the Danish goalkeeper saved at full stretch.

The visitors gained their victory with three excellent second half goals – the first of which came after 4 minutes. Morten Olsen's long ball out of defence was headed on by Elkjaer for Laudrup to race clear. O'Leary got back to cover but Laudrup shook him off and had plenty of time to steer his shot wide of McDonagh into the corner of the net. Ten minutes later Sivebaek, deep in his own half, played a one-two with Laudrup to find space up the Irish left. He cut infield at full speed, used Elkjaer to draw off Lawrenson, beat Moran and Beglin with ease before chipping the ball over McDonagh for a fine individual goal. Soon after Jesper Olsen found Molby free on the Irish right and the latter had a chip shot tipped over by McDonagh. Elkjaer had a free kick just over before Denmark scored their fourth. Arnesen put Sivebaek free again on the Irish left and his cross was side-footed down by Berggreen into the path of Elkjaer whose flashing shot from an acute angle found the top corner of the net. Two late chances fell to Ireland in the closing stages as Denmark relaxed. Robinson had a volley from outside the box saved at the second attempt by Rasmussen and Beglin had a shot wide after beating Sivebaek. Both O'Leary and McGrath were booked for fouls.

Match No. 221 — WALES — Home

Wednesday 26th March 1986 – Dublin

REP. OF IRELAND (0) 0
WALES (1) 1 Rush 17

Ref: Hope (Scotland) **Ground:** Lansdowne Road **Att:** 16,500

Ireland: Gerry Petyon (Fulham 21), David Langan (Oxford United 19), David O'Leary (Arsenal 40), John Anderson (Newcastle United 7), Jim Beglin (Liverpool 12), Ray Houghton (Oxford United 1), Liam Brady (Inter. Milan 57), Paul McGrath (Manchester United 8), Ronnie Whelan (Liverpool 16), John Aldridge (Oxford United 1), Michael Robinson (Queens Park Rangers 23). **Subs:** Mick McCarthy (Manchester City 12) for Anderson (50 mins), Pat Byrne (Shamrock Rovers 6) for Robinson (66 mins). **Captain:** Liam Brady. **Manager:** Jack Charlton (1). **Formation:** 4-4-2.

Wales: N. Southall, R. James, J. Jones, J. Charles, K. Jackett, D. Phillips, P. Nicholas, C. Blackmore, S. Lowndes, I. Rush, A. Davies. **Subs:** D. Saunders for Davies (60 mins), T Norman for Southall (66 mins).

On the 60th anniversary of its first ever full international, the Republic of Ireland began a new phase with this first game under the control of Englishman Jack Charlton. It is only with the benefit of hindsight that this epoch can be seen for there was little to indicate that Ireland was to enter its most successful era on Charlton's debut.

After 5 minutes a free kick by Brady was headed on by Robinson for Whelan to send a volley just past the post. In the first Welsh attack of the match they forced a corner off O'Leary and from Phillips's flag kick James headed on for the unmarked Rush to head home. The only other Welsh attack of note came five minutes later when Rush and Davies combined to get Lowndes free only for the latter's shot to be turned over the bar by Peyton. At the other end Whelan chested down a Houghton cross in the box and his volley was headed just over by Robinson while Aldrige had a shot on the turn saved by Southall. Coming up to the break a Nicholas free kick found the unmarked Charles but he headed over.

The home side dominated the second half and after 14 minutes a corner by Whelan was headed on by Robinson for, first, Houghton then Aldridge to have shots blocked with Aldridge shooting his rebounded effort against the foot of the post. Soon after Southall was injured on landing after coming for a high ball and was replaced. His deputy, Norman, was soon in action saving a shot on the turn by Houghton (who had moved up into the attack when Robinson went off). In the final ten minutes Ireland had three chances – Byrne, after beating Charles, had a powerful shot saved for a corner, McGrath's header from Brady's corner was also saved while Aldridge raced onto a long ball from O'Leary only to curl his shot against the upright. Aldridge's misfortune would be a recurring feature of future games.

John Aldridge made his international debut against Wales.

Match No. 222 URUGUAY Home

Wednesday 23rd April 1986 – Dublin

REP. OF IRELAND (1) 1 Daly 38 (pen)
URUGUAY (1) 1 Paz 22

Ref: Martin (England) **Ground:** Lansdowne Road **Att:** 14,000

Ireland: Patrick Bonner (Glasgow Celtic 10), David Langan (Oxford United 20), Mick McCarthy (Manchester City 13), Barry Murphy (Bohemians 1), Chris Hughton (Tottenham Hotspur 29), Ray Houghton (Oxford United 2), Gerry Daly (Shrewsbury Town 45), Liam O'Brien (Shamrock Rovers 1), Tony Galvin (Tottenham Hotspur 12), Frank Stapleton (Manchester United 49), John Aldridge (Oxford United 2). **Subs:** John Byrne (Queens Park Rangers 4) for Stapleton (67 mins), Peter Eccles (Shamrock Rovers 1) for Hughton (80 mins). **Captain:** Frank Stapleton. **Manager:** Jack Charlton (2). **Formation:** 4-3-3.

Uruguay: F. Alvez, V. Djogo, M. Saralegui, C Vega, N. Gutierrez, E. Rivero, J. Barrios, R. Paz, J. Salazor, V. Ramos, W. Cabrera.

The Irish started well with Daly back-heeling a free kick to Houghton whose shot from 25 yards flashed wide. Another Irish free kick from Daly was layed off to McCarthy who forced Alvez into his first save with a powerful shot which was turned out for a corner. After 22 minutes Cabrera was fouled by Murphy about 25 yards from goal and from the resulting free kick Paz shot low and hard to Bonner's right. The Irish goalkeeper had the free covered but the ball deflected off the body of McCarthy and rolled into the net with Bonner unable to adjust in time. It was the visitors only threatening moment on the Irish goal. Four minutes later a long throw-in from McCarthy found Stapleton in the box and his flick header beat Alvez but struck the outside of the far post and went out. Then Hughton's long ball into the area was headed down by Stapleton for Galvin to send a volley just wide. After 38 minutes Ireland got a deserved equaliser. Stapleton was pushed by his marker Saralegui when going for a high ball and a free kick was awarded. Houghton took it quickly and sent a high ball into the area but as Aldridge went for it he was elbowed in the face by Gutierrez. The referee immediately pointed to the spot and, despite Uruguayan protests and delaying antics on the part of Alvez, Daly sent the goalkeeper the wrong way to keep up his 100% penalty record for Ireland. The half ended with a Hughton shot which was well off target.

The second half was not as good as the first and the only chances came Ireland's way. Six minutes after the restart O'Brien had a shot deflected wide by Saralegui while Aldridge headed into the side netting following an excellent cross from Galvin. Byrne had a late opportunity for a winner but, after outwitting two defenders, he shot inches wide. The Uruguayans, who were on their way to establish a reputation as a 'dirty' side in Mexico '86, indulged in some rough play which earned a booking for their centre forward Cabrera. The game however was generally free of the scenes of misbehaviour associated with Uruguay in the world cup finals.

Match No. 223 ICELAND Away

Sunday 25th May 1986 Reykjavik

ICELAND (1) 1 Gudjohnsen 40
REP. OF IRELAND (1) 2 McGrath 34, Daly 84

Ref: Worrall (England) **Ground:** Laugardalsvöllur **Att:** 4,246

Iceland: B. Sigurdsson, G. Gislason, L. Olafsson, V. Torkelsson, A. M. Jonsson, H. Askelsson, R. Margeirsson, P. Ormslev, S. Jonsson, P. Petursson, A. Gudjohnsen. **Subs:** G. Steinsson for Askelsson (62 mins), O. Tordarson for S. Jonsson (67 mins), G. Bergsson for A. M. Jonsson (79 mins).

Ireland: Patrick Bonner (Glasgow Celtic 11), John Anderson (Newcastle United 8), Kevin Moran (Manchester United 20), Mick McCarthy (Manchester City 14), Chris Hughton (Tottenham Hotspur 30), Ray Houghton (Oxford United 3), Paul McGrath (Manchester United 9), Mick Kennedy (Portsmouth 1), Tony Galvin (Tottenham Hotspur 13), Frank Stapleton (Manchester United 50), John Aldridge (Oxford

United 3). **Subs:** Pat Byrne (Shamrock Rovers 7) for Hughton (half-time), Gerry Daly (Shrewsbury Town 46) for McGrath (70 mins), Niall Quinn (Arsenal 1) for Aldridge (84 mins). **Captain:** Frank Stapleton. **Manager:** Jack Charlton (3). **Formation:** 4-3-3.

Ireland were invited to take part in a tournament to celebrate the 200th anniversary of the founding of the city of Reykjavik. This tournament, which also involved Czechoslovakia, was to provide Ireland with its first-ever trophy and Charlton with a basic outline of his first choice team. That team included a central defensive partnership of McCarthy and Moran which would serve the manager for the next four years and a forward line which would take Ireland to the European Championship finals.

Ireland began well with Anderson having a shot saved and Galvin shooting into the side netting in the first 10 minutes. Iceland then had three good openings with Petursson wasting the first by shooting wide when sent clear. Bonner brought off a good save to deny Gudjohnsen however a bad kick out by the Irish goalkeeper gave Petursson another chance but Moran reacted quickest to dispossess the striker before he could get a shot in. Aldridge had a weak header saved before Ireland took the lead on 34 minutes. Houghton took a free kick on the left side of the Icelandic box and sent a high ball over to the right side where McCarthy ran in to head it back across the face of the goal for McGrath to volley home from 7 yards. Three minutes later Anderson almost increased Ireland's lead with a fierce shot which just went over. Five minutes before half-time Gudjohnsen got the ball out by the Irish left hand touchline and sent over a cross for the incoming Petursson. Bonner went to meet the ball at the near post but he over-estimated its flight and the ball slipped through his fingers into the net.

Hughton was not fully fit and was replaced during the break with Byrne going to right back and Anderson taking over at left back. Ireland dominated the play in the second half. Galvin beat three men and shot wide early on as did Kennedy after playing a one-two with Stapleton. After 10 minutes Stapleton headed down a long ball from Anderson to Houghton. Houghton turned quickly on it and sent a shot just the wrong side of the post. Two minutes later Moran and Galvin set up Stapleton for a shot which hit the crossbar. McGrath went off with a hamstring injury and his replacement, Daly, scored the winner with 6 minutes left. A corner from Kennedy was cleared out to Daly whose volley was blocked back out to him by an Icelandic defender. Daly again sent in another volley from outside the box which flew past a host of players and the sprawled goalkeeper, who had gone down to save the first effort. Late in the game another substitute, Quinn, was sent clear by Houghton only to lob his shot over the bar.

Match No. 224 — CZECHOSLOVAKIA — Neutral

Tuesday 27th May 1986 – Reykjavik

CZECHOSLOVAKIA (0) 0
REP. OF IRELAND (0) 1 Stapleton 82

Ref: Olsen (Iceland) **Ground:** Laugardalsvöllur **Att:** 1,000

CSSR: L. Miklosko, S. Levy, J.Chovanec, F. Stracka, J. Fiala, I. Hasek, J. Berger, K. Kula, M. Siva, M. Luhovy, L. Vizek. **Subs:** L. Kubik for Luhovy (56 mins), I. Knoflicek for Siva (75 mins), J. Novak for Vizek (80 mins).

Ireland: Gerry Peyton (Fulham 22), Pat Byrne (Shamrock Rovers 8), Kevin Moran (Manchester United 21), Mick McCarthy (Manchester City 15), John Anderson (Newcastle United 9), Michael Robinson (Queens Park Rangers 24), Ray Houghton (Oxford United 4), Paul McGrath (Manchester United 10), Tony Galvin (Tottenham Hotspur 14), John Aldridge (Oxford United 4), Niall Quinn (Arsenal 2). **Subs:** Mick Kennedy (Portsmouth 2) for Anderson (half-time), Frank Stapleton (Manchester United 51) for Quinn (55 mins), Gerry Daly (Shrewsbury Town 47) for Robinson (67 mins). **Captain:** Mick McCarthy. **Manager:** Jack Charlton (4). **Formation:** 4-3-3.

Ireland duly won their first trophy with this victory in the Reykjavik 200 tournament and also achieved another first – their first win when wearing their second colours of white shirts, green shorts and white stockings. To date that is the only victory when Ireland wore such a strip.

Ireland opened strongly with McGrath having two good openings. A free kick by Houghton found Aldridge free in the area and when he crossed in McGrath met it with a firm header which the goalkeeper saved. Houghton and Anderson set up McGrath for a second crack at goal but again Miklosko made a good save to keep out his powerful shot. The Czechs had few chances in the first half although Peyton did very well to save a shot from Siva. Five minutes before the break Quinn got in at the end of a free kick from Moran but his shot from an acute angle just went the wrong side of the far post.

Anderson did not re-appear for the second half and Kennedy took his place at left back. The Czechs had an early chance to take the lead but Hasek's close range header went wide. After 15 minutes a cross from McGrath was handled by Stracka on the edge of the area and a harsh penalty decision went Ireland's way. Aldridge took the spot kick but his poor effort was turned around the post by Miklosko. Ten minutes later a long throw-in by McCarthy was headed on by Stapleton for McGrath to have a shot on the turn just over. Then a long clearance by the Czech goalkeeper was headed on by Kubik for Knoflicek to race completely clear. As Peyton advanced the Czech substitute placed the ball wide of him but also wide of the goal. With 8 minutes to go McGrath and Galvin pressured Kubik into losing possession on the half-way line and Stapleton raced away with the ball. Ignoring the obvious pass to Aldridge, Stapleton ran to the edge of the box and unleashed a thunderbolt of a shot which flew into the roof of the net. There was one booking – Galvin for a foul on Levy in the second half.

Match No. 225 BELGIUM Away

Wednesday 10th September 1986 – Brussels (European Championship)

BELGIUM (1) 2 Claesen 13, Scifo 69
REP. OF IRELAND (1) 2 Stapleton 17, Brady (89) pen.

Ref: Igna (Romania) **Ground:** Heysel Stadium **Att:** 22,212

Belgium: J. M. Pfaff, G. Grun, F. Vander Elst, S. Demol, L. Clysters, P. Vervoort, V. Scifo, J. Ceulemans, F. Vercauteren, N. Claesen, P. Desmet.

Ireland: Patrick Bonner (Glasgow Celtic 12), David Langan (Oxford United 21), Mark Lawrenson (Liverpool 36), Kevin Moran (Manchester United 22), Chris Hughton (Tottenham Hotspur 31), Ray Houghton (Oxford United 5), Paul McGrath (Manchester United 11), Liam Brady (Ascoli 58), Tony Galvin (Tottenham Hotspur 15), Frank Stapleton (Manchester United 52), John Aldridge (Oxford United 5). **Subs:** Ronnie Whelan (Liverpool 17) for Galvin (79 mins), Jim Beglin (Liverpool 13) for Hughton (81 mins). **Captain:** Frank Stapleton. **Manager:** Jack Charlton (5). **Formation:** 4-4-2.

Belgium had had an excellent World Cup in Mexico and returned home heros having finished the tournament in fourth place. They were favourites to qualify from Group 7 but most teams suffer a backlash following a successful World Cup and Ireland hoped to capitalise on this. However this backlash was not to be decisive factor in determining the group winners rather the new style of play Charlton imposed on Ireland for this his first competitive game in change. It was also the first competitive international at the Heysel Stadium since the tragic events at the 1985 European Champions Cup Final.

Both sides started tamely testing each others defence and it was not until the 13th minute that Belgium forced the first corner. From that corner Claesen shot home at the near post from close range to open the scoring. Four minutes later Ireland were level. Aldridge had a shot blocked out to Galvin and his pin-point cross was sent to the corner of the net by a full-length diving header from Stapleton. Two minutes later Galvin headed a Brady free kick down to Moran but Pfaff made a brave save at the defenders feet. Play in the first half was generally scrappy and it was not until the latter stages that either goal was threatened. Desmet beat Lawrenson and shot across goal with the ball just going wide. Scifo had a long-range shot also just wide while, 6 minutes before the break, Stapleton and Galvin combined for Brady to have a shot across the area which was just missed by the two Irish forwards.

The second half saw Belgium have the majority of the play. But it was Ireland who had the best of the early chances. Brady had a shot wide and Galvin a curling effort over in the first five minutes. After 9 minutes McGrath sent a powerful header across goal from Brady's free kick. Aldridge got on the end of it but Pfaff saved well on his line even though the Irish forward was offside. Two minutes later a long pass from Ceulemans allowed Desmet to get past Moran but, with only Bonner to beat, he shot too close to the goalkeeper and Bonner made a great save. Bonner again came to Ireland's rescue with another save from a Vercauteren free kick while sweeper Demol blazed hopelessly wide from close range following a cross from Scifo. After 24 minutes Vercauteren took a corner quickly and, from the edge of the box, Scifo sent a header in off the far post. The home side then settled back on that lead and as the game entered its final 10 minutes Claesen shot wide. With two minutes to go Moran headed a long Belgium clearance to Beglin. The substitute sent it forward to Stapleton who was upended in the box by Pfaff. With just 20 seconds left Brady sent the goalkeeper the wrong way from the penalty spot to level the scores. Galvin and Scifo were booked in the first half.

Match No. 226 — SCOTLAND — Home

Wednesday 15th October 1986 – Dublin (European Championship)

REP. OF IRELAND (0) 0
SCOTLAND (0) 0

Ref: Halle (Norway) **Ground:** Lansdowne Road **Att:** 49,203

Ireland: Patrick Bonner (Glasgow Celtic 13), David Langan (Oxford United 22), Mick McCarthy (Manchester City 16), Kevin Moran (Manachester United 23), Jim Beglin (Liverpool 14), Ray Houghton (Oxford United 6), Paul McGrath (Manchester United 12), Liam Brady (Ascoli 59), Kevin Sheedy (Everton 9), Frank Stapleton (Manchester United 53), John Aldridge (Oxford United 6). **Subs:** Gerry Daly (Shrewsbury Town 48) for Moran (71 mins). **Captain:** Frank Stapleton. **Manager:** Jack Charlton (6). **Formation:** 4-4-2.

Scotland: J. Leighton, R. Stewart, R. Gough, A. Hansen, D. Narey, G Strachan, P. McStay, R. Aitken, M. MacLeod, G. Sharp, M. Johnston.

A poor match on a poor surface saw Scotland, with three central defenders at the back, come to defend for a point. Few openings were created as both sides used the aerial option to negate the 'heavy' pitch.

In the first half-hour McGrath and Strachan had shots over and Aldridge a powerful shot saved after getting past Gough and Strachan. The best chance of the game came after 34 minutes when a cross from Houghton was punched down to Sheedy by Leighton but the Irish midfielders volley was headed off the line by Hansen.

After the interval McCarthy headed a Brady corner over and McGrath had a header saved from another Brady cross. Moran went off injured after 71 minutes and McGrath dropped back to defence to cover when Daly came on. Three minutes later Aldridge challenged Leighton for a cross from Langan and when the ball fell loose Stapleton blasted over in front of goal. Daly had a long-range shot saved, Stapleton a header over and Aldridge a shot over as the game drew to a close. Daly was shown the yellow card for a foul on McStay in the second half.

Match No. 227 — POLAND — Away

Wednesday 12th November 1986 – Warsaw

POLAND (1) 1 Koniarek 43
REP. OF IRELAND (0) 0

Ref: Nemeth (Hungary) **Ground:** Legia Stadium **Att:** 9,000

Poland: J. Kazimierski, M. Ostrowski, P. Krol, K. Przybys, D. Wdowczyk, A. Rudy, W. Prusik, J. Karas, J. Urban, J. Furtok, M. Koniarek. **Subs:** J. Wandzik for Kazimierski (half-time), R. Tarasiewicz for Rudy (half-time), D. Dziekanowski for Karas (half-time), M. Lesniak for Furtok (half-time).

Ireland: Patrick Bonner (Glasgow Celtic 14), David Langan (Oxford United 23), Mick McCarthy (Manchester City 17), Kevin Moran (Manchester United 24), Jim Beglin (Liverpool 15), Ray Houghton (Oxford United 7), Paul McGrath (Manchester United 13), Liam Brady (Ascoli 60), Kevin Sheedy (Everton 10), Frank Stapleton (Manchester United 54), John Aldridge (Oxford United 7). **Captain:** Liam Brady. **Manager:** Jack Charlton (7). **Formation:** 4-4-2.

Ireland dominated the game for long periods but fell to goal which could be attributed to defensive lapses on the part of the entire defence.

The visitors had their chances of scoring but the lack of a finishing touch cost them the match. Stapleton had a shot over before Sheedy, after a fine run had taken him past two players, smacked a shot against a post and out. Sheedy and Brady had other chances with free kicks, which were off target, before Poland scored a breakway goal. A long clearance by the goalkeeper found Rudy breaking up the left wing. The Pole outpaced McCarthy and sent in a harmless looking low cross which was left by Moran and Langan for Beglin. Before the ball got to the full back in nipped Koniarek to totally mis-hit his shot into the net. Just before the break McCarthy shot over from close range.

Twelve minutes into the second half Koniarek set up Lesniak for a great chance but Bonner made a brilliant save at the far post. Bonner was in action soon after saving a shot from Tarasiewicz while McCarthy and Aldridge missed good chances at the other end. Eleven minutes from the end a corner from Brady landed at the feet of the unmarked Stapleton who was unable to get in a telling finish before the Polish defence closed and cleared. In the closing minutes Stapleton headed over and Sheedy shot wide while, with two minutes to go, McGrath's header from Langan's cross was well saved by Wandzik. Three players were shown the yellow card – Ostrowski and Tarasiewicz for Poland and McCarthy for Ireland.

Match No. 228 SCOTLAND Away

Wednesday 18th February 1987 – Glasgow (European Championship)

SCOTLAND (0) 0

REP. OF IRELAND (1) 1 Lawrenson 6

Ref: Van Ettekoven (Holland) **Ground:** Hampden Park **Att:** 45,081

Scotland: J. Leighton, R. Stewart, R. Gough, A. Hansen, M. Malpas, G. Strachan, R. Aitken, P. Nevin, B. McClair, M. Johnston, D. Cooper. **Subs:** P. McStay for Cooper (half-time), A. McCoist for Malpas (68 mins).

Ireland: Patrick Bonner (Glasgow Celtic 15), Paul McGrath (Manchester United 14), Mick McCarthy (Manchester City 18), Kevin Moran (Manchester United 25), Ronnie Whelan (Liverpool 18), Ray Houghton (Oxford United 8), Mark Lawrenson (Liverpool 37), Liam Brady (Ascoli 61), Tony Galvin (Tottenham Hotspur 16), Frank Stapleton (Manchester United 55), John Aldridge (Liverpool 8). **Subs:** John Byrne (Queens Park Rangers 5) for Brady (60 mins). **Captain:** Frank Stapleton. **Manager:** Jack Chartlon (8). **Formation:** 4-4-2.

A spate of injuries forced Jack Charlton into an experimental move of playing McGrath and Whelan in unaccustomed roles as full-backs. This experiment proved to be a masterstroke as it released Lawrenson, a nominal full back, to have an outstanding game in the centre of the field.

Two minutes into the match a throw-in from Galvin found Houghton whose cross was headed just wide by Aldridge. Three minutes later a lovely move saw Houghton, Whelan and Brady combine to set Galvin running up the left wing. The Irish winger outpaced Stewart and crossed over for Aldridge to send a near post header just over. Ireland's fine start got its reward a minute later. Following a foul on Stapleton, Aldridge took a quick free kick and found Lawrenson running through the centre. Lawrenson held off Gough and shot low into the corner of the net. Scotland had few chances in the first half with the best of them being a McClair shot blocked, a Strachan shot saved and a mis-hit effort by McClair wide. Hansen made two goal-line interceptions to prevent a further Irish goal and Houghton nearly scored with a lob from long range after a bad throw out by Leighton.

Scotland reverted to a 4-3-3 formation for the second half and in the first ten minutes McStay had two shots wide and Johnston a shot deflected away. After 15 minutes Brady went off injured with Byrne going on up front and Stapleton dropping back into midfield. Aldridge had the ball in the Scots net but was offside in doing so. A minute later Bonner punched a Nevin cross off Johnston's head. Bonner denied Johnston five minutes later when he saved the latters bicycle kick but was beaten by Johnston after 39 minutes only for McCarthy to clear off the line. Byrne headed a Houghton cross straight at Leighton before McCarthy cleared his lines again; this time from a shot by McCoist. Three minutes from the end Lawrenson broke from defence to accept a pass from Galvin deep in the Scottish half. Lawrenson's cross was back heeled by Aldridge for the unmarked Byrne who totally fluffed his shot well off target. A minute later a Houghton pass found McGrath running into the box but his low shot was taken off the line by Stewart. Ireland's two centre backs, Moran and McCarthy, were booked during the course of the first half.

Match No. 229 BULGARIA Away

Wednesday 1st April 1987 – Sofia (European Championship)

BULGARIA (1) 2 Sadkov 40, Tanev 81 (pen)
REP. OF IRELAND (0) 1 Stapleton 51

Ref: Valente (Portugal) **Ground:** Vasil Levski Stadium **Att:** 35,247
Buglaria: B. Michailov, P. Nikolov, N. Iliev, G. Dimitrov, K. Gezinski, A. Sadkov, H. Kolev, P.Simeovov, B. Iskrenov, N. Sirakov, L. Tanev. **Subs:** P. Alexandrov for Iskrenov (61 mins), I. Voinov for Simeovov (65 mins).

Ireland: Patrick Bonner (Glasgow Celtic 16), John Anderson (Newcastle United 10), Mick McCarthy (Manchester City 19), Kevin Moran (Manchester United 26), Chris Hughton (Tottenham Hotspur 32), Ronnie Whelan (Liverpool 19), Paul McGrath (Manchester United 15), Liam Brady (West Ham United 62), Tony Galvin (Tottenham Hotspur 17), Frank Stapleton (Manchester United 56), John Aldridge (Liverpool 9). **Subs:** Niall Quinn (Arsenal 3) for Stapleton (84 mins). **Captain:** Frank Stapleton/Mick McCarthy. **Manager:** Jack Charlton (9). **Formation:** 4-4-2.

Previous Irish visits to Bulgaria had provided for many controversial incidents. Disallowed goals, sendings off and poor refereeing had been the hallmark of the two earlier meetings so, by contrast, this was a tame affair. However one feature remained – the rain which fell constantly during this (and previous) games.

The Irish came for a draw and with Bulgaria's short passing game destroyed because of the rain-sodden pitch the first half had little to offer. After 3 minutes Galvin shot wide following a McGrath cross but it was another 23 minutes before another goal threat was forthcoming when Sirakov raced clear on a through ball only for Bonner to come well outside his box and clear. The final 15 minutes of the half saw a flurry of activity with Whelan's chip shot just over after a lovely interchange with Aldridge. Kolev, with a free kick, and Nikolov, with a long-range shot, were both off target before Bulgaria went into the lead. Sirakov and McCarthy chased a long ball from Dimitrov on the Irish right. The Irishman appeared to have won the race but Sirakov dived in and gained possession with McCarthy sent flying. Sirakov played it inside to Sadkov who controlled it before shooting low into the corner of the net. Two minutes before the break McGrath had a shot blocked on the edge of the box and when the rebound came to Galvin he curled a shot just around the post.

The Irish abandoned caution in the second half and began at a furious pace. After 2 minutes Brady found Aldridge free in the area and he crossed in for Whelan to have a powerful shot brilliantly parried away by Michailov. The ball came to Stapleton whose shot was kicked off the line by the goalkeeper and when Galvin latched on to this rebound his cross was headed wide by Aldridge. Four minutes later McGrath's header was cleared back out to him by Dimitrov. McGrath's second header was headed on by Whelan for Stapleton to turn and volley a shot past Michailov into the far corner of the net. In the next four minutes Kolev had a free kick saved by Bonner, Whelan had a shot over, Kolev a shot wide and Galvin another shot over. Both sides number 10s had efforts cleared off the line by the No. 3s. After 21 minutes Brady released Galvin whose cross from the by-line was headed past Michailov by Aldridge only for Iliev to clear his lines. Then, 8 minutes later, Sirakov met a Kolev corner with a stooping header which was cleared off the line by Hughton. Brady had a shot just wide and McCarthy cleared a dangerous Alexandrov cross before Bulgaria got a second goal. Voinov and Alexandrov combined to send Sirakov racing in on goal. Moran came across with the intention of taking Sirakov down outside the box but both players slid into the box and the referee gave the penalty which was converted by Tanev. Five minutes from the end a Brady free kick was cleared out to Galvin whose volley was saved by Michailov. The match had a confusing ending when another Brady free kick was cleared to Whelan whose cross was palmed off Quinn's head by the goalkeeper. The ball came to Brady who shot through a forest of legs only for it to hit Quinn and go wide. The referee had blown however and amid some confusion called for the ball to end an exciting second half.

Aldridge, McGrath and Brady were booked as was Voinov for Bulgaria. Brady's booking, for argueing about the penalty decision, was to have repercussions later when UEFA took this (and a future sending off) into consideration while making a decision which was to cost Brady a place in the finals.

Match No. 230 — BELGIUM — Home

Wednesday 29th April 1987 – Dublin (European Championship)

REP. OF IRELAND (0) 0
BELGIUM (0) 0

Ref: Holzmann (Austria) **Ground:** Lansdowne Road **Att:** 44,600

Ireland: Patrick Bonner (Glasgow Celtic 17), John Anderson (Newcastle United 11), Mick McCarthy (Manchester City 20), Kevin Moran (Manchester United 27), Ronnie Whelan (Liverpool 20), Ray Houghton (Oxford United 9), Paul McGrath (Manchester United 16), Liam Brady (West Ham United 63), Tony Galvin (Tottenham Hotspur 18), Frank Stapleton (Manchester United 57), John Aldridge (Liverpool 10). **Subs:** John Byrne (Queens Park Rangers 6) for Brady (77 mins). **Captain:** Frank Stapleton. **Manager:** Jack Charlton (10). **Formation:** 4-4-2.

Belgium: J. M. Pfaff, E. Gerets, G. Grün, L. Clysters, P. Albert, P. Vervoort, V. Scifo, J. Ceulemans, F. Vercauteren, N. Claesen, P. Desmet. **Subs:** P. Janssen for Albert (66 mins).

The match opened brightly with Stapleton heading on Anderson's free kick into the patch of Brady after 75 seconds. Brady, in the clear about 7 yards out, tried to shoot across Pfaff but the Belgian goalkeeper saved with his foot. Bonner was forced into action at the far end when he saved a shot from Claesen after Ceulemans had a shot deflected. From the resulting corner Vervoort had a shot wide. After 6 minutes Houghton and Stapleton combined to send Aldridge racing free of Albert only for Grün to hustle him off the ball in the box with the referee waving away Irish protests for a penalty. The game settled down then with few openings. McGrath, Anderson, Houghton and Brady all had shots off target while Aldridge had a header over as the half drew to a close. A minute before the break Vercauteren had a shot turned around the post for a corner by Bonner. From the flag kick Claesen had another shot saved for a corner and when this kick came across Albert's header was kicked over the bar by Galvin. The referee blew for half-time before this corner could be taken.

Ireland had another early chance at the start of the second half when Aldridge's header from Brady's free kick was saved by Pfaff. After 4 minutes Pfaff saved a Stapleton header but was beaten three minutes later when McCarthy's header, from a Whelan free kick, was kicked off the goalline by Grün. Bonners only save of the half came four minutes later when he easily dealt with a long range shot from Scifo. Belgium restricted the home side to a few half-chances as the game progressed. Both Albert and Brady had to leave the field with injuries and Vercauteren was booked after fouling Houghton. The other 'highlights' of a poor game were a McCarthy header saved one-handedly by Pfaff, a Moran header wide, a Byrne volley over and a McGrath header saved easily by Pfaff.

Match No. 231 **BRAZIL** **Home**

Saturday 23rd May 1987 – Dublin

REP. OF IRELAND (1) 1 Brady 33
BRAZIL (0) 0

Ref: Sandoz (Switzerland) **Ground:** Lansdowne Road **Att:** 17,000

Ireland: Patrick Bonner (Glasgow Celtic 18), John Anderson (Newcastle United 12), Mick McCarthy (Glasgow Celtic 21), Kevin Moran (Manchester United 28), Ronnie Whelan (Liverpool 21), Liam O'Brien (Manchester United 2), Paul McGrath (Manchester United 17), Liam Brady (West Ham United 64), Kevin O'Callaghan (Portsmouth 21), John Byrne (Queens Park Rangers 7), John Aldridge (Liverpool 11). **Subs:** David Langan (Oxford United 24) for Whelan (60 mins), Ken De Mange (Liverpool 1) for McCarthy (64 mins), Niall Quinn (Arsenal 4) for O'Brien (80 mins). **Captain:** Mick McCarthy. **Manager:** Jack Charlton (11). **Formation:** 4-3-3.

Brazil: Carlos, Josimar, Ricardo II, Geraldao, Nelsinho, Silas, Valdo, Douglas, Edu I, Muller, Mirandinha. **Subs:** Rai for Edu I (65 mins), Romario for Mirandinha (67 mins), Joao Paulo for Muller (74 mins).

A poor crowd turned up to see Ireland record their first win over Brazil in three attempts. For John Anderson, Kevin O'Callaghan and especially Liam Brady it was a sweet victory as they were the only survivors of the side between 7-0 by Brazil five years earlier.

The early stages of the game were played at a slow pace with both sides 'feeling' each other out. Muller had a shot saved and Nelsinho and McGrath had others shots off target before Ireland scored with the first real opening. Brady accepted a Whelan pass and turned inside two players before passing the ball to Aldridge. Aldridge flicked it into Bryne and, even though the ball came loose in a challenge by Geraldao, Brady picked up the rebound in the box. Brady shaped for a cross to the far post and the goalkeeper advanced three yards off his line in anticipation of this. However Brady quickly changed feet and sent a low shot inside Carlos's near post with the goalkeeper wrongfooted. Soon after Muller burst up the Irish left past three players but his hard cross was cut out by Bonner. Then Byrne headed a long clearance into the path of the onrushing McGrath whose parting shot was only just over. Geraldao had a long range free kick wide and both Byrne and O'Brien failed to connect with an O'Callaghan cross when only a few yards from goal.

The Irish dominated the first half but the visitors improved in the second. Early in the half Valdo had a shot blocked with Mirandinha shooting the rebound over. Muller had a shot across goal following a pass from Douglas but missed a great chance when he sent a free header wide after Valdo and Josimar had combined up the Irish left. A tremendous shot from Silas was blocked by Moran out to Aldridge but his backpass was intercepted by Mirandinha who was held up by Bonner long enough for the defence to get back and clear. Langan came on at right back with Anderson moving to the left back spot of Whelan and De Mange replaced the injured McCarthy whose place in defence was taken by McGrath. Valdo had a shot saved by Bonner before a long ball from Brady allowed O'Callaghan to trick his way past Josimar and Geraldao for a free run on goal. Carlos advanced to lessen the angle and made a good save to deny the Irish winger. The Brazilian goalkeeper made another fine save at the feet of Aldridge soon after when Quinn had headed a Byrne cross into his path. Near the end Romario came close to an equaliser twice when, first, Bonner saved his shot and then he scuffed another shot wide.

John Anderson played in both full back positions against Brazil.

Match No. 232 **LUXEMBOURG** **Away**

Thursday 28th May 1987 – Luxembourg (European Championship)

LUXEMBOURG (0) 0
REP. OF IRELAND (1) 2 Galvin 44, Whelan 64

Ref: Peduzzi (Switzerland) **Ground:**Municipal Stadium **Att:** 4,290

Luxembourg: J. Van Rijswijck, L. Schonckert, H. Meunier, C. Weis, M. Bossi, J. Girres, G. Hellers, J. P. Barboni, T. Malget, R. Langers, B. Reiter. **Subs:** G Jeitz for Reiter (69 mins), M. Thome for Girres (87 mins).

Ireland: Patrick Bonner (Glasgow Celtic 19), John Anderson (Newcastle United 13), Mick McCarthy (Glasgow Celtic 22), Kevin Moran (Manchester United 29), Ronnie Whelan (Liverpool 22), Ray Houghton (Oxford United 10), Paul McGrath (Manchester United 18), Liam Brady (West Ham United 65), Tony Galvin (Tottenham Hotspur 19), Frank Stapleton (Manchester United 58), John Aldridge (Liverpool 12). **Subs:** John Byrne (Queens Park Rangers 8) for Moran (half-time), David Langan (Oxford United 25) for Anderson (52 mins). **Captain:** Frank Stapleton. **Manager:** Jack Charlton (12). **Formation:** 4-3-3.

Ireland went in search of goals and began well with Houghton having a header saved after 75 seconds. But a combination of a strong defence and poor finishing were to deny the Irish a large victory. After 12 minutes Girres had a shot saved by Bonner while in the space of 6 minutes McGrath headed wide twice when well placed. Langers tested Bonner again with a powerful shot which was well held. Just before the half hour a perfect set-piece free kick from Brady gave Stapleton a free header which the Irish striker somehow managed to put wide. Another free kick 4 minutes later, this time by Houghton, was headed down by McCarthy for Aldridge to chip Van Rijswijck but the ball landed on the crossbar and went out. A minute later a good run by Houghton gave Aldridge another chance but his shot was saved by the goalkeeper. Galvin had a shot blocked and Malget missed a 'sitter' in front of goal before the visitors scored a minute before the break. Aldridge and Hellers tangled in going for a cross from Anderson which resulted in Hellers being grounded and Aldridge crossing over for Galvin to place the ball home with his right foot. In injury time Galvin almost returned the compliment to Aldridge when his knock on was headed by Aldridge into the goalkeepers arms.

Ireland's John Aldridge gets between Luxembourg's Hubert Meunier and Marcel Bossi to knock a shot over John Van Rijswijck but onto the crossbar. In the background is Mick McCarthy. (Photo: Luxemborger Wort)

Byrne came on for the injured Moran at half-time with McGrath dropping back to partner McCarthy in defence. Anderson had to go off injured soon after the restart with Charlton forced to use his second permitted substitute, Langan. After Byrne had curled a shot wide Luxembourg had their best spell of the game forcing three openings. After 10 minutes Weis had a shot saved and a minute later Langers got away from McCarthy with his ball to Reiter forcing McGrath to make a splendid saving tackle. Two minutes later still Langers had a shot wide. That though was the height of the Luxembourg threat. Aldridge had a header saved from Galvin's cross before Galvin set up Whelan for a 30 yard shot which found the bottom corner of the net. Seven minutes from the end Stapleton headed a Langan cross down to Aldridge who netted only for the referee to disallow the goal for a marginal offside decision. An angry Aldridge was booked for arguing about the ruling and, as this was his second yellow card in the Championship, he would miss the next game.

Match No. 233 LUXEMBOURG Home

Wednesday 9th September 1987 – Dublin (European Championship)

REP. OF IRELAND (1) 2 Stapleton 31, McGrath 74
LUXEMBOURG (1) 1 Krings 29

Ref: Cooper (Wales) **Ground:** Lansdowne Road **Att:** 18,000

Ireland: Gerry Peyton (AFC Bournemouth 23), David Langan (Oxford United 26), Kevin Moran (Manchester United 30), Paul McGrath (Manchester United 19), Ashley Grimes (Luton Town 17), Ray Houghton (Oxford United 11), Ronnie Whelan (Liverpool 23), Liam Brady (West Ham United 66), Tony Galvin (Sheffield Wednesday 20), Frank Stapleton (Ajax 59), John Byrne (Queens Park Rangers 9). **Subs:** Niall Quinn (Arsenal 5) for Galvin (55 mins). **Captain:** Frank Stapleton. **Manager:** Jack Charlton (13). **Formation:** 4-3-3.

Luxembourg: J. Van Rijswijck, L. Schonckert, H. Meunier, C. Weis, M. Bossi, T. Malget, G. Hellers, T. Scholten, J. P. Barboni, R. Langers, A. Krings. **Subs:** G. Dresch for Scholten (65 mins), G. Jeitz for Barboni (81 mins).

Ireland, as in the previous game, began well with Moran having a header saved from Houghton's cross after 45 seconds. In further attacks Stapleton scooped a close range shot over after Galvin had flicked on a Brady cross, Houghton had a shot blocked with Whelan shooting the rebound wide and Galvin shot over another close range effort when Stapleton headed a Houghton cross back across the goalmouth. Luxembourg defended in depth relying on quick breakways one of which saw a defensive header fall for Langers who put Krings clear with just Peyton to beat. However the Irish goalkeeper did well to parry Krings's shot and then recovered quickly to palm the rebound off Langers head. Five minutes later a cross from Langers bounced off McGrath and Whelan to Krings who shot low into the corner of the net from 10 yards. The Irish replied quickly with Stapleton heading a curling cross from Grimes into the net.

It was Luxembourg who made the better start to the second half with Krings heading a Langers cross wide and then using his hand to put Scholten's cross into the net although the referee did not fall for that. Quinn came on for Galvin with Houghton taking up a left wing role. The substitute was soon in action heading a Brady corner straight at the goalkeeper and another Brady cross wide. Peyton made another good one-on-one save to stop Hellers before Ireland increased the pressure in the final quarter. After 71 minutes Byrne's header from Houghton's cross was turned onto a post by Van Rijswijck with the ball rebounding back into the goalkeepers arms. Another Houghton cross was headed wide by Stapleton before Ireland scored with 16 minutes to go. Quinn headed down a Byrne cross and McGrath send a flashing volley from the edge of the area into the back of the net. Three Luxembourg players, Malget, Hellers and Barboni, and one Irish player, Quinn, were booked in the second half.

Match No. 234 **BULGARIA** **Home**

Wednesday 14th October 1987 – Dublin (European Championship)

REP. OF IRELAND (0) 2 McGrath 52, Moran 84
BULGARIA (0) 0

Ref: Keizer (Holland) **Ground:** Lansdowne Road **Att:** 26,000

Ireland: Patrick Bonner (Glasgow Celtic 20), Paul McGrath (Manchester United 20), Mick McCarthy (Glasgow Celtic 23), Kevin Moran (Manchester United 31), Ronnie Whelan (Liverpool 24), Ray Houghton (Oxford United 12), Mark Lawrenson (Liverpool 38), Liam Brady (West Ham United 67), Tony Galvin (Sheffield Wednesday 21), Frank Stapleton (Ajax 60), John Aldridge (Liverpool 13). **Subs:** Niall Quinn (Arsenal 6) for Aldridge (77 mins). John Byrne (Queens Park Rangers 10) for Galvin (77 mins). **Captain:** Frank Stapleton. **Manager:** Jack Charlton (14). **Formation:** 4-4-2.

Bulgaria: A. Ananiev, P. Nikolov, N. Iliev, G. Dimitrov, P. Petrov, P. Simeonov, A. Sadkov, I. Voinov, H. Stoitchkov, N. Sirakov, B. Iskrenov. **Subs:** I. Valov for Ananiev (55 mins), P. Alexandrov for Voinov (65 mins).

Sending-off: Liam Brady (Ireland) 85 mins.

Ireland's 50th European Championship game completed their programme in Group 7 but, with a home game still to come, Bulgaria, were expected to qualify for the finals in Germany. Things, however, did not turn out as expected and this merited win was the launching pad which rocketed Irish soccer into a new era.

After 4 minutes a cross from Lawrenson was badly mis-punched by Ananiev to the feet of the unmarked Stapleton. But, with the goal at his mercy, Stapleton's weak effort from 6 yards was cleared off the line by Nikolov. Soon after a long ball from McCarthy was headed on by Stapleton for Aldridge to have a shot from an acute angle saved by Ananiev. Bulgaria's best chance of the match came when Voinov's header allowed Sirakov to break clear in the box only for Bonner to make a magnificent save at his feet. Brady had a long-range shot saved by Ananiev at the butt of the upright as the home side increased the pressure in the last 15 minutes. Stapleton headed a Galvin cross wide, Moran had an overhead kick saved by Ananiev, Galvin's curling shot went wide and Stapleton had another header wide this time from a cross by Houghton.

Paul McGrath scorer of Ireland's first goal against Bulgaria.

Seven minutes after the restart Ireland got the goal their play deserved. A long throw-in by McCarthy was returned back out to him by Brady. McCarthy beat Stoitchkov before crossing over for Stapleton to pressure Ananiev into palming the ball down to McGrath who volleyed into the roof of the net from 7 yards. Brady was booked soon after for a foul on Nikolov and Valov replaced Ananiev in the Bulgarian goal. Valov was soon in action saving a shot from Aldridge following a cross from Houghton. Ireland then seemed to lose control of the game with Bulgaria having chances when Sirakov and Stoitchkov were denied by Bonner and Sadkov had a shot well over. Brady brought another save out of Valov before Charlton replaced Galvin and Aldridge with Byrne and Quinn. The two substitutes had a hand in Ireland's second goal 6 minutes from the end. A throw-in by Houghton was controlled by Byrne before his cross was headed back to him by Quinn. Byrne, on the by-line, then crossed over for Moran to head powerfully into the net from 2 yards. A minute later Brady retaliated when fouled by Sadkov and referee Jan Keizer sent him off. It was the death knell to Brady's international career for this, combined with an injury, would force him to miss the European Championship finals and restrict him to only five more caps before his retirement. An ill-tempered game also saw the bookings of Aldridge and Nikolov.

Match No. 235 ISRAEL Home

Tuesday 10th November 1987 – Dublin

REP. OF IRELAND (2) 5 Byrne 12, D. Kelly, 41, 56, 71 (pen), Quinn 83
ISRAEL (0) 0

Ref: Midgley (England) **Ground:** Dalymount Park **Att:** 9,500

Ireland: Kelham O'Hanlon (Rotherham United 1), Chris Morris (Glasgow Celtic 1), Mick McCarthy (Glasgow Celtic 24), Kevin Moran (Manchester United 32), Chris Hughton (Tottenham Hotspur 33), Ray Houghton (Liverpool 13), Mark Lawrenson (Liverpool 39), John Byrne (Queens Park Rangers 11), Kevin Sheedy (Everton 11), Niall Quinn (Arsenal 7), David Kelly (Walsall 1). **Subs:** Liam O'Brien (Manchester United 3) for Houghton (74 mins). **Captain:** Mark Lawrenson. **Manager:** Jack Charlton (15). **Formation:** 4-4-2.

Israel: B. Ginzburg, A. Cohen, E. Davidi, M. Shimonov, N. Klinger, E. Cohen, A. Ovadia, Y. Amar, U. Malmilian, D. Briyalovsky, S. Tikva. **Subs:** E. Yani for Ovadia (half-time), M. Eizenberg for Tikva (half-time).

Jack Charlton's first game at Dalymount Park provided him with his biggest victory to date. In a one-sided game Ireland did all the attacking and after 12 minutes a long ball from Hughton was headed down by Quinn for Byrne. Byrne took it on a few paces before cracking a low shot from 25 yards to the back of the net with the help of a defelction from Davidi. The home side continued to press with Houghton giving Kelly the chance to cross to the far post where Byrne's downward header was saved by Ginzburg. The Israeli goalkeeper was kept busy punching another Kelly cross off the head of Quinn and saving a McCarthy header while in between these efforts Houghton shot over after Quinn had knocked down a Morris cross. Four minutes from half time Ireland scored again when Kelly took advantage of a very bad throw out by Ginzburg and closed in to squeeze the ball between the back-peddling goalkeeper and his left hand post. In a rare attack Malmilian almost got through to score but just on half-time Sheedy's header put Houghton clear in the box but his shot just went the wrong side of the post.

Eleven minutes into the second half Sheedy and Houghton combined for Kelly to head home the latters cross in off the post. Houghton had a shot saved and another over before Yani got into trouble on the edge of his own area and rugby tackled Sheedy to the ground in the box. The referee awarded a penalty, amid much Israeli protests, and Kelly sent the goalkeeper the wrong way from the spot-kick to complete his hat-trick. Seven minutes from the end a free kick by Morris was headed powerfully home by Quinn. In the final few minutes Lawrenson and Byrne exchanged passes and Byrne's cross was headed against the post by O'Brien with Klinger denying Kelly a fourth goal with a last-ditch tackle from the rebound. In the last minute Malmilian and Briyalovsky got Eizenberg in for a shot which O'Hanlon did well to save. Davidi, Klinger and Ginzburg were all booked during the second half.

The following day Scotland travelled to Bulgaria with Irish hopes resting on a Scottish victory. That looked unlikely as Bulgaria played for a draw but three minutes from the end Gary Mackay ran onto a pass from Steve Clarke and neatly placed his shot wide of the goalkeeper into the corner of the net. Ireland had qualified for a major finals competition for the first time and Gary Mackay became an instant hero in Ireland.

Match No. 236 ROMANIA Home

Wednesday 23rd March 1988 – Dublin

REP. OF IRELAND (1) 2 Moran 31, D. Kelly 89
ROMANIA (0) 0

Ref: Martin (England) **Ground:** Lansdowne Road **Att:** 15,000

Ireland: Patrick Bonner (Glasgow Celtic 21), Chris Morris (Glasgow Celtic 2), Mick McCarthy (Glasgow Celtic 25), Kevin Moran (Manchester United 33), Ashley Grimes (Luton Town 18), Tony Galvin (Sheffield Wednesday 22), John Byrne (Queens Park Rangers 12), John Sheridan (Leeds United 1), Kevin Sheedy

(Everton 12), Frank Stapleton (Derby County 61), David Kelly (Walsall 2). **Subs:** John Anderson (Newcastle United 14) for McCarthy (half-time), Niall Quinn (Arsenal 8) for Stapleton (53 mins), Liam O'Brien (Manchester United 4) for Galvin (65 mins). **Captain:** Frank Stapleton. **Manager:** Jack Charlton (16). **Formation:** 4-4-2.

Romania: D Moraru, M. Popa, M. Rednic, I. Andone, N. Stanescu, I. Sabau, M. Coras, L. Boloni, D Mateut, C. Vaiscovici, R. Camataru. **Subs:** H. Lasconi for Vaiscovici (half-time).

The wind spoilt what should have been an entertaining game and Ireland's first match in their build-up to Euro '88 had few highlights other than the goals.

The first goal came after Stapleton had two headers, from crosses by Kelly and Galvin, easily saved and a shot from Popa, from a poorly cleared corner, just wide. Sheridan's corner from the left was parried away by Moraru but the lurking Moran fastened onto the loose ball and shot powerfully home. This was just about the only clear-cut chance of the half.

The second half was slightly better with Sheridan having a shot wide while Morris miscued his shot badly with the goal at his mercy following a cross from Grimes. Soon after another Morris effort was just wide. Romania's best chance came when Boloni's long range free kick was just tipped over by Bonner at full stretch. Quinn had two headers easily saved and O'Brien was also denied by Moraru, before Ireland scored again in the last minute. Sheedy took a high ball from Sheridan on the run, beat Sabau and crossed over to the far post where Kelly scored with a simple downward header.

Match No. 237 — YUGOSLAVIA — Home

Wednesday 27th April 1988 – Dublin

REP. OF IRELAND (1) 2 McCarthy 24, Moran 65
YUGOSLAVIA (0) 0

Ref: Smith (Scotland) **Ground:** Lansdowne Road **Att:** 12,000

Ireland: Patrick Bonner (Glasgow Celtic 22), Chris Morris (Glasgow Celtic 3), Mick McCarthy (Glasgow Celtic 26), Kevin Moran (Manchester United 34), Chris Hughton (Tottenham Hotspur 34), Ray Houghton (Liverpool 14), Paul McGrath (Manchester United 21), John Sheridan (Leeds United 2), Mark Kelly (Portsmouth 1), Frank Stapleton (Derby County 62), David Kelly (Walsall 3). **Subs:** John Anderson (Newcastle United 15) for Hughton (55 mins), John Byrne (Queens Park Rangers 13) for D. Kelly (79 mins), Liam O'Brien (Manchester United 5) for M. Kelly (89 mins). **Captain:** Frank Stapleton. **Manager:** Jack Charlton (17). **Formation:** 4-3-3.

Yugoslavia: D. Lekovic, B. Miljus, F. Hadzibegic, M. Elsner, L. Radanovic, M. Baljic, M. Jankovic, M. Bazdarevic, M. Mlinaric, Z. Vujovic, H. Skoro. **Subs:** D. Brnovic for Mlinaric (78 mins), Boban for Jankovic (78 mins).
Sending-off: Marko Elsner (Yugoslavia) 88 mins.

An improved performance saw Ireland extend their unbeaten run to eight. The Yugoslavs, like the Rumanians, did not show in attack but indulged in some rough play which resulted in four of their players, Hadzibegic, Elsner, Bazdarevic and Skoro being booked with Elsner receiving his marching orders for a foul on Mark Kelly.

With the visitors reliant on a five-man defence chances were very few but a free kick from McCarthy was headed down by Stapleton for Sheridan to volley wide. However the Irish unlocked the heavily manned defence with two superb corner kicks from Sheridan. The first, after 24 minutes, caught goalkeeper Lekovic out when he seemed to punch the ball into his own net under pressure from McCarthy. The goal was credited to McCarthy. Skoro had a shot over in a rare attack and Stapleton had a header easily saved in further play. Just before the break David Kelly's cross eluded everybody as it went across the goalmouth with Morris and McGrath unable to convert.

After 58 minutes Mark and David Kelly headed a Morris cross to Stapleton whose volley was well held by Lekovic. Houghton had a chip shot over and McCarthy a curling shot wide before another accurate Sheridan corner was headed powerfully home by Moran. Another Sheridan corner was headed over by McCarthy who had a second header from a Houghton free kick saved by the goalkeeper. Boban had a great chance for an equaliser near the end but shot wide. Two minutes before the final whistle Elsner hacked down Mark Kelly as he was going through and was sent off. Mark Kelly was forced to go off and his replacement, O'Brien, did not even get a touch of the ball before the referee blew for full time. As well as the four Yugoslavs, David Kelly was booked for fighting.

Match No. 238 — POLAND — Home

Sunday 22nd May 1988 – Dublin

REP. OF IRELAND (3) 3 Sheedy 12, Cascarino 30, Sheridan 40
POLAND (0) 1 Warzycha 66

Ref: Roberts (Wales) **Ground:** Lansdowne Road **Att:** 18,500

Ireland: Gerry Peyton (AFC Bournemouth 24), Chris Morris (Glasgow Celtic 4), Paul McGrath (Manchester United 22), Kevin Moran (Manchester United 35), Chris Hughton (Tottenham Hotspur 35), Tony Galvin (Sheffield Wednesday 23), Ronnie Whelan (Liverpool 25), John Sheridan (Leeds United 3), Kevin Sheedy (Everton 13), John Aldridge (Liverpool 14), Tony Cascarino (Millwall 4). **Subs:** Niall Quinn (Arsenal 9) for McGrath (54 mins), John Byrne (Queens Park Rangers 14) for Whelan (56 mins), Liam O'Brien (Manchester United 6) for Galvin (63 mins), Mark Kelly (Portsmouth 2) for Sheridan (63 mins). **Captain:** Kevin Moran. **Manager:** Jack Charlton (18). **Formation:** 4-4-2.

Poland: J. Wandzik, D. Kubicki, R. Wojciki, D. Lukasik, W. Cisek, W. Prusik, R. Komornicki, J. Urban, J. Ziober, D. Dziekanowski, R. Kosecki. **Subs:** W. Bendkowski for Lukasik (26 mins), G. Stengel for Wandzik (half-time), R. Warzycha for Kosecki (half-time), R. Tarasiewicz for Komornicki (half-time).

Poland's first game at Lansdowne Road ended with their heaviest defeat at the hands of Ireland. The Irish victory should have been bigger and Warzycha's goal put a more respectable look on the scoreline for the visitors.

After 12 minutes Wandzik was penalised for handling the ball outside his area and from the resulting free kick Sheedy shot low and hard around the wall into the corner of the net. Poland lost their centre back Lukasik with a head injury after 26 minutes and his replacement, Bendkowski, was only just on the field when Aldridge headed a Sheridan free kick down to Cascarino with Wandzik making a brave save at his feet. On the half hour Wandzik made a complete hash of coming to collect a free kick from Whelan and the ball bounced through to Cascarino who nodded it into the empty net. Ten minutes later a long ball from Morris found Aldridge whose cross was left by Cascarino for the unmarked Sheridan who controlled it in space before finding the roof of the net with a rising shot. Just before half-time Dziekanowski got through the Irish defence only to shoot wide.

Urban had a shot over early in the second half but it was Ireland who still dominated. Hughton played a one-two with Sheedy before crossing over for Aldridge to have a header saved and a Sheedy cross to the far post was met by a Morris shot which was saved for a corner by Stengel. Quinn replaced McGrath and played as a central defender and Byrne replaced Whelan in a straight swop before another Dziekanowski shot went wide. O'Brien and Mark Kelly then came on with Sheedy moving into centre midfield in a 4-3-3 formation. These changes disrupted Ireland and Poland took advantage to score. A Kubicki throw-in found Urban in the box and he shook off Quinn before passing in for Warzycha to shoot home. Ireland came back with Aldridge heading a Morris cross over while a header from Cascarino hit the crossbar. After 75 minutes a ball from Sheedy allowed Aldridge to chip the ball over Stengel into the net but Aldridge's misfortune continued when the referee ruled the goal out for offside. In the last minute a shot from Bendkowski went just wide.

Match No. 239 NORWAY Away

Wednesday 1st June 1988 – Oslo

NORWAY (0) 0
REP. OF IRELAND (0) 0

Ref: Sorensen (Denmark) **Ground:** Ullevaal Stadium **Att:** 9,494

Norway: E. Thorstvedt, H. Hansen, R. Bratseth, E. Johnsen, G. Halle, K. P. Loken, S. Brandhaug, O. Berg, K. Osvold, J. Andersen, J. Berg. **Subs:** G. Sorloth for Andersen (61 mins), C. Backhe for Loken (75 mins).

Ireland: Patrick Bonner (Glasgow Celtic 23), Chris Morris (Glasgow Celtic 5), Mick McCarthy (Glasgow Celtic 27), Kevin Moran (Manchester United 36), Chris Hughton (Tottenham Hotspur 36), Ray Houghton (Liverpool 15), Paul McGrath (Manchester United 23), Ronnie Whelan (Liverpool 26), Tony Galvin (Sheffield Wednesday 24), Frank Stapleton (Derby County 63), John Aldridge (Liverpool 15). **Subs:** Tony Cascarino (Millwall 5) for Stapleton (62 mins), John Sheridan (Leeds United 4) for Galvin (74 mins). **Captain:** Frank Stapleton. **Manager:** Jack Charlton (19). **Formation:** 4-4-2.

Ireland's final game before the European Championship Finals in West Germany could best be summed up as a tame friendly. The first half was basically a kick around with only two real chances both of which fell to the visitors. Galvin's cross to the far post was headed back by Stapleton for McGrath to have a powerful shot brilliantly saved by Thorstvedt after 37 minutes and in injury time Stapleton headed McCarthy's long ball into the path of Aldridge whose shot was saved well again by the Norwegian goalkeeper.

The second half was a bit more lively with Bratseth having a shot saved by Bonner and Anderson mis-hitting a shot wide. Galvin and McGrath set up Whelan for a shot off target while Johnsen headed a corner over. After 70 minutes Hughton played a one-two with Whelan before crossing over for Cascarino whose downward header was saved. In the next two minutes Cascarino had another header saved while McCarthy denied Sorloth a shooting chance with a fine tackle in the box. From the resultant corner the ball was cleared out to Houghton whose crossfield pass found Cascarino running into the box and his low cross was turned into the net by Galvin. The referee disallowed the goal for offside. In the closing 15 minutes Cascarino had a low shot saved and Aldridge a header from Whelan's cross saved. In the last minute Hansen had a cross-cum-shot turned over by Bonner but the referee blew for full time before the corner could be taken.

Match No. 240 ENGLAND Neutral

Sunday 12th June 1988 Stuttgart (European Championship Finals)

ENGLAND (0) 0
REP. OF IRELAND (1) 1 Houghton 5

Ref: Kirschen (East Germany) **Ground:** Neckarstadion **Att:** 55,500

England: P. Shilton, G. Stevens, M. Wright, T. Adams, K. Sansom, N. Webb, B. Robson, C. Waddle, P. Beardsley, G. Lineker, J. Barnes. **Subs:** G. Hoddle for Webb (60 mins), M. Hateley for Beardsley (82 mins).

Ireland: Patrick Bonner (Glasgow Celtic 24), Chris Morris (Glasgow Celtic 6), Mick McCarthy (Glasgow Celtic 28), Kevin Moran (Manchester United 37), Chris Hughton (Tottenham Hotspur 37), Ray Houghton (Liverpool 16), Paul McGrath (Manchester United 24), Ronnie Whelan (Liverpool 27), Tony Galvin (Sheffield Wednesday 25), Frank Stapleton (Derby County 64), John Aldridge (Liverpool 16). **Subs:** Niall Quinn (Arsenal 10) for Stapleton (63 mins), Kevin Sheedy (Everton 14) for Galvin (76 mins). **Captain:** Frank Stapleton/Kevin Moran. **Manager:** Jack Charlton (20). **Formation:** 4-4-2.

In a match which was almost a repeat of the 1957 Dalymount meeting between the two countries, Ireland achieved one of their greatest-ever victories. As in the previous clash, Ireland had a great

The Irish team line out in Stuttgart before their European Championship match with England.

Ray Houghton (far right) *runs away to celebrate, after heading Ireland into a fifth minute lead against England.*

start and an early goal, while England played better after the break but unlike the '57 game a header in the dying seconds of the game failed to find the net. . .

Ireland's good start saw McGrath scuff a shot which was easily saved by Shilton after two minutes. The next chance also fell to Ireland and this time they scored. After 5 minutes a long free kick by Moran was challenged for by Stevens, Stapleton and Wright, with the ball falling down to Galvin. The Irish winger's hooked cross was miskicked into the air by Sansom and Aldridge headed it to Houghton who sent a looping header into the corner of the net. Bonner was in action soon after saving at the feet of Lineker from a header by Sansom but it was the Irish who ran the first half. After 19 minutes a throw-in by Hughton was headed clear by Stevens only for Morris to latch onto the ball and send a first-time shot through a ruck of players with Shilton turning the ball around the post for a corner. Seven minutes later England should have had a penalty when Barnes was taken down in the area by Moran but the referee waved play on. Waddle shot into the side netting and Lineker had another shot saved by Bonner but it was Ireland who finished the half on the up when Houghton broke through England's offside trap only for Shilton to save at his feet.

The second half was a different story with an English onslaught which should have given them victory. After 3 minutes a long ball from Sansom put Lineker in the clear but his shot was saved by Bonner with Beardsley shooting the rebound over. Barnes curled a free kick wide, Beardsley curled another shot wide after a jinky run and Webb was also wide with another shot in a nine minute spell. After 14 minutes Robson sent Lineker clear again to chip the ball over Bonner but the shot just clipped the bar as it went over. A minute later Whelan also clipped the crossbar with a shot from the edge of the box after a McCarthy free kick was not properly cleared. Hoddle had a free kick saved for a corner before Quinn replaced Stapleton with Moran taking the captain's armband. Barnes and Stevens had further efforts off target before Adams and Hoddle combined to get Lineker free again but this time his shot screwed across goal and just past the far post. Two minutes later Aldridge knocked a long ball down to Houghton whose curling shot went wide with Quinn just failing to get his head to the ball. Bonner denied Barnes and Beardsley with good saves but made an even better one to stop a Robson shot after Lineker had set up the English captain. On the half hour Robson set up Lineker for another shot which Bonner saved with his foot at the expense of a corner. Two minutes later Bonner saved at Lineker's feet with Moran kicking the rebound out for a corner. From the flag kick Hoddle sent a flashing volley just wide. Seven minutes from the end Ireland staged a mini-recovery with Aldridge heading a Houghton cross over and Whelan way off target with a free kick from a good position. In the last minute Barnes was wide with a low shot after Robson had headed the ball down to him. Then, in injury time, history almost repeated itself when Lineker got his head to a Hoddle free kick with Bonner hopelessly out of position. But the Irish goalkeeper made a magnificent twisting save to turn the ball onto a post and out for an inconsequential corner. This time the Irish roar was not silenced.

Match No. 241 — USSR — Neutral

Wednesday 15th June 1988 – Hanover (European Championship Finals)

USSR (0) 1 Protasov 74
REP. OF IRELAND (1) 1 Whelan 38

Ref: Aladren (Spain) **Ground:** Niedersachen Stadium **Att:** 45,290

USSR: R. Dasayev, V. Khidiatulin, O. Kuznetsov, T. Sulakvelidze, A. Demianenko, S. Aleinikov, A. Zavarov, A. Mikhailichenko, V. Rats, I. Belanov, O. Protasov. **Subs:** S. Gotsmanov for Sulakvelidze (half-time), V. Chanov for Dasayev (68 mins).

Ireland: Patrick Bonner (Glasgow Celtic 25), Chris Morris (Glasgow Celtic 7), Mick McCarthy (Glasgow Celtic 29), Kevin Moran (Manchester United 38), Chris Hughton (Tottenham Hotspur 38), Ray Houghton (Liverpool 17), Ronnie Whelan (Liverpool 28), Kevin Sheedy (Everton 15), Tony Galvin (Sheffield Wednesday 26), Frank Stapleton (Derby County 65), John Aldridge (Liverpool 17). **Subs:** Tony Cascarino (Millwall 6) for Stapleton (80 mins). **Captain:** Frank Stapleton/Mick McCarthy. **Manager:** Jack Charlton (21). **Formation:** 4-4-2.

Ray Houghton, Ronnie Whelan, John Aldridge and Paul McGrath celebrate a great start against England.

Ronnie Whelan volleys the ball home after 38 minutes against USSR, to give Ireland the lead.

Both sides went into this game with 1-0 victories in their previous outings and knowing that a second victory could see them through to the semi-finals. Ireland's pressure game, which had worked so well in the first-half of the English match, worked even better against the Soviets but the victory eluded them when some poor finishing and a Soviet equaliser with their only real shot on target gave them a share of the points. However the equaliser could not detract from a superb display from the Irish.

Five minutes into the game a Sheedy shot bounced up into the air and down for Houghton to have a side footed effort brilliantly pushed onto a post by Dasayev although the flag was raised for offside. Another Sheedy shot, a few minutes later, went over the bar while Houghton skipped past three tackles before his shot was again saved by Dasayev. The only Soviet shot of note during this half came after 28 minutes when Kuznetsov's powerful effort just went wide. Stapleton and Sheedy, with two long range shots, had further efforts on goal before Ireland took a deserved lead. A long throw-in by McCarthy sailed right over to the far post where Whelan met the ball with a spectacular bicycle kick which gave Dasayev no chance. Just before half-time Aldridge headed a Morris cross onto the top of the net.

Ireland almost got a repeat of their first half score soon after the start of the second when another long throw-in by McCarthy was headed out to Whelan for a shot which Dasayev did well to turn over the bar. After 53 minutes Zavarov had a shot blocked on the edge of the box and a minute later Ireland could have had a penalty when Galvin was tackled feet first by Dasayev in going for a Sheedy through ball. After 65 minutes Galvin took a cross from Stapleton on the run but his control let him down and he crashed into the goalkeeper. Dasayev was injured and half a minute later a superb Galvin cross was blasted wide by Aldridge with the Soviet goalkeeper helpless. He was replaced by Chanov and sixteen minutes minutes from the end a long ball out of defence was flicked past Moran by Belanov leaving Protasov in the clear to shoot under Bonner for the equaliser.

Match No. 242 — HOLLAND — Neutral

Saturday 18th June 1988 – Gelsenkirchen (European Championship Finals)

HOLLAND (0) 1 Kieft 81
REP. OF IRELAND (0) 0

Ref: Brummier (Austria) **Ground:** Parkstadion **Att:** 70,800

Holland: H. Van Breukelen, B. Van Aerle, R. Koeman, F. Rijkaard, A. Van Tiggelen, J. Wouters, A. Muhren, R. Gullit, E. Koeman, M. Van Basten, G. Vanenburg. **Subs:** W. Kieft for E. Koeman (49 mins), J. Bosman for Muhren (78 mins).

Ireland: Patrick Bonner (Glasgow Celtic 26), Chris Morris (Glasgow Celtic 8), Mick McCarthy (Glasgow Celtic 30), Kevin Moran (Manchester United 39), Chris Hughton (Tottenham Hotspur 39), Ray Houghton (Liverpool 18), Paul McGrath (Manchester United 25), Ronnie Whelan (Liverpool 29), Tony Galvin (Sheffield Wednesday 27), Frank Stapleton (Derby County 66), John Aldridge (Liverpool 18). **Subs:** Kevin Sheedy (Everton 16) for Morris (half-time), Tony Cascarino (Millwall 7) for Stapleton (82 mins). **Captain:** Frank Stapleton/Ray Houghton. **Manager:** Jack Charlton (22). **Formation:** 4-4-2.

Needing only a draw to remain in the competition, Ireland adopted a basic defensive posture which allowed the Dutch to dominated the play. The Dutch needed a win to progress but could not break down the Irish defence until the Dutch manager brought on two extra forwards, one of which scored a goal which could be described as a fluke.

The game began at a slow pace but after 7 minutes Van Tiggelen's powerful long-range shot forced Bonner into a good save when he tipped the ball over the bar for the first of ten Dutch corners in the match. Two minutes after this another long-range shot, this time by Vanenburg, went wide. Ireland only won one corner during the entire match but from this McGrath got a free header which hit the upright with Vanenburg, on the goal-line, preventing Aldridge from scoring from the rebound. Ten minutes later another Van Tiggelen long-range effort went over while a cross from Van Basten was headed just wide by Erwin Koeman. After 28 minutes Van Breukelen

HOLLAND 1 – IRELAND 0

Paul McGrath is first to head the ball and clear the danger from this Dutch attack.

Dutch substitute Kieft celebrates his late winning goal against Ireland.
Kevin Sheedy (No. 15) *holds his head in disbelief.*

saved a looping header from Stapleton under pressure from Galvin. In the final ten minutes Bonner was forced to come outside his area to make saving tackles (sic!) on Van Basten and Gullit, Ronald Koeman had a 'fresh air' shot in front of goal, Muhren had a powerful long-range shot wide and, in injury time, Van Basten had a low shot saved by Bonner.

Morris was injured in the first half and did not re-appear for the second. Instead Sheedy went into midfield and McGrath took over at right-back. The Dutch continued their attacks in this half and, after 6 minutes, Wouters broke up the Irish left, linked at Gullit, and smacked a shot off the frame of the goal. At the other end Sheedy and Aldridge set up Galvin for a shot which went into the side netting. Two minutes later Bonner came off his line to try and get a cross from Vanenburg but McCarthy headed it out to Wouters whose chip shot landed on the top of the net with Bonner backpeddling. After 24 minutes Vanenburg shot just over from a pass by Ronald Koeman, while, after 33 minutes, Houghton weaved past two men to curl a shot wide. With 9 minutes to go a cross by Wouters was headed out by McGrath to Ronald Koeman. The Dutchman's shot was driven into the ground and spun up wildly to Kieft whose header, lacking power, seemed destined to go wide. But the ball spun viciously off the turf and bounced into the net. Van Basten had being clearly in an offside position at the time but the goal stood. Charlton immediately replaced the tiring Stapleton with Cascarino with Houghton taking the captains armband. Six minutes from the finish Cascarino headed a Galvin cross wide while, in a further three minutes, Van Basten just failed to get a touch in front of goal to finish off a Rijkaard-Gullit move. The only booking of the match was Wouters who fouled Bonner.

Match No. 243 — NORTHERN IRELAND — Away

Wednesday 14th September 1988 – Belfast (World Cup)

NORTHERN IRELAND (0) 0
REP. OF IRELAND (0) 0

Ref: Vautraut (France) **Ground:** Windsor Park **Att:** 24,000

Northern Ireland: A. McKnight, M. Donaghy, J. McClelland, A. McDonald, N. Worthington, S. Penney, D. Wilson, M. O'Neill, K. Black, J. Quinn, C. Clarke. **Subs:** A. Rogan for Donaghy (half-time).

Ireland: Gerry Peyton (AFC Bournemouth 25), Chris Morris (Glasgow Celtic 9), Mick McCarthy (Glasgow Celtic 31), Kevin Moran (Sporting Gijon 40), Chris Hughton (Tottenham Hotspur 40), Ray Houghton (Liverpool 19), Paul McGrath (Manchester United 26), Ronnie Whelan (Liverpool 30), Kevin Sheedy (Everton 17), John Aldridge (Liverpool 19), Tony Cascarino (Millwall 8). **Captain:** Kevin Moran. **Manager:** Jack Charlton (23). **Formation:** 4-4-2.

Jack Charlton's World Cup campaign began with this game at Windsor Park. After Euro '88, expections for Italia '90 were high in the Republic but against Northern Ireland, who had qualified for the last two World Cups, things were not going to be easy.

After 3 minutes Whelan had a shot blocked out to Hughton who slung a high ball out to Moran, whose header was flicked onto a post by Cascarino with McKnight saving the rebound on the line. Another Cascarino header was just wide after 12 minutes while a minute later Cascarino crossed in for Aldridge to head over. At the other end Quinn headed narrowly wide before McGrath and Houghton combined to send Cascarino racing clear with McKnight saving with his legs. Whelan and Black had further efforts on goal before Peyton, in injury time, made a great save to push a Clarke header, from a Wilson free kick, around the post.

Worthington and Clarke had shots over before the visitors had the best chance of the game. Whelan's through ball found Houghton racing into the box. Houghtons first shot was stopped by McKnight but he latched onto the rebound, rounded the goalkeeper only for his second shot to be kicked off the line by O'Neill. Headers by Cascarino and Sheedy were saved and over respectively with another shot by Sheedy also over. In the last 10 minutes Wilson almost got through but his control let him down while a Moran volley was saved by McKnight. A typical British cup-tie game saw McDonald and Whelan booked.

Match No. 244 — TUNISIA — Home

Wednesday 19th October 1988 – Dublin (P J O'Driscoll Testimonial)

REP. OF IRELAND (3) 4 Cascarino 26, 44, Aldridge 45, Sheedy 87
TUNISIA (0) 0

Ref: Snoddy (N. Ireland) **Ground:** Lansdowne Road **Att:** 12,000

Ireland: Gerry Peyton, (AFC Bournemouth 26), Chris Morris (Glasgow Celtic 10), Mick McCarthy (Glasgow Celtic 32), John Anderson (Newcastle United 16), Stephen Staunton (Liverpool 1), Ray Houghton (Liverpool 20), Liam O'Brien (Manchester United 7), Kevin Sheedy (Everton 18), Mark Kelly (Portsmouth 3), Tony Cascarino (Millwall 9), John Aldridge (Liverpool 20). **Subs:** Pat Scully (Arsenal 1) for Morris (half-time), David Kelly (West Ham United 4) for Houghton (half-time), Niall Quinn (Arsenal 11) for Aldridge (70 mins), Ken De Mange (Hull City 2) for Cascarino (70 mins). **Captain:** Mick McCarthy. **Manager:** Jack Charlton (24). **Formation:** 4-3-3.

Tunisia: N. Chouchane, H. Ouahchi, N. Bousnina, K. Benyahia, M. Ali-Mahjoubi, I. Mizouri, Nabil Maaloul, Taoufik, Baoueb, Yahnadi, Rannane. **Subs:** Ben Massoud for Mizouri (41 mins), H. Abid for Taoufik (60 mins), Jabali for Yahnadi (73 mins).

Ireland totally dominated in a poor game but poor finishing prevented the home side from running up a bigger margin of victory. Early on Houghton set up Sheedy but he shot over as did Aldridge from a pass by Sheedy. A cross from Mark Kelly gave Sheedy another good chance but again his shot went over the top while a free kick from Houghton was volleyed just wide by McCarthy. After 26 minutes a cross from Houghton came back to him from Sheedy and he headed it down for Cascarino to shoot home from close range. Sheedy had another shot deflected out for a corner, Aldridge headed a Houghton cross over and O'Brien shot over when it seemed easier to score as half-time approached. A minute into stoppage time a cross from Staunton was headed home by the unmarked Cascarino. Then 2½ minutes minutes into the added time Houghton, from a pass by Sheedy, set up Aldridge for a simple tap-in from 3 yards for his first goal in 1,738 minutes of international football.

The second half had little to offer after a good start. The four substitutes used by Charlton saw Scully partner McCarthy in defence, with Anderson at right back and David Kelly and Niall Quinn taking over from Aldridge and Cascarino at the front. De Mange came on at central midfield releasing David Kelly to go up front. Sheedy had two early shots over and wide while David Kelly had a volleyed shot from a cross by Mark Kelly saved at the expense of a corner by Chouchane. Tunisia's only attack of note came after 65 minutes when a cross from Nabil Maaloul was headed on by Yahnadi for Baoueb to take the ball on the run and force an excellent save out of Peyton who got both hands to the powerful close-range shot to turn it away. Six minutes later a corner from Mark Kelly was headed powerfully down by McCarthy for Scully to shoot off a post and wide. Quinn headed a Staunton free kick over before Sheedy accepted a pass from De Mange to score with a low shot from the edge of the box.

The game was a testimonial for FAI General Secretary Peadar O'Driscoll who retired in November.

Match No. 245 — SPAIN — Away

Wednesday 16th November 1988 – Seville (World Cup)

SPAIN (0) 2 Manolo 52, Butragueno 65
REP. OF IRELAND (0) 0

Ref: Sauchenko (USSR) **Ground:** Benito Villamarin Stadium **Att:** 50,000

Spain: Zubizarreta, Quique, Gorriz, Sanchis, Andrinua, Jimenez, Michel, Roberto, Martin Vazquez, Butragueno, Manolo. **Subs:** Ramon for Manolo (67 mins), Solana for Quique (84 mins).

Ireland: Patrick Bonner (Glasgow Celtic 27), Chris Morris (Glasgow Celtic 11), Mick McCarthy (Glasgow Celtic 33), David O'Leary (Arsenal 41), Stephen Staunton (Liverpool 2), Ray Houghton (Liverpool 21), Kevin Moran (Sporting Gijon 41), John Sheridan (Leeds United 5), Tony Galvin (Sheffield Wednesday 28),

Tony Cascarino (Millwall 10), John Aldridge (Liverpool 21). **Subs:** Niall Quinn (Arsenal 12) for Aldridge (64 mins), Liam O'Brien (Newcastle United 8) for Sheridan (81 mins). **Captain:** Kevin Moran. **Manager:** Jack Charlton (25). **Formation:** 4-4-2.

Spain began well and after 56 seconds a header by Manolo was cleared off the line by Staunton following a corner by Michel. Despite a hectic opening five minutes Ireland settled down well and after 6 minutes a great cross from Galvin was headed just wide by Cascarino. Spain, though, dominated the play and after Roberto headed wide from a free kick, Butragueno beat 3 men, passed out to Michel but was unable to get to the return due to Morris's interception. The ball fell to Quique whose shot was well saved by Bonner. The Irish goalkeeper also denied Michel, three minutes later, and saved another shot from Roberto on 41 minutes. The half ended with a Galvin shot which went wide.

Seven minutes into the second half a cross from Martin Vazquez found Manolo unmarked in the box and, even though his first shot was parried by Bonner, he pounced on the rebound to blast the ball into the roof of the net. Ten minutes later Manolo had the ball in the net again but this score was ruled out for offside. Spain scored again when Quique got the better of Staunton in a race for possession and crossed over for the unmarked Butragueno to shoot home. After 73 minutes a cross from Quinn was punched out to Staunton by Zubizarreta. The Irish full backs attempted chip shot back came to Quinn whose header was knocked out for a corner by a defender. Spain came close to adding to their total when Michel shot narrowly wide and Ramon headed over. Houghton was booked in the second half.

Match No. 246 — FRANCE — Home

Tuesday 7th February, 1989 – Dublin

REP. OF IRELAND (0) 0
FRANCE (0) 0

Ref: Lloyd (Wales) **Ground:** Dalymount Park **Att:** 22,000

Ireland: Patrick Bonner (Glasgow Celtic 28), Chris Morris (Glasgow Celtic 12), Mick McCarthy (Glasgow Celtic 34), Paul McGrath (Manchester United 27), Chris Hughton (Tottenham Hotspur 41), Ray Houghton (Liverpool 22), Ronnie Whelan (Liverpool 31), Andy Townsend (Norwich City 1), Liam Brady (West Ham United 68), Frank Stapleton (Le Havre 67), Tony Cascarino (Millwall 11). **Sub:** John Aldridge (Liverpool 22) for Stapleton (75 mins). **Captain:** Mick McCarthy. **Manager:** Jack Charlton (26). **Formation:** 4-4-2.

France: J. Bats, S. Kastendeuch, F. Silvestre, P. Battiston, L. Sonor, M. Amaros, L. Blanc, F. Sauzee, J. P. Durand, J. P. Papin, J. P. Paille. **Subs:** J. Toure for Paille (half-time), A. Roche for Silvestre (73 mins), P. Vercruysee for Blanc (66 mins).

Ireland's 80th game at Dalymount Park was a dull affair but that had more to do with the rain-sodden pitch than the players themselves. After 26 minutes Blanc latched onto a through ball but his shot was saved by Bonner. Five minutes later Brady sent a side-footed shot wide following a cross from Houghton. The half ended with Whelan and Silvestre having efforts over.

There was little improvement in the second half with the best efforts being a Toure header saved, a Houghton shot blocked by Stapleton (sic), a Whelan shot saved and a Papin shot saved.

Match No. 247 — HUNGARY — Away

Wednesday 8th March 1989 – Budapest (World Cup)

HUNGARY (0) 0
REP. OF IRELAND (0) 0

Ref: Petrovic (Yugoslavia) **Ground:** NEP Stadium **Att:** 33,966

Hungary: P. Disztl, I. Kozma, Z. Bognar, L. Disztl, E. Kovacs, J. Sass, J. Gregor, L. Detari, G. Hajszan, F. Meszaros, J. Kiprich. **Subs:** G. Bognar for Meszaros (half-time), I. Boda for Gregor (77 mins).

Ireland: Patrick Bonner (Glasgow Celtic 29), Chris Morris (Glasgow Celtic 13), Mick McCarthy (Glasgow Celtic 35), Kevin Moran (Sporting Gijon 42), Chris Hughton (Tottenham Hotspur 42), Ray Houghton (Liverpool 23), Paul McGrath (Manchester United 28), Ronnie Whelan (Liverpool 32), Kevin Sheedy (Everton 19), Tony Cascarino (Millwall 12), John Aldridge (Liverpool 23). **Subs:** Niall Quinn (Arsenal 13) for Cascarino (79 mins), Liam Brady (West Ham United 69) for Aldridge (79 mins). **Captain:** Kevin Moran. **Manager:** Jack Charlton (27). **Formation:** 4-4-2.

Another scoreless draw but the Irish played well and deserved a win. In the first five minutes a timely tackle from Houghton prevented Sass from getting a shot in at goal while a shot from Whelan was saved by Peter Disztl. Aldridge just failed to make contact with a Hughton through ball and shot wide from another through ball from Whelan. Houghton had a shot wide before the best chance of the game fell to McGrath whose overhead kick, from an Aldridge head back was brilliantly turned over by the Hungarian goalkeeper. Bonner, in the other goal, had to make two saves, both with his legs, to stop a shot from Sass and a through ball from Hajszan from getting to Meszaros.

After 48 minutes a long ball from Detari put Kiprich away but the Hungarian captain shot a good chance wide. A minute later Detari had a deflected shot saved by Bonner. Houghton had a shot blocked and Morris another shot saved while Bonner saved a shot from Gregor and Kovacs headed a Kiprich cross over as the game petered out with both sides settling for a point.

Match No. 248 — SPAIN — Home

Wednesday 26th April 1989 – Dublin (World Cup)

REP. OF IRELAND (1) 1 Michel (og) 15
SPAIN (0) 0

Ref: Brummier (Austria) **Ground:** Lansdowne Road **Att:** 49,600

Ireland: Patrick Bonner (Glasgow Celtic 30), Chris Hughton (Tottenham Hotspur 43), Mick McCarthy (Glasgow Celtic 36), Kevin Moran (Sporting Gijon 43), Stephen Staunton (Liverpool 3), Ray Houghton (Liverpool 24), Paul McGrath (Manchester United 29), Ronnie Whelan (Liverpool 33), Kevin Sheedy (Everton 20), Frank Stapleton (Le Havre 68), Tony Cascarino (Millwall 13). **Subs:** Andy Townsend (Norwich City 2) for Stapleton (67 mins). **Captain:** Mick McCarthy. **Manager:** Jack Charlton (28). **Formation:** 4-4-2.

Spain: Zubizarreta, Quique, Gorriz, Sanchis, Serna, Jimenez, Michel, Roberto, Martin Vazquez, Manolo, Butragueno. **Subs:** Eusebio for Quique (69 mins), Julio Salinas for Butragueno (69 mins).

This was the twenty-first meeting between the two nations and Ireland's record against Spain was poor with only three wins. One of those victories came in a previous World Cup campaign when an own goal by Iribar gave Ireland hope for qualifying for the 1966 World Cup Finals. That did not happen but, nearly 24 years later, another Spanish own goal again gave Ireland hope and this time their expectations were to be realized.

On a heavy pitch and backed by a vociferous crowd, Ireland made a great start. After Houghton had a weak shot saved Ireland went into the lead on 15 minutes. A long kick out by Bonner was headed on by Cascorino for Houghton to beat Sanchis and cross low into the goalmouth. Whelan touched it on for Stapleton only for Michel to intercept and turn the ball into his own net. Houghton had another shot saved by Zubizarreta who also saved a Sheedy header and a strong back pass from one of his own players as Irish pressure increased. After 34 minutes a free kick from Whelan just curled around the post but coming up to half time it was Spain who came close to scoring when, first, Bonner was out quickly to cut out a through ball for Butragueno, then made a brilliant save to turn Martin Vazquez's free kick out for a corner. Just on half-time Cascarino sent Houghton through to net but the goal was ruled out for offside. In injury time another shot from Martin Vazquez was well over.

Spain almost got on level terms soon after the start of the second half but Manolo wasted a good chance by shooting well wide after beating Moran. Four minutes later a McGrath shot just went wide with Zubizarreta caught wrong footed and the Spanish goalkeeper was again caught out when a long range free kick from Houghton just went wide. Sheedy and Cascarino had further efforts over before Townsend replaced Stapleton and played as an attacking midfielder. This 4-5-1 formation was to be used in later games by Charlton to good effect. Serna came close with two efforts soon after but it was Ireland who finished the strongest. Sheedy had a header saved, McGrath had the ball in the net again but the goal was again ruled out for pushing by Cascarino and Whelan had a shot well over. Three players were booked in an, at times, rough game – McCarthy and Stapleton for Ireland and Julio Salinas for Spain.

Match No. 249 — MALTA — Home

Sunday 28th May 1989 – Dublin (World Cup)

REP. OF IRELAND (1) 2 Houghton 32, Moran 54
MALTA (0) 0

Ref: Dos Santos (Portugal) **Ground:** Lansdowne Road **Att:** 48,928

Ireland: Patrick Bonner (Glasgow Celtic 31), Chris Hughton (Tottenham Hotspur 44), David O'Leary (Arsenal 42), Kevin Moran (Sporting Gijon 44), Stephen Staunton (Liverpool 4), Ray Houghton (Liverpool 25), Paul McGrath (Manchester United 30), Ronnie Whelan (Liverpool 34), Kevin Sheedy (Everton 21), Frank Stapleton (Le Havre 69), Tony Cascarino (Millwall 14). **Subs:** John Aldridge (Liverpool 24) for Stapleton (27 mins), Andy Townsend (Norwich City 3) for Houghton (69 mins). **Captain:** Kevin Moran. **Manager:** Jack Charlton (29). **Formation:** 4-4-2.

Malta: D. Cluett, J. Galea, J. Buttigieg, S. Vella, A. Azzopardi, E. Camilleri, M. Gregory, C. Busuttil, R. Vella, M. Degiorgio, C. Scerri. **Subs:** D. Carabott for Azzopardi (65 mins).

In the first 15 minutes of this basically one-sided contest, O'Leary had a shot over and Cascarino had three good chances. His first saw Cluett get down well to turn his low shot around the post for a corner. Cascarino followed this with a shot wide and another shot over. Houghton also had a chip shot over and Stapleton headed wide after Sheedy had gone on a good run up the Maltese right. Stapleton was injured in making this effort and was replaced by Aldridge. After 29 minutes Cascarino had another header over but, three minutes later, the Irish striker headed down a high ball from Moran for Houghton to shoot powerfully home. Just on the break Whelan had a chip shot over.

Ireland's first corner of the second half ended with their second goal when Moran stole in unmarked to head Sheedy's flag kick past Cluett. The rest of the half saw Ireland press for more goals but the Maltese brought everybody back to defend. So it is surprising to note that the last 3 chances of the game fell to the visitors when Buttigieg shot over and, with eight minutes to go, Busuttil forced Bonner into action to tip over his long range shot. From the resulting corner Buttigieg shot wide. Three Maltese were booked in the first half – Silvio Vella, Cluett and Raymond Vella; and two Irishmen in the second – O'Leary and Whelan.

Match No. 250 — HUNGARY — Home

Sunday 4th June 1989 – Dublin (World Cup)

REP. OF IRELAND (1) 2 McGrath 33, Cascarino 80
HUNGARY (0) 0

Ref: Nervik (Norway) **Ground:** Lansdowne Road **Att:** 49,600

Ireland: Patrick Bonner (Glasgow Celtic 32), Chris Hughton (Tottenham Hotspur 45), David O'Leary (Arsenal 43), Kevin Moran (Sporting Gijon 45), Stephen Staunton (Liverpool 5), Ray Houghton (Liverpool 26), Paul McGrath (Manchester United 31), Andy Townsend (Norwich City 4), Kevin Sheedy (Everton 22), John Aldridge (Liverpool 25), Tony Cascarino (Millwall 15). **Subs:** Liam Brady (West Ham United 70) for Aldridge (74 mins), Chris Morris (Glasgow Celtic 14) for McGrath (79 mins). **Captain:** Kevin Moran. **Manager:** Jack Charlton (30). **Formation:** 4-4-2.

Hungary: P. Disztl, I. Kozma, Z. Bognar, L. Disztl, I. Garaba, J. Keller, L. Detari, Fitos, T. Csehi, F. Meszaros, I. Boda. **Subs:** G. Bognar for Csehi (66 mins), I. Vincze for Meszaros (71 mins).

A week after beating Malta 2-0, Ireland secured another 2-0 win this time over Hungary – the only team left in the group who could really threaten Ireland's chances of qualification. It was Ireland's 40th game at Lansdowne and their first victory over Hungary.

Again Ireland made a tremendous start. Sheedy had a chip shot off target and Cascarino a shot which was saved by the goalkeeper's legs in the first five minutes. After 8 minutes Laszlo Disztl played a one-two with Meszaros to get in a shot which forced Bonner to make the first of two crucial saves which was to have an influence on the final score. On 14 minutes Cascarino and Aldridge headed on a long ball from Moran only for McGrath to shoot wide. Three minutes later Peter Disztl again saved with his legs to deny Houghton and soon after Keller was forced to clear his lines after an Aldridge effort had eluded Peter Disztl. Aldridge had another shot well saved by the goalkeeper before Ireland opened the scoring. Staunton and Sheedy combined on the Hungarian right for Staunton to cross over from the by-line. Fitos got his head to the ball but it fell to McGrath on the edge of the area and he volleyed it into the back of the net. Keller, McGrath and Cascarino finished the half with efforts which were off target.

After 47 minutes a header from Moran was saved on the line by Peter Disztl. A break by Sheedy set up Ireland's next chance which saw Townsend shoot a good chance wide when the ball was headed back to him. Brady was brought on to restrict Hungary with a 4-5-1 formation (and later Morris was added to midfield when McGrath went off injured). With 15 minutes to go the visitors forced their first corner from which Detari's cross was volleyed over by the unmarked Garaba. Three minutes later Detari squared a free kick to Garaba who fired in a powerful long range shot which Bonner did very well to turn onto a post and out. That was the turning point of the game for, two minutes later, with Hungary caught up-field, Ireland scored again. Cascarino and Townsend combined to send Houghton away. Garaba came across to cover and got to the ball first but Hougton pushed him and he fell to the ground. A free kick was expected but the referee waved play on and Houghton cut in along the by-line to have his cross deflected over Peter Didsztl by his brother, Laszlo, leaving Cascarino an easy task to nod the ball home. Townsend and Detari were booked during the game.

Match No. 251 — WEST GERMANY — Home

Wednesday 6th September 1989 – Dublin

REP. OF IRELAND (1) 1 Stapleton 10
WEST GERMANY (1) 1 Dorfner 32

Ref: Vander Wijngaert (Belgium) **Ground:** Lansdowne Road **Att:** 48,000

Ireland: Patrick Bonner (Glasgow Celtic 33), Chris Morris (Glasgow Celtic 15), Mick McCarthy (Olympique Lyon 37), David O'Leary (Arsenal 44), Stephen Staunton (Liverpool 6), Ronnie Whelan (Liverpool 35), Paul McGrath (Aston Villa 32), Liam Brady (West Ham United 71), Tony Galvin (Swindon Town 29), Frank Stapleton (Blackburn Rovers 70), John Aldridge (Liverpool 26). **Subs:** Andy Townsend (Norwich City 5) for Brady (35 mins), John Byrne (Le Havre 15) for Stapleton (74 mins), Tony Cascarino (Millwall 16) for Aldridge (74 mins). **Captain:** Mick McCarthy. **Manager:** Jack Charlton (31). **Formation:** 4-4-2.

Germany: B. Illgner, S. Reuter, K. Augenthaler, G. Buchwald, H. Pflügler, A. Möller, H. Dorfner, P. Littbarski, O. Thon, T. Hässler, R. Wohlfarth. **Subs:** R. Aumann for Illgner (half-time), A. Reinhardt for Buchwald (half-time), U. Bein for Dorfner (84 mins).

Ireland opened strongly with Whelan heading a Staunton cross over the bar. A minute later a long spectacular shot from Stapleton almost caught out Illgner but the goalkeeper recovered well to save. After 10 minutes Stapleton latched onto a back pass from Hässler and hooked the ball into the net. That goal equaled Don Givens total of 19 goals for Ireland. Germany came back with Möller shooting a pass from Hässler wide and Bonner saving a shot from Thon with O'Leary clearing the rebound. After 32 minutes a good run by Hässler up the Irish left took him past challenges from Brady and Staunton to leave him clear on the edge of the box. The winger squared the ball across for the inrushing Dorfner to hit a first time shot from outside the box which flew into the net giving

Bonner no chance. Charlton then decided to take off Brady and by doing so ended an international career of one of Ireland's best players. His last appearance for Ireland would be his testimonial eight months later.

Ireland had the better of the second half with Whelan heading a Townsend cross over, Galvin having a shot saved by Aumann and headers from McCarthy and McGrath off target. However the best chance for a winner fell to the visitors when Möller ran half the length of the field, evading tackles from Morris and McCarthy, to cross low across the goal with Bonner saving well to prevent it from reaching Wohlfarth. Five minutes from the end Whelan got onto the end of a through ball from Morris but his chip shot, from a difficult angle, hit the crossbar with Littbarski putting the rebound out ahead of Byrne. Townsend and McGrath were booked for fouls.

Match No. 252 — NORTHERN IRELAND — Home

Wednesday 11th October 1989 – Dublin (World Cup)

REP. OF IRELAND (1) 3 Whelan 42, Cascarino 47, Houghton 56
NORTHERN IRELAND (0) 0

Ref: D'Elia (Italy) **Ground:** Lansdowne Road **Att:** 46,800

Rep. of Ireland: Patrick Bonner (Glasgow Celtic 34), Chris Morris (Glasgow Celtic 16), Mick McCarthy (Olympique Lyon 38), Kevin Moran (Sporting Gijon 46), Stephen Staunton (Liverpool 7), Ray Houghton (Liverpool 27), Ronnie Whelan (Liverpool 36), Andy Townsend (Norwich City 6), Kevin Sheedy (Everton 23), John Aldridge (Real Sociedad 27), Tony Cascarino (Millwall 17). **Subs:** David O'Leary (Arsenal 45) for Staunton (77 mins). **Captain:** Mick McCarthy. **Manager:** Jack Charlton (32). **Formation:** 4-4-2.

Northern Ireland: G. Dunlop, G. Fleming, A. McDonald, M. Donaghy, N. Worthington, D. Wilson, D. McCreery, N. Whiteside, M. O'Neill, C. Clarke, R. Dennison. **Subs:** C. O'Neill for McCreery (71 mins), K. Wilson for M. O'Neill (79 mins).

A very important game for the Republic as victory against the North would almost certainly secure a place in Italia '90. Tension was high and it was Northern Ireland, using a 4-3-3 formation, who had the better of the opening exchanges. The Republic had two headers, from Whelan and Aldridge, off target in the first 15 minutes but it was the more settled North who came closest to scoring mid-way through the half. After 24 minutes a free kick from Worthington was headed down by Clarke for Michael O'Neill to beat McCarthy and have a shot parried by Bonner with McCarthy clearing the rebound for a throw-in. From the throw-in Fleming got Michael O'Neill in again to cross over. Bonner palmed the ball down to the feet of Dennison but, from only a few yards out, the winger could not force it home and McCarthy cleared. The Republic continued to struggle but with three minutes to go to the break they got the breakthrough. A cross from Staunton was punched away by Dunlop on the edge of the area. The ball fell to Whelan who placed a low shot through a crowded goalmouth into the back of the net.

Forty seconds after the start of the second half a cross from Danny Wilson came to Dennison whose shot was deflected over by Clarke. After 47 minutes a first-time pass from Whelan found Sheedy on the left of the North's box and his high cross was headed powerfully home by Cascarino. Two minutes later Whelan, Aldridge, Houghton and Morris combined in a move the length of the pitch which ended with Aldridge's header, from Morris's cross, going just the wrong side of the post. After 53 minutes Aldridge was again out of luck when his header from Sheedy's corner hit the upright but three minutes later the Republic got a third goal with a brilliant move. Townsend and Houghton combined to find Sheedy in space who, in turn, found Houghton on the edge of the box. Houghton side-stepped the challenge of Donaghy and placed his shot wide of Dunlop to the back of the net. After 72 minutes Aldridge had a header saved by Dunlop and soon after Clarke forced Bonner into action to save his shot. Clarke had the last chance of the game when his shot was again saved by Bonner. Two players from each side were booked; Whiteside and Worthington for the North and Aldridge and Morris for the South. During the second half Staunton was injured and was replaced by O'Leary who went to central defence with Moran moving out to left back.

Match No. 253 **MALTA** **Away**

Wednesday 15th November 1989 – Valetta (World Cup)

MALTA (0) 0
REP. OF IRELAND (1) 2 Aldridge 30, 67 (Pen)

Ref: Vilenberg (Holland) **Ground:** Ta'Qali Stadium **Att:** 25,000

Malta: R. Cini, S. Vella, J. Buttigieg, J. Galea, A. Azzopardi, J. Zerafa, C. Scerri, M. Degiorgio, M. Gregory, D. Carabott, C. Busuttil. **Subs:** H. Suda for Azzopardi (68 mins), J. Zarb for Zerafa (68 mins).

Ireland: Patrick Bonner (Glasgow Celtic 35), Paul McGrath (Aston Villa 33), David O'Leary (Arsenal 46), Kevin Moran (Sporting Gijon 47), Stephen Staunton (Liverpool 8), Ray Houghton (Liverpool 28), Ronnie Whelan (Liverpool 37), Andy Townsend (Norwich City 7), Kevin Sheedy (Everton 24), John Aldridge (Real Sociedad 28), Tony Cascarino (Millwall 18). **Subs:** Chris Morris (Glasgow Celtic 17) for Moran (33 mins). **Captain:** Ronnie Whelan. **Manager:** Jack Charlton (33). **Formation:** 4-4-2.

Ireland's position was such that a defeat at the hands of Malta would not necessarily deprive them of a place in the World Cup finals. However a point would secure them a berth and with Malta also in search of a point to establish a new points record in a group, the competitive 'edge' would not be lacking.

Malta, in fact, had the first shot on goal with Degiorgio's effort going well wide. Four minutes after this Cascarino had a header saved by Cini. After 18 minutes a long kick out by Bonner allowed Houghton to break clear of the offside trap but he elected to pass in to Sheedy instead of shooting and Buttigieg cleared the danger. A quick free kick by Houghton almost got Cascarino in for a goal but his low shot was deflected out for a corner by Cini. From the corner by Houghton, Cascarino was again denied by Cini when his powerful header was tipped over by the goalkeeper. On the half hour another corner by Houghton was headed on at the near post by O'Leary for Aldridge to steal in at the far post and nod the ball over the line. Cascarino volleyed over before Moran went off injured. McGrath took over at central defence with Morris going to right back.

Soon after the start of the second half Aldridge had a close range effort saved by Cini after Cascarino had headed down a Houghton free kick and another Cascarino knock down gave Sheedy the chance to shoot wide. After 51 minutes Carabott headed a Degiorgio cross over while four minutes later O'Leary made a great interception to stop Busuttil, at the expense of a corner. From the flag kick Scerri had a long range shot saved by Bonner. Sheedy and Morris volleyed over before Whelan hooked on a quick throw-in from Houghton to Townsend who broke free. As he worked his way into the box he was taken down from behind by Carabott and from the resulting penalty Aldridge scored his second goal. Sheedy and Carabott had shots over and Aldridge was denied a hat-trick when his header, from Houghton's corner, was kicked off the line by Degiorgio. Houghton and Galea were booked in the course of the game.

Ireland, after 13th attempts in 25 years, had at last made it to the finals of the World Cup.

Ireland's Andy Townsend and Ray Houghton attempt to tackle Malta's Joe Galea in front of a sea of green in Valetta.
(Photo: via the Malta FA)

International Record	P	W	D	L	F	A
1980-1989	76	31	19	26	96	78
Home	38	21	11	6	70	26
Away	33	7	7	19	22	50
Neutral	5	3	1	1	4	2

International Record	P	W	D	L	F	A
1926-1989	253	89	54	110	347	406
Home	125	58	30	37	218	163
Away	118	26	23	69	118	233
Neutral	10	5	1	4	11	10

World Cup Record	P	W	D	L	F	A
	62	19	14	29	78	104
Home	31	15	8	8	56	40
Away	30	4	6	20	22	63
Neutral	1	0	0	1	0	1

European Championship Record	P	W	D	L	F	A
	53	19	13	21	71	71
Home	25	13	7	5	48	25
Away	25	5	5	15	21	44
Neutral	3	1	1	1	2	2

Number of players capped by Ireland	333
Number of goalscorers for Ireland	104 (+ 6 own goals)
Number of Nations played	42

Leading Goalscorers		Most Capped Players	
Don Givens	19	Liam Brady	71
Frank Stapleton		Frank Stapleton	70
Noel Cantwell	14	Johnny Giles	59
Gerry Daly	13	Don Givens	56
Jimmy Dunne		Mick Martin	52
Liam Brady	9	Paddy Mulligan	50
Dermot Curtis	8	Gerry Daly	48
Tony Grealish		Alan Kelly	47
Arthur Fitzsimons	7	Kevin Moran	
Paddy Moore		David O'Leary	46
Alf Ringstead		Tony Grealish	45
Andy McEvoy	6	Chris Hughton	
Con Martin		Ray Treacy	42
Kevin Moran		Charlie Hurley	40
Tony Cascarino	5	Mark Lawrenson	39
George Cummins		Mick McCarthy	38
Fionan Fagan		Ronnie Whelan	37
Johnny Giles		Noel Cantwell	36
Mark Lawrenson		Patrick Bonner	35
Eamonn Rogers		Steve Heighway	34
Ray Treacy		Tony Dunne	33
Davy Walsh		Paul McGrath	

Penalties awarded to Ireland 41 (32 scored, 5 saved, 4 missed)

Penalties awarded against Ireland 19 (14 scored, 4 saved, 1 missed)

Hat-tricks for Ireland

John Joe Flood	3 goals	v Belgium	1929
Paddy Moore	4 goals	v Belgium	1934
Don Givens	3 goals	v USSR	1974
Don Givens	4 goals	v Turkey	1975
David Kelly	3 goals	v Israel	1985

Hat-tricks against Ireland

Kalle Palmer, Sweden	3 goals	1929
Jef Mermans, Belgium	3 goals	1950
Adolf Huber, Austria	3 goals	1952
Milos Milutinovic, Yugoslavia	3 goals	1955
Tommy Taylor, England	3 goals	1957
Jesus Maria Pereda, Spain	3 goals	1965
Josef Adamec, Czechoslovakia	3 goals	1969
Thomas Parits, Austria	3 goals	1971

Irish Captains

30	Johnny Giles, Frank Stapleton
23	Noel Cantwell
21	Charlie Hurley
19	Johnny Carey
17	Tony Grealish
13	Paddy Mulligan
12	Liam Brady, Peter Farrell
8	Charlie Turner
7	Mick McCarthy
6	Kevin Moran
5	Shay Brennan, Jimmy Dunne, Paddy Gaskins, Con Martin, Mick Martin
4	Tony Dunne, William Glen
2	Tommy Eglington, Mick O'Brien, Pat Saward
1	Frank Brady, John Burke, Harry Chatton, John Dempsey, Seamus Dunne, Al Finucane, John Joe Flood, Mick Foley, Theo Foley, Alan Kelly, Mark Lawrenson, Jack McCarthy, Gerry Mackey, Mick Meagan, David O'Leary, Ronnie Whelan.

Own goals for Ireland

Josef Posipal, West Germany	1951
Karl Koller, Austria	1963
Jose Angel Iribar, Spain	1965
Joey Jones, Wales	1979
Phillippe Mahut, France	1981
Miguel Gonzaelez Michel, Spain	1989

Own goals by Irish players

Seamus Dunne for Sweden	1960
Andy McEvoy for Belgium	1965
Al Finucane for Czechoslovakia (H)	1967
John Dempsey for Czechoslovakia (A)	1967
Jimmy Dunne II for Austria	1971
Mick Martin for Turkey	1974
David O' Leary for Poland	1981
Mick Martin for Spain	1982

Irish Players sent-off

John Dempsey v Hungary	1969
Don Givens v Ecuador	1972
Turlough O'Connor v Chile	1972
Don Givens v Chile	1974
Terry Mancini v USSR	1974
Mick Martin v Turkey	1975
Mick Martin v Bulgaria	1977
Noel Campbell v Bulgaria	1977
Liam Brady v Bulgaria	1987

Leading goalscorer against Ireland

5	Wlodzimierz Lubanski, Poland
4	Josef Adamec, Czechoslovakia
	Preben Elkjaer-Larsen, Denmark
	Reider Kvammen, Norway
	Andrej Kvasnak, Czechoslovakia
	Jef Mermans, Belgium
	Telmo Zarraonandia Montaya "Zarra", Spain

Match No. 254 WALES Home

Wednesday 28th March 1990 – Dublin

REP. OF IRELAND (0) 1 Slaven 86
WALES (0) 0

Ref: Gunn (England) **Ground:** Lansdowne Road **Att:** 41,350

Ireland: Patrick Bonner (Glasgow Celtic 36), Chris Morris (Glasgow Celtic 18), Mick McCarthy (Millwall 39), Kevin Moran (Blackburn Rovers 48), Stephen Staunton (Liverpool 9), John Byrne (Le Havre 16), John Sheridan (Sheffield Wednesday 6), Ronnie Whelan (Liverpool 38), Andy Townsend (Norwich City 8), Bernie Slaven (Middlesbrough 1), Tony Cascarino (Aston Villa 19). **Subs:** Kevin Sheedy (Everton 25) for Whelan (half-time), Chris Hughton (Tottenham Hotspur 46) for Staunton (67 mins), David O'Leary (Arsenal 47) for Moran (75 mins). **Captain:** Ronnie Whelan. **Manager:** Jack Charlton (34). **Formation:** 4-4-2.

Wales: N. Southall, G. Hall, A. Melville, G. Maguire, M. Aizlewood, D. Philips, B. Horne, P. Nicholas, A. Davies, M. Allen, I. Rush.

Ireland's first victory over Wales and their 25th at Lansdowne Road was not spectacular. It began well with Cascarino, Whelan and Byrne all having efforts off target in the first 6 minutes. Further chances fell to Byrne and Cascarino before Wales forced their first corner after 26 minutes. Nicholas's flag kick came to Melville who headed on for Rush who, in turn, had a header turned out by Bonner. A minute later Southall saved at the feet of Sheridan when the latter was through. Slaven then headed over from a difficult angle before Southall made a brilliant one-handed save to keep out a header by Cascarino from a cross by Slaven. A minute before the break Slaven shot over from Sheridan's pass.

After 49 minutes Davies shot over following a pass by Nicholas. Byrne had a shot deflected out for a corner and from the flag kick Cascarino's header struck the crossbar. Hall, Maguire and Phillips had other shots off target for Wales as had Sheedy, Slaven and Cascarino for Ireland. The only goal came when a long kick out from Bonner allowed Slaven to cut through the Welsh cover and round Southall. His shot, from a difficult angle, was handled on the line by Maguire, and a penalty was awarded. Sheedy took the kick but his Everton club mate, Southall, guessed the right way and saved. However the ball squirmed out of his grasp and Slaven followed up to score. Seconds later the ball was in the net again via Cascarino but the Irish striker was offside and the goal ruled out. All substitutes used replaced injured players.

Match No. 255 USSR Home

Wednesday 25th April 1990 – Dublin

REP. OF IRELAND (0) 1 Staunton 59
USSR (0) 0

Ref: Kleinaitis (USA) **Ground:** Lansdowne Road **Att:** 43,990

Ireland: Gerry Peyton (AFC Bournemouth 27), Chris Morris (Glasgow Celtic 19), Mick McCarthy (Millwall 40), David O'Leary (Arsenal 48), Stephen Staunton (Liverpool 10), Gary Waddock (Millwall 20), Paul McGrath (Aston Villa 34), Andy Townsend (Norwich City 9), Kevin Sheedy (Everton 26), David Kelly (Leicester City 5), Niall Quinn (Manchester City 14). **Subs:** Chris Hughton (Tottenham Hotspur 47) for Morris (73 mins), Kevin Moran (Blackburn Rovers 49) for O'Leary (77 mins). **Captain:** Mick McCarthy. **Manager:** Jack Charlton (35). **Formation:** 4-4-2.

USSR: A. Uvarov, S. Fokin, O. Kuznetsov, V. Khidiatulin, A. Zigmantovich, S. Gorlukovich, V. Tshenko, A. Borodjuk, V. Broshin, I. Belanov, V. Ljuty. **Subs:** Y. Savichev for Ljuty (70 mins), F. Cherenkov for Broshin (76 mins).

A forgettable first half yielded just three chances of note on a bumpy pitch. After two minutes a mistake by Gorlukovich allowed Waddock to beat Uvarov on the by-line but his shot struck an upright. After 33 minutes a long throw-in by McCarthy was headed down by Quinn for Kelly but

Uvarov saved well at the latters feet. The best chance of the half came after 41 minutes when Kelly played a one-two with Townsend to get to the by-line but his high cross from there was just missed by Quinn at the far post.

It could only improve in the second half and within 70 seconds Peyton was forced into action for the first time when saving a deflected free kick from Kuznetsov. Another Soviet free kick, this time from Fokin, found the head of Tshenko and Peyton was almost caught out but saved well. A third free kick resulted in the only goal of the game when Staunton curled the ball over the wall and just inside the post, giving Uvarov no chance. After 65 minutes Sheedy teed-up a cross from Waddock for Townsend whose pile-driver was well saved by Uvarov, who saved a long range shot from Morris seconds later. A mistake by McCarthy presented Savichev with a great chance but his attempted chip went wide. After 80 minutes Townsend knocked a short-free kick to Staunton who had another shot saved by Uvarov. Four minutes later Peyton was forced to tip over a strong pass back from Townsend and from the resulting corner Savichev had a cross-shot taken off the line by Townsend. Three minutes from the end a through ball from Savichev put Belanov clear but his shot went narrowly wide. There were three bookings; Townsend and Kelly for Ireland and Uvarov for the visitors.

Match No. 256 — FINLAND — Home

Wednesday 16th May 1990 – Dublin (Liam Brady Testimonial)

REP. OF IRELAND (0) 1 Sheedy 84
FINLAND (0) 1 V. Tauriainen 75

Ref: Gifford (Wales) **Ground:** Lansdowne Road **Att:** 31,556

Ireland: Patrick Bonner (Glasgow Celtic 37), Chris Hughton (Tottenham Hotspur 48), Mick McCarthy (Millwall 41), David O'Leary (Arsenal 49), Stephen Staunton (Liverpool 11), Ray Houghton (Liverpool 29), Paul McGrath (Aston Villa 35), Liam Brady (West Ham United 72), John Byrne (Le Havre 17), Tony Cascarino (Aston Villa 20), Bernie Slaven (Middlesbrough 2). **Subs:** Andy Townsend (Norwich City 10) for Brady (26 mins), John Aldridge (Real Sociedad 29) for Slaven (56 mins), Kevin Sheedy (Everton 27) for Byrne (63 mins), Chris Morris (Glasgow Celtic 20) for Staunton (67 mins). **Captain:** Liam Brady/Mick McCarthy. **Manager:** Jack Charlton (36). **Formation:** 4-4-2.

Finland: O. Huttunen, J. Vuorela, A. Heikkinen, H. Jantti, Sulonen, M. Kanvera,M. Myyry, P. Tauriainen, J. Litmanen, P. Jurvienen, M. Paatelainen. **Subs:** M. Aaltonen for Myyry (58 mins), V. Tauriainen for Litmanen (70 mins), Turenen for Jantti (86 mins).

The Liam Brady testimonial formed part of the preparations for Italia '90 and, as such, it would be more than just a 'kick around'. Brady, in agreement with Charlton, would only play for 20 minutes and after 26 minutes and 50 seconds his international career came to an end. His international career had spaned nearly 26 years and up to his sending off against Bulgaria in 1987 he only missed 21 games of which only 3 were competitive matches. He had played in all Ireland World Cup games between 1976 and 1985 but would not appear in their first-ever finals. He has rightly being acclaimed as Ireland's greatest-ever player.

The game itself got off to a flying start with the visitors having two great chances in the first five minutes. First, after 75 seconds, Kanvera got through the Irish cover but his shot was saved by the legs of Bonner. Then Paatelainen got away from McCarthy but scuffed his shot from a good position and Bonner saved easily. Houghton and Litmanen had further efforts well over but after 13 minutes Byrne's shot was blocked out for a corner and from Brady's flag kick, O'Leary had a near post header brilliantly turned over by Huttunen. The Finnish goalkeeper was in action three more times before the break to deny Ireland a deserved lead. First he saved a volley from Byrne when Cascarino and Townsend headed on a cross from Houghton. He then saved a Townsend header when Cascarino and Slaven had headed on a long ball. In injury time, Huttunen had a bit of luck when Slaven mis-cued a hooked shot from close range and he adjusted well to save.

The second half flagged somewhat despite an early Slaven shot which sailed wide following a quick free kick from Houghton. After 71 minutes Aldridge shot just over after Cascarino had headed down a cross from Morris and the visitors seemed to pose little danger as the game went on. However, after 75 minutes, a throw-in from Heikkinen was headed out by McCarthy to Vesa Tauriainen on the edge of the box. The substitute took the ball down before sending a superb dipping volley into the far corner of the net. This set-back seemed to 'wake' Ireland and, after McGrath had two efforts over, they equalised with 6 minutes left. A cross from Houghton was deflected over to the unmarked Aldridge by the head of Paatelainen. Aldridge's shot was turned onto the crossbar by Huttunen but Sheedy followed up to head the rebound home.

All the Irish substitutions were straight swops except when Morris came on as right back with Hughton switching to left back.

Match No. 257 — TURKEY — Away

Sunday 27th May 1990 – Izmir

TURKEY (0) 0
REP. OF IRELAND (0) 0

Ref: Kerkof (USSR) **Ground:** Kamal Attaturk Stadium **Att:** 35,000

Turkey: Engin, Riza, Kemal, B. Gokhan, Ogun, Tugay, Unal, Oguz, Mustafa, Feyyaz, Metin. **Subs:** Savas for Feyyaz (66 mins), Hayrettin for Mustafa (66 mins), Mehmet for Unal (73 mins), K. Gokhan for Kemal (86 mins).

Ireland: Patrick Bonner (Glasgow Celtic 38), Chris Morris (Glasgow Celtic 21), Mick McCarthy (Millwall 42), David O'Leary (Arsenal 50), Stephen Staunton (Liverpool 12), Gary Waddock (Millwall 21), Paul McGrath (Aston Villa 36), Andy Townsend (Norwich City 11), Kevin Sheedy (Everton 28), Tony Cascarino (Aston Villa 21), John Aldridge (Real Sociedad 30). **Subs:** John Sheridan (Sheffield Wednesday 7) for Townsend (half-time), Chris Hughton (Tottenham Hotspur 49) for Staunton (51 mins), John Byrne (Le Havre 18) for Waddock (51 mins), Bernie Slaven (Middlesbrough 3) for O'Leary (67 mins). **Captain:** Mick McCarthy. **Manager:** Jack Charlton (37). **Formation:** 4-4-2.

A game arranged to get the players accustomed to the heat of Italy served its purpose – thanks to the hottest day in Turkey for half a century. The 106° temperature meant the match was basically a kick-around with few chances.

After 8 minutes a cross from Tugay found Metin at the far post but his return shot from a difficult angle was stopped on the line by O'Leary. After 14 minutes Engin saved a looping header from Cascarino while Unal, with a shot, and McGrath, with a header, had efforts off target. The other chances of the half saw shots from Oguz and Tugay saved and a shot from Feyyaz wide.

On the hour another Cascarino header was saved by Engin and at the other end Mustafa shot over. After 84 minutes Slaven headed in a cross from Byrne but the goal was disallowed for an earlier foul by Aldridge on Kemal. Late in the game Tugay had a long range shot wide.

All the substitutions were straight swops except when Slaven replaced O'Leary. Slaven took over in midfield with McGrath dropping back to defence. For Gary Waddock his replacement signalled the end of his involvement with the Irish world cup squad.

Match No. 258 — MALTA — Away

Saturday 2nd June 1990 – Valetta

MALTA (0) 0
REP. OF IRELAND (1) 3 Quinn 43, Townsend 77, Stapleton 87

Ref: Azzopardi (Malta) **Ground:** Ta'Qali Stadium **Att:** 3,000

Malta: R. Cini, S. Vella, K. Laferla, J. Buttigieg, J. Galea, M. Gregory, R. Vella, M. Degiorgio, D. Carabott, B. Licari, J. Zerafa. **Subs:** J. Delia for S. Vella (62 mins), J. Zarb for Gregory (70 mins), E. Camilleri for Galea (80 mins).

Ireland: Gerry Peyton (AFC Bournemouth 28), Chris Hughton (Tottenham Hotspur 50), David O'Leary (Arsenal 51), Kevin Moran (Blackburn Rovers 50), Stephen Staunton (Liverpool 13), John Byrne (Le Havre 19), Alan McLoughlin (Swindon Town 1), John Sheridan (Sheffield Wednesday 8), Bernie Slaven

Rival captains Raymond Vella (Malta) and Kevin Moran (Ireland) shake hands before the friendly in Valetta in 1990. (Photo: via Malta FA)

(Middlesbrough 4), Niall Quinn (Manchester City 15), David Kelly (Leicester City 6). **Subs:** Frank Stapleton (Blackburn Rovers 71) for Kelly (62 mins), Andy Townsend (Norwich City 12) for Slaven (71 mins). **Captain:** Kevin Moran. **Manager:** Jack Charlton (38). **Formation:** 4-4-2.

Ireland returned to Malta to prepare for the World Cup Finals and as part of the build-up a shadow team played this friendly against their hosts.

Ireland dominated the game with Cini denying McLoughlin a debut goal after two minutes when he tipped over the latters volley. The Maltese goalkeeper also did well to save a pile-driver from Sheridan. McLoughlin, Kelly and Slaven had other chances before Ireland scored, two minutes from the break. Sheridan and O'Leary combined to send Hughton up the Maltese left and his pin-point cross was headed home by Quinn.

The same domination continued in the second half with efforts by Quinn, McLoughlin, Stapleton and Staunton all coming near. But Ireland got two more goals, both by substitutes, to achieve their biggest away win under Jack Charlton to date. After 77 minutes McLoughlin headed on a kick out from Peyton to Quinn and his pass allowed Townsend to shoot powerfully into the roof of the net from an oblique angle. Seven minutes from the end Sheridan rounded the goalkeeper and crossed over for Stapleton to head home easily. It was his 20th goal for Ireland and one which broke Don Givens record total for Ireland.

Match No. 259 — ENGLAND — Neutral

Monday 11th June 1990 Cagliari (World Cup Finals)

ENGLAND (1) 1 Lineker 8
REP. OF IRELAND (0) 1 Sheedy 72

Ref: Schmidhuber (West Germany) **Ground:** Sant'Elia Stadium **Att:** 35,238

England: P. Shilton, G. Stevens, D. Walker, T. Butcher, S. Pearce, C. Waddle, P. Gascoigne, B. Robson, J. Barnes, P. Beardsley, G. Lineker. **Subs:** S. McMahon for Beardsley (69 mins), S. Bull for Lineker (83 mins).

Ireland: Patrick Bonner (Glasgow Celtic 39), Chris Morris (Glasgow Celtic 22), Mick McCarthy (Millwall 43), Kevin Moran (Blackburn Rovers 51), Stephen Staunton (Liverpool 14), Ray Houghton (Liverpool 30), Paul McGrath (Aston Villa 37), Andy Townsend (Norwich City 13), Kevin Sheedy (Everton 29), Tony Cascarino (Aston Villa 22), John Aldridge (Real Sociedad 31). **Subs:** Alan McLoughlin (Swindon Town 2) for Aldridge (64 mins). **Captain:** Mick McCarthy. **Manager:** Jack Charlton (39). **Formation:** 4-4-2.

Packie Bonner can only watch as Gary Lineker's chested effort goes out of his reach.

Kevin Sheedy dispossesses Steve McMahon (on the ground), *and fires home the equaliser against England in Cagliari.*

Fifty-six years after making her world cup debut the Republic of Ireland had finally played its first match in the finals of the games biggest competition. In Feburary 1934 Ireland had drawn its first world cup game in its first finals game the result was also a draw.

The first half was played in a strong breeze, and it was Ireland who had the first shot on target when Sheedy's low effort was easily saved by Shilton. After 7 minutes Robson got a free header to a Gascoigne free kick but it went well wide. A minute later England took the lead thanks to slackness in the Irish side. A throw in from Staunton was headed to touch by Stevens but, with the Irish players expecting a throw-in, Waddle kept the ball in play. The defence was thus discommoded when Waddle's cross found Lineker and he chested it past Bonner and bundled it into the net. Ireland's response was to take the play to the English with Sheedy having a shot wide and McGrath having a header saved by Shilton. Coming up to the break Ireland wasted a good free kick chance when McGrath shot wide and Lineker had a shot deflected over by Moran following a low cross from Pearce.

The second half was played during a thunder storm and rain. Ireland continued to have the best of things and after 48 minutes a low shot from Cascarino was saved by Shilton. Eight minutes later McGrath sent a rising shot over but in a poor game the most exciting piece of action came from England when Waddle's run up the Irish left took him past Staunton and Townsend. As he cut into the box he was taken down by Moran but no penalty was awarded. Pearce had a long-range shot saved by Bonner before McLoughlin came on for Ireland and McMahon for England. Both substitutions altered their teams formation to 4-5-1 but it was England's replacement who presented Ireland with their equaliser. A long kick out by Bonner was headed down by Butcher, under pressure from Cascarino, for Sheedy. Sheedy's first time ball was intercepted by McMahon on the edge of his own area but, under pressure from Townsend and Sheedy, McMahon lost control and Sheedy thumped a low shot into the bottom corner of the net. England almost went back in front two minutes later when Butcher got a free header to a Gascoigne free kick but the defender headed badly wide. In the end a draw was a fair result and to complete a miserable night for McMahon he was booked for retaliation.

Match No. 260 — EGYPT — Neutral

Sunday 17th June 1990 – Palermo (World Cup Finals)

EGYPT (0) 0
REP. OF IRELAND (0) 0

Ref: Van Langenhove (Belgium) **Ground:** Della Favorita Stadium **Att:** 33,288

Egypt: A. Shobeir, I. Hassan, H. Yakan, H. Ramzy, R. Yassein, I. Youssef, El Kass, M. Abdul Ghani, M. Tolba, O. Oraby, H. Hassan. **Subs:** T. Abouzeid for Tolba (59 mins), G. Abdelhamid for El Kass (76 mins).

Ireland: Patrick Bonner (Glasgow Celtic 40), Chris Morris (Glasgow Celtic 23), Mick McCarthy (Millwall 44), Kevin Moran (Blackburn Rovers 52), Stephen Staunton (Liverpool 15), Ray Houghton (Liverpool 31), Paul McGrath (Aston Villa 38), Andy Townsend (Norwich City 14), Kevin Sheedy (Everton 30), Tony Cascarino (Aston Villa 23), John Aldridge (Real Sociedad 32). **Subs:** Alan McLoughlin (Swindon Town 3) for Aldridge (64 mins). Niall Quinn (Manchester City 16) for Cascarino (84 mins). **Captain:** Mick McCarthy. **Manager:** Jack Charlton (40), Formation 4-4-2.

Ireland having salvaged a point from England, travelled from Sardinia to Sicily full of confidence. 'For now sits expectation in the air' (Henry V, Act II Chor. 8) but, as in Shakespeare's play, over-optimism did not bring success. It did not mean failure either because Ireland completely dominated but in a poor game only created four openings.

After two minutes McCarthy shot well over but it was not until the 23rd minute that they had their next chance when Staunton's shot was blocked out for a corner. The first real opening came four minutes from the break when Houghton's corner was cleared but to Sheedy whose return header was controlled on his chest by Cascarino before having a volley saved by Shobeir. His opposite number, Bonner, was not tested at all.

Paul McGrath and Tony Cascarino try to force home a corner for Ireland, to break the deadlock against Egypt.

Paul McGrath fails to stop Ruud Gullit from putting Holland in front after 10 minutes.

No joy for Van Basten as the Irish clear their lines.

Three minutes after the restart Sheedy took down a cross from Houghton only to have his volley saved by Shobeir. A long-range free kick by Abdul Ghani went well over but was Egypt's first shot on goal. After 69 minutes a Sheedy through ball put Houghton free in the box but the Egyptian goalkeeper made a good close-range save. Five minutes later a Houghton pass found Staunton free on the edge of the box but his shot just went the wrong side of the far post. Seven minutes from the end Abdul Ghani shot wide from a cross by Hassam Hassan while Staunton had a cross-cum-shot tipped over by Shobeir, four minutes from full time.

Morris was booked for a foul in the second half as was Shobeir for time-wasting. The Irish had used a 4-5-1 formation with the introduction of McLoughlin while Quinn's use was as a straight-swop for Cascarino.

Match No. 261 — HOLLAND — Neutral

Thursday 21st June 1990 – Palermo (World Cup Finals)

HOLLAND (1) 1 Gullit 10
REP. OF IRELAND (0) 1 Quinn 71

Ref: Vautrot (France) **Ground:** Della Favorita Stadium **Att:** 33,288

Holland: H. Van Breukelen, B. Van Aerle, R. Koeman, F. Rijkaard, A. Van Tiggelen, R. Gullit, J. Wouters, H. Gillhaus, R. Witschge, M. Van Basten, W. Kieft. **Subs:** H. Fräser for Witschge (59 mins), J. Van Loen for Kieft (79 mins).

Ireland: Patrick Bonner (Glasgow Celtic 41), Chris Morris (Glasgow Celtic 24), Mick McCarthy (Millwall 45), Kevin Moran (Blackburn Rovers 53), Stephen Staunton (Liverpool 16), Ray Houghton (Liverpool 32), Paul McGrath (Aston Villa 39), Andy Townsend (Norwich City 15), Kevin Sheedy (Everton 31), John Aldridge (Real Sociedad 33), Niall Quinn (Manchester City 17). **Subs:** Ronnie Whelan (Liverpool 39) for Sheedy (62 mins), Tony Cascarino (Aston Villa 24) for Aldridge (62 mins). **Captain:** Mick McCarthy. **Manager:** Jack Charlton (41). **Formation:** 4-4-2.

Both sides needed a point to stay in the competition but a victory was a priority as the result from the England-Egypt game could influence who could qualify or whether the qualifiers would be drawn by lot. In the end England beat Egypt 1-0 and both sides went through to Round Two.

Both goalkeepers were in action early with Bonner saving a Koeman shot and Van Breukelen an Aldridge shot. But it was Bonner who was beaten first. After 10 minutes Koeman knocked a short free kick to Gullit who played a one-two with Kieft before shooting low into the corner of the net. A minute later Van Breukelen was beaten when Aldridge headed home a Staunton cross but the goal was ruled out for a marginal offside decision. After 19 minutes Gullit got a free header to a Van Basten cross but the ball went wide while Sheedy volleyed over five minutes later. Gillhaus came close with two headers as did Staunton and Townsend with shots as the half came to an end.

After 35 seconds of the restart McGrath had a shot saved by the Dutch goalkeeper while Aldridge and Quinn both got in each others way in trying to convert a Staunton cross after 48 minutes. Gullit and Sheedy had shots wide before Gullit had another shot deflected out for a corner by Staunton. From Witschge's flag kick, Kieft had a header cleared off the line by Townsend. Gillhaus and Kieft had other shots wide before Ireland equalised after 71 minutes. A long kick out by Bonner was kicked back across his own goal by Van Aerle. Van Breukelen tried to save it but the ball spun out of his grasp and Quinn, following up, shot it into the net. Soon after news of England's goal filtered through to the players and both teams settled for a draw playing out the remaining minutes with no threat to either goal. There was one booking – Rijkaard of Holland.

Both Ireland and Holland finished the group with identical records so lots were drawn to see who they would play in Round Two. Ireland drew Rumania and Holland drew West Germany.

Irish hopes are kept alive, Quinn scores after 71 minutes. He celebrates but Van Breukelen is despondent.

Bonner dives to save Timofte's penalty in the penalty shoot-out with Romania.

Match No. 262 **ROMANIA** **Neutral**

Monday 25th June 1990 – Genoa (World Cup Finals)

ROMANIA (0) 0
REP. OF IRELAND (0) 0

(After extra time – Ireland win 5-4 on penalties)

Ref: Wright (Brazil) **Ground:** Luigi Ferraris Stadium **Att:** 31,818

Romania: S. Lung, M. Rednic, I. Andone, G. Popesca, I. Lupescu, M. Klein, G. Hagi, I. Sabau, J. Rotariu, G. Balint, F. Raducioiu. **Subs:** D. Lupu for Raducioiu (74 mins), D. Timofte for Sabau (97 mins).

Ireland: Patrick Bonner (Glasgow Celtic 42), Chris Morris (Glasgow Celtic 25), Mick McCarthy (Millwall 46), Kevin Moran (Blackburn Rovers 54), Stephen Staunton (Liverpool 17), Ray Houghton (Liverpool 33), Paul McGrath (Aston Villa 40), Andy Townsend (Norwich City 16), Kevin Sheedy (Everton 32), John Aldridge (Real Sociedad 34), Niall Quinn (Manchester City 18). **Subs:** Tony Cascarino (Aston Villa 25) for Aldridge (22 mins), David O'Leary (Arsenal 52) for Staunton (93 mins). **Captain:** Mick McCarthy. **Manager:** Jack Charlton (42). **Formation:** 4-4-2.

Ireland, in their first finals, had qualified for Round Two but having avoided tournament favourites West Germany in the lots they faced potentially tricky opponents in Romania. For Romania, in their fifth finals, it was a chance to get to the quarter finals for the first time. With both sides playing excellent football, despite the heat, it turned out to be an intriguing match.

Romania opened strongly and after three minutes a good move saw Hagi play a one-two with Sabau up the Irish left before crossing over for Sabau to shoot wide. Sabau set up the next chance when his good run allowed Balint to get in a shot which Bonner saved. Hagi had two further efforts, one of which was well saved by Bonner, and Townsend also had a shot saved before Aldridge was injured in a tackle on Hagi for which he was booked. Cascarino replaced Aldridge in a straight swop. A minute later danger-man Hagi got away from Morris and had a shot across goal which went wide. Sheedy and Hagi both had long range shots but it was Ireland who finished the half on the attack. Two minutes from the break Sheedy had a shot saved one-handedly by Lung after Cascarino had headed down a cross from McGrath and, in injury time, a Quinn header from a Houghton cross went just wide.

Ireland had a better start to the second half with Cascarino having a weak shot saved by Lung after 53 minutes. A minute later Cascarino headed over from 6 yards from a good cross by Quinn. Raducioiu and Hagi followed this with shots off target before Bonner brought off a great save to stop a shot from Raducioiu from going in. After 74 minutes Hagi got past Staunton and cut inside to have another shot well saved by Bonner. Again the half ended with Ireland to the fore. Cascarino glanced a header wide from Sheedy's free kick, Quinn headed wide from a cross by Morris and McGrath headed over Sheedy's corner kick.

For the first time Ireland played extra time and after 70 seconds Staunton sent a free kick just wide. A minute and a half later another long-range shot from Hagi was turned out for a corner by Bonner. After 3 minutes O'Leary replaced Staunton at left back while, a minute later, a good run from Sheedy took him past three players and when his cross was cleared out to Houghton the latter headed over. Timofte replaced Sabau after 7 minutes and three minutes later was one of two Romanians who had a shot blocked in the Irish box before Rotariu shot over. Andone had a header wide after 13 minutes while both Townsend and Hagi had shots off target soon after the turn-around. The last shot of this draining contest was by Sheedy whose effort went wide five minutes before full-time.

The game was over but a winner was needed so a penalty shoot-out was put into operation. Critics of this method of deciding the winners of a match point to other criteria which should be used. A replay, corners (Romania 9, Ireland 4) and yellow cards (Ireland 2: Aldridge, McGrath), Romania 2 (Hagi, Lupu) have all being submitted as replacements but should these criteria also end level you would be back to square one. Like or dislike it the penalty shoot-out is, at least, a 'footballing' solution.

Where's Dave O'Leary?
Dave O'Leary's penalty against Romania puts Ireland into the World Cup Quarter Finals – the celebrations have begun.

The first penalty was taken by Hagi who shot high into the left corner even though Bonner guessed correctly. Sheedy equalised when he blased his spot kick over Lung into the roof of the net. Lupu again beat Bonner low to his left although Bonner had gone the right way. Houghton sent Lung the wrong way to equalise. Rotariu put Romania 3-2 ahead with Bonner again guessing correctly but Lung was sent the wrong way by Townsend to tie the scores again. Bonner again guessed correctly for Lupescu's penalty and got his fingers to the ball but was unable to stop it from going in. Ireland's fourth penalty was mis-hit by Cascarino but it went under Lung into the net. It was now up to the two substitutes. Timofte sent his penalty low to Bonner's right and, as he had done for all the rest, Ireland's goalkeeper guessed correctly but this time turned the ball away with a magnificent save. The pressure was now on O'Leary but, despite never having taken a penalty before, he sent Lung the wrong way with a perfect spot-kick. Ireland had made it to the quarter finals despite having not won a game and having set a new World Cup Finals record of four successive draws.

Match No. 263 — ITALY — Away

Saturday 30th June 1990 – Rome (World Cup Finals)

ITALY (1) 1 Schillaci 37
REP. OF IRELAND (0) 0

Ref: Silva Valente (Portugal) **Ground:** Stadio Olimpico **Att:** 73,303

Italy: W. Zenga, G. Bergomi, R. Ferri, F. Baresi, L. De Agostini, P. Maldini, R. Donadoni, F. De Napoli, G. Giannini, S. Schillaci, R. Baggio. **Subs:** C. Ancelotti for Giannini (62 mins), A. Serena for Baggio (70 mins).

Ireland: Patrick Bonner (Glasgow Celtic 43), Chris Morris (Glasgow Celtic 26), Mick McCarthy (Millwall 47), Kevin Moran (Blackburn Rovers 55), Stephen Staunton (Liverpool 18), Ray Houghton (Liverpool 34), Paul McGrath (Aston Villa 41), Andy Townsend (Norwich City 17), Kevin Sheedy (Everton 33), John Aldridge (Real Sociedad 35), Niall Quinn (Manchester City 19). **Subs:** Tony Cascarino (Aston Villa 26) for Quinn (52 mins), John Sheridan (Sheffield Wednesday 9) for Aldridge (78 mins). **Captain:** Mick McCarthy. **Manager:** Jack Charlton (43). **Formation:** 4-4-2.

Ireland provided another gritty performance but against the World Cup hosts Italy, a team which had won all previous Ireland-Italy meetings, they suffered their first finals defeat and so ended their participation in Italia '90. Ireland gave Italy a tough time but with only two headers on target never really threatened the Italian goal.

Ireland's first header on target, and the first real chance of the game, came after 11 minutes when McGrath's effort, from Sheedy's corner, was saved by Zenga. Seven minutes earlier Ferri had a long-range free kick deflected out for a corner. After 24 minutes Quinn got his head to a McGrath cross only for Zenga to produce a flying save. A minute later Schillaci headed a cross from Donadoni wide. Quinn, Maldini and De Agostini had further efforts off target, Baggio had the ball in the net from a Donadoni pass but the score was ruled out for offside. Three minutes later Baggio and Giannini set up Donadoni for a scorching shot which Bonner parried but only to the feet of Schillaci who steered it into the goal. De Napoli and Quinn were both wide with other shots and a minute before the break Schillaci shot over in front of goal when a cross by De Agostini went across the Irish goalmouth.

The second half saw more Irish pressure but, as in the first, the better chances fell to Italy. One of those came after 52 minutes when a bullet-like free kick by Schillaci came down off the underside of the cross bar onto the goal-line and bounced back out into play for Schillaci to shoot over. McGrath had a long-range shot wide ten minutes later. After 65 minutes Staunton's free kick was deflected over for another corner. This corner was cleared but promptly returned to the Italian box where Aldridge almost got in on a Houghton header but the referee stopped play for offside.

After 78 minutes a cross from Donadoni gave Serena a great chance but he headed wide with a free header. Charlton again altered his formation to 4-5-1 with the introduction of Sheridan soon

Bonner parries Donadoni's shot – Schillaci reacts quickest to hit home the rebound – The Italians celebrate a place in the semi-finals

after. After 82 minutes a through ball from Baresi put Serena in the clear but Bonner made a great save with his legs. Baresi and Donadoni came close for Italy in the closing stages but Schillaci was denied a second goal in the last minute when he got clear on a through ball from De Napoli and scored only for the goal to be ruled out for a marginal offside decision. Ireland's World Cup ended with them on the offensive and the last shot was by Sheridan in injury time but unfortunately well off target. It was Ireland's 30th World Cup defeat but for Irish fans the result was secondary as they celebrated the end of the event which had gripped a nation.

De Agostini and Moran were booked in a game which saw 48 free kicks awarded.

Match No. 264 MOROCCO Home

Wednesday 12th September 1990 – Dublin

REP. OF IRELAND (0) 1 D. Kelly 74
MOROCCO (0) 0

Ref: McKnight (N. Ireland) **Ground:** Dalymount Park **Att:** 19,450

Ireland: Patrick Bonner (Glasgow Celtic 44), Denis Irwin (Manchester United 1), Mick McCarthy (Millwall 48), David O'Leary (Arsenal 53), Stephen Staunton (Liverpool 19), Ray Houghton (Liverpool 35), Ronnie Whelan (Liverpool 40), Andy Townsend (Chelsea 18), Mark Kelly (Portsmouth 4), David Kelly (Leicester City 7), Niall Quinn (Manchester City 20). **Subs:** Tony Cascarino (Aston Villa 27) for Quinn (59 mins), John Sheridan (Sheffield Wednesday 10) for Townsend (65 mins), Alan McLoughlin (Swindon Town 4) for M. Kelly (70 mins). **Captain:** Mick McCarthy. **Manager:** Jack Charlton (44). **Formation:** 4-3-3.

Morocco: El Brazi, Jbilou, Benabicha, Khairi, Mouhcine, Naybat, Raghib, Daoudi, Mjid, Nader, El Ghrissi. **Subs:** El Khalej for Jbilou (76 mins).

Ireland's first game after their World Cup Finals exploits was a 'bringing back down to earth' experience. Dalymount Park was a sharp contrast to the Italian stadia Ireland had used in the Finals and the crowd now contained a large proportion of people making their soccer 'debut'. Sadly the enthusiasm shown by these new supporters and indeed the 'genuine' fan was not to be realised as the success of the international team mitigated against them. Few of these fans would get tickets and although the future of soccer in this country was now secure its high profile threatened to alienate the people who were its foundation and supporters.

The game itself was a 'bringing back down to earth' experience for the Irish team also. Morocco were not the glamour team to celebrate Ireland's homecoming but a side with a similar playing style to Turkey – Ireland's first opponents in the forthcoming European Championship. Five minutes into the game the visitors almost went ahead when a high back pass from O'Leary beat Bonner and bounced out for a corner via the crossbar. From the flag kick Jbilou had a shot easily saved by Bonner. Ireland then had the better of the play and after 8 minutes a glancing header by Quinn, from Whelan's free kick, just went wide. Mark Kelly had a bicycle kick turned around the post by El Brazi while Houghton (twice) and David Kelly came close between the 21st and 24th minutes. The half ended with shots from Nader and Daoudi going wide.

Ireland made a poor start to the second half with Bonner in action early to force El Ghrissi's shot out for a corner. Further shots from Daoudi and Raghib came close but marked the last threat to Bonners goal. Ireland's only response where headers by Cascarino and McLoughlin until the 72nd minute when David Kelly's chip shot came back off the crossbar with Jbilou clearing Cascarino's header off the line from the rebound. Two minutes later Cascarino headed down a Whelan cross into the path of David Kelly who scored with a hooked shot at the near post. The visitors showed a bit more attacking spirit after this setback but it was Ireland, with shots from Houghton and Sheridan, who came closest to scoring again.

Match No. 265 TURKEY Home

Wednesday 17th October 1990 – Dublin (European Championship)

REP. OF IRELAND (2) 5 Aldridge 15, 57, 70 (pen), O'Leary 39, Quinn 65
TURKEY (0) 0

Ref: Fredriksen (Sweden) **Ground:** Lansdowne Road **Att:** 46,000

Ireland: Patrick Bonner (Glasgow Celtic 45), Denis Irwin (Manchester United 2), Mick McCarthy (Millwall 49), David O'Leary (Arsenal 54), Chris Hughton (Tottenham Hotspur 51), Ray Houghton (Liverpool 36), Andy Townsend (Chelsea 19), John Sheridan (Sheffield Wednesday 11), Stephen Staunton (Liverpool 20), John Aldridge (Real Sociedad 36), Niall Quinn (Manchester City 21). **Subs:** Tony Cascarino (Aston Villa 28) for Quinn (68 mins). Kevin Moran (Blackburn Rovers 56) for Townsend (73 mins). **Captain:** Mick McCarthy. **Manager:** Jack Charlton (45). **Formation:** 4-4-2.

Turkey: Engin, Riza, Kemal, K. Gokhan, Ercan, Tugay, Oguz, Mehmet, Bulent, Hami, Sercan. **Subs:** Tanju for Sercan (half-time), Metin for Ercan (half-time).

Turkey made a bright start with Bonner in action early on saving a deflected shot from Hami and kicking away a through ball for Sercan while Hami had a shot wide after a neat interchange with Sercan. Ireland showed with a shot from Sheridan, which went wide, and a header from Aldridge, which was saved. After 15 minutes Aldrige set up Hughton for a shot which was deflected by Ercan and spun under Engins body. Aldridge pounced on the loose ball and scored from three yards. In further play Houghton had a shot wide and Engin saved at Quinn's feet following a one-two with Houghton. Turkey should have had a penalty after 34 minutes when Bonner brought down Sercan when he was clean through and from this let-off Ireland profited. A free kick from Sheridan was headed goalwards by McCarthy but deflected by the unfortunate Ercan straight to O'Leary who shot home. Two minutes from the break a long kick out by Bonner was headed down by Quinn for Townsend to have a shot well saved by Engin.

Ireland made the better start to the second period and after 4 minutes Sheridan had a shot just wide. A pass from Sheridan, after 57 minutes found O'Leary free in the box, and the latter passed to Aldridge who shot home powerfully. Sheridan then had a header saved by Engin before the Turkish goalkeeper was beaten for the fourth time when Quinn volleyed home after Aldridge had headed down an Irwin cross. After 70 minutes a shot from Aldrige was handled by Gokhan and a penalty was awarded. Despite a delay of two minutes due to Turkish protests Aldridge scored from the spot – the first success from the penalty spot in Ireland-Turkey meetings. In the last 6 minutes Tanju volleyed over and Aldridge had a shot deflected onto the crossbar by Kemal. Five players, Townsend and Cascarino for Ireland and Bulent, Engin and Riza for Turkey, were booked during the match.

Match No. 266 ENGLAND Home

Wednesday 14th November 1990 – Dublin (European Championship)

REP. OF IRELAND (0) 1 Cascarino 79
ENGLAND (0) 1 Platt 67

Ref: D'Elia (Italy) **Ground:** Lansdowne Road **Att:** 45,000

Ireland: Patrick Bonner (Glasgow Celtic 46), Chris Morris (Glasgow Celtic 27), Mick McCarthy (Millwall 50), David O'Leary (Arsenal 55), Stephen Staunton (Liverpool 21), Ray Houghton (Liverpool 37), Paul McGrath (Aston Villa 42), Ronnie Whelan (Liverpool 41), Andy Townsend (Chelsea 20). John Aldridge (Real Sociedad 37), Niall Quinn (Manchester City 22). **Subs:** Tony Cascarino (Aston Villa 29) for Quinn (61 mins), Alan McLoughlin (Swindon Town 5) for Whelan (74 mins). **Captain:** Mick McCarthy. **Manager:** Jack Charlton (46). **Formation:** 4-4-2.

England: C. Woods, L. Dixon, T. Adams, M. Wright, D. Walker, S. Pearce, D. Platt, S. McMahon, G. Cowans, G. Lineker, P. Beardsley.

In a scrappy game few chances were created despite early promise with a shot from Dixon which went wide. After 10 minutes Quinn had a header easily saved by Woods but in an immediate counter-attack Lineker shot over when put through by Pearce. A minute later another Lineker shot was deflected over by McCarthy while Aldridge headed over a Houghton free kick. The home side should have had a penalty after 33 minutes when Townsend was pushed off the ball by Dixon but the referee was unsighted. Woods only decent save came after 35 minutes when he punched over Whelan's free kick. Bonner was untroubled.

The second half was more of the same but the conditions almost led to a goal when McCarthy's free kick from the half-way line caught on the wind and went just over with Woods almost caught out. After 67 minutes a move started and finished by Platt gave England the lead. Platt headed down an English clearance for Lineker to lay the ball off for McMahon who broke into the Irish half before passing out to the overlapping Dixon. The full-back's low cross eluded McCarthy, Lineker and Whelan but came to the unmarked Platt at the far post who side-footed home. Three minutes later a long pass from Dixon found Beardsley who beat Morris to have a shot saved by Bonner. Whelan and McCarthy had efforts wide before Ireland equalised. McLoughlin set up Staunton for a cross which was headed beyond Woods by Cascarino. Three minutes from the end a mistake by Pearce almost let in Houghton for a winner but he scuffed his shot and Woods saved easily. O'Leary, Whelan and Beardsley were booked during the game.

Match No. 267 — WALES — Away

Wednesday 6th February 1991 – Wrexham

WALES (0) 0

REP. OF IRELAND (1) 3 Quinn 23, 66, Byrne 86

Ref: McKnight (N. Ireland) **Ground:** Racecourse Ground **Att:** 9,168

Wales: N. Southall, G. Hall, E. Young, K. Ratcliffe, P. Bodin, M. Aizlewood, C. Pascoe, P. Nicolas, B. Horne, D. Saunders, I. Rush. **Subs:** G. Speed for Young (half-time), M. Allen for Rush (52 mins).

Ireland: Patrick Bonner (Glasgow Celtic 47), Denis Irwin (Manchester United 3), Kevin Moran (Blackburn Rovers 57), Paul McGrath (Aston Villa 43), Stephen Staunton (Liverpool 22), John Byrne (Brighton 20), Alan McLoughlin (Southampton 6), Andy Townsend (Chelsea 21), Kevin Sheedy (Everton 34), Bernie Slaven (Middlesbrough 5), Niall Quinn (Manchester City 23). **Subs:** David Kelly (Leicester City 8) for Slaven (67 mins). **Captain:** Kevin Moran. **Manager:** Jack Charlton (47). **Formation:** 4-4-2.

On a pitch which more resembled an ice-rink Ireland turned in a superior team performance and recorded their first win against Wales on Welsh soil. An early effort from Sheedy was stopped

Ireland's scorers John Byrne and Niall Quinn are prevented from getting to the ball by Peter Nicolas and Gary Speed of Wales. Ian Rush looks on. (Photo: via the Welsh FA)

by Southall who also denied Quinn eight minutes later. McLoughlin and Byrne tested the Welsh goalkeeper with further efforts before Quinn rose highest to send a looping header out of Southalls reach and into the net following a cross from Sheedy. Four minutes before the break a tremendous 30 yard free kick from Irwin was touched out for a corner by Southall. Just before the break Saunders produced Wales only chance when his shot was tipped over by Bonner.

McLoughlin was just wide with an early effort in the second half and Staunton shot over after beating three men. After 66 minutes Irwin and Byrne won the ball for McLoughlin to send a high cross into the box where Quinn beat Ratcliffe to shoot past Southall. Soon after coming on Kelly had a shot saved by the Welsh goalkeeper but four minutes from the end a through ball from Sheedy found Byrne running in on goal and he shot home the third goal. Near the end a bad back pass almost got Kelly in for a fourth but he shot wide.

Match No. 268 — ENGLAND — Away

Wednesday 27th March 1991 – London (European Championship)

ENGLAND (1) 1 Staunton (og) 9
REP. OF IRELAND (1) 1 Quinn 27

Ref: Rothlisberger (Switzerland) **Ground:** Wembley Stadium **Att:** 83,000

England: D. Seaman, L. Dixon, T. Adams, M. Wright, D. Walker, S. Pearce, B. Robson, D. Platt, J. Barnes, G. Lineker, P. Beardsley. **Subs:** L. Sharpe for Adams (half-time), I. Wright for Lineker (76 mins).

Ireland: Patrick Bonner (Glasgow Celtic 48), Denis Irwin (Manchester United 4), David O'Leary (Arsenal 56), Kevin Moran (Blackburn Rovers 58), Stephen Staunton (Liverpool 23), Ray Houghton (Liverpool 38), Paul McGrath (Aston Villa 44), Andy Townsend (Chelsea 22), Kevin Sheedy (Everton 35), John Aldridge (Real Sociedad 38), Niall Quinn (Manchester City 24). **Subs:** Tony Cascarino (Aston Villa 30) for Aldridge (72 mins). **Captain:** Kevin Moran. **Manager:** Jack Charlton (48). **Formation:** 4-4-2.

A crowd of 83,000, paying a British record of £1¼ million for an international, saw England create the first chance of the match when Barnes's flick on was cleared by Staunton ahead of Platt. After 9 minutes a cross from Pearce was back-headed by Staunton to Dixon whose shot from outside the area seemed to be covered by Bonner but deflected off Staunton and went in by the near post. Ireland responded well and from their first corner McGrath had a shot kicked off the line by Beardsley with Moran pouncing on the loose ball to smack a shot off the upright. Irish pressure continued and it had its reward after 27 minutes when a lovely curling cross from McGrath was side footed home by Quinn. Ten minutes later a last-ditch tackle by Mark Wright denied Sheedy a chance while two minutes from half-time a brilliant Irish attack involving Aldridge, Townsend and Houghton ended with Seaman saving at Houghton's feet.

After 59 minutes Quinn and Aldridge combined to put Sheedy running in on goal but the ball fell on the midfielder's weaker right foot and he shot a great chance wide. Twenty minutes later Cascarino almost got in for another chance but Pearce made a saving tackle at the expense of a corner. More Irish pressure should have yielded a winner when Cascarino headed down a McGrath ball into the path of Houghton. Houghton took the ball on the run but with only the goalkeeper to beat he shot inches wide. There was one booking – McGrath for a foul on Robson.

Match No. 269 — POLAND — Home

Wednesday 1st May 1991 – Dublin (European Championship)

REP. OF IRELAND (0) 0
POLAND (0) 0

Ref: Blankenstein (Holland) **Ground:** Lansdowne Road **Att:** 48,000

Ireland: Patrick Bonner (Glasgow Celtic 49), Denis Irwin (Manchester United 5), David O'Leary (Arsenal 57), Kevin Moran (Blackburn Rovers 59), Stephen Staunton (Liverpool 24), Ray Houghton (Liverpool 39),

Paul McGrath (Aston Villa 45), Andy Townsend (Chelsea 23), Kevin Sheedy (Everton 36), John Aldridge (Real Sociedad 39), Niall Quinn (Manchester City 25). **Subs:** Bernie Slaven (Middlesbrough 6) for Aldridge (68 mins), Tony Cascarino (Aston Villa 31) for Quinn (71 mins). **Captain:** Kevin Moran. **Manager:** Jack Charlton (49). **Formation:** 4-4-2.

Poland: J. Wandzik, D. Kubicki, P. Soczynski, C. Jakolceiwcz, D. Wdowczyk, R. Warzycha, R. Tarasiewicz, R. Szewckyk, P. Czachowski, J. Urban, J. Furtok. **Subs:** K. Warzycha for Urban (89 mins), R. Kosecki for Furtok (90 mins).

Poland had a bright opening with Czachowski heading over in the first minute and Robert Warzycha shooting wide after five minutes. The Polish goalkeeper was forced to save twice at the feet of Aldridge and Houghton, the second save at the expense of a corner. From this flag kick Sheedy crossed over with Moran clashing with Wandzik. The ball ran free to Quinn whose shot was handled by Soczynski with Aldridge following up to net. However the referee disallowed the score for Moran's foul on the goalkeeper. Wdowczyk had a shot turned over by Bonner after 13 minutes. Six minutes later an Irish free kick caught out the Polish defence but McGrath's side-footed volley just went past the far post. The Poles were caught again by another quick Irish free but this time Houghton's shot was well saved by Wandzik.

The second half began with Aldridge, Urban and McGrath all having shots blocked and Moran having a header kicked off the line with Wandzik beaten. Chances were few in this period and the only other efforts of note were headers by Aldridge and Cascarino which went over and a shot from Kosecki, in injury time, which went wide. Three Poles Szewckyk, Czachowski and Robert Warzycha, were booked in this second half.

Match No. 270 — CHILE — Home

Wednesday 22nd May 1991 – Dublin

REP. OF IRELAND (0) 1 D. Kelly 81
CHILE (0) 1 Estay 64

Ref: Roduit (Switzerland) **Ground:** Lansdowne Road **Att:** 32,230

Ireland: Gerry Peyton (AFC Bournemouth 29), Chris Hughton (West Ham United 52), David O'Leary (Arsenal 58), Kevin Moran (Blackburn Rovers 60), Stephen Staunton (Liverpool 25), Ray Houghton (Liverpool 40), Roy Keane (Nottingham Forest 1), John Sheridan (Sheffield Wednesday 12), Andy Townsend (Chelsea 24), Kevin Sheedy (Everton 37), David Kelly (Leicester City 9),. **Subs:** Paul McGrath (Aston Villa 46) for O'Leary (7 mins), Alan McLoughlin (Southampton 7) for Houghton (63 mins), Tony Cascariño (Aston Villa 32) for Sheedy (70 mins). **Captain:** Kevin Moran. **Manager:** Jack Charlton (50). **Formation:** 4-5-1.

Chile: P. Toledo, A. Romero, L. Abarca, R. Fuentes, F. Guevara, J. Vera, R. Gomez, N. Parraguez, F. Estay, L. Guarda, H. Rubio. **Subs:** M. Miranda for Guevara (15 mins), J. Contreras for Vera (63 mins), A. Gonzalez for Guarda (78 mins).

This game had a dramatic opening for, with 24 seconds gone, Keane headed over a Sheedy cross and then, in another 40 seconds Ireland were reduced to ten men when O'Leary went off following a clash of heads with Moran. Hughton took over at centre-back and Houghton went to right-back before McGrath came on after 7 minutes. After this hectic start the game settled down but few openings were created. After 21 minutes a header from Kelly was cleared off the goal-line. Two minutes later Estay got free but his shot struck an upright. The only other chance of the half fell to Staunton whose volley was saved at the second attempt by Toledo.

Staunton was also denied by Toledo five minutes after the restart but within three minutes two Chilians shot across the face of the Irish goal in quick succession. Houghton and Kelly came close for Ireland before a mistake by Moran allowed Rubio and Guarda to set up Estay for an easy tap in goal. Both goalkeepers were subsequently in action with Toledo saving McLoughlin's volley and Peyton a shot from Gonzalez. The equaliser came when a corner from Sheridan was flicked into the far corner of the net by the head of Kelly. In the end a draw was a fair result from an entertaining game.

Match No. 271 USA Away

Saturday 1st June 1991 – Boston

USA (0) 1 Wynalda 68
REP. OF IRELAND (0) 1 Cascarino 55

Ref: Arrowsmith (Canada) **Ground:** Foxboro Stadium **Att:** 51,273

USA: T. Meola, J. Agoos, J. Michallik, M. Balboa, B. Savage, S. Trittschuh, C. Henderson, B. Quinn, B. Murray, P. Vermes, E. Wynalda. **Subs:** H. Perez for Vermes (59 mins), Snyder for Quinn (84 mins).

Ireland: Patrick Bonner (Glasgow Celtic 50), Denis Irwin (Manchester United 6), Mick McCarthy (Millwall 51), Kevin Moran (Blackburn Rovers 61), Stephen Staunton (Liverpool 26), Ray Houghton (Liverpool 41), Paul McGrath (Aston Villa 47), Andy Townsend (Chelsea 25), Kevin Sheedy (Everton 38), David Kelly (Leicester City 10), Tony Cascarino (Aston Villa 33). **Subs:** John Sheridan (Sheffield Wednesday 13) for Irwin (65 mins). **Captain:** Mick McCarthy. **Manager:** Jack Charlton (51). **Formation:** 4-4-2.

Ireland dominated the game for long periods but their failure to convert goalscoring opportunities meant that they would have to settle for a fourth consecutive draw.

In the opening ten minutes Cascarino missed a 'sitter' when he headed a Kelly cross wide from close range, Sheedy had a shot deflected for a corner and Henderson came close for the United States. The Irish had the majority of the play but it was the Americans who came closest to scoring when Murray headed a Henderson cross against the post.

The second half was again controlled by Ireland but, after Sheedy and McCarthy had gone close, they finally scored. A long kick out by Bonner caught the Americans trying to play offside and Cascarino sent a low shot from outside the area into the corner of the net. Sheridan replaced Irwin with McGrath moving to right back after 65 minutes and minutes later a flashing header from Townsend was saved by Meola. After 68 minutes a Henderson header was missed by Moran and Wynalda broke free to chip the ball over the advancing Bonner. In the last minute a Sheedy cross fell to Cascarino but his volley was blocked by Trittschuh with the goal gaping.

Match No. 272 HUNGARY Away

Wednesday 11th September 1991 – Györ

HUNGARY (0) 1 K. Kovacs 59
REP. OF IRELAND (0) 2 D. Kelly 61, Sheedy 69

Ref: Vassilakis (Greece) **Ground:** Raba ETO Stadium **Att:** 4,000

Hungary: Z. Petry, T. Monos, P. Lipcsei, L. Disztl, E. Lorincz, T. Csehi, I. Kozma, L. Detari, E. Kovacs, I. Vincze, K. Kovacs. **Subs:** B. Berczy for E. Kovacs (54 mins), D. Eszenyi for Vincze (64 mins), V. Rugovics for Monos (73 mins).

Ireland: Patrick Bonner (Glasgow Celtic 51), Denis Irwin (Manchester United 7), David O'Leary (Arsenal 59), Mick McCarthy (Millwall 52), Terry Phelan (Wimbledon 1), Ray Houghton (Liverpool 42), Roy Keane (Nottingham Forest 2), John Sheridan (Sheffield Wednesday 14), Kevin Sheedy (Everton 39), Niall Quinn (Manchester City 26), David Kelly (Leicester City 11). **Subs:** Alan McLoughlin (Southampton 8) for Sheridan (half-time), John Aldridge (Tranmere Rovers 40) for Kelly (64 mins), Chris Morris (Glasgow Celtic 28) for Phelan (82 mins). **Captain:** Mick McCarthy. **Manager:** Jack Charlton (52). **Formation:** 4-4-2.

The game got off to a slow start and it was not until the 16th minute that either goal was threatened. Then a cross from Kalman Kovacs went right across the face of the goal with Phelan knocking the ball out for a corner. From the flag kick Csehi sent a free header well over. Keane volleyed over from Sheridan's free kick after 33 minutes but just before the break Kelly twice came close. On 45 minutes a free kick by Phelan was headed down by Quinn to Kelly who shot wide and, in injury time, Keane played a one-two with Irwin before crossing over for Kelly to have a diving header saved by Petry.

The second half opened with two long-range shots – one by Keane which was well off target and the other by Vincze which was easily saved by Bonner. A third long-range shot, this time by

Detari after 59 minutes, was only parried by Bonner to the unmarked Kalman Kovacs who shot into the empty net from seven yards. Straight from the restart Ireland forced a corner and from this flag kick Sheedy crossed over for Kelly to head home. Eight minutes later a long throw-in by McCarthy was headed on by Quinn for Sheedy to volley home off he underside of the crossbar. The ball bounced back into play but Aldridge headed it into the net. The goal was Sheedy's as the ball had originally crossed the line from his volley. A minute later Hungary almost got an equaliser but Bonner managed to turn Berczy's shot out for a corner. After 77 minutes Detari sent a free kick just over the bar and two minutes later Aldridge had a header saved when Quinn headed on a Sheedy corner. There were two bookings – McCarthy and Lorincz.

Match No. 273 — POLAND — Away

Wednesday 16th October 1991 – Poznan (European Championship)

POLAND (0) 3 Czachowski 53, Furtok 76, Urban 86
REP. OF IRELAND (1) 3 McGrath 10, Townsend 61, Cascarino 68

Ref: Goethels (Belgium) **Ground:** KKS Lech Stadium **Att:** 17,000

Poland: J. Wandzik, D. Kubicki, P. Soczynski, D. Wdowczyk, R. Kosecki, P. Czachowski, R. Tarasiewicz, J. Nawrocki, J. Urban, J. Furtok, J. Ziober. **Subs:** A. Lesiak for Kubicki (32 mins), D. Skrzypczak for Nawrocki (79 mins).

Ireland: Patrick Bonner (Glasgow Celtic 52), Denis Irwin (Manchester United 8), David O'Leary (Arsenal 60), Kevin Moran (Blackburn Rovers 62), Stephen Staunton (Aston Villa 27), Chris Morris (Glasgow Celtic 29), Roy Keane (Nottingham Forest 3), Paul McGrath (Aston Villa 48), Andy Townsend (Chelsea 26), Kevin Sheedy (Everton 40), Tony Cascarino (Glasgow Celtic 34). **Subs:** Terry Phelan (Wimbledon 2) for Staunton (56 mins). **Captain:** Kevin Moran. **Manager:** Jack Charlton (53). **Formation:** 4-5-1.

Before this game Jack Charlton said that the best result for the group would be a draw and his 4-5-1 formation appeared to be defensively orientated. Looks proved deceptive as both Keane and Townsend were used in an attacking role which was demonstrated after seven minutes. Bonner's

The Irish team which drew 3-3 with Poland in 1991.
Left to right: *Kevin Moran, Patrick Bonner, Denis Irwin, Stephen Staunton, Andy Townsend, Roy Keane, Chris Morris, Paul McGrath, Kevin Sheedy, Tony Cascarino and David O'Leary. (Photo: PAP/CAF)*

long kick out was headed on by Cascarino for Townsend to burst through and have a shot saved by Wandzik. Ireland's next attack yielded a goal when Sheedy dummied Kubicki on the edge of the box and crossed over for McGrath to head home. Urban had a shot saved and Czachowski had a penalty claim turned down before Cascarino had a header saved by Wandzik following a Sheedy corner. Nawrocki and Wdowczyk came close for Poland but an Irish breakway saw Keane and Townsend combine for the latter to round Wandzik and put the ball in the net. The goal was ruled out for a marginal offside decision. Urban sent a free header over the bar, McGrath had a shot deflected over and Sheedy also topped the goal with a shot. Just before half time Furtok had a deflected shot wide and Cascarino had the ball in the net again but that too was from an offside position.

Poland began the second half well with two shots from Kosecki, one of which forced Bonner into a good save. After 53 minutes an attempted clearance by McGrath fell to Czachowski who shot low into the net. Eight minutes later a long kick out by Bonner was headed on by Cascarino for Townsend to send a bullet-like shot from the edge of the box into the corner of Wandzik's goal. Townsend almost got in for a second goal when he dispossessed Wdowczyk but Wandzik, in a one-on-one situation, made a good save to turn the shot out for a corner. From the corner by Irwin, Keane headed the ball down to Cascarino who hooked the ball home. Ireland, it seemed, were in complete command but fourteen minutes from time a deflected shot from Kosecki caught Bonner wrongfooted and he could only palm the ball into the path of Furtok who tapped the ball home. A minute later Bonner saved a long-range shot from Tarasiewicz while, at the other end, a shot from Sheedy went over. Four minutes from the end a mistake in defence allowed Urban to score with a diving header as Bonner came to collect a cross from Czachowski. The game ended with Bonner saving twice to deny the Poles a winner. Staunton and Furtok were booked in the course of the game.

Match No. 274 — TURKEY — Away

Wednesday 13th November 1991 – Istanbul (European Championship)

TURKEY (1) 1 Riza 12 (pen)
REP. OF IRELAND (1) 3 Byrne 7, 56, Cascarino 53

Ref: Petrovic (Yugoslavia) **Ground:** Inonu Stadium **Att:** 40,000

Turkey: Hayrettin, Ogun, Recep, Gokhan, Turhan, Riza, Oguz, Orhan, Tugay, Feyyaz, Hami. **Subs:** Ridvan for Feyyaz (half-time), Bulent for Recep (69 mins).

Ireland: Patrick Bonner (Glasgow Celtic 53), Chris Hughton (West Ham United 53), David O'Leary (Arsenal 61), Mick McCarthy (Millwall 53), Terry Phelan (Wimbledon 3), John Byrne (Sunderland 21), Paul McGrath (Aston Villa 49), Stephen Staunton (Aston Villa 28), Kevin Sheedy (Everton 41), Tony Cascarino (Glasgow Celtic 35), John Aldridge (Tranmere Rovers 41). **Captain:** Mick McCarthy. **Manager:** Jack Charlton (54). **Formation:** 4-4-2.

An injury-hit Irish side needed a combination of results to qualify for the European Championship Finals – a victory over Turkey and a Polish win over England. At the break half the combination (a Polish win) was on the cards. At full time the second half of the combination was completed but an English equaliser 14 minutes from time in Posnan denied Ireland a final berth they deserved. This disappointment over-shadowed another marvellous performance which resulted in Ireland completing a qualifying group undefeated for the first time.

Turkey began well with, first, Phelan, then, McCarthy forced to clear dangerous-looking crosses while Hami had a shot well off target. After 7 minutes a long throw-in from McCarthy was not cleared by Gokhon who headed down for Byrne to volley home. Four minutes later Turhan dispossed Cascarino in the centre circle and sent Orhan away. Bonner came out to get the ball but only succeeded in taking down Orhan and Riza scored from the spot kick after Bonner was booked for the foul. Aldridge and Riza had further efforts saved before McGrath and Sheedy combined to get Aldridge in for a shot which was parried by Hayrettin with Byrne following up to net. However the referee had already blown for offside. After 25 minutes Byrne volleyed over but in a hectic last five minutes Feyyaz had a back-heeled shot saved by Bonner, Byrne was denied by a marvellous save on the part of Hayrettin, Aldridge had another shot saved and Orhan shot over.

Ireland made a great start to the second half with two goals in the first eleven minutes; the first being the result of a brilliant move. A Turkish free kick was cleared by McGrath to Aldridge who combined with Byrne and Sheedy up the Turkish left before the latter found McGrath again. He sent the ball up to Staunton who crossed over to the far post where Byrne met it with a powerful downward header. Hayrettin kept the ball out with his outstretched leg but Cascarino followed up to shoot the loose ball into the net. Three minutes later McGrath headed a Sheedy corner back across goal for Byrne to nod it home on the goal-line. Sheedy had a shot on the turn just over and Aldridge deflected a lovely curling cross from Byrne just wide as the game approached a conclusion. Ridvan and Hami had parting shots off target for Turkey. Both Staunton and Recep joined Bonner in the referee's notebook.

Match No. 275 — WALES — Home

Wednesday 19th February 1992 – Dublin

REP. OF IRELAND (0) 0
WALES (0) 1 Pembridge 70

Ref: Mumenthaler (Switzerland) **Ground:** RDS **Att:** 15,100

Ireland: Patrick Bonner (Glasgow Celtic 54), Chris Morris (Glasgow Celtic 30), David O'Leary (Arsenal 62), Liam Daish (Cambridge United 1), Denis Irwin (Manchester United 9), John Byrne (Sunderland 22), Roy Keane (Nottingham Forest 4), Terry Phelan (Wimbledon 4), Andy Townsend (Chelsea 27), Kevin Sheedy (Everton 42), Tony Cascarino (Chelsea 36). **Subs:** Alan McLoughlin (Southampton 9) for Townsend (half-time), John Aldridge (Tranmere Rovers 42) for Phelan (55 mins), Niall Quinn (Manchester City 27) for Cascarino (68 mins). **Captain:** Andy Townsend/David O'Leary. **Manager:** Jack Charlton (55). **Formation:** 4-5-1.

Wales: N. Southall, D. Phillips, E. Young, M. Aizlewood, K. Symons, M. Bowen, B. Horne, G. Speed, M. Pembridge, D. Saunders, M. Hughes. **Subs:** C. Blackmore for Speed (half-time), P. Bodin for Young (62 mins), G. Hodges for Pembridge (81 mins), A. Neilson for Saunders (86 mins).

Ireland's first home defeat in nearly six years was at the hands of the last team to win in Dublin – Wales. The unusual setting of the RDS lacked atmosphere and it was a poor game overall. It was the visitors who had the better of the first half. Shots from Horne and Saunders came close for Wales while a header from Keane went over in the first ten minutes. After 14 minutes Bonner was forced into a good save to keep out a swerving 25 yard shot from Horne and then did equally well to save further shots from Phillips and Saunders. Despite this the best chance of the half fell to Ireland when Keane headed an Irwin free kick to Cascarino whose close-range shot was brilliantly parried by Southall.

Keane and Cascarino opened the second half with headed efforts which were close but Daish mis-kicked in front of an open goal with Sheedy following up with a shot which went just wide. Phelan went off injured and Ireland reverted to a 4-4-2 formation with the introduction of Aldridge after 55 minutes. Bonner saved further shots from Hughes and Saunders but after 70 minutes he was beaten when O'Leary failed to cut out a long kick out by Southall and Pembridge ran on to score. A minute later a shot from McLoughlin was tipped over by Southall who also kept out a Sheedy volley after 80 minutes. Byrne and Hughes almost capitalised on defensive mistakes in the last ten minutes and Keane had the ball in the net with three minutes to go but was offside. In the last minute both Hughes and Keane had efforts off target.

Match No. 276 — SWITZERLAND — Home

Wednesday 25th March 1992 – Dublin

REP. OF IRELAND (1) 2 Coyne 27, Aldridge 88 (pen)
SWITZERLAND (1) 1 Whelan (og), 25

Ref: Dominquez (USA) **Ground:** Lansdowne Road **Att:** 23,601

Ireland: Patrick Bonner (Glasgow Celtic 55), Chris Morris (Glasgow Celtic 31), Paul McGrath (Aston Villa 50), David O'Leary (Arsenal 63), Terry Phelan (Wimbledon 5), Eddie McGoldrick (Crystal Palace 1), Roy Keane (Nottingham Forest 5), Ronnie Whelan (Liverpool 42), Stephen Staunton (Aston Villa 29), Tommy Coyne (Glasgow Celtic 1), Tony Cascarino (Chelsea 37). **Subs:** Liam Daish (Cambridge United 2) for O'Leary (half-time), Liam O'Brien (Newcastle United 9) for McGoldrick (half-time), Kevin Sheedy (Newcastle United 43) for Staunton (54 mins), John Aldridge (Tranmere Rovers 43) for Coyne (80 mins). **Captain:** Paul McGrath. **Manager:** Jack Charlton (56). **Formation:** 4-4-2.

Switzerland: M. Brunner, C. Ohrel, A. Egli, P. Schepull, H. Gamperle, B. Piffaretti, A. Geiger, T. Bickel, A. Sutter, K. Turkyilmaz, S. Chapuisat. **Subs:** M. Pascolo for Brunner (39 mins), R. Rothenbuhler for Ohrel (50 mins), M. Heldmann for Bickel (65 mins), X. Dietlin for Chapuisat (83 mins).

Ireland's 50th game at Lansdowne Road resulted in their first home victory in five starts with Aldridge, a hat-trick scorer in the last home win, scoring the winner from the penalty spot.

After four minutes Swiss goalkeeper Brunner was injured in challenging McGrath for a McGoldrick free kick but managed to recover in time to save a shot by Whelan from the rebound. Despite receiving treatment Brunner was replaced by Pascolo later in the match. Coyne, Cascarino and Staunton came close to scoring in the next fifteen minutes before Chapuisat had the ball in the net but was well offside in scoring. However from a free kick, for a foul on Chapusiat, Switzerland took the lead when Sutter's kick spun in off the top of Whelan's head. Soon after Piffaretti came close to increasing that lead but his low 35 yard shot was saved by Bonner. Seconds later Ireland were level when Staunton's through ball put Coyne free of the offside trap and he chipped the ball over the advancing Brunner. On the half hour Cascarino had a shot wide but it was the Swiss, with a Piffaretti corner which hit the crossbar and a Sutter shot which was blocked by McGrath, who finished the half on the up.

Both O'Leary and McGoldrick were replaced during the break due to injuries and, after Keane and Staunton had shots wide, one of the substitutes, O'Brien, had a header saved by Pascolo following a cross from a third substitute, Sheedy. Turkyilmaz and Whelan had free kicks saved and Coyne fluffed a great chance before Ireland got the winner with two minutes to go. Keane put O'Brien clear in the box and when his unselfish pass came to Aldridge he was taken down by Gamperle. Aldridge scored from the spot by using his famous 'shuffle' although Pascolo nearly saved. Gamperle was booked for the foul on Aldridge as was Keane for an off-the-ball incident with Chapuisat and Turkyilmaz.

Match No. 277 — USA — Home

Wednesday 29th April 1992 – Dublin

REP. OF IRELAND (0) 4 Townsend 46, Irwin 51, Quinn 68, Cascarino 86
USA (0) 1 Wynalda 88

Ref: Piraux (Belgium) **Ground:** Lansdowne Road **Att:** 27,000

Ireland: Gerry Peyton (Everton 30), Chris Morris (Glasgow Celtic 32), Paul McGrath (Aston Villa 51), David O'Leary (Arsenal 64), Denis Irwin (Manchester United 10), Eddie McGoldrick (Crystal Palace 2), Alan McLoughlin (Portsmouth 10), Andy Townsend (Chelsea 28), Stephen Staunton (Aston Villa 30), Tommy Coyne (Glasgow Celtic 2), Niall Quinn (Manchester City 28). **Subs:** Mike Milligan (Oldham Athletic 1), for Irwin (62 mins), Brian Carey (Manchester United 1) for O'Leary (72 mins), Tony Cascarino (Chelsea 38) for Quinn (72 mins), John Aldridge (Tranmere Rovers 44) for Coyne (82 mins). **Captain:** Paul McGrath. **Manager:** Jack Charlton (57). **Formation:** 4-4-2.

USA: T. Meola, B. Savage, D. Armstrong, M. Balboa, J. Doyle, F. Clavijo, E. Wynalda, J. Harkes, H. Perez, B. Quinn, P. Vermes. **Subs:** D. Kinnear for Perez (68 mins), Z. Ibsen for Savage (72 mins), T. Eck for Vermes (81 mins).

Ireland were in the driving seat for most of the game. Niall Quinn had an early shot over but, after 5 minutes, Wynalda broke from the half-way line and sent a low shot, from outside the box, just past Peyton's right hand past. This and another Balboa shot well off target were all the visitors had to offer in the first half. After 9 minutes Coyne had a long range shot saved by Meola while, in another six minutes, Townsend shot a good chance over. The American goalkeeper saved a Staunton header after 21 minutes and made another save to turn a low shot from Townsend around the post. Both efforts were a result of McGoldrick crosses and another cross by the midfielder after half an hour was met by Niall Quinn at the far post but Balboa headed off the line with Meola beaten. In injury time McGrath shot over from Irwin's corner.

Twenty-three seconds after the restart Ireland were in front when a long kick out by Peyton was back-headed by Niall Quinn into the path of Townsend who unleashed a powerful 30 yard shot which swerved into the back of the net. Townsend almost got through for a second goal after 51 minutes but he was taken down by Balboa on the edge of the area. The American sweeper was booked and from the resulting free kick Irwin curled the ball over the wall and just inside Meola's right hand upright for the second goal. Niall Quinn almost got a third three minutes later but he headed over Irwin's cross. Irwin was injured and replaced by Milligan who went to central midfield with Townsend taking over on the left when Staunton dropped back to left-back. After 66 minutes McGoldrick's shot from an acute angle just tipped the crossbar but two minutes later another of his crosses was headed on by Milligan for Niall Quinn to steal in at the far post and net. Coyne was only just off target with a long range shot after 71 minutes but, with four minutes left, Aldridge received the ball from McLoughlin on the touchline and passed inside for Cascarino who ran at a hesitant defence, beat four men, and shot powerfully home. Two minutes later Brian Quinn, Wynalda and Eck combined in a neat interchange of passing which sent Wynalda racing away into the Irish box to beat Peyton with a rising shot from a difficult angle. In the last minute Peyton was in action again stopping a shot from Balboa who was joined in the referee's notebook by Townsend.

Match No. 278 — ALBANIA — Home

Tuesday 26th May 1992 – Dublin (World Cup)

REP. OF IRELAND (0) 2 Aldridge 60, McGrath 79
ALBANIA (0) 0

Ref: Uilenberg (Holland) **Ground:** Lansdowne Road **Att:** 29,727

Ireland: Patrick Bonner (Glasgow Celtic 56), Denis Irwin (Manchester United 11), Paul McGrath (Aston Villa 52), David O'Leary (Arsenal 65), Stephen Staunton (Aston Villa 31), Ray Houghton (Liverpool 43), Andy Townsend (Chelsea 29), Roy Keane (Nottingham Forest 6), Kevin Sheedy (Newcastle United 44), Niall Quinn (Manchester City 29), John Aldridge (Tranmere Rovers 45). **Subs:** Mick McCarthy (Millwall 54) for Sheedy (51 mins), Tommy Coyne (Glasgow Celtic 3) for Aldridge (83 mins). **Captain:** Paul McGrath. **Manager:** Jack Charlton (58). **Formation:** 4-4-2.

Albania: A. Dani, H. Zmijani, K. Peqini, R. Vata, E. Abazi, A. Quendro, A. Vasi, S. Kushta, S. Demollari, A. Zela, A. Raklli. **Subs:** A. Pali for Quendro (71 mins), B. Sokoli for Zela (80 mins).

Albania arrived in a poor state due to the political problems in their country and in fact had only 9 senior players. The deficiency was made up by under 21 players, three of whom had played in the under 21 game the night before. All seemed set for a massacre but looks can be deceptive and a well-disciplined defensive formation frustrated the Irish for long periods.

Interestingly it was the visitors who had the first scoring opportunity when Raklli headed wide. However that was their only first half effort whereas Ireland brought two saves out of Dani in the first 12 minutes with shots from Irwin and Houghton. After 16 minutes Quinn headed against the crossbar with Dani stranded but the Albanian goalkeeper made further saves from Houghton and Keane. Sheedy, Townsend, Quinn and Houghton were all off target with more efforts before Aldridge had a shot saved by Dani in the 38th minute and headed over the rebound.

The second half started like the first with Kushta having a shot saved by Bonner. An injury to Sheedy forced a reshuffle in the Irish team with McCarthy coming on to join O'Leary in defence with McGrath moving to central midfield and 9 minutes later Ireland were ahead. Houghton, Townsend and Quinn were all involved in the move which ended with Aldridge heading in a curling cross from Keane. Six minutes later Aldridge should have had a second but headed wide from a Staunton cross. Both Keane and Quinn had headers saved in quick succession by Dani at the expense of corners. From the second of these Quinn shot home but was adjudged to be offside. Ireland's second goal came when McGrath headed powerfully home from McCarthy's long throw-in. Dani was booked for time-wasting.

Match No. 279 — USA — Away

Saturday 30th May 1992 – Washington (US Cup)

USA (0) 3 Balboa 54, Ramos 72, Harkes 87
REP. OF IRELAND (0) 1 McCarthy 51

Ref: Seiffert (Canada) **Ground:** RFK Stadium **Att:** 35,696

USA: T. Meola, P. Caligiuri, T. Dooley, M. Balboa, J. Doyle, J. Harkes, T. Ramos, B. Quinn, H. Perez, B. Murray, P. Vermes. **Subs:** C. Henderson for Murray (half-time), R. Wegerle for Vermes (half-time), E. Stewart for Perez (57 mins), F. Clavijo for Henderson (59 mins), J. Michallik for Ramos (78 mins)

Ireland: Gerry Peyton (Everton 31), Chris Morris (Glasgow Celtic 33), Mick McCarthy (Millwall 55), Kevin Moran (Blackburn Rovers 63), Terry Phelan (Wimbledon 6), Ray Houghton (Liverpool 44), Roy Keane (Nottingham Forest 7), Paul McGrath (Aston Villa 53), Andy Townsend (Chelsea 30), Stephen Staunton (Aston Villa 32), Niall Quinn (Manchester City 30). **Subs:** Tommy Coyne (Glasgow Celtic 4) for Staunton (60 mins), Denis Irwin (Manchester United 12) for Morris (78 mins), Alan McLoughlin (Portsmouth 11) for Keane (80 mins). **Captain:** Paul McGrath. **Manager:** Jack Charlton (59). **Formation:** 4-5-1.

Instead of playing in the European Championships Finals in Sweden, Ireland were on the other side of the world taking part in a World Cup rehearsal tournament – the US Cup. Thus a feeling of apathy on the part of the Irish was bound to be realised when, instead of one of the European elite teams, they were faced with a team they had beaten 4-1 a month earlier.

The first half belonged to the home side but, due to the constant rain, scoring chances were at a minimum. The two best chances fell to the Americans. After 32 minutes Harkes and Vermes combined to get Dooley in but Peyton made an excellent save at the American's feet. Shortly before the interval Peyton came to Ireland's rescue when he parried a shot from Vermes with the follow-up from Harkes being blocked by the defence.

Six minutes after the break Ireland managed to get an effort on target when McCarthy's header found the top of the net following a Staunton corner. Three minutes later Dooley headed a Perez free kick to Doyle who squared the ball into the unmarked Balboa who shot low into the net. Meola saved at Niall Quinn's feet before Charlton reverted to a 4-4-2 formation on the hour, with the introduction of Coyne. After 63 minutes Peyton deflected a long range shot from Ramos onto a post but could do nothing 9 minutes later when the same player volleyed home Clavijo's cross. Three minutes from the end Wegerle's back-heel put Dooley in to chip the ball over Peyton for Harkes to shoot home. Niall Quinn and Phelan were booked.

Match No. 280 — ITALY — Neutral

Thursday 4th June, 1992 – Boston (US Cup)

ITALY (1) 2 Signori 17, Costacurta 63 (pen)
REP. OF IRELAND (0) 0

Ref: D'Aquila (USA) **Ground:** Foxboro Stadium **Att:** 34,797

Italy: W. Zenga, P. Maldini, A. Costacurta, F. Baresi, A. Carboni, A. Bianchi, L. Fusi, R. Galia, R. Mancini, P. Casiraghi, G. Signori. **Subs:** G. Venturin for Fusi (half-time), M. Mannini for Carboni (51 mins), A. Lombardo for Bianchi (73 mins), R. Ferri for Baresi (77 mins), G. Vialli for Mancini (80 mins)

Ireland: Patrick Bonner (Glasgow Celtic 57), Denis Irwin (Manchester United 13), Mick McCarthy (Millwall 56), David O'Leary (Arsenal 66), Stephen Staunton (Aston Villa 33), Eddie McGoldrick (Crystal Palace 3), Paul McGrath (Aston Villa 54), Andy Townsend (Chelsea 31), Ray Houghton (Liverpool 45), Niall Quinn (Manchester City 31), John Aldridge (Tranmere Rovers 46). **Subs:** Alan McLoughlin (Portsmouth 12) for McCarthy (half-time), Gerry Peyton (Everton 32) for Irwin (63 mins), Tommy Coyne (Glasgow Celtic 5) for Quinn (72 mins), David Kelly (Newcastle United 12) for Aldridge (78 mins), Terry Phelan (Wimbledon 7) for McGoldrick (80 mins). **Captain:** Mick McCarthy/Paul McGrath. **Manager:** Jack Charlton (60). **Formation:** 4-4-2.
Sending-off: Patrick Bonner (Ireland) 63 mins.

A competitive match began with a goal from the first chance of note when Fusi tapped a free to Signori who shot powerfully home. That was only one of two shots on targets in the half. The other was a shot from Houghton which was saved at the expense of a corner.

At half-time McLoughlin came on at midfield with McGrath replacing the injured McCarthy at the back. Two minutes after the restart Townsend shot across goal after being put through by Staunton. On 63 minutes a through ball from Mancini put Signori clear and as he tried to go around Bonner the goalkeeper took him down. The referee sent the Irishman off and Peyton came on in goal with Irwin going off. From the resulting penalty Peyton was sent the wrong way by Costacurta. Soon after Peyton saved a shot from Maldini while at the other end McGoldrick shot over. There was a hectic final 15 minutes with McLoughlin having a looping header off the crossbar, Casiraghi shooting over in front of goal, Peyton saving a shot from Lombardo, Coyne shooting just over, Lombardo denied again by Peyton and Vialli having two late chances easily saved. There were four bookings – McGrath and McCarthy for Ireland and Galia and Costacurta for Italy,

Match No. 281 — PORTUGAL — Neutral

Sunday 7th June, 1992 – Boston (US Cup)

PORTUGAL (0) 0
REP. OF IRELAND (1) 2 Staunton 39, Coyne 90

Ref: Dias (USA) **Ground:** Foxboro Stadium **Att:** 41,227

Portugal: Vitor Baia, Joao Pinto I, Rui Filipe, F. Couto, Samuel, Leal, Figo, Semedo, Vitor Paneira, J. Couto, Cadete. **Subs:** Joao Pinto II for J. Couto (half-time), L. Filipe for Vitor Paneira (half-time), Domingos for Figo (half-time), Sousa for Semedo (62 mins), Jaime Magalhaes for Leal (71 mins)

Ireland: Gerry Peyton (Everton 33), Chris Morris (Glasgow Celtic 34), Mick McCarthy (Millwall 57), David O'Leary (Arsenal 67), Stephen Staunton (Aston Villa 34), Ray Houghton (Liverpool 46), Paul McGrath (Aston Villa 55), Alan McLoughlin (Portsmouth 13), Terry Phelan (Wimbledon 8), Niall Quinn (Manchester City 32), David Kelly (Newcastle United 13). **Subs:** Tommy Coyne (Glasgow Celtic 6) for Kelly (59 mins), John Aldridge (Tranmere Rovers 47) for Quinn (87 mins), Eddie McGoldrick (Crystal Palace 4) for Phelan (90 mins). **Captain:** Mick McCarthy. **Manager:** Jack Charlton (61). **Formation:** 4-4-2.

The US Cup's 'Wooden Spoon' match brought together two sides which had not played each other for 20 years and that was in another tournament.

Ireland had the better of the opening half with Quinn having a header easily saved and Houghton well off target with a shot. Figo had a shot also way off before Kelly headed over from in front of goal. A minute later Staunton repeated an event which had not been done since 1949 when he scored direct from a corner kick to put Ireland ahead. The half ended with Quinn having a shot over.

Steve Staunton, Ray Houghton and Paul McGrath. Three Republic of Ireland International players playing for Aston Villa.

Alan Kernaghan played his first match for Ireland in the 4-0 success over Latvia.

David Kelly replaced John Aldridge in the 0-0 draw with Denmark in Copenhagen.

In between a host of substitutions during the second period, Kelly had a header easily saved, McLoughlin shot over as did Houghton and Quinn shot wide. It was all Portugal in the last 15 minutes with Ireland restricted to breakaways. Two headers from Domingos Oliveira went wide as did a shot from Fernando Couto. Peyton then saved at the feet of Cadete before Houghton put Aldridge racing clear. Vitor Baia saved but in the ensuing melee Houghton had a header back-heeled towards goal by Coyne with Samuel clearing the ball away from an empty goal. One and a half minutes into injury time Staunton found Houghton in the box and his curling cross was dispatched into the net by a diving header from Coyne. McLoughlin, McGrath and Morris were all booked during the game.

Match No. 282 — LATVIA — Home

Wednesday 9th September, 1992 – Dublin (World Cup)

REP. OF IRELAND (1) 4 Sheedy 31, Aldridge 59, 81 (pen), 88
LATVIA (0) 0

Ref: Frisk (Sweden) **Ground:** Lansdowne Road **Att:** 32,000

Ireland: Patrick Bonner (Glasgow Celtic 58), Denis Irwin (Manchester United 14), Alan Kernaghan (Middlesbrough 1), Paul McGrath (Aston Villa 56), Stephen Staunton (Aston Villa 35), Roy Keane (Nottingham Forest 8), Andy Townsend (Chelsea 32), Ronnie Whelan (Liverpool 43), Kevin Sheedy (Newcastle United 45), Niall Quinn (Manchester City 33), John Aldridge (Tranmere Rovers 48). **Subs:** Tommy Coyne (Glasgow Celtic 7) for Quinn (61 mins), Terry Phelan (Manchester City 9) for Sheedy (76 mins). **Captain:** Andy Townsend. **Manager:** Jack Charlton (62). **Formation:** 4-4-2.

Latvia: K. Igoshnin, R. Bulders, O. Alexeenko, E. Gnedoi, Abzhinov, A. Glasov, Astafjev, D. Sprogis, J. Popkov, A. Linards, A. Jeliseev. **Subs:** R. Sidorov for Astafiev (36 mins), G. Gilis for Popkov (63 mins)

Ireland's 21st World Cup victory was rather easily achieved in a one-sided game. They forced the first of 15 corners after 21 seconds and had the first of 26 goal attempts after 2 minutes when Quinn weakly volleyed wide. There were further shots off target by Keane (twice) and McGrath before Quinn forced Igoshnin into his first save with a header. McGrath then extracted another save from Igoshnin before Aldridge hooked a shot over after Quinn had headed down a Sheedy cross. Latvia's only goal attempt came on the half-hour with Popkov's free kick well off target. A minute later a cross from Keane was headed on by Quinn for Sheedy to shoot home. The half's final ten minutes saw chances by Townsend, Quinn, Aldridge and Staunton all off target.

The Irish were in complete control after the break and after Irwin had forced Igoshnin into another save with a free kick. They increased their lead when Aldridge headed home a Sheedy free kick. Sheedy then shot wide and Igoshnin saved from Townsend and Aldridge before Phelan came on at left-back with Staunton moving to midfield in place of Sheedy. After 81 minutes Coyne was pushed in the back by Bulders and Aldridge scored from the resulting penalty. Keane had another good chance wide before Aldridge headed home a cross by Irwin to complete Ireland's second World Cup hat-trick. Kernaghan was booked for Ireland as was Astafiev and Gnedoi for the visitors. Aldridge's penalty was Ireland's 50th.

Match No. 283 — DENMARK — Away

Wednesday 14th October, 1992 – Copenhagen (World Cup)

DENMARK (0) 0
REP. OF IRELAND (0) 0

Ref: Wojcik (Poland) **Ground:** Parken Stadium **Att:** 40,100

Denmark: P Schmeichel, J. Sivebaek, M. Rieper, L. Olsen, T. Piechnik, J. Heintze, K. Vilfort, H. Larsen, J. Jensen, B. Laudrup, F. Povlsen. **Sub:** B. Christiansen for Povlsen (76 mins)

Ireland: Patrick Bonner (Glasgow Celtic 59), Denis Irwin (Manchester United 15), Alan Kernaghan (Middlesbrough 2), Kevin Moran (Blackburn Rovers 64), Terry Phelan (Manchester City 10), Ray Houghton (Aston Villa 47), Roy Keane (Nottingham Forest 9), Andy Townsend (Chelsea 33), Eddie McGoldrick (Crystal Palace 5), Niall Quinn (Manchester City 34), John Aldridge (Tranmere Rovers 49). **Sub:** David Kelly (Newcastle United 14) for Aldridge (72 mins). **Captain:** Andy Townsend. **Manager:** Jack Charlton (63). **Formation:** 4-4-2.

Despite an excellent performance, Ireland failed to produce a shot on target although there were a few near things. In the first 5 minutes Povlsen had a shot saved by Bonner and Townsend flashed a shot wide. After 10 minutes McGoldrick worked his way into a good position but shot over as did Townsend 7 minutes later. The best chance of the half came when Denmark broke from an Irish corner with Laudrup having a shot saved by Bonner. Houghton and McGoldrick switched wings after 36 minutes and almost at once McGoldrick crossed in for Aldridge to head over. Just on half-time Houghton shot over from McGoldrick's corner.

After 52 minutes Laudrup worked his way into the Irish box but his shot from a tight angle was saved by Bonner. Soon after Phelan headed clear with the defence stretched. After 68 minutes Sivebaek shot over and a minute later Kernaghan made a saving tackle to stop Larsen. Two Kelly headed chances went wide late in the game. Quinn and Kernaghan were booked for Ireland with Piechnik cautioned for Denmark.

Match No. 284 — SPAIN — Away

Wednesday 18th November, 1992 – Seville (World Cup)

SPAIN (0) 0
REP. OF IRELAND (0) 0

Ref: Constantin (Belgium) **Ground:** Sanchez Pizjuan **Att:** 52,000

Spain: Zubizarreta, Ferrer, Lopez, Solozabal, Goikoetxea, Michel, Hierro, Amor, Martin Vazquez, Butragueno, Julio Salinas. **Subs:** Bakero for Julio Salinas (51 mins), Beguiristain for Butragueno (60 mins)

Ireland: Patrick Bonner (Glasgow Celtic 60), Denis Irwin (Manchester United 16), Paul McGrath (Aston Villa 57), Kevin Moran (Blackburn Rovers 65), Terry Phelan (Manchester City 11), Ray Houghton (Aston Villa 48), Roy Keane (Nottingham Forest 10), Andy Townsend (Chelsea 34), Stephen Staunton (Aston Villa 36), John Aldridge (Tranmere Rovers 50), Niall Quinn (Manchester City 35). **Captain:** Andy Townsend. **Manager:** Jack Charlton (64). **Formation:** 4-4-2.
Sending-off: Juan Lopez (Spain) 58 mins.

Another excellent display by Ireland should have brought victory but a combination of poor finishing and poor refereeing decisions denied the Irish. Still, the draw was the first undefeated Irish visit to Spain since 1946.

The first 20 minutes saw three bookings (McGrath, Moran and Goikoetxea) and a snatched shot from Houghton go wide. After 22 minutes Aldridge flicked on a through ball from Townsend to put Quinn clear with just the goalkeeper to beat. Quinn's low shot was just deflected wide by Zubizarreta for a corner. It was a good chance squandered as was a Martin Vazquez shot 11 minutes later. That shot was deflected away by Moran with Butragueno just behind him to apply a finish had the ball reached him.

Bonner was in action early in the second half saving shots from Hierro and Butragueno before Lopez was sent off for a 'professional' foul on Aldridge when the Irishman had got half a yard on him. From the resulting free kick Irwin had a shot blocked. After 72 minutes Staunton, Keane and Quinn combined to put Aldridge in. He rounded Zubizarreta and scored but the referee had already blown for offside. Six minutes later a timely tackle from Solozabal prevented Townsend from getting in a shot on goal. Three minutes from the end a long ball from Martin Vazquez floated over Moran's head for Bakero's outstretched leg to send the ball over the bar.

Match No. 285 — WALES — Home

Wednesday 17th February 1993 – Dublin

REP. OF IRELAND (0) 2 Sheedy 75, Coyne 80
WALES (1) 1 Hughes 18

Ref: Karlsson (Sweden) **Ground:** Tolka Park **Att:** 9,500

Ireland: Patrick Bonner (Glasgow Celtic 61), Chris Morris (Middlesbrough 35), Brian Carey (Manchester United 2), David O'Leary (Arsenal 68), Eddie McGoldrick (Crystal Palace 6), John Byrne (Millwall 23), Roy Keane (Nottingham Forest 11), Alan McLoughlin (Portsmouth 14), Liam O'Brien (Newcastle United 10), David Kelly (Newcastle United 15), Tony Cascarino (Chelsea 39). **Subs:** Ronnie Whelan (Liverpool 44) for O'Leary (6 mins), Alan Kelly (Sheffield United 1) for Bonner (half-time), Kevin Sheedy (Newcastle United 46) for Whelan (half-time), Tommy Coyne (Glasgow Celtic 8) for D. Kelly (69 mins), Bernie Slaven (Middlesbrough 7) for Cascarino (82 mins). **Captain:** David O'Leary/John Byrne. **Manager:** Jack Charlton (65) (Maurice Setters). **Formation:** 4-4-2.

Wales: N. Southall, D. Phillips, E. Young, M. Aizlewood, K. Symons, P. Bodin, G. Williams, B. Horne, M. Pembridge, G. Speed, M. Hughes. **Subs:** C. Coleman for Young (half-time), M. Allen for Williams (73 mins), T. Roberts for Southall (84 mins)

One minute and forty-seven seconds into the game which marked Ireland's return to Tolka Park, the home side lost its captain when O'Leary was injured in a challenge with Speed. The game was held up for five minutes as he received treatment but was stretchered off to be replaced by Whelan. Whelan went into midfield as Keane dropped back to central defence. When the game restarted both Hughes and Whelan exchanged shots both of which went wide. After 18 minutes an Irish attack broke down and Horne sent Pembridge away. Pembridge's cross eventually reached Phillips via Speed and when the full back's shot was palmed out by Bonner, Hughes was on hand to steer the ball home from 7 yards. Ten minutes later Cascarino headed wide from a Byrne corner while the latter had a shot saved by Southall, after 37 minutes. Three minutes later Hughes had a shot on the turn saved by Bonner. In injury time Cascarino shot wide, O'Brien had a shot saved and Pembridge shot over.

The second half also had a dramatic start when Coleman brought McLoughlin down in the box after a minute and forty-five seconds. A penalty was awarded but Kelly's effort hit the underside of the crossbar and bounced back into play. The ball eventually reached Sheedy at the far post but his shot was blocked by Southall. After 63 minutes Bodin shot over a great chance when free in the box and two minutes later, Southall saved a shot from O'Brien. With 15 minutes left a free kick from O'Brien was headed down by Coyne for the in-rushing Byrne. Byrne's shot was parried by Southall to Sheedy who shot home the loose ball. Five minutes later another O'Brien free kick, this time a superb curling effort, forced Southall into making a good save but Coyne was quickly up to head in the winner when the ball was loose. In the closing minutes Sheedy shot over and Slaven had two close range efforts wide.

Setters used a total of five substitutes which altered the team line-up to: A. Kelly, Morris, Keane, Carey, McGoldrick, Byrne, McLoughlin, O'Brien, Sheedy, Coyne, Slaven.

Match No. 286 — NORTHERN IRELAND — Home

Wednesday 31st March 1993 – Dublin (World Cup)

REP. OF IRELAND (3) 3 Townsend 19, Quinn 21, Staunton 28
NORTHERN IRELAND (0) 0

Ref: Roethlisberger (Switzerland) **Ground:** Lansdowne Road **Att:** 33,000

Rep. of Ireland: Patrick Bonner (Glasgow Celtic 62), Denis Irwin (Manchester United 17), Paul McGrath (Aston Villa 58), Kevin Moran (Blackburn Rovers 66), Terry Phelan (Manchester City 12), Ray Houghton

(Aston Villa 49), Roy Keane (Nottingham Forest 12), Andy Townsend (Chelsea 35), Stephen Staunton (Aston Villa 37), Niall Quinn (Manchester City 36), Tommy Coyne (Tranmere Rovers 9). **Subs:** Tony Cascarino (Chelsea 40) for Coyne (78 mins), Eddie McGoldrick (Crystal Palace 7) for Quinn (84 mins). **Captain:** Andy Townsend. **Manager:** Jack Charlton (66). **Formation:** 4-4-2.

Northern Ireland: T. Wright, M. Donaghy, G. Taggart, A. McDonald, N. Worthington, M. O'Neill, J. Magilton, S. Morrow, M. Hughes, I. Dowie, P. Gray. **Subs:** J. Quinn for Magilton (50 mins), K. Black for O'Neill (73 mins).

Northern Ireland kicked off and almost forced Bonner into an error after 5 minutes when Gray charged down an attempted clearance. But that was about as good as it got for the visitors in a half completely dominated by the Republic. On 9 minutes Townsend sent a powerful shot just past a post while twice in the following 6 minutes Wright had to save at the feet of Coyne. After 19 minutes Irwin put Townsend in and he played a one-two with Niall Quinn before guiding a low shot past Wright and into the corner of the net. Two minutes later a superb curling cross from Houghton was side-footed home by Niall Quinn. After 28 minutes another Houghton cross was headed goalwards by Niall Quinn. Wright did well to turn it out for a corner but from the flag kick Staunton's corner was missed by Dowie at the near post and flew into the net. On the half-hour Niall Quinn shot over then headed just past the far post when a cross from Houghton was headed at him by McGrath. Coyne also had a header wide three minutes later and Northern Ireland's only attempt on goal came with three minutes left when Magilton shot wide.

Northern Ireland's performance improved in the second half when their formation was altered to a 4-2-4 line-up with the introduction of Jimmy Quinn. Gray and Taggart shot over before Niall Quinn had a shot saved by Wright. Donaghy forced Bonner into his first save after 56 minutes but six minutes later Wright saved a header from Niall Quinn. The other Quinn, Jimmy, had two shots off target soon after before an attempted chip shot from Houghton went over. Further efforts from Hughes and Niall Quinn followed before the half's best chance fell to Keane whose volley from Cascarino's cross was superbly turned over by Wright. From the resulting corner Staunton drilled over a low cross which McGrath shot wide. McGoldrick's introduction altered the Republic's formation to a 4-5-1 but it was the visitors who had the last two chances with a Hughes free kick over and a McDonald header saved by Bonner.

Match No. 287 — DENMARK — Home

Wednesday 28th April 1993 – Dublin (World Cup)

REP. OF IRELAND (0) 1 Quinn 74
DENMARK (1) 1 Vilfort 26

Ref: Harrel (France) **Ground:** Lansdowne Road **Att:** 33,000

Ireland: Patrick Bonner (Glasgow Celtic 63), Denis Irwin (Manchester United 18), Paul McGrath (Aston Villa 59), Alan Kernaghan (Middlesbrough 3), Eddie McGoldrick (Crystal Palace 8), Ray Houghton (Aston Villa 50), Andy Townsend (Chelsea 36), Roy Keane (Nottingham Forest 13), Stephen Staunton (Aston Villa 38), John Aldridge (Tranmere Rovers 51), Niall Quinn (Manchester City 37). **Subs:** Tony Cascarino (Chelsea 41) for Aldridge (63 mins). **Captain:** Andy Townsend. **Manager:** Jack Charlton (67). **Formation:** 4-4-2.

Denmark: P. Schmeichel, J. Friis-Hansen, M. Rieper, L. Olsen, J. Kjeldbjerg, B. Steen Nielsen, K. Vilfort, J. Jensen, L. Elstrup, B. Laudrup, F. Pingel. **Subs:** B. Kristensen for Pingel (60 mins).

A poorly refereed game was constantly interrupted with free kick awards which not only made constructive play difficult but also led to few scoring chances. Indeed, Denmark only managed two shots on goal in the entire match – the first of which from Brian Steen Nielsen went over. Ireland did little better but after 14 minutes Townsend found Houghton free in the box but the latter screwed his shot just past the far post. Laudrup went on two mazy runs but both times he was stopped by saving tackles from McGrath and Keane while at the other end a fine Irish move culminated with Schmeichel saving a volleyed effort from Aldridge. Denmark secured the lead when a mistake in the Irish defence saw McGrath head a long ball from Olsen down to Vilfort. McGrath should have left the ball for Bonner and with the goalkeeper now of his line Vilfort controlled the ball with one foot and with the other sent a beautifully flighted chip shot over Bonner into the back of the net. Just on half-time Houghton had the ball in the Danish net with a shot from an acute angle but he was offside at the time.

The second half saw no improvement in the overall play but there was almost an improvement on the Danish lead after five minutes. Pingel outpaced McGoldrick on the left and crossed over for Vilfort to head the ball down for Elstrup. As the Dane steadied himself for a shot, Kernaghan came in from behind and effected a clearing tackle which appeared to catch Elstrup by surprise, as he had fallen a penalty could have been awarded. Ireland had little to offer save a Staunton shot which Schmeichel grabbed and a Keane shot which went over. So it came as a surprise when they equalised with 16 minutes to go. Houghton played a short corner to Staunton whose cross was flicked into the far corner of net by the head of Quinn. Two minutes from the end Quinn had a shot on the turn saved by Schmeichel. Two Irishmen, McGoldrick and Keane, and two Danes, Olsen and Kristensen were booked.

Match No. 288 — ALBANIA — Away

Wednesday 26th May 1993 – Tirana (World Cup)

ALBANIA (1) 1 Kushta 7
REP. OF IRELAND (1) 2 Staunton 12, Cascarino 77

Ref: Cinciripini (Italy) **Ground:** Qemal Stafa Stadium **Att:** 10,000

Albania: P. Musta, H. Zmijani, A. Lekbello, R. Vata, S. Shala, I. Shulku, K. Peqini, S. Kushta, S. Demollari, A. Milori, A. Raklli. **Subs:** I. Fortuzi for Zmijani (56 mins), A. Bano for Raklli (76 mins).

Ireland: Patrick Bonner (Glasgow Celtic 64), Denis Irwin (Manchester United 19), Kevin Moran (Blackburn Rovers 67), Alan Kernaghan (Middlesbrough 4), Terry Phelan (Manchester City 13), Ray Houghton (Aston Villa 51), Roy Keane (Nottingham Forest 14), Andy Townsend (Chelsea 37), Stephen Staunton (Aston Villa 39), John Aldridge (Tranmere Rovers 52), Niall Quinn (Manchester City 38). **Subs:** Tony Cascarino (Chelsea 42) for Aldridge (74 mins). **Captain:** Andy Townsend. **Manager:** Jack Charlton (68). **Formation:** 4-4-2.

Although Townsend had an early strike deflected into Musta's arms, it was Alblania who made the better start with Raklli having a shot deflected wide and Kushta securing the lead after seven minutes. An Irish free kick was headed out by Lekbello to Demollari who immediately sent a long ball into the Irish half. Both Kushta and Kernaghan chased it with the Albanian outpacing Kernaghan before beating Bonner at his near post with a powerful shot on the run. Five minutes later Ireland were level when Staunton scored directly from a free kick past a badly formed 'wall'. An overall poor first half saw little other highlights save for shots from Vata and Staunton which did not unduly trouble the respective goalkeepers and a booking for Staunton for taking a free kick too quickly!

The second half was better and, after early shots from Milori and Irwin, Quinn forced Musta into a good save with a 35-yard shot. After 63 minutes a Moran header fell to Fortuzi but the substitute volleyed wide. A minute later Musta brought off another fine save to push away a Keane shot then, seven minutes later, denied Quinn by pushing his header over the bar. After 74 minutes Cascarino replaced Aldridge and three minutes later headed a corner from Staunton into the net for the lead goal. Two minutes later Quinn shook off his marker to get his head to a Houghton cross but his effort went wide of an open goal. The names of Peqini, Lekbello and Musta joined that of Staunton in the referee's notebook.

Match No. 289 **LATVIA** **Away**

Wednesday 9th June 1993 – Riga (World Cup)

LATVIA (0) 0
REP. OF IRELAND (2) 2 Aldridge 14, McGrath 42

Ref: Jol (Holland) **Ground:** Dauvadas Stadium **Att:** 7,000

Latvia: O. Karavajev, A. Sarando, E. Gnedoi, J. Sevlakovs, R. Bulders, G. Erglis, V. Astafjev, V. Ivanov, J. Popkov, A. Linards, V. Babicev. **Subs:** A. Jeilejev for Babicev (half-time), J. Gorjacilov for Sarando (54 mins).

Ireland: Patrick Bonner (Glasgow Celtic 65), Denis Irwin (Manchester United 20), Paul McGrath (Aston Villa 60), Alan Kernaghan (Middlesbrough 5), Terry Phelan (Manchester City 14), Ray Houghton (Aston Villa 52), Roy Keane (Nottingham Forest 15), Andy Townsend (Chelsea 38), Stephen Staunton (Aston Villa 40), Niall Quinn (Manchester City 39), John Aldridge (Tranmere Rovers 53). **Subs:** Tony Cascarino (Chelsea 43) for Quinn (72 mins), John Sheridan (Sheffield Wednesday 15) for Aldridge (80 mins). **Captain:** Andy Townsend. **Manager:** Jack Charlton (69). **Formation:** 4-4-2.

Ireland were in complete control of this match and despite an interchange of chances early on – Linards shot easily shot, Quinn headed wide and Erglis shot wide – their first goal emphasised their superiority. Keane fed Irwin on the overlap and when his cross came over Aldridge timed his run perfectly to head the ball home. The home side's response to this was a shot from Popkov which was deflected over. On the half hour Quinn chested down a Staunton free kick but his shot went just wide. Then, from a Staunton corner, Quinn had a header blocked on the line by Popkov who also prevented Aldridge from scoring on the rebound. After 42 minutes Staunton played a free kick short to Houghton who had time to look up and pick out McGrath with a pinpoint cross which the Irish defender headed low into the corner of the net.

For the second half both Keane and Townsend switched positions and it was the Irish captain who had the first chance when Quinn headed a long ball down to him but Karavajev turned his shot onto the crossbar and out for a corner. Popkov shot wide after 55 minutes and McGrath had a header saved from Staunton's corner three minutes later. Staunton shot over a great chance soon after while Astafjev forced Bonner into his only save of the half a minute later. After 70 minutes Aldridge had a point-blank shot saved by Karavajev with Keane following-up on the loose ball to shoot against an upright. Seven minutes later Aldridge shot over another great chance following a break by Keane and Houghton. Karavajev made yet another point-blank save to keep out a shot from Staunton with ten minutes to go. Sheridan's introduction meant Ireland adopted a 4-5-1 formation for that final ten minutes.

Match No. 290 **LITHUANIA** **Away**

Wednesday 16th June 1993 – Vilnius (World Cup)

LITHUANIA (0) 0
REP. OF IRELAND (1) 1 Baltusnikas (OG) 40

Ref: Philippi (Luxembourg) **Ground:** Zalgirls Stadium **Att:** 5,000

Lithuania: V. Martinkenas, T. Ziukas, V. Baltusnikas, S. Baranauskas, R. Mazeikis, V. Buzmakovas, A. Skarbalius, V. Urbonas, I. Kirilovas, I. Stumbrys, V. Slekys. **Subs:** R. Zdancius for Skarbalius (half-time), T. Ranelis for Urbonas (67 mins).

Ireland: Patrick Bonner (Glasgow Celtic 66), Denis Irwin (Manchester United 21), Paul McGrath (Aston Villa 61), Alan Kernaghan (Middlesbrough 6), Terry Phelan (Manchester City 15), Ray Houghton (Aston Villa 53), Roy Keane (Nottingham Forest 16), Andy Townsend (Chelsea 39), Stephen Staunton (Aston Villa 41), Niall Quinn (Manchester City 40), John Aldridge (Tranmere Rovers 54). **Subs:** Ronnie Whelan (Liverpool 45) for Aldridge (77 mins). **Captain:** Andy Townsend. **Manager:** Jack Charlton (70). **Formation:** 4-4-2.

Ireland ended a long season in the best possible way with this third successive away victory which put them two points clear at the top of Group Three. These three away victories equalled a record set over fifty-six years ago.

Early Lithuanian pressure saw them force two corners in the first 75 seconds and Skarbalius have a shot saved in a further 15 seconds. Both sides had shots blocked before a long range shot from Urbonas went wide after 17 minutes. Ireland's first real chance almost brought them a first goal but Keane's shot from McGrath's head down was kicked off the line by Baltusnikas. Six minutes later a Kernaghan pile-driver was beaten away by Martinkenas. Urbonas and Mazeikis had efforts off target while Aldridge headed just wide from Irwins's corner. After 32 minutes Urbonas had a shot deflected over by Irwin but 8 minutes later Ireland scored. A free kick from Staunton was deflected into the roof of his own net by Baltusnikas. Just on half-time a corner from Staunton was almost forced home by Ziukas but this time Martinkenas made a good save to prevent the own goal.

Both Aldridge and Baltusnikas had shots over before a 57th minute shot from Irwin was saved by Martinkenas. A minute later Aldridge was denied a certain goal, from Houghton's through ball, by a last-ditch tackle and when the ball came to Quinn he shot wide. After 75 minutes a free kick from Baranauskas hit the bottom of a post, rebounded out off Bonner's head and was cleared by Kernaghan. The introduction of Whelan again altered the Irish formation to 4-5-1 which saw Ireland end on the up. Both Houghton and Kirilovas had shots saved before Keane and Staunton had efforts over the bar. The only bookings were for Irishmen – McGrath and Houghton, the latter again for taking a free kick too quickly!

Goalscoring Disputes

The following is a list of the disputed goals:

Match No. 3 – Belgium 1928 – One report credits Lacey with the first Irish goal.

Match No. 7 – Spain 1931 – The fourth Spanish goal was scored by Arocha or Samitier. Spanish records credit the latter.

Match No. 13 – Germany 1935 – Difficult to credit the Irish goal. Gaskins (some sources say Leo Dunne) took a free kick from long range which either went in directly or was deflected into the net by the head of Ellis or a German defender.

Match No. 16 – Hungary 1936 – the second Irish goal was scored by Madden, Donnelly or O'Reilly. I have gone with the best description I could find of the goal.

Match No. 17 – Luxembourg 1936 – Goalscorers sometimes given as Dunne (3), Donnelly and O'Reilly.

Match No. 18 – Germany 1936 –The fourth Irish goal was credited as an own goal but Donnelly has since claimed it. See page 107 of the *Book of Irish goalscorers* by Sean Ryan and Stephen Burke (Irish Soccer Co-op 1985).

Match No. 19 – Hungary 1936 – the second Hungarian goal was scored by either Vincze of Cseh. Hungarian records favour Cseh.

Match No. 25 – Poland 1938 – conflicting reports give the goalscorers as Piontek (4) and Wodarz (2) and Piontek (2), Wodarz (2), Wilmowski and Wasiewicz with Polish records favouring the latter.

Match No. 39 – Belgium 1949 – the first Belgium goal was scored by either Mees (Irish newspapers) or Lamberechts (Belgian records).

Match No. 51 – West Germany 1951 – the German reports credited Morlock with the first and Fritz Walter with the second, while some Irish newspaper reports credit Walter with the first and Morlock with the second.

Facts

	P	W	D	L	F	A
International Record	290	107	69	114	402	430
Home	141	68	35	38	247	171
Away	132	33	29	70	140	244
Neutral	17	6	5	6	15	15
World Cup Record	76	25	21	30	95	109
Home	35	18	9	8	66	41
Away	36	7	8	21	27	65
Neutral	5	0	4	1	2	3
(See Appendix A)						
European Championship Record	59	21	17	21	84	77
Home	28	14	9	5	54	26
Away	28	6	7	15	28	49
Neutral	3	1	1	1	2	2
(See Appendix B)						

No. of Players capped by Ireland 345
No. of Goalscorers for Ireland .... 110 (+ 7 own goals)
No. of Nations played 47

Penalties awarded to Ireland 51 (40 scored, 6 saved, 5 missed)
Penalties awarded against Ireland 26 (20 scored, 5 saved, 1 missed)

Record Win	8-0	v Malta	16 November 1983
(Away)	5-1	v Luxembourg	9 May 1936
Heaviest Defeat	0-7	v Brazil	27 May 1982
(Home)	0-5	v Spain	13 December 1931
Record Competitive Win (Away)	3-0	v Iceland (1983)	
Heaviest Competitive Defeat (Home)	3-5	v France (1953)	
	1-4	v Austria (1971)	
	1-4	v Denmark (1985)	

Most Capped Player	Liam Brady, 72 caps
Leading Goalscorer	Frank Stapleton, 20 goals
Most Goals in a Game	4: Paddy Moore and Don Givens
Most No. of Scorers in One Match	6 v Malta 1983
Most No. of Substitutes used in One Match	5 v Mexico 1984
	v Italy 1992
	v Wales 1993

Internationals Played

	ALBANIA				
278	26 May	1992	Dublin	WC	W 2-0
288	26 May	1993	Triana	WC	W 2-1
	ALGERIA				
193	28 April	1982	Algiers		L 0-2
	ARGENTINA				
49	13 May	1951	Dublin		L 0-1
181	16 May	1980	Dublin		L 0-1
	AUSTRIA				
53	7 May	1952	Vienna		L 0-6
56	25 March	1953	Dublin		W 4-0
74	14 March	1958	Vienna		L 1-3
88	8 April	1962	Dublin		L 2-3
92	25 Sept.	1963	Vienna	EC	D 0-0
93	13 Oct.	1963	Dublin	EC	W 3-2
105	22 May	1966	Vienna		L 0-1
115	10 Nov.	1968	Dublin		D 2-2
131	30 May	1971	Dublin	EC	L 1-4
132	10 Oct.	1971	Linz	EC	L 0-6
	BELGIUM				
3	12 Feb.	1928	Liege		W 4-2
4	20 April	1929	Dublin		W 4-0
5	11 May	1930	Brussels		W 3-1
9	26 Feb.	1934	Dublin	WC	D 4-4
39	24 April	1949	Dublin		L 0-2
47	10 May	1950	Brussels		L 1-5
100	24 March	1965	Dublin		L 0-2
106	25 May	1966	Liege		W 3-2
183	15 Oct.	1980	Dublin	WC	D 1-1
187	25 March	1981	Brussels	WC	L 0-1
225	10 Sept.	1986	Brussels	EC	D 2-2
230	29 April	1987	Dublin	EC	D 0-0

Austria's Walter Skocik gets in a header despite Alan Kelly's attempted punch during the 1966 Austria-Ireland game in Vienna. (Photo: Votavafota)

Ireland's captain Charlie Hurley shakes hands with Austria's Walter Glechner before the 1966 encounter. Hurley and Noel Cantwell were co-managers of the Irish team. (Photo: Votavafoto)

BRAZIL

144	5 May	1974	Rio de Janeiro		L 1-2
195	27 May	1982	Uberlandia		L 0-7
231	23 May	1987	Dublin		W 1-0

BULGARIA

162	1 June	1977	Sofia	WC	L 1-2
163	12 Oct.	1977	Dublin	WC	D 0-0
171	19 May	1979	Sofia	EC	L 0-1
175	17 Oct.	1979	Dublin	EC	W 3-0
229	1 April	1987	Sofia	EC	L 1-2
234	14 Oct.	1987	Dublin	EC	W 2-0

CHILE

79	30 March	1960	Dublin		W 2-0
135	21 June	1972	Recife		L 1-2
146	12 May	1974	Santiago		W 2-1
194	22 May	1982	Santiago		L 0-1
270	22 May	1991	Dublin		D 1-1

CHINA, PEOPLE'S REPUBLIC OF

207	3 June	1984	Sapparo		W 1-0

CYPRUS

179	26 March	1980	Nicosia	WC	W 3-2
185	19 Nov.	1980	Dublin	WC	W 6-0

CZECHOSLOVAKIA

24	18 May	1938	Prague		D 2-2
76	5 April	1959	Dublin	EC	W 2-0
77	10 May	1959	Bratislava	EC	L 0-4
86	8 Oct.	1961	Dublin	WC	L 1-3
87	29 Oct.	1961	Prague	WC	L 1-7
111	21 May	1967	Dublin	EC	L 0-2
112	22 Nov.	1967	Prague	EC	W 2-1
117	4 May	1969	Dublin	WC	L 1-2
121	7 Oct.	1969	Prague	WC	L 0-3
174	26 Sept.	1979	Prague		L 1-4
188	29 April	1981	Dublin		W 3-1
224	27 May	1986	Reykjavik		W 1-0

DENMARK

68	3 Oct.	1956	Dublin	WC	W 2-1
72	2 Oct.	1957	Copenhagen	WC	W 2-0
116	4 Dec.	1968	Dublin	WC	D 1-1
	(abandoned after 51 minutes)				
118	27 May	1969	Copenhagen	WC	L 0-2
122	15 Oct.	1969	Dublin	WC	D 1-1
167	24 May	1978	Copenhagen	EC	D 3-3
170	2 May	1979	Dublin	EC	W 2-0
211	14 Nov.	1984	Copenhagen	WC	L 0-3
220	13 Nov.	1985	Dublin	WC	L 1-4
283	14 Oct.	1992	Copenhagen	WC	D 0-0
287	28 April	1993	Dublin	WC	D 1-1

ECUADOR

134	19 June	1972	Natal		W 3-2

EGYPT

260	17 June	1990	Palermo	WC	D 0-0

ENGLAND

33	30 Sept.	1946	Dublin		L 0-1
44	21 Sept.	1949	Liverpool		W 2-0
70	8 May	1957	London	WC	L 1-5
71	19 May	1957	Dublin	WC	D 1-1
98	24 May	1964	Dublin		L 1-3
156	8 Sept.	1976	London		D 1-1
169	25 Oct.	1978	Dublin	EC	D 1-1
178	6 Feb.	1980	London	EC	L 0-2
214	26 March	1985	London		L 1-2
240	12 June	1988	Stuttgart	EC	W 1-0
259	11 June	1990	Cagliari	WC	D 1-1
266	14 Nov.	1990	Dublin	EC	D 1-1
268	27 March	1991	London	EC	D 1-1

FINLAND

43	8 Sept.	1949	Dublin	WC	W 3-0
45	9 Oct.	1949	Helsinki	WC	D 1-1
256	16 May	1990	Dublin		D 1-1

Ronnie Whelan being closed down by Platini of France in the World Cup match in Dublin in 1981.

FRANCE

21	23 May	1937	Paris		W 2-0
55	16 Nov.	1952	Dublin		D 1-1
57	4 Oct.	1953	Dublin	WC	L 3-5
59	25 Nov.	1953	Paris	WC	L 0-1
138	15 Nov.	1972	Dublin	WC	W 2-1
141	19 May	1973	Paris	WC	D 1-1
158	17 Nov.	1976	Paris	WC	L 0-2
160	30 March	1977	Dublin	WC	W 1-0
184	28 Oct.	1980	Paris	WC	L 0-2
192	14 Oct.	1981	Dublin	WC	W 3-2
246	7 Feb.	1989	Dublin		D 0-0

GERMANY (including West Germany)

13	8 May	1935	Dortmund		L 1-3
18	17 Oct.	1936	Dublin		W 5-2
30	23 May	1939	Bremen		D 1-1
51	17 Oct.	1951	Dublin		W 3-2
52	4 May	1952	Cologne		L 0-3
64	28 May	1955	Hamburg		L 1-2
69	25 Nov.	1956	Dublin		W 3-0
80	11 May	1960	Dusseldorf		W 1-0
104	4 May	1966	Dublin		L 0-4
125	9 May	1970	Berlin		L 1-2
149	11 March	1975	Dublin	"B"	W 1-0
172	22 May	1979	Dublin		L 1-3
189	21 May	1981	Bremen	"B"	L 0-3
251	6 Sept.	1989	Dublin		D 1-1

HOLLAND

8	8 May	1932	Amsterdam		W 2-0
10	8 April	1934	Amsterdam	WC	L 2-5
14	8 Dec.	1935	Dublin		L 3-5
62	1 May	1955	Dublin		W 1-0
67	10 May	1956	Rotterdam		W 4-1
182	10 Sept.	1980	Dublin	WC	W 2-1
191	9 Sept.	1981	Rotterdam	WC	D 2-2
197	22 Sept.	1982	Rotterdam	EC	L 1-2
203	12 Oct.	1983	Dublin	EC	L 2-3
242	18 June	1988	Gelsenkirchen	EC	L 0-1
261	21 June	1990	Palermo	WC	D 1-1

HUNGARY

11	15 Dec.	1934	Dublin		L 2-4
16	3 May	1936	Budapest		D 3-3
19	6 Dec.	1936	Dublin		L 2-3
28	19 March	1939	Cork		D 2-2
29	18 May	1939	Budapest		D 2-2
119	8 June	1969	Dublin	WC	L 1-2
123	5 Nov.	1969	Budapest	WC	L 0-4
247	8 March	1989	Budapest	WC	D 0-0
250	4 June	1989	Dublin	WC	W 2-0
272	11 Sept.	1991	Gyor		W 2-1

ICELAND

89	12 Aug.	1962	Dublin	EC	W 4-2
90	2 Sept.	1962	Reykjavik	EC	D 1-1
198	13 Oct.	1982	Dublin	EC	W 2-0
202	21 Sept.	1983	Reykjavik	EC	W 3-0
223	25 May	1986	Reykjavik		W 2-1

IRAN

133	18 June	1972	Recife		W 2-1

ISRAEL

205	4 April	1984	Tel Aviv		L 0-3
213	27 Feb.	1985	Tel Aviv		D 0-0
235	10 Nov.	1987	Dublin		W 5-0

ITALY

1	21 March	1926	Turin		L 0-3
2	27 April	1927	Dublin	"B"	L 1-2
129	8 Dec.	1970	Florence	EC	L 0-3
130	10 May	1971	Dublin	EC	L 1-2
212	5 Feb.	1985	Dublin		L 1-2
263	30 June	1990	Rome	WC	L 0-1
280	4 June	1992	Boston		L 0-2

LATVIA

282	9 Sept.	1992	Dublin	WC	W 4-0
289	9 June	1993	Riga	WC	W 2-0

LITHUANIA

290	16 June	1993	Vilnius	WC	W 1-0

LUXEMBOURG

17	9 May	1936	Luxembourg		W 5-1
58	28 Oct.	1953	Dublin	WC	W 4-0
60	7 March	1954	Luxembourg	WC	W 1-0
232	28 May	1987	Luxembourg	EC	W 2-0
233	9 Sept.	1987	Dublin	EC	W 2-1

MALTA

200	30 March	1983	Valetta	EC	W 1-0
204	16 Nov.	1983	Dublin	EC	W 8-0
249	28 May	1989	Dublin	WC	W 2-0
253	15 Nov.	1989	Valetta	WC	W 2-0
258	2 June	1990	Valetta		W 3-0

MEXICO

208	8 Aug.	1984	Dublin		D 0-0

MOROCCO

264	12 Sept.	1990	Dublin		W 1-0

NORTHERN IRELAND

168	20 Sept.	1978	Dublin	EC	D 0-0
177	21 Nov.	1979	Belfast	EC	L 0-1
243	14 Sept.	1988	Belfast	WC	D 0-0
252	11 Oct.	1989	Dublin	WC	W 3-0
286	31 March	1993	Dublin	WC	W 3-0

NORWAY

22	10 Oct.	1937	Oslo	WC	L 2-3
23	7 Nov.	1937	Dublin	WC	D 3-3
48	26 Nov.	1950	Dublin		D 2-2
50	30 May	1951	Oslo		W 3-2
61	7 Nov.	1954	Dublin		W 2-1
63	25 May	1955	Oslo		W 3-1
83	6 Nov.	1960	Dublin		W 3-1
97	13 May	1964	Oslo		W 4-1
142	6 June	1973	Oslo		D 1-1

154	24 March	1976	Dublin		W 3-0
166	21 May	1978	Oslo		D 0-0
210	17 Oct.	1984	Oslo	WC	L 0-1
215	1 May	1985	Dublin	WC	D 0-0
239	1 June	1988	Oslo		D 0-0

POLAND

25	22 May	1938	Warsaw		L 0-6
27	13 Nov.	1938	Dublin		W 3-2
73	11 May	1958	Katowice		D 2-2
75	5 Oct.	1958	Dublin		D 2-2
96	10 May	1964	Cracow		L 1-3
99	25 Oct.	1964	Dublin		W 3-2
113	15 May	1968	Dublin		D 2-2
114	30 Oct.	1968	Katowice		L 0-1
124	6 May	1970	Poznan		L 1-2
126	23 Sept.	1970	Dublin		L 0-2
140	16 May	1973	Wroclaw		L 0-2
143	21 Oct.	1973	Dublin		W 1-0
155	26 May	1976	Poznan		W 2-0
161	24 April	1977	Dublin		D 0-0
165	12 April	1978	Lodz		L 0-3
190	23 May	1981	Bydgoszcz		L 0-3
206	23 May	1984	Dublin		D 0-0
227	12 Nov.	1986	Warsaw		L 0-1
238	22 May	1988	Dublin		W 3-1
269	1 May	1991	Dublin	EC	D 0-0
273	16 Oct.	1991	Poznan	EC	D 3-3

PORTUGAL

31	16 June	1946	Lisbon		L 1-3
35	4 May	1947	Dublin		L 0-2
36	23 May	1948	Lisbon		L 0-2
40	22 May	1949	Dublin		W 1-0
136	25 June	1972	Recife		L 1-2
281	7 June	1992	Boston		W 2-0

RUMANIA

236	23 March	1988	Dublin		W 2-0
262	25 June	1990	Genoa	WC	D 0-0

SCOTLAND

84	3 May	1961	Glasgow	WC	L 1-4
85	7 May	1961	Dublin	WC	L 0-3
91	9 June	1963	Dublin		W 1-0
120	21 Sept.	1969	Dublin		D 1-1
226	15 Oct.	1986	Dublin	EC	D 0-0
228	18 Feb.	1987	Glasgow	EC	W 1-0

SPAIN

6	26 April	1931	Barcelona		D 1-1
7	13 Dec.	1931	Dublin		L 0-5
32	23 June	1946	Madrid		W 1-0
34	2 March	1947	Dublin		W 3-2
37	30 May	1948	Barcelona		L 1-2
42	12 June	1949	Dublin		L 1-4
54	1 June	1952	Madrid		L 0-6
66	27 Nov.	1955	Dublin		D 2-2
94	11 March	1964	Seville	EC	L 1-5
95	8 April	1964	Dublin	EC	L 0-2
101	5 May	1965	Dublin	WC	W 1-0
102	27 Oct.	1965	Seville	WC	L 1-4
103	10 Nov.	1965	Paris	WC	L 0-1
107	23 Oct.	1966	Dublin	EC	D 0-0
109	7 Dec.	1966	Valencia	EC	L 0-2
159	9 Feb.	1977	Dublin		L 0-1
199	17 Nov.	1982	Dublin	EC	D 3-3
201	27 April	1983	Zaragosa	EC	L 0-2
216	26 May	1985	Cork		D 0-0
245	16 Nov.	1988	Seville	WC	L 0-2
248	26 April	1989	Dublin	WC	W 1-0
284	18 Nov.	1992	Seville	WC	D 0-0

Switzerland v Ireland 1937.
Ireland's goalkeeper Tommy Breen saves from Bickel of Switzerland as Con Moulson and Charlie Turner look on.

SWEDEN

41	2 June	1949	Stockholm	WC	L 1-3
46	13 Nov.	1949	Dublin	WC	L 1-3
78	1 Nov.	1959	Dublin		W 3-2
81	18 May	1960	Malmo		L 1-4
127	14 Oct.	1970	Dublin	EC	D 1-1
128	28 Oct.	1970	Malmo	EC	L 0-1

SWITZERLAND

12	5 May	1935	Basel		L 0-1
15	17 March	1936	Dublin		W 1-0
20	17 May	1937	Berne		W 1-0
26	18 Sept.	1938	Dublin		W 4-0
38	5 Dec.	1948	Dublin		L 0-1
150	11 May	1975	Dublin	EC	W 2-1
152	21 May	1975	Berne	EC	L 0-1
180	30 April	1980	Dublin		W 2-0
217	2 June	1985	Dublin	WC	W 3-0
218	11 Sept.	1985	Berne	WC	D 0-0
276	25 March	1992	Dublin		W 2-1

TRINIDAD AND TABAGO

196	30 May	1982	Port of Spain		L 1-2

TUNISIA

244	19 Oct.	1988	Dublin		W 4-0

TURKEY

108	16 Nov.	1966	Dublin	EC	W 2-1
110	22 Feb.	1967	Ankara	EC	L 1-2
148	20 Nov.	1974	Izmir	EC	D 1-1
153	29 Oct.	1975	Dublin	EC	W 4-0
157	13 Oct.	1976	Ankara		D 3-3
164	5 April	1978	Dublin		W 4-2
257	27 May	1990	Izmir		D 0-0
265	17 Oct.	1990	Dublin	EC	W 5-0
274	13 Nov.	1991	Istanbul	EC	W 3-1

URUGUAY

145	8 May	1974	Montevideo		L 0-2
222	23 April	1986	Dublin		D 1-1

USA

176	29 Oct.	1979	Dublin		W 3-2
271	1 June	1991	Boston		D 1-1
277	29 April	1992	Dublin		W 4-1
279	30 May	1992	Washington		L 1-3

USSR

137	18 Oct.	1972	Dublin	WC	L 1-2
139	13 May	1973	Moscow	WC	L 0-1
147	30 Oct.	1974	Dublin	EC	W 3-0
151	18 May	1975	Kiev	EC	L 1-2
209	12 Sept.	1984	Dublin	WC	W 1-0
219	16 Oct.	1985	Moscow	WC	L 0-2
241	15 June	1988	Hanover	EC	D 1-1
255	25 April	1990	Dublin		W 1-0

WALES

82	28 Sept.	1960	Dublin		L 2-3
173	11 Sept.	1979	Swansea		L 1-2
186	24 Feb.	1981	Dublin		L 1-3
221	26 March	1986	Dublin		L 0-1
254	28 March	1990	Dublin		W 1-0
267	6 Feb.	1991	Wrexham		W 3-0
275	19 Feb.	1992	Dublin		L 0-1
285	17 Feb.	1993	Dublin		W 2-1

YUGOSLAVIA

65	19 Sept.	1955	Dublin		L 1-4
237	27 April	1988	Dublin		W 2-0

Irish goalkeeper Jimmy O'Neill waits while a Garda moves the crowd back.

Other Statistics

IRISH GOALSCORERS

Frank Stapleton
Ireland's top goalscorer
with 20 goals

	Scoring Games	WC	Goals EC	FR	Tot.	Pens
20						
Frank Stapleton (H12,A8)	19	5	10	5	20	1
19						
Don Givens (H13,A6)	13	3	9	7	19	
14						
Noel Cantwell (H11,A3)	10	0	6	8	14	5
13						
Gerry Daly (H8,A5)	12	3	5	5	13	3
Jimmy Dunne (H4,A9)	10	2	0	11	13	
12						
John Aldridge (H9,A3)	7	7	3	2	12	4
11						
Tony Cascarino (H7,A4)	10	3	3	5	11	
10						
Niall Quinn (H5,A5)	9	3	2	5	10	
9						
Liam Brady (H6,A3)	8	1	4	4	9	2
Kevin Sheedy (H7,A2)	9	3	1	5	9	
8						
Dermot Curtis (H4,A4)	7	3	0	5	8	
Tony Grealish (H7,A1)	8	3	3	2	8	
7						
Arthur Fitzsimons (H5,A2)	5	2	0	5	7	
David Kelly (H6,A1)	5	0	0	7	7	1
Paul McGrath (H4,A3)	7	3	3	1	7	
Paddy Moore (H4,A3)	4	5	0	2	7	
Alf Ringstead (H4,A3)	6	1	0	6	7	
6						
Andy McEvoy (H3,A3)	5	1	2	3	6	
Con Martin (H5,A1)	5	3	0	3	6	4
Kevin Moran (H6,A0)	5	1	1	4	6	
5						
George Cummins (H0,A5)	4	2	0	3	5	
Fionan Fagan (H3,A2)	4	0	0	5	5	2
Johnny Giles (H4,A1)	5	2	0	3	5	1
Mark Lawrenson (H3,A2)	4	2	3	0	5	
Eamonn Rogers(H3,A2)	5	1	1	3	5	1
Ray Treacy (H4,A1)	4	1	2	2	5	
Davy Walsh (H4,A1)	4	2	0	3	5	
4						
Paddy Bradshaw (H3,A1)	3	0	0	4	4	
John Byrne (H1,A3)	3	0	2	2	4	
Tom Davis (H3,A1)	3	0	0	4	4	2
Joey Donnelly (H3,A1)	3	0	0	4	4	
John Joe Flood (H3,A1)	2	0	0	4	4	
Paul McGee (H1,A3)	3	2	0	2	4	

	Scoring Games	WC	Goals EC	FR	Tot.	Pens
Mick Martin (H2,A2)	4	1	2	1	4	
Michael Robinson (H2,A2)	4	3	1	0	4	
Stephen Staunton (H2,A2)	4	2	0	2	4	
Andy Townsend (H2,A2)	4	1	1	2	4	
Liam Tuohy (H3,A1)	4	0	3	1	4	
3						
Johnny Carey (H3,A0)	3	0	0	3	3	1
Paddy Coad (H2,A1)	3	0	0	3	3	1
Jimmy Conway (H2,A1)	3	0	1	2	3	
Tommy Coyne (H2,A1)	3	0	0	3	3	
Peter Farrell (H0,A3)	3	1	0	2	3	
Joe Haverty (H1,A2)	3	1	0	2	3	
Ray Houghton (H2,A1)	3	2	1	0	3	
Kevin O'Flanagan (H1,A2)	2	1	0	2	3	
Reg Ryan (H3,A0)	3	2	0	1	3	2
Gary Waddock (H2,A1)	3	0	2	1	3	
Mickey Walsh (H2,A1)	3	1	1	1	3	
Ronnie Whelan (H1,A2)	3	1	2	0	3	
2						
Terry Conroy (H2,A0)	2	2	0	0	2	
Miah Dennehy (H1,A1)	2	0	0	2	2	
Tommy Eglington (H2,A0)	2	1	0	1	2	
Plev Ellis (H1,A1)	2	0	0	2	2	
Bill Fallon (H2,A0)	2	0	0	2	2	
Sean Fallon (H1,A1)	2	0	0	2	2	
Peter Fitzgerald (H2,A0)	1	0	0	2	2	
Ambrose Fogarty (H1,A1)	2	1	1	0	2	
Johnny Gavin (H2,A0)	2	2	0	0	2	1
Matthy Geoghegan (H1,A1)	2	1	0	1	2	
Alfie Hale (H2,A0)	2	0	0	2	2	
Eoin Hand (H0,A2)	2	0	1	1	2	
Fred Horlacher (H2,A0)	1	0	0	2	2	
Charlie Hurley (H0,A2)	1	0	0	2	2	
Jimmy Kelly (H0,A2)	1	0	0	2	2	
Mick Leech (H0,A2)	2	0	0	2	2	

	Scoring Games	Goals WC	EC	FR	Tot.	Pens
Mick McCarthy (H1,A1)	2	0	0	2	2	
Turlough O'Connor (H0,A2)	2	0	1	1	2	
Frank O'Farrell (H2,A0)	2	1	0	1	2	
Joe O'Reilly (H0,A2)	2	0	0	2	2	
Jimmy White (H0,A2)	1	0	0	2	2	
1						
Paddy Ambrose (H0,A1)	1	0	0	1	1	
John Anderson (H1,A0)	1	0	0	1	1	
Paddy Bermingham (H1,A0)	1	0	0	1	1	1
Johnny Browne (H0,A1)	1	0	0	1	1	
David Byrne (H1,A0)	1	0	0	1	1	
Tommy Carroll (H1,A0)	1	0	1	0	1	1
John Dempsey (H1,A0)	1	0	0	1	1	
Tom Donnelly (H1,A0)	1	0	0	1	1	
Bobby Duffy (H0,A1)	1	0	0	1	1	
Harry Duggan (H1,A0)	1	1	0	0	1	
Jack Fitzgerald (H1,A0)	1	0	0	1	1	
Bob Fullam (H1,A0)	1	0	0	1	1	
Johnny Fullam (H0,A1)	1	0	0	1	1	
Tony Galvin (H0,A1)	1	0	1	0	1	
Dessie Glynn (H1,A0)	1	0	0	1	1	
Ashley Grimes (H1,A0)	1	0	1	0	1	
Jimmy Holmes (H1,A0)	1	0	0	1	1	1
Chris Hughton (H1,A0)	1	1	0	0	1	
Denis Irwin (H1,A0)	1	0	0	1	1	
Davy Jordan (H0,A1)	1	0	0	1	1	
Billy Lacey (H0,A1)	1	0	0	1	1	
Jimmy McCann (H1,A0)	1	0	0	1	1	
Terry Mancini (H0,A1)	1	0	0	1	1	
Jackie Mooney (H1,A0)	1	0	0	1	1	
Tommy Moroney (H0,A1)	1	0	0	1	1	
Paddy Mulligan (H0,A1)	1	0	0	1	1	
Kevin O'Callaghan (H1,A0)	1	0	1	0	1	
Eamonn O'Keefe (H0,A1)	1	0	0	1	1	
David O'Leary (H1,A0)	1	0	1	0	1	
Frank O'Neill (H1,A0)	1	0	1	0	1	
Jack O'Reilly (H0,A1)	1	0	0	1	1	
Gerry Ryan (H1,A0)	1	0	0	1	1	
John Sheridan (H1,A0)	1	0	0	1	1	
Bernie Slaven (H1,A0)	1	0	0	1	1	
Josiah Sloan (H0,A1)	1	0	0	1	1	
Johnny Squires (H0,A1)	1	1	0	0	1	
Fred Strahan (H1,A0)	1	0	0	1	1	
Jack Sullivan (H0,A1)	1	0	0	1	1	1
Joe Waters (H0,A1)	1	0	0	1	1	

GOALSCORING RECORDS

First Goal Scored	Bob Fullam v Italy 'B' 1927 Lansdowne Road
First Away Goal Scored	Jimmy White v Belgium 1928 Liege
Most Number of Goals in a Game	4: Paddy Moore v Belgium 1934 Don Givens v Turkey 1975
Most Number of Scorers in a Game	6: v Malta 1983
Longest Run of Scoring in Consecutive Games	4: Fionan Fagan 1960
Longest Run of Scoring in Consecutive Appearances	5: Jimmy Dunne 1930-37
Fastest Goal Scored by Ireland	20 seconds: Paddy Bradshaw v Switzerland 1938
Goals Direct from a Corner	3: Johnny Gavin v Finland 1949 Stephen Staunton v Portugal 1992 Stephen Staunton v N. Ireland 1993
Goals Direct from a Free Kick	5: Eamonn Rogers v Ecuador 1972 Kevin Sheedy v Poland 1988 Stephen Staunton v USSR 1990 Denis Irwin v USA 1992 Stephen Staunton v Albania 1993

IRISH HAT-TRICKS

John Joe Flood	3 goals	v Belgium	1929
Paddy Moore	4 goals	v Belgium	1934
Don Givens	3 goals	v USSR	1974
Don Givens	4 goals	v Turkey	1975
David Kelly	3 goals	v Israel	1987
John Aldridge	3 goals	v Turkey	1990
John Aldridge	3 goals	v Latvia	1992

Quickest hat-trick 9 minutes: Don Givens v Turkey 1975

GOALS SCORED

Total Goals Scored	402
Total Scored First Half	185
Total Scored Second Half	217

Karl Koller of Austria who scored an own goal for Ireland in the European Championship in 1963.

OWN GOALS

Josef Posipal	West Germany	1951
Karl Koller	Austria	1963
Jose Angel Iribar	Spain	1965
Joey Jones	Wales	1979
Phillippe Mahut	France	1981
Miguel Gonzaelez Michel	Spain	1989
Virginijus Baltusnikas	Lithuania	1993

CONSECUTIVE RUNS

Longest Run of Consecutive Wins (overall) 8; 1987-1988: **Home** 8; 1987-1988: **Away** 3; 1936-37, 1993.

Longest Run of Consecutive Draws (overall) 4; 1978 and 1990: **Home** 3; 1968, 1986-87 and 1990-91: **Away** 4; 1990.

Longest Run of Consecutive Defeats (overall) 5; 1934-35, 1947-49, 1961-62, 1970-71, 1982: **Home** 3; 1947-49, 1961-62, 1971-72; **Away** 9; 1968-1971.

Longest Consecutive Run Without Defeat (overall) 17; 1989-1990: **Home** 25; 1986-1991: **Away** 8; 1989-1990.

Longest Consecutive Run Without a Win (overall) 20; 1968-1971: **Home** 13; 1967-1972: **Away** 12: 1976-1980.

Longest Consecutive Run Without Conceding a Goal (overall) 5; 1989: **Home** 5;1988-1989: **Away** 4: 1989-1990.

Longest Consecutive Run Without Scoring (overall) 3: 1952, 1965-66, 1982, 1988-89: **Home** 3; 1947-49: **Away** 4; 1952-53, 1968-69, 1980-81, 1988-89.

Longest Run of Consecutive Appearances on Irish Team 24; Johnny Carey (1937-1949), Mick Martin (1973-1977), Stephen Staunton (1989-1991), Andy Townsend (1989-1991).

Longest Run of Consecutive Clean Sheets in Consecutive Games 5; Patrick Bonner (1989) 507 minutes.

Longest Run of Consecutive Clean Sheets in Consecutive Appearances 8; Patrick Bonner (1987-88) 803 minutes.

Jimmy Holmes the youngest player to be capped for Ireland.

Youngest and Oldest
Youngest player capped by Ireland:
Jimmy Holmes 17 yrs, 6 mths, 19 days
Youngest player to score for Ireland:
Johnny Giles 19 yrs, 9 mths, 26 days.

Oldest player to play for Ireland:
Billy Lacey 41 yrs, 7 mths, 3 days
Oldest player to make his debut for Ireland:
Billy Lacey 37 yrs, 7 mths, 3 days.

Years and Seasons
Most Number of Games played in a Year: 13 in 1990
Best Record in a Calander Year: 1989 P8 W5 D3 L0 F11 A1
Worst Record in a Calander Year: 1961 P4 W0 D0 L4 F3 A17
Most Goals Scored in a Year: 16 in 1936
Most Goals Conceded in a Year: 17 in 1961 and 1982.

Most Number of Games Played in a Season: 13 in 1989/90
Best Season Record: 1975/76 P3 W3 D0 L0 F9 A0
Worst Season Record: 1961/62 P3 W0 D0 L3 F4 A13
Most Goals Scored in a Season: 19 in 1991/92
Most Goals Conceded in a Season: 17 in 1951/52.

RELATIONS

Brothers

5 sets of brothers have played for Ireland: Ray and Liam Brady, Tony and Pat Dunne, Fran and Ray O'Brien, David and Pierce O'Leary, Michael and Kevin O'Flanagan.

Fathers and Sons

Jack (1926) and Fionan (1955/61) Fagan, Jimmy (1930/39) and Tommy (1956/57) Dunne, John 'Kit' (1949/51) and Mick (1971/73) Lawlor, Con (1946/56) and Mick (1971/83) Martin, Ronnie (1964) and Ronnie (1981-) Whelan, Don (1954/57) and Terry (1979/81) Donovan, Alan (1957/73) and Alan (1993-) Kelly.

Others

Frank Brady was the grand-uncle of Ray and Liam Brady; Jimmy 'Snowy' Dunne was an uncle of Christy Doyle; Denis 'Dinny' Doyle was an uncle of Jackie Mooney; Phil Kelly was a cousin of Peter Farrell.

HOME GROUNDS RECORDS

Lansdowne Road

First Game .... 27 April 1927 v Italy 'B' L1-2
Record Win .... 6-0 v Cyprus 19 November 1980
Record Defeat .... 1-4 v Denmark 13 November 1985
Record Attendance........................ 53,000 v France 1981
Lowest Attendance........................ 10,000 v Czechoslovakia 1981

	P	W	D	L	F	A
Record at	55	32	15	8	96	38

Leading Scorer at .... Frank Stapleton 11 goals

Dalymount Park

First Game .... 20 April 1929 v Belgium W 4-0
Record Win .... 8-0 v Malta 16 November 1983
Record Defeat .... 0-5 v Spain 13 December 1931
Record Attendance .... 47,600 v England 1957
Lowest Attendance .... 5,000 v Mexico 1984

	P	W	D	L	F	A
Record at	81	35	18	28	146	126

Leading Scorer at .... Noel Cantwell, Don Givens 11 goals

Tolka Park

First Game .... 24 February 1981 v Wales L1-3
Record Win .... 2-1 v Wales 17 February 1993
Record Defeat .... 1-3 v Wales 24 February 1981
Record Attendance .... 15,000 v Wales 1981
Lowest Attendance .... 9,500 v Wales 1993

	P	W	D	L	F	A
Record at	2	1	0	1	3	4

Leading Scorer at .... Tommy Coyne, Tony Grealish, Kevin Sheedy 1 each

Other Grounds

The Mardyke .... 19 March 1939 v Hungary D2-2
Flower Lodge .... 26 May 1985 v Spain D0-0
The RDS .... 19 February 1992 v Wales L0-1

Noel Cantwell scorer of 11 International goals at Dalymount Park.

PLAYERS RECORDS

Players who have Scored on their International Debuts

Jimmy White	2 goals	v Belgium	1928
Jack Sullivan	Pen.	v Belgium	1928
David Byrne		v Belgium	1929
Jimmy Dunne	2 goals	v Belgium	1930
Paddy Moore		v Spain	1931
Joe O'Reilly		v Holland	1932
Johnny Squires		v Holland (WC)	1934
Joey Donnelly		v Hungary	1934
Paddy Bermingham	Pen.	v Hungary	1934
Tom Davis	2goals(1P)	v Germany	1936
Matty Geoghegan		v Germany	1936
Kevin O'Flanagan		v Norway (WC)	1937
Paddy Bradshaw	2 goals	v Switzerland	1938
Jack O'Reilly		v Portugal	1946
Tommy Moroney		v Spain	1948
Johnny Gavin		v Finland (WC)	1949
Bobby Duffy		v Belgium	1950
Dessie Glynn		v West Germany	1951
Jack Fitzgerald		v Holland	1955
Joe Haverty		v Holland	1956
Dermot Curtis		v Denmark (WC)	1956
Jimmy McCann		v West Germany	1956
Johnny Giles		v Sweden	1959
Jackie Mooney		v Poland	1964
Turlough O'Connor		v Czechoslovakia (EC)	1967
Mickey Walsh		v Norway	1976
Frank Stapleton		v Turkey	1976
Joe Waters		v Turkey	1976
Paul McGee		v Turkey	1978
David Kelly	3goals(1P)	v Israel	1987
Bernie Slaven		v Wales	1990
Tommy Coyne		v Switzerland	1992

Irish Players Sent Off

John Dempsey	v Hungary	1969
Don Givens	v Ecuador	1972
Turlough O'Connor	v Chile	1972
Don Givens	v Chile	1974
Terry Mancini	v USSR	1974
Mick Martin	v Turkey	1975
Mick Martin	v Bulgaria	1977
Noel Campbell	v Bulgaria	1977
Liam Brady	v Bulgaria	1987
Patrick Bonner	v Italy	1992

Own Goals Scored by Irish Players

Seamus Dunne	Sweden	1960
Andy McEvoy	Belgium	1965
Al Finucane	Czechoslovakia	1967
John Dempsey	Czechoslovakia	1967
Jimmy Dunne	Austria	1971
Mick Martin	Turkey	1974
David O'Leary	Poland	1981
Mick Martin	Spain	1982
Stephen Staunton	England	1991
Ronnie Whelan	Switzerland	1992

Number of Games Played Without Conceding a Goal: 90; **Home** 56; **Away** 34.

Number of Games Played Without Scoring a Goal: 85; **Home** 28; **Away** 57.

Birthdays

Packie Bonner made his international debut on his 21st birthday but conceded 3 goals to Poland in 1981.

Gerry Daly celebrated his 26th birthday with a goal against Switzerland in 1980 and **Kevin Moran**, who made his debut in the Switzerland game, scored his first two goals for Ireland on his 25th birthday a year later against Czechoslovakia.

Other players who celebrated birthdays when playing for Ireland were: **Shay Brennan** was 33 on 6 May 1970 when playing against Poland. **Ray Treacy** was 26 on 18 June 1972 when playing against Ecuador. **Tony Grealish** was 27 on 21 September 1983 when playing against Iceland. **Mick McCarthy** was 30 on 7 February 1989 when playing against France.

Irish Players Landmarks

E. Weir was the 100th player to be capped by Ireland; A. McEvoy was the 200th player to be capped by Ireland; E. Deacy was the 300th player to be capped by Ireland.

J. Carey was the 25th different Irish player to score for Ireland; F. Fagan was the 50th different Irish player to score for Ireland; L. Brady was the 75th different Irish player to score for Ireland; M. McCarthy was the 100th different Irish player to score for Ireland.

P. Ellis scored Ireland's 25th goal (v Holland 1935); K. O'Flanagan scored Ireland's 50th goal (v Norway 1937); J. Gavin scored Ireland's 75th goal (v Finland 1949); R. Ryan scored Ireland's 100th goal (v Luxembourg 1953, a penalty); G. Cummins scored Ireland's 125th goal (v Denmark 1957); L. Tuohy scored Ireland's 150th goal (v Austria 1962); F. O'Neill scored Ireland's 175th goal (v Turkey 1966) (Note: It was also Ireland's 100th goal at Dalymount Park); M. Leech scored Ireland's 200th goal (v Portugal 1972); D. Givens scored Ireland's 225th goal (v Poland 1976) and also Ireland's 250th goal (v USA 1979); L. Brady scored Ireland's 275th goal (v Trinidad and Tabago 1982); F. Stapleton scored Ireland's 300th goal (v Switzerland 1985); D. Kelly scored Ireland's 325th goal (v Romania 1988); K. Sheedy scored Ireland's 350th goal (v Finland 1990); T. Cascarino scored Ireland's 375th goal (v Turkey 1991); J. Aldridge scored Ireland's 400th goal (v Latvia 1993).

League of Ireland

Irish teams composed entirely of League of Ireland players

21 March 1926	v Italy	A	0	3
12 February 1928	v Belgium	A	4	2
8 December 1935	v Holland	A	3	5

Note: The team that played Holland on 8 May 1932 included Kelly of Derry City which was then an Irish League club.

Players who have scored for Ireland when at League of Ireland Clubs.

5
Jimmy Dunne

4
Paddy Bradshaw, Joey Donnelly, John Joe Flood

3
Paddy Coad, Kevin O'Flanagan

2
Plev Ellis, Matty Geoghegan, Alfie Hale, Fred Horlacher, Mick Leech, Paddy Moore, Joe O'Reilly, Ray Treacy, Jimmy White.

1
Paddy Ambrose, Paddy Bermingham, David Byrne, Dermot Curtis, Tom Donnelly, Bobby Duffy, Jack Fitzgerald, Bob Fullam, Johnny Fullam, Johnny Giles, Dessie Glynn, Billy Lacey, Jimmy McCann, Mick Martin, Jackie Mooney, Turlough O'Connor, Frank O'Neill, Jackie O'Reilly, Johnny Squires, Fred Strahan, Jack Sullivan, Liam Tuohy.

Total Goals 63

Frank O'Neill
most capped League of Ireland player.

Most Capped League of Ireland Players

20
Frank O'Neill

18
Joe O'Reilly

11
Paddy Coad, Al Finucane, William O'Neill.

10
Joey Donnelly, Johnny Fullam, Paddy Mulligan, Ronnie Nolan

9
Jimmy Dunne, Johnny Giles, Alfie Hale

8
Pat Byrne, William Glen, Eamonn Gregg, Mick Leech

7
Plev Ellis, Paddy Gaskins, Joe Haverty, Fred Horlacher, Kevin O'Flanagan, Pierce O'Leary

6
Mick Hoy, Tommy McConville, Mick Martin, Turlough O'Connor

5
Paddy Ambrose, Paddy Bradshaw, John Joe Flood, Tommy Godwin, William Harrington, Jackie Hennessy, Mick Lawlor, Paddy Moore, Fred Strahan, Liam Tuohy

Captain Most Times

30
Johnny Giles, Frank Stapleton

23
Noel Cantwell

22
Mick McCarthy

21
Charlie Hurley

19
Johnny Carey

17
Tony Grealish

13
Liam Brady, Paddy Mulligan

12
Peter Farrell, Kevin Moran

9
Andy Townsend

8
Charlie Turner

5
Shay Brennan, Jimmy Dunne, Paddy Gaskins, Con Martin, Mick Martin.

Goalscoring Captains

Tony Grealish scored two goals while captaining the Irish team.

6
Frank Stapleton

5
Noel Cantwell

2
Jimmy Dunne
Tony Grealish
Charlie Hurley

1
Johnny Carey
Tommy Eglington
Johnny Giles
Paul McGrath
Kevin Moran
Andy Townsend

Captains Substituted

Captain	Replacement Captain		
Noel Cantwell		v Sweden	1960
Charlie Hurley		v Hungary	1969
Johnny Giles		v USSR	1973
Johnny Giles		v Switzerland	1975
Johnny Giles		v Poland	1978
Tony Grealish		v Argentina	1980
Tony Grealish		v Spain	1982
Tony Grealish		v Holland	1983
Frank Stapleton		v Poland	1984
Frank Stapleton		v Israel	1985
Frank Stapleton		v Uruguay	1986
Frank Stapleton	Mick McCarthy	v Bulgaria	1987
Mick McCarthy		v Brazil	1987
Frank Stapleton		v Rumania	1988
Frank Stapleton		v Norway	1988
Frank Stapleton	Kevin Moran	v England	1988
Frank Stapleton	Mick McCarthy	v USSR	1988
Frank Stapleton	Ray Houghton	v Holland	1988
Ronnie Whelan		v Wales	1990
Liam Brady	Mick McCarthy	v Finland	1990
Andy Townsend	David O'Leary	v Wales	1992
Mick McCarthy	Paul McGrath	v Italy	1992
David O'Leary	John Byrne	v Wales	1993

Captain on International Debut

Mick Foley	v Italy	1926
John Burke	v Belgium	1929
Paddy Gaskins	v Belgium	1934
Peter Farrell	v Portugal	1946

LEAGUE CLUB PLAYERS

ENGLISH LEAGUE – 181 PLAYERS

Arsenal – 11 Players
L. Brady (26), J. Devine (8), J. Dunne (3), J. Haverty (15), T. Mancini (1), K. O'Flanagan (3), D. O'Leary (68), N. Quinn (13), P. Scully (1), J. Sloan (2), F. Stapleton (24).

Aston Villa – 11 Players
T. Cascarino (15), E. Deacy (4), T. Donovan (2), A. Hale (1), R. Houghton (7), P. McGrath (30), C. Martin (24), T. Muldoon (1), P. Saward (13), S. Staunton (15), D. Walsh (6).

Barnsley – 1 Player
C. Dowdall (1).

Birmingham City – 6 Players
T. Carroll (9), G. Daly (5), D. Givens (13), J. Higgins (1), D. Langan (11), S. McDonagh (1).

Blackburn Rovers – 6 Players
J. Haverty (3), A. McEvoy (17), M. McGrath (18), K. Moran (20), E. Rogers (14), F. Stapleton (2).

Blackpool – 1 Player
Mickey Walsh (4).

Bolton Wanderers – 3 Players
Tony Dunne (9), C. Hurley (1), S. McDonagh (9).

Bournemouth – 2 Players
T. Godwin (2), G. Peyton (7).

Bradford City – 1 Player
M. McGrath (4).

Brentford – 1 Player
B. Gorman (3).

Brighton and Hove Albion – 7 Players
J. Byrne (1), T. Grealish (11), G. Howlett (1), J. Kinnear (1), M. Lawrenson (14), M. Robinson (13), G. Ryan (17).

Bristol Rovers – 2 Players
J. Haverty (1), M. O'Mahoney (6).

Bury – 1 Player
B. Gorman (10).

Cambridge United – 1 Player
L. Daish (2).

Cardiff City – 2 Players
T. Farquharson (4), R. Healey (2).

Charlton Athletic – 2 Players
E. Rogers (5), R. Treacy (15).

Chelsea – 5 Players
T. Cascarino (8), J. Dempsey (12), P. Mulligan (11), A. Townsend (22), R. Whittaker (1).

Chester – 1 Player
P. Fitzgerald (2).

Coventry City – 4 Players
J. Brown (2), G. Daly (16), A. Grimes (2), J. Holmes (16).

Crystal Palace – 3 Players
E. McGoldrick (8), P. Mulligan (14), J. Murphy (3)

Three ROI Internationals and One NI International at Blackburn Rovers in the 1960s.
Left to right: *Andy McEvoy, Ian Lawther, Joe Haverty and Mick McGrath.*

Derby County – 8 Players
G. Daly (17), F. Fagan (6), D. Langan (4), T. Macken (1), M. O'Brien (1), G. Ryan (1), R. Ryan (2), F. Stapleton (6).

Doncaster Rovers – 3 Players
C. Giles (1), A. Hale (3), J. Lawlor (2).

Everton – 15 Players
T. Clinton (3), P. Corr (4), D. Donovan (5), T. Eglington (22), P. Farrell (26), J. Kendrick (1), S. McDonagh (4), M. Meagan (4), E. O'Keefe (1), Jimmy O'Neill (17), G. Peyton (4), K. Sheedy (42), A. Stevenson (6), Mickey Walsh (1), Mike Walsh (4).

Exeter City – 1 Player
D. Curtis (1).

Fulham – 7 Players
J. Conway (19), J. Dempsey (7), J. Dunne (1), J. Lawler (8), T. O'Connor (1), S. O'Driscoll (3), G. Peyton (22).

Gillingham – 3 Players
T. Cascarino (3), S. McDonagh (2), D. Richardson (2).

Grimsby Town – 1 Player
J. Waters (2).

Hartlepools United – 1 Player
A. Fogarty (1).

Huddersfield Town – 3 Players
B. Hayes (2), M. Meagan (12), P. Saward (4).

Hull City – 1 Player
K. de Mange (1).

Ipswich Town – 3 Players
T. Carroll (8), D. Curtis (9), K. O'Callaghan (17).

Leeds United – 7 Players
J. Chandler (2), H. Duggan (4), P. Fitzgerald (3), J. Giles (32), C. Martin (3), N. Peyton (5), J. Sheridan (5).

Leicester City – 2 Players
T. Godwin (6), D. Kelly (7).

Lincoln City – 3 Players
A. Fitzsimons (1), C. Moulson (2), G. Moulson (3).

Liverpool – 9 Players
J. Aldridge (19), J. Beglin (15), K. de Mange (1), S. Heighway (33), R. Houghton (34), M. Lawrenson (23), M. Robinson (5), S. Staunton (26), R. Whelan (45).

Luton Town – 7 Players
T. Aherne (14), G. Cummins (19), S. Dunne (15), D. Givens (8), T. Grealish (17), A. Grimes (2), B. McNally (3).

Manchester City – 7 Players
J. Conway (1), L. Dunne (2), F. Fagan (2), M. McCarthy (20), T. Phelan (7), N. Quinn (27), W. Walsh (9).

Manchester United – 20 Players
T. Breen (2), S. Brennan (18), N. Cantwell (19), B. Carey (2), J. Carey (29), J. Carolan (2), G. Daly (16), Tony Dunne (24), P. Dunne (5), J. Giles (11), D. Givens (7), A. Grimes (14), D. Irwin (21), P. McGrath (31), M. Martin (14), K. Moran (39), L. O'Brien (6), P. Roche (7), F. Stapleton (34), L. Whelan (4).

Middlesbrough – 6 Players
P. Desmond (4), A. Fitzsimons (25), J. Hartnett (2), A. Kernaghan (6), C. Morris (1), B. Slaven (7).

Millwall – 8 Players
J. Byrne (1), T. Cascarino (15), E. Dunphy (22), J. Haverty (5), C. Hurley (1), M. McCarthy (19), P. Saward (1), G. Waddock (2).

Newcastle United – 6 Players
J. Anderson (11), D. Kelly (4), M. Martin (22), L. O'Brien (3), K. Sheedy (4), L. Tuohy (3).

Newport County – 1 Player
H. Duggan (1).

Northampton Town – 1 Player
T. Foley (9).

Norwich City – 4 Players
J. Devine (5), J. Gavin (5), M. O'Brien (1), A. Townsend (17).

Nottingham Forest – 3 Players
M. Dennehy (7), N. Kelly (1), R. Keane (16).

Notts County – 5 Players
B. Fallon (7), E. Gannon (1), S. McDonagh (7), C. Moulson (3), R. O'Brien (5).

Oldham Athletic – 2 Players
T. Davis (2), M. Milligan (1).

Orient – 1 Player
T. Grealish (7).

Oxford United – 4 Players
J. Aldridge (7), R. Houghton (12), M. Kearns (1), D. Langan (11).

Peterborough United – 1 Player
O. Conmy (5).

Portsmouth – 6 Players
E. Hand (20), M. Kelly (4), M. Kennedy (2), J. McAlinden (2), A. McLoughlin (5), K. O'Callaghan (4).

Port Vale – 1 Player
E. O'Keefe (4).

Eoin Hand
one of six Portsmouth players to play for Ireland.

Preston North End – 8 Players
J. Anderson (5), J. Fullam (1), A. Kelly (45), M. Lawrenson (1), P. McGee (6), F. O'Farrell (2), John O'Neill (1), R. Treacy (8).

Queen's Park Rangers – 8 Players
R. Brady (6), J. Byrne (14), D. Givens (27), P. McGee (9), T. Mancini (4), M. Robinson (6), G. Waddock (19), Mickey Walsh (3).

Rotherham United – 1 Player
K. O'Hanlon (1).

Sheffield United – 3 Players
J. Dunne (1), A. Kelly (1), A. Ringstead (20).

Sheffield Wednesday – 4 Players
B. Fallon (2), T. Galvin (9), E. Gannon (10), J. Sheridan (9).

Shrewsbury Town – 1 Player
G. Daly (4).

Southampton – 6 Players
T. Byrne (14), J. Dunne (2), A. Hayes (1), F. Kiernan (3), A. McLoughlin (4), T. Traynor (8).

Southend United – 3 Players
G. McKenzie (9), T. Scannell (1), C. Turner (7).

Stoke City – 2 Players
T. Conroy (26), B. O'Callaghan (6).

Sunderland – 5 Players
J. Byrne (2), J. Feenan (2), A. Fogarty (10), C. Hurley (38), S. McDonagh (1).

Swansea Town – 3 Players
N. Dwyer (10), T. Keane (4), J. O'Driscoll (3).

Tottenham Hotspur – 5 Players
T. Galvin (19), J. Gavin (2), J. Holmes (13), C. Hughton (51), J. Kinnear (25).

Tranmere Rovers – 3 Players
J. Aldridge (15), T. Coyne (1), T. Davis (2).

Walsall – 5 Players
M. Dennehy (1), R. Griffiths (1), M. Kearns (15), D. Kelly (3), M. O'Brien (1).

Watford – 1 Player
M. O'Brien (1).

West Bromwich Albion – 7 Players
J. Giles (7), T. Grealish (10), M. Martin (10), P. Mulligan (15), R. Ryan (14), R. Treacy (5), D. Walsh (14).

West Ham United – 10 Players
L. Brady (11), N. Cantwell (17), N. Dwyer (4), C. Hughton (2), F. Kearns (1), D. Kelly (1), D. McGowan (3), T. Moroney (11), F. O'Farrell (7), C. Turner (3).

Wimbledon – 1 Player
T. Phelan (8).

Wolverhampton Wanderers – 4 Players
M. Daly (2), D. Jordan (2), M. Kearns (2), P. Kelly (2).

York City – 1 Player
E. Dunphy (1).

Note: The list above includes Welsh clubs that played in the English Football League.

SCOTTISH LEAGUE – 20 PLAYERS

Aberdeen – 2 Players
P. Moore (4), Joe O'Reilly (2).

Bo'ness – 1 Player
C. Martin (1).

Glasgow Celtic – 11 Players
P. Bonner (66), T. Cascarino (2), T. Coyne (8), S. Fallon (8), J. Foley (5), C. Gallagher (2), J. Haverty (1), P. Kavanagh (2), M. McCarthy (16), C. Morris (34), P. Turner (2).

Clyde – 2 Players
A. Murphy (1), E. Weir (3).

Dumbarton – 1 Player
H. Chatton (1).

Falkirk – 1 Player
P. Gallagher (1).

Hibernian – 2 Players
P. Farrell (2), M. Gallagher (1).

LEAGUE OF IRELAND – 176 PLAYERS

Bohemians – 20 Players
P. Andrews (1), J. Bermingham (1), W. Browne (3), S. Byrne (1), H. Cannon (2), P. Ellis (7), E. Gregg (8), F. Horlacher (7), B. Jordan (2), J. McCarthy (3), B. McGuire (1), M. Martin (6), B. Murphy (1), T. O'Connell (1), Turlough O'Connor (2), K. O'Flanagan (7) , M. O'Flanagan (1), P. O'Kane (3), J. Robinson (1), J. White (1).

Brideville – 2 Players
Joe O'Reilly (5), C. Reid (1).

Bray Unknowns – 1 Player
J. Byrne (1).

Cork – 9 Players
T. Burke (1), H. Chatton (1), H. Connolly (1), C. Dowdall (1), J. Foley (2), W. Harrington (5), F. McLoughlin (1), O. Madden (1), T. O'Keeffe (1).

Cork Athletic – 1 Player
F. Burke (1).

Cork Bohemians – 1 Player
J. Lynch (1).

Cork Hibernians – 2 Players
M. Dennehy (2), J. Herrick (2).

Cork United – 3 Players
E. Courtney (1), J. McGowan (1), Jackie O'Reilly (2).

Dolphin – 6 Players
P. Byrne (1), L. Doyle (1), J. Kendrick (3), G. Lennox (2), J. Robinson (1), A. Stevenson (1).

Drogheda United – 3 Players
J. Clarke (1), M. Meagan (1), C. Muckian (1).

Drumcondra – 13 Players
F. Brennan (1), P. Byrne (1), K. Clarke (2), T. Coffey (1), T. Donnelly (1), D. Glynn (2), J. Grace (1), B. Henderson (2), F. Hutchinson (2), A. Kelly (2), J. Lawlor (1), P. Meehan (1), M. Swan (1).

Synan Braddish won two caps while playing with Dundalk.

Dundalk – 11 Players
S. Braddish (2), J. Donnelly (10), R. Egan (1), M. Fairclough (2), M. Hoy (6), D. Lunn (2), T. McConville (1), T. Murray (1), T. O'Connell (1), Turlough O'Connor (4), W. O'Neill (11).

Evergreen United – 1 Player
T. Moroney (1).

Fordsons – 6 Players
P. Barry (2), F. Brady (2), J. Connolly (1), C. Dowdall (1), F. McLoughlin (1), J. Sullivan (1).

Jacobs – 1 Player
F. Collins (1).

Limerick/Limerick United – 6 Players
T. Cuneen (1), S. Cusack (1), A. Finucane (11), K. Fitzpatrick (1), W. Hayes (1), J. Walsh (1).

St. James's Gate – 8 Players
P. Bermingham (1), P. Bradshaw (5), P. Gaskins (2), M. Geoghegan (2), B. Kennedy (3), C. Lennon (3), Joe O'Reilly (13), A. Rigby (3).

St. Patrick's Athletic – 6 Players
N. Campbell (1), Tommy Dunne (3), S. Gibbons (4), J. Hennessy (1), D. Lowry (1), R. Whelan (2).

Shamrock Rovers – 62 Players
P. Ambrose (5), E. Bailham (1), T. Breen (3), L. Buckley (1), J. Burke (1), D. Byrne (1), P. Byrne (8), M. Clarke (1), P. Coad (11), J. Daly (2), P. Daly (1), T. Donnelly (1), D. Doyle (1), B. Duffy (1), J. Dunne (9), T. Eglington (2), P. Eccles (1), E. Fagan (1), J. Fagan (1), P. Farrell (2), T. Foy (2), B. Fullam (2), J. Fullam (10) , J. J. Flood (5), P. Gaskins (5), B. Gilbert (1), J. Giles (9), W. Glen (8), T. Godwin (5), J. Golding (2), T. Hamilton (2), J. Herrick (1), M. Kearin (1), J. Keogh (1), S. Keogh (1), F. Kiernan (2),

Mick Smyth one of sixty-two Shamrock Rovers players to play for Ireland.

O. Kinsella (2), A. Kirkland (1), M. Lawlor (5), M. Leech (8), J. McCann (1), M. McCarthy (1), J. McDonagh (3), G. Mackey (3), J. Maguire (1), J. Mooney (2), P. Moore (5), P. Mulligan (10), L. Munroe (1), R. Nolan (10), L. O'Brien (1), L. O'Byrne (1), Tommy O'Connor (4), P. O'Leary (7), F. O'Neill (20), N. Peyton (1), D. Richardson (1), M. Smyth (1), N. Synnott (3), R. Treacy (3), L. Tuohy (5), J. Williams (1).

Shelbourne – 22 Players
E. Barber (2), D. Byrne (1), P. Byrne (1), B. Carroll (2), H. Chatton (1), M. Colfer (2), D. Curtis (2), C. Doyle (1), P. Dunning (2), M. Foley (1), E. Gannon (3), M. Gannon (1), J. Haverty (7), J. Hennessy (4), J. Kinsella (1), B. Lacey (3), G. Malone (1), B. Newman (1), P. Roche (1), J. Squires (1), F. Strahan (5), F. Watters (1).

Sligo Rovers – 1 Player
P. Monahan (2).

Waterford – 8 Players
T. Arrigan (1), S. Brennan (1), J. Fitzgerald (2), A. Hale (9), T. McConville (5), T. O'Keeffe (2), T. Taylor (1), P. Thomas (2).

IRISH LEAGUE - 6 PLAYERS

Belfast Celtic – 3 Players
T. Aherne (2), B. McMillan (2), J. Vernon (2).

Coleraine – 1 Player
D. Byrne (1).

Derry City – 1 Player
J. Kelly (4).

Glentoran – 1 Player
C. Martin (3).

BELGIAN LEAGUE – 1 PLAYER

Waregem – 1 Player
L. Buckley (1).

FRENCH LEAGUE – 3 PLAYERS

Le Havre – 2 Players
J. Byrne (5), F. Stapleton (3).

Olympique Lyon – 1 Player
M. McCarthy (2).

GERMAN LEAGUE – 1 PLAYER

Fortuna Cologne – 1 Player
N. Campbell (10).

DUTCH LEAGUE – 1 PLAYER

Ajax – 1 Player
F. Stapleton (2).

ITALIAN LEAGUE – 1 PLAYER

Ascoli – 1 Player
L. Brady (4).

Internazionale Milan – 1 Player
L. Brady (12).

Juventus – 1 Player
L. Brady (10).

Sampdoria – 1 Player
L. Brady (9).

PORTUGESE LEAGUE – 1 PLAYER

FC Porto – 1 Player
Mickey Walsh (13).

SPANISH LEAGUE – 3 PLAYERS

Sporting Gijon – 1 Player
K. Moran (8).

RC Santander – 1 Player
A. Campbell (3).

Real Sociedad – 1 Player
J. Aldridge (13)

SWISS LEAGUE – 1 PLAYER

Neuchatel Xamax – 1 Player
D. Givens (1).

USA and CANADIAN LEAGUES – 4 PLAYERS

Minnesota Kicks – 1 Player
S. Heighway (1).

Philadelphia Furies – 1 Player
F. O'Brien (3).

Wichita Wings – 1 Player
S. McDonagh (1)

Vancouver Whitecaps – 1 Player
J. Holmes (1).

GOALKEEPER RECORDS

	Caps	Clean Sheets	Goals Conceded
Patrick Bonner	66	36	42
Alan Kelly (Snr)	47	5	80
Gerry Peyton	33	13	34
Seamus McDonagh	25	9	40
Mick Kearns	18	7	19
Jimmy O'Neill	17	4	33
Noel Dwyer	14	2	34
Tommy Godwin	13	4	22
George McKenzie	9	1	20
Paddy Roche	8	3	11
Jim Foley	7	0	22
Tommy Breen	5	2	5
Pat Dunne	5	1	10
William Harrington	5	1	10
Fred Kiernan	5	0	14
Tom Farquharson	4	1	7
George Moulson	3	0	5
Harry Cannon	2	0	5
Ron Healey	2	1	1
Con Martin	2	2	0
Peter Thomas	2	1	2
Frank Collins	1	0	2
Edward Courtney	1	0	3
Kevin Fitzpatrick	1	0	3
Willie Hayes	1	0	2
Alan Kelly (Jnr)	1	1	0
Dinny Lowry	1	0	3
Mick McCarthy	1	1	0
Kelham O'Hanlon	1	1	0
Ted Scannell	1	1	0
Mick Smyth	1	1	0
Maurice Swan	1	0	1
Tommy Taylor	1	1	0

Irish Goalkeepers Penalty Records

	Pens Faced	Pens Saved	Pens Conced.	Oth.
Tom Farquharson	1	1	0	–
Jim Foley	1	0	1	–
William Harrington	2	0	2	–
Tommy Breen	1	1	0	–
George McKenzie	2	0	1	†
Tommy Godwin	1	0	1	–
Jimmy O'Neill	1	0	1	–
Alan Kelly (Snr)	4	0	4	–
Paddy Roche	1	1	0	‡
Mick Kearns	1	1	0	–
Gerry Peyton	2	0	2	–
Seamus McDonagh	1	0	1	–
Patrick Bonner	8	1	7	–

† 1 Missed
‡ Taker followed-up to score

Paddy Roche
three clean sheets in his eight appearances
for the Republic of Ireland.

Other Facts about Goalkeepers

- Alan Kelly (Snr) is the only goalkeeper to have captained Ireland.
- No Irish goalkeeper has scored for Ireland. However Con Martin scored 6 goals for Ireland as an out-field player.
- Packie Bonner is the only Irish goalkeeper to have been sent-off.
- Imrich Stacho of Czechoslovakia scored a penalty against Jimmy O'Neill in 1959. Stacho thus became the only goalkeeprer to score against an Irish goalkeeper!
- The youngest goalkeeper to play for Ireland was Mick Kearns who made his debut against Poland in 1970 when he was aged 19 years, 9 months and 28 days.
- Of the record 80 goals conceded by Alan Kelly (Snr) 4 were scored by Irishmen! (Own Goals). Three of the 42 conceded by Packie Bonner were also own goals.
- Tommy Godwin (2), Fred Kiernan, Jimmy O'Neill, Alan Kelly, Pat Dunne, Kevin Fitzpatrick and Paddy Roche have all had hat-tricks scored against them.

Irish Penalties

	Taken	Scored	Saved	Missed
Total	**51**	**40**	**6**	**5**
Jack Sullivan	1	1	0	0
Paddy Bermingham	1	1	0	0
Joe O'Reilly	1	0	1	0
Tom Davis	2	2	0	0
Billy Hayes	1	0	0	1
Paddy Coad	1	1	0	0
Con Martin	5	4	0	1
Johnny Carey	1	1	0	0
Reg Ryan	3	2	1A	0
Johnny Gavin	1	1	0	0
Noel Cantwell	6	5	0	1
Fionan Fagan	2	2	0	0
Johnny Giles	1	1	0	0
Tommy Carroll	1	1	0	0
Eamonn Rogers	1	1	0	0
Jimmy Holmes	2	1	1	0
Don Givens	1	0	1	0
Gerry Daly	3	3	0	0
Ray Treacy	1	0	0	1
Liam Brady	2	2	0	0
Frank Stapleton	1	1	0	0
John Aldridge	5	4	1	0
David Kelly	2	1	0	1
Kevin Sheedy	2	1	1B	0
Ray Houghton	1	1	0	0
Andy Townsend	1	1	0	0
Tony Cascarino	1	1	0	0
David O'Leary	1	1	0	0

A = Ryan followed-up to score
B = Slaven followed-up to score

SUBSTITUTES

Irish Substitutes – Most Used as sub . . .

18
Tony Cascarino

13
Niall Quinn

11
John Byrne
Gerry Daly

10
Kevin O'Callaghan
Mickey Walsh
Ronnie Whelan

9
Alan McLoughlin
Gerry Ryan

8
John Aldridge

7
Miah Dennehy
Kevin Sheedy
Ray Treacy

6
Tommy Coyne
Liam O'Brien
John Sheridan

5
Don Givens
Paul McGee
Paul McGrath
Turlough O'Connor
Andy Townsend

Most Often Replaced

21
John Aldridge

18
Frank Stapleton

13
Tony Galvin
Don Givens

12
Niall Quinn

9
David O'Leary
Michael Robinson
Ronnie Whelan

8
Gerry Daly
Stephen Staunton

7
Liam Brady
Kevin Moran

6
Tony Grealish
Chris Hughton
Kevin Sheedy

5
Tony Cascarino
Terry Conroy
Steve Heighway
David Kelly
Ray Treacy

Super Subs – Goalscoring Substitutes

Paddy Coad	v Norway	1951
Alfie Hale	v Poland	1968
Turlough O'Connor	v Ecuador	1972
Jimmy Conway	v W. Germany 'B'	1975
Don Givens	v USA	1979
John Anderson	v USA	1979
Mickey Walsh	v Iceland	1983
Gerry Daly	v Iceland	1986
Frank Stapleton	v Czechoslovakia	1986
Kevin Sheedy	v Finland	1990
Andy Townsend	v Malta	1990
Frank Stapleton	v Malta	1990
Tony Cascarino	v England	1990
John Aldridge	v Switzerland	1992 (P)
Tony Cascarino	v USA	1992
Tommy Coyne	v Portugal	1992
Kevin Sheedy	v Wales	1993
Tommy Coyne	v Wales	1993
Tony Cascarino	v Albania	1993

Quickest goal by a substitute

3 Mins: John Anderson v USA 1979;
Tony Cascarino v Albania 1993.

Irish Substitutions used 315
Players Used as Subs 110
Players Replaced 93
Irish teams in which no substitutions were used 119

Irish Players Capped

	Total	WC	EC	FR	Capt	Sub	Replaced
Liam Brady	72	22	27	23	13	2	7
Frank Stapleton	71	20	26	25	30	3	18
David O'Leary	68	23	15	30	2	4	9
Kevin Moran	67	23	19	25	12	3	7
Patrick Bonner	66	22	17	27	0	0	1
Paul McGrath	61	22	15	24	4	5	4
Johnny Giles	59	15	19	25	30	0	3
Mick McCarthy	57	15	12	30	22	2	3
Don Givens	56	16	16	24	0	5	13
John Aldridge	54	20	15	19	0	8	21
Ray Houghton	53	21	14	18	0	0	4
Chris Hughton	53	15	15	23	0	4	6
Mick Martin	52	10	15	27	5	0	4
Paddy Mulligan	50	13	14	23	13	2	0
Gerry Daly	49	12	12	25	0	11	8
Alan Kelly (Snr)	47	11	17	19	1	0	4
Kevin Sheedy	46	18	10	18	0	7	6
Tony Grealish	45	13	12	20	17	1	6
Ronnie Whelan (Jnr)	45	16	14	15	2	10	9
Tony Cascarino	43	20	8	15	0	18	5
Ray Treacy	42	9	11	22	0	7	5
Stephen Staunton	41	19	6	16	0	0	8
Charlie Hurley	40	10	13	17	21	0	1
Niall Quinn	40	15	8	17	0	13	12
Andy Townsend	39	19	5	15	9	5	4
Mark Lawrenson	38	15	15	8	1	1	3
Noel Cantwell	36	12	8	16	23	0	1
Chris Morris	35	11	5	19	0	4	4
Steve Heighway	34	11	14	9	0	0	5
Tony Dunne	33	6	14	13	4	1	1
Gerry Peyton	33	7	5	21	0	3	1
Joe Haverty	32	11	4	17	0	0	1
Jimmy Holmes	30	7	9	14	0	1	0
Con Martin	30	7	0	23	5	1	3
Johnny Carey	29	5	0	24	19	0	0
Tony Galvin	29	5	13	11	0	2	13
Peter Farrell	28	5	0	23	12	1	0
Terry Conroy	26	6	8	12	0	2	5
Arthur Fitzsimons	26	8	1	17	0	0	0
Joe Kinnear	26	5	9	12	0	2	0
David Langan	26	9	4	13	0	2	3
Seamus McDonagh	25	10	7	8	0	0	1
Tommy Eglington	24	4	0	20	2	0	0
Michael Robinson	24	10	6	8	0	1	9
John Byrne	23	0	6	17	0	11	2
Eamonn Dunphy	23	6	10	7	0	1	2
Mick McGrath	22	4	5	13	0	0	0
Denis Irwin	21	9	4	8	0	1	3
Kevin O'Callaghan	21	4	7	10	0	10	3
Gary Waddock	21	2	7	12	0	3	3
Mickey Walsh	21	5	8	8	0	10	3
Jimmy Conway	20	4	6	10	0	2	3
Eoin Hand	20	5	6	9	0	1	0
Frank O'Neill	20	9	5	6	0	2	0

	Total	WC	EC	FR	Capt	Sub	Replaced
Joe O'Reilly	20	4	0	16	0	0	0
Alf Ringstead	20	4	2	14	0	0	0
Davy Walsh	20	5	0	15	0	0	1
Shay Brennan	19	8	5	6	5	1	0
George Cummins	19	5	2	12	0	0	0
John Dempsey	19	4	6	9	1	0	0
Eamonn Rogers	19	7	4	8	0	0	3
Ashley Grimes	18	1	6	11	0	2	2
Mick Kearns	18	3	4	11	0	2	1
Gerry Ryan	18	3	1	14	0	9	1
Pat Saward	18	5	3	10	2	0	0
Tommy Carroll	17	5	1	11	0	0	4
Dermot Curtis	17	5	2	10	0	0	0
Andy McEvoy	17	5	6	6	0	0	0
Mick Meagan	17	3	8	6	1	0	0
Jimmy O'Neill	17	4	2	11	0	0	1
Tommy Aherne	16	4	0	12	0	0	0
John Anderson	16	0	3	13	0	4	3
Roy Keane	16	9	1	6	0	0	1
Reg Ryan	16	4	0	12	0	0	0
Jim Beglin	15	6	2	7	0	1	1
Jimmy Dunne	15	2	0	13	5	0	0
Seams Dunne	15	5	0	10	1	0	0
David Kelly	15	1	0	14	0	4	5
Paul McGee	15	2	7	6	0	5	3
Terry Phelan	15	7	2	6	0	3	3
John Sheridan	15	3	1	11	0	6	3
Tony Byrne	14	4	5	5	0	1	2
Noel Dwyer	14	4	0	10	0	1	1
Eddie Gannon	14	4	0	10	0	0	0
Alan McLoughlin	14	2	1	11	0	9	0
John Devine	13	3	5	5	0	0	1
Tommy Godwin	13	6	0	7	0	0	0
Bill Gorman	13	1	0	12	0	0	0
Alfie Hale	13	2	5	6	0	4	0
Tommy Moroney	12	4	0	8	0	0	0
Noel Campbell	11	3	1	7	0	3	1
Paddy Coad	11	1	0	10	0	1	0
Al Finucane	11	4	6	1	1	1	0
Ambrose Fogarty	11	3	5	3	0	1	0
Johnny Fullam	11	2	1	8	0	1	0
William O'Neill	11	1	0	10	0	0	0
Miah Dennehy	10	2	1	7	0	7	1
Joey Donnelly	10	1	0	9	0	0	0
Ronnie Nolan	10	4	1	5	0	0	0
Liam O'Brien	10	1	0	9	0	6	1
Kevin O'Flanagan	10	1	0	9	0	0	0
Charlie Turner	10	2	0	8	8	0	0
Tommy Coyne	9	3	0	6	0	6	3
Bill Fallon	9	0	0	9	0	0	0
Theo Foley	9	2	2	5	1	0	1
George McKenzie	9	2	0	7	0	0	1
Paddy Moore	9	2	0	7	0	0	0
Frank O'Farrell	9	2	1	6	0	0	0
Willie Walsh	9	1	0	8	0	0	0
Pat Byrne	8	1	0	7	0	4	2
Fionan Fagan	8	1	0	7	0	0	0

	Total	WC	EC	FR	Capt	Sub	Replaced
Sean Fallon	8	0	0	8	0	0	0
William Glen	8	0	0	8	4	0	0
Eamonn Gregg	8	0	4	4	0	2	0
Joseph 'Robin' Lawlor	8	2	0	6	0	0	0
Mick Leech	8	4	1	3	0	1	3
Eddie McGoldrick	8	3	0	5	0	2	2
Paddy Roche	8	0	7	1	0	0	0
Tommy Traynor	8	1	5	2	0	0	0
Liam Tuohy	8	0	5	3	0	0	0
Plev Ellis	7	0	0	7	0	0	0
Jim Foley	7	2	0	5	0	0	0
Paddy Gaskins	7	2	0	5	5	0	0
Johnny Gavin	7	4	0	3	0	0	0
Fred Horlacher	7	1	0	6	0	1	0
Turlough O'Connor	7	1	2	4	0	5	0
Pierce O'Leary	7	1	3	3	0	1	1
Bernie Slaven	7	0	1	6	0	3	3
Alex Stevenson	7	0	0	7	0	0	0
Ray Brady	6	0	4	2	0	0	0
Mick Hoy	6	1	0	5	0	0	0
Alan Kernaghan	6	6	0	0	0	0	0
Tommy McConville	6	4	1	1	0	0	0
Brendan O'Callaghan	6	0	0	6	0	1	2
Matt O'Mahoney	6	0	0	6	0	0	0
Noel Peyton	6	0	1	5	0	1	1
Paddy Ambrose	5	0	0	5	0	0	0
Paddy Bradshaw	5	0	0	5	0	0	0
Tommy Breen	5	0	0	5	0	0	0
Oliver Conmy	5	1	2	2	0	0	0
Don Donovan	5	1	0	4	0	0	0
Harry Duggan	5	1	0	4	0	0	0
Pat Dunne	5	3	1	1	0	0	0
Peter Fitzgerald	5	3	0	2	0	0	0
John Joe Flood	5	0	0	5	1	0	0
William Harrington	5	0	0	5	0	1	0
Jackie Hennessy	5	1	0	4	0	0	1
Phil Kelly	5	3	0	2	0	0	0
Fred Kiernan	5	0	0	5	0	0	0
Mick Lawlor	5	0	3	2	0	1	2
Terry Mancini	5	0	1	4	0	0	0
Con Moulson	5	0	0	5	0	0	0
Ray O'Brien	5	0	0	5	0	1	0
Eamonn O'Keefe	5	1	0	4	0	1	1
Fred Strahan	5	0	0	5	0	0	0
Peter Corr	4	1	0	3	0	0	0
Tom Davis	4	0	0	4	0	0	0
Eamonn Deacy	4	0	0	4	0	1	1
Peter Desmond	4	3	0	1	0	0	0
Tom Farquharson	4	0	0	4	0	0	0
Shay Gibbons	4	1	0	3	0	0	0
Tom Keane	4	1	0	3	0	0	0
Jimmy Kelly	4	1	0	3	0	0	0
Mark Kelly	4	0	0	4	0	1	2
Joe Kendrick	4	2	0	2	0	0	0
Mick O'Brien	4	0	0	4	2	0	0
Tommy O'Connor	4	3	0	1	0	0	0
Kieran O'Regan	4	0	1	3	0	1	1

	Total	WC	EC	FR	Capt	Sub	Replaced
Mike Walsh	4	0	1	3	0	0	0
Liam Whelan	4	3	0	1	0	0	0
Willie Browne	3	0	2	1	0	0	0
David Byrne	3	1	0	2	0	0	0
Paddy Byrne	3	1	0	2	0	0	0
Alan Campbell	3	0	0	3	0	1	0
Harry Chatton	3	1	0	2	1	0	0
Tommy Clinton	3	2	0	1	0	0	0
Charlie Dowdall	3	0	0	3	0	0	0
Tommy Dunne	3	1	0	2	0	0	0
John Herrick	3	1	1	1	0	2	0
Billy Kennedy	3	2	0	1	0	0	0
Billy Lacey	3	0	0	3	0	0	0
John 'Kit' Lawlor	3	0	0	3	0	0	0
Charlie Lennon	3	0	0	3	0	0	0
Jack McCarthy	3	0	0	3	1	0	0
Jacko McDonagh	3	0	1	2	0	3	0
Daniel McGowan	3	1	0	2	0	0	0
Gerry Mackay	3	2	0	1	1	0	0
Bernard McNally	3	1	2	0	0	0	0
George Moulson	3	0	0	3	0	0	0
Jerry Murphy	3	1	0	2	0	0	1
Fran O'Brien	3	1	1	1	0	1	0
Jackie O'Driscoll	3	1	0	2	0	0	0
Sean O'Driscoll	3	0	0	3	0	1	1
Paddy O'Kane	3	0	0	3	0	0	0
Tim O'Keeffe	3	1	0	2	0	0	0
Damien Richardson	3	0	1	2	0	2	1
Alf Rigby	3	0	0	3	0	0	0
Jerehmiah Robinson	3	0	0	3	0	0	0
Noel Synnott	3	0	1	2	0	0	0
E. Weir	3	0	0	3	0	0	0
Eric Barber	2	1	0	1	0	0	0
Paddy Barry	2	0	0	2	0	0	0
Synan Braddish	2	0	0	2	0	1	0
Frank Brady	2	0	0	2	1	0	0
Johnny Brown	2	0	0	2	0	0	0
Liam Buckley	2	0	0	2	0	1	0
Harry Cannon	2	0	0	2	0	0	0
Brian Carey	2	0	0	2	0	1	0
Joe Carolan	2	0	0	2	0	0	0
Brendan Carroll	2	1	0	1	0	0	1
Jeff Chandler	2	0	0	2	0	1	1
Kevin Clarke	2	0	0	2	0	0	0
Martin Colfer	2	0	0	2	0	0	0
Liam Daish	2	0	0	2	0	1	0
Jimmy Daly	2	0	0	2	0	0	0
Maurice Daly	2	0	0	2	0	0	0
Ken De Mange	2	0	0	2	0	2	0
Tom Donnelly	2	1	0	1	0	0	0
Terry Donovan	2	0	0	2	0	1	1
Leo Dunne	2	0	0	2	0	0	0
Paddy Dunning	2	0	2	0	0	0	0
Mick Fairclough	2	0	0	2	0	2	0
P. Farrell	2	0	0	2	0	0	0
Johnny Feenan	2	0	0	2	0	0	0
Jack Fitzgerald	2	0	0	2	0	0	0

	Total	WC	EC	FR	Capt	Sub	Replaced
Tom Foy	2	1	0	1	0	0	0
Bob Fullam	2	0	0	2	0	0	0
Charlie Gallagher	2	0	2	0	0	0	0
Matty Geoghegan	2	1	0	1	0	0	0
Desmond Glynn	2	0	0	2	0	0	0
Joseph Golding	2	0	0	2	0	0	0
Tommy Hamilton	2	0	2	0	0	0	0
Jim Hartnett	2	1	0	1	0	0	0
Billy Hayes	2	0	0	2	0	0	0
Ron Healey	2	0	1	1	0	1	0
Benny Henderson	2	0	0	2	0	0	0
Fred Hutchinson	2	0	0	2	0	0	0
Billy Jordan	2	2	0	0	0	0	1
Davy Jordan	2	0	0	2	0	0	0
Peter Kavanagh	2	0	0	2	0	0	0
Mick Kennedy	2	0	0	2	0	1	0
Owen Kinsella	2	1	0	1	0	0	0
George Lennox	2	0	0	2	0	0	0
Dicky Lunn	2	0	0	2	0	0	0
Jimmy McAlinden	2	0	0	2	0	0	0
F. McLoughlin	2	0	0	2	0	0	0
Billy McMillan	2	0	0	2	0	0	0
Paddy Monahan	2	0	0	2	0	0	0
Jackie Mooney	2	0	0	2	0	0	0
Tony O'Connell	2	0	1	1	0	1	0
Jackie O'Reilly	2	0	0	2	0	0	0
Josiah Sloan	2	0	0	2	0	0	0
Peter Thomas	2	0	0	2	0	0	1
Paddy Turner	2	0	1	1	0	0	0

The 1951-52 Everton squad featuring five Irish internationals: Jimmy O'Neill (back row, 5th left), *George Cummins* (standing on right), *Peter Farrell* (seated, 4th left), *Tommy Eglington* (seated, 5th left) and *Tommy Clinton* (seated far right).

	Total	WC	EC	FR	Capt	Sub	Replaced
Jackie Vernon	2	0	0	2	0	0	0
Johnny Walsh	2	0	0	2	0	0	0
Joe Waters	2	0	1	1	0	1	0
Ronnie Whelan (Snr)	2	0	1	1	0	1	0
Paddy Andrews	1	0	0	1	0	0	0
Tom Arrigan	1	1	0	0	0	0	0
Eddie Bailham	1	0	0	1	0	0	0
Jimmy Bermingham	1	0	0	1	0	0	0
Paddy Bermingham	1	0	0	1	0	0	0
Fran Brennan	1	0	0	1	0	0	0
Florrie Burke	1	0	0	1	0	0	0
John Burke	1	0	0	1	1	0	0
Tom Burke	1	1	0	0	0	0	0
Jack Byrne	1	0	0	1	0	0	0
Sean Byrne	1	0	0	1	0	0	0
Jerome Clarke	1	0	0	1	0	1	0
Mattie Clarke	1	0	0	1	0	0	0
Jimmy Coffey	1	1	0	0	0	0	0
Frank Collins	1	0	0	1	0	0	0
Hugh Connolly	1	0	0	1	0	0	0
James Connolly	1	0	0	1	0	0	0
Ed Courtney	1	0	0	1	0	0	1
Tim Cuneen	1	0	0	1	0	0	1
Sean Cusack	1	0	0	1	0	0	0
Pat Daly	1	1	0	0	0	1	0
Christy Doyle	1	0	1	0	0	0	0
Dinny Doyle	1	0	0	1	0	0	0
Larry Doyle	1	0	0	1	0	0	0
Bobby Duffy	1	0	0	1	0	0	0
Jimmy Dunne	1	0	1	0	0	0	0
Peter Eccles	1	0	0	1	0	1	0
Robert Egan	1	0	0	1	0	0	0
Eamonn Fagan	1	0	0	1	0	1	0
Jack Fagan	1	0	0	1	0	0	0
Kevin Fitzpatrick	1	1	0	0	0	0	0
Mick Foley	1	0	0	1	1	0	0
Matt Gallagher	1	1	0	0	0	0	0
Patsy Gallagher	1	0	0	1	0	0	0
Mick Gannon	1	0	1	0	0	0	0
Bobby Gilbert	1	0	0	1	0	0	0
Christy Giles	1	0	0	1	0	0	0
Joe Grace	1	0	0	1	0	0	0
R. Griffiths	1	0	0	1	0	0	0
Austin Hayes	1	0	1	0	0	0	1
Willie Hayes	1	0	0	1	0	0	0
Jim Higgins	1	0	0	1	0	0	0
Gary Howlett	1	0	0	1	0	1	0
MIck Kearin	1	0	1	0	0	0	1
Fred Kearns	1	1	0	0	0	0	0
Alan Kelly (Jnr)	1	0	0	1	0	1	0
Noel Kelly	1	1	0	0	0	0	0
John Keogh	1	0	0	1	0	1	0
Shay Keogh	1	0	0	1	0	0	0
Joe Kinsella	1	0	0	1	0	0	0
Alec Kirkland	1	0	0	1	0	0	0
Dinny Lowry	1	0	0	1	0	1	0
Miah Lynch	1	1	0	0	0	0	0

	Total	WC	EC	FR	Capt	Sub	Replaced
Jimmy McCann	1	0	0	1	0	0	0
Mick McCarthy	1	0	0	1	0	0	0
John McGowan	1	0	0	1	0	0	0
Bill McGuire	1	0	0	1	0	0	0
Tony Macken	1	0	0	1	0	0	0
Owen Madden	1	0	0	1	0	0	0
Jim Maguire	1	0	0	1	0	0	0
Gerry Malone	1	0	0	1	0	0	0
C. Martin	1	0	0	1	0	0	0
Paddy Meehan	1	1	0	0	0	0	0
Michael Milligan	1	0	0	1	0	1	0
Cathal Muckian	1	0	0	1	0	0	0
Tommy Muldoon	1	0	0	1	0	0	0
Liam Munroe	1	1	0	0	0	0	0
Albie Murphy	1	0	0	1	0	0	0
Barry Murphy	1	0	0	1	0	0	0
Terry Murray	1	0	0	1	0	0	0
Billy Newman	1	1	0	0	0	0	1
Lar O'Byrne	1	0	0	1	0	0	0
Michael O'Flanagan	1	0	0	1	0	0	0
Kelham O'Hanlon	1	0	0	1	0	0	0
John O'Neill	1	0	0	1	0	0	0
Charlie Reid	1	0	0	1	0	0	0
Ted Scannell	1	1	0	0	0	0	0
Pat Scully	1	0	0	1	0	1	0
Mick Smyth	1	0	0	1	0	1	0
Johnny Squires	1	1	0	0	0	0	0
Jack Sullivan	1	0	0	1	0	0	0
Maurice Swan	1	0	0	1	0	1	0
Tommy Taylor	1	0	0	1	0	1	0
Fran Watters	1	0	0	1	0	0	0
Jimmy White	1	0	0	1	0	0	0
Joe Williams	1	1	0	0	0	0	0
Richard Whittaker	1	0	1	0	0	0	0

Lubanski (Poland)
five goals against Ireland.

OPPOSITION RECORDS

Leading Goalscorers Against Ireland

5
Wlodzimierz Lubanski (Poland)

4
Josef Adamec (Czechoslovakia)
Preben Elkjaer (Denmark)
Ruud Gullit (Holland)
Andrej Kvasnak (Czechoslovakia)
Reidar Kvammen (Norway)
Jef Mermans (Belgium)
Telmo Zarraonandia Montoya 'Zarra' (Spain)

3
Arocha (Spain)
Johnny Atyeo (England)
Eberhard Bakhuys (Holland)
Basora (Spain)
Ralph Brand (Scotland)
B. Cemil Turan (Turkey)
Adolf Huber (Austria)
Igoa (Spain)
Milos Milutinovic (Yugoslavia)
Kalle Palmer (Sweden)
Thomas Parits (Austria)
Jesus Maria Pereda (Spain)
Leonard Piontek (Poland)
Michel Platini (France)
Ernest Pol (Poland)
Dr. Gyorgy Sarosi (Hungary)
Adolf Scherer (Czechoslovakia)
Jaap Smit (Holland)
Zigfryd Szoltysik (Poland)
Tommy Taylor (England)

Opposition Records Against Ireland

Players Sent-off when Playing Against Ireland

Lajos Szucs	Hungary	1969
Carlos Reynoso	Chile	1974
Vladimir Kaplichny	USSR	1974
Alpaslan Eratli	Turkey	1975
Krasimir Borisov	Bulgaria	1977
Andrej Jeliazkov	Bulgaria	1977
Greg Villa	USA	1979
Marko Elsner	Yugoslavia	1988
Juan Lopez	Spain	1992

Hat-tricks Against Ireland

Kalle Palmer	Sweden	1949
Jef Mermans	Belgium	1950
Adolf Huber	Austria	1952
Milos Milutinovic	Yugoslavia	1955
Tommy Taylor	England	1957
Jesus Maria Pereda	Spain	1965
Josef Adamec	Czechoslovakia	1969
Thomas Parits	Austria	1971

Quickest Hat-trick against Ireland
4 minutes: Adolf Huber

Adolf Huber who scored the quickest ever hat-trick against Ireland, for Austria in 1952.

Adolfo Baloncieri, the captain of the Italian team in 1926, scored the first-ever goal against the Republic of Ireland in their first game on 21st March 1926. It was his 8th goal out of a total of 25 he was to score for Italy. He was capped 47 times.

Landmarks

Reidar Kvammen (Norway) scored the 50th goal Ireland conceded; Angel Labruna (Argentina) scored the 100th goal Ireland conceded; Ernest Pol (Poland) scored the 150th goal Ireland conceded; Zigfryd Szoltysik (Poland) scored the 200th goal Ireland conceded; Marian Kozerski (Poland) scored the 250th goal Ireland conceded; Isa Erturk (Turkey) scored the 300th goal Ireland conceded; Arnold Muhren (Holland) scored the 350th goal Ireland conceded; Armin Krings (Luxembourg) scored the 400th goal Ireland conceded.

SCORELINES

Wins		Home	Away
1-0	24	14	10
2-0	20	11	9
2-1	15	9	6
3-0	11	8	3
3-1	6	3	3
3-2	12	8	4
4-0	7	7	0
4-1	3	1	2
4-2	3	2	1
5-0	2	2	0
5-1	1	0	1
5-2	1	1	0
6-0	1	1	0
8-0	1	1	0

Draws		Home	Away
0-0	24	11	13
1-1	27	14	13
2-2	11	6	5
3-3	6	2	4
4-4	1	1	0

Defeats		Home	Away
0-1	23	7	16
0-2	19	6	13
1-2	21	6	15
0-3	10	1	9
1-3	11	5	6
2-3	5	4	1
0-4	3	1	2
1-4	8	4	4
2-4	1	1	0
0-5	1	1	0
1-5	3	0	3
2-5	1	0	1
3-5	2	2	0
0-6	4	0	4
0-7	1	0	1
1-7	1	0	1

INTERESTING NOTES

- Shamrock Rovers had at least one player in all but three of Ireland's first 50 internationals. The club has also provided nearly 20% of Ireland's players.
- Ireland's record for unchanged starting line-ups is 3 games – set during the 1990 World Cup Finals. The Irish starting eleven was unaltered for the games against Holland, Rumania and Italy. On 12 other occasions Ireland's team was unchanged for two successive games, the last time being the games against Latvia and Lithuania in 1993.
- Kevin O'Callaghan is (so far) the only Irish player to star in a film. He was one of a number of soccer players picked by director John Huston to star in the in 1981 movie 'Escape to Victory'. In the flick the Irish winger played a goalkeeper who got his arm broken by Michael Caine so that Sylvester Stallone could play in goal for the Allies team!
- Stanley Matthews (England), Denis Law (Scotland), Bobby Charlton (England), Gerd Müller (Germany), Eusebio (Portugal), Diego Maradona (Argentina), Ally McCoist (Scotland) and Jean-Pierre Papin (France) have all played against Ireland but despite being prolific goalscorers they had never managed to score against Ireland.
- Gerry Daly and Don Givens scored their Irish goals under four different managers.
- Both Jack Charlton and Mick Kearns were born in England on the day of an Ireland game. On 8 May 1935 John 'Jack' Charlton was born in Ashington while the Irish team was losing 1-3 to Germany in Dortmund. Mick Kearns was born in Banbury on 26 November 1950 the same day as the Republic of Ireland were drawing 2-2 at home to Norway.
- The shortest Ireland career lasted 10 minutes when Peter Eccles played his one and so far only game for Ireland against Uruguay in 1986. Eamonn Fagan (11 minutes), Jerome Clarke (12 minutes) and Tommy Taylor (25 minutes) also had short introductions to international football.
- Both Tony Grealish and Kevin Sheedy have scored goals at three different home grounds – Dalymount Park, Lansdowne Road and Tolka Park.
- Terry Yorath of Wales has played, scored, captained and managed a team against the Rep. of Ireland. He played twice in 2 wins over Ireland and has managed the Welsh national side on 4 occasions against Ireland. His record as manager against Ireland reads P4 W1 D0 L3 F2 A6. Michel Platini has also played, scored, captained and managed for a team against Ireland. He played in 4 games against Ireland (2 wins and 2 defeats), scored in three, captained the team on 2 occasions and managed the French team which drew 0-0 with Ireland in 1989.
- Ireland's record against all previous World Cup holders is P5 W1 D0 L4 F6 A7. Our only victory was against Germany (West) in 1956. Ireland's record against the European Champions is P11 W1 D4 L6 F6 A18. Our only win was over the 1964 champions Spain in 1965.
- The most number of goals scored by an Irish striker against one nation is 5 by Don Givens in 3 games against Turkey.
- When a player has played 25 times for Ireland he is awarded a 25-cap statutte. 43 players have received this statutte (Tommy Eglington, 24 caps, was awarded one in special circumstances) and the quickest to qualify for this honour was Andy Townsend who made his 25 appearances in 2 years, 3 months and 25 days. Another honour, the gold medal, is awarded to a player who has played 50 times for Ireland and the quickest to this award (of the 14 who have done so) is John Aldridge in 6 years, 7 months and 25 days.

John Aldridge
one of fourteen players to receive the gold medal for fifty appearances for the Republic of Ireland.

Players Capped
(in alphabetical order)

Alb = Albania	Ger = Germany	PRC = Peoples Republic of China
Alg = Algeria	Hol = Holland	Rom = Romania
Arg = Argentina	Hun = Hungary	Scot = Scotland
Aus = Austria	Ice = Iceland	Spa = Spain
Bel = Belgium	Is = Israel	Swe = Sweden
Bra = Brazil	Lat = Latvia	Swit = Switzerland
Bul = Bulgaria	Lith = Lithuania	Trin = Trinidad and Tabago
Cy = Cyprus	Lux = Luxembourg	Tun = Tunisia
CSSR = Czechoslovakia	Mal = Malta	Tu = Turkey
Den = Denmark	Mex = Mexico	Uru = Uruguay
Ecu = Ecuador	Mor = Morocco	Wal = Wales
Egy = Egypt	N.I = Northern Ireland	W.G = West Germany
Eng = England	Nor = Norway	Yugo = Yugoslavia
Fin = Finland	Pol = Poland	
Fra = France	Port = Portugal	

* = on loan to another club (given at bottom of players caps record).

AHERNE, THOMAS "Bud"
16 Caps
1946 Belfast Celtic – Port, Spa.
1949 Luton Town – Fin, Eng, Fin, Swe.
1950 Luton Town – Bel, Nor.
1951 Luton Town – Arg, Nor, W.G.
1952 Luton Town – W.G, Aus, Spa, Fra.
1953 Luton Town – Fra.

ALDRIDGE, JOHN WILLIAM
54 Caps (12 goals)
1986 Oxford United – Wal, Uru, Ice, CSSR, Bel, Scot, Pol.
1987 Liverpool – Scot, Bul, Bel, Bra, Lux, Bul.
1988 Liverpool – Pol, Nor, Eng, USSR, Hol, N.I, Tun, Spa.
1989 Liverpool – Fra (sub), Hun, Mal (sub), Hun, W.G.
Real Sociedad – N.I, Mal.
1990 Real Sociedad – Fin (sub), Tu, Eng, Egy, Hol, Rom, Italy, Tu, Eng.
1991 Real Sociedad – Eng, Pol.
Tranmere Rovers – Hun (sub), Tu.
1992 Tranmere Rovers– Wal (sub), Swit (sub), USA (sub), Alb, Italy, Port (sub), Lat, Den, Spa.
1993 Tranmere Rovers – Den, Alb, Lat, Lith.

AMBROSE, PADDY
5 Caps (1 goal)
1954 Shamrock Rovers – Nor.
1955 Shamrock Rovers – Hol.
1964 Shamrock Rovers – Pol, Nor, Eng.

ANDERSON, JOHN
16 Caps (1 goal)
1979 Preston North End – CSSR (sub), USA (sub).
1982 Preston North End – Chile, Bra, Trin.
1984 Newcastle United – PRC.
1986 Newcastle United – Wal, Ice, CSSR.
1987 Newcastle United – Bul, Bel, Bra, Lux.
1988 Newcastle United – Rom (sub), Yugo (sub), Tun.

ANDREWS, PADDY
1 Cap
1935 Bohemians – Hol.

ARRIGAN, TOM
1 Cap
1937 Waterford – Nor.

BAILHAM, EDDIE
1 Cap
1964 Shamrock Rovers – Eng.

BARBER. ERIC
2 Caps
1965 Shelbourne – Spa.
1966 Shelbourne – Bel.

BARRY, PADDY (Patrick)
2 Caps
1928 Fordson – Bel.
1929 Fordson – Bel.

BEGLIN, JIM (James Martin)
15 Caps
1984 Liverpool – PRC, Mex, Den.
1985 Liverpool – Italy, Is, Eng, Nor, Swit, Swit, USSR, Den.
1986 Liverpool – Wal, Bel (sub), Scot, Pol.

BERMINGHAM, JIMMY
1 Cap
1929 Bohemians – Bel.

BERMINGHAM, PADDY
1 Cap (1 goal)
1934 St. James's Gate – Hun.

Packie Bonner – 66 caps.

BONNER, PATRICK JOSEPH "Packie"
66 Caps
1981 Glasgow Celtic – Pol.
1982 Glasgow Celtic – Alg.
1983 Glasgow Celtic – Mal.
1984 Glasgow Celtic – Is, PRC.
1985 Glasgow Celtic – Italy, Is, Eng, Nor.
1986 Glasgow Celtic – Uru, Ice, Bel, Scot, Pol.
1987 Glasgow Celtic – Scot, Bul, Bel, Bra, Lux, Bul.
1988 Glasgow Celtic – Rom, Yugo, Nor, Eng, USSR, Hol, Spa.
1989 Glasgow Celtic – Fra, Hun, Spa, Mal, Hun, W.G, N.I, Mal.
1990 Glasgow Celtic – Wal, Fin, Tu, Eng, Egy, Hol, Rom, Italy, Mor, Tu, Eng.
1991 Glasgow Celtic – Wal, Eng, Pol, USA, Hun, Pol, Tu.
1992 Glasgow Celtic – Wal, Swit, Alb, Italy, Lat, Den, Spa.
1993 Glasgow Celtic – Wal, N.I, Den. Alb, Lat, Lith.

BRADDISH, SYNAN
2 Caps
1978 Dundalk – Tu (sub), Pol.

BRADSHAW, PADDY
5 Caps (4 goals)
1938 St. James's Gate – Swit, Pol.
1939 St. James's Gate – Hun, Hun, Ger.

BRADY, FRANK
2 Caps
1926 Fordsons – Italy.
1927 Fordsons – Italy "B"

BRADY, LIAM (William L.)
72 Caps (9 goals)
1974 Arsenal – USSR, Tu.
1975 Arsenal – W.G. "B", Swit, USSR, Swit, Tu.
1976 Arsenal – Nor, Pol, Eng, Tu, Fra.
1977 Arsenal – Spa, Fra, Bul, Bul.
1978 Arsenal – Nor, N.I, Eng.
1979 Arsenal – Den, Bul, W.G, Wal, Bul.
1980 Arsenal – Eng, Cy.
Juventus – Hol, Bel, Fra, Cy.
1981 Juventus – Bel, Hol, Fra.
1982 Juventus – Chile, Bra, Trin.
Sampdoria – Hol, Ice, Spa.
1983 Sampdoria – Mal, Ice, Hol, Mal.
1984 Sampdoria – Is, Pol.
Internazionale Milan – USSR, Nor, Den.
1985 Internazionale Milan – Italy, Eng, Nor, Spa, Swit, Swit, USSR, Den.
1986 Internazionale Milan – Wal.
Ascoli – Bel, Scot, Pol.
1987 Ascoli – Scot.
West Ham United – Bul, Bel, Bra, Lux, Lux, Bul.
1989 West Ham United – Fra, Hun (sub), Hun (sub), W.G.
1990 West ham United – Fin.

BRADY, RAY (T. R.)
6 Caps
1963 Queen's Park Rangers – Aus, Aus.
1964 Queen's Park Rangers – Spa, Spa, Pol, Nor.

BREEN, TOMMY
5 Caps
1937 Manchester United – Swit, Fra.
1946 Shamrock Rovers – Eng.
1947 Shamrock Rovers – Spa, Port.

BRENNAN, FRAN
1 Cap
1965 Drumcondra – Bel.

BRENNAN, SHAY (Seamus A.)
19 Caps
1965 Manchester United – Spa, Spa.
1966 Manchester United – Aus, Bel, Spa, Tu, Spa.
1969 Manchester United – CSSR, Den, Hun, Scot, CSSR, Den, Hun.
1970 Manchester United – Hun (sub), W.G, Pol, Swe.
Waterford – Italy.

BROWN, JOHNNY
2 Caps (1 goal)
1937 Coventry City – Swit, Fra.

BROWNE, WILLIE
3 Caps
1963 Bohemians – Aus.
1964 Bohemians – Spa, Eng.

BUCKLEY, LIAM
2 Caps
1984 Shamrock Rovers – Pol (sub).
KSV Waregem – Mex.

BURKE, FLORRIE
1 Cap
1951 Cork Athletic – W.G.

BURKE, JOHN
1 Cap
1929 Shamrock Rovers – Bel.

BURKE, TOM
1 Cap
1934 Cork – Bel.

BYRNE, DAVID "Babby"
3 Caps (1 goal)
1929 Shelbourne – Bel.
1931 Shamrock Rovers – Spa.
1934 Coleraine – Bel.

BYRNE, JACK "Squib"
1 Cap
1928 Bray Unknowns – Bel.

Shay Brennan won 19 caps.

John Byrne – 23 caps.

BYRNE, JOHN FREDERICK
23 Caps (4 goals)
1985 Queen's Park Rangers – Itlay Is (sub), Eng (sub).
1986 Queen's Park Rangers – Uru (sub).
1987 Queen's Park Rangers – Scot (sub), Bel (sub), Bra, Lux (sub), Lux, Bul (sub), Is.
1988 Queen's Park Rangers – Rom, Yugo (sub), Pol (sub).
Le Havre – W.G. (sub).
1990 Le Havre – Wal, Fin, Tu (sub), Mal.
1991 Brighton – Wal.
Sunderland – Tu.
1992 Sunderland – Wal.
1993 Millwall – Wal.

BYRNE, PADDY "Babs"
3 Caps
1931 Dolphin – Spa.
1932 Shelbourne – Hol.
1934 Drumcondra – Hol.

BYRNE, PAT J.
8 Caps
1984 Shamrock Rovers – Pol, PRC, Mex.
1985 Shamrock Rovers – Spa (sub), Den (sub).
1986 Shamrock Rovers – Wal (sub), Ice (sub), CSSR.

BYRNE, SEAN
1 Cap
1931 Bohemians – Spa.

BYRNE, TONY (Anthony B.)
14 Caps
1969 Southampton – Den.
1970 Southampton – Pol, W.G, Pol, Swe, Swe, Italy.
1971 Southampton – Italy, Aus.
1972 Southampton – Fra.
1973 Southampton – USSR (sub), Fra, Nor, Pol.

CAMPBELL, ALAN
3 Caps
1985 R.C.Santander – Italy (sub), Is, Spa.

CAMPBELL, NOEL
11 Caps
1971 St. Patrick's Athletic – Aus (sub).
1972 Fortuna Köln – Iran, Ecu, Chile, Port, USSR, Fra (sub).
1975 Fortuna Köln – W.G. "B"
1976 Fortuna Köln – Nor.
1977 Fortuna Köln – Spa, Bul (sub).

CANNON, HARRY
2 Caps
1926 Bohemians – Italy.
1928 Bohemians – Bel.

CANTWELL, NOEL
36 Caps (14 goals)
1953 West Ham United – Lux.
1955 West Ham United – Spa.
1956 West Ham United – Hol, Den, W.G.
1957 West Ham United – Eng, Eng, Den.
1958 West Ham United – Pol, Aus, Pol.
1959 West Ham United – CSSR. CSSR, Swe.
1960 West Ham United – Chile, Swe, Nor.
1961 Manchester United – Scot, Scot, CSSR, CSSR.
1962 Manchester United – Aus, Ice, Ice.
1963 Manchester United – Scot, Aus.
1964 Manchester United – Spa, Eng, Pol.
1965 Manchester United – Spa, Spa, Spa.
1966 Manchester United – Aus, Bel, Spa.
1967 Manchester United – Tu.

CAREY, BRIAN P.
2 Caps
1992 Manchester United – USA (sub).
1993 Manchester United – Wal.

CAREY, JOHNNY J. (Jackie)
29 Caps (3 goals)
1937 Manchester United – Nor.
1938 Manchester United – CSSR, Pol Swit, Pol.
1939 Manchester United – Hun, Hun, Ger.
1946 Manchester United – Port, Spa, Eng.
1947 Manchester United – Spa, Port.
1948 Manchester United – Port, Spa, Swit.
1949 Manchester United – Bel, Port, Swe, Spa, Fin, Eng, Fin, Swe.
1950 Manchester United – Nor.
1951 Manchester United – Arg, Nor.
1952 Manchester United – Fra, Aus.

CAROLAN, JOE
2 Caps
1959 Manchester United – Swe.
1960 Manchester United – Chile.

Johnny Carey – 29 caps.

CARROLL, BRENDAN J.
2 Caps
1949 Shelbourne – Bel, Fin.

CARROLL, TOMMY R.
17 Caps (1 goal)
1968 Ipswich Town – Pol, Pol, Aus, Den.
1969 Ipswich Town – CSSR.
1970 Ipswich Town – Pol, W.G, Swe.
1972 Birmingham City – Iran, Ecu, Chile, Port, USSR.
1973 Birmingham City – USSR, Pol, Fra, Nor.

CASCARINO, TONY (Anthony Guy)
43 Caps (11 goals)
1985 Gillingham – Swit, USSR, Den.
1988 Millwall – Pol, Nor (sub), USSR (sub), Hol (sub), N.I, Tun, Spa.
1989 Millwall – Fra, Hun, Spa, Mal, Hun, W.G. (sub), N.I, Mal.
1990 Aston Villa – Wal, Fin, Tu, Eng, Egy, Hol (sub), Rom (sub), Italy (sub), Mor (sub), Tu (sub), Eng (sub).
1991 Aston Villa – Eng (sub), Pol (sub), Chile (sub), USA. Glasgow Celtic – Pol, Tu.
1992 Chelsea – Wal, Swit, USA (sub).
1993 Chelsea – Wal, N.I (sub), Den (sub), Alb (sub), Lat (sub).

Tommy Carroll playing for Birmingham City gets in a sliding tackle.

CHANDLER, JEFF
2 Caps
1979 Leeds United – CSSR (sub), USA.

CHATTON, HARRY A.
3 Caps
1931 Shelbourne – Spa.
Dumbarton – Spa.
1934 Cork – Hol.

CLARKE, JEROME
1 Cap
1978 Drogheda United – Pol (sub).

CLARKE, KEVIN
2 Caps
1948 Drumcondra – Port, Spa.

CLARKE, MATTIE
1 Cap
1950 Shamrock Rovers – Bel.

CLINTON, TOMMY J.
3 Caps
1951 Everton – Nor.
1953 Everton – Fra.
1954 Everton – Lux.

COAD, PADDY
11 Caps (3 goals)
1946 Shamrock Rovers – Eng.
1947 Shamrock Rovers – Spa, Port.
1948 Shamrock Rovers – Port, Spa, Swit.
1949 Shamrock Rovers – Bel, Port, Swe.
1951 Shamrock Rovers – Nor (sub).
1952 Shamrock Rovers – Spa.

COFFEY, JIMMY
1 Cap
1949 Drumcondra – Fin.

COLFER, MARTIN D.
2 Caps
1950 Shelbourne – Bel.
1951 Shelbourne – Nor.

COLLINS, FRANK
1 Cap
1927 Jacobs – Italy "B".

CONMY, OLIVER M.
5 Caps
1965 Peterborough United – Bel.
1967 Peterborough United – CSSR, CSSR.
1968 Peterborough United – Pol.
1969 Peterborough United – CSSR.

CONNOLLY, HUGH
1 Cap
1936 Cork – Ger.

CONNOLLY, JAMES "Sally"
1 Cap
1926 Fordsons – Italy.

CONROY, TERRY (G. A.)
26 Caps (2 goals)
1969 Stoke City – CSSR, Den, Hun.
1970 Stoke City – Pol, W.G, Pol, Swe, Swe, Italy.
1972 Stoke City – USSR, Fra.
1973 Stoke City – USSR, Nor, Pol.
1974 Stoke City – Bra, Uru, Chile, Tu.
1975 Stoke City – W.G. "B" (sub), Swit, USSR, Swit, Tu (sub).
1976 Stoke City – Pol, Eng, Tu.

CONWAY, JIMMY P.
20 Caps (3 goals)
1966 Fulham – Spa, Tu, Spa.
1967 Fulham – CSSR.
1968 Fulham – Aus (sub).
1969 Fulham – Hun, Scot, CSSR, Den, Hun.
1970 Fulham – Pol, W.G.
1971 Fulham – Italy, Aus.
1974 Fulham – Uru, Chile.
1975 Fulham – W.G. "B" (sub).
1976 Fulham – Nor, Pol.
1977 Manchester City – Pol.

CORR, PETER J.
4 Caps
1949 Everton – Port, Spa, Eng, Swe.

COURTNEY, EDWARD "Ned"
1 Cap
1946 Cork United – Port.

COYNE, TOMMY
9 Caps (3 goals)
1992 Glasgow Celtic – Swit, USA, Alb, USA (sub), Italy (sub), Port (sub), Lat (sub).
1993 Glasgow Celtic – Wal (sub).
Tranmere Rovers – N.I.

CUMMINS, GEORGE P.
19 Caps (5 goals)
1953 Luton Town – Lux.
1954 Luton Town – Lux, Nor.
1955 Luton Town – Nor, W.G, Yugo, Spa.
1957 Luton Town – Den.
1958 Luton Town – Pol, Aus, Pol.
1959 Luton Town – CSSR, CSSR, Swe.
1960 Luton Town – Chile, W.G, Swe.
1961 Luton Town – Scot, Scot.

CUNEEN, TIM (Timothy)
1 Cap
1951 Limerick – Nor.

CURTIS, DERMOT P.
17 Caps (8 goals)
1956 Shelbourne – Den, W.G.
1957 Bristol City – Eng, Eng, Den.
1958 Bristol City – Pol, Aus.
Ipswich Town – Pol.
1959 Ipswich Town – Swe.
1960 Ipswich Town – Chile, W.G, Swe, Nor.
1961 Ipswich Town – Scot.
1962 Ipswich Town – Aus, Ice.
1963 Exeter City – Aus.

CUSACK, SEAN
1 Cap
1952 Limerick – Fra.

DAISH, LIAM
2 Caps
1992 Cambridge United – Wal, Swit (sub).

DALY, GERRY A.
48 Caps (13 goals)
1973 Manchester United – Pol (sub), Nor.
1974 Manchester United – Bra (sub), Uru (sub).
1975 Manchester United – W.G. "B", Swit (sub).
1976 Derby County – Eng, Tu, Fra.
1977 Derby County – Fra, Bul, Bul.
1978 Derby County – Tu, Den, N.I, Eng.
1979 Derby County – Den, Bul, N.I.
1980 Derby County – Eng, Cy, Swit, Arg.
Coventry City – Hol, Bel, Cy.

George Cummins
scored 5 goals in his 19 appearances.

Gerry Daly
came on as sub against Poland in his first international.

1981 Coventry City – Wal, Bel, CSSR, W.G. "B", Pol (sub).
1982 Coventry City – Alg, Chile, Bra, Trin, Hol.
1983 Coventry City – Spa* (sub), Mal*.
1984 Coventry City – Is (sub).
Birmingham City – Mex (sub).
1985 Birmingham City – Nor, Spa, Swit, Swit.
1986 Shrewsbury Town – Uru, Ice (sub), CSSR (sub), Scot (sub), **on loan to Leicester City*

DALY, JIMMY
2 Caps
1932 Shamrock Rovers – Hol.
1935 Shamrock Rovers – Swit.

DALY, MAURICE
2 Caps
1978 Wolverhampton Wanderers – Tu, Pol.

DALY, PAT
1 Cap
1949 Shamrock Rovers – Fin (sub).

DAVIS, TOM L.
4 Caps (4 goals)
1936 Oldham Athletic – Ger, Hun.
1938 Tranmere Rovers – CSSR, Pol.

DEACY, EAMONN "Chick"
4 Caps
1982 Aston Villa – Alg (sub), Chile, Bra, Trin.

DE MANGE, KEN (Kenneth J. P. P.)
2 Caps
1987 Liverpool – Bra (sub).
1988 Hull City – Tun (sub).

DEMPSEY, JOHN T.
19 Caps (1 goal)
1966 Fulham – Spa.
1967 Fulham – CSSR, CSSR.
1968 Fulham – Pol, Pol, Aus, Den.
1969 Chelsea – CSSR, Den, Hun.
1970 Chelsea – W.G, Pol, Swe, Swe, Italy.
1972 Chelsea – Iran, Ecu, Chile, Port.

DENNEHY, MIAH (Jeremiah)
10 Caps (2 goals)
1972 Cork Hibernians – Ecu (sub), Chile.
1973 Nottingham Forest – USSR (sub), Pol, Fra, Nor, Pol (sub).
1974 Nottingham Forest – Tu (sub).
1975 Nottingham Forest – W.G. "B" (sub).
1976 Walsall – Pol (sub).

DESMOND, PETER
4 Caps
1949 Middlesbrough – Fin, Eng, Fin, Swe.

DEVINE, JOHN
13 Caps
1979 Arsenal – CSSR, N.I.
1981 Arsenal – CSSR, W.G. "B", Hol.
1982 Arsenal – Alg, Spa.
1983 Arsenal – Mal.
Norwich City – Ice, Hol.
1984 Norwich City – Is, USSR, Nor.

Tom Davis
scored four goals in his four International matches.

John Devine played his first international in 1979 against Czechoslovakia.

DONNELLY, JOEY
10 Caps (4 goals)
1934 Dundalk – Hun.
1935 Dundalk – Swit, Ger, Hol.
1936 Dundalk – Swit, Hun, Lux, Ger, Hun.
1937 Dundalk – Nor.

DONNELLY, TOM
2 Caps (1 goal)
1937 Drumcondra – Nor.
1938 Shamrock Rovers – Swit.

DONOVAN, DON C.
5 Caps
1954 Everton – Nor.
1955 Everton – Hol, Nor, W.G.
1957 Everton – Eng.

DONOVAN, TERRY
2 Caps
1979 Aston Villa – CSSR.
1981 Aston Villa – W.G. "B" (sub).

DOWDALL, CHARLIE
3 Caps
1928 Fordsons – Bel.
1929 Barnsley – Bel.
1931 Cork – Spa.

DOYLE, CHRISTY
1 Cap
1959 Shelbourne – CSSR.

DOYLE, DENIS "Dinny"
1 Cap
1926 Shamrock Rovers – Italy.

DOYLE, LARRY
1 Cap
1931 Dolphin – Spa.

DUFFY, BOBBY
1 Cap (1 goal)
1950 Shamrock Rovers - Bel.

DUGGAN, HARRY A.
5 Caps (1 goal)
1927 Leeds United – Italy "B".
1930 Leeds United – Bel.
1936 Leeds United – Hun, Lux.
1937 Newport County – Nor.

DUNNE, JIMMY "Snowy"
15 Caps (13 goals)
1930 Sheffield United – Bel.
1936 Arsenal – Swit, Hun, Lux.
1937 Southampton – Swit, Fra.
Shamrock Rovers – Nor, Nor.
1938 Shamrock Rovers – CSSR, Pol, Swit, Pol.
1939 Shamrock Rovers – Hun, Hun, Ger.

DUNNE, JIMMY C.
1 Cap
1971 Fulham – Aus.

DUNNE, LEO "Ducky"
2 Caps
1935 Manchester City – Swit, Ger.

Don Donovan and his son Terry, both played for the Republic of Ireland.

Seamus Dunne
an own goal on his last appearance.

DUNNE, PAT A. J.
5 Caps
1965 Manchester United – Spa, Spa, Spa.
1966 Manchester United – W.G, Tu.

DUNNE, SEAMUS
15 Caps
1952 Luton Town – Fra.
1953 Luton Town – Aus, Fra, Lux.
1955 Luton Town – Spa.
1956 Luton Town – Hol, Den, W.G.
1957 Luton Town – Eng, Den.
1958 Luton Town – Pol, Aus, Pol.
1960 Luton Town – W.G, Swe.

Tommy Dunne
won 3 caps for Ireland.

DUNNE, TOMMY
3 Caps
1956 St. Patrick's Athletic – Hol, Den, W.G.

DUNNE, TONY (Anthony)
33 Caps
1962 Manchester United – Aus, Ice.
1963 Manchester United – Scot, Aus.
1964 Manchester United – Spa, Pol, Nor, Eng, Pol.
1965 Manchester United – Spa, Spa, Spa.
1966 Manchester United – Aus, Bel, Spa, Tu, Spa.
1968 Manchester United – Pol, Den.
1969 Manchester United – Hun, Hun.
1970 Manchester United – Swe.
1971 Manchester United – Italy, Aus.
1974 Bolton Wanderers – Bra (sub), Uru, Chile, Tu.
1975 Bolton Wanderers – W.G. "B", Swit, USSR, Swit, Tu.

DUNNING, PADDY
2 Caps
1970 Shelbourne – Swe, Italy.

DUNPHY, EAMONN M.
23 Caps
1965 York City – Spa.
1966 Millwall – W.G, Tu, Spa.
1967 Millwall – Tu, CSSR, CSSR.
1968 Millwall – Pol, Pol, Aus, Den.
1969 Millwall – Den, Hun, Den, Hun.
1970 Millwall – Pol, W.G. (sub), Pol, Swe, Swe, Italy.
1971 Millwall – Italy, Aus.

Tony Dunne
13 years service to the Irish team.

Eamonn Dunphy
won 23 caps in his 6 years with Ireland.

DWYER, NOEL M.
14 Caps
1959 West Ham United – Swe.
1960 West Ham United – Chile, W.G, Swe.
Swansea Town – Wal, Nor.
1961 Swansea Town – Scot, Scot, CSSR, CSSR.
1964 Swansea Town – Pol (sub), Nor, Eng, Pol.

ECCLES, PETER
1 Cap
1986 Shamrock Rovers – Uru (sub).

EGAN, ROBERT
1 Cap
1929 Dundalk – Bel.

EGLINGTON, TOMMY J.
24 Caps (2 goals)
1946 Shamrock Rovers – Port, Spa.
Everton – Eng.
1947 Everton – Spa, Port.
1948 Everton – Port, Swit.
1949 Everton – Port, Swe.
1950 Everton – Nor.
1951 Everton – Arg, W.G.
1952 Everton – W.G, Aus, Spa, Fra.
1953 Everton – Aus, Fra, Lux, Fra.
1954 Everton – Nor.
1955 Everton – Hol, W.G, Spa.

ELLIS, PLEV (Plevna)
7 Caps (2 goals)
1935 Bohemians – Swit, Ger, Hol.
1936 Bohemians – Swit, Lux, Ger, Hun.

FAGAN, EAMONN
1 Cap
1973 Shamrock Rovers – Nor (sub).

FAGAN, FIONAN
8 Caps (5 goals)
1954 Manchester City – Nor.
1959 Manchester City – Swe.
1960 Derby County – Chile, W.G, Swe, Wal, Nor.
1961 Derby County – Scot.

FAGAN JACK "Kruger"
1 Cap
1926 Shamrock Rovers – Italy.

FAIRCLOUGH, MICK
2 Caps
1982 Dundalk – Chile (sub), Trin (sub).

FALLON, BILL (Willie)
9 Caps (2 goals)
1934 Notts County – Hun.
1936 Notts County – Hun, Hun.
1937 Notts County – Swit, Fra.
1938 Notts County – Swit, Pol.
1939 Sheffield Wednesday – Hun, Ger.

FALLON, SEAN
8 Caps (2 goals)
1950 Glasgow Celtic – Nor.
1951 Glasgow Celtic – W.G.
1952 Glasgow Celtic – W.G, Aus, Spa, Fra.
1955 Glasgow Celtic – Nor, W.G.

FARQUHARSON, TOM G.
4 Caps
1929 Cardiff City – Bel.
1930 Cardiff City – Bel.
1931 Cardiff City – Spa, Spa.

FARRELL, PADDY
2 Caps
1937 Hibernian – Swit, Fra.

FARRELL, PETER D.
28 Caps (3 goals)
1946 Shamrock Rovers – Port, Spa.
1947 Everton – Spa, Port.
1948 Everton – Port, Spa, Swit.
1949 Everton – Port (sub), Spa, Eng, Fin, Swe.
1951 Everton – Arg, Nor, W.G.
1952 Everton – W.G, Aus, Spa, Fra.
1953 Everton – Aus, Fra, Fra.
1954 Everton – Nor.
1955 Everton – Hol,W.G, Yugo, Spa.
1957 Everton – Eng.

FEENAN, JOHNNY J.
2 Caps
1937 Sunderland – Swit, Fra.

FINUCANE, AL
11 Caps
1967 Limerick – Tu, CSSR.
1969 Limerick – CSSR, Den, Hun, Scot, CSSR.
1970 Limerick – Swe, Italy.
1971 Limerick – Italy (sub), Aus.

FITZGERALD, JACK (F. J.)
2 Caps (1 goal)
1955 Waterford – Hol.
1956 Waterford – Hol.

FITZGERALD, PETER J.
5 Caps (2 goals)
1960 Leeds United – Wal, Nor.
1961 Leeds United – Scot.
Chester – CSSR, CSSR.

FITZPATRICK, KEVIN
1 Cap
1969 Limerick – CSSR.

FITZSIMONS, ARTHUR G.
26 Caps (7 goals)
1949 Middlesbrough – Fin.
1950 Middlesbrough – Bel.
1951 Middlesbrough – W.G.
1952 Middlesbrough – W.G, Aus, Spa, Fra.
1953 Middlesbrough – Aus, Fra, Lux, Fra.
1955 Middlesbrough – Hol, Nor, W.G, Yugo, Spa.
1956 Middlesbrough – Hol, Den, W.G.
1957 Middlesbrough – Eng, Eng, Den.
1958 Middlesbrough – Pol, Aus, Pol.
1959 Lincoln City – CSSR.

FLOOD, JOHN JOE
5 Caps (4 goals)
1926 Shamrock Rovers – Italy.
1929 Shamrock Rovers – Bel.
1930 Shamrock Rovers – Bel.
1931 Shamrock Rovers – Spa, Spa.

FOGARTY, AMBROSE
11 Caps (2 goals)
1960 Sunderland – W.G, Swe.
1961 Sunderland – Scot, CSSR, CSSR.
1962 Sunderland – Ice, Ice.
1963 Sunderland – Scot (sub), Aus, Aus.
1964 Hartlepools United – Spa.

FOLEY, JIM "Fox"
7 Caps
1934 Cork – Bel, Hol.
Glasgow Celtic – Hun.
1935 Glasgow Celtic – Swit, Ger.
1936 Glasgow Celtic – Ger, Hun.

FOLEY, MICK "Boxer"
1 Cap
1926 Shelbourne – Italy.

Theo Foley
won 9 caps in 4 years.

FOLEY, THEO C,
9 Caps
1964 Northampton Town – Spa, Pol, Nor, Pol.
1965 Northampton Town – Bel, Spa, Spa.
1966 Northampton Town – W.G.
1967 Northampton Town – CSSR.

FOY, TOMMY
2 Caps
1937 Shamrock Rovers – Nor.
1939 Shamrock Rovers – Hun.

FULLAM, BOB
2 Caps (1 goal)
1926 Shamrock Rovers – Italy.
1927 Shamrock Rovers – Italy "B".

FULLAM, JOHNNY
11 Caps
1960 Preston North End – Nor.
1964 Shamrock Rovers – Spa, Pol, Nor.
1966 Shamrock Rovers – Aus, Bel.
1968 Shamrock Rovers – Pol, Pol, Aus, Den.
1969 Shamrock Rovers – CSSR (sub).

GALLAGHER, CHARLIE
2 Caps
1967 Glasgow Celtic – Tu, CSSR.

GALLAGHER, MATT
1 Cap
1954 Hibernian – Lux.

GALLAGHER, PATSY
1 Cap
1931 Falkirk – Spa.

GALVIN, TONY
29 Caps (1 goal)
1982 Tottenham Hotspur – Hol.
1983 Tottenham Hotspur – Mal, Hol (sub).
1984 Tottenham Hotspur – Is (sub), Mex, USSR, Nor, Den.
1985 Tottenham Hotspur – Italy, Nor, Spa,
1986 Tottenham Hotspur – Uru, Ice, CSSR, Bel.
1987 Tottenham Hotspur – Scot, Bul, Bel, Lux.
Sheffield Wednesday – Lux, Bul.
1988 Sheffield Wednesday – Rom, Pol, Nor, Eng, USSR, Hol, Spa.
1989 Swindon Town – W.G.

GANNON, EDDIE
14 Caps
1948 Notts County – Swit.
1949 Sheffield Wednesday – Bel, Port, Swe, Spa, Fin.
1950 Sheffield Wednesday – Nor.
1952 Sheffield Wednesday – W.G, Aus.
1953 Sheffield Wednesday – Lux, Fra.
1954 Shelbourne – Nor.
1955 Shelbourne – Nor, W.G.

Tony Galvin
his only goal for Ireland was away to Luxembourg in 1987.

GANNON, MICK
1 Cap
1971 Shelbourne – Aus.

GASKINS, PADDY (Peader)
7 Caps
1934 Shamrock Rovers – Bel, Hol, Hun.
1935 Shamrock Rovers – Swit, Ger.
1938 St. James's Gate – CSSR, Pol.

GAVIN, JOHNNY T.
7 Caps (2 goals)
1949 Norwich City – Fin, Fin.
1952 Norwich City – Fra.
1954 Norwich City – Lux.
1955 Tottenham Hotspur – Hol, W.G.
1956 Norwich City – Den.

GEOGHEGAN, MATT
2 Caps (2 goals)
1936 St. James's Gate – Ger.
1937 St. James's Gate – Nor.

GIBBONS, SHAY
4 Caps
1952 St. Patrick's Athletic – W.G.
1953 St. Patrick's Athletic – Lux.
1955 St. Patrick's Athletic – Yugo, Spa.

GILBERT, BOBBY
1 Cap
1966 Shamrock Rovers – W.G.

GILES, CHRISTY
1 Cap
1950 Doncaster Rovers – Nor.

GILES, JOHNNY (Michael John)
59 Caps (5 goals)
1959 Manchester United – Swe.
1960 Manchester United – Chile, Wal, Nor.
1961 Manchester United – Scot, Scot, CSSR, CSSR.
1962 Manchester United – Aus, Ice.
1963 Manchester United – Scot.
Leeds United - Aus, Aus.
1964 Leeds United - Spa, Spa, Pol, Nor, Eng.
1965 Leeds United - Spa, Spa, Spa.
1966 Leeds United - Aus, Bel, Spa, Tu.
1967 Leeds United - Tu.
1968 Leeds United - Aus, Den.
1969 Leeds United - CSSR, Scot.
1970 Leeds United - Pol, W.G.
1971 Leeds United - Italy.
1972 Leeds United - Fra.
1973 Leeds United - USSR.
1974 Leeds United - Bra, Uru, Chile, USSR, Tu.
1975 Leeds United - Swit, USSR, Swit.
West Bromwich Albion – Tu.
1976 West Bromwich Albion – Eng, Tu, Fra.

John Giles
player, captain and manager of the Republic of Ireland.

1977 West Bromwich Albion – Fra, Pol, Bul.
Shamrock Rovers – Bul.
1978 Shamrock Rovers – Tu, Pol, Nor, Den, N.I.
1979 Shamrock Rovers – Den, Bul, W.G.

GIVENS, DON J.
56 Caps (19 goals)
1969 Manchester United – Den, Hun, Scot, CSSR, Den, Hun.
1970 Manchester United – Pol.
Luton Town – W.G, Swe, Italy.
1971 Luton Town – Italy, Aus.
1972 Luton Town – Iran, Ecu, Port.
Queen's Park Rangers – Fra.
1973 Queen's Park Rangers – USSR, Pol, Fra, Nor, Pol.
1974 Queen's Park Rangers – Bra, Uru, Chile, USSR, Tu.
1975 Queen's Park Rangers – W.G. "B", Swit, USSR, Swit, Tu.
1976 Queen's Park Rangers – Nor, Pol, Eng, Tu, Fra.
1977 Queen's Park Rangers – Spa, Fra, Bul, Bul.
1978 Queen's Park Rangers – Nor, Den.
Birmingham City – N.I. (sub), Eng.
1979 Birmingham City – Den, Bul, W.G, USA (sub), N.I. (sub).
1980 Birmingham City – Swit, Arg, Hol, Bel, Cy (sub).
1981 Birmingham City – Wal.
Neuchatel Xamax – Fra (sub).

GLEN, WILLIAM "Sacky"
8 Caps
1927 Shamrock Rovers – Italy "B".
1929 Shamrock Rovers – Bel.
1930 Shamrock Rovers – Bel.
1931 Shamrock Rovers – Spa.
1935 Shamrock Rovers – Hol.
1936 Shamrock Rovers – Swit, Hun, Lux.

GLYNN, DESMOND
2 Caps (1 goal)
1951 Drumcondra – W.G.
1955 Drumcondra – Nor.

GODWIN, TOMMY F.
13 Caps
1949 Shamrock Rovers – Port, Swe, Spa, Fin, Eng.
Leicester City – Fin, Swe.
1950 Leicester City – Bel, Nor.
1956 Leicester City – Hol.
1957 Leicester City – Eng.
A.F.C. Bournemouth – Den.
1958 A.F.C. Bournemouth Pol.

GOLDING, JOSEPH "Lye"
2 Caps
1928 Shamrock Rovers – Bel.
1930 Shamrock Rovers – Bel.

Don Givens
scorer of the quickest hat-trick for Ireland – nine minutes, against Turkey in 1975.

Bill Gorman
won 13 caps for Ireland.

GORMAN, BILL (William Charles)
13 Caps
1936 Bury – Swit, Hun, Lux, Ger, Hun.
1937 Bury – Nor, CSSR.
1938 Bury – Pol, Swit, Pol.
1939 Brentford – Hun.
1946 Brentford – Eng.
1947 Brentford – Port.

GRACE, JOE
1 Cap
1926 Drumcondra – Italy.

GREALISH, TONY
45 Caps (8 goals)
1976 Orient – Nor, Pol.
1978 Orient – Nor, Den, N.I, Eng.
1979 Orient – W.G.
Luton Town – Wal, CSSR, Bul, USA, N.I.
1980 Luton Town – Eng, Cy, Swit, Arg, Hol, Bel, Fra, Cy.
1981 Luton Town – Wal, Bel, W.G. "B", Pol.
Brighton – Hol.
1982 Brighton – Alg, Chile, Bra, Trin, Hol, Ice, Spa.
1983 Brighton – Spa, Ice, Hol.
1984 West Bromwich Albion – Pol, PRC, Mex, USSR, Nor, Den.
1985 West Bromwich Albion – Spa (sub), Swit, USSR, Den.

GREGG, EAMONN
8 Caps
1978 Bohemians – Pol, Den (sub), Eng (sub).
1979 Bohemians – Den, Bul, W.G, Wal, CSSR.

GRIFFITHS, R.
1 Cap
1934 Walsall – Hun.

GRIMES, ASHLEY (Augustine Ashley)
18 Caps (1 goal)
1978 Manchester United – Tu, Pol, Nor (sub).
1979 Manchester United – Bul, USA, N.I.
1980 Manchester United – Eng, Cy.
1981 Manchester United – CSSR, W.G. "B" (sub),Pol.
1982 Manchester United – Alg, Spa.
1983 Manchester United – Spa.
1984 Coventry City – Is, Pol.
1987 Luton Town – Lux.
1988 Luton Town – Rom.

HALE, ALFIE
13 Caps (2 goals)
1962 Aston Villa – Aus.
Doncaster Rovers – Ice.
1964 Doncaster Rovers – Spa, Spa.
1966 Waterford – Spa.
1968 Waterford – Pol (sub), Pol, Aus, Den.
1969 Waterford – Scot, CSSR.
1970 Waterford – Pol (sub).
1971 Waterford – Aus (sub).

Ashley Grimes
scored his only goal for Ireland on his 13th appearance.

Alfie Hale
13 caps and 2 goals for Ireland.

HAMILTON, TOMMY
2 Caps
1959 Shamrock Rovers – CSSR, CSSR.

HAND, EOIN K.
20 Caps (2 goals)
1969 Portsmouth – CSSR (sub).
1970 Portsmouth – Pol, W.G, Pol.
1971 Portsmouth – Aus.
1972 Portsmouth – USSR, Fra.
1973 Portsmouth – USSR, Pol, Fra, Pol.
1974 Portsmouth – Bra, Uru, Chile, Tu.
1975 Portsmouth – W.G. "B", Swit, USSR, Swit, Tu.

HARRINGTON, WILLIAM
5 Caps
1935 Cork – Hol.
1936 Cork – Swit, Hun, Lux.
1938 Cork – Pol (sub).

HARTNETT, JIM B.
2 Caps
1949 Middlesbrough – Spa.
1954 Middlesbrough – Lux.

HAVERTY, JOE
32 Caps (3 goals)
1956 Arsenal – Hol, Den, W.G.
1957 Arsenal – Eng, Eng, Den.
1958 Arsenal – Pol, Aus, Pol.
1959 Arsenal – Swe.
1960 Arsenal – Chile, Wal, Nor.
1961 Arsenal – Scot, Scot.
Blackburn Rovers – CSSR, CSSR.
1963 Blackburn Rovers – Scot.
Millwall – Aus.
1964 Millwall – Spa, Pol, Nor, Eng.
Glasgow Celtic – Pol.
1965 Bristol Rovers – Spa.
Shelbourne – Spa, Spa.
1966 Shelbourne – W.G, Aus, Bel, Tu, Spa.

HAYES, AUSTIN W. P.
1 Cap
1979 Southampton – Den.

HAYES, BILLY (William E.)
2 Caps
1946 Huddersfield Town – Eng.
1947 Huddersfield Town – Port.

HAYES, WILLIE (William J.)
1 Cap
1949 Limerick – Bel.

HEALEY, RON
2 Caps
1977 Cardiff City – Pol.
1980 Cardiff City – Eng (sub).

Joe Haverty
played with 6 different clubs while winning his 32 caps.

Steve Heighway
34 caps but never scored for Ireland.

HEIGHWAY, STEVE (Steven Derek)
34 Caps
1970 Liverpool – Pol, Swe, Swe.
1971 Liverpool – Italy, Aus.
1972 Liverpool – USSR.
1974 Liverpool – USSR, Tu.
1975 Liverpool – W.G. "B", USSR, Tu.
1976 Liverpool – Nor, Eng, Fra.
1977 Liverpool – Spa, Fra, Bul, Bul.
1978 Liverpool – Nor, Den, N.I.
1979 Liverpool – Bul, Bul, USA, N.I.
1980 Liverpool – Eng, Cy, Arg, Bel, Fra, Cy.
1981 Liverpool – Wal, Bel.
Minnesota Kicks – Hol.

HENDERSON, BENNY "Rosie" (Bernard)
2 Caps
1948 Drumcondra – Port, Spa.

HENNESSY, JACKIE
5 Caps
1964 Shelbourne – Pol.
1965 Shelbourne – Bel, Spa.
1966 Shelbourne – W.G.
1968 St. Patrick's Athletic – Aus.

HERRICK, JOHN
3 Caps
1971 Cork Hibernians – Aus.
1972 Cork Hibernians – Chile (sub).
1973 Shamrock Rovers – Fra (sub).

HIGGINS, JIM
1 Cap
1951 Birmingham City – Arg.

HOLMES, JIMMY (James Paul)
30 Caps (1 goal)
1971 Coventry City – Aus (sub).
1972 Coventry City – Fra.
1973 Coventry City – USSR, Pol, Fra, Nor, Pol.
1974 Coventry City – Bra, USSR.
1975 Coventry City – Swit, Tu.
1976 Coventry City – Nor, Pol, Eng, Tu, Fra.
1977 Tottenham Hotspur – Spa, Fra, Pol, Bul, Bul.
1978 Tottenham Hotspur – Tu, Pol, Nor, Den, N.I, Eng.
1979 Tottenham Hotspur – Den, Bul.
1981 Vancouver Whitecaps – Wal.

HORLACHER, FRED (Alfred F.)
7 Caps (2 goals)
1930 Bohemians – Bel.
1931 Bohemians – Spa.
1932 Bohemians – Hol.'
1934 Bohemians – Hol (sub), Hun.
1935 Bohemians – Hol.
1936 Bohemians – Swit.

HOUGHTON, RAY (Raymond James)
53 Caps (3 goals)
1986 Oxford United – Wal, Uru, Ice, CSSR, Bel, Scot, Port.
1987 Oxford United – Scot, Bel, Lux, Lux, Bul.
Liverpool – Is.
1988 Liverpool – Yugo, Nor, Eng, USSR, Hol, N.I, Tun, Spa.
1989 Liverpool – Fra, Hun, Spa, Mal, Hun, N.I, Mal.
1990 Liverpool – Fin, Eng, Egy, Hol, Rom, Italy, Mor, Tu, Eng.
1991 Liverpool – Eng, Pol, Chile, USA, Hun.
1992 Liverpool – Alb, USA, Italy, Port.
Aston Villa – Den, Spa.
1993 Aston Villa – N.I, Den, Alb, Lat, Lith.

HOWLETT, GARY
1 Cap
1984 Brighton – PRC (sub).

HOY, MICK
6 Caps
1937 Dundalk – Nor.
1938 Dundalk – Swit, Pol.
1939 Dundalk – Hun, Hun, Ger.

HUGHTON, CHRIS
53 Caps (1 goal)
1979 Tottenham Hotspur – USA.
1980 Tottenham Hotspur – Eng, Swit, Arg, Hol, Bel, Fra, Cy.
1981 Tottenham Hotspur – Wal, Bel, Pol, Fra.
1982 Tottenham Hotspur – Hol, Spa.
1983 Tottenham Hotspur – Mal. Spa, Ice, Hol, Mal.
1984 Tottenham Hotspur – Mex (sub), USSR, Nor.
1985 Tottenham Hotspur – Italy, Is, Eng, Spa, Swit, USSR.
1986 Tottenham Hotspur – Uru, Ice, Bel.
1987 Tottenham Hotspur – Bul, Is.
1988 Tottenham Hotspur – Yugo, Pol, Nor, Eng, USSR, Hol, N.I.
1989 Tottenham Hotspur – Fra, Hun, Spa, Mal, Hun.
1990 Tottenham Hotspur – Wal (sub), USSR (sub), Fin Tu (sub), Mal, Tu.
1991 West Ham United – Chile, Tu.

Chris Hughton, versatile full-back who won 53 caps.

HURLEY, CHARLIE (Charles J.)
40 Caps (2 goals)
1957 Millwall – Eng.
Sunderland – Den.
1958 Sunderland – Pol, Aus.
1959 Sunderland – CSSR, CSSR, Swe.
1960 Sunderland – Chile, W.G, Swe, Wal, Nor.
1961 Sunderland – Scot, Scot, CSSR, CSSR.
1962 Sunderland – Aus, Ice, Ice.
1963 Sunderland – Scot, Aus, Aus.
1964 Sunderland – Spa, Spa, Pol, Nor.
1965 Sunderland – Spa.
1966 Sunderland – W.G, Aus, Bel, Tu, Spa.
1967 Sunderland – Tu, CSSR, CSSR.
1968 Sunderland – Pol, Pol, Den.
1969 Sunderland – CSSR.
Bolton Wanderers – Hun.

HUTCHINSON, FREDDIE
2 Caps
1935 Drumcondra – Swit, Ger.

Charlie Hurley receives his statuette for winning 25 caps.

IRWIN, DENIS (Joseph)
21 Caps (1 goal)
1990 Manchester United – Mor, Tu.
1991 Manchester United – Wal, Eng, Pol, USA, Hun, Pol.
1992 Manchester United – Wal, USA, Alb, USA (sub), Italy, Lat, Den, Spa.
1993 Manchester United – N.I, Den, Alb, Lat, Lith.

JORDAN, BILLY
2 Caps
1934 Bohemians – Hol.
1937 Bohemians – Nor.

JORDAN, DAVY
2 Caps (1 goal)
1937 Wolverhampton Wanderers – Swit, Fra.

KAVANAGH, PETER J.
2 Caps
1931 Glasgow Celtic – Spa, Spa.

KEANE, ROY (Maurice)
16 Caps
1991 Nottingham Forest – Chile, Hun, Pol.
1992 Nottingham Forest – Wal, Swit, Alb, USA, Lat, Den, Spa.
1993 Nottingham Forest – Wal, N.I, Den, Alb, Lat, Lith.

KEANE, TOM "Rory"
4 Caps
1948 Swansea – Swit.
1949 Swansea – Port, Swe, Spa.

KEARIN, MICK
1 Cap
1971 Shamrock Rovers – Aus.

KEARNS, FRED T.
1 Cap
1954 West Ham United – Lux.

KEARNS, MICK
18 Caps
1970 Oxford United – Pol (sub).
1973 Walsall – Pol (sub).
1974 Walsall – Uru, Chile.
1976 Walsall – Nor, Pol, Eng, Tu, Fra.
1977 Walsall – Spa, Fra, Bul.
1978 Walsall – Nor, Den, N.I, Eng.
1979 Wolverhampton Wanderers – USA, N.I.

KELLY, ALAN (Senior) (J. A.)
47 Caps
1956 Drumcondra – W.G.
1957 Drumcondra – Eng.
1962 Preston North End – Aus, Ice, ice.
1963 Preston North End – Scot, Aus, Aus.
1964 Preston North End – Spa, Spa, Pol.
1965 Preston North End – Bel.
1966 Preston North End – Aus, Bel, Spa, Spa.
1967 Preston North End – Tu, CSSR, CSSR.
1968 Preston North End – Pol, Pol, Aus, Den.
1969 Preston North End – CSSR, Den, Hun, Scot, Den, Hun.
1970 Preston North End – Pol, W.G, Pol, Swe, Swe, Italy.
1971 Preston North End – Italy, Aus.
1972 Preston North End – Iran, Ecu, Chile, Port, USSR, Fra.
1973 Preston North End – USSR, Pol, Fra, Nor.

Alan Kelly
only one cap to date, against Wales in 1993.

KELLY, ALAN (Junior)
1 Cap
1993 Sheffield United – Wal (sub).

KELLY, DAVID T.
15 Caps (7 goals)
1987 Walsall – Is.
1988 Walsall – Rom, Yugo.
West Ham United – Tun (sub).
1990 Leicester City – USSR, Mal, Mor.
1991 Leicester City – Wal (sub), Chile, USA, Hun.
1992 Newcastle United – Italy (sub), Port, Den (sub).
1993 Newcastle United – Wal.

KELLY, JIMMY
4 Caps (2 goals)
1932 Derry City – Hol.
1934 Derry City – Bel.
1936 Derry City – Swit, Lux.

KELLY, MARK J.
4 Caps
1988 Portsmouth – Yugo, Pol (sub), Tun.
1990 Portsmouth – Mor.

Mick Kennedy won 2 caps in 1986.

KELLY, NOEL
1 Cap
1954 Nottingham Forest – Lux

KELLY, PHIL (J. P. V.)
5 Caps
1960 Wolverhampton Wanderers – Wal, Nor.
1961 Wolverhampton Wanderers –Scot, CSSR, CSSR.

KENDRICK, JOE
4 Caps
1927 Everton – Italy "B".
1934 Dolphin – Bel, Hol.
1935 Dolphin – Hol.

KENNEDY, BILLY
3 Caps
1932 St. James's Gate – Hol.
1934 St. James's Gate – Bel, Hol.

KENNEDY, MICK (Michael F.)
2 Caps
1986 Portsmouth – Ice, CSSR (sub).

KEOGH, JOHN
1 Cap
1966 Shamrock Rovers – W.G. (sub).

KEOGH, SHAY
1 Cap
1958 Shamrock Rovers – Pol.

KERNAGHAN, ALAN N.
6 Caps
1992 Middlesbrough – Lat, Den.
1993 Middlesbrough – Den, Alb, Lat, Lith.

KIERNAN, FRED W.
5 Caps
1951 Shamrock Rovers – Arg. Nor.
Southampton – W.G.
1952 Southampton – W.G, Aus.

KINNEAR, JOE P.
26 Caps
1967 Tottenham Hotspur – Tu, CSSR.
1968 Tottenham Hotspur – Pol, Aus.
1969 Tottenham Hotspur – CSSR, Den, Hun.
1970 Tottenham Hotspur – Pol, Swe (sub).
1971 Tottenham Hotspur – Italy.
1972 Tottenham Hotspur – Iran, Ecu, Chile, Port, USSR, Fra.
1973 Tottenham Hotspur – Pol.
1974 Tottenham Hotspur – Bra, Uru, Chile, USSR, Tu.
1975 Tottenham Hotspur – W.G. "B", Swit, USSR.
Brighton – Tu (sub).

KINSELLA, JOE
1 Cap
1928 Shelbourne – Bel.

KINSELLA, OWEN
2 Caps
1932 Shamrock Rovers – Hol.
1937 Shamrock Rovers – Nor.

KIRKLAND, ALEC
1 Cap
1927 Shamrock Rovers – Italy "B".

LACEY, BILLY
3 Caps (1 goal)
1927 Shelbourne – Italy "B".
1928 Shelbourne – Bel.
1930 Shelbourne – Bel.

LANGAN, DAVID FRANCIS
26 Caps
1978 Derby County – Tu, Nor.
1980 Derby County – Swit, Arg.
Birmingham City – Hol, Bel, Fra, Cy.
1981 Birmingham City – Wal, Bel, CSSR, W.G. "B", Pol, Hol, Fra.
1985 Oxford United – Nor Spa, Swit.
1986 Oxford United – Wal, Uru, Bel, Scot, Pol.
1987 Oxford United – Bra (sub), Lux (sub), Lux.

David Langan
made his debut against Turkey in 1978.

LAWLER, JOSEPH "Robin" (Joseph F.)
8 Caps
1953 Fulham – Aus, Lux, Fra.
1954 Fulham – Nor.
1955 Fulham – Hol, Nor, W.G, Yugo.

LAWLOR, JOHN "Kit" (John Christopher)
3 Caps
1949 Drumcondra – Bel.
1950 Doncaster Rovers – Nor.
1951 Doncaster Rovers – Arg.

LAWLOR, MICK (Michael Gerard)
5 Caps
1970 Shamrock Rovers – Pol, Swe, Swe, Italy (sub).
1973 Shamrock Rovers – Pol.

LAWRENSON, MARK THOMAS
38 Caps (5 goals)
1977 Preston North End – Pol.
Brighton – Bul.
1978 Brighton – Pol, Nor (sub), Den, N.I, Eng.
1980 Brighton – Eng, Cy, Swit, Hol, Bel, Fra, Cy.
1981 Brighton – Pol.
Liverpool – Hol, Fra.
1982 Liverpool – Hol, Ice, Spa.
1983 Liverpool – Mal, Spa, Ice, Hol, Mal,
1984 Liverpool – Is, USSR, Nor, Den.
1985 Liverpool – Italy, Eng, Nor, Swit, USSR, Den.
1986 Liverpool – Bel.
1987 Liverpool – Scot, Bul.

LEECH, MICK
8 Caps (2 goals)
1969 Shamrock Rovers – CSSR, Den, Hun.
1971 Shamrock Rovers – Aus.
1972 Shamrock Rovers – Iran, Ecu, Port, USSR (sub).

LENNON, CHARLIE
3 Caps
1934 St. James's Gate – Hun.
1935 St. James's Gate – Swit, Ger.

LENNOX, GEORGE
2 Caps
1931 Dolphin – Spa, Spa.

LOWRY, DINNY
1 Cap
1962 St. Patrick's Athletic – Aus (sub).

LUNN, DICK
2 Caps
1938 Dundalk – Swit, Pol.

LYNCH, MIAH (Jeremiah)
1 Cap
1934 Cork Bohemians – Bel.

Mark Lawrenson
five goals in his thirty eight Internationals.

Jimmy McAlinden
won 2 caps for the Republic of Ireland in 1946.

McALINDEN, JIMMY
2 Caps
1946 Portsmouth – Port, Spa.

McCANN, JIMMY "Maxie"
1 Cap (1 goal)
1956 Shamrock Rovers – W.G.

McCARTHY, JACK
3 Caps
1926 Bohemians – Italy.
1928 Bohemians – Bel.
1930 Bohemians – Bel.

McCARTHY, MICK
1 Cap
1932 Shamrock Rovers – Hol.

McCARTHY, MICK
57 Caps (2 goals)
1984 Manchester City – Pol, PRC, Mex, Den.
1985 Manchester City – Italy, Is, Eng, Spa, Swit, Swit, USSR.
1986 Manchester City – Wal (sub), Uru, Ice, CSSR, Scot, Pol.
1987 Manchester City – Scot, Bul, Bel.
Glasgow Celtic – Bra, Lux, Bul, Is.
1988 Glasgow Celtic –Rom, Yugo, Nor, Eng, USSR, Hol, N.I, Tun, Spa.
1989 Glasgow Celtic – Fra, Hun, Spa.
Olympique Lyon – W.G, N.I.
1990 Millwall – Wal, USSR, Fin, Tu, Eng, Egy, Hol, Rom, Italy, Mor, Tu, Eng.
1991 Millwall – USA, Hun, Tu.
1992 Millwall – Alb (sub), USA, Italy, Port.

Jimmy McCann
scored on his one and only appearance for Ireland.

McCONVILLE, TOMMY
6 Caps
1971 Dundalk – Aus.
1972 Waterford – USSR, Fra.
1973 Waterford – USSR, Pol, Fra.

McDONAGH, JACKO (Jim)
3 Caps
1983 Shamrock Rovers – Mal (sub).
1984 Shamrock Rovers – Pol (sub), Mex (sub).

McDONAGH, SEAMUS (James Martin)
25 Caps
1981 Everton – Wal, Bel, CSSR, W.G. "B".
Bolton Wanderers – Hol, Fra.
1982 Bolton Wanderers – Chile, Bra, Hol, Ice, Spa.
1983 Bolton Wanderers – Mal, Spa.
Notts County – Ice, Hol.
1984 Notts County – Pol, Mex, USSR.
Birmingham City – Nor.
Notts County – Den.
1985 Gillingham – Spa, Swit.
Sunderland – Swit.
Notts County – USSR.
Wichita Wings – Den.

McEVOY ANDY (M. A.)
17 Caps (6 Goals)
1961 Blackburn Rovers – Scot, Scot.
1963 Blackburn Rovers – Scot, Aus.
1964 Blackburn Rovers – Spa, Spa, Pol, Nor, Eng, Pol.
1965 Blackburn Rovers – Bel, Spa, Spa, Spa.
1966 Blackburn Rovers – Spa, Tu.
1967 Blackburn Rovers – CSSR.

McGEE, PAUL G.
15 Caps (4 goals)
1978 Queen's Park Rangers – Tu, Nor (sub), Den (sub), N.I, Eng.
1979 Queen's Park Rangers – Den (sub), Bul (sub), CSSR, Bul.
Preston North End – USA, N.I.
1980 Preston North End – Cy, Swit, Arg, Bel (sub).

McGOLDRICK, EDDIE (Edward John)
8 Caps
1992 Crystal Palace – Swit, USA, Italy, Port (sub), Den.
1993 Crystal Palace – Wal, N.I. (sub), Den.

McGOWAN, DANIEL
3 Caps
1949 West Ham United – Port, Swe, Swe.

Mick McCarthy
captain of Ireland on 22 occasions.

SeamusMcDonagh
9 clean sheets in 25 appearances.

McGOWAN, JOHN
1 Cap
1947 Cork United – Spa.

McGRATH, MICK
22 Caps
1958 Blackburn Rovers – Aus, Pol.
1959 Blackburn Rovers – CSSR, CSSR, Swe.
1960 Blackburn Rovers – W.G, Swe, Wal.
1961 Blackburn Rovers – CSSR, CSSR.
1963 Blackburn Rovers – Scot, Aus, Aus.
1964 Blackburn Rovers – Eng, Pol.
1965 Blackburn Rovers – Bel, Spa, Spa.
1966 Bradford City – W.G, Aus, Bel.
1967 Bradford City – Tu.

McGRATH, PAUL
61 Caps (7 goals)
1985 Manchester United – Italy (sub), Is, Eng, Nor (sub), Swit (sub), Swit (sub), Den.
1986 Manchester United – Wal, Ice, CSSR, Bel, Scot, Pol.
1987 Manchester United – Scot, Bul, Bel, Bra, Lux, Lux, Bul.
1988 Manchester United – Yugo, Pol, Nor, Eng, Hol, N.I.
1989 Manchester United – Fra, Hun, Spa, Mal, Hun.
Aston Villa – W.G, Mal.
1990 Aston Villa – USSR, Fin, Tu, Eng, Egy, Hol, Rom, Italy, Eng.
1991 Aston Villa – Wal, Eng, Pol, Chile (sub), USA, Pol, Tu.
1992 Aston Villa – Swit, USA, Alb, USA, Italy, Port, Lat, Spa.
1993 Aston Villa – N.I, Den. Lat, Lith.

McGUIRE, BILL
1 Cap
1935 Bohemians – Hol.

McKENZIE, GEORGE
9 Caps
1937 Southend United – Nor, Nor.
1938 Southend United – CSSR, Pol, Swit, Pol.
1939 Southend United – Huh, Hun, Ger.

McLOUGHLIN, ALAN
14 Caps
1990 Swindon Town– Mal, Eng (sub), Egy (sub), Mor (sub), Eng (sub).
1991 Southampton – Wal, Chile (sub), Hun (sub).
1992 Southampton – Wal* (sub).
Portsmouth – USA, USA (sub), Italy (sub), Port.
1993 Portsmouth – Wal.
**on loan to Portsmouth.*

Eddie McGoldrick won 8 caps in 1992 and 1993.

Paul McGrath has scored 7 times in his 61 appearances.

McLOUGHLIN, F.
2 Caps
1930 Fordsons – Bel.
1931 Cork – Spa.

McMILLAN, BILLY
2 Caps
1946 Belfast Celtic – Port, Spa.

McNALLY, BRENDAN (J. B.)
3 Caps
1959 Luton Town – CSSR.
1961 Luton Town – Scot.
1962 Luton Town – Ice.

MACKEN, TONY
1 Cap
1977 Derby County – Spa.

MACKEY, GERRY
3 Caps
1956 Shamrock Rovers – Den, W.G.
1957 Shamrock Rovers – Eng.

MADDEN, OWEN
1 Cap
1936 Cork – Hun.

MAGUIRE, JIM
1 Cap
1929 Shamrock Rovers – Bel.

MALONE, GERRY
1 Cap
1949 Shelbourne – Bel.

Gerry Mackey
captained Ireland in only his second international match, against West Germany.

MANCINI, TERRY J.
5 Caps (1 goal)
1973 Queen's Park Rangers – Pol.
1974 Queen's Park Rangers – Bra, Uru, Chile.
Arsenal – USSR.

MARTIN, C.
1 Cap
1927 Bo'ness – Italy "B".

MARTIN, CON J.
30 Caps (6 goals)
1946 Glentoran – Port (sub), Spa, Eng.
1947 Leeds United – Spa.
1948 Leeds United – Port, Spa.
Aston Villa – Swit.
1949 Aston Villa – Bel, Port, Swe, Spa, Fin, Eng, Fin, Swe.
1950 Aston Villa – Bel.
1951 Aston Villa – Arg.

Con Martin
scored 5 of his 6 international goals at Dalymount Park.

1952 Aston Villa – W.G, Aus, Spa.
1953 Aston Villa – Fra, Fra.
1954 Aston Villa – Lux, Nor.
1955 Aston Villa – Hol, Nor, W.G, Yugo, Spa.
1956 Aston Villa – Hol.

MARTIN, MICK P.
52 Caps (4 goals)
1971 Bohemians – Aus.
1972 Bohemians – Iran, Ecu, Chile, Port, USSR.
1973 Manchester United – USSR, Pol, Fra, Nor, Pol.
1974 Manchester United – Bra, Uru, Chile, USSR, Tu.
1975 Manchester United – W.G. "B", Swit, USSR, Swit.
West Bromwich Albion – Tu.
1976 West Bromwich Albion – Nor, Pol, Eng, Tu, Fra.
1977 West Bromwich Albion – Spa, Fra, Pol, Bul.
1979 Newcastle United – Den, Bul, W.G, Wal, CSSR, Bul, USA, N.I.
1980 Newcastle United – Fra.
1981 Newcastle United – Bel, CSSR, W.G. "B", Hol, Fra.
1982 Newcastle United – Alg, Chile, Bra, Trin, Hol, Spa.
1983 Newcastle United – Mal, Spa.

Mick Meagan
played his last match for Ireland against Scotland in 1969.

MEAGAN, MICK K.
17 Caps
1961 Everton – Scot.
1962 Everton – Aus, Ice.
1964 Everton – Spa.
1965 Huddersfield Town – Bel, Spa, Spa.
1966 Huddersfield Town – Aus, Bel, Spa, Tu, Spa.
1967 Huddersfield Town – Tu, CSSR, CSSR.
1968 Huddersfield Town – Pol.
1969 Drogheda United – Scot.

MEEHAN, PADDY "Wooderer"
1 Cap
1934 Drumcondra – Hol.

Mick Milligan
came on as substitute against USA for his only international appearance.

MILLIGAN, MICHAEL (Joseph)
1 Cap
1992 Oldham Athletic – USA (sub).

MONAHAN, PADDY "Monty"
2 Caps
1935 Sligo Rovers – Swit, Ger.

MOONEY, JACKIE
2 Caps (1 goal)
1964 Shamrock Rovers – Pol.
1965 Shamrock Rovers – Bel.

MOORE, PADDY
9 Caps (7 goals)
1931 Shamrock Rovers – Spa.
1932 Shamrock Rovers – Hol.
1934 Aberdeen – Bel, Hol, Hun.
1935 Aberdeen – Ger.
Shamrock Rovers – Hol.
1936 Shamrock Rovers – Ger, Hun.

MORAN, KEVIN RICHARD
67 Caps (6 goals)
1980 Manchester United – Swit, Arg, Bel, Fra, Cy.
1981 Manchester United – Wal (sub), Bel, CSSR, W.G. "B", Pol, Fra.
1982 Manchester United – Alg, Ice.
1983 Manchester United – Ice, Hol, Mal.
1984 Manchester United – Is, Mex.
1985 Manchester United – Den.
1986 Manchester United – Ice, CSSR, Bel, Scot, Pol.
1987 Manchester United – Scot, Bul, Bel, Bra, Lux, lux, Bul, Is.
1988 Manchester United – Rom, Yugo, Pol, Nor, Eng, USSR, Hol.
Sporting Gijon – N.I, Spa.
1989 Sporting Gijon – Hun, Spa, Mal, Hun, N.I, Mal.

Kevin Moran
scored his first 2 goals for Ireland against Czechoslovakia on his 25th birthday.

1990 Blackburn Rovers – Wal, USSR (sub), Mal, Eng, Egy, Hol, Rom, Italy, Tu (sub).
1991 Blackburn Rovers – Wal, Eng, Pol, Chile, USA, Pol.
1992 Blackburn Rovers – USA, Den, Spa.
1993 Blackburn Rovers – N.I, Alb.

MORONEY, TOMMY
12 Caps (1 goal)
1948 West Ham United – Spa.
1949 West Ham United – Port, Swe, Spa, Fin, Eng, Fin.
1950 West Ham United – Bel, Nor.
1951 West Ham United – Nor, W.G.
1953 Evergreen United – Fra.

MORRIS, CHRIS B.
35 Caps
1987 Glasgow Celtic – Is.
1988 Glasgow Celtic – Rom, Yugo, Pol, Nor, Eng, USSR, Hol, N.I, Tun, Spa.
1989 Glasgow Celtic – Fra, Hun, Hun (sub), W.G, N.I, Mal (sub).
1990 Glasgow Celtic – Wal, USSR, Fin (sub), Tu, Eng, Egy, Hol, Rom, Italy, Eng.
1991 Glasgow Celtic – Hun (sub), Pol.
1992 Glasgow Celtic – Wal, Swit, USA, USA, Port.
1993 Middlesbrough – Wal.

MOULSON, CON
5 Caps
1936 Lincoln City – Hun, Lux.
Notts County – Hun.
1937 Notts County – Swit, Fra.

MOULSON, GEORGE B.
3 Caps
1948 Lincoln City – Port, Spa, Swit.

Cathal Muckian
his only international match was against Poland in 1978.

MUCKIAN, CATHAL P.
1 Cap
1978 Drogheda United – Pol.

MULDOON, TOMMY
1 Cap
1927 Aston Villa – Italy "B".

Tommy Muldoon
one of 11 Aston Villa players to win an international cap.

Paddy Mulligan played the last of his 50 caps in 1979.

MULLIGAN, PADDY M.
50 Caps (1 goal)
1969 Shamrock Rovers – CSSR, Den Hun, Scot, CSSR, Den.
Chelsea – Hun.
1970 Chelsea – Pol, W.G, Pol, Swe.
1971 Chelsea – Italy, Aus.
1972 Chelsea – Iran, Ecu, Chile, Port.
Crystal Palace – Fra.
1973 Crystal Palace – USSR, Pol, Fra, Nor, Pol.
1974 Crystal Palace – Bra, Uru, Chile, USSR, Tu.
1975 Crystal Palace – Swit, USSR, Swit,
West Bromwich Albion – Tu.
1976 West Bromwich Albion – Pol, Eng, Tu, Fra.
1977 West Bromwich Albion – Fra, Pol, Bul, Bul.
1978 West Bromwich Albion – Nor, Den, Eng.
1979 West Bromwich Albion – Den, Bul (sub), W.G.
Shamrock Rovers – Wal, CSSR, Bul, USA (sub).

MUNROE, LIAM "Mousie" (William J.)
1 Cap
1953 Shamrock Rovers – Lux.

MURPHY, ALBIE (Albert)
1 Cap
1955 Clyde – Yugo.

MURPHY, BARRY
1 Cap
1986 Bohemians – Uru.

MURPHY, JERRY
3 Caps
1979 Crystal Palace – Wal, USA.
1980 Crystal Palace – Cy.

MURRAY, TERRY
1 Cap
1950 Dundalk – Bel.

NEWMAN, BILLY
1 Cap
1969 Shelbourne – Den.

NOLAN, RONNIE
10 Caps
1956 Shamrock Rovers – Den W.G.
1957 Shamrock Rovers – Eng.
1958 Shamrock Rovers – Pol.
1960 Shamrock Rovers – Chile, W.G, Swe.
1961 Shamrock Rovers – CSSR, CSSR.
1962 Shamrock Rovers – Ice.

O'BRIEN, FRAN "Maggot"
3 Caps
1979 Philadelphia Furies – CSSR.
1980 Philadelphia Furies – Eng, Cy (sub).

O'BRIEN, LIAM FRANCIS
10 Caps
1986 Shamrock Rovers – Uru.
1987 Manchester United – Bra, Ice (sub).
1988 Manchester United – Rom (sub), Yugo (sub), Pol (sub), Tun.
Newcastle United – Spa (sub).
1992 Newcastle United – Swit (sub).
1993 Newcastle United – Wal.

Jerry Murphy one of only 3 Crystal Palace players to play for Ireland.

O'BRIEN, MICK T.
4 Caps
1927 Derby County – Italy "B".
1929 Walsall – Bel.
1930 Norwich City – Bel.
1932 Watford – Hol.

O'BRIEN, RAY (Raymond Christopher)
5 Caps
1976 Notts County – Nor, Pol.
1977 Notts County – Spa, Pol.
1980 Notts County – Arg.

O'BYRNE, LAR B.
1 Cap
1949 Shamrock Rovers – Bel.

O'CALLAGHAN, BRENDAN RICHARD
6 Caps
1979 Stoke City – W.G. (sub), Wal, USA.
1981 Stoke City – Wal.
1982 Stoke City – Bra, Trin.

O'CALLAGHAN, KEVIN
21 Caps (1 goal)
1981 Ipswich Town – CSSR, W.G. "B", Pol.
1982 Ipswich Town – Alg, Chile, Bra, Trin (sub), ice (sub), Spa.
1983 Ipswich Town – Mal (sub), Spa (sub), Ice, Hol, Mal.
1984 Ipswich Town – Mex (sub), Nor (sub), Den (sub).
1985 Portsmouth – Eng (sub), Swit (sub), USSR (sub).
1987 Portsmouth – Bra.

Kevin O'Callaghan
scored his only goal for Ireland in the 8-0 victory over Malta.

O'CONNELL, TONY
2 Caps
1966 Dundalk – Spa.
1970 Bohemians – Pol (sub).

O'CONNOR, TOMMY
4 Caps
1949 Shamrock Rovers – Fin, Eng, Fin, Swe.

O'CONNOR, TURLOUGH
7 Caps (2 goals)
1967 Fulham – CSSR.
1971 Dundalk – Aus.
1972 Dundalk – Iran (sub), Ecu (sub), Chile.
Bohemians – Fra (sub).
1973 Bohemians – Pol (sub),

O'DRISCOLL, JOHN "Jackie"
3 Caps
1948 Swansea – Swit.
1949 Swansea – Bel, Swe.

O'DRISCOLL, SEAN
3 Caps
1982 Fulham – Chile, Bra, Trin (sub).

O'FARRELL, FRANK
9 Caps (2 goals)
1952 West Ham United – Aus.
1953 West Ham United – Aus, Fra.
1955 West Ham United – Hol, Nor, Yugo.
1956 West Ham United – Hol.
1957 Preston North End – Den.
1959 Preston North End – CSSR.

O'FLANAGAN, KEVIN P.
10 Caps (3 goals)
1937 Bohemians – Nor.
1938 Bohemians – CSSR, Pol, Pol.
1939 Bohemians – Hun, Hun, Ger.
1946 Arsenal – Eng.
1947 Arsenal – Spa, Port.

O'FLANAGAN, MICHAEL
1 Cap
1946 Bohemians – Eng.

O'HANLON, KELHAM G.
1 Cap
1987 Rotherham United – Is.

O'KANE, PADDY
3 Caps
1934 Bohemians – Hun.
1935 Bohemians – Swit, Ger.

O'KEEFE, EAMONN
5 Caps (1 goal)
1981 Everton – Wal.
1984 Port Vale – PRC, Mex, USSR (sub).
1985 Port Vale – Eng.

Frank O'Farrell
won 9 caps for Ireland and went on to become manager of Manchester Utd.

David O'Leary
his only goal for Ireland was against Turkey in 1990.
(apart from the penalty shoot-out against Romania 1990!)

O'KEEFFE, TIM (Timothy Jim)
3 Caps
1934 Cork – Bel.
1938 Waterford – CSSR, Pol.

O'LEARY, DAVID ANTHONY
68 Caps (1 goal)
1976 Arsenal – Eng, Fra.
1977 Arsenal – Spa, Fra, Bul, Bul.
1978 Arsenal – Nor, Den, Eng.
1979 Arsenal – Bul, W.G, Wal, Bul, N.I.
1980 Arsenal – Eng, Cy, Hol.
1981 Arsenal – CSSR, W.G. "B", Pol, Hol, Fra.
1982 Arsenal – Hol, Ice.
1983 Arsenal – Spa.
1984 Arsenal – Is, Pol, PRC, USSR, Nor, Den.
1985 Arsenal – Is, Eng (sub), Nor, Spa, Swit, Swit, USSR, Den.
1986 Arsenal – Wal.
1988 Arsenal – Spa.
1989 Arsenal – Mal, Hun, W.G, N.I. (sub), Mal.
1990 Arsenal – Wal (sub), USSR, Fin, Tu, Mal, Rom (sub), Tu, Eng.
1991 Arsenal – Eng, Pol, Chile, Hun, Pol, Tu.
1992 Arsenal – Wal, Swit, USA, Alb, Italy, Port.
1993 Arsenal – Wal.

O'LEARY, PIERCE CHRISTOPHER
7 Caps
1979 Shamrock Rovers – CSSR, Bul, USA, N.I.
1980 Shamrock Rovers – Eng (sub), Arg. Hol.

O'MAHONEY, MATT (Matthew Thomas)
6 Caps
1938 Bristol Rovers – CSSR, Pol, Swit, Pol.
1939 Bristol Rovers – Hun, Ger.

Matt O'Mahoney
one of only two Bristol Rovers players to play for Ireland.

O'NEILL, FRANK S.
20 Caps (1 goal)
1961 Shamrock Rovers – CSSR, CSSR.
1964 Shamrock Rovers – Pol.
1965 Shamrock Rovers – Bel, Spa, Spa, Spa.
1966 Shamrock Rovers – W.G, Aus, Spa, Tu, Spa.
1967 Shamrock Rovers – Tu.
1968 Shamrock Rovers – Pol, Aus, Den.
1969 Shamrock Rovers – CSSR, Den (sub), Hun (sub).
1971 Shamrock Rovers – Aus.

O'NEILL, JIMMY
17 Caps
1952 Everton – Spa, Fra.
1953 Everton – Aus, Fra, Lux, Fra.
1954 Everton – Nor.
1955 Everton – Hol, Nor, W.G, Yugo, Spa.
1956 Everton – Den.
1958 Everton – Aus, Pol.
1959 Everton – CSSR, CSSR.

O'NEILL, JOHN "Sonny"
1 Cap
1960 Preston North End – Wal.

O'NEILL, WILLIAM
11 Caps
1935 Dundalk – Hol.
1936 Dundalk – Swit, Hun, Lux, Ger, Hun.
1937 Dundalk – Swit, Fra, Nor.
1939 Dundalk – Hun, Ger.

Jimmy O'Neill
won his 17 International caps as an Everton player.

O'REILLY, JACK
2 Caps (1 goal)
1946 Cork United – Port, Spa.

O'REILLY, JOE
20 Caps (2 goals)
1932 Brideville – Hol.
1934 Aberdeen – Bel, Hol.
1935 Brideville – Hol,
1936 Brideville – Swit, Hun, Lux.
St. James's Gate – Ger, Hun.
1937 St. James's Gate – Swit, Fra, Nor, Nor.
1938 St. James's Gate – CSSR, Pol, Swit, Pol.
1939 St. James's Gate – Hun, Hun, Ger.

O'REGAN, KIERAN
4 Caps
1983 Brighton – Mal.
1984 Brighton – Pol, Mex.
1985 Brighton – Spa (sub).

Gerry Peyton
13 clean sheets in 33 International matches.

PEYTON, GERRY (Gerard Joseph)
33 Caps
1977 Fulham – Spa (sub), Bul.
1978 Fulham – Tu, Pol.
1979 Fulham – Den, Bul, W.G, Wal, CSSR, Bul.
1980 Fulham – Eng, Cy, Swit, Arg, Hol, Bel, Fra, Cy.
1982 Fulham – Trin.
1984 Fulham – Mex (sub).
1986 Fulham – Wal, CSSR.
1987 A.F.C. Bournemouth – Lux.
1988 A.F.C. Bournemouth – Pol, N.I, Tun.
1990 A.F.C. Bournemouth – USSR, Mal.
1991 A.F.C. Bournemouth – Chile
1992 Everton – USA*, USA, Italy (sub), Port.
** on loan to Norwich City*

PEYTON, NOEL
6 Caps
1956 Shamrock Rovers – W.G.
1960 Leeds United – W.G, Swe (sub), Wal.
1962 Leeds United – Ice, Scot.

PHELAN, TERRY
15 Caps
1991 Wimbledon – Hun, Pol (sub), Tu.
1992 Wimbledon – Wal, Swit, USA, Italy (sub), Port.
Manchester City – Lat (sub), Den, Spa.
1993 Manchester City – N.I, Alb, Lat, Lith.

QUINN, NIALL JOHN
40 Caps (10 goals)
1986 Arsenal – Ice (sub), CSSR.
1987 Arsenal – Bul (sub), Bra (sub), Lux (sub), Bul (sub), Is.
1988 Arsenal – Rom (sub), Pol (sub), Eng (sub), Tun (sub), Spa (sub).
1989 Arsenal – Hun (sub).
1990 Manchester City – USSR, Mal, Egy (sub), Hol, Rom, Italy, Mor, Tu, Eng.
1991 Manchester City – Wal, Eng, Pol, Hun.
1992 Manchester City – Wal (sub), USA, Alb, USA, Italy, Port, Lat, Den. Spa.
1993 Manchester City – N.I, Den, Alb, Lat, Lith.

Niall Quinn
10 goals in 40 appearances.

REID, CHARLIE
1 Cap
1931 Brideville – Spa.

RICHARDSON, DAMIEN J.
3 Caps
1971 Shamrock Rovers – Aus (sub).
1973 Gillingham – Nor (sub).
1979 Gillingham – CSSR.

RIGBY, ALF
3 Caps
1934 St. James's Gate – Hun.
1935 St. James's Gate – Swit, Ger.

RINGSTEAD, ALF
20 Caps (7 goals)
1951 Sheffield United – Arg, Nor, W.G.
1952 Sheffield United – W.G, Aus, Spa.
1953 Sheffield United – Aus, Fra.
1955 Sheffield United – Nor, Yugo, Spa.
1956 Sheffield United – Hol.
1957 Sheffield United – Eng, Eng, Den.
1958 Sheffield United – Pol, Aus, Pol.
1959 Sheffield United – CSSR, CSSR.

ROBINSON, JEREMIAH "Sam"
2 Caps
1928 Bohemians – Bel.
1931 Dolphin – Spa.

ROBINSON, MICHAEL JOHN
24 Caps (4 goals)
1980 Brighton – Fra, Cy.
1981 Brighton – Bel, W.G. "B", Pol, Hol, Fra.
1982 Brighton – Alg, Chile, Hol, Ice, Spa.
1983 Brighton – Mal.
Liverpool – Ice, Hol.
1984 Liverpool – Is, USSR, Nor.
1985 Queen's Park Rangers – Nor, Spa, Swit, Den (sub).
1986 Queen's Park Rangers – Wal, CSSR.

ROCHE, PADDY J.
8 Caps
1971 Shelbourne – Aus.
1974 Manchester United – USSR, Tu.
1975 Manchester United – W.G. "B", Swit, USSR, Swit, Tu.

ROGERS, EAMONN
19 Caps (5 goals)
1967 Blackburn Rovers – CSSR.
1968 Blackburn Rovers – Pol, Pol, Aus, Den.
1969 Blackburn Rovers – CSSR, Den, Hun, Scot, Den, Hun.
1970 Blackburn Rovers – Italy.
1971 Blackburn Rovers – Italy, Aus.
1972 Charlton Athletic – Iran, Ecu, Chile, Port, USSR.

RYAN, GERRY
18 Caps (1 goal)
1978 Derby County – Tu.
Brighton – Eng.
1979 Brighton – W.G, Wal.
1980 Brighton – Cy (sub), Swit, Arg (sub), Fra (sub).
1981 Brighton – W.G. "B" (sub), Pol (sub), Hol (sub).
1982 Brighton – Alg (sub), Chile (sub), Bra (sub), Trin.
1984 Brighton – Pol, PRC, Mex.

RYAN, REG A.
16 Caps (3 goals)
1949 West Bromwich Albion – Swe.
1950 West Bromwich Albion – Bel, Nor.
1951 West Bromwich Albion – Arg, Nor, W.G.
1952 West Bromwich Albion – W.G, Aus, Spa, Fra.
1953 West Bromwich Albion – Aus, Fra, Lux, Fra.
1954 Derby County – Nor.
1955 Derby County – Spa.

SAWARD, PAT
18 Caps
1954 Millwall – Lux.
1957 Aston Villa – Eng, Eng, Den.
1958 Aston Villa – Pol, Aus, Pol.
1959 Aston Villa – CSSR, Swe.
1960 Aston Villa – Chile, W.G, Swe, Wal, Nor.
1961 Huddersfield Town – Scot.
1962 Huddersfield Town – Aus, Ice, Ice.

Pat Saward
won 18 caps for Ireland.

Kevin Sheedy
scored one of his 9 goals direct from a corner kick against Poland in 1988.

SCANNELL, TED
1 Cap
1954 Southend United – Lux.

SCULLY, PAT J.
1 Cap
1988 Arsenal – Tun (sub).

SHEEDY, KEVIN
46 Caps (9 goals)
1983 Everton – Hol (sub), Mal.
1984 Everton – Den.
1985 Everton – Italy, Is, Swit, Swit, Den.
1986 Everton – Scot, Pol.
1987 Everton – Is.
1988 Everton – Rom, Pol, Eng (sub), USSR, Hol (sub), N.I, Tun.
1989 Everton – Hun, Spa, Mal, Hun, N.I, Mal.
1990 Everton – Wal (sub), USSR, Fin (sub), Tu, Eng, Egy, Hol, Rom, Italy.
1991 Everton – Wal, Eng, Pol, Chile, USA, Hun, Pol, Tu.
1992 Everton – Wal.
Newcastle United – Swit (sub), Alb, Lat,
1993 Newcastle United – Wal (sub).

SHERIDAN, JOHN JOSEPH
15 Caps (1 goal)
1988 Leeds United – Rom, Yugo, Pol, Nor (sub), Spa.
1990 Sheffield Wednesday – Wal, Tu (sub), Mal, Italy (sub), Mor (sub), Tu.
1991 Sheffield Wednesday – Chile, USA (sub), Hun.
1993 Sheffield Wednesday – Lat (sub).

SLAVEN, BERNIE
7 Caps (1 goal)
1990 Middlesbrough – Wal, Fin, Tu (sub), Mal.
1991 Middlesbrough – Wal, Pol (sub).
1993 Middlesbrough – Wal (sub).

SLOAN, JOSIAH WALTER "Paddy"
2 Caps (1 goal)
1946 Arsenal – Port, Spa.

SMYTH MICK "Smudger"
1 Cap
1968 Shamrock Rovers – Pol (sub).

SQUIRES, JOHNNY
1 Cap (1 goal)
1934 Shelbourne – Hol.

STAPLETON, FRANK (Francis Anthony)
71 Caps (20 goals)
1976 Arsenal – Tu, Fra.
1977 Arsenal – Spa, Bul, Bul.
1978 Arsenal – Nor, Den, N.I, Eng (sub).
1979 Arsenal – Den, W.G, Wal, Bul, N.I.
1980 Arsenal – Eng, Cy, Hol, Bel, Fra, Cy.
1981 Arsenal – Bel, CSSR, W.G. "B", Pol.
Manchester United – Hol, Fra.
1982 Manchester United – Alg, Hol, Ice, Spa.
1983 Manchester United – Mal, Spa, Ice, Hol, Mal.
1984 Manchester United – Is, Pol, PRC, Nor, Den.
1985 Manchester United – Italy, Is, Eng, Nor, Swit, Swit, USSR, Den.
1986 Manchester United – Uru, Ice, CSSR (sub), Bel, Scot, Pol.
1987 Manchester United – Scot, Bul, Bel, Lux.
Ajax – Lux, Bul.
1988 Derby County – Rom, Yugo, Nor, Eng, USSR, Hol.
1989 Le Havre – Fra, Spa, Mal.
Blackburn Rovers – W.G.
1990 Blackburn Rovers – Mal (sub).

STAUNTON, STEPHEN
41 Caps (4 goals)
1988 Liverpool – Tun, Spa.
1989 Liverpool – Spa, Mal, Hun, W.G, N.I, Mal.
1990 Liverpool – Wal, USSR, Fin, Tu, Mal, Eng, Egy, Hol, Rom, Italy, Mor, Tu, Eng.
1991 Liverpool – Wal, Eng, Pol, Chile, USA.
Aston Villa – Pol, Tu.
1992 Aston Villa – Swit, USA, Alb, USA, Italy, Port, Lat, Spa.
1993 Aston Villa – N.I, Den, Alb, Lat, Lith.

John Sheridan
scored his only goal for Ireland against Poland in 1988.

STEVENSON, ALEX E.
7 Caps
1932 Dolphin – Hol.
1946 Everton – Eng.
1947 Everton – Spa, Port.
1948 Everton – Port, Spa, Swit.

STRAHAN, FRED
5 Caps (1 goal)
1964 Shelbourne – Pol, Nor, Eng, Pol.
1966 Shelbourne – W.G.

SULLIVAN, JACK
1 Cap (1 goal)
1928 Fordsons – Bel.

SWAN MAURICE M. G.
1 Cap
1960 Drumcondra – Swe (sub).

SYNNOTT, NOEL
3 Caps
1978 Shamrock Rovers – Tu, Pol, N.I.

TAYLOR, TOMMY
1 Cap
1958 Waterford – Pol (sub).

THOMAS, PETER
2 Caps
1973 Waterford – Pol.
1974 Waterford – Bra.

Andy Townsend
39 caps in 5 years.

TOWNSEND, ANDY (Andrew David)
39 Caps (4 goals)
1989 Norwich City – Fra, Spa (sub), Mal (sub), Hun, W.G. (sub), N.I, Mal.
1990 Norwich City – Wal, USSR, Fin (sub), Tu, Mal (sub), Eng, Egy. Hol, Rom, Italy.
Chelsea – Mor, Tu, Eng.
1991 Chelsea – Wal, Eng, Pol, Chile, USA, Pol.
1992 Chelsea – Wal, USA, Alb, USA, Italy, Lat, Den, Spa.
1993 Chelsea – N.I, Den. Alb, Lat, Lith.

TRAYNOR, TOMMY J.
8 Caps
1954 Southampton – Lux.
1962 Southampton – Aus, Ice, Ice.
1963 Southampton – Scot, Aus, Aus.
1964 Southampton – Spa.

TREACY, RAY
42 Caps (5 goals)
1966 West Bromwich Albion – W.G, Spa.
1967 West Bromwich Albion – CSSR.
Charlton Athletic – CSSR.
1968 Charlton Athletic – Pol, Pol.
1969 Charlton Athletic – CSSR, Den, Scot, Den, Hun (sub).
1970 Charlton Athletic – Pol (sub), W.G. (sub), Pol, Swe (sub), Swe, Italy.
1971 Charlton Athletic – Aus.
1972 Swindon Town – Iran, Ecu, Chile, Port, USSR, Fra.
1973 Swindon Town – USSR, Pol, Fra, Nor, Pol.
1974 Preston North End – Bra, USSR.
1975 Preston North End – W.G "B", Swit, Swit, Tu.
1976 Preston North End – Nor (sub), Pol (sub).
1977 West Bromwich Albion – Fra, Pol.
1978 Shamrock Rovers – Tu, Pol.
1979 Shamrock Rovers – CSSR (sub).

Liam Tuohy
one of 62 Shamrock Rovers players to play for Ireland.

TUOHY, LIAM "Rasher"
8 Caps (4 goals)
1955 Shamrock Rovers – Yugo.
1959 Shamrock Rovers – CSSR, CSSR.
1962 Newcastle United – Aus, Ice, Ice.
1963 Shamrock Rovers – Aus.
1965 Shamrock Rovers Bel.

TURNER, CHARLIE J.
10 Caps
1936 Southend – Swit, Ger, Hun.
1937 Southend – Swit, Fra, Nor, Nor.
1938 West Ham United – CSSR, Pol.
1939 West Ham United – Hun.

TURNER, PADDY (A.)
2 Caps
1963 Glasgow Celtic – Scot.
1964 Glasgow Celtic – Spa.

VERNON, JACKIE
2 Caps
1946 Belfast Celtic – Port, Spa.

WADDOCK, GARY
21 Caps (3 goals)
1980 Queen's Park Rangers – Swit, Arg.
1981 Queen's Park Rangers – Wal, Pol (sub).
1982 Queen's Park Rangers – Alg, Hol (sub), Ice.
1983 Queen's Park Rangers – Mal, Spa, Ice, Hol, Mal (sub).

Gary Waddock
had a five year gap (1985-90) in his international career.

1984 Queen's Park Rangers – Is.
1985 Queen's Park Rangers – Italy, Is, Eng, Nor, Spa, USSR.
1990 Millwall – USSR, Tu.

WALSH, DAVY J.
20 Caps (5 goals)
1946 West Bromwich Albion – Port, Spa.
1947 West Bromwich Albion – Spa, Port.
1948 West Bromwich Albion – Port, Spa, Swit.
1949 West Bromwich Albion – Port, Swe, Spa, Eng, Fin, Swe.
1950 West Bromwich Albion – Nor.
1951 Aston Villa – Arg, Nor.
1952 Aston Villa – Spa.
1953 Aston Villa – Aus, Fra, Fra.

WALSH, JOHNNY
1 Cap
1982 Limerick United – Trin.

WALSH, MICKEY (Michael Anthony)
21 Caps (3 goals)
1976 Blackpool – Nor, Pol, Fra (sub).
1977 Blackpool – Pol.
1978 Everton – N.I (sub).
1979 Queen's Park Rangers – Den (sub), Bul, W.G (sub).
1981 F.C. Porto – Bel (sub), CSSR.
1982 F.C. Porto – Alg (sub), Hol (sub), Spa (sub).
1983 F.C. Porto – Spa, Ice (sub), Mal.
1984 F.C. Porto – Pol, PRC, USSR, Nor (sub), Den.

WALSH, MIKE (Michael T.)
4 Caps
1982 Everton – Chile, Bra, Trin, Ice*
**on loan to Norwich City*

Davy Walsh
scored 5 goals in 20 appearances for Ireland.

Mickey Walsh
scored on his international debut against Norway in 1976.

WALSH, WILLIE
9 Caps
1946 Manchester City – Eng.
1947 Manchester City – Spa, Port.
1948 Manchester City – Port, Spa.
1949 Manchester City – Bel, Eng, Swe.
1950 Manchester City – Bel.

WATERS, JOE
2 Caps (1 goal)
1976 Grimsby Town – Tu.
1979 Grimsby Town – N.I (sub).

WATTERS, FRAN
1 Cap
1926 Shelbourne – Italy.

WEIR, E.
3 Caps
1939 Clyde – Hun, Hun, Ger.

WHELAN, LIAM "Billy"
4 Caps
1956 Manchester United – Hol, Den.
1957 Manchester United – Eng, Eng.

WHELAN, RONNIE (Senior)
2 Caps
1963 St. Patrick's Athletic – Aus.
1964 St. Patrick's Athletic – Eng (sub).

Ronnie Whelan won his 45 caps as a Liverpool player.

Liam Whelan one of 20 Manchester Utd. players to play for the Republic of Ireland.

WHELAN, RONNIE ANDREW (Junior)
45 Caps (3 goals)
1981 Liverpool – CSSR (sub), Hol (sub), Fra.
1982 Liverpool – Ice.
1983 Liverpool – Mal, Spa.
1984 Liverpool – Is, USSR, Nor.
1985 Liverpool – Italy (sub), Is, Eng, Nor (sub), Swit (sub), USSR (sub).
1986 Liverpool – Wal, Bel (sub).
1987 Liverpool – Scot, Bul, Bel, Bra, Lux, Lux, Bul.
1988 Liverpool – Pol, Nor, Eng, USSR, Hol, N.I.
1989 Liverpool – Fra, Hun, Spa, Mal, W.G, N.I, Mal.
1990 Liverpool – Wal, Hol (sub), Mor, Eng.
1992 Liverpool – Swit, Lat,
1993 Liverpool – Wal (sub), Lit (sub).

WHITE, JIMMY J.
1 Cap (2 goals)
1928 Bohemians – Bel.

WILLIAMS, JOE
1 Cap
1937 Shamrock Rovers – Nor.

WHITTAKER, RICHARD "Dick"
1 Cap
1959 Chelsea – CSSR.

AW = Away Wins; D = Draws; HW = Home wins; GP = Games played; GS = Goals scored; GD = Goal difference.

Appendix A

IRELAND'S WORLD CUP GROUPS

1930 World Cup
Did not enter.

1934 World Cup - Group 11

25Feb.'34	Dublin	Ireland	4-4	Belgium
8April'34	Amsterdam	Holland	5-2	Ireland
29April'34	Antwerp	Belgium	2-4	Holland

	P	W	D	L	F	A	GD	Pts
Holland	2	2	0	0	9	4	+5	4
Belgium	2	0	1	1	6	8	-2	1
Ireland	2	0	1	1	6	9	-3	1

GP3 HW 1 AW1 D1 GS21
Leading Group Goalscorer: Moore (Ireland) 5
Irish Appearances (+Goals) Players Used: 17
T. Burke 1, D. Byrne 1, P. Byrne 1, H. Chatton 1, J. Foley 2, P. Gaskins 2, F. Horlacher 1, B. Jordan 1, J. Kelly 1, J. Kendrick 2, B. Kennedy 2, M. Lynch 1, P. Meehan 1, P. Moore 2(5), T. O'Keeffe 1, J. O'Reilly 2, J. Squires 1(1).

Holland and Belgium qualified for the finals in Italy where both were knocked out in the First Round.

1938 World Cup – Group 2

10 Oct. '37	Oslo	Norway	3-2	Ireland
7 Nov. '37	Dublin	Ireland	3-3	Norway

Norway qualified 6-5 on aggregate

GP2 HW1 AW0 D1 GS10
Leading Goalscorer: Kvammen (Norway) 4
Irish appearances (+Goals) Players Used: 18
T. Arrigan 1, J. Carey 1, J. Donnelly 1, T. Donnelly 1, H. Duggan 1(1), J. Dunne 2(2), T. Foy 1, M. Geoghegan 1(1), B. Gorman 1, M. Hoy 1, B. Jordan 1, O. Kinsella 1, G. McKenzie 2, K. O'Flanagan 1(1), W. O'Neill 1, J. O'Reilly 2, C. Turner 2, J. Williams 1.

In the finals in France the Norwegians were knocked out in the First Round by the eventual winners, Italy.

1950 World Cup – Group 5

2 June '49	Stockholm	Sweden	3-1	Ireland
8 Sept. '49	Dublin	Ireland	3-0	Finland
9 Oct. '49	Helsinki	Finland	1-1	Ireland
13 Nov. '49	Dublin	Ireland	1-3	Sweden

The games between Sweden and Finland were not played

	P	W	D	L	F	A	GD	Pts
Sweden	2	2	0	0	6	2	+4	4
Ireland	4	1	1	2	6	7	-1	3
Finland	2	0	1	1	1	4	-3	1

GP4 HW2 AW1 D1 GS13
Leading Group Goalscorers: Martin (Ireland), Palmer (Sweden) 3.
Irish Appearances (+Goals) Players Used: 23
T. Aherne 3, J. Carey 4, B. Carroll 1, P. Coad 1, J. Coffey 1, P. Corr 1, P. Daly 1, P. Desmond 3, T. Eglington 1, P. Farrell 2(1), A. Fitzsimons 1, E. Gannon 2, J. Gavin 2(1), T. Godwin 4, T. Keane 1, D. McGowan 1, C. Martin 4(3), T. Moroney 3, T. O'Connor 3, J. O'Driscoll 1, R. Ryan 1, D Walsh 3(1), W. Walsh 1.

Sweden qualified for the finals in Brazil where they finished third in the Final Pool.

1954 World Cup – Group 4

20 Sept '53	Luxembourg	Luxembourg	1-6	France
4 Oct '53	Dublin	Ireland	3-5	France
28 Oct '53	Dublin	Ireland	4-0	Luxembourg
25 Nov '53	Paris	France	1-0	Ireland
17 Dec '53	Paris	France	8-0	Luxembourg
7 Mar '54	Luxembourg	Luxembourg	0-1	Ireland

	P	W	D	L	F	A	GD	Pts
France	4	4	0	0	20	4	+16	8
Ireland	4	2	0	2	8	6	+2	4
Luxembourg	4	0	0	4	1	19	-18	0

GP6 HW3 AW3 D0 GS29
Leading Group Goalscorer: Fontaine (France), 3
Irish Appearances (+Goals) Players Used: 27

T. Aherne 1, N. Cantwell 1, T. Clinton 2, G. Cummins 2(1), S. Dunne 2, T. Eglington 3(1), P. Farrell 2, A. Fitzsimons 3(2), M. Gallagher 1, E. Gannon 2, J. Gavin 1, S. Gibbons 1, J. Hartnett 1, F. Kearns 1, N. Kelly 1, J. Lawler 2, C. Martin 3, T. Moroney 1, L. Munroe 1, F. O'Farrell 1(1), J. O'Neill 3, A. Ringstead 1, R. Ryan 3(2), P. Saward 1, T. Scannell 1, T. Traynor 1, D. Walsh 2(1).

France qualified for the finals in Switzerland where they were knocked out in the First Pool games.

1958 World Cup – Group 1

3 Oct '56	Dublin	Ireland	2-1	Denmark
5 Dec '56	Wolverhampton	England	5-2	Denmark
8 May '57	London	England	5-1	Ireland
15 May '57	Copenhagen	Denmark	1-4	England
19 May '57	Dublin	Ireland	1-1	England
2 Oct '57	Copenhagen	Denmark	0-2	Ireland

	P	W	D	L	F	A	GD	Pts
England	4	3	1	0	15	5	+10	7
Ireland	4	2	1	1	6	7	-1	5
Denmark	4	0	0	4	4	13	-9	0

GP6 HW3 AW2 D1 GS25
Leading Group Goalscorer: Taylor (England), 8
Irish Appearances (+Goals) Players Used: 20
N. Cantwell 4, G. Cummins 1(1), D. Curtis 4(3), D. Donovan 1, S. Dunne 3, T. Dunne 1, P. Farrell 1, A. Fitzsimons 4, J. Gavin 1(1), T. Godwin 2, J. Haverty 4, C. Hurley 2, A. Kelly 1, G. Mackey 2, R. Nolan 2, F. O'Farrell 1, J. O'Neill 1, A. Ringstead 3(1), P. Saward 3, L. Whelan 3.

England qualified for the finals in Sweden where they were knocked out after a First Pool play-off.

1962 World Cup – Group 8

3 May '61	Glasgow	Scotland	4-1	Ireland
7 May '61	Dublin	Ireland	0-3	Scotland
14 May '61	Bratislava	Czechoslovakia	4-0	Scotland
26 Sept '61	Glasgow	Scotland	3-2	Czechoslovakia
8 Oct '61	Dublin	Ireland	1-3	Czechoslovakia
29 Oct '61	Prague	Czechoslovakia	7-1	Ireland

	P	W	D	L	F	A	GD	Pts
Czechoslovakia	4	3	0	1	16	5	+11	6
Scotland	4	3	0	1	10	7	+3	6
Ireland	4	0	0	4	3	17	-14	0

Play-off
29 Nov '61 Brussels Czechoslovakia 4-2 Scotland

GP7 HW4 AW2 D0 GS35
Leading Group Goalscorer: Kvasnak (Czechoslavakia), 6
Irish Appearances (+Goals) Players Used: 18
N. Cantwell 4; G. Cummins 2, D. Curtis 1, N. Dwyer 4, F. Fagan 1, P. Fitzgerald 3, A. Fogarty 3(1), J. Giles 4(1), J. Haverty 4(1), C. Hurley 4, P. Kelly 3, A. McEvoy 2, M. McGrath 2, B. McNally 1, M. Meagan 1, R. Nolan 2, F. O'Neill 2, P. Saward 1.

Czechoslovakia qualified for the finals in Chile where they progressed to the Final only to be beaten 3-1 by Brazil.

1966 World Cup – Group 9

5 May '65	Dublin	Ireland	1-0	Spain
27 Oct '65	Seville	Spain	4-1	Ireland

	P	W	D	L	F	A	GD	Pts
Spain	2	1	0	1	4	2	+2	2
Ireland	2	1	0	1	2	4	-2	2

Syria Withdrew

Play-off
10 Nov '65 Paris Spain 1-0 Ireland

GP3 HW2 AW0 D0 GS7
Leading Group Goalscorer: Pereda (Spain), 3
Irish Appearances (+Goals) Players Used: 15

E. Barber 1, S. Brennan 2, N.Cantwell 3, P. Dunne 3, Tony Dunne 3, E. Dunphy 1, T. Foley 2, J. Giles 3, J. Haverty 3, J. Hennessy 1, C. Hurley 1, A. McEvoy 3(1), M. McGrath 2, M. Meagan 2, F. O'Neill 3.

Spain qualified for the finals in England where they were knocked out after the First Pool games.

1970 World Cup – Group 2

25 Sept '68	Copenhagen	Denmark	0-3	Czechoslovakia
20 Oct '68	Bratislava	Czechoslovakia	1-0	Denmark
4 Dec '68	Dublin	Ireland	1A1*	Denmark
4 May '69	Dublin	Ireland	1-2	Czechoslovakia
25 May '69	Budapest	Hungary	2-0	Czechoslovakia
27 May '69	Copenhagen	Denmark	2-0	Ireland
8 June '69	Dublin	Ireland	1-2	Hungary
15 June '69	Copenhagen	Denmark	3-2	Hungary
14 Sept '69	Prague	Czechoslovakia	3-3	Hungary
7 Oct '69	Prague	Czechoslovakia	3-0	Ireland
15 Oct '69	Dublin	Ireland	1-1	Denmark
22 Oct '69	Budapest	Hungary	3-0	Denmark
5 Nov '69	Budapest	Hungary	4-0	Ireland

* Abandoned game not counted in statistics but in Irish Appearances (+ goals)

	P	W	D	L	F	A	GD	Pts
Hungary	6	4	1	1	16	7	+9	9
Czechoslovakia	6	4	1	1	12	6	+6	9
Denmark	6	2	1	3	6	10	-4	5
Ireland	6	0	1	5	3	14	-11	1

Play-off
3 Dec '69 Marseilles Czechoslovakia 4-1 Hungary

GP13 HW7 AW3 D2 GS42
Leading Group Goalscorer: Bene (Hungary), 6
Irish Appearances (+Goals) Players Used: 25

S. Brennan 6, T. Byrne 1, T. Carroll 2, O. Conmy 1, T. Conroy 3, J. Conway 4, J. Dempsey 4, Tony Dunne 3, E. Dunphy 5, A. Finucane 4, K. Fitzpatrick 1, J. Fullam 2, J. Giles 2(1), D. Givens 5(2), A. Hale 2, E. Hand 1, C. Hurley 3, A. Kelly 6, J. Kinnear 3, M. Leech 3, P. Mulligan 6, B. Newman 1, F. O'Neill 4, E. Rogers 6(1), R. Treacy 4.

Czechoslovakia qualified for the finals in Mexico where they were knocked out after the First Round Pool games.

1974 World Cup – Group 9

13 Oct '72	Paris	France	1-0	USSR
18 Oct '72	Dublin	Ireland	1-2	USSR
15 Nov '72	Dublin	Ireland	2-1	France
13 May '73	Moscow	USSR	1-0	Ireland
19 May '73	Paris	France	1-1	Ireland
26 May '73	Moscow	USSR	2-0	France

	P	W	D	L	F	A	GD	Pts
USSR	4	3	0	1	5	2	+3	6
Ireland	4	1	1	2	4	5	-1	3
France	4	1	1	2	3	5	-2	3

GP6 HW4 AW1 D1 GS12
Leading Group Goalscorers: Conroy (Ireland), Onishenko (USSR), 2
Irish Appearances (+Goals) Players Used: 20
T. Byrne 3, N. Campbell 2, T. Carroll 3, T. Conroy 3(2), M. Dennehy 2, J. Giles 2, D. Givens 3, E. Hand 4, S. Heighway 1, J. Herrick 1, J. Holmes 3, A. Kelly 4, J. Kinnear 2, M. Leech 1, T. McConville 4, M. Martin 3(1), P. Mulligan 3, T. O'Connor 1, E. Rogers 1, R. Treacy 4(1).

USSR qualified for a play-off with Chile but withdrew after a scoreless first leg in Moscow.

1978 World Cup – Group 5

9 Oct '76	Sofia	Bulgaria	2-2 France
17 Nov '76	Paris	France	2-0 Ireland
30 Mar '77	Dublin	Ireland	1-0 France
1 June '77	Sofia	Bulgaria	2-1 Ireland
12 Oct '77	Dublin	Ireland	0-0 Bulgaria
16 Nov '77	Paris	France	3-1 Bulgaria

	P	W	D	L	F	A	GD	Pts
France	4	2	1	1	7	4	+3	5
Bulgaria	4	1	2	1	5	6	-1	4
Ireland	4	1	1	2	2	4	-2	3

GP6 HW4 AW0 D2 GS14
Leading Group Goalscorer: Platini (France), 3
Irish Appearances (+Goals) Players Used: 16
L. Brady 4(1), N. Campbell 1, G. Daly 4, J. Giles 4, D. Givens 4(1), S. Heighway 4, J. Holmes 4, M. Kearns 3, M. Lawrenson 1, M. Martin 3, P. Mulligan 4, D. O'Leary 4, G. Peyton 1, F. Stapleton 3, R. Treacy 1, M. Walsh 1.

France qualified for the finals in Argentina where they were knocked out after the First Round Pool games.

1982 World Cup – Group 2

26 Mar '80	Nicosia	Cyprus	2-3 Ireland
10 Sept '80	Dublin	Ireland	2-1 Holland
11 Oct '80	Limassol	Cyprus	0-7 France
15 Oct '80	Dublin	Ireland	1-1 Belgium
28 Oct '80	Paris	France	2-0 Ireland
19 Nov '80	Dublin	Ireland	6-0 Cyprus
19 Nov '80	Brussels	Belgium	1-0 Holland
21 Dec '80	Nicosia	Cyprus	0-2 Belgium
18 Feb '81	Brussels	Belgium	3-2 Cyprus
22 Feb '81	Groningen	Holland	3-0 Cyprus
25 Mar '81	Brussels	Belgium	1-0 Ireland
25 Mar '81	Rotterdam	Holland	1-0 France
29 April '81	Paris	France	3-2 Belgium
29 April '81	Nicosia	Cyprus	0-1 Holland
9 Sept '81	Rotterdam	Holland	2-2 Ireland
9 Sept '81	Brussels	Belgium	2-0 France
14 Oct '81	Dublin	Ireland	3-2 France
14 Oct '81	Rotterdam	Holland	3-0 Belgium
18 Nov '81	Paris	France	2-0 Holland
5 Dec '81	Paris	France	4-0 Cyprus

	P	W	D	L	F	A	GD	Pts
Belgium	8	5	1	2	12	9	+3	11
France	8	5	0	3	20	8	+12	10
Ireland	8	4	2	2	17	11	+6	10
Holland	8	4	1	3	11	7	+4	9
Cyprus	8	0	0	8	4	29	-25	0

GP20 HW14 AW4 D2 GS64
Leading Group Goalscorers: Platini (France), E. Vandenbergh (Belgium), 5
Irish Appearances (+Goals) Players Used:24
L. Brady 8, G. Daly 5(3), J. Devine 1, T. Grealish 7(2), A. Grimes 1, D. Givens 4, S. Heighway 6, C. Hughton 6(1), D. Langan 7, M. Lawrenson 7(2), S. McDonagh 3, P. McGee 2(2), M. Martin 4, K. Moran 5, J. Murphy 1, F. O'Brien 1, D. O'Leary 4,P. O'Leary 1, G. Peyton 5, M. Robinson 5(3), G. Ryan 3, F. Stapleton 8(3), M. Walsh 1, R. Whelan 2.

Belgium and France qualified for the finals in Spain. Belgium got as far as the Second Round Pool games. France finished fourth overall after being knocked out in a semi-final penalty shoot-out.

1986 World Cup – Group 6

12 Sept '84	Dublin	Ireland	1-0 USSR
12 Sept '84	Oslo	Norway	0-1 Switzerland
26 Sept '84	Copenhagen	Denmark	1-0 Norway
10 Oct '84	Oslo	Norway	1-1 USSR
17 Oct '84	Oslo	Norway	1-0 Ireland
17 Oct '84	Berne	Switzerland	1-0 Denmark
14 Nov '84	Copenhagen	Denmark	3-0 Ireland
17 April '85	Berne	Switzerland	2-2 USSR
1 May '85	Dublin	Ireland	0-0 Norway
2 May '85	Moscow	USSR	4-0 Switzerland
2 June '85	Dublin	Ireland	3-0 Switzerland
5 June '85	Copenhagen	Denmark	4-2 USSR
11 Sept '85	Berne	Switzerland	0-0 Ireland
25 Sept '85	Moscow	USSR	1-0 Denmark
9 Oct '85	Copenhagen	Denmark	0-0 Switzerland
16 Oct '85	Oslo	Norway	1-5 Denmark
19 Oct '85	Moscow	USSR	2-0 Ireland
30 Oct '85	Moscow	USSR	1-0 Norway
13 Nov '85	Dublin	Ireland	1-4 Denmark
13 Nov '85	Lucerne	Switzerland	1-1 Norway

	P	W	D	L	F	A	GD	Pts
Denmark	8	5	1	2	17	6	+11	11
USSR	8	4	2	2	13	8	+5	10
Switzerland	8	2	4	2	5	10	-5	8
Ireland	8	2	2	4	5	10	-5	6
Norway	8	1	3	4	4	10	-6	5

GP20 HW11 AW3 D6 GS44

Leading Group Goalscorer: Elkjaer (Denmark), 8

Irish Appearances (+Goals) Players Used: 25

J. Beglin 6, P. Bonner 1, L. Brady 8, P. Byrne 1, T. Cascarino 3, G. Daly 3, J. Devine 2, T. Galvin 4, T. Grealish 6(1), C. Hughton 4, D. Langan 2, M. Lawrenson 7, M. McCarthy 4, S. McDonagh 7, P. McGrath 4, K. Moran 1, K. O'Callaghan 4, E. O'Keefe 1, D. O'Leary 8, M. Robinson 5, K. Sheedy 4(1), F. Stapleton 7(2), G. Waddock 2, M. Walsh 3(1), R. Whelan 5.

Denmark and the USSR qualified for the finals in Mexico where both were knocked out in the Second Round.

1990 World Cup – Group 6

21 May '88	Belfast	N. Ireland	3-0	Malta
14 Sept '88	Belfast	N. Ireland	0-0	Rep. of Ireland
19 Oct '88	Budapest	Hungary	1-0	N. Ireland
16 Nov '88	Seville	Spain	2-0	Rep. of Ireland
11 Dec '88	Valetta	Malta	2-2	Hungary
21 Dec '88	Seville	Spain	4-0	N. Ireland
22 Jan '89	Valetta	Malta	0-2	Spain
8 Feb '89	Belfast	N. Ireland	0-2	Spain
8 Mar '89	Budapest	Hungary	0-0	Rep of Ireland
23 Mar '89	Seville	Spain	4-0	Malta
12 April '89	Budapest	Hungary	1-1	Malta
26 April '89	Dublin	Rep of Ireland	1-0	Spain
26 April '89	Valetta	Malta	0-2	N. Ireland
28 May '89	Dublin	Rep.ofIreland	2-0	Malta
4 June '89	Dublin	Rep.ofIreland	2-0	Hungary
6 Sept '89	Belfast	N. Ireland	1-2	Hungary
11 Oct '89	Dublin	Rep.ofIreland	3-0	N. Ireland
11 Oct '89	Budapest	Hungary	2-2	Spain
15 Nov '89	Valetta	Malta	0-2	Rep. of Ireland
15 Nov '89	Seville	Spain	4-0	Hungary

	P	W	D	L	F	A	GD	Pts
Spain	8	6	1	1	20	3	+17	13
Rep. of Ireland	8	5	2	1	10	2	+8	12
Hungary	8	2	4	2	8	12	-4	8
N. Ireland	8	2	1	5	6	12	-6	5
Malta	8	0	2	6	3	18	-15	2

GP20 HW10 AW5 D5 GS47

Leading Group Goalscorers: Manolo and Michel (both Spain), 5

Irish Appearances (+Goals) Players Used: 21

J. Aldridge 7(2), P. Bonner 7, L. Brady 2, T. Cascarino 8(2), T. Galvin 1, R. Houghton 8(2), C. Hughton 5, M. McCarthy 5, P. McGrath 6(1), K. Moran 8(1), C. Morris 6, L. O'Brien 1, D. O'Leary 5, G. Peyton 1, N. Quinn 2, K. Sheedy 7, J. Sheridan 1, F. Stapleton 2, S. Staunton 6, A. Townsend 5, R. Whelan 6(1).

Spain and the Republic of Ireland qualified for the finals in Italy.

1990 World Cup Finals

Panel (Manager – Jack Charlton P38 W21 D12 L5 F50 A16)

Squad No		Club	Birthplace	Date	Position	Caps	Goals
1	Patrick Bonner	Glasgow Celtic	Burtonport	24/5/1960	GK	38	0
2	Chris Morris	Glasgow Celtic	Newquay	24/12/1963	FB	21	0
3	Stephen Staunton	Liverpool	Drogheda	19/1/1969	FB	13	1
4	Mick McCarthy	Millwall	Barnsley	7/2/1959	CD	42	1
5	Kevin Moran	Blackburn Rovers	Dublin	29/4/1956	CD	50	6
6	Ronnie Whelan	Liverpool	Dublin	25/9/1961	MF	38	3
7	Paul McGrath	Aston Villa	Ealing	4/12/1959	CD/MF	36	4
8	Ray Houghton	Liverpool	Glasgow	9/1/1962	MF	29	3
9	John Aldridge	Real Sociedad	Liverpool	18/9/1958	CF	30	3
10	Tony Cascarino	Aston Villa	St. Paul's Cray	1/9/1962	CF	21	5
11	Kevin Sheedy	Everton	Builth Wells	21/10/1959	MF	28	5
12	David O'Leary	Arsenal	Stoke Newington	2/5/1958	CD	51	0
13	Andy Townsend	Norwich City	Maidstone	23/7/1963	MF	12	1
14	Chris Hughton	Tottenham Hotspur	West Ham	11/12/1958	FB	50	1
15	Bernie Slaven	Middlesbrough	Paisley	13/11/1960	CF	4	1
16	John Sheridan	Sheffield Wednesday	Stretford	1/10/1964	MF	8	1
17	Niall Quinn	Manchester City	Dublin	6/10/1966	CF	15	2
18	Frank Stapleton	Blackburn Rovers	Dublin	10/7/1956	CF	71	20
19	David Kelly	Leicester City	Birmingham	25/11/1965	CF	6	4
20	John Byrne	Le Havre	Manchester	1/2/1961	MF/CF	19	1
21	Alan McLoughlin	Swindon Town	Manchester	20/4/1967	MF	1	0
22	Gerry Peyton	AFC Bournemouth	Birmingham	20/5/1956	GK	28	0

1990 – Final Group F

11 June	Cagliari	England	1-1	Ireland
12 June	Palermo	Holland	1-1	Egypt
16 June	Cagliari	England	0-0	Holland
17 June	Palermo	Egypt	0-0	Ireland
21 June	Palermo	Holland	1-1	Ireland
21 June	Cagliari	England	1-0	Egypt

	P	W	D	L	F	A	GD	Lots	Pts
England	3	1	2	0	2	1	+1	–	4
Ireland	3	0	3	0	2	2	0	1	3
Holland	3	0	3	0	2	2	0	2	3
Egypt	3	0	2	1	1	2	-1	–	2

Round Two

1990				Full-time	Ext.-time	Pen
23 Jun	Naples	Cameroon	v Colombia	0-0	2-1	
23 Jun	Bari	Czechoslovakia	v Costa Rica	4-1		
24 Jun	Turin	Argentina	v Brazil	1-0		
24 Jun	Milan	West Germany	v Holland	2-1		
25 Jun	Genoa	Romania	v Ireland	0-0	0-0	4-5
25 Jun	Rome	Italy	v Uruguay	2-0		
26 Jun	Verona	Yugoslavia	v Spain	1-1	2-1	
26 Jun	Bologna	England	v Belgium	0-0	1-0	
Quarter Finals						
30 Jun	Florence	Argentina	v Yugoslavia	0-0	0-0	3-2
30 Jun	Rome	Italy	v Ireland	1-0		
1 Jul	Milan	West Germany	v CSSR	1-0		
1 Jul	Naples	England	v Cameroon	2-2	3-2	
Semi Finals						
3 Jul	Naples	Italy	v Argentina	1-1	1-1	3-4
4 Jul	Turin	West Germany	v England	1-1	1-1	4-3
Third & Fourth Place Play-off						
7 July	Bari	Italy	v England	2-1		
Final						
8 July	Rome	West Germany	v Argentina	1-0		

Leading Finals Goalscorer: Schillaci (Italy), 6
Irish Appearances (+Goals) Players Used: 16
J. Aldridge 5, P. Bonner 5, T. Cascarino 5, R. Houghton 5, M. McCarthy 5, P. McGrath 5, A. McLoughlin 2, K. Moran 5, C. Morris 5, D. O'Leary 1, N. Quinn 4(1), K. Sheedy 5(1), J. Sheridan 1, S. Staunton 5, A. Townsend 5, R. Whelan 1.

1994 World Cup – Group 3

22 April '92	Seville	Spain	3-0	Albania
28 Apr. '92	Belfast	N. Ireland	2-2	Lithuania
26 May '92	Dublin	Rep.of Ireland	2-0	Albania
3 June '92	Tirana	Albania	1-0	Lithuania
12 Aug. '92	Riga	Latvia	1-2	Lithuania
26 Aug. '92	Riga	Latvia	0-0	Denmark
9 Sept. '92	Dublin	Rep. of Ireland	4-0	Latvia
9 Sept. '92	Belfast	N. Ireland	3-0	Albania
23 Sept. '92	Riga	Latvia	0-0	Spain
23 Sept '92	Vilnius	Lithuania	0-0	Denmark
14 Oct '92	Belfast	N. Ireland	0-0	Spain
14 Oct. '92	Copenhagen	Denmark	0-0	Rep. of Ireland
28 Oct. '92	Vilnius	Lithuania	1-1	Latvia
11 Nov '92	Tirana	Albania	1-1	Latvia
18 Nov. '92	Seville	Spain	0-0	Rep. of Ireland
18 Nov. '92	Belfast	N. Ireland	0-1	Denmark
16 Dec. '92	Seville	Spain	5-0	Latvia
17 Feb. '93	Tirana	Albania	1-2	N. Ireland
24 Feb. '93	Seville	Spain	5-0	Lithuania
31 Mar. '93	Dublin	Rep. of Ireland	3-0	N. Ireland
31 Mar. '93	Copenhagen	Denmark	1-0	Spain
14 Apr. '93	Copenhagen	Denmark	2-0	Latvia
14 Apr. '93	Vilnius	Lithuania	3-1	Albania
28 Apr. '93	Seville	Spain	3-1	N. Ireland
28 Apr. '93	Dublin	Rep. of Ireland	1-1	Denmark
15 May '93	Riga	Latvia	0-0	Albania
25 May '93	Vilnius	Lithuania	0-1	N. Ireland
26 May '93	Tirana	Albania	1-2	Rep. of Ireland
2 June '93	Riga	Latvia	1-2	N. Ireland
2 June '93	Copenhagen	Denmark	4-0	Albania
2 June '93	Vilnius	Lithuania	0-2	Spain
9 June '93	Riga	Latvia	0-2	Rep. of Ireland
16 June '93	Vilnius	Lithuania	0-1	Rep. of Ireland
25 Aug. '93		Denmark		Lithuania
8 Sept '93		Albania		Denmark
8 Sept. '93		N. Ireland		Latvia
8 Sept. '93		Rep. of Ireland		Lithuania
22 Sept. '93		Albania		Spain
13 Oct. '93		Rep. of Ireland		Spain
13 Oct. '93		Denmark		N. Ireland
17 Nov. '93		N. Ireland		Rep. of Ireland
17 Nov. '93		Spain		Denmark

	P	W	D	L	F	A	GD	Pts
Rep. of Ireland	9	6	3	0	15	2	+13	15
Spain	9	5	3	1	18	2	+16	13
Denmark	8	4	4	0	9	1	+8	12
N. Ireland	9	4	2	3	11	11	0	10
Lithuania	10	2	3	5	8	15	-7	7
Latvia	11	0	5	6	4	19	-15	5
Albania	10	1	2	7	5	20	-15	4

GP33 HW13 AW9 D11 GS70
Leading Group Goalscorer: Aldridge (Rep. of Ireland), 5
Irish Appearances (+Goals) Players Used: 21
J. Aldridge 8(5), P. Bonner 9, T. Cascarino 4(1), T. Coyne 3, R. Houghton 8, D. Irwin 9, R. Keane 9, D. Kelly 1, A. Kernaghan 6, M. McCarthy 1, E. McGoldrick 3, P. McGrath 7(2), K. Moran 4, D. O'Leary 1, T. Phelan 7, N. Quinn 9(2), K. Sheedy 2(1), J. Sheridan 1, S. Staunton 8(2), A. Townsend 9(1), R. Whelan 2.

World Cup Facts

Record Win

Home	6-0	v Cyprus	19 November 1980
Away	3-2	v Cyprus	26 March 1980

Record Defeat

Away	1-7	v Czechoslovakia	29 October 1961
Home	1-4	v Denmark	13 November 1985
	3-5	v France	4 October 1953

Leading World Cup Goalscorer: John Aldridge, 7
Most Goals in a World Cup Match: 4 Paddy Moore v Belgium 26/2/1934
Most World Cup Appearances: 23 Kevin Moran and David O'Leary

Appendix B

IRELAND'S EUROPEAN CHAMPIONSHIP GROUPS

1960 European Championship – Preliminary Round

5 Apr '59	Dublin	Ireland	2-0	Czechoslovakia
10 May '59	Bratislava	Czechoslovakia	4-0	Ireland

Czechosovakia won 4-2 on aggregate.

GP2 HW2 AW0 D0 GS6

Leading Tournament Goalscorers: Bubernik (Czechoslovakia), Fontaine (France), Vincent (France), 5

Irish Appearances (+Goals) Players Used: 14

N. Cantwell 2(1), G. Cummins 2, C. Doyle 1, A. Fitzsimons 1, T. Hamilton 2, C. Hurley 2, B. McNally 1, M. McGrath 2, F. O'Farrell 1, J. O'Neill 2, A. Ringstead 2, P. Saward 1, L. Tuohy 2(1), R. Whittaker 1.

Czechoslovakia progressed to the semi-finals where they lost to the USSR. They finished third overall after beating France in the 3/4 place game.

1964 European Championship – First Round

12 Aug '62	Dublin	Ireland	4-2	Iceland
2 Sept '62	Reykjavik	Iceland	1-1	Ireland

Ireland won 5-3 on aggregate.

Second Round

23 Sept '63	Vienna	Austria	0-0	Ireland
13 Oct '63	Dublin	Ireland	3-2	Austria

Ireland won 3-2 on aggregate.

Quarter Finals

11 Mar '64	Seville	Spain	5-1	Ireland
8 Apr '64	Dublin	Ireland	0-2	Spain

Spain won 7-1 on aggregate.

GP6 HW3 AW1 D2 GS21

Leading Tournament Goalscorers: O. Madsen (Denmark), 11

Irish Appearances (+Goals) Players Used: 24

R. Brady 4, W. Browne 2, N. Cantwell 4(4), D. Curtis 2, Tony Dunne 3, A. Fogarty 5(1), T. Foley 1, J. Fullam 1, J. Giles 5, A. Hale 3, J. Haverty 2, C. Hurley 6, A. Kelly 6, A. McEvoy 3(1), M. McGrath 2, B. McNally 1, M. Meagan 2, R. Nolan 1, N. Peyton 1, P. Saward 2, T. Traynor 5, L. Tuohy 3(2), P. Turner 1, R. Whelan 1.

Spain went on to reach the Final where they beat the USSR 2-1.

1968 European Championship – Group 1

23 Oct '66	Dublin	Ireland	0-0	Spain
19 Nov '66	Dublin	Ireland	2-1	Turkey
7 Dec '66	Valencia	Spain	2-0	Ireland
1 Feb '67	Istanbul	Turkey	0-0	Spain
22 Feb '67	Ankara	Turkey	2-1	Ireland
21 May '67	Dublin	Ireland	0-2	Czechoslovakia
31 May '67	Bilbao	Spain	2-0	Turkey
18 Jun '67	Bratislava	Czechoslovakia	3-0	Turkey
1 Oct '67	Prague	Czechoslovakia	1-0	Spain
22 Oct '67	Madrid	Spain	2-1	Czechoslovakia
15 Nov '67	Ankara	Turkey	0-0	Czechoslovakia
22 Nov '67	Prague	Czechoslovakia	1-2	Ireland

	P	W	D	L	F	A	GD	Pts
Spain	6	3	2	1	6	2	+4	8
Czechoslovakia	6	3	1	2	8	4	+4	7
Ireland	6	2	1	3	5	8	-3	5
Turkey	6	1	2	3	3	8	-5	4

GP12 HW7 AW2 D3 GS22

Leading Group Goalscorers: Adamec (Czechoslovakia), Ogun (Turkey), Pirri (Spain), 2

Irish Appearances (+Goals) Players Used: 25

S. Brennan 3, N. Cantwell 2(1), O. Conmy 2, J. Conway 4, J. Dempsey 3, P. Dunne 1, Tony Dunne 3, E. Dunphy 5, A. Finucane 2, T. Foley 1, C. Gallagher 2, J. Giles 3, A. Hale 1, J. Haverty 2, C. Hurley 5, A. Kelly 5, J. Kinnear 2, A. McEvoy 3(1), M. McGrath 1, M. Meagan 6, T. O'Connell 1, T. O'Connor 1(1), F. O'Neill 4(1), E. Rogers 1, R. Treacy 3(1).

Spain qualified for the Quarter Finals where they were beaten over two legs by England.

1972 European Championship – Group 6

14 Oct '70	Dublin	Ireland	1-1	Sweden
28 Oct '70	Stockholm	Sweden	1-0	Ireland
30 Oct '70	Vienna	Austria	1-2	Italy
8 Dec '70	Florence	Italy	3-0	Ireland
10 May '71	Dublin	Ireland	1-2	Italy
26 May '71	Stockholm	Sweden	1-0	Austria
30 May '71	Dublin	Ireland	1-4	Austria
9 Jun '71	Stockholm	Sweden	0-0	Italy
4 Sept '71	Vienna	Austria	1-0	Sweden
9 Oct '71	Milan	Italy	3-0	Sweden
10 Oct '71	Linz	Austria	6-0	Ireland
20 Nov '71	Rome	Italy	2-2	Austria

	P	W	D	L	F	A	GD	Pts
Italy	6	4	2	0	12	4	+8	10
Austria	6	3	1	2	14	6	+8	7
Sweden	6	2	2	2	3	5	-2	6
Ireland	6	0	1	5	3	17	-14	1

GP12 HW6 AW3 D3 GS32

Leading Group Goalscorer: Parits (Austria), 4

Irish Appearances (+Goals) Players Used: 34

S. Brennan 2, T. Byrne 5, N. Campbell 1, T. Carroll 1(1), T. Conroy 3, J. Conway 2(1), J. Dempsey 3, J. Dunne 1, Tony Dunne 3, P. Dunning 2, E. Dunphy 5, A. Finucane 4, M. Gannon 1, J. Giles 1, D. Givens 4, A. Hale 1, E. Hand 1, S. Heighway 4, J. Herrick 1, J. Holmes 1, M. Kearin 1, A. Kelly 5, J. Kinnear 2, M. Lawlor 3, M. Leech 1, T. McConville 1, M. Martin 1, P. Mulligan 3, T. O'Connor 1, F. O'Neill 1, D. Richardson 1, P. Roche 1, E. Rogers 3(1), R. Treacy 4.

Italy qualified for the Quarter Finals where they were beaten over two legs by Belgium.

1976 European Championship – Group 8

30 Oct '74	Dublin	Ireland	3-0	USSR
20 Nov '74	Izmir	Turkey	1-1	Ireland
1 Dec '74	Izmir	Turkey	2-1	Switzerland
2 Apr '75	Kiev	USSR	3-0	Turkey
30 Apr '75	Zurich	Switzerland	1-1	Turkey
10 May '75	Dublin	Ireland	2-1	Switzerland
18 May '75	Kiev	USSR	2-1	Ireland
21 May '75	Berne	Switzerland	1-0	Ireland
12 Oct '75	Zurich	Switzerland	0-1	USSR
29 Oct '75	Dublin	Ireland	4-0	Turkey
12 Nov '75	Kiev	USSR	4-1	Switzerland
23 Nov '75	Izmir	Turkey	1-0	USSR

	P	W	D	L	F	A	GD	Pts
USSR	6	4	0	2	10	6	+4	8
Ireland	6	3	1	2	11	5	+6	7
Turkey	6	2	2	2	5	10	-5	6
Switzerland	6	1	1	4	5	10	-5	3

GP12 HW9 AW1 D2 GS31
Leading Group Goalscorer: Givens (Ireland), 8
Irish Appearances (+Goals) Players Used:16
L. Brady 6, T. Conroy 5, G. Daly 1, M. Dennehy 1, Tony Dunne 5, J. Giles 6, D. Givens 6(8), E. Hand 5(1), S. Heighway 4, J. Holmes 3, J. Kinnear 5, T. Mancini 1, M. Martin 6(1), P. Mulligan 6, P. Roche 6, R. Treacy 4(1).

The USSR qualified for the Quarter Finals where they were beaten over two legs by Czechoslovakia.

1980 European Championships – Group 1

24 May '78	Copenhagen	Denmark	3-3	Rep. of Ireland
20 Sept '78	Dublin	Rep. of Ire.	0-0	N. Ireland
20 Sept '78	Copenhagen	Denmark	3-4	England
11 Oct '78	Copenhagen	Denmark	2-2	Bulgaria
25 Oct '78	Dublin	Rep. of Ire.	1-1	England
25 Oct '78	Belfast	N. Ireland	2-1	Denmark
29 Nov '78	Sofia	Bulgaria	0-2	N. Ireland
7 Feb '79	London	England	4-0	N. Ireland
2 May '79	Dublin	Rep. of Ire.	2-0	Denmark
2 May '79	Belfast	N. Ireland	2-0	Bulgaria
19 May '79	Sofia	Bulgaria	1-0	Rep. of Ireland
6 Jun '79	Sofia	Bulgaria	0-3	England
6 Jun '79	Copenhagen	Denmark	4-0	N. Ireland
12 Sept '79	London	England	1-0	Denmark
17 Oct '79	Dublin	Rep. of Ire.	3-0	Bulgaria
17 Oct '79	Belfast	N. Ireland	1-5	England
31 Oct '79	Sofia	Bulgaria	3-0	Denmark
21 Nov '79	Belfast	N. Ireland	1-0	Rep. of Ireland
22 Nov '79	London	England	2-0	Bulgaria
6 Feb '80	London	England	2-0	Rep. of Ireland

	P	W	D	L	F	A	GD	Pts
England	8	7	1	0	22	5	+17	15
N. Ireland	8	4	1	3	8	14	-6	9
Rep. of Ireland	8	2	3	3	9	8	+1	7
Bulgaria	8	2	1	5	6	14	-8	5
Denmark	8	1	2	5	13	17	-4	4

GP20 HW12 AW4 D4 GS58
Leading Group Goalscorer: Keegan (England), 7
Irish Appearances (+Goals) Players Used: 27
L. Brady 6, G. Daly 7(3), J. Devine 1, J. Giles 4, D. Givens 6(1), T. Grealish 6(2), E. Gregg 4, A. Grimes 3, A. Hayes 1, R. Healey 1, S. Heighway 6, J. Holmes 5, C. Hughton 1, M. Kearns 4, M. Lawrenson 4, P. McGee 7, M. Martin 4(1), P. Mulligan 5, F. O'Brien 1, D. O'Leary 6, P. O'Leary 3, G. Peyton 4, G. Ryan 1, F. Stapleton 7(2), N. Synnott 1, M. Walsh 3, J. Waters 1.

England qualified for the finals in Italy where they were knocked out after the Quarter Final Group games.

1984 European Championship – Group 7

5 Jun '82	Messina, Italy	Malta	2-1	Iceland
1 Sept '82	Reykjavik	Iceland	1-1	Holland
22 Sept '82	Rotterdam	Holland	2-1	Ireland
13 Oct '82	Dubin	Ireland	2-0	Iceland
27 Oct '82	Malaga	Spain	1-0	Iceland
17 Nov '82	Dublin	Ireland	3-3	Spain
19 Dec '82	Aachen, W.Germany	Malta	0-6	Holland
16 Feb '83	Seville	Spain	1-0	Holland
30 Mar '83	Valetta	Malta	0-1	Ireland
27 Apr '83	Zaragoza	Spain	2-0	Ireland
15 May '83	Valetta	Malta	2-3	Spain
29 May '83	Reykjavik	Iceland	0-1	Spain
5 Jun '83	Reykjavik	Iceland	1-0	Malta
7 Sept '83	Groningen	Holland	3-0	Iceland
21 Sept '83	Reykjavik	Iceland	0-3	Ireland
12 Oct '83	Dublin	Ireland	2-3	Holland
16 Nov '83	Rotterdam	Holland	2-1	Spain
16 Nov '83	Dublin	Ireland	8-0	Malta
17 Dec '83	Rotterdam	Holland	5-0	Malta
21 Dec '83	Seville	Spain	12-1	Malta

	P	W	D	L	F	A	GD	Pts
Spain	8	6	1	1	24	8	+16	13
Holland	8	6	1	1	22	6	+16	13
Ireland	8	4	1	3	20	10	+10	9
Iceland	8	1	1	6	3	13	-10	3
Malta	8	1	0	7	5	37	-32	2

GP20 HW11 AW7 D2 GS74
Leading Group Goalscorer: Santillana (Spain), 6
Irish Appearances (+Goals) Players Used: 23
P. Bonner 1, L. Brady 7(3), G. Daly 3(2), J. Devine 4, T. Galvin 3, T. Grealish 6(1), A. Grimes 2(1), C. Hughton 7, M. Lawrenson 8(2), J. McDonagh 1, S. McDonagh 7, M. Martin 4, K. Moran 4, K. O'Callaghan 7(1), D. O'Leary 3, K. O'Regan 1, M. Robinson 6(1), K. Sheedy 2(1), F. Stapleton 8(5), G. Waddock 7(2), Mickey Walsh 5(1), Mike Walsh 1, R. Whelan 3.

Spain qualified for the finals in France and went on to contest the Final but lost 2-0 to France.

1988 European Championship – Group 7

10 Sept '86	Brussels	Belgium	2-2	Ireland
10 Sept '86	Glasgow	Scotland	0-0	Bulgaria
14 Oct '86	Luxembourg	Luxembourg	0-6	Belgium
15 Oct '86	Dublin	Ireland	0-0	Scotland
12 Nov '86	Glasgow	Scotland	3-0	Luxembourg
19 Nov '86	Brussels	Belgium	1-1	Bulgaria
18 Feb '87	Glasgow	Scotland	0-1	Ireland
1 Apr '87	Sofia	Bulgaria	2-1	Ireland
1 Apr '87	Brussels	Belgium	4-1	Scotland
29 Apr '87	Dublin	Ireland	0-0	Belgium
30 Apr '87	Luxembourg	Luxembourg	1-4	Bulgaria
20 May '87	Sofia	Bulgaria	3-0	Luxembourg
28 May '87	Luxembourg	Luxembourg	0-2	Ireland
9 Sept '87	Dublin	Ireland	2-1	Luxembourg
23 Sept '87	Sofia	Bulgaria	2-0	Belgium
14 Oct '87	Dublin	Ireland	2-0	Bulgaria
14 Oct '87	Glasgow	Scotland	2-0	Belgium
11 Nov '87	Brussels	Belgium	3-0	Luxembourg
11 Nov '87	Sofia	Bulgaria	0-1	Scotland
12 Nov '87	Esch	Luxembourg	0-0	Scotland

	P	W	D	L	F	A	GD	Pts
Ireland	8	4	3	1	10	5	+5	11
Bulgaria	8	4	2	2	12	6	+6	10
Belgium	8	3	3	2	16	8	+8	9
Scotland	8	3	3	2	7	5	+2	9
Luxembourg	8	0	1	7	2	23	-21	1

GP20 HW9 AW5 D6 GS47
Leading Group Goalscorer: Claesen (Belgium), 7

Irish Appearances (+Goals) Players Used: 21
J. Aldridge 7, J. Anderson 3, J. Beglin 2, P. Bonner 7, L. Brady 8(1), J. Byrne 5, G. Daly 1, T. Galvin 7(1), A. Grimes 1, R. Houghton 7, C. Hughton 2, D. Langan 4, M. Lawrenson 3(1), M. McCarthy 6, P. McGrath 8(2), K. Moran 8(1), G. Peyton 1, N. Quinn 3, K. Sheedy 1, F. Stapleton 8(3), R. Whelan 7(1).

Ireland qualified for the finals in West Germany.

1988 Final Group B

12 June	Stuttgart	England	0-1	Ireland
12 June	Cologne	USSR	1-0	Holland
15 June	Dusseldorf	Holland	3-1	England
15 June	Hanover	USSR	1-1	Ireland
18 June	Gelsenkirchen	Holland	1-0	Ireland
18 June	Frankfurt	USSR	3-1	England

	P	W	D	L	F	A	GD	Pts
USSR	3	2	1	0	5	2	+3	5
Holland	3	2	0	1	4	2	+2	4
Ireland	3	1	1	1	2	2	-	3
England	3	0	0	3	2	7	-5	0

Leading Finals Goalscorer: Van Basten (Holland), 5
Irish Appearances (+Goals) Players Used: 14
J. Aldridge 3, P. Bonner 3, T. Cascarino 2, T. Galvin 3, R. Houghton 3(1), C. Hughton 3, M. McCarthy 3, P. McGrath 2, K. Moran 3, C. Morris 3, N. Quinn 1, K. Sheedy 3, F. Stapleton 3, R. Whelan 3(1).

Both the USSR and Holland qualified for the semi-finals and later both contested the Final, which the Dutch won 2-0.

1988 European Championship Finals

Panel (Manager – Jack Charlton P19 W11 D5 L3 F27 A10)

Squad No		Club	Birthplace	Date	Position	Caps	Goals
1	Patrick Bonner	Glasgow Celtic	Burtonport	24/5/1960	GK	23	0
2	Chris Morris	Glasgow Celtic	Newquay	24/12/1963	FB	5	0
3	Chris Hughton	Tottenham Hotspur	West Ham	11/12/1958	FB	36	1
4	Mick McCarthy	Glasgow Celtic	Barnsley	7/2/1959	CD	27	1
5	Kevin Moran	Manchester United	Dublin	29/4/1956	CD	36	5
6	Ronnie Whelan	Liverpool	Dublin	25/9/1961	MF	26	1
7	Paul McGrath	Manchester United	Ealing	4/12/1959	CD/MF	23	3
8	Ray Houghton	Liverpool	Glasgow	9/1/1962	MF	15	0
9	John Aldridge	Liverpool	Liverpool	18/9/1958	CF	15	0
10	Frank Stapleton	Derby County	Dublin	10/7/1956	CF	63	18
11	Tony Galvin	Sheffield Wednesday	Huddersfield	24/11/1956	W	24	1
12	Tony Cascarino	Millwall	St. Paul's Cray	1/9/1962	CF	5	1
13	Liam O'Brien	Manchester United	Dublin	5/9/1964	MF	6	0
14	David Kelly	Walsall	Birmingham	25/11/1965	CF	3	4
15	Kevin Sheedy	Everton	Builth Wells	21/10/1959	MF	13	3
16	Gerry Peyton	AFC Bournemouth	Birmingham	20/5/1956	GK	24	0
17	John Byrne	Le Havre	Manchester	1/2/1961	MF/CF	14	1
18	John Sheridan	Leeds United	Stretford	1/10/1964	MF	4	1
19	John Anderson	Newcastle United	Dublin	7/11/1959	FB	15	1
20	Niall Quinn	Arsenal	Dublin	6/10/1966	CF	9	1

1992 European Championship – Group 7

17 Oct '90	Dublin	Ireland	5-0	Turkey
17 Oct '90	London	England	2-0	Poland
14 Nov '90	Dublin	Ireland	1-1	England
14 Nov '90	Istanbul	Turkey	0-1	Poland
27 Mar '91	London	England	1-1	Ireland
17 Apr '91	Warsaw	Poland	3-0	Turkey
1 May '91	Dublin	Ireland	0-0	Poland
1 May '91	Izmir	Turkey	0-1	England
16 Oct '91	Poznan	Poland	3-3	Ireland
16 Oct '91	London	England	1-0	Turkey
13 Nov '91	Istanbul	Turkey	1-3	Ireland
13 Nov '91	Poznan	Poland	1-1	England

	P	W	D	L	F	A	GD	Pts
England	6	3	3	0	7	3	+4	9
Ireland	6	2	4	0	13	6	+7	8
Poland	6	2	3	1	8	6	+2	7
Turkey	6	0	0	6	1	14	-13	0

GP12 HW4 AW3 D5 GS29

Leading Group Goalscorers: Aldridge, Cascarino (Ireland), 3

Irish Appearances (+Goals) Players Used: 22

J. Aldridge 5(3), P. Bonner 6, J. Byrne 1(2), T. Cascarino 6(3), R. Houghton 4, C. Hughton 2, D. Irwin 4, R. Keane 1, M. McCarthy 3, P. McGrath 5(1), A. McLoughlin 1, K. Moran 4, C. Morris 2, D. O'Leary 6(1), T. Phelan 2, N. Quinn 4(2), K. Sheedy 4, J. Sheridan 1, B. Slaven 1, S. Staunton 6, A. Townsend 5(1), R. Whelan 1.

England qualified for the finals in Sweden where they were knocked out after the Quarter Final Group games.

European Championships Facts

Record Win

Home	8-0	v Malta	16 November 1983
Away	3-0	v Iceland	21 September 1983

Record Defeat

Away	0-6	v Austria	10 October 1971
Home	1-4	v Austria	30 May 1971

Leading European Championship Goalscorer: Frank Stapleton, 10

Most Goals in a European Championship Match: 4 Don Givens v Turkey 29/10/1975

Most European Championships Appearances: 27 Liam Brady.

APPENDIX C

1972 COPA INDEPENDENCIA DO BRASIL (Independence Cup, Brazil)

GROUP 1

11 June	Salvador	Argentina	2-0	Africa
11 June	Salvador	France	5-0	CONCACAF
15 June	Maceio	France	2-0	Africa
15 June	Salvador	Columbia	4-3	CONCACAF
18 June	Salvador	Argentina	7-0	CONCACAF
18 June	Salvador	France	3-2	Columbia
22 June	Salvador	Africa	0-0	CONCACAF
22 June	Salvador	Argentina	4-1	Columbia
25 June	Salvador	Africa	3-0	Columbia
25 June	Salvador	Argentina	0-0	France

	P	W	D	L	F	A	GD	PTS
Argentina	4	3	1	0	13	1	+12	7
France	4	3	1	0	10	2	+8	7
Africa	4	1	1	2	3	4	-1	3
Columbia	4	1	0	3	7	13	-6	2
CONCACAF	4	0	1	3	3	16	-13	1

Argentina qualified for Quarter Final Group B

GROUP 2

11 June	Natal	Portugal	3-0	Eduador
11 June	Recife	Iran	1-2	Ireland
14 June	Recife	Portugal	3-0	Iran
14 June	Natal	Chile	2-1	Ecuador
18 June	Recife	Portugal	4-1	Chile
18 June	Natal	Ecuador	2-3	Ireland
21 June	Recife	Ecuador	1-1	Iran
21 June	Recife	Chile	2-1	Ireland
25 June	Recife	Chile	2-1	Iran
25 June	Recife	Portugal	2-1	Ireland

	P	W	D	L	F	A	GD	PTS
Portugal	4	4	0	0	12	2	+10	8
Chile	4	3	0	1	7	7	0	6
Ireland	4	2	0	2	7	7	0	4
Ecuador	4	0	1	3	4	9	-5	3
Iran	4	0	1	3	3	8	-5	1

Portugal qualified for Quarter Final Group B

GROUP 3

11 June	Curitiba	Peru	3-0	Bolivia
11 June	Campo Grande	Paraguay	4-1	Venezuela
14 June	Curitiba	Yugoslavia	10-0	Venezuela
14 June	Campo Grande	Paraguay	1-0	Peru
18 June	Campo Grande	Bolivia	1-1	Yugoslavia
18 June	Manaus	Peru	1-0	Venezuela
21 June	Manaus	Bolivia	2-2	Venezuela

22 June	Manaus	Yugoslavia	2-1	Paraguay
25 June	Manaus	Paraguay	6-1	Bolivia
25 June	Manaus	Yugoslavia	2-1	Peru

	P	W	D	L	F	A	GD	PTS
Yugoslavia	4	3	1	0	15	3	+12	7
Paraguay	4	3	0	1	12	4	+8	6
Peru	4	2	0	2	5	3	+2	4
Bolivia	4	0	2	2	4	12	-8	2
Venezuela	4	0	1	3	3	17	-14	1

Yugoslavia qualified for Quarter Final Group A

QUARTER FINAL GROUP A

28 June	Rio de Janeiro	Brazil	0-0	Czechoslovakia
29 June	Belo Horizonte	Scotland	2-2	Yugoslavia
2 July	Sao Paulo	Brazil	3-0	Yugoslavia
2 July	Porto Alegre	Czechoslovakia	0-0	Scotland
5 July	Rio de Janeiro	Brazil	1-0	Scotland
6 July	Sao Paulo	Yugoslavia	2-1	Czechoslovakia

	P	W	D	L	F	A	GD	PTS
Brazil	3	2	1	0	4	0	+4	5
Yugoslavia	3	1	1	1	4	6	-2	3
Scotland	3	0	2	1	2	3	-1	2
Czechoslovakia	3	0	2	1	1	2	-1	2

Brazil qualified for the Final. Yugoslavia qualified for a 3/4 place play-off.

QUARTER FINAL GROUP B

29 June	Sao Paulo	USSR	1-0	Uruguay
29 June	Rio de Janeiro	Portugal	3-1	Argentina
2 July	Sao Paulo	Portugal	1-1	Uruguay
2 July	Belo Horizonte	Argentina	1-0	USSR
6 July	Belo Horizonte	Portugal	1-0	USSR
6 July	Porto Alegre	Argentina	1-0	Uruguay

	P	W	D	L	F	A	GD	PTS
Portugal	3	2	1	0	5	2	+3	5
Argentina	3	2	0	1	3	3	0	4
USSR	3	1	0	2	1	2	-1	2
Uruguay	3	0	1	2	1	3	-2	1

Portugal qualified for the Final. Argentina qualified for a 3/4 place play-off.

3/4 PLACE PLAY-OFF

9 July Rio de Janeiro Yugoslavia 4-2 Argentina

FINAL

9 July Rio de Janeiro Brazil 1-0 Portugal

Leading tournament goalscorer: Bejevic (Yugoslavia) 13

Irish appearances (+ goals) Players used: 14.
T. Carroll 4, N. Campbell 4, J. Dempsey 4, M. Dennehy 2, D. Givens 3 (1), J. Herrick 1, A. Kelly 4, J. Kinnear 4, M. Leech 3 (2), M. Martin 4 (1), P. Mulligan 4, T. O'Connor 4 (1), E. Rogers 4 (2), R. Treacy 4.

APPENDIX D

1984 JAPAN CUP KIRIN WORLD SOCCER COMPETITION

GROUP A

27 May	Tokyo	Toulouse FC	1-0	Japan
29 May	Hiroshima	PR China	3-2	Toulouse FC
31 May	Omiya	Japan	1-0	PR China

	P	W	D	L	F	A	GD	PTS
PR China	2	1	0	1	3	3	0	2
Toulouse FC	2	1	0	1	3	3	0	2
Japan	2	1	0	1	1	1	0	2

GROUP B

27 May	Matsuyama	Japan Univer.	0-0	Ireland
30 May	Kobe	SC Internacional	3-0	Japan Univer.
1 June	Nayoya	SC Internacional	0-0	Ireland

	P	W	D	L	F	A	GD	PTS
SC Internacional Porto Alegre, Brazil	2	1	1	0	3	0	+3	3
Ireland	2	0	2	0	0	0	0	2
Japan Universities	2	0	1	1	0	3	-3	1

SEMI-FINALS

3 June	Sapparo	PR China	0-1	Ireland
3 June	Yokohama	SC Internacional	4-1	Toulouse FC

FINAL

5 June Tokyo SC Internacional 2-1 Ireland

Irish Appearances (+ goals) Players used: 18.
J. Anderson 2, J. Beglin 4, P. Bonner 1, L. Buckley 1, P. Byrne 3, T. Grealish 4, A. Grimes 2, G. Howlett 2, M. McCarthy 4, J. McDonagh 2, S. McDonagh 3, E. O'Keefe 3 (1), D. O'Leary 2, K. O'Regan 2, G. Ryan 4, F. Stapleton 4 (1), J. Walsh 1, M. Walsh 4.

APPENDIX E

1986 ICELANDIC TOURNAMENT (Reykjavik 200)

25 May	Reykjavik	Iceland	1-2 Ireland
27 May	Reykjavik	Czechoslovakia	0-1 Ireland
29 May	Reykjavik	Iceland	1-2 Czechoslovakia

	P	W	D	L	F	A	GD	PTS
Ireland	2	2	0	0	3	1	+2	4
Czechoslovakia	2	1	0	1	2	2	0	2
Iceland	2	0	0	2	2	4	-2	0

Irish Appearances (+ goals) Players used 16.
J. Aldridge 2, J. Anderson 2, P. Bonner 1, P. Byrne 2, G. Daly 2 (1), T. Galvin 2, R. Houghton 2, C. Hughton 1, M. Kennedy 2, M. McCarthy 2, P. McGrath 2 (1), K. Moran 2, G. Peyton 1, N. Quinn 2, M. Robinson 1, F. Stapleton 2 (1).

APPENDIX F

1992 US CUP

30 May	Washington	USA	3-1 Ireland
31 May	Connecticut	Italy	0-0 Portugal
3 June	Chicago	USA	1-0 Portugal
4 June	Boston	Italy	2-0 Ireland
6 June	Chicago	USA	1-1 Italy
7 June	Boston	Portugal	0-2 Ireland

	P	W	D	L	F	A	GD	PTS
USA	3	2	1	0	5	2	+3	5
Italy	3	1	2	0	3	1	+2	4
Ireland	3	1	0	2	3	5	-2	2
Portugal	3	0	1	2	0	3	-3	1

Irish Appearances (+ goals) Players used: 19. J. Aldridge 2, P. Bonner 1, T. Coyne 3 (1), R. Houghton 3, D. Irwin 2, R. Keane 1, D. Kelly 2, M. McCarthy 3 (1), E. McGoldrick 2, P. McGrath 3, A. McLoughlin 3, K. Moran 1, C. Morris 2, D. O'Leary 2, G. Peyton 3, T. Phelan 3, N. Quinn 3, S. Staunton 3 (1), A. Townsend 2.

The Irish team which played the Japan Universities team in the 1984 Japan Cup.
Back Row (left to right): *Jim Beglin, Ashley Grimes, Jacko McDonagh, Mickey Walsh, Seamus McDonagh and Mick McCarthy.*
Front Row (left to right): *Pat Byrne, Kieran O'Regan, Gerry Ryan, Tony Grealish and Frank Stapleton.*

APPENDIX G

RECORD OF IRISH MANAGER'S

MICK MEAGAN – 1969-1971

Born – Dublin 29 May 1934. 17 Republic of Ireland Caps.

	P	W	D	L	F	A
Overall Record	12	0	3	9	7	26
Home	6	0	3	3	5	11
Away	6	0	0	6	2	15
Record in World Cup	3	0	1	2	1	8
European Championship	5	0	1	4	3	11

Players Used: 30
Debuts Under: 10
Most Appearances: Alan Kelly, Eamonn Dunphy, 11
Leading Goalscorer: Don Givens, 3
Captain Most Times: Shay Brennan, 5

Biggest Win: None
Heaviest Defeat: 0-4 v Hungary

Appearances under (+ goals): S. Brennan 9, T. Byrne 9, N. Campbell 1, T. Carroll 3 (1), O. Conmy 1, T. Conroy 9, J. Conway 9 (1), J. Dempsey 5, J. Dunne 1, Tony Dunne 4, E. Dunphy 11, P. Dunning 2, A. Finucane 5, K. Fitzpatrick 1, J. Fullam 1, J. Giles 4, D. Givens 10 (3), A. Hale 3, E. Hand 4, S. Heighway 5, J. Holmes 1, M. Kearns 1, A. Kelly 11, J. Kinnear 6, M. Lawlor 4, M. Meagan 1, P. Mulligan 9 (1), T. O'Connell 1, E. Rogers 6 (1), R. Treacy 10.

LIAM TUOHY – 1971-1973

Born – Dublin 27 April 1933. 8 Republic of Ireland Caps.

	P	W	D	L	F	A
Overall Record	10	3	1	5	11	20
Home	2	1	0	1	3	3
Away	8	2	1	6	8	17
Record in World Cup	4	1	1	2	4	5
European Championship	1	0	0	1	0	6

Players Used: 30
Debuts Under: 9
Most Appearances: Alan Kelly, Mick Martin, Paddy Mulligan, Ray Treacy, 9
Leading Goalscorers: Terry Conroy, Mick Leech, Mick Martin Eamonn Rogers, 2
Captain Most Times: Paddy Mulligan, 6

Biggest Win: 3-2 v Ecuador
Heaviest Defeat: 0-6 v Austria.

Appearances under (+ goals): T. Byrne 3, N. Campbell 6, T. Carroll 8, T. Conroy 3 (2), G. Daly 1, J. Dempsey 4, M. Dennehy 5, A. Finucane 1, M. Gannon 1, J. Giles 2, D. Givens 7 (1), A. Hale 1, E. Hand 5, S. Heighway 1, J. Herrick 3, J. Holmes 4, M. Kearin 1, A. Kelly 9, J. Kinnear 6, M. Lawlor 1, M. Leech 5 (2), T. McConville 6, M. Martin 9 (2), P. Mulligan 9, T. O'Connnor 7 (1), F. O'Neill 1, D. Richardson 1, P. Roche 1, E. Rogers 5 (2), R. Treacy 9 (1).

SEAN THOMAS – 1973

Born –

In charge for only 1 game, a friendly away to Norway which finished 1-1

Players Used: 13

Debut Under: 1

Goalscorer: Miah Dennehy

Captain: Paddy Mulligan

Appearances Under (+ goals): T. Byrne, 1, T. Carroll 1, T. Conroy 1, G. Daly 1, M. Dennehy 1 (1), E. Fagan 1, D. Givens 1, J. Holmes 1, A. Kelly 1, M. Martin 1, P. Mulligan 1, D. Richardson 1, R. Treacy 1.

JOHNNY GILES – 1973-1980

Born – Dublin 6 January 1940. 59 Republic of Ireland Caps.

	P	W	D	L	F	A
Overall Record	37	14	9	14	49	45
Home	17	11	4	2	29	10
Away	20	3	5	12	20	35
Record in World Cup	5	2	1	2	5	6
European Championship	14	5	4	5	20	13

Players Used: 53
Debuts Under: 33
Most Appearances: Mick Martin, Paddy Mulligan, 28
Leading Goalscorer: Don Givens, 13
Captain Most Times: Johnny Giles, 24

Biggest Win: 4-0 v Turkey
Heaviest Defeat: 1-4 v Czechoslovakia

Appearances Under (+ goals): J. Anderson 2 (1), S. Braddish 2, L. Brady 26 (2), T. Byrne 1, N. Campbell 4, J. Chandler 2, J. Clarke 1, T. Conroy 14, J. Conway 6 (2), G. Daly 19 (5), M. Daly 2, M. Dennehy 5 (1), J. Devine 2, T. Donovan 1, Tony Dunne 9, J. Giles 24 (1), D. Givens29 (13), T. Grealish 14 (3), E. Gregg 8, A. Grimes 8, A. Hale 1, E. Hand 10 (2), A. Hayes 1, R. Healey 2, S. Heighway 21, J. Holmes 23, C. Hughton 2, M. Kearns 16, J. Kinnear 10, D. Langan 2, M. Lawrenson 9 (1), T. Macken 1, T. Mancini 5 (1), M. Martin 28 (2), C. Muckian 1, P. Mulligan 28, J. Murphy 3, P. McGee 12 (4), F. O'Brien 3, R. O'Brien 4, B. O'Callaghan 3, D. O'Leary 16, P. O'Leary 5, G. Peyton 12, D. Richardson 1, P. Roche 7, G. Ryan 5 (1), F. Stapleton 16 (3), N. Synnott 3, P. Thomas 2, R. Treacy 14 (3), M. Walsh 8 (1), J. Waters 2 (1).

ALAN KELLY – 1980

Born – Dublin 5 July 1936. 47 Republic of Ireland Caps.

In charge for only 1 game, a friendly at home to Switzerland which Ireland won 2-0.

Players Used: 11

Debuts Under: 2

Goalscorers: Gerry Daly, Don Givens, 1

Captain: Tony Grealish

Appearances Under (+ goals): G. Daly 1 (1), D. Givens 1 (1), T. Grealish 1, C. Hughton 1, D. Langan 1, M. Lawrenson 1, P. McGee 1, K. Moran 1, G. Peyton 1, G. Ryan 1, G. Waddock 1.

EOIN HAND – 1980-1985

Born – Dublin 30 March 1946. 19 Republic of Ireland Caps.

	P	W	D	L	F	A
Overall Record	40	11	9	20	47	59
Home	19	8	6	5	37	21
Away	21	3	3	15	10	38
Record in World Cup	15	5	4	6	19	19
European Championship	8	4	1	3	20	10

Players Used: 49

Debuts Under: 24

Most Appearances: Frank Stapleton, 32

Leading Goalscorer: Frank Stapleton, 11

Captain Most Times: Tony Grealish, 16

Biggest Win: 8-0 v Malta

Heaviest Defeat: 0-7 v Brazil

Appearances Under (+ goals): J. Anderson 4, J. Beglin 11, P. Bonner 9, L. Brady 30 (5), L. Buckley 2, J. Byrne 3, P. Byrne 5, A. Campbell 3, T. Cascarino 3, G. Daly 22 (5), E. Deacy 4, J. Devine 11, T. Donovan 1, M. Fairclough 2, T. Galvin 11, D. Givens 6, T. Grealish 30 (5), A. Grimes 8 (1), S. Heighway 7, J. Holmes 1, G. Howlett 1, C. Hughton 25 (1), D. Langan 15, M. Lawrenson 25 (3), M. McCarthy 11, J. McDonagh 3, S. McDonagh 25, P. McGee 2, P. McGrath 7, M. Martin 14, K. Moran 18 (2), R. O'Brien 1, B. O'Callaghan 3, K. O'Callaghan 20 (1), S. O'Driscoll 3, E. O'Keefe 5 (1), D. O'Leary 23, P. O'Leary 2, K. O'Regan 4, G. Peyton 7, M. Robinson 22 (4), G. Ryan 12, K. Sheedy 8 (2), F. Stapleton 32 (11), G. Waddock 18 (3), J. Walsh 1, Mickey Walsh 13 (2), Mike Walsh 4, R. Whelan 15.

Jack Charlton

JACK CHARLTON OBE – 1986-

Born – Ashington 8 May 1935. 35 England Caps.

	P	W	D	L	F	A
Overall Record	70	36	25	9	99	39
Home	34	22	10	2	60	13
Away	36	14	15	7	39	26
Record in World Cup	22	11	9	2	27	7
European Championship	17	7	8	2	25	13

Players Used: 52
Debuts Under: 28
Most Appearances: Patrick Bonner, 57
Leading Goalscorer: John Aldridge, 12
Captain Most Times: Mick McCarthy, 22

Biggest Win: 5-0 v Israel and Turkey
Heaviest Defeat: 1-3 v USA

Appearances Under (+ goals): J. Aldridge 54 (12),J. Anderson 10, J. Beglin 4, P. Bonner 57, L. Brady 16 (2), J. Byrne 20 (4), P. Byrne 3, B. Carey 2, T. Cascarino 40 (11), T. Coyne 9 (3), L. Daish 2, G. Daly 4 (2), K. DeMange 2, P. Eccles 1, T. Galvin 18 (1), A. Grimes 2, R. Houghton 53 (3), C. Hughton 25, D. Irwin 21 (1), R. Keane 16, A. Kelly 1, D. Kelly 15 (7), M. Kelly 4, M. Kennedy 2, A. Kernaghan 6, D. Langan 8, M. Lawrenson 4 (1), M. McCarthy 46 (2), E. McGoldrick 8, P. McGrath 54 (7), A. McLoughlin 14, M. Milligan 1, K. Moran 48 (4), C. Morris 35, B. Murphy 1, L. O'Brien 10, K. O'Callaghan 1, K. O'Hanlon 1, D. O'Leary 29 (1), G. Peyton 13, T. Phelan 15, N. Quinn 40 (10), M. Robinson 2, P. Scully 1, K. Sheedy 38 (7), J. Sheridan 15 (1), B. Slaven 7 (1), F. Stapleton 23 (6), S. Staunton 41 (4), A. Townsend 39 (4), G. Waddock 2, R. Whelan 30 (3).

APPENDIX H

IRELAND'S UNOFFICIAL MATCHES

23 Feb	'24 Free State XI	v Glasgow Celtic	A	L	0-3
24 March	'26 Nomads	v Cercle Athletique	B	D	1-1
6 May	'36 Free State XI	v Rhineland XI	C	L	1-4
14 April	'46 FAI XI	v Irish Defence Forces	A	L	1-2
27 April	'47 FAI XI	v Irish Defence Forces	A	D	1-1
8 May	'47 FAI XI	v RAF	A	W	3-1
2 May	'48 FAI XI	v Irish Defence Forces	A	W	5-2
20 April	'53 FAI XI	v Glasgow Celtic	A	W	3-2
12 May	'71 Rep. of Ireland XI	v Munster FA	D	L	2-4
24 May	'71 FAI XI	v England XI	E	D	1-1
5 Jan	'72 FAI XI	v W. German Olympic XI	A	W	3-0
3 July	'73 Shamrock Rovers All-Ireland XI	v Brazil	E	L	3-4
4 Sept	'74 Rep. of Ireland	Manchester United	F	W	2-0
4 Feb	'75 Rep of Ireland	v Cambridge United	G	L	1-3
23 May	'75 Rep. of Ireland	v Cork City XI	H	W	8-2
14 Oct	'75 Rep. of Ireland	v W. Brom. Albion	I		
10 Feb	'76 Rep. of Ireland	v W. Brom. Albion	I	W	1-0
[1] 28 April	'76 Johnny Giles XI	v Don Revies XI	E	D	0-0
[2] 8 July	'76 Johnny Giles XI	v Munster FA	H		
[3] 26 March	'77 Rep. of Ireland	v Leeds United	J	W	5-2
[4] 26 June	'77 Paddy Mulligan XI	v Finn Harps	K	D	3-3
21 Sept	'77 Rep. of Ireland	v League of Ireland	A	W	2-1
[5] 29 May	'79 ShamrockRoversXI	v Argentina	E	D	0-0
[6] 5 Aug	'80 Rep. of Ireland XI	v Nottingham Forest	A	L	0-2
13 Nov	'81 Rep. of Ireland	v Liverpool	L	L	0-1
1 June	'82 Rep. of Ireland	v ASL	M	W	3-1
[7] 10 Aug	'82 Rep. of Ireland	v Manchester United	A	L	2-4
[8] 5 Aug	'83 Rep. of Ireland	v Kevin Keegan XI	A	L	2-4
[9] 27 May	'84 Rep. of Ireland	v Japanese Universities	N	D	0-0
[9] 1 June	'84 Rep. of Ireland	v SC Internacional	N	D	0-0
[9] 5 June	'84 Rep. of Ireland	v SC Internacional	N	L	1-2
[10] 7 Aug	'85 Rep. of Ireland	v Glen Hoddle XI	A	W	2-1
18 Aug	'86 Jack Charlton XI	v Liverpool	H	L	1-2
17 May	'88 Rep. of Ireland	v International XI	E	L	1-2
27 May	'88 Rep. of Ireland	v Munster FA	0	W	5-2
[11] 23 May	'89 Rep. of Ireland	v League of Ireland	L	L	0-1
[12] 5 June	'89 Rep. of Ireland	v Dundalk XI	P	D	2-2
[13] 12 May	'91 Rep. of Ireland XI	v Glasgow Celtic	Q	L	2-3
[14] 9 Aug	'91 Rep. of Ireland	v Manchester United	F	D	1-1
9 Aug	'92 Rep. of Ireland	v Manchester United	E	L	0-2
[15] 29 May	'93 Rep. of Ireland	v Hungary	E	L	2-4

Notes: [1]Johnny Giles Testimonial, [2] Ray O'Halloran Testimonial,[3] Paul Madeley Testimonial, [4] Peter Hutton Benefit, [5] UNICEF Benefit, [6] Paddy Mulligan Testimonial, [7] Don Givens Testimonial, [8] MIck Martin Testimonial, [9] Japan Cup, [10] Jimmy Holmes Testimonial, [11] Ray Treacy Testimonial, [12] Barry Kehoe Testimonial, [13] Patrick Bonner Testimonial, [14] Sir Matt Busby Testimonial, [15] David O'Leary Testimonial.

A = Dalymount Park, B = Stade Bergeyrne, C = Cologne, D = Market's Field, E = Lansdowne Road, F = Old Trafford, G = Abbey Stadium, H = Flower Lodge, I = Bisham Abbey, J = Elland Road, K = Finn Park, L = Tolka Park, M = Port of Spain, N = Japan, 0 = Turner's Cross, P = Oriel Park, Q = Parkhead.

It should be noted that the list of games is incomplete.

Three of these unofficial matches are considered to be full internationals by the opposition. So for the sake of continuity the statistics of these games are included below.

3rd July, 1973 – Dublin

SHAMROCK ROVERS ALL-IRELAND XI (1) 3 Martin 28, Dougan 74, Conroy 78
BRAZIL (2) 4 Paulo Cesar Lima 10 (pen), 51, Jairzinho 43, Valdemiro 61

Ref: Byrne (Dublin) **Ground:** Lansdowne Road **Att:** 34,000

Shamrock Rovers XI: Pat Jennings (Tottenham Hotspur), David Craig (Newcastle United), Paddy Mulligan (Crystal Palace), Alan Hunter (Ipswich Town), Tommy Carroll (Birmingham City), Martin O'Neill (Nottingham Forest), Johnny Giles (Leeds United), Mick Martin (Manchester United), Terry Conroy (Stoke City), Derek Dougan (Wolverhampton Wanderers), Don Givens (Queen's Park Rangers). **Subs:** Liam O'Kane (Nottingham Forest), for Carroll (66 mins), Byran Hamilton (Ipswich Town) for Givens (66 mins), Miah Dennehy (Nottingham Forest) for Conroy (88 mins). **Captain:** Johnny Giles. **Manager:** Liam Tuohy. **Formation:** 4-3-3.

Brazil: Leao, Luis Pereira, Ze Maria, Clodoaldo, Piazza, Marco Anonio, Paulo Cesar Lima, Rivelino, Jairzinho, Valdomiro, Dirceu.

29th May, 1979 – Dublin (UNICEF benefit game)

SHAMROCK ROVERS
IRELAND XI (0) 0
ARGENTINA (0) 0

Ref: Valentine (Scotland) **Ground:** Lansdowne Road **Att:** 25,000

Shamrock Rovers XI: Gerry Peyton (Fulham) Eamonn Gregg (Bohemians), David O'Leary (Arsenal), Mick Martin (Newcastle United), Paddy Mulligan (West Bromwich Albion), Tony Grealish (Orient), Johnny Giles (Shamrock Rovers), Liam Brady (Arsenal), Mickey Walsh (Queen's Park Rangers), Frank Stapleton (Arsenal), Don Givens (Birmingham City). **Subs:** Paul McGee (Queen's Park Rangers) for Givens (66 mins), Brendan O'Callaghan (Stoke City) for Stapleton (82 mins). **Captain:** Johnny Giles. **Manager:** Johnny Giles. **Formation:** 4-3-3.

Argentina: Fillol, Villaverde, Olguin, Oviedo, Trossero, Tarantini, Houseman, Barbas, Reinaldi, Valencia, Perotti. **Subs:** Gallego for Tarantini (37 mins), Maradona for Perotti (half-time), Outes for Reinaldi (half-time).

29th May, 1993 – Dublin (David O'Leary testimonial)

REP. OF IRELAND (2) 2 Keane 1, Quinn 4
HUNGARY (0) 4 Hamor 49, 65, Balog 83, Urban 87

Ref: Lloyd (Wales) **Ground:** Lansdowne Road **Att:** 25,000

Ireland: Alan Kelly (Sheffield United), Chris Morris (Middlesbrough), David O'Leary (Arsenal), Alan Kernaghan (Middlesbrough), Stephen Staunton (Aston Villa), Eddie McGoldrick (Crystal Palace), Ronnie Whelan (Liverpool), Roy Keane (Nottingham Forest), Kevin Sheedy (Newcastle United), David Kelly (Newcastle United), Niall Quinn (Manchester City). **Subs:** Alan McLoughlin (Portsmouth) for Keane (14 mins), Phil Babb (Coventry City) for Kernaghan (33 mins), Phil Hardy (Wrexham) for Staunton (37 mins), Tony Cascarino (Chelsea) for D. Kelly (51 mins), John Byrne (Millwall) for Whelan (70 mins). **Captain:** David O'Leary. **Manager:** Jack Charlton. **Formation:** 4-4-2.

Hungary: Z. Petry, J. Csabi, E. Lorincz, A. Telek, A. Kereszturi, J. Banfi, I. Pisont, F. Urban, G. Marton, D. Eszenyi, F. Orosz. **Subs:** T. Balog for Banfi (half-time), I. Hamor for Eszenyi (half-time).

APPENDIX I

League of Ireland Representative side v International sides.

As these games are often considered to be full internationals by the opposition and the League of Ireland side to be a Republic of Ireland selection a list of these games are included to prevent further confusion.

2 May	'52 Dublin	v USA	W 4-0	12 May	'82 Gisborne	v New Zealand	D 0-0
27 Nov	'70 Dublin	v Australia	W 1-0	16 May	'82 Dunedin	v New Zealand	W 2-1
20 April	'78 Buenos Aires	v Argentina	L 1-3	19 May	'82 Invercargill	v New Zealand	L 0-1
23 June	'79 Kuala Lumpar	v Malaysia	L 0-1	28 April	'86 Baghdad	v Iraq	L 0-1
25 June	'79 Singapore	v Singapore	W 4-1	29 Aug	'86 Singapore	v Saudi Arabia	D 1-1
12 Oct	'79 Dublin	v New Zealand	W 2-1	1 Sept	'86 Singapore	v Saudi Arabia	L 0-3
1 May	'80 Buenos Aires	v Argentina	L 0-1	7 Aug	'88 Los Angeles	v El Salvador	
23 Sept	'81 Maceio	v Brazil	L 0-6	19 June	'89 Trinidad	v Ecuador	D 1-1
8 May	'82 Auckland	v New Zealand	L 0-1	20 June	'89 Port of Spain	v Trinidad and Tabago	L 0-1
9 May	'82 Rotorva	v New Zealand	L 0-1	18 Aug	'93 Dublin	v RCS	L 1-4

APPENDIX J

Thirty-four players have played for both Northern Ireland and the Republic of Ireland.
The Northern Ireland record of those players appear below.

AHERNE, T.
4 Caps
1946 Belfast Celtic – Eng.
1947 Belfast Celtic – Scot.
1949 Belfast Celtic – Wal.
1950 Luton Town – Wal.

BREEN, T.
9 Caps
1935 Belfast Celtic - Eng, Wal.
1936 Belfast Celtic – Scot, Eng.
1937 Manchester United – Wal, Eng, Scot.
1938 Manchester United – Scot.
1939 Manchester United – Wal.

BROWN, J.
10 Caps (1 goal)
1935 Wolverhampton
Wanderers – Eng, Wal, Eng.
1936 Coventry City – Eng.
1937 Coventry City – Wal, Scot.
1938 Coventry City – Wal.
Birmingham City – Scot, Eng.
1939 Birmingham City – Wal.

CAREY, J.
7 Caps
1946 Manchester United – Eng, Scot.
1947 Manchester United – Wal, Eng.
1948 Manchester United – Eng, Scot.
1949 Manchester United – Wal.

CHATTON, H.
3 Caps
1924 Partick Thistle – Eng.
1925 Partick Thistle – Scot, Eng.

DAVIS, T.
1 Cap (1 goal)
1936 Oldham Athletic – Eng.

DUGGAN, H.
8 Caps
1929 Leeds United – Eng.
1930 Leeds United – Eng.
1931 Leeds United – Wal.
1932 Leeds United – Eng.
1933 Leeds United – Eng.
1934 Leeds United – Scot.
1935 Leeds United – Wal, Scot.

DUNNE, J.
7 Caps (4 Goals)
1928 Sheffield United – Wal.
1930 Sheffield United – Eng.
1931 Sheffield United – Wal, Scot, Eng.
1932 Sheffield United – Eng, Wal.

EGLINGTON, T.
6 Caps
1946 Everton – Scot.
1947 Everton – Wal, Scot, Eng.
1948 Everton – Wal, Eng.

FARQUHARSON, T.
7 Caps
1923 Cardiff City – Scot, Wal, Eng.
1924 Cardiff City – Scot, Wal, Eng.
1925 Cardiff City – Scot.

FARRELL, PADDY
1 Cap
1938 Hibernian – Wal.

FARRELL, PETER
7 Caps
1946 Everton – Scot.
1947 Everton – Wal, Scot, Eng.
1948 Everton – Wal, Eng.
1949 Everton – Wal.

GALLAGHER, P.
11 Caps
1919 Glasgow Celtic – Eng.
1920 Glasgow Celtic – Scot.
1922 Glasgow Celtic – Scot.
1923 Glasgow Celtic – Scot, Wal.
1924 Glasgow Celtic – Scot, Wal, Eng.
1925 Glasgow Celtic – Scot, Wal.
1927 Falkirk – Scot.

GORMAN, B.
4 Caps
1946 Brentford – Eng, Scot.
1947 Brentford – Wal.
1948 Brentford – Wal.

HAYES, BILLY
4 Caps
1937 Huddersfield Town – Eng, Scot.
1938 Huddersfield Town – Scot, Eng.

KAVANAGH, P.
1 Cap
1929 Glasgow Celtic – Eng.

KEANE, T.
1 Cap
1948 Swansea Town – Scot.

KELLY, J.
11 Caps (4 goals)
1931 Derry City – Eng, Wal.
1932 Derry City – Scot, Eng, Wal.
1933 Derry City – Wal.
1935 Derry City – Eng, Scot.
1936 Derry City – Wal, Scot, Eng.

LACEY, B.
23 Caps (3 goals)
1909 Everton – Eng, Scot, Wal.
1910 Everton – Eng, Scot, Wal.
1911 Everton – Wal, Eng, Scot.
1912 Everton – Eng.
1913 Liverpool – Wal.
1914 Liverpool – Wal, Eng, Scot.
1919 Liverpool – Eng.
1920 Liverpool – Scot, Wal, Eng.
1921 Liverpool – Scot, Wal, Eng.
1922 Liverpool – Scot.
1924 New Brighton – Eng.

McALINDEN, J.
4 Caps
1937 Belfast Celtic – Scot.
1938 Belfast Celtic – Scot.
1946 Portsmouth – Eng.
1948 Southend United – Eng.

MADDEN, O.
1 Cap
1937 Norwich City – Eng.

MARTIN, C.
1 Cap
1925 Bo'ness – Scot.

MARTIN, CON
6 Caps
1946 Glentoran – Scot.
1947 Leeds United – Scot, Eng.
1948 Leeds United – Wal.
Aston Villa – Eng.
1950 Aston Villa – Wal.

MOORE, P.
1 Cap
1932 Aberdeen – Eng.

O'BRIEN, M.
10 Caps
1921 Queen's Park Rangers – Scot.
1922 Leicester City – Scot, Wal.
1924 Leicester City – Scot, Wal.
Hull City – Eng.
1925 Hull City – Scot, Wal.
1926 Hull City – Wal.
1927 Derby County – Wal.

O'DRISCOLL, J.
3 Caps
1948 Swansea Town – Eng, Scot.
1949 Swansea Town – Wal.

O'MAHONEY, M.
1 Cap
1938 Bristol Rovers – Scot.

RYAN R.
1 Cap
1950 West Bromwich Albion – Wal.

SLOAN, J.
1 Cap
1947 Arsenal – Wal.

STEVENSON, A.
17 Caps (5 goals)
1933 Glasgow Rangers – Scot, Eng, Wal.
1934 Everton – Scot.
1935 Everton – Eng, Scot.
1936 Everton – Wal, Eng.
1937 Everton – Wal, Eng.
1938 Everton – Wal, Scot, Eng.
1939 Everton – Wal.
1946 Everton – Scot.
1947 Everton – Wal, Scot.

VERNON, J.
17 Caps
1946 Belfast Celtic – Eng, Scot.
1947 West Bromwich Albion – Wal, Scot, Eng.
1948 West Bromwich Albion – Wal, Eng, Scot.
1949 West Bromwich Albion – Wal, Scot, Eng.
1950 West Bromwich Albion – Eng, Scot, Wal.
1951 West Bromwich Albion – Fra, Scot, Eng.

WALSH, D.
9 Caps (5 goals)
1946 West Bromwich Albion – Scot.
1947 West Bromwich Albion – Wal, Scot, Eng.
1948 West Bromwich Albion – Wal, Eng, Scot.
1949 West Bromwich Albion – Wal.
1950 West Bromwich Albion – Wal.

WALSH, W.
5 Caps
1947 Manchester City – Scot, Eng.
1948 Manchester City – Wal, Eng, Scot.

WEIR, E.
1 Cap
1939 Clyde – Wal.

APPENDIX K

Acknowledgements

Individuals
Ken Avis
Shay Blair
Liam Brady
Liam Buckley
Darren Butler
Denis Byrne
Dierdre Cooney
Mrs. Joan Curtis
Gerry Desmond
Christy Doyle
Tommy Eglington
George W. Forster
Ted Green
Phillip Greene
Mike Jay
Alan Kernaghan
Mark Lawrenson
Frank Lynch
Jim McAlister
Mick McCarthy
Eddie McGoldrick
Con Martin
Ria Matthews
Tony Matthews
Richard Middleton
Mike Milligan
Cathal Muckian
Gunther Nagy
Stephen Staunton
Renata Symanska
Walter Steenhaut
Gary Waddock
Mickey Walsh
Terry Weir
Michael White
Izabela Wojciechowska
Mr. A Woolway

Clubs
Aberdeen
Aston Villa
Barnsley
Birmingham City
Blackburn Rovers
Blackpool
AFC Bournemouth
Brighton & Hove Albion
Bristol Rovers
Bury
Chelsea
Coventry City
Crystal Palace
Derby County
Doncaster Rovers
Everton
Falkirk
Gillingham
Glasgow Celtic
Glasgow Rangers
Hibernian
Ipswich Town
Luton Town
Manchester United
Middlesbrough
Norwich City
Notts County
Nottingham Forest
Partick Thistle
Portsmouth
Preston North End
Shelbourne
Southampton
Southend United
Stoke City
Swansea City
Tranmere Rovers
Walsall
Watford
West Ham United
Wolverhampton Wanderers

Newspapers, Magazines, Photographic Agencies
Aberdeen Journals
Aftenposten a/s
ANP Photo
Belfast Telegraph
Belga
Breedon Books
The Bulletin
Cork Examiner
Croydon Advertiser
Elf
Evening Argus
Evening Mail
Evening Herald
Evening Press
Irish Independent
Irish News
Irish Press
Irish Times
Journal de Geneve
Keystone Press
Lancashire Evening Telegraph
Le Soir
Luxemburger Wort
The News
90 Minutes
The Sentinel
Soccer Magazine
Soccer Reporter
The Star
Sunday Independent
Sunday Press
Sunday Tribune
Sunday World
Sunderland Echo
Tages-Anzeiger
The Times
Votovafoto
Watford Observer
Western Mail
West Lancs Evening Gazette
World Soccer

Others
Austrian Embassy
Austrian Football Association
Belgian Embassy
Belgian Football Association
Dutch Football Association
Football Association of Ireland
Luxembourg Footbal Association
Malta Football Association
Norwegian Embassy
Israeli Embassy
Polish Embassy
Portuguese Embassy
Spainish Embassy
Swedish Embassy
Swiss Embassy
Swiss Football Association
Turkish Embassy
UEFA
United States Soccer Federation
Welsh Football Association